Windows 10
Inside Out
Second Edition

Ed Bott
Carl Siechert
Craig Stinson

PUBLISHED BY
Microsoft Press
A division of Microsoft Corporation
One Microsoft Way
Redmond, Washington 98052-6399

Library of Congress Control Number: 2016940206
ISBN: 978-1-5093-0485-1

Printed and bound in the United States of America.

1 16

Microsoft Press books are available through booksellers and distributors worldwide. If you need support related to this book, email Microsoft Press Support at mspinput@microsoft.com. Please tell us what you think of this book at http://aka.ms/tellpress.

This book is provided "as-is" and expresses the author's views and opinions. The views, opinions and information expressed in this book, including URL and other Internet website references, may change without notice.

Some examples depicted herein are provided for illustration only and are fictitious. No real association or connection is intended or should be inferred.

Microsoft and the trademarks listed at http://www.microsoft.com on the "Trademarks" webpage are trademarks of the Microsoft group of companies. All other marks are property of their respective owners.

Acquisitions and Developmental Editor: Rosemary Caperton
Editorial Production: Curtis Philips, Publishing.com
Technical Reviewer: Randall Galloway; Technical Review services provided by Content Master, a member of CM Group, Ltd.
Copyeditor: Roger LeBlanc
Proofreader: Teresa Nolan Barensfeld
Indexer: William Meyer
Cover: Twist Creative • Seattle

To our many friends and colleagues from the Microsoft Press family.
Thanks for the memories.

Contents at a glance

Appendixes

Table of contents

What do you think of this book? We want to hear from you!

Microsoft is interested in hearing your feedback so we can improve our books and learning resources for you. To participate in a brief survey, please visit:

What do you think of this book? We want to hear from you!

Microsoft is interested in hearing your feedback so we can improve our books and learning resources for you. To participate in a brief survey, please visit:

http://aka.ms/tellpress

Introduction

We're back! (Again.)

The three authors responsible for this edition began working together in 2001. Like many of you, we took a break a few years ago, watching from the sidelines as Microsoft released Windows 8 and Windows 8.1. We returned for Windows 10 because, quite frankly, we were excited by the possibilities of "Windows as a Service." As we predicted in the first edition of this book, published shortly after the initial release of Windows 10 in 2015, you can expect Windows 10 to evolve rapidly.

That forecast has been borne out by our experience over the past year, as we researched and wrote what turned out to be a very significant revision to the original edition. Microsoft released two major updates to Windows 10: one in November 2015, the other (the Anniversary Update) in July 2016. This edition incorporates all of the features from both of those updates.

Much of what is in Windows 10 is familiar, especially its core features. The fundamentals of NTFS security and the registry, for example, have remained reassuringly consistent throughout many generations of Windows. But there's also plenty that's new in Windows 10, some of it obvious (the new Start experience) and some not so obvious (Windows Hello). The two feature updates included significant additions and helped plug gaps in the original release.

The challenge of writing a book like this one is that Microsoft plans to keep changing Windows 10, releasing new features once or twice each year instead of every few years. Fortunately, our friends at Microsoft Press have a plan for dealing with those changes. This edition is part of the brand-new Current Book Service, which means you can expect a web-based update shortly after major updates are released over the next 12 to 18 months. (Later in this chapter, we explain how to register this title with the Current Book Service program so that you can access those updates.)

Who this book is for

This book offers a well-rounded look at the features most people use in Windows. It serves as an excellent starting point for anyone who wants a better understanding of how the central features in Windows 10 work. If you're a Windows expert-in-training, or if your day job involves IT responsibilities, or if you're the designated computer specialist managing computers and networks in a home or small business, you'll discover many sections we wrote just for you. And if you consider yourself a Windows enthusiast—well, we hope you'll find enough fun and interesting tidbits to hold your attention because, after all, we're unabashed enthusiasts ourselves.

Assumptions about you

This book was written for people who have some experience with Windows and are comfortable with and even curious about the technical details of what makes Windows work. It touches only briefly on some of the basic topics that you'll find covered in more detail elsewhere. (For those, we recommend other Microsoft Press titles, such as *Windows 10 Step by Step* or *Windows 10 Plain & Simple*.)

Whether your experience comes from using Windows 8.1 or Windows 7, we expect that you're comfortable finding your way around the desktop, launching programs, using copy and paste operations, and finding information in a web browser. We don't assume that you're a hardware tinkerer, hacker, hardcore gamer, or developer.

How this book is organized

Part 1, "Getting started with Windows 10," offers an overview of what's new in this version, with details on installing and configuring Windows 10, personalizing the Windows experience, connecting to the internet and local networks, and keeping your user accounts and devices secure.

Part 2, "Working and playing with Windows 10," covers the essentials of using and managing Universal Windows Platform (UWP) apps and desktop programs, with details on built-in productivity tools (including Mail) and the entertainment apps that help you enjoy your collection of digital photos and music. This section covers Cortana, the personal assistant that's integrated into Windows 10, as well as the occasionally complicated relationship between Microsoft Edge, the new default browser, and Internet Explorer. Finally, it explains how to organize your folders and files, on local drives or in the cloud using OneDrive, and how to find those files when you need them.

Part 3, "System maintenance and troubleshooting," starts with a detailed guide to the different types of hardware you can use with Windows 10, with storage devices getting their own chapter. Additional chapters cover routine maintenance tasks and explore tools and techniques for measuring and improving your computer's performance. The section closes with advice on how to back up your important files, how to recover quickly from problems, and how to troubleshoot issues when they arise.

Part 4, "Windows 10 for experts and IT pros," goes into detail about advanced system-management tools and explains how to set up an advanced network so that you can safely share files, printers, internet connections, and other resources. Other topics include Windows PowerShell scripting and the powerful Hyper-V virtualization technology built in to the Pro, Enterprise, and Education editions of Windows 10.

Finally, we provide two appendixes of reference information: a concise look at the differences between Windows 10 editions and an overview of help and support resources.

Acknowledgments

For this edition of the book, like many before it, we're fortunate to have an expert production team led by Curtis Philips of Publishing.com. Along with technical editor Randall Galloway, copyeditor Roger LeBlanc, and proofreader Teresa Barensfeld, our favorite team asked the right questions and made excellent suggestions to cover our lapses. And, as usual, they made it all happen quickly and efficiently, despite all the curveballs that we would throw them.

And we've saved a special tip of the hat to our friends and colleagues at Microsoft Press, several of whom left the company as part of a reorganization while we are in the middle of this project. This book would never have gotten into your hands without the assistance of product manager Rosemary Caperton and director of publishing Anne Hamilton, and we're grateful to have the assistance of Kim Spilker going forward.

Current Book Service

This book is part of our new Current Book Service, which provides content updates for major technology changes and improvements related to Windows 10. As Microsoft releases significant updates, sections of this book will be updated or new sections will be added to address the changes. The updates will be delivered to you via a free Web Edition of this book, which can be accessed with any internet connection at MicrosoftPressStore.com.

Register this book at MicrosoftPressStore.com to receive access to the latest content as an online Web Edition. If you bought this book through MicrosoftPressStore.com, you do not need to register; this book and any updates are already in your account.

How to register your book

If you have not registered your book, follow these steps:

1. Go to *https://microsoftpressstore.com/register*.

2. Sign in or create a new account.

3. Enter the ISBN found on the copyright page of this book.

4. Answer the questions as proof of purchase.

5. The Web Edition will appear under the Digital Purchases tab on your Account page. Click Launch to access your product.

Find out about updates

Sign up for the What's New newsletter at *https://www.microsoftpressstore.com/newsletters/* to receive an email alerting you of the changes each time this book's Web Edition has been updated. The email address you use to sign up for the newsletter must be the same email address used for your MicrosoftPressStore.com account in order to receive the email alerts. If you choose not to sign up, you can periodically check your account at MicrosoftPressStore.com to find out if updates have been made to the Web Edition.

This book will receive periodic updates to address significant software changes for 12 to 18 months following first publication date. After the update period has ended, no more changes will be made to the book, but the final update to the Web Edition will remain available in your account on MicrosoftPressStore.com.

The Web Edition can be used on tablets that use current web browsers. Simply log in to your MicrosoftPressStore.com account and access the Web Edition from the Digital Purchases tab.

Visit *https://www.microsoftpressstore.com/CBS* for more information about the Current Book Service.

Errata, updates, and book support

We've made every effort to ensure the accuracy of this book. You can access updates to this book—in the form of a list of submitted errata and their related corrections—at

https://aka.ms/Win10InsideOut/errata

If you discover an error that is not already listed, please submit it to us at the same page.

If you need additional support, email Microsoft Press Book Support at

mspinput@microsoft.com

Please note that product support for Microsoft software and hardware is not offered through the previous addresses. For help with Microsoft software or hardware, go to

https://support.microsoft.com

Free ebooks from Microsoft Press

From technical overviews to in-depth information on special topics, the free ebooks from Microsoft Press cover a wide range of topics. These ebooks are available in PDF, EPUB, and Mobi for Kindle formats, ready for you to download at

https://aka.ms/mspressfree

Check back often to see what is new!

We want to hear from you

At Microsoft Press, your satisfaction is our top priority, and your feedback our most valuable asset. Please tell us what you think of this book at

https://aka.ms/tellpress

We know you're busy, so we've kept it short with just a few questions. Your answers go directly to the editors at Microsoft Press. (No personal information will be requested.) Thanks in advance for your input!

Stay in touch

Let's keep the conversation going! We're on Twitter: *https://twitter.com/MicrosoftPress*.

What's new in Windows 10

They don't make PCs like they used to.

We don't mean that as a figure of speech, but rather as a statement of fact that helps to explain why Microsoft Windows 10 exists.

Every year, Microsoft's hardware partners sell hundreds of millions of PCs running the latest version of Windows. Many of those PCs still follow traditional form factors: towers designed to fit under a desk, all-in-one PCs that pack the electronics behind a desktop display, and clamshell-shaped laptops with full keyboards and trackpads.

But the fastest-growing group—and by far the most interesting—have diverged from those familiar designs. The defining characteristic of these next-generation Windows devices is a touchscreen. On touchscreen-equipped laptops, you can choose to perform a task by tapping the screen or by using the keyboard and trackpad. In the case of a tablet running Windows 10, the touchscreen offers the only way to navigate between and within apps.

NOTE

The core code that makes up Windows 10 runs on a broad assortment of hardware, ranging from mobile phones and pocket-size tablets to oversize, touch-enabled smart displays mounted on the walls of corporate conference rooms. In this book, we focus primarily on devices designed to perform the functions associated with traditional PCs.

Then there's the most intriguing category of all: so-called *hybrid devices*, equipped with a touchscreen and a keyboard that can be detached or folded out of the way. The touch-enabled displays in Lenovo's perfectly named Yoga series, for example, can rotate 360 degrees, turning a laptop into a tablet with the keyboard behind the display.

On Microsoft's popular Surface Pro series, the Type Cover clicks into place magnetically, allowing the keyboard to flip open for typing and then flip closed to cover the screen. With the Type Cover attached and the adjustable kickstand extended, the Surface Pro looks and acts like a laptop. When you remove the Type Cover and close the kickstand, the Surface Pro becomes a tablet you can control with a finger or a pen.

Windows 10 is the engine that powers all of those next-generation devices as well as the large population of traditional PC designs still in use.

On a touchscreen, you swipe and tap to interact with objects on the screen and use an on-screen keyboard to enter and edit text. For devices with detachable keyboards, Windows 10 includes features designed to ease the transition between the traditional PC way of working and the new Tablet Mode. In the case of PCs that aren't touch-enabled, Windows 10 offers the familiar keyboard-and-mouse experience, with no compromises.

We offer details on how to master the new user experience on traditional PCs and touchscreen-equipped devices in Chapter 3, "Using Windows 10." Our coverage of customization options is in Chapter 4, "Personalizing Windows 10."

The new generation of hardware isn't just defined by peripherals. Modern devices designed for Windows 10 incorporate new features that enhance the security of the startup process. If you've mastered the ins and outs of BIOS setup on a legacy PC, you need to learn how to configure its replacement, the Unified Extensible Firmware Interface (UEFI). That hardware design, in turn, enables an additional security feature called Secure Boot, which protects your Windows 10 PC from an insidious form of malware called *rootkits*. We discuss these features in much greater detail in Chapter 7, "Securing Windows 10 devices."

In this chapter, we offer a high-level overview of Windows 10, with a special emphasis on features that are new or changed since the initial release.

The Windows 10 user experience

How you react to Windows 10 is determined in no small part by how you feel about its predecessor.

With the launch of Windows 8 in October 2012, Microsoft removed the familiar touchstones of the Windows user experience—the Start button and Start menu—and replaced them with a radically redesigned Start screen created for use with touch-enabled devices. It also introduced a new class of touch-friendly apps, delivered through a new Windows Store.

The innovations in Windows 8 were essential for tablets and other touch-oriented devices. But that new design also inspired some passionate and often blunt feedback from Windows users who weren't pleased with the often confusing changes to an operating system they had spent years mastering.

Microsoft reacted to that feedback by reworking the user experience in Windows 10, bringing back the Start menu from Windows 7, combining it with live tiles and other features that were introduced in Windows 8, and tossing in some impressive all-new capabilities. The result should feel significantly more natural for anyone upgrading from Windows 7.

If you skipped Windows 8 and stuck with Windows 7, as we suspect many of our readers did, you have some catching up to do. If you're coming to Windows 10 after learning how to use Windows 8 and Windows 8.1, you have a different kind of adjusting to do.

Ironically, if you skipped Windows 8, you missed several major iterations of the Windows user experience that some people found difficult to use on conventional PCs with a keyboard and mouse. By contrast, the Windows 10 user experience feels very much like a smooth evolution of Windows 7. The Anniversary Update adds a few more changes to the overall user experience without altering its fundamental design.

On a conventional PC, equipped with a keyboard and a mouse or trackpad, Windows 10 starts at the Windows desktop. If you're making the move from Windows 7, this environment, shown in Figure 1-1, should be familiar.

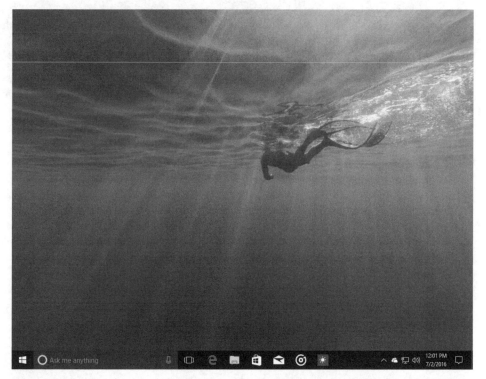

Figure 1-1 After you sign in to Windows 10, you're greeted with the familiar desktop and taskbar.

In the lower left corner is a stylized Windows logo. Clicking that button opens what Windows designers call the *Start experience*, an example of which is shown in Figure 1-2.

Figure 1-2 In Windows 10, Start combines the scrolling list of shortcuts from Windows 7 (left) with live tiles like those from the Windows 8 Start screen (right).

That configuration addresses one of the biggest complaints about Windows 8, which organized programs on a Start screen that occupied the entire display. The new Start experience can be resized to occupy nearly the entire display. If you prefer the Windows 8–style full-screen option, it's available by switching to Tablet Mode, which works even on traditional PCs.

Although the basic arrangement of Start in Windows 10 has remained consistent, the Anniversary Update introduces some subtle but significant changes. The new design incorporates a scrolling All Apps list that is permanently available, while the power button and shortcuts to frequently used folders shrink to a slim column of icons on the left, with a so-called hamburger button at the top that reveals labels for those icons. That change echoes the design of the built-in Windows 10 apps, including Groove Music, Photos, Mail, and Calendar.

About Windows 10 versions

Windows 10 had an eventful first year. In the 12 months after its initial public release on July 29, 2015, the number of active devices running Windows 10 grew to roughly 400 million. That figure was powered partly by new PC sales, but it was helped even more substantially by a yearlong free upgrade offer that applied to nearly every device running Windows 7 or Windows 8.1.

In November 2015, Microsoft released the first feature update and introduced a new versioning scheme. Version 1511 contains a slew of changes, many of them aimed at enterprise customers, including changes to Windows Update that allow administrators to delay installation of updates.

On August 2, 2016, Microsoft publicly released the Windows 10 Anniversary Update, more prosaically known as version 1607. It includes new security features as well as major improvements to some signature features in Windows 10, including Cortana and the Microsoft Edge browser. The Anniversary Update also marks the debut of the Windows Ink platform for pen-equipped devices.

The new versioning system starts with a four-digit release date in the format *yymm*, where the first two digits represent the year and the last two represent the month. Thus, version 1511 is from November 2015, and version 1607 was completed in July 2016. A separate build number keeps track of update versions. The initial release of Windows 10, for example, was build 10240, version 1511 was build 10586, and version 1607 was build 14393. Each monthly cumulative update is appended to that build number.

To see which Windows 10 version is installed on a device, go to Settings > System > About. The example that follows shows a PC running Windows 10 version 1607 with the August 23, 2016, cumulative update (OS Build 14393.82) installed.

The visual design of Windows 10 uses flat icons and a monochromatic color scheme in the notification area and in the Settings app, as shown in Figure 1-3.

Figure 1-3 The visual design and arrangement of the Windows 10 Settings app are characteristic of the overall design of the operating system.

The Settings app debuted in 2012 with Windows 8. Since that time, Microsoft's designers and engineers have been methodically moving user controls from the old Control Panel to their new home. With the Anniversary Update, that work takes a major step forward. Several major groups of options, including the networking controls shown next, have now moved almost entirely to Settings. New iconography appears throughout the app, replacing the generic gear icons used in previous versions.

The pieces of Windows 8 that didn't survive

The Windows 8 user interface was radically different from any previous version of Windows. Maybe too radical, based on the clear feedback Microsoft received from customers.

That feedback inspired a thorough rethinking of the Windows user experience, which in turn led to the design you see in Windows 10. In the process, these signature Windows 8 elements were retired:

- **Charms menu.** This vertical row of five buttons, with the Windows logo key at the center, appeared on the right side of Windows 8 PCs in response to a swipe from the right edge or the mouse moving to the upper right corner of the display. Its five functions have been broken up and moved to the new Start and to Action Center, which now appears where the Charms once did with a swipe from the right or a click of the Notifications icon.

- **Hot corners.** For PCs without a touchscreen, a key navigation principle in Windows 8 involved moving the mouse to a corner and pausing until something happened. Moving the mouse pointer to the upper left corner and then sliding down, for example, exposed a column of thumbnails for switching between running apps. In Windows 10, moving the mouse to a corner does nothing special, and app switching has been moved to the Task View button and its keyboard shortcuts.

- **Start screen.** The Start screen, filled with colorful live tiles, was the first thing a new Windows 8 user saw. Over time, with Windows 8.1 and a subsequent update, the Start screen was modified to make it less jarring. In Windows 10, the desktop is the default first step, and live tiles appear as part of Start. If you miss the Windows 8–style Start screen, you can restore the experience by configuring Start to run in a full screen or by switching to Tablet Mode.

Our experience suggests the learning curve for Windows 10 is not that steep. But it's ironic that one of the biggest challenges in making the transition from Windows 8 is unlearning these now-missing elements.

Windows 10 isn't just an evolution of features you already knew, however; you'll also find plenty of new capabilities to explore.

Cortana, for example, is the Windows 10 "intelligent personal assistant," who takes over the search box if you give her permission and then delivers news headlines, reminders, and answers based on your schedule and your interests. Which interests exactly? That's under your control, using the Notebook shown in Figure 1-4 to tailor your preferences. Cortana recognizes your voice and can also be, in turn, a calculator, package tracker, translator, and source of real-time sports updates, to list just a few skills from Cortana's resume.

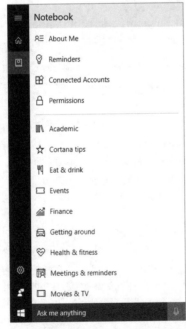

Figure 1-4 With Cortana enabled, clicking in the search box displays personalized reminders and alerts based on settings you specify in the Cortana Notebook.

➤ We explain how to use and customize this feature in Chapter 9, "Cortana and the web."

Another major addition, new in Windows 10 and significantly refined as part of the Anniversary Update, is Action Center. This pane appears on the right side when you swipe in from the right on a touchscreen or click the Notifications icon, which appears to the right of the system clock. A badge over that icon shows how many new notifications are available. In addition, you can now tweak notification settings on an app-by-app basis, with more intelligent grouping options. The top of the pane contains notifications from apps (new messages, weather alerts, alarms, reminders), while the bottom contains handy buttons for performing common tasks, as shown in Figure 1-5.

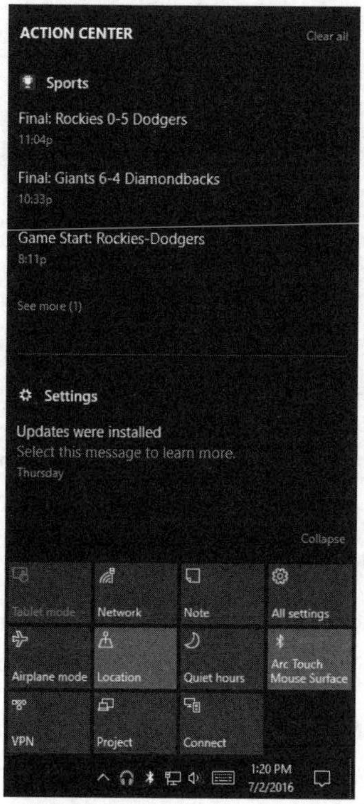

Figure 1-5 These buttons, which appear beneath notifications in Action Center, allow quick access to system settings.

The new universal apps for Windows 10 are delivered through the Windows Store, just as their predecessors in Windows 8 were, but that's where the resemblance ends. In Windows 10, these so-called *modern apps* can work in resizable windows alongside conventional Windows desktop applications.

On a tablet, for example, the editing capabilities in the new Photos app work best in full screen. On a large desktop display (or two), the full-screen view is overkill and the app is perfectly usable in a window, as shown in Figure 1-6.

Figure 1-6 The editing controls in the universal Photos app are designed so that they work well in a resizable window on desktop PCs with a large display, a keyboard, and a mouse.

For a more thorough look at how modern apps work, see Chapter 8, "Using and managing apps and desktop programs."

Fundamental changes in core features

If you're among the substantial population that has stuck with Windows 7 for the past few years, avoiding Windows 8 and waiting for Windows 10 to mature, you missed some interesting and deep-seated changes to some core features in Windows. We go into detail about three of those features in this book.

- **File Explorer.** It's no longer called Windows Explorer; beginning with Windows 8, the name officially changed to File Explorer. The addition of a Microsoft Office–style ribbon, shown in Figure 1-7, makes a number of formerly obscure operations more discoverable and dramatically improves search capabilities by adding a Search Tools tab when you click in the search box. Windows 10 adds a Quick Access region in the navigation pane. We cover File Explorer in exhaustive detail in Chapter 12, "Managing files on PCs and in the cloud."

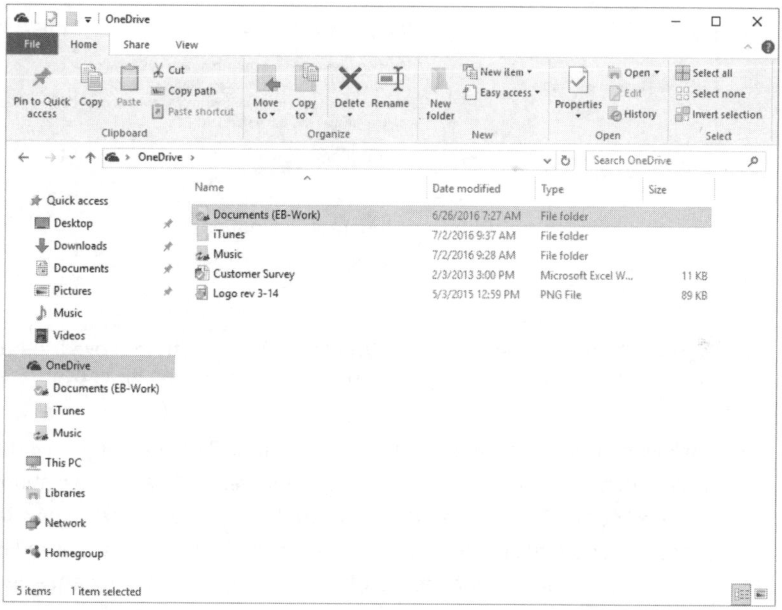

Figure 1-7 For anyone upgrading from Windows 7, File Explorer has an all-new ribbon, and OneDrive is included by default in the navigation pane.

- **Backup and recovery.** If you ever had to reinstall an older version of Windows, you know how tedious and time-consuming the process can be. Windows 8 introduced "push-button reset" options that automate the process of a clean install, with the option to keep your data or wipe it clean. Windows 10 refines those options impressively, as we explain in Chapter 16, "Backup, restore, and recovery." It also adds the ability to undo a Windows 10 feature update and restore a previous build, as shown in Figure 1-8.

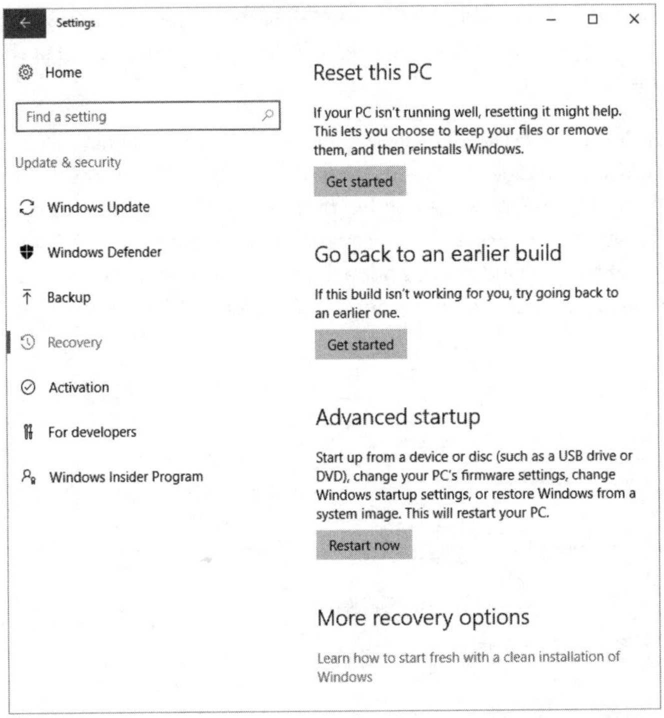

Figure 1-8 The Recovery options in Windows 10 are greatly improved compared with the Windows 8.1 equivalents, using less disk space and requiring fewer post-reset updates.

- **Task Manager.** This is another familiar Windows 7 utility that received a major makeover in Windows 8. Those same fundamental improvements (and a few minor tweaks) are visible in Windows 10: more information about running processes, a new tab for managing processes, and detailed performance information, as shown in Figure 1-9. For an in-depth look at the new Task Manager, see Chapter 15, "System maintenance and performance."

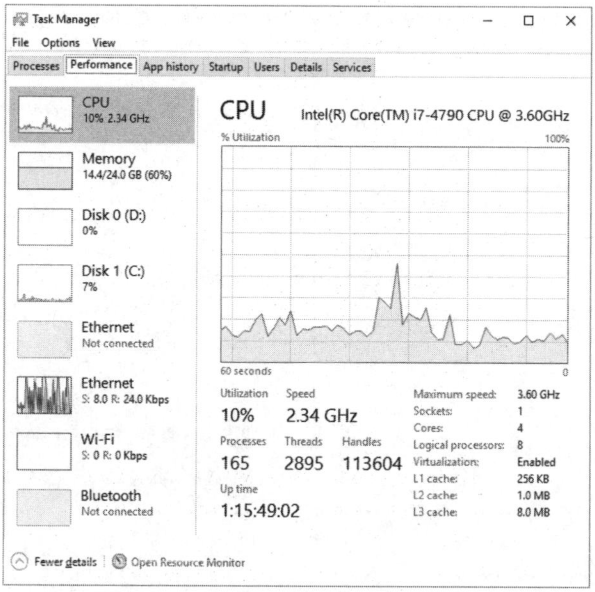

Figure 1-9 The Task Manager Performance tab in Windows 10 offers more information, more clearly organized, than its Windows 7 predecessor.

Windows 10, the web, and cloud services

Internet Explorer has been a part of Windows for more than two decades. In Windows 10, Internet Explorer is included, but it's no longer the default web browser. Instead, that honor goes to a new browser, Microsoft Edge.

Microsoft Edge is touch friendly, with a minimal list of controls. Among its unique features is a Reading View button that reformats and rearranges the text of a cluttered webpage to make a less distracting reading experience. You can see this feature in action in Figure 1-10, with side-by-side Microsoft Edge windows displaying the same page in its original view (left) and in reading view (right).

Microsoft Edge uses a new rendering engine designed with interoperability as a much higher priority than backward compatibility. Internet Explorer is still available for situations where its unique features are essential. We explain the differences between Internet Explorer and Microsoft Edge, as well as how to configure each one to match your preferences, in Chapter 9.

The version of Microsoft Edge that was included with the initial release of Windows 10 was functional but lacked features that most experienced Windows users expect in a web browser. After a year's worth of development, Microsoft Edge has become more polished and powerful. The major update to Microsoft Edge included as part of the Windows 10 Anniversary Update adds support for browser extensions, which are delivered through the Store. Figure 1-11 shows some of those extensions in use.

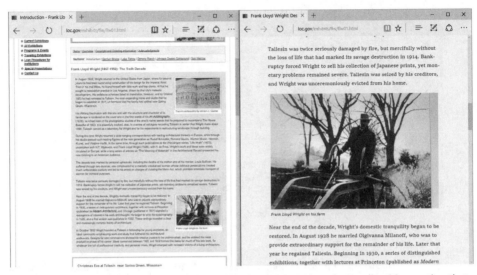

Figure 1-10 The Microsoft Edge web browser has simple controls and a Reading View option that reformats text and removes clutter from webpages.

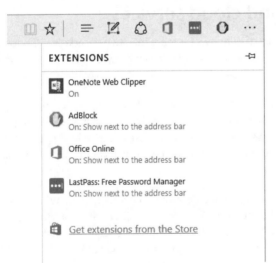

Figure 1-11 Effective with the Windows 10 Anniversary Update, the Microsoft Edge browser supports extensions like the four shown here, which add features and connect to other apps and services.

Of course, a web browser isn't the only way to connect to shared resources online. When you sign in using a Microsoft account, Windows 10 automatically connects to shared files in the OneDrive service. You can also connect to business-class services using Office 365 and Azure Active Directory.

The OneDrive synchronization client installed with Windows 10 supports connections to cloud storage from the consumer version of OneDrive and OneDrive for Business, with synced files and folders available in File Explorer. A universal OneDrive app, released at the same time as the Anniversary Update, offers an alternative view that shows all cloud-based files, including those not synced locally.

For more information about how OneDrive and Windows 10 work together, see Chapter 12.

Working and playing with Windows 10

If you're looking for familiar names in the list of apps included with Windows 10, you'll find plenty of old favorites—Windows Media Player, Notepad, and Paint, for example.

But much more interesting are the new universal apps that are designed to work on any device running Windows 10. Because these apps are updated automatically via the Windows Store, they can incorporate new features and fix bugs without requiring a separate installation. You also can use these apps to access files stored in the cloud and to sync settings and data between Windows 10 devices without having to reconfigure accounts or import data.

Windows 10 includes a lengthy list of productivity, entertainment, and news apps as part of a default installation. These apps have matured dramatically since the initial release of Windows 10, thanks in part to improvements in the underlying Universal Windows Platform. (You'll find more details about universal apps and how they differ from legacy desktop programs in Chapter 8.)

Chief among the productivity apps are Mail and Calendar, which work with various internet services, including Microsoft's Outlook.com and Office 365 services as well as Google's Gmail and Apple's iCloud. Figure 1-12 shows a month of appointments in the Calendar app.

A universal OneNote app is installed with Windows 10. Other Microsoft Office apps are available in the Windows Store, including touch-friendly versions of Word, Excel, and PowerPoint that are included as part of a standard installation in some editions of Windows 10.

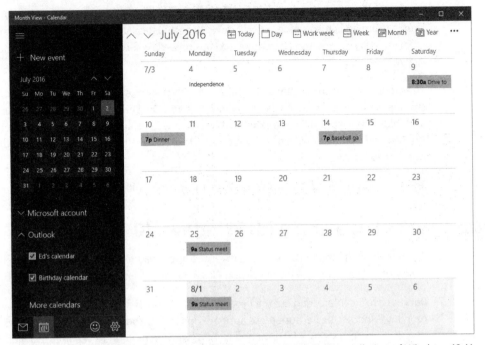

Figure 1-12 The Calendar app, shown here, is included with a default installation of Windows 10. You can switch to the companion Mail app with a click of the icon in the lower left corner.

For more information about work-oriented apps and utilities in Windows 10, see Chapter 10, "Productivity and communication tools."

Windows 10 is also a solid platform for entertainment apps, with connections to digital music and video services that also work on Xbox consoles and mobile devices. With the Groove Music app for Windows 10, shown in Figure 1-13, you can stream or download tracks and albums from your personal music collection, stored on a local drive or in the cloud, using OneDrive.

Another hidden gem among the new entertainment features in Windows 10 is built-in support for the Miracast standard (sometimes called screen mirroring), which allows you to send a video signal to a larger screen. Miracast support is built in to some newer TVs and Blu-ray players, and is also available using a device that plugs in to an HDMI input. Using Miracast, you can tune in to an online video clip and project it to the big screen, with full support for surround sound. The Anniversary Update expands the capabilities of this feature significantly, adding the option to project to another Windows 10 PC.

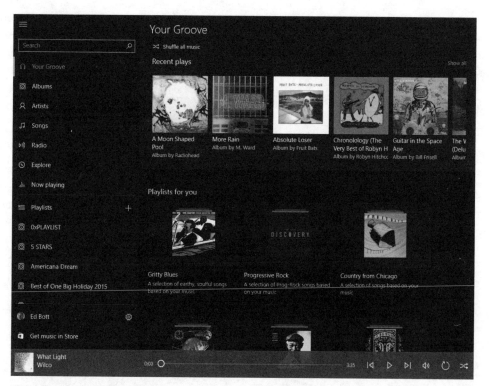

Figure 1-13 Using the Windows 10 Music app, you can connect via the cloud to a music collection stored in OneDrive's Music folder.

More updates, more often

For decades, the cadence of Windows went something like this: Roughly every three years, a new version of Windows came out. New PCs included the latest Windows version; owners of existing PCs could choose to pay for an upgrade to the new Windows version (or choose not to upgrade). The cycle began anew with the next new Windows version.

That's all history now.

Before the initial release of Windows 10, Microsoft declared its intention to treat Windows as a service. In the first year after that release, the first wave of Windows 10 customers had a chance to see "Windows as a service" in action, with two major feature updates that in earlier days would have qualified as new Windows versions.

Any device running Windows 10 Home, Pro, Enterprise, or Education is eligible for feature updates. (The sole exception is the Long Term Servicing Branch of Windows 10 Enterprise, which we discuss in "Servicing options for Windows" in Chapter 21, "Managing Windows 10 in business.") Instead of waiting two or three years to be included in a new Windows version or a service pack, new features are delivered automatically, through Windows Update. That's a major change from previous Windows versions, which delivered only security and reliability updates through these Microsoft-managed channels.

The new update process also allows Windows users to choose how soon they want to receive those updates.

Previously, Microsoft developed and tested new Windows features privately, occasionally offering the public an advance look in the form of preview versions before releasing them publicly.

Beginning with Windows 10, those preview releases are built into the development cycle. As new features make their way into Windows, they're delivered to different "flights," starting with internal testers in Microsoft's engineering group, and then working out to customers who have opted to receive preview releases. Each new flight reaches a larger number of people, with fixes for bugs discovered in previous flights incorporated into later ones. Figure 1-14 shows, conceptually, how the flight process works.

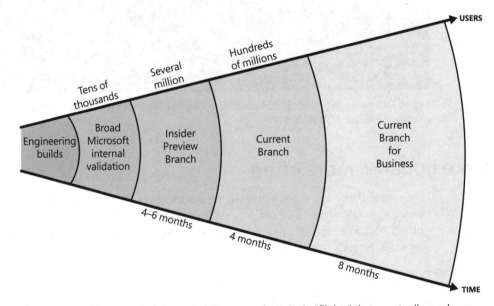

Figure 1-14 For Windows 10, Microsoft delivers new features in "flights" that eventually reach consumers in the Current Branch.

The first public release of a feature update, installed by PC manufacturers and available to the general public through Windows Update, goes to the Current Branch. That release represents program code that has been thoroughly tested as part of the preview cycle and corresponds to what have traditionally been General Availability releases of new Windows versions or service packs.

IT managers and administrators on enterprise networks can choose a more cautious approach to feature updates by configuring PCs under their management to receive feature updates after they're released to the Current Branch for Business, typically about four months after an update has gone to the Current Branch.

For earlier access to new Windows 10 feature updates, anyone can sign up for the Windows Insider Program at *https://insider.windows.com*. This program, which started in October 2014, offers its members (who are referred to as *Windows Insiders*) full access to preview releases of Windows 10, along with frequent updates. In exchange, Microsoft's developers receive unprecedented levels of feedback that shape the development effort in real time. That feedback comes from automated data collection (known as *telemetry*) and a Feedback app, shown in Figure 1-15, which is installed with every release, including those that go to the Current Branch.

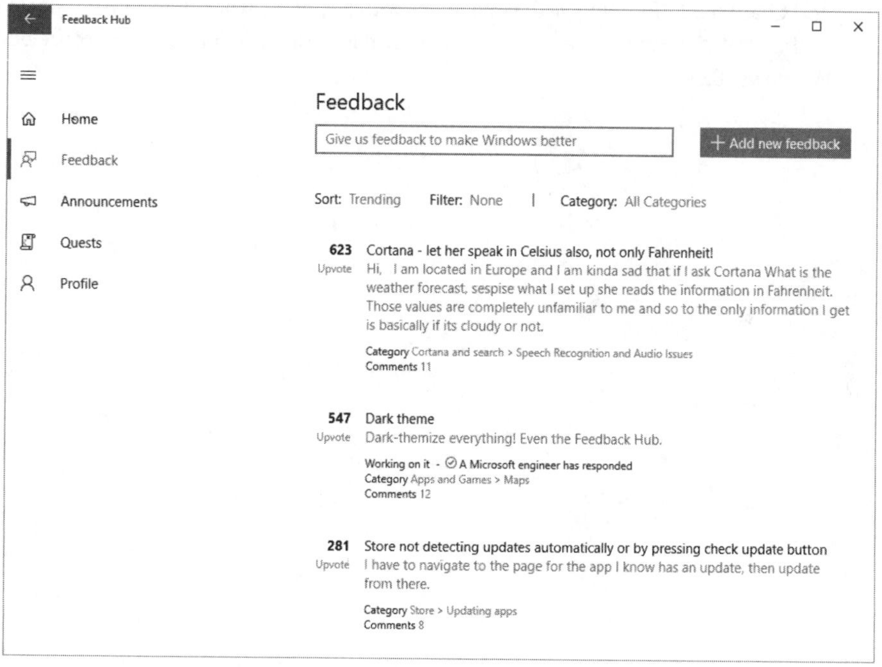

Figure 1-15 This Windows Feedback app allows anyone using Windows 10 to report bugs and offer suggestions directly to Microsoft.

➤ For more details on how the Windows Insider Program works, see Chapter 23, "What's next for Windows 10?"

CHAPTER 1

Windows 10 for IT pros and experts

The intended scope of this book covers consumers and small businesses using Windows 10. We would need hundreds of additional pages to cover the concerns of IT pros and network administrators responsible for integrating Windows 10 devices into Windows domains using Active Directory.

But if you fall into the "IT pro" classification, we haven't completely forgotten about you. In particular, we suggest you look at Part 4, "Windows 10 for experts and IT pros," where we have assembled information of special interest to power users and administrators.

In those chapters, you'll find information on arcane but incredibly useful topics such as editing the Windows registry, troubleshooting performance-related issues, and automating routine tasks.

For those who really want to polish their expert skills, we especially recommend Chapter 21 and Chapter 22, "Running virtual machines with Hyper-V," which offers in-depth coverage of the powerful Hyper-V virtualization platform included with Pro and Enterprise editions of Windows 10.

Installing, configuring, and deploying Windows 10

How do you get to Microsoft Windows 10? That depends on where you start.

On new devices that come with Windows 10 already installed, all you need to do is press the power button. On a PC that's currently running Windows 7 or Windows 8.1, you have multiple options for upgrading. If you're sitting in front of a PC that has no operating system installed, your only choice is to boot from installation media and perform a clean install.

Among some PC traditionalists, it's a badge of honor to wipe a newly purchased PC clean and then set up Windows from scratch. Even if you're not so fastidious, a clean install is sometimes unavoidable: It's the only option for PCs you build yourself and for virtual machines, and it's sometimes the fastest way to get back up and running after a disk failure.

Beyond the mechanics of installation, there are also the sometimes confusing details of licensing and activation. Adding an extra complication to that topic is the free upgrade offer Microsoft made available for the first year after Windows 10 debuted. (That offer ended on July 29, 2016, one year after the initial release of Windows 10.) PCs upgraded during that period acquired a digital license (sometimes referred to as a *digital entitlement*) for a specific edition of Windows 10. Knowing which license is attached to a particular PC is essential for choosing the right upgrade path.

The same Windows 10 setup program is used for both upgrades and clean installs. For upgrades, the installer is streamlined, offering a minimum of options. Booting from Windows 10 installation media offers a much more complete set of options: choosing a specific physical disk for use in dual-boot (or multi-boot) scenarios, creating and formatting partitions, and setting up unattended installations, for example.

In this chapter, we cover both options. We don't include step-by-step instructions to document every possible upgrade or clean installation scenario. Given the nearly infinite number of combinations of PC hardware, providing comprehensive instructions would be impossible. And besides, we're confident our readers can make their way through a setup wizard without handholding.

Instead, this chapter concentrates on the big picture, starting with licensing and activation details, and then breaking each type of Windows setup into its major steps and explaining what happens (and what can go wrong) in each one. We finish with a checklist to run through after completing an upgrade or clean install.

But first, some suggestions on how to make the setup process as smooth as possible.

Before you start

If you're lucky, your Windows 10 upgrade or clean install will be uneventful and the results will be trouble free. You can increase the odds of this ideal outcome by taking some common-sense precautions first.

At the top of this list is checking the hardware on which you plan to install Windows 10 to confirm that it meets the minimum requirements (note that this list is unchanged from the system requirements for Windows 7):

- Processor: 1 gigahertz (GHz) or faster

- RAM: 1 gigabyte (GB) (32-bit) or 2 GB (64-bit)

- Free disk space (system drive): 16 GB

- Graphics card: Microsoft DirectX 9 graphics device with WDDM driver

> ### NOTE
> The free disk space requirement varies, and Microsoft is continuing to work on improving upgrade scenarios for low disk space. On devices with small amounts of built-in storage, you might be able to upgrade with as little as 10 free gigabytes. As you approach that threshold, however, you might find that setup fails in unpredictable ways. If you're stuck, check the Microsoft Community forums (*http://answers.microsoft.com*) to see whether there's a workaround for your situation.

Those are fairly modest requirements, and virtually every PC sold in the past six years with Windows 7 or a later version preinstalled should qualify. Note that some older devices that are at or near the minimum for one or more of these hardware components might not perform acceptably.

For online upgrades to Windows 10, you also need internet access. (In fact, reliable internet access is a prerequisite for most tasks we describe in this book.) A Microsoft account is recommended but is not required.

Inside OUT

RIP, Windows Media Center

One of the signature features of Windows for many years has been Windows Media Center. This feature, which debuted with headline billing in a special edition of Windows XP in 2002, enabled a so-called 10-foot interface for using Windows PCs as an entertainment hub in a living room. Media Center grew steadily from its original design, adding support for high-definition TV and digital cable tuners, to become the centerpiece of the Windows 7 Home Premium, Professional, and Ultimate editions.

After Windows 7 launched, the Windows Media Center team was disbanded and development of the feature ceased. In Windows 8 and 8.1, the Media Center functionality was available as an extra-cost add-on, but it was a simple port of the Windows 7 version, with no new features.

With Windows 10, Windows Media Center is officially retired. When you run Windows 10 Setup to upgrade a PC that has the Windows Media Center feature enabled, it will be uninstalled, and the feature will be completely unavailable after the upgrade is complete. There's no registry magic or secret to enable the feature on Windows 10, either. If Media Center is a make-or-break feature for you, avoid the Windows 10 upgrade on that PC.

Check for potential compatibility problems

In broad terms, any device that is already running Windows 8.1 should be compatible with Windows 10, as should any apps or device drivers installed on that device. There are, however, exceptions to this rule—some of them minor, others more serious. Your likelihood of encountering (usually minor) compatibility issues goes up when upgrading Windows 7 (with Service Pack 1).

NOTE

Throughout this book, we refer to Windows 8.1 and not to Windows 8. That's deliberate. Windows 8 is no longer a supported operating system, and we assume most of our readers long ago upgraded to Windows 8.1. If you find yourself in front of a PC running Windows 8, you can upgrade directly to Windows 10—there's no need to upgrade to Windows 8.1.

The Windows 10 setup program includes a compatibility checker that alerts you to any potential compatibility issues before performing the actual installation. We describe its workings in the section, "Upgrading to Windows 10."

Before you run the setup program, though, it's worth taking inventory of your critical apps and devices and checking with the developer or manufacturer to confirm that those products are supported under Windows 10. Pay special attention to any app or device originally designed and developed before the release of Windows 7 in 2009.

Inside OUT

Use dynamic updates

When you upgrade an existing Windows version using Windows Update, the setup program automatically checks for and downloads dynamic updates. When you start the upgrade process from installation media, you're asked whether you want to get the latest updates. If you have an active internet connection, be sure to take advantage of this option.

Dynamic updates can include any or all of the following: critical updates to the setup program itself; improved or new versions of boot-critical drivers for storage, display, and network hardware detected on your system; and compatibility updates (also known as *shims*) for programs you're currently running. Rolling these updates in at the beginning of the process increases the likelihood that your Windows 10 upgrade will be successful. After completing installation, you'll still need to connect to Windows Update to check for critical updates for Windows and the most recent drivers for detected hardware.

Back up your data and settings

Having an up-to-date backup of important files is, of course, good advice for any time. But it's especially important when you're upgrading an operating system.

The simplest way to back up files is to sync them to the cloud. OneDrive sync capabilities are built in to Windows 8.1; a sync utility for Windows 7 is available for download from *https://onedrive.com/download*. Move or copy your files into the OneDrive folder and wait for them to be fully synchronized before proceeding.

With large file collections or slow internet connections—or if you just prefer not putting your files in cloud storage—a sufficiently large USB flash drive or an external hard drive makes a perfectly good target for a local backup. If you're upgrading from Windows 7, you can use its built-in backup program; individual files and folders from those backups can be restored in Windows 10 by using the helpfully labeled Backup And Restore (Windows 7) option in Control Panel. For a complete look at your options, see Chapter 16, "Backup, restore, and recovery."

If you're upgrading from Windows 8.1 and you signed in with a Microsoft account, your personalized settings are already being synced to OneDrive. From Windows 7, there's no easy way to back up those settings. Although you can find third-party utilities that promise to accomplish this task, it's probably faster (and less risky) to re-create that handful of settings than it is to mess with transfer utilities.

Build (or buy) installation media

For every Windows 10 installation scenario, you need access to installation media. To do a clean install on modern hardware, the most common choice is a bootable USB flash drive or, on older hardware, a bootable DVD. For upgrades and reinstallations, you can use the same physical media or download an ISO file, which you can then mount directly or use to create your own installation media.

NOTE

The ISO name is ancient, by modern computing standards, dating back to the mid-1980s. And, strictly speaking, it's also meaningless. The name is shorthand for the file system originally used with CD-ROM media, which was designated ISO 9660 by the standards-setting body that published it. These days, an ISO image file is just as likely to use the UDF file system (ISO/IEC 13346), which is commonly found on larger-capacity optical media such as DVDs and Blu-ray Discs.

Physical copies of Windows 10 are available in packages in which the installer is on a bootable USB flash drive or a DVD. If you don't have one of those, you can use Microsoft's Media Creation Tool, which downloads the files capable of installing Home or Pro editions and then allows you to create a bootable USB flash drive or save the resulting file in ISO format.

NOTE

IT pros, developers, and service providers with access to subscription programs such as MSDN or the Microsoft Partner Program can download ISO files in a variety of configurations after signing in to the online portal for the respective service. Volume License customers will find ISO files for Pro and Enterprise editions at the Volume Licensing Service Center.

No subscription is required to download installation media in ISO format through the Microsoft Tech Bench Upgrade Program. Full documentation can be found at *https://www.microsoft.com/software-download/techbench*.

The Media Creation Tool, MediaCreationTool.exe, is actually a bootstrap version of the Windows 10 Setup program and shares its look and feel. It's a small file (less than 20 MB in size) that takes only seconds to download from *https://www.microsoft.com/software-download/windows10*. After running the tool and accepting a license agreement, you should see a screen that offers the option to create installation media for another PC. Select that option to reach the step shown in Figure 2-1.

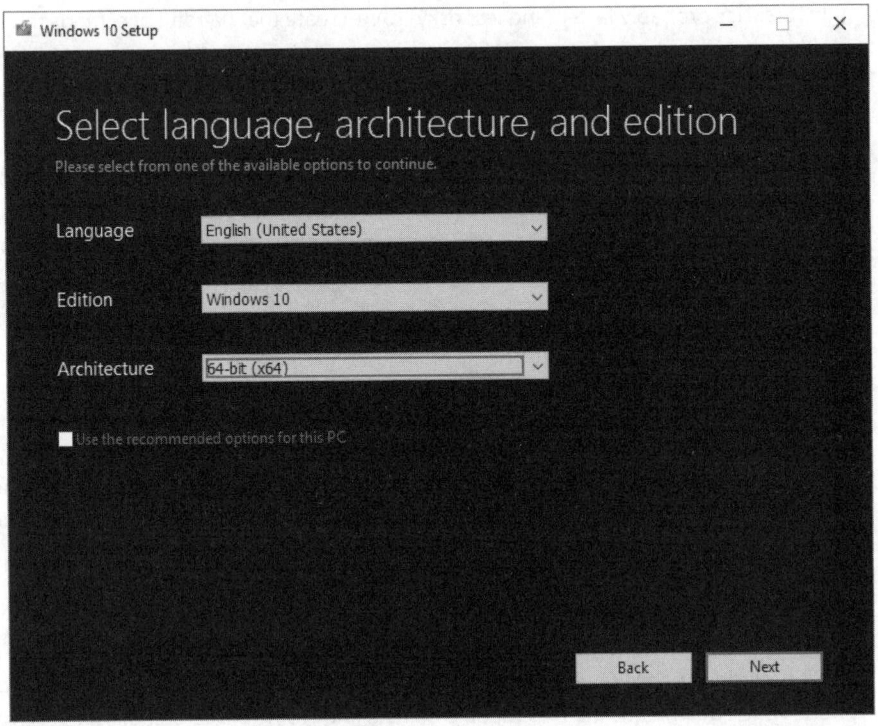

Figure 2-1 Clear the small check box beneath these three options to make additional options available for each.

By default, the Use The Recommended Options For This PC check box is selected, and the entries for Language, Architecture, and Edition match the current configuration. If you want to change any of those choices, clear the check box.

Choosing the correct installer involves finding the specific combination of three factors that match your needs:

- **Language.** Windows 10 is available in a large number of languages—more than 100, covering nearly 200 countries and regions. Choose the base language that's appropriate for your installation. You can add language interface packs to translate text that's displayed in commonly used wizards, dialog boxes, menus, and other items in the user interface; however, you can't change the parent language except by reinstalling Windows using an edition built for that language.

- **Edition.** For installing or upgrading a desktop PC, laptop, or hybrid device, select Windows 10 from this menu in the Media Creation Tool; you use this option to install either Windows 10 Home or Windows 10 Pro. (The Windows 10 Home Single Language edition generally is found only in emerging markets; Windows 10 N is a version created to fulfill an antitrust settlement that lacks some media features. We assume most of our readers have no need for either of these editions. Large organizations with volume license contracts can install Windows 10 Enterprise or Education as an upgrade. We describe the differences between the editions in Appendix A, "Windows 10 editions at a glance."

- **Architecture.** Windows 10 is available in 32-bit and 64-bit distributions. Most modern CPUs support either version, and your preference should be for the 64-bit version. In general, 32-bit versions of Windows are appropriate for systems with 2 GB (or less) of RAM, with no option to add memory. Choose a 64-bit version if your system includes 4 GB or more of memory or if you rely on one or more programs that are available only in 64-bit editions. (And note that all your 32-bit programs, including new and old versions of Microsoft Office, will work fine on a 64-bit copy of Windows, so you needn't have any fears in that regard.) If you clear the Use The Recommended Updates For This PC check box in the Media Creation Tool, you can choose Both. That downloads a larger ISO file capable of installing either architecture.

If your goal is to purchase a physical or electronic copy of Windows for installation on a new PC or in a virtual machine, the intricacies of Windows licensing require several additional decisions beyond those we just described.

You can choose from the following license types:

- **Full.** A full license is sold directly to consumers as an electronic distribution or a packaged product. With a full license, Windows can be installed on a computer that was not sold with Windows originally, or it can be used as an upgrade. A full license can be transferred to a different computer as long as the underlying copy of Windows is no longer being used in the original location.

- **OEM.** An OEM (original equipment manufacturer) license is one that's included with a new computer. This license is locked to the computer on which it's installed and cannot be transferred to a new computer. OEM System Builder packages are intended for use by small PC makers but are often used by consumers and hobbyists in place of a more expensive full license. The system builder is required to provide support for OEM Windows along with the device on which it is installed.

- **Volume.** Volume licenses are sold in bulk to corporate, government, nonprofit, and educational customers and are typically deployed by using enterprise-management tools. A volume license is available as an upgrade only.

You need a full license to install Windows in a virtual machine, on a Mac or other computer that does not come with Windows preinstalled, or in a dual-boot or multi-boot setup. That condition can be satisfied with a full (retail or OEM) license of Windows 10 or a full license for an earlier Windows version that was upgraded to Windows 10 during the first-year free-upgrade offer.

NOTE

You need to understand that the legal and contractual restrictions imposed by license agreements are completely independent of technical restrictions related to installation. If you upgrade a system to Windows 10 from Windows 7 and then the system's hard disk fails, you can perform a clean install of Windows 10 and still be properly licensed. Conversely, it's technically possible to install and activate Windows on a computer that doesn't have an underlying license, but that successful activation doesn't translate to a license. This distinction is especially crucial for businesses (even small ones) that could be the target of a software audit to verify proper licensing.

If you already have an ISO file and a PC running Windows 10, you can create your own installation media with ease.

You can't simply copy installation files to a flash drive and use it to perform a clean install. First, you have to make the disk bootable. When creating a bootable drive, you need to consider two factors:

- **Partitioning scheme: MBR or GPT?** You can use either scheme with a Unified Extensible Firmware Interface (UEFI) system; older BIOS-based systems might be able to recognize only MBR partitions. (For an explanation of the difference, see Chapter 14, "Managing disks and drives.")

- **Disk format: NTFS or FAT32?** If you plan to install Windows on a modern UEFI-based system (such as the Microsoft Surface Pro and Surface Book families), the boot files *must* reside on a FAT32 partition. If the drive is formatted using another file system, the PC will not recognize the device as bootable.

One of the simplest ways to create a bootable install drive is to use the built-in Recovery Media Creator tool, RecoveryDrive.exe. Just as in previous Windows versions, this tool is able to create a bootable drive that includes the recovery partition provided by the OEM. If you perform a clean install or remove that recovery partition for space purposes, the recovery drive can be used only for simple repair operations.

To run the tool, search for the Create A Recovery Drive option in Control Panel or Settings. Figure 2-2 shows this tool in operation.

If you downloaded an ISO file containing the Windows installation files, you can burn that file to a DVD (assuming the target system has an optical drive from which it can start). Or you can create a blank recovery drive using Windows 8.1 or Windows 10, skipping the option to copy system files to the drive; then double-click the ISO file to mount it as a virtual DVD. Use File Explorer to drag all files and folders from the virtual DVD to the USB recovery drive.

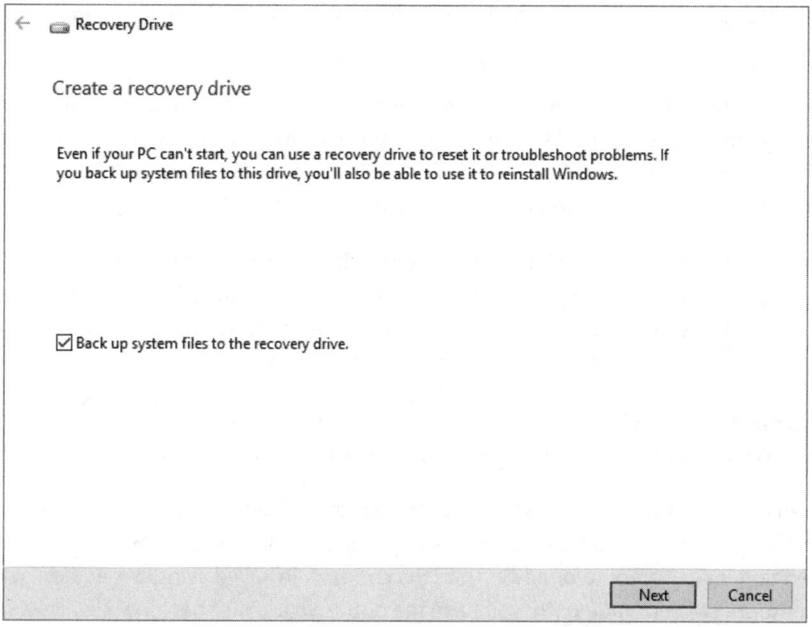

Figure 2-2 Choose the option to back up system files if you want to create a recovery drive using a Windows 10 image preinstalled by an OEM that you can use to reset the current system.

NOTE

Although it's not necessary for most purposes involving Windows 10, some people and organizations want maximum flexibility in creating installable media. If that description fits you, we recommend the free, open source utility Rufus, available at *https://rufus. akeo.ie/*. It allows precise control over partitioning, formatting, and copying installation files to a USB flash drive.

Choose your installation method

Microsoft strongly encourages in-place upgrades for anyone running Windows 7 (with Service Pack 1) or Windows 8.1. An upgrade retains all your data files, installed programs, and settings, at the risk of creating some compatibility issues. But you also have options when you perform an upgrade by starting Windows Setup from within an earlier Windows version. These options allow you to start from scratch, with or without your personal data files; you need to reinstall your programs and re-create or transfer settings from another system.

You need to boot from the Windows 10 media and choose a custom installation if either of the following conditions is true:

- **You need to adjust the layout of the system disk.** The Windows 10 installation program includes disk-management tools you can use to create, delete, format, and extend (but not shrink) partitions on hard disks installed in your computer. Knowing how these tools work can save you a significant amount of time when setting up Windows.

- **You want to install Windows 10 alongside another operating system.** If you want to set up a multi-boot system, you need to understand how different startup files work so that you can manage your startup options effectively. We discuss this option later in this chapter, in the section "Configuring a multi-boot system."

If the system on which you plan to install Windows 10 is already running Windows 7, Windows 8.1, or Windows 10, you can start the setup program from within Windows.

When running setup from within Windows, you can upgrade from Windows 7 or Windows 8.1, transferring settings and desktop programs to the new installation—provided that the Windows 10 edition is equivalent to or newer than the currently installed Windows edition. If you attempt an unsupported upgrade path, you have the option to transfer personal files only. Table 2-1 shows the supported upgrade paths.

Table 2-1 Supported Upgrade Paths by Edition

Current version	Supported upgrade
Windows 7 Starter, Home Basic, Home Premium	Windows 10 Home
Windows 7 Professional, Ultimate	Windows 10 Pro
Windows 8.1	Windows 10 Home
Windows 8.1 Pro, Windows 8.1 Pro for Students	Windows 10 Pro
Windows Phone 8.1	Windows 10 Mobile

Starting Setup from within Windows does not offer the option to perform a custom install. However, performing an upgrade and choosing Nothing from the list of what you want to keep has the same effect as performing a clean install. After Windows 10 is installed, the Reset option is the preferred way to accomplish the task of repairing a Windows installation that isn't working properly.

Note that the installation media must match the architecture of the installed Windows version. You cannot run the 64-bit setup program on a PC running a 32-bit version of Windows, or vice versa. In addition, you cannot make any changes to the layout of a disk when running Setup from within Windows; you must use existing partitions, and Setup will not recognize or use unallocated space on an attached hard drive.

If you boot from the Windows 10 installation media, you can delete existing partitions, create new partitions from free space, extend an existing disk partition to unallocated space, or designate a block of unallocated space as the setup location. (We describe these actions later in this chapter.) After booting from the Windows installation media, you cannot upgrade an existing Windows installation. Your only option is a custom install.

Using either setup option, you can install Windows 10 on the same volume as an existing Windows version. (You'll find step-by-step instructions in "Performing a clean install" later in this chapter.)

Later in this chapter, we explain the best ways to perform a Windows 10 upgrade or a clean install. But first, a brief discussion of a complex and confusing topic: Windows licensing and activation.

Windows licensing and activation

For more than a dozen years, desktop versions of Windows have included a set of anti-piracy and anti-tampering features. In the past, Microsoft has used different names for these capabilities: Windows Activation Technologies and Windows Genuine Advantage, for example. In Windows 10, these features are collectively referred to as the *Software Protection Platform*.

The various checks and challenges in Windows 10, in essence, are enforcement mechanisms for the Windows 10 license agreement, which is displayed during the process of installing or deploying the operating system. (You must provide your consent to complete setup.) We're not lawyers, so we won't attempt to interpret the terms of this legal document. We do recommend you read the license agreement, which is written in relatively plain language compared to many such documents we've read through the years. In this section, we explain how the activation and validation mechanisms in Windows 10 affect your use of the operating system.

Product activation happens shortly after you sign in on a new PC running Windows 10. Typically, this involves a brief communication between your PC and Microsoft's licensing servers. If everything checks out, your copy of Windows is activated silently, and you never have to deal with product keys or activation prompts.

The activation process is completely anonymous and does not require that you divulge any personal information. If you choose to register your copy of Windows 10, this is a completely separate (and optional) task.

After you successfully activate your copy of Windows 10, you're still subject to periodic anti-piracy checks from Microsoft. This process, called *validation*, verifies that your copy of Windows has not been tampered with to bypass activation. It also allows Microsoft to revoke the activation for a computer when it determines after the fact that the activation was the result of product tampering or that a product key was stolen or used in violation of a volume licensing agreement.

Validation takes two forms: an internal tool that regularly checks licensing and activation files to determine that they haven't been tampered with and an online tool that restricts access to some downloads and updates.

If your system fails validation, your computer continues to work, but you'll see some differences: personalization options are unavailable, an "activate now" reminder on a black desktop background tells you your copy of Windows is "Not Genuine," and an Activate Now dialog box appears periodically. In addition, your access to Windows Update is somewhat restricted; you won't be able to download optional updates, new drivers, or certain other programs from the Microsoft Download Center until your system passes the validation check.

NOTE

A device that has failed Windows validation can still be used. All Windows functions (with the exception of personalization options) work normally, all your data files are accessible, and all your programs work as expected. The nagging reminders are intended to strongly encourage you to resolve the underlying issue. Some forms of malware can damage system files in a way that resembles tampering with activation files. Another common cause of activation problems is a lazy or dishonest repair technician who installs a stolen or "cracked" copy of Windows instead of using your original licensed copy.

Links in the Windows Activation messages lead to online support tools, where you might be able to identify and repair the issue that's affecting your system. This wiki article at Microsoft's Answers forum also offers troubleshooting advice: *https://bit.ly/trouble-shoot-activation*. Finally, Microsoft offers free support for activation issues via online forums and by telephone.

The activation mechanism is designed to enforce license restrictions by preventing the most common form of software piracy: casual copying. Typically, a Windows 10 license entitles you to install the operating system software on a single computer. (You can find a link to the license terms for the currently installed edition by visiting Settings > System > About.) If you're trying to activate Windows 10 using a product key that has previously been activated on a second (or third or fourth) device, you might be unable to activate the software automatically.

In the remainder of this section, we describe the activation rules associated with the following distinct types of Windows 10 licenses:

- **OEM license.** On new PCs sold with Windows 10 preinstalled by large system makers, information about the edition is stored in the system firmware. Activation of that edition is automatic. System Builder OEM licenses are available from smaller PC makers and require a product key.

- **Retail license.** This type of package, which is available with or without installation media, requires a product key to activate. It can be used on a new PC or as an upgrade on a PC running an older version of Windows.

- **Volume license.** For large customers, Microsoft sells upgrades to Enterprise and Education editions. These can be activated by a product key. Smaller businesses can purchase Windows 10 Enterprise licenses as part of an Office 365 Enterprise subscription and activate by signing in with that subscription.

- **Digital license.** PCs that were upgraded from Windows 7 or Windows 8.1 during the year-long free upgrade offer receive a digital entitlement that is associated with the upgraded hardware on Microsoft's activation servers. The details of a digital license can be linked to a Microsoft account, as we describe later in this section.

The first three license types should be familiar to anyone who has worked with Windows in recent years. The final item on that list deserves more explanation.

Managing digital licenses

In the first year after the initial release of Windows 10, Microsoft made upgrades from Windows 7 and Windows 8.1 free. As part of that year-long campaign, it also added a new license type. On PCs upgraded using that free offer, the Windows activation server generated a Windows 10 license certificate (Microsoft calls it a *digital entitlement*) for the corresponding edition (Home or Pro). That digital license is stored in conjunction with your unique installation ID on Microsoft's activation servers. (You can read more details about this and other license types at *https://support.microsoft.com/en-us/help/12440/windows-10-activation*.)

The unique installation ID is essentially a fingerprint of your PC, based on a cryptographic hash derived from your hardware. That hash, reportedly, is not reversible and not tied to any other Microsoft services. So although it defines your device, it doesn't identify you. But it does make it possible to store activation status for that device online.

Once that online activation status is recorded, you can wipe your drive clean, boot from Windows 10 installation media, install a clean copy (skipping right past the prompts for a product key), and at the end of the process you'll have a properly activated copy of Windows 10.

CHAPTER 2

At any time, you can check the activation status of your device by going to Settings > Update & Security > Activation, as shown in Figure 2-3.

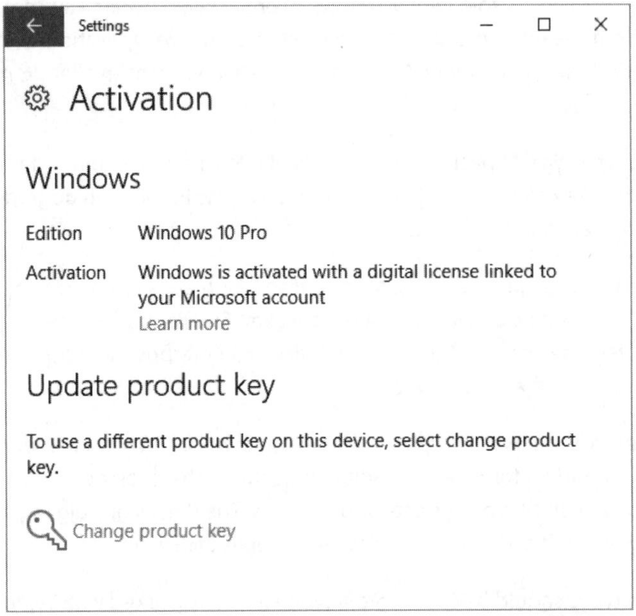

Figure 2-3 Most Windows 10 PCs will be automatically activated, with the successful activation status shown in this dialog box.

Troubleshooting activation problems

When you install Windows 10 on a new PC, it attempts to contact Microsoft's licensing servers and activate automatically within three days. If the activation process fails, you can activate Windows by connecting to a Microsoft activation server over the internet or by making a toll-free call to an interactive telephone activation system.

Under most circumstances, activation over the internet takes no more than a few seconds. If you need to use the telephone, the process takes longer because you have to enter a 50-digit identification key (either by using the phone's dial pad or by speaking to a customer service representative) and then input the 42-digit confirmation ID supplied in response.

The Windows 10 Anniversary Update, version 1607, introduces an additional option—an activation troubleshooter. If Windows doesn't activate automatically, you're reminded of this fact with a Windows Is Not Activated link at the bottom of every page in Settings. Checking the activation status shows more details. Figure 2-4, for example, shows the Activation page for a PC that had its motherboard replaced after being activated. After reinstalling Windows 10 Pro, it displayed the error shown here.

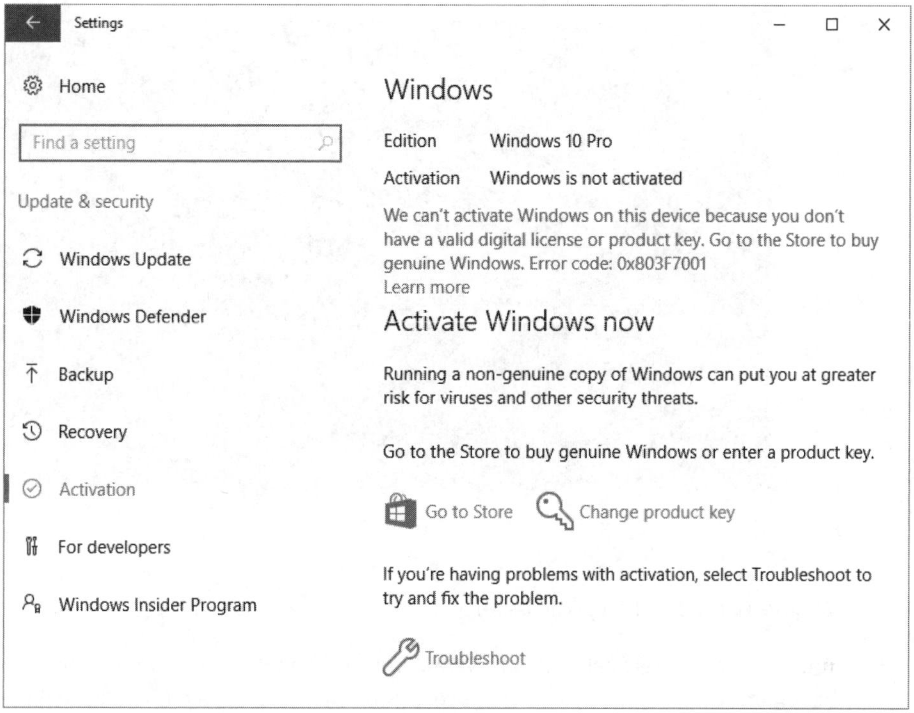

Figure 2-4 In the event of an activation error, you can use options on this Settings page to buy a new license, enter a product key, or use a troubleshooting tool.

The activation troubleshooter can resolve some simple problems and is especially well suited for activation errors that result from hardware changes or from situations where you inadvertently installed the wrong Windows edition (Home instead of Pro, for example). In fact, if the troubleshooter is unable to resolve your issue, it offers an I Changed Hardware On This Device Recently option:

Why are hardware changes an issue?

You're allowed to reinstall and reactivate Windows 10 on the same hardware an unlimited number of times. During the activation process, Windows transmits a hashed file that serves as a "fingerprint" of key components in your system. When you reinstall Windows 10 and attempt to activate the same edition of Windows 10 you activated previously, the activation server calculates a fingerprint on the fly, using your current hardware setup, and compares the value against the one stored in its database. If you're reinstalling Windows 10 on hardware that is essentially the same, the fingerprints will match and activation will be automatic.

Just as with earlier Windows versions, the activation process is designed to prevent attempts to tamper with the activation files or to "clone" an activated copy of Windows and install it on another computer. What happens if you upgrade the hardware in your computer? When you activate your copy of Windows 10, a copy of the hardware fingerprint is stored on your hard disk and checked each time you start your computer. If you make substantial changes to your system hardware, you might be required to reactivate your copy of Windows.

You can upgrade almost all components in a system without requiring a new license. Replacing the motherboard on a PC is the most certain way to trigger the activation mechanism, because the activation server assumes you tried to install your copy of Windows on a second computer. If you replaced a defective or failed motherboard with one that is the same model or the manufacturer's equivalent, you do not need to acquire a new operating system license and you should be able to reactivate your copy of Windows.

To help with this scenario, the activation troubleshooter relies on another feature that's new with the Anniversary Update: the capability to save a digital license for Windows 10 and link it to your Microsoft account. This step isn't mandatory, but it's handy if you make major changes to a system with a digital license and need to reactivate.

If the PC in question has a valid digital license that has been previously associated with a Microsoft account, you can run the activation troubleshooter to make the match that Microsoft's activation servers can't. Click the Troubleshoot link at the bottom of that Settings page to launch a tool that tries to find the activation record for the PC you're using. If you're not signed in with a Microsoft account, you need to do so, using the account you used previously to activate this PC.

Figure 2-5 shows the activation troubleshooter in action. After signing in with the Microsoft account to which the previous device activation was linked, you'll see a list of linked devices. Select the name associated with the device you're having troubles with and then click Activate.

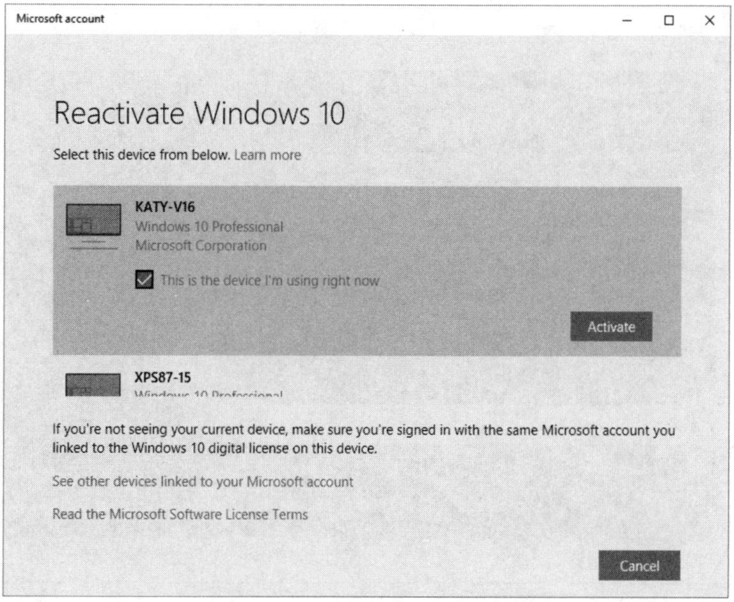

Figure 2-5 Using the activation troubleshooter, you can choose a digital license from a previously activated device to resolve issues that occur if you make significant hardware changes.

If all else fails, your only remaining option is to contact the telephone-based activation support center, explain the circumstances, and—assuming that the support representative accepts your claim—manually enter a new activation code. (If you upgrade your PC with a new motherboard, that is considered a new PC and might require a new license.)

Entering a product key

The 25-character alphanumeric product key is certainly not dead, although you're increasingly less likely to need such a key to work with Windows 10. On OEM PCs, Windows can retrieve the embedded product key from the computer's firmware and activate automatically.

If you're building your own PC or installing Windows 10 in a new virtual machine, you still need a product key for use with a retail Windows 10 package or an OEM System Builder license. You also need a product key to upgrade a PC running Windows 7 or Windows 8.1 performed after the expiration of the free upgrade offer.

If you skip the opportunity to enter a product key during a clean install, or if the key you enter fails activation (perhaps because it has been used on another PC), you can use the Change Product Key button to set things right, using the dialog box shown in Figure 2-6.

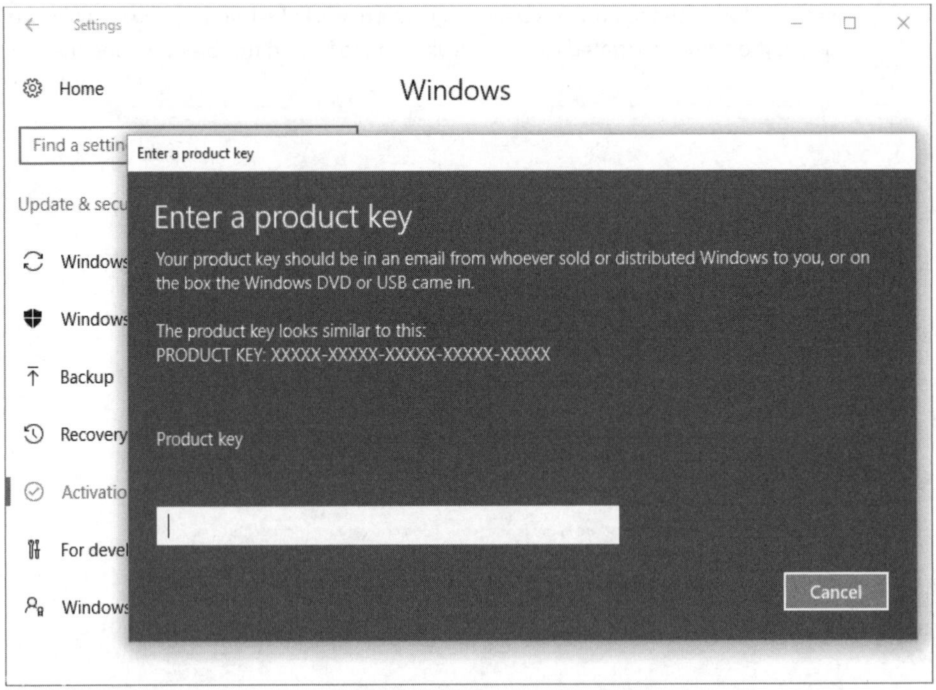

Figure 2-6 When you enter the 25-character alphanumeric product key, Windows automatically checks it and prompts you to complete activation.

Here are some key facts you should know about this procedure:

- **The product key is entered automatically on any copy of Windows that is preinstalled on a new PC by a large computer maker.** This configuration is called System Locked Preinstallation (SLP). Using this configuration, you can reinstall Windows from recovery media without entering a product key.

- **Your product key matches your edition of Windows.** If you purchase a boxed copy of Windows 10 from a retail outlet, the installation media (a DVD or a USB flash drive) contains a configuration file that automatically installs the edition you purchased: Home or Pro. The product key works only with that edition.

- **Some upgraded Windows 10 PCs don't require a product key.** If you upgraded a properly activated copy of Windows 7 or Windows 8.1 before the expiration date of the free upgrade offer, you don't need to enter a product key. A record of the edition you're licensed to use, Home or Pro, is stored with your hardware ID on Microsoft's activation servers. That digital license can be associated with your Microsoft account for later use.

- **Product keys are not tied to a specific architecture.** You can use the same key to activate a 32-bit or 64-bit Windows 10 edition on your hardware (assuming the hardware is compatible with the architecture you choose, of course).

- **You are not required to enter a product key when performing a clean install of Windows 10.** You're prompted to enter a valid product key when you perform a clean installation of Windows 10 on a system, as shown in Figure 2-7. If you enter a product key and click Next, Setup continues. If you are reinstalling Windows 10 on a PC that has previously been activated, click I Don't Have A Product Key, just to the left of the Next button.

The other common use for a product key is to perform a version upgrade of Windows 10—from Home to Pro, for example. On a PC running Windows 10 Home, open the Activation page in Settings, click the Change Product Key button, and enter a valid product key for Windows 10 Pro. After your product key is accepted, the upgrade proceeds quickly, with no changes to existing apps or files.

Beginning with the Anniversary Update, version 1607, you can use the Change Product Key option to upgrade from Windows 10 Pro to Enterprise edition as well.

CHAPTER 2

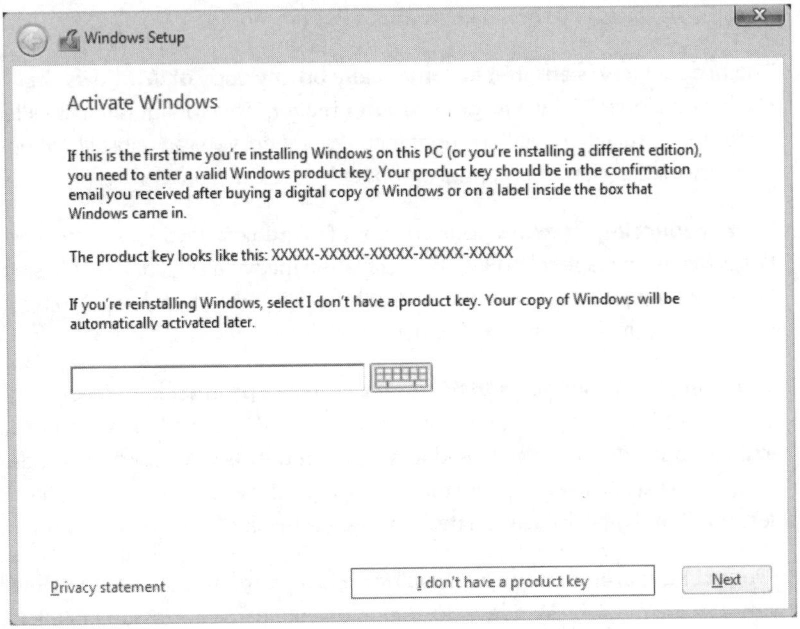

Figure 2-7 When you enter the 25-character alphanumeric product key, Windows automatically checks it and prompts you to complete activation.

Activation requirements for OEM installations

When you purchase a new computer with Windows 10 already installed by the manufacturer, the licensing procedures are different, as are the rules for activation. In the arcane parlance of Windows, system makers are known as *original equipment manufacturers*, or OEMs. To make matters more confusing, not all OEMs are created equal; instead, they're divided into two classes:

- Large system builders (which Microsoft refers to as *named* or *multinational* OEMs or, informally, as *royalty OEMs*) are allowed to install and preactivate Windows using System Locked Preinstallation (SLP), as mentioned earlier. The information in the system BIOS or firmware identifies the Windows version and edition (Home or Pro, typically). A new computer from one of these large companies might contain a sticker that certifies your installation, but unlike in earlier versions of Windows, that sticker contains no product key. The OEM uses a single master key to activate large numbers of computers. You can reinstall the same Windows edition using any installation source, including recovery media from the same computer.

- Smaller firms that build PCs can also preinstall Windows. These OEM versions are called *System Builder copies* and require activation. The rules of the System Builder program require the PC manufacturer to use specific tools to preinstall Windows with the unique product key for that copy; you accept a license agreement and activate the software when you first turn on the PC. In addition, the manufacturer is required to supply the purchaser with the Windows 10 media (typically a DVD) and affix a product key sticker to the PC's case. If you need to reinstall Windows on this computer, you must enter the product key and activate again (unless you associate your license with a Microsoft account, as described in the following section).

The license agreement for a retail copy of Windows 10 allows you to transfer it to another computer, provided that you completely remove it from the computer on which it was previously installed. An OEM copy, by contrast, is tied to the computer on which it was originally installed. You can reinstall an OEM copy of Windows an unlimited number of times on the same computer. However, you are prohibited by the license agreement from transferring that copy of Windows to another computer.

Product activation and corporate licensing

Businesses that purchase licenses through a Microsoft Volume Licensing (VL) program receive VL media and product keys that require activation under a different set of rules from those that apply to retail or OEM copies. Under the terms of a volume license agreement, each computer with a copy of Windows 10 must have a valid license and must be activated.

Beginning with the Anniversary Update to Windows 10, Microsoft also makes it possible to upgrade to Windows 10 Enterprise from Windows 10 Pro by purchasing an Office 365 E3 subscription. For more details, see *https://bit.ly/E3-plan-enterprise-license*.

Enterprise editions of Windows 10 can be installed using Multiple Activation Keys, which allow activations on a specific number of devices within an organization, or they can use Key Management servers to activate computers within their organization. If you encounter activation issues with Windows 10 Pro or Enterprise in a VL deployment, contact the person in your organization who manages your VL agreement—the "Benefits Administrator," as this person is called.

Managing Windows activation from the command prompt

Windows 10 includes a command-line tool you can use to examine the licensing status of a PC, change its product key, and perform other activation-related tasks. Although this feature is primarily intended for automating license administration activities, you can also run the Windows Software Licensing Management Tool interactively. Open a Command Prompt window with administrative privileges and then run the command **slmgr.vbs**. If it's run without parameters, this command shows its full syntax in a series of dialog boxes.

CHAPTER 2

One common use of this tool is to display the current licensing status for a device, using the syntax **slmgr.vbs /dli**. Figure 2-8, for example, shows the status of a device that has been properly activated with a digital license.

```
┌─────────────────────────────────────────────┐
│  Windows Script Host                    ✕    │
│                                               │
│                                               │
│   Name: Windows(R), Professional edition      │
│   Description: Windows(R) Operating System, RETAIL channel │
│   Partial Product Key: 3V66T                  │
│   License Status: Licensed                    │
│                                               │
│                          ┌──────────┐         │
│                          │    OK    │         │
│                          └──────────┘         │
└─────────────────────────────────────────────┘
```

Figure 2-8 This output from the Windows Software Licensing Management Tool shows a system that is properly licensed. If you see an error code here, you need to do some troubleshooting.

For a much more detailed display of information, use the same command with a switch that produces verbose output: **slmgr.vbs /dlv**. To see all available switches, enter the **slmgr.vbs** command by itself.

How Windows 10 Setup works

The Windows 10 Setup program works in multiple stages, the details of which vary depending on whether you're performing an in-place upgrade or a clean install. The process is extremely robust and is capable of recovering from a failure at any stage.

Setup performs basic system compatibility checks to confirm that the system has sufficient free disk space for both the installation and recovery options, that required CPU features are available, and that both memory and graphics hardware meet minimum requirements. During this phase, Setup also inventories hardware and confirms that critical drivers are available (storage and networking, for example). If any critical drivers are unavailable, setup stops and rolls back.

In either type of installation, the lengthiest stage occurs with Setup running offline in the Windows Recovery Environment, during which it backs up the previous Windows installation (if one exists) into a Windows.old folder and applies the new Windows 10 image.

The final stages of installation run after a restart, with the final stage consisting of the user signing in and either creating a new profile or migrating an existing one as part of the upgrade.

Setup does its magic using two folders:

- **C:\$Windows.~BT** is a hidden folder that contains the files used during both the online and offline phases of setup. When you launch Setup from installation media, such as a mounted ISO file or a bootable DVD or USB flash drive, the initial phase of setup creates this folder and copies the setup files to it for temporary use, eliminating the possibility of a setup failure caused by prematurely removing or unmounting the installation media.

- **C:\Windows.old** is created only when you perform an upgrade or do a clean install on a volume that already contains a Windows installation. This folder does double duty. During upgrades, it's used as a transfer location to hold files and settings that are moving from the old installation to the new one. After setup is complete, this folder holds system files from the previous Windows installation as well as any user files that were not migrated during setup.

NOTE

Effective with version 1607, these temporary installation files are deleted automatically after 10 days. Your previous Windows installation is saved indefinitely in Windows.old, allowing you to roll back to the previous version or recover files if necessary. On systems with limited storage, you can use the Disk Cleanup utility to remove these files manually. We describe this process in more detail in "Managing disk space" in Chapter 15, "System maintenance and performance."

If you poke around in the root of the system drive, you might notice one additional hidden folder with a similar name: $Windows.~WS. This folder is created by the Media Creation Tool when you download Windows 10 installation files.

Upgrading to Windows 10

The streamlined wizard that walks you through a Windows 10 upgrade should be familiar if you used Windows 8 or 8.1. If most of your experience is with Windows 7, we predict you'll be pleasantly surprised by the improvements in speed (especially on systems with a large number of files) and the reduction in complexity of the entire setup process.

In Windows 10, the upgrade process is optimized for software distribution over the internet. During the first year after the initial release of Windows 10, Microsoft offered free upgrades using Windows Update and the well-tested Background Intelligent Transfer Service. With that option no longer available, your choices are to download an installer file and either run it immediately or create installation media for later use (or for upgrading multiple PCs).

No major upgrade is ever risk free, of course, but the Windows 10 installer is designed to be robust enough to roll back gracefully in the case of a failure.

When you kick off a Windows 10 upgrade, the setup program performs a series of tasks. First, it runs a compatibility check, which determines whether your PC, peripheral devices, and installed Windows apps will work with Windows 10. (See "Checking compatibility" later in this section for details about warnings that might appear.)

Inside OUT

Upgrade directly from an ISO file

The ISO disc image format was originally devised to make it possible to share DVDs as files, without having to put shiny discs in the mail and wait a few days or weeks. Over time, they've evolved into a virtual alternative that doesn't require discs at all. Beginning with Windows 8, File Explorer supports the capability to mount ISO files directly. (For Windows 7, you need a third-party utility program. We previously recommended Virtual CloneDrive, but the company that created it is out of business, and we hesitate to send you to download sites that might not be trustworthy. If you have a Windows 8.1 or Windows 10 system handy, consider mounting the ISO file and copying its contents to a removable drive.)

Obviously, this option won't work for a clean install on a freshly formatted drive, but it's ideal for upgrades. Double-click a saved ISO file in File Explorer to map its contents to a virtual disk, which appears as a DVD drive in the Devices And Drives area of File Explorer, as in Figure 2-9.

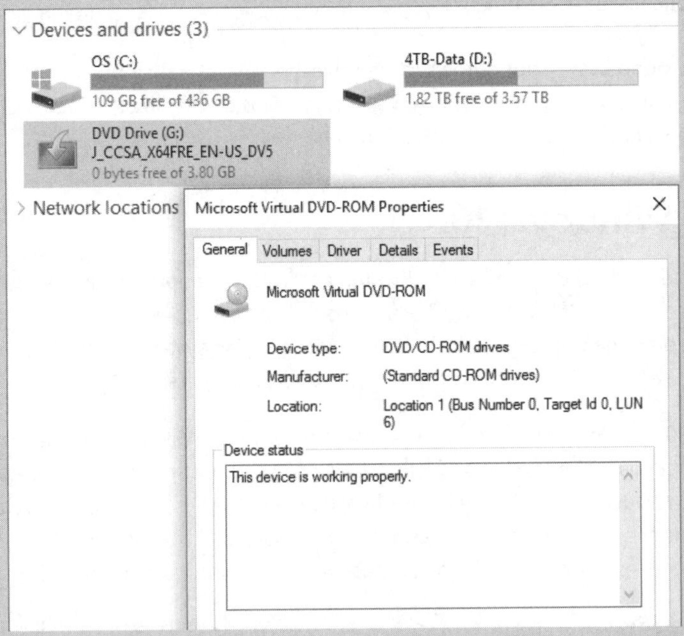

Figure 2-9 In this File Explorer window, drives C and D are physical drives, but drive G is a virtual drive created by double-clicking and mounting an ISO disc image file.

Double-click to open the mounted disk, and then run Setup to kick off an upgrade. When you no longer need the virtual drive, right-click its File Explorer icon and click Eject.

Using Windows installation media

When you start an online upgrade from within Windows 8.1, the upgrade keeps all your data files and migrates settings, Windows apps, and desktop programs. Upgrades from Windows 7 preserve data files and desktop programs but do not migrate personalized settings such as your desktop background.

If you have Windows 10 installation media, you can also start the upgrade process from within Windows. Open the DVD or USB flash drive in File Explorer and double-click Setup. The resulting wizard walks you through several steps that aren't part of the streamlined online upgrade. The most important of these is the option to transfer files, apps, and settings, a topic we cover shortly.

Checking compatibility

A comprehensive compatibility checker is built into the Windows 10 setup program (replacing the Upgrade Advisor from Windows 7), and it runs as one of the first steps when you kick off an upgrade. A more limited version runs on a clean install, checking for issues such as a BIOS that needs updating or a disk controller or network adapter that has no supported driver.

In most cases, this appraisal turns up nothing, and setup continues without interruption. If this routine finds any issues, however, it notifies you with a warning dialog box. Setup will refuse to continue if your device doesn't have enough RAM or free disk space. Other causes of hard blocks include a CPU or a BIOS that is not supported, as well as the presence of a hard-disk controller or networking device that lacks a driver. When the compatibility checker turns up any hard blocks, setup ends immediately, with a message like the one shown in Figure 2-10.

For less severe issues, Setup might warn you that specific apps or devices might not work correctly or will have reduced functionality in Windows 10. You might be given the option to fix the issue and try the upgrade again. In these cases, the compatibility checker offers instructions to deal with specific issues:

- You might need to install updates to your current version of Windows before continuing. If you're upgrading from Windows Update, this task is handled automatically.

- You might need to suspend disk encryption before upgrading.

- Some apps must be uninstalled before the upgrade can continue. (In some cases, they can be reinstalled after the upgrade is complete.)

- Some apps must be updated to a newer version before the upgrade can be completed.

- After the upgrade, you might need to reinstall language packs.

CHAPTER 2

If the upgrade process ends prematurely for any of these reasons, Setup generally cleans up after itself, although you might have to manually remove some leftovers.

Figure 2-10 A hard block, such as too little memory or an unsupported CPU or network device, will prevent you from installing Windows 10 on a PC.

Transferring files, apps, and settings

When you upgrade to Windows 10 on a volume that already contains a copy of Windows, you must choose what you want to do with user files, settings, and apps. To choose an alternative option, run Setup from installation media or an ISO file. Figure 2-11 shows your options when upgrading from Windows 7 to Windows 10.

Here's what happens with each option:

- **Keep Personal Files And Apps.** All Windows desktop programs and user accounts are migrated. After the upgrade is complete, you need to sign in with your Microsoft account to install apps from the Windows Store and sync saved settings. When upgrading from Windows 8.1, this option includes the capability to preserve settings.

NOTE

This option is unavailable if you're installing a Windows edition that is not a supported upgrade path from the current edition.

- **Keep Personal Files Only.** This option is the equivalent of a repair installation. Each user's personal files are available in a new user profile that otherwise contains only default apps and settings.

- **Nothing.** Choose this option if you want to perform a clean install, with your existing installation moved to Windows.old. Note that the descriptive text, "Everything will be deleted," is misleading. Your personal files, as well as those belonging to other user accounts in the current installation, are not deleted. Instead, they are moved to the Windows.old folder, where you can recover them by using File Explorer.

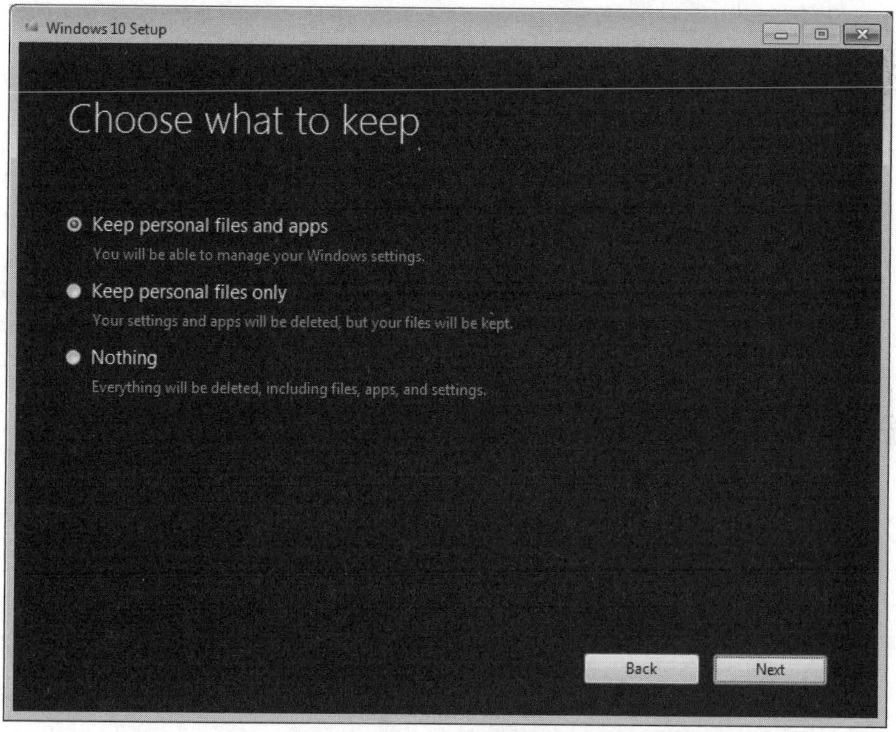

Figure 2-11 When you start a Windows 10 upgrade from installation media, you see the full range of options shown here.

After the initial prep work, Setup restarts in offline mode, displaying a progress screen that is simpler than the one from the initial release of Windows 10.

In this mode, you can't interact with the PC at all. Your PC is effectively offline as the following actions occur.

Windows Setup first moves the following folders from the existing Windows installation on the root of the system drive into Windows.old:

- Windows

- Program Files

- Program Files (x86)

- Users

- ProgramData

During this offline phase, Setup extracts registry values and program data from the Windows. old folder, based on the type of upgrade, and then prepares to add this data to the corresponding locations in the new Windows 10 installation. Third-party hardware drivers are also copied from the old driver store in preparation for the new installation.

Next, Setup lays down a new set of system folders for Windows 10 using the folder structure and files from the compressed Windows image. After that task is complete, Setup moves program files, registry values, and other settings it gathered earlier.

Moving folders minimizes the number of file operations that have to take place, making upgrade times consistent even when individual user accounts contain large numbers of files. (By contrast, the Windows 7 setup program moved files individually, which led to some painfully long upgrades.)

To further speed things up, Windows 10 Setup uses hard link operations to move files and folders from the transport location to the new Windows 10 hierarchy. Not having to physically move the file improves performance and also allows for easy rollback if something goes wrong during setup.

Folders associated with individual user accounts are moved when they meet the following criteria:

- Every file in the folder and all of its subfolders are preserved, with no rules defined to exclude some files or subfolders.

- The entire folder is placed within the fresh Windows 10 installation unchanged.

- The target Windows 10 destination doesn't already exist, and thus there's no need to merge an existing folder in the target destination with one from the source operating system.

CHAPTER 2

This activity is accompanied by several restarts and can take as long as a few hours, depending on your hardware, although an upgrade on most modern hardware goes much faster. At the conclusion of this process, you're confronted with a sign-in screen like the one shown in Figure 2-12.

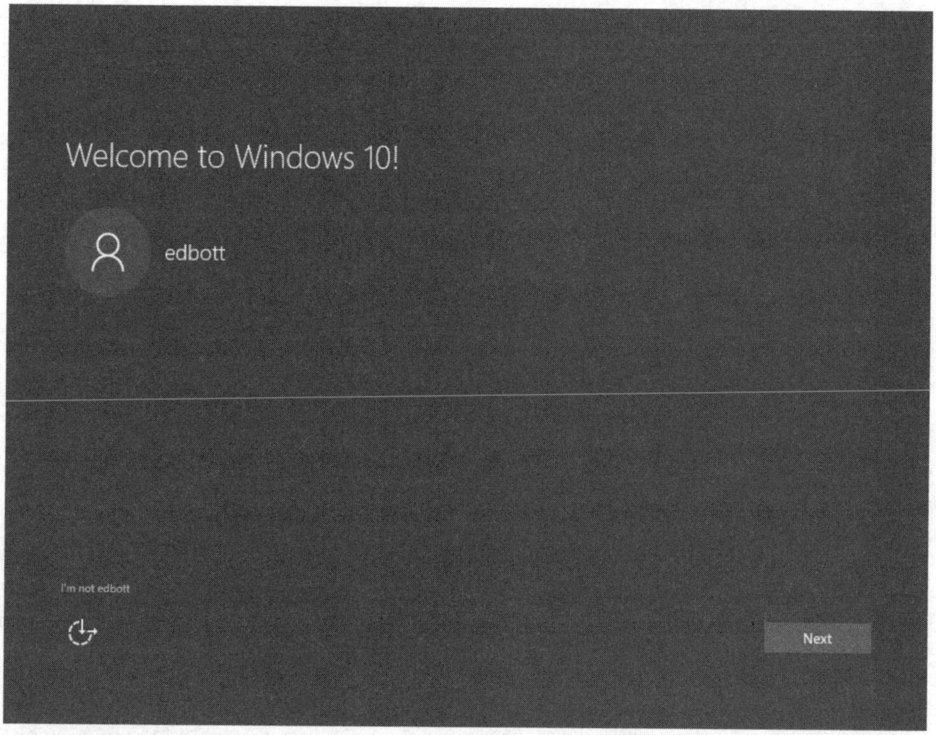

Welcome to Windows 10!

   edbott

I'm not edbott

Next

Figure 2-12 In the final stage of setup, signing in with a Microsoft account restores synced settings that were previously saved to OneDrive and makes it possible to restore apps from the Store as well.

By signing in with a Microsoft account, you can continue setting up Windows 10 by using synced settings. The most current version of each preinstalled app is downloaded and installed from the Store before you sign in.

If you're upgrading from Windows 7 or from a Windows 8.1 PC that was configured to use a local user account, you need to sign in using the credentials for that account. After that, you'll have the option to link your account to a Microsoft account or to continue using a local account.

For more information about your options when setting up a user account, see Chapter 6, "Managing user accounts, passwords, and credentials."

CHAPTER 2

Performing a clean install

For some veteran Windows users, a clean install is the only option worth considering. Historically, that option means starting up from a bootable USB flash drive containing the Windows 10 installation files and removing all traces of the currently installed Windows version before proceeding with setup.

This is still a perfectly valid installation method, one we'll describe in more detail shortly. But it's no longer the only option, nor is it always the best. For a system that's already running any modern version of Windows, you'll find it much easier to start Setup from within Windows, choose an upgrade install, and choose the option to keep Nothing. After you use Disk Cleanup Manager to remove the old Windows installation, the result is virtually identical to an old-fashioned clean install.

> **NOTE**
> For a thorough discussion of how the push-button reset option works, see Chapter 16.

Inside OUT

Setup and your hard disk

In this section, we describe the steps for a clean installation on the simplest of all PC configurations: a single hard disk containing unallocated space ready to be automatically partitioned for use as the system drive. Out in the real world, especially among Windows enthusiasts, we know that disk configurations can be much more complex.

On most desktop PCs and on some notebooks, you can connect multiple physical disk drives. You can choose to install Windows 10 to a volume on any IDE or SATA drive (including eSATA drives, which attach to the system via an external cable but appear to Windows as an ordinary internal drive). You cannot, however, install Windows to an external drive connected via USB or IEEE 1394 (FireWire), or to any form of removable media. (The sole exception is the Windows To Go feature, which requires specially built USB drives and an installed copy of Windows 10 Enterprise edition.)

With a new hard disk or an existing one, you might have any of several good reasons to tinker with disk partitions. You might prefer to segregate your operating-system files from your data files by placing them on separate volumes, for example, or you might be planning to set up a dual-boot or multi-boot system. In any event, it's always easier to make partitioning decisions before setup than it is to resize and rearrange volumes after they're in use.

For a full inventory of all disk-management tools and techniques available in Windows 10, see Chapter 14.

That neat option isn't possible if you're starting with a brand-new hard disk or you want to install a 64-bit Windows 10 edition on a device that's currently running 32-bit Windows, or you want to clean up a messy OEM's partition layout on the system disk, or . . . you get the idea.

For those scenarios, you need to boot into the Windows 10 setup program from a USB flash drive (or a DVD drive, if your PC is equipped with one of those increasingly rare peripherals). You might need to read the manual for your device to learn the magic combination of key-strokes and firmware settings that make it possible to start up using a bootable Windows 10 disc or drive.

After the setup process begins, you can follow the instructions as outlined in this section.

When you boot from that media, you pass through a few introductory screens—choosing a language, accepting a license agreement—and eventually reach the Windows Setup window shown in Figure 2-13. Although you're prompted to choose an installation type—Upgrade or Custom—that's actually a trick question.

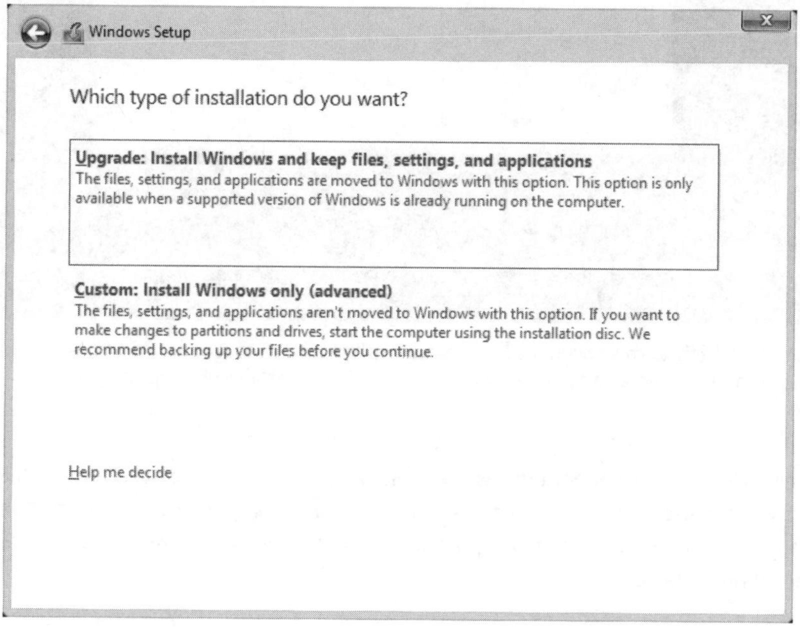

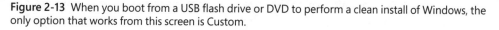

Figure 2-13 When you boot from a USB flash drive or DVD to perform a clean install of Windows, the only option that works from this screen is Custom.

Choosing the Upgrade option raises an error message; you can upgrade Windows only if you start Setup from within Windows.

The Custom option allows you to continue, and you're presented with a list of available disks and volumes. Figure 2-14 shows what you see on a system with a single drive that already contains an installation of Windows 10.

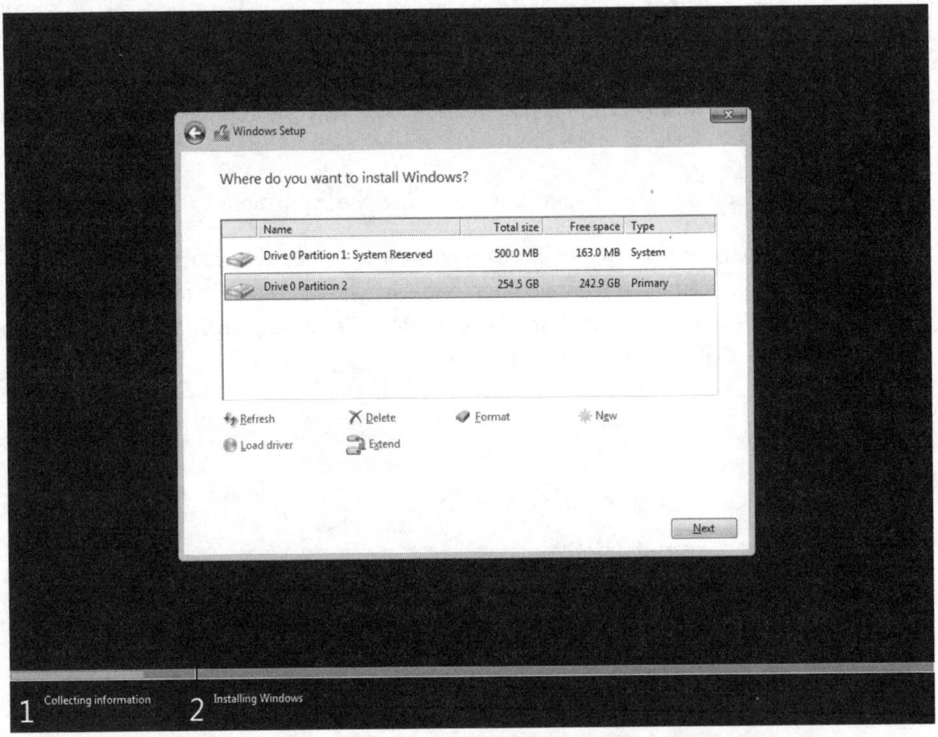

Figure 2-14 In this simple scenario, with a single physical disk that contains a current Windows 10 installation, click Delete to remove existing partitions and install Windows using the entire physical drive.

You can use the tools beneath the list of available drives to manage partitions on the selected drive. You can use these tools to delete an existing partition (for a truly fresh start on a drive that already contains files), create a new partition, format a partition, or extend a partition to include adjacent unallocated space.

➤ **For more information about managing disks using the full array of Windows tools, see Chapter 14.**

When you click Next, the setup process switches into a lengthy unattended phase in which it lays down the clean Windows 10 image. When that's complete, you get to choose default settings for all new accounts. The default settings are explained in detail in the screen shown in Figure 2-15, which encourages you to click Use Express Settings to move on quickly. Click the Customize button to open additional pages where you can adjust any of these settings.

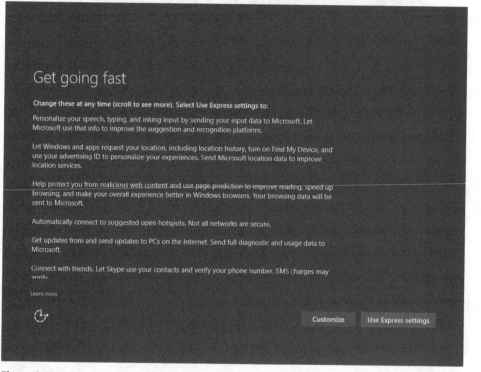

Figure 2-15 When you do a clean install, these default options allow you to configure a user account quickly, without fussing over individual options.

If you do a clean install using bootable media for Windows 10 Pro, you're faced with one additional choice immediately after this phase of setup. The dialog box shown in Figure 2-16 asks you who owns your PC. (For an installation of Windows 10 Enterprise, the dialog box asks whether you want to join Azure AD or join a domain.)

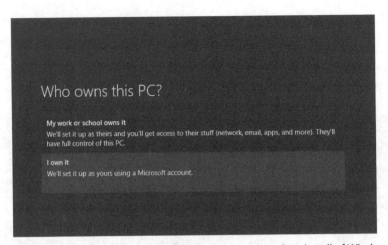

Figure 2-16 This option is available only when you do a clean install of Windows 10 Pro.

Choosing the first option (My Work Or School Owns It) and clicking Next leads you through a slightly confusing series of dialog boxes you use to set up a device for access to online services (from Microsoft and others). The credentials are managed in Azure Active Directory and can be linked to services such as an Office 365 account at a workplace or university.

If you own the device, or if it is a company PC that will be joined to a Windows domain managed by your organization, choose the I Own It option.

> ➤ **For more information about setting up user accounts, during or after setup, see Chapter 6.**

Inside OUT

How Windows 10 divides a disk

If you install Windows 10 on a UEFI-based system with a single unformatted disk, Setup creates a default disk layout. Three of its partitions are visible in the Disk Management console, as shown here.

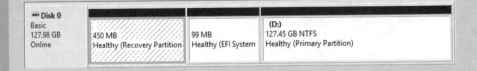

The small (450-MB) recovery partition at the start of the disk in this example (which might be different on your PC) contains the Windows Recovery Environment, which allows the system to boot for repair and recovery operations. (For more information, see "Troubleshooting in Safe Mode" in Chapter 17, "Troubleshooting.")

The EFI system partition is even smaller, at 99 MB. It contains the files required for the system to start up, including the Windows Hardware Abstraction Layer and the boot loader (NTLDR).

The largest partition is the primary partition, formatted using NTFS, which contains Windows system files, the paging file, and all user profiles.

A fourth partition, required for every GPT disk, is hidden and not visible in Disk Management. This partition, labeled MSR (Reserved), resides between the EFI system partition and the primary partition and is used for post-installation tasks, such as converting a basic disk to a dynamic disk. It's visible when you use DiskPart or the partitioning tools available with a custom installation.

PC makers have the option to add custom OEM partitions to this layout, with those volumes containing files that are part of a custom installation. In addition, some PCs contain a second recovery partition, at the end of the drive, that contains files you can use to restore the original system configuration.

To make adjustments to existing disk partitions, boot from Windows 10 installation media (DVD or bootable USB flash drive) and run through Windows Setup until you reach the Where Do You Want To Install Windows page of the Windows Setup window, shown earlier in Figure 2-14. The collection of tools below the list of disks and partitions is shown in Figure 2-17.

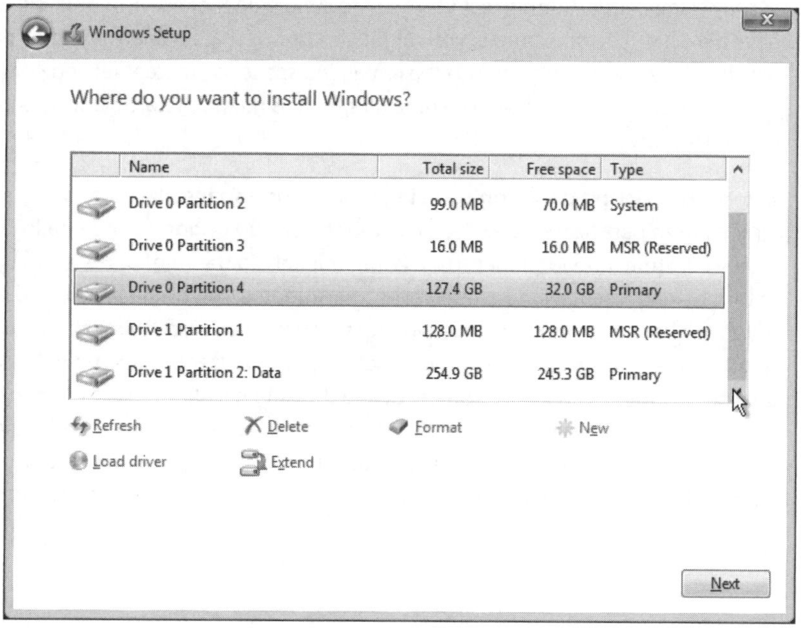

Figure 2-17 Use the disk-management tools in this phase of the Windows 10 setup process to manage disk partitions for more efficient data storage and multi-boot configurations.

The system shown in Figure 2-17 includes two physical disks. The first, Drive 0, has a standard partition layout, with a Windows installation on Partition 4. The second physical disk, Drive 1, has been partitioned but still has most of its space free.

You can accomplish any of the following tasks here:

- **Select an existing partition or unallocated space on which to install Windows 10.** Setup is simple if you already created and formatted an empty partition in preparation for setting up Windows, or if you plan to install Windows 10 on an existing partition that currently contains data or programs but no operating system, or if you want to use unallocated space on an existing disk without disturbing the existing partition scheme. Select the partition or unallocated space, and click Next.

- **Delete an existing partition.** Select a partition, and then click Delete. This option is useful if you want to perform a clean installation on a drive that currently contains an earlier version of Windows. Because this operation deletes data irretrievably, you must respond to an "Are you sure?" confirmation request. After deleting the partition, you can select the unallocated space as the destination for your Windows 10 installation or create a new partition. Be sure to back up any data files before choosing this option.

- **Create a new partition from unallocated space.** Select a block of unallocated space on a new drive or on an existing drive after deleting partitions, and click New to set up a partition in that space.

  By default, Windows Setup offers to use all unallocated space on the current disk. You can specify a smaller partition size if you want to subdivide the disk into multiple drives. If you have a 4-TB drive, for example, you might choose to create a relatively small partition on which to install Windows and use the remaining space to create a second volume with its own drive letter on which to store data files such as music, pictures, documents, and videos or TV shows.

- **Extend an existing partition by using unallocated space.** If you're not happy with your existing partition scheme, you can use the Extend option to add unallocated space to any partition, provided that space is immediately to the right of the existing partition in Disk Management, with no intervening partitions. If you originally divided a 128-GB notebook hard disk into two equal volumes, you might decide to rejoin the two partitions to give your system drive more breathing room. After backing up your data files to an external drive or to cloud storage, delete the data partition, select the partition you want to make larger, and click Extend. Choose the total size of the extended partition in the Size box (the default is to use all available unallocated space), and click Apply. You can now continue with your installation, restoring your data files after setup is complete.

CAUTION

In both the Disk Management console and the disk-management tools available via Windows Setup, it can be confusing to tell which partition is which. Confusion, in this case, can have drastic consequences if you inadvertently wipe out a drive full of data instead of writing over an unwanted installation of Windows. One good way to reduce the risk of this sort of accident is to label drives well.

Alert observers will no doubt notice that one option is missing from that list. Unfortunately, Setup does not allow you to shrink an existing disk partition to create unallocated space on which to install a fresh copy of Windows 10. The option to shrink a volume is available from the Disk Management console after Windows 10 is installed, but if you want to accomplish this task before setup, you need to use third-party disk-management tools.

Configuring a multi-boot system

If your computer already has any version of Windows installed and you have a second disk partition available (or enough unallocated space to create a second partition), you can install a clean copy of Windows 10 without disturbing your existing Windows installation. At boot time, you choose your Windows version from a startup menu, like the one shown in Figure 2-18. Although this is typically called a *dual-boot system*, it's more accurate to call it a *multi-boot configuration*, because you can install multiple copies of Windows or other PC-compatible operating systems.

Having the capability to choose your operating system at startup is handy if you have a program or device that simply won't work under Windows 10. When you need to use the legacy program or device, you can boot into your earlier Windows version without too much fuss. This capability is also useful for software developers and IT professionals who need to be able to test how programs work under different operating systems using physical (not virtual) hardware.

TROUBLESHOOTING

After installing Windows 7, you see a text-based boot menu

The preferred way to build a multi-boot system is to install the most recent version last. That option uses the graphical boot menu. If you install Windows 7 as a second operating system on a PC that is currently running Windows 10, you get Windows 7's black and white, text-based boot menu. To restore the graphical menu, start Windows 10, open an Administrative Command Prompt, and run the following command: **bcdboot c:\windows**. Restart and you should see the familiar blue-and-white menu.

CHAPTER 2

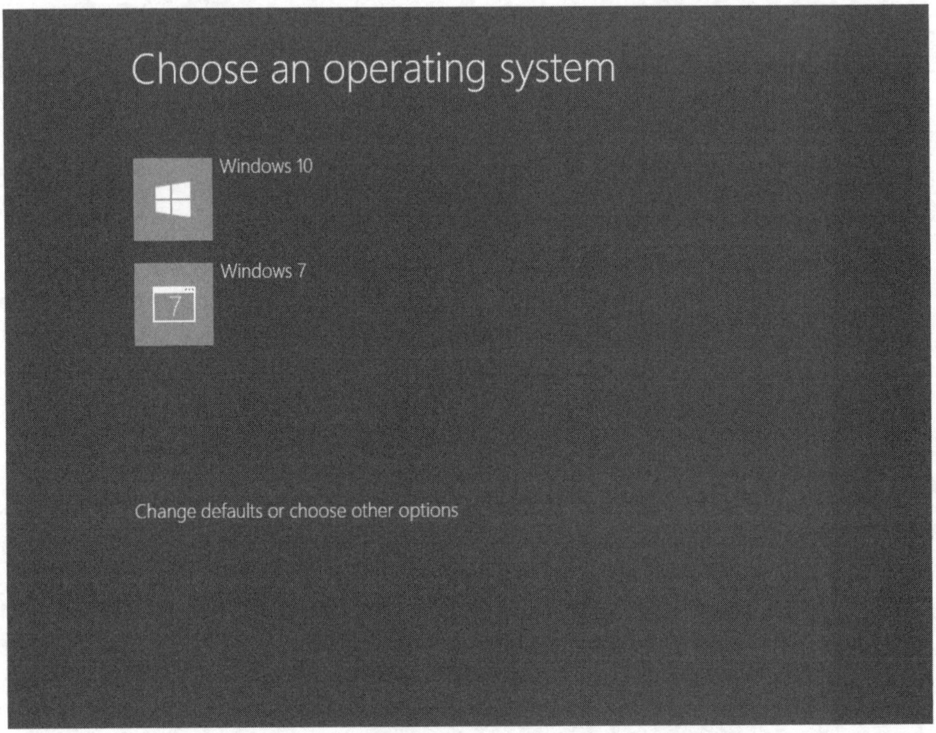

Figure 2-18 This system is configured to allow a choice of operating systems at startup.

For experienced Windows users, installing a second copy of Windows 10 in its own partition can also be helpful as a way to experiment with a potentially problematic program or device driver without compromising a working system. After you finish setting up the second, clean version of Windows 10, you'll see an additional entry on the startup menu that corresponds to your new installation. (The newly installed version is the default menu choice; it runs automatically if 30 seconds pass and you haven't made a choice.) Experiment with the program or driver and see how well it works. If, after testing thoroughly, you're satisfied that the program is safe to use, you can add it to the Windows 10 installation you use every day.

To add a separate installation of Windows 10 to a system on which an existing version of Windows is already installed, first make sure you have an available volume (or unformatted disk space) separate from the volume that contains the system files for your current Windows version.

Inside OUT

Use virtual machines instead of hassling with multi-boot menus

You can create truly elaborate multi-boot configurations using Windows versions that date back a decade or more. But unless you're running a hardware testing lab, there's no good reason to do that. The much simpler, smoother alternative is to use virtual hardware that faithfully re-creates the operating environment. During the course of researching and writing this book, we installed Windows 10 in virtual machines to capture details of several crucial tasks and processes that can't easily be documented on physical hardware, and we saved many hours compared to how long those tasks would have taken had we set up and restored physical hardware.

We strongly recommend Microsoft's Hyper-V virtualization software, which is a standard feature in Windows 10 Pro, Enterprise, and Education and on current Windows Server versions. (For more information about Client Hyper-V in Windows 10, see Chapter 22, "Running virtual machines with Hyper-V.")

To run Windows 10 on a Mac, try Parallels, available at *https://parallels.com*. For other operating systems, check out VMware (*https://vmware.com*), which offers excellent virtualization software for use on desktop Windows machines and servers, and the free VirtualBox package from Oracle (*https://virtualbox.org*).

Using any of these solutions, you can install even the most ancient Windows version. Backing up a machine's configuration and restoring it is as simple as copying a file. You will, of course, need a license for every operating system you install in a virtual machine. If you have a license to use Windows for evaluation purposes, the option to run Windows in a virtual machine can be a tremendous timesaver.

The target volume can be a separate partition on the same physical disk as the current Windows installation, or it can be on a different hard disk. If your system contains a single disk with a single volume used as drive C, you cannot create a multi-boot system unless you add a new disk or use software tools to shrink the existing partition and create a new partition from the free space. (The Disk Management console, Diskmgmt.msc, includes this capability on all supported versions of Windows; you can also use third-party software for this task. For details, see "Shrinking a volume" in Chapter 14.) The new partition does not need to be empty; if it contains system files for another Windows installation, they will be moved to Windows.old. Run Setup, choose the Custom (Advanced) option, and select the disk and partition you want to use for the new installation.

The setup program automatically handles details of adding the newly installed operating system to the Boot Configuration Data store.

And how do you edit and configure the Boot Configuration Data store? Surprisingly, the only official tool is a command-line utility called Bcdedit. Bcdedit isn't an interactive program; instead, you perform tasks by appending switches and parameters to the Bcdedit command line. To display the complete syntax for this tool, open an elevated Command Prompt window (using the Run As Administrator option) and type the command **bcdedit /?**.

For everyday use, most Bcdedit options are esoteric, unnecessary—and risky. In fact, the only option that we remember using more than once in the past four years is the command to change the text for each entry in the boot menu. By default, the setup program adds the generic entry "Windows 10" for each installation. If you set up a dual-boot system using two copies of Windows 10 (one for everyday use, one for testing), you'll find it hard to tell which is which because the menu text will be the same for each. To make the menu more informative, follow these steps:

1. Start your computer, and choose either entry from the boot menu. After startup is complete, make a note of which installation is running.

2. Right-click Start, or press Windows key+X, and choose Command Prompt (Admin) from the Quick Link menu. Click Yes in the User Account Control box to open an elevated Command Prompt window.

3. Type the following command: **bcdedit /set {current} description "*Menu description goes here*"** (substituting your own description for the placeholder text, and making sure to include the quotation marks). Press Enter.

4. Restart your computer, and note that the menu description you just entered now appears on the menu. Select the other menu option.

5. Repeat steps 2 and 3, again adding a menu description to replace the generic text and distinguish this installation from the other one.

A few startup options are available when you click or tap Change Defaults Or Choose Other Options at the bottom of the boot menu. Doing so leads to the Options menu shown here:

You can choose which installation is the default operating system (this is where descriptive menu choices come in handy) and change the timer that determines how long you want to display the list of operating systems. The default is 30 seconds; you can choose 5 seconds (allowing the default operating system to start virtually automatically) or 5 minutes, if you want to ensure you have a choice even if you're distracted while the system is restarting. These options write data directly to the Boot Configuration Data store.

Inside OUT

Installing Windows 10 and Linux in a multi-boot configuration

It's possible to install Windows 10 and Linux in a multi-boot configuration that works much like the Windows multi-boot setup described on the preceding pages. You can set it up to use the Windows 10 boot menu, or you can use a Linux boot loader (most commonly, GRUB) if you prefer. The procedure is a bit more complex than the procedure for installing another version of Windows, and it varies somewhat depending on which Linux distribution you use and which Linux tools (such as partition editors, boot loaders, and the like) you prefer. It's generally easier to set up such a system if the Windows partition is set up first, but it can be done either way: Windows and then Linux, or Linux and then Windows.

An internet search for "dual boot Linux Windows" turns up plenty of detailed instructions, and if you add the name of your Linux distribution to the search input, you're likely to find the specific steps needed to make it work with Windows 10.

For slightly more control over the boot menu timer, use the System Configuration utility, Msconfig.exe. You can use the Boot tab to change the default operating system and set the Timeout interval in any amount between 3 and 999 seconds.

Tweaking and tuning your Windows 10 installation

When Windows Setup completes, you're signed in and ready to begin using Windows 10. For upgrades and clean installs alike, we suggest following this simple checklist to confirm that basic functionality is enabled properly:

- **Look for missing device drivers.** Open Device Management, and look for any devices that have a yellow exclamation mark over the icon or any devices that are listed under the Other category. This is also a good time to install any custom drivers supplied by the device maker and not available through Windows Update. For more information on working with device drivers, see "How device drivers and hardware work together" in Chapter 13, "Hardware."

- **Adjust display settings.** You'll want to confirm that the display is set for its native resolution and that any additional tasks, such as color calibration, have been completed.

- **Check your network connection.** If you skipped network setup during a clean install, you can complete the task now. Open the Network folder in File Explorer to switch from a public network to a private network and allow local file sharing.

- **Verify security settings.** If you use third-party security software, install it now and get the latest updates.

- **Check Windows Update.** You'll get the latest updates automatically within the next 24 hours. Doing the update manually lets you avoid a scheduled overnight restart.

- **Change default programs.** Use this opportunity to set your preferred browser, email client, music playback software, and so on.

- **Adjust power and sleep settings.** The default settings are usually good enough, but they're rarely a perfect match for your preferences. Now is a good time to adjust when your device sleeps and whether it requires a password when it wakes.

Using Windows 10

Regardless of your upgrade path—from Microsoft Windows 7 or from Windows 8.1—your day-to-day experience changes significantly with Windows 10.

The change is more striking if you're moving from a conventional PC or laptop to a touchscreen device. Even if you still have access to a keyboard and mouse or trackpad, the addition of touch fundamentally changes how you interact with Windows and with apps. With a phone or small tablet added to the mix, you have still more options to explore.

In this chapter, we look at the things you tap, click, drag, and drop to make Windows do your bidding. Some, like the taskbar and notification icons, are similar enough to their predecessors that you might miss subtle but significant changes. Our coverage also includes a section on the unique ways to interact with a tablet running Windows 10.

Although there's only a fine and fuzzy line of demarcation between the ways you tailor Windows to make your work more productive and the customizations you perform to make the system more esthetically pleasing (good esthetics do enhance productivity, we're convinced), we focus in this chapter primarily on productivity issues, saving matters of esthetics for Chapter 4, "Personalizing Windows 10."

A disclaimer, right up front: In this chapter and the next, we are writing about a user experience that's evolving from month to month and that will continue to do so even after the release of Windows 10 Anniversary Edition, version 1607. The screenshots and step-by-step instructions you see here are based on version 1607. It's certainly possible, perhaps probable, that some features we describe here will change in the runup to the next big feature update as Microsoft continues to deliver on its promise of "Windows as a service."

If you see subtle differences between what's on these pages and what's on your screen, that's the likely reason. We hope our descriptions make it possible for you to incorporate those changes into your learning.

An overview of the Windows 10 user experience

Before we dive into detailed descriptions of individual features, please join us for a brief tour of Windows 10. Our goal is to introduce the different parts of Windows, new and old, so that we can be sure you're on the same page . . . or at least looking at the same arrangement of pixels.

Figure 3-1 shows the basic building blocks of Windows 10 and offers a hint of its signature visual style.

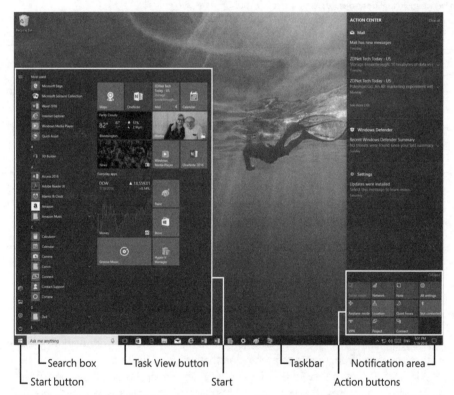

Figure 3-1 Start and Action Center are at the core of the Windows 10 experience, with the familiar desktop front and center for conventional PCs.

When you first start up a conventional PC running Windows 10, you see the familiar Windows 7–style desktop and taskbar. Clicking the Start button—the Windows logo in the lower left corner—opens Start, which is conceptually similar to its predecessor but differs dramatically in the details.

How the cloud changes your experience

One noteworthy difference between the initial Windows 10 experience and the traditional Windows experience that reached its zenith with Windows 7 is the amount of personalization you see when you sign in on a new PC or device. If you use a Microsoft account you've already used on a different device, the customized settings saved with your account appear automatically on the new device, making it feel familiar right away.

On a clean install or a refresh, you can create a local account, which gives you the standard default layout and themes, as defined by Microsoft. If you sign in to a corporate network, your personalized settings roam according to policies defined by your network administrator. (If your organization allows you to, you can attach a Microsoft account to your domain account, and both your personal and work settings roam together as you switch between devices.)

When you allow your Microsoft account to sync settings between devices, you don't have to go through a tedious process of tweaking the default settings to match those preferences; instead, your visual themes, browser settings, and saved Wi-Fi passwords appear exactly as you expect. If your Microsoft account is connected to OneDrive, your online files, photos, and music collection will be available too. We discuss these features in more detail in "Syncing your settings between computers" in Chapter 4.

A click on the right side of the taskbar opens Action Center, which is also shown in Figure 3-1. This pane, which uses the full height of your display, contains notifications from apps and services as well as action buttons that allow quick access to settings.

As with previous versions, Windows 10 offers multiple ways to switch between tasks. The Task View button, a new addition to the Windows 10 taskbar, produces the view shown in Figure 3-2, which also illustrates another new feature: virtual desktops. We discuss both features in more detail later in this chapter.

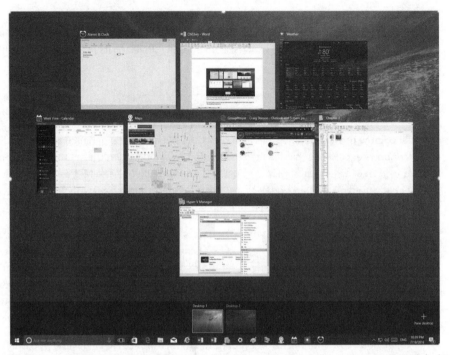

Figure 3-2 Use Task View to switch quickly between available windows; the new virtual desktop feature allows you to group windows.

Navigating Windows 10

Touchscreens might represent the future of computing, but the present is still ruled by more-or-less conventional desktop and laptop PCs, each equipped with a keyboard and a mouse or touchpad. For that type of device, the desktop is where you'll likely spend most of your time, and it's what we concentrate on in this section. We discuss Tablet Mode separately, later in this chapter. (See "Using Windows 10 on a touchscreen device.")

Using and customizing Start

What in earlier versions was called the Start menu is now known simply as Start. Start is divided into three segments. At the very left is a thin column, near the bottom of which appear the current user's name and picture and icons for File Explorer, Settings, and Power. You can display descriptive labels alongside each of those icons by clicking the hamburger menu at the top.

Next to this thin column is a wider column that includes a list of your most used apps at the top and a scrolling list of all your apps below. Here in this All Apps list, you'll find the names and launch icons for your programs, listed in alphabetical order. You can move through the list by swiping directly on a touchscreen, using two-finger scrolling gestures on a touchpad, or using the scroll wheel with a mouse. Often the quickest way to get from one part of the list to another is by clicking any of the letter headings. That produces an index menu, like this:

You can click or tap any letter or symbol in this menu to jump to the associated part of the All Apps list.

CHAPTER 3

Inside OUT

Hold the suggestions

Below the Most Used list and above the All Apps list, you might occasionally find a suggestion from the Store. Windows tries to make these suggestions congruent with your usage habits, and you might find them welcome. If you don't, it's easy to eliminate them. Go to Settings > Personalization > Start. Then deselect Occasionally Show Suggestions In Start.

Obviously, you can launch any item in the All Apps list by tapping or clicking it. Alternatively, if you're comfortable typing, you can skip all the scrolling and simply type the beginning characters of an item you want in the Search box, directly to the right of the Start button.

(See Figure 3-1.) What you're looking for will soon appear at the top of the Search results. This approach is especially handy when you're not sure exactly where in the All Apps list the item you desire is located. (Where's Notepad, for example? Its default location is within the Windows Accessories folder, several clicks or taps away from the top of the list. You'll get to it quicker by typing.)

Inside OUT

Change your Start picture

The picture that appears on the left side of Start is the one associated with your user account (the one that also appears on the Welcome screen). If you're not happy with that picture, click it, and then click Change Account Settings. That takes you to the Settings page for your account, where you can choose a different picture or snap one with a webcam.

The remainder of Start consists of tiles. This is the remnant of the Start screen that filled the desktop in Windows 8. As in Windows 8, tiles can be live or not. The live ones update their appearance periodically with relevant content. Windows gives you some tiles to get you going, but, of course, this part of Start is completely customizable, as we discuss shortly.

You can change the size and shape of Start by dragging it up (to a maximum height that is 100 pixels below the top of the display), to the right, or both ways. Resizing Start doesn't change the width of the left columns, and making it wider can be done only in increments corresponding to the width of two Wide tiles. (More on that shortly.)

Customizing the contents of Start

If you're accustomed to the extensive array of customization options for items on the Start menu in earlier Windows versions, you'll need to make some adjustments. You can remove programs from the Most Used section, but you can't pin program shortcuts to the left side of Start.

You can add or remove shortcuts from the narrow column of options at the left edge of Start. In addition to the default File Explorer and Settings menu items, locations available for this section include your personal folder, the default folders from your user profile (Documents, Downloads, Music, Pictures, and Videos), and the Network folder. You can also add a HomeGroup shortcut. To see the entire list, go to Settings > Personalization > Start, and then click or tap Choose Which Folders Appear On Start.

Inside OUT

Master the powerful "other" Start menu

Here's some good news for anyone who misses the system shortcuts from earlier iterations of the Start menu. Most of those tools are available as part of a hidden menu, called
the Quick Link menu, that appears when you right-click the Start button or press Windows
key+X, as shown here:

Programs and Features

Power Options

Event Viewer

System

Device Manager

Network Connections

Disk Management

Computer Management

Command Prompt

Command Prompt (Admin)

Task Manager

Control Panel

File Explorer

Search

Run

Shut down or sign out   >

Desktop

Most of the major system management and troubleshooting tools are on that list, including
Disk Management, Event Viewer, and the Computer Management console.

Windows traditionalists will appreciate the fact that the Shut Down Or Sign Out menu item
is here, along with links to Control Panel and Task Manager. Our personal favorite is the
Command Prompt (Admin) shortcut, which eliminates one minor hassle when it's time to
get work done the old-fashioned way, by typing commands directly. If you're a PowerShell
aficionado, you can use an option in Settings > Personalization > Taskbar to replace the two
Command Prompt options with PowerShell equivalents.

CHAPTER 3

Inside OUT

Which programs are included in the Most Used list?

The list of most-used programs—the items that appear below the pinned programs on the left side of Start—is controlled by Windows. In previous Windows versions, this list included only shortcuts to executable files you open, such as .exe files and .msc files. Windows 10 continues this behavior.

Several types of items are excluded by default, so you won't see things like setup programs, installer and uninstaller packages, Control Panel modules, and MMC consoles. You can find a list of what's excluded in the AddRemoveApps value of the registry key HKLM\Software\ Microsoft\Windows\CurrentVersion\Explorer\FileAssociation. We do not recommend trying to edit these values manually.

Pin any Windows app to Start by right-clicking the program's entry in the All Apps list or by dragging it from that list and dropping it on the right side of Start. Pin an item to the taskbar by right-clicking it in the All Apps list, clicking More, and then clicking Pin To Taskbar. You can pin items in both places.

Adding and arranging tiles

Anything that appears on the All Apps menu can be dragged to the right side of Start and placed as a tile. Tiles, which were found on a separate Start screen in Windows 8.1, behave much the same way in Windows 10, but they are constrained to Start.

Clicking a tile has the same effect as clicking a Start program shortcut or a pinned taskbar button. What makes tiles different is the variety of sizes and their ability to display information or notifications from the app, making a tile *live*.

To pin a program as a tile to the right side of Start, drag it into position. As an alternative, right-click its entry in All Apps or the Most Used list on the left side of Start, and then click or tap Pin To Start. The item will take up residence as a medium-sized tile in the first available empty space, from where you can move and resize it as needed.

To remove a program from the right side of Start, right-click it and then click Unpin From Start.

You can adjust the size of any tile by right-clicking the tile to see the menu shown in Figure 3-3.

Note that not all tiles support the full range of sizes shown in this figure. Windows desktop programs, for example, offer only the Small and Medium options.

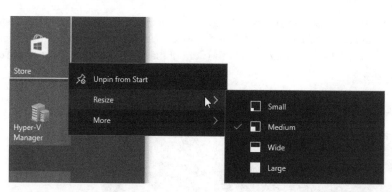

Figure 3-3 These options are available for most programs acquired from the Windows Store. Not all apps support this full list of sizes.

On a touchscreen, you can accomplish the same tile customization tasks with a long press on the tile. That produces the two options shown in white circles on the right side of the tile in Figure 3-4. Tapping the top option unpins the tile, while tapping the ellipsis at the bottom right reveals a menu with Resize and Live Tile items.

Figure 3-4 On a touchscreen, a long press on any tile produces these controls, which lead to options identical to those on the right-click menu.

> ### NOTE
> **Options for a specific app might allow additional customization of the live tile. The Photos app, for example, allows you to choose a specific image for its tile.**

Right-clicking the tile for a Windows desktop program produces a menu with an extra set of options: Run As Administrator, for example.

Tiles can be arranged into groups, with or without custom group names. Drag tiles, one at a time, into the position you prefer. If the position you choose is sufficiently far from the edge of an existing group, your tile ends up in a new group of its own. You can move it back to an existing group or add other tiles to the new group.

A slim bar sits above every group of tiles. Click (as we have in Figure 3-5) to display a text box where you can type a group name of your choosing. (We created a group named Microsoft Office here.) Click the horizontal lines to the right of the name box to drag the entire group to a new location.

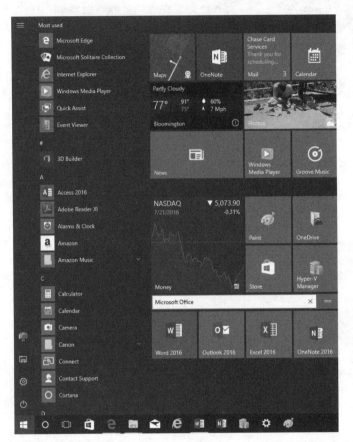

Figure 3-5 Click above any group of tiles to give that group a descriptive label.

Using and customizing the taskbar

The taskbar is that strip of real estate along one screen edge (bottom by default) that contains, from left to right, the Start button, the search box, the Task View button, program buttons, notification icons, and a clock. The taskbar made its first appearance in Windows 95. In the years since, it has slowly evolved without changing its basic shape.

The Windows 10 taskbar continues to serve the same basic functions as its progenitors—launching programs, switching between programs, and providing notifications—with only subtle changes in functionality.

Every running program with a user interface has a corresponding taskbar button. When you close that program, the button vanishes as well, unless you pinned it to the taskbar. A faint line appears underneath the icon for a running program, and the program with the current focus has a subtle but noticeable transparent shadow to identify it.

The Windows 10 taskbar offers a limited selection of customization options, most of which are available through Settings > Personalization > Taskbar (or right-clicking an empty space on the taskbar or the Task View button and clicking Settings). Figure 3-6 shows the first group of options on that Settings page.

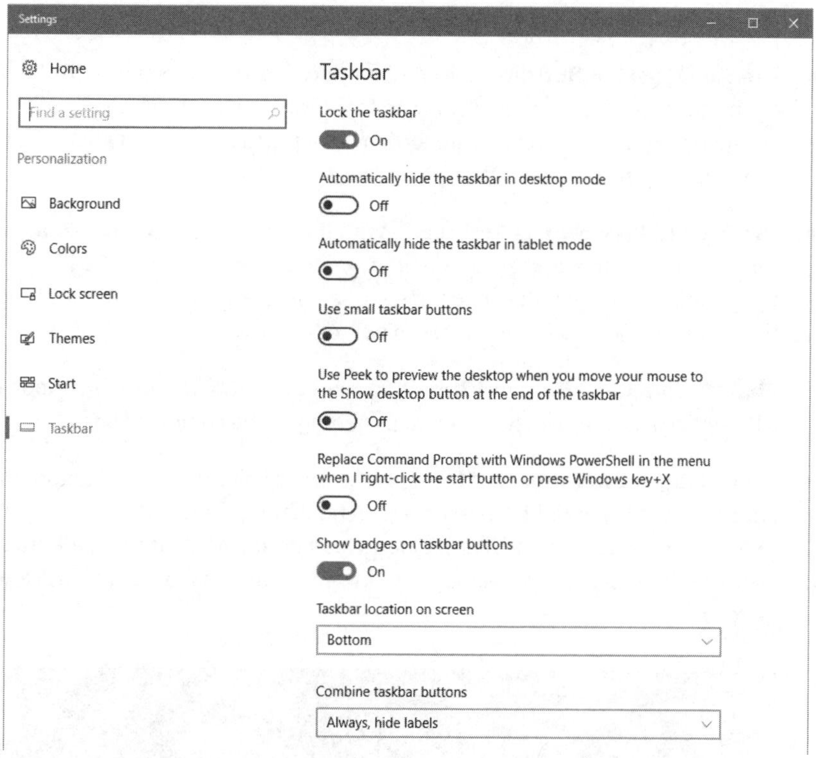

Figure 3-6 For most people, the default options here will be acceptable, especially Lock The Taskbar, which prevents you from accidentally dragging the taskbar to the side of the monitor.

Here is a rundown of the options shown in Figure 3-6:

- **Lock The taskbar.** On by default, this option prevents you from accidentally dragging the taskbar to the side of the monitor. Note that the shortcut menu that appears when you right-click the taskbar also includes Lock The Taskbar. It's there so that you can easily switch in and out of the locked mode when you need to adjust the size or position of the taskbar. Also note that locking the taskbar does not prevent you from rearranging taskbar icons.

- **Automatically Hide The Taskbar...** By default, the taskbar remains visible at all times. If that's inconvenient for any reason, you can tell it to get out of the way. The Settings page provides separate Hide options for Desktop and Tablet modes. With either option set, the taskbar retreats into the edge of the desktop whenever a window has the focus. To display the hidden taskbar, move the mouse pointer to the edge of the desktop where the taskbar normally resides.

- **Use Small Taskbar Buttons.** Select this option if you want to reduce the height of taskbar buttons, making them similar in size to buttons in earlier Windows versions. In our experience, buttons of this size are too small for practical use. If you have the eyesight of a hawk, your opinion might differ.

- **Use Peek To Preview The Desktop...** With this option on, moving your mouse to the extreme edge of the taskbar (beyond the Action Center button) hides all open windows temporarily, giving you the opportunity to see the underlying desktop. This option is off by default; we don't see a good reason not to turn it on.

- **Replace Command Prompt With Windows PowerShell...** Turn this option on if you're a PowerShell user. You'll save some steps getting to the command line.

- **Show Badges On Taskbar Buttons.** Badges are small circular notifications that can appear on the lower right corner of certain taskbar buttons. In the following illustration, for example, badges on the Alarm Clock, Weather, and Mail buttons indicate that an alarm has been set, that a weather alert is in effect, and that a stack of mail is waiting to be read.

- **Taskbar Location On Screen.** The taskbar appears at the bottom of the screen by default. As you would expect, the alternatives are top, left, and right. You don't have to visit Settings to change positions, however. Simply unlock the taskbar and drag it.

- **Combine Taskbar Buttons.** The default setting for Combine Taskbar Buttons is Always, Hide Labels. This setting instructs Windows to always group multiple windows from a single application (such as Microsoft Word documents) into a single taskbar button. The Hide Labels setting for this option is left over from an old Windows version; Windows 10 does not display labels (window titles) for taskbar buttons. With either of the other settings (When Taskbar Is Full or Never), Windows gives each window its own separate taskbar button. It groups windows only when the taskbar becomes too crowded or continues to shrink the size of taskbar buttons as you open more windows. We recommend the default setting here.

➤ **If you have more than one display attached to a Windows 10 PC, some extra customization options are available for the taskbar. See "Configuring the taskbar with multiple displays," later in this chapter, for details.**

Pinning programs to the taskbar

Pinning a taskbar button makes it easy to find and run favorite programs without the need to open Start or use the search box to find the program's shortcut. To pin a program to the taskbar, simply drag its icon or a shortcut (from Start, from the desktop, or from any other folder) to the taskbar. Alternatively, right-click a program icon wherever you find it and then click Pin To Taskbar.

To remove a pinned program from the taskbar, right-click the pinned icon and then click Unpin This Program From Taskbar. This command also appears on other shortcuts to the program, including those on the desktop and on Start.

You can use taskbar buttons to launch a program that's not currently running or to switch from one running program to another. You can also click a taskbar button to minimize an open window or to restore a minimized window. If those features sound too obvious, here's a trick you might not know: You can open a new instance of a program that's already running—a new Microsoft Word document, for example, or a fresh File Explorer window—by right-clicking the taskbar button and then clicking the program name.

Using Jump Lists for quick access to documents and folders

A Jump List is the official name of the menu that appears when you right-click a taskbar button. Each taskbar Jump List includes commands to open the program, to pin the program to the taskbar (or unpin it), and to close all open windows represented by the button.

In addition, for programs developed to take advantage of this feature, Jump Lists can include shortcuts to common tasks that can be performed with that program, such as Open New Tab on an Internet Explorer window. For Microsoft Office programs, Adobe Acrobat, and other, similarly document-centric programs, Jump Lists also typically include links to recently opened files.

CHAPTER 3

Figure 3-7 shows the default Jump List for File Explorer.

Figure 3-7 Right-click a taskbar button, such as File Explorer, to see a Jump List showing recently opened files and folders with the option to pin items for quick access.

Individual files and folders can't be pinned directly to the taskbar, but you can add them to Jump Lists by using the following techniques:

- To pin a document to the taskbar, drag its icon or a shortcut to any empty space on the taskbar. If the taskbar already has a button for the program associated with the document, Windows adds the document to the Pinned section of the program's Jump List. If the document's program is not on the taskbar, Windows pins the program to the taskbar and adds the document to the program's Jump List.

- To pin a folder to the taskbar, drag its icon or a shortcut to the taskbar. Windows adds the folder to the Pinned section of the Jump List for File Explorer.

- To open a pinned document or folder, right-click the taskbar button and then click the name of the document or folder.

- To remove a pinned document or folder from the Jump List, right-click the taskbar button and point to the name of the document or folder to be removed. Click the pushpin icon that appears.

Changing the order of taskbar buttons

To change the order of buttons on the taskbar, simply drag them into position. Pinned program icons retain their order between sessions, allowing you to quickly find your most used programs in their familiar (to you) location.

Inside OUT

Use shortcut keys for taskbar buttons

The first 10 taskbar buttons are accessible by keyboard as well as by mouse. Press Windows key+1 for the first, Windows key+2 for the second, and so on (using 0 for the tenth). Using one of these shortcuts is equivalent to clicking the corresponding taskbar button: If the button's program isn't running, it starts; if it has a single open window, you switch to that window; if it has multiple open windows, Windows displays previews of all windows and switches to the first window. Hold down the Windows key and tap the number key repeatedly to cycle between all open windows for that program.

Note that when you change the order of a taskbar button, you also change the Windows key+number combination that starts that particular program.

Another useful shortcut key is Windows key+T, which brings focus to the first item on the taskbar. At that point, you can repeatedly press Windows key+T, Shift+Windows key+T, or the arrow keys to select other taskbar buttons. When a taskbar button is selected, you can press Spacebar to "click" the button, press the Menu key to display its Jump List, or press Shift+F10 to display its shortcut menu.

Changing the taskbar's size and appearance

The default height of the taskbar is enough to display one button. (If you switch to small buttons, the taskbar automatically shrinks its height to fit.) You can enlarge it—and given the typical size and resolution of computer displays these days, enlarging it is often a great idea. Before you can change the taskbar's dimensions, you need to unlock it. Right-click an unoccupied area of the taskbar; if a check mark appears next to the Lock The Taskbar command, click the command to clear the check mark. Then position the mouse along the border of the taskbar farthest from the edge of the screen. When the mouse pointer becomes a two-headed arrow, drag toward the center of the screen to expand the taskbar. Drag the same border in the opposite direction to restore the original size.

Moving the taskbar

The taskbar docks by default at the bottom of the screen, but you can move it to any other edge. You do this by selecting the Taskbar Location On Screen option in Settings > Personalization > Taskbar.

As an alternative, you can manipulate the taskbar directly. Unlock it, and then drag any unoccupied part of the taskbar in the direction you want to go. (Don't drag the edge of the taskbar closest to the center of the screen; doing that changes the taskbar's size, not its position.)

Adding toolbars to the taskbar

A seldom-used feature of the taskbar is its ability to host other toolbars. Optional toolbars date back to much older versions of Windows, offering shortcuts to folders, documents, and applications. Third parties can also write add-ons that operate entirely within the confines of the taskbar. Built-in toolbars you can choose to install include the following:

- **Address.** The Address toolbar provides a place where you can type an internet address or the name and path of a program, document, or folder. When you press Enter or click the Go button, Windows takes you to the internet address, starts the program, opens the document, or displays the folder in a File Explorer window. The Address toolbar is functionally equivalent to the Run command in Start or the address bar in File Explorer or the Microsoft Edge browser.

- **Links.** The Links toolbar provides shortcuts to internet sites; its contents are drawn from the Favorites Bar in Internet Explorer.

- **Desktop.** The Desktop toolbar provides access to all the icons currently displayed on your desktop. In addition, it includes links to your Libraries, HomeGroup, This PC, Network, Control Panel, and other user profile folders. When you click the toolbar's double arrow, a cascading menu of all the folders and files on your system appears.

To install a new toolbar or remove one you're currently using, right-click any unoccupied part of the taskbar or any existing toolbar. Click Toolbars on the menu that appears, and then choose from the ensuing submenu. A check mark beside a toolbar's name means that it's already displayed on the taskbar. Clicking a selected toolbar name removes that toolbar.

In addition, any folder on your system can become a toolbar. To create a new toolbar, right-click an existing toolbar or a spot on the taskbar, click Toolbars, and then click New Toolbar. In the next dialog box, navigate to a folder and click Select Folder.

The folder's name becomes the name of the new toolbar, and each item within the folder becomes a tool.

Configuring the taskbar with multiple displays

If your computer has more than one monitor attached, you have additional options for configuring the taskbar: You can show it on just the main display or on all displays, and you can vary its appearance on each display. To review these options, right-click the taskbar and choose Settings. The following illustration shows the multiple-display options. You'll find them at the bottom of the page at Settings > Personalization > Taskbar.

> **Multiple displays**
>
> Show taskbar on all displays
>
> ⬤ On
>
> Show taskbar buttons on
>
> | All taskbars   ⌄ |
>
> Combine buttons on other taskbars
>
> | Always, hide labels   ⌄ |

Selecting the first option shows a taskbar on each monitor. If you set it to Off, the taskbar appears only on the main display. (You specify the "main display" in Settings > System > Display. For details, see "Configuring displays" in Chapter 13, "Hardware.")

The Show Taskbar Buttons On setting determines where the taskbar button for a particular app appears—on all taskbars or only the one where that app's window resides.

The last setting specifies how taskbar buttons are combined on displays other than the main display.

Customizing the notification area

Windows displays icons around the perimeter of the desktop too: in the notification area (the right side of the taskbar), in Action Center, and on Start. The notification area can display a set of system icons and another set of icons, some of which supply notifications in the form of pop-up messages, while others don't "notify" you of anything and simply offer shortcuts to associated programs. The system icons, which appear at the right end of a horizontally displayed taskbar, include the date and time, icons that indicate network and battery status, a shortcut for setting speaker volume, and the like. The other set of icons, to the left of the system icons, mostly relate to functionality that's specific to your own system—your applications and peripherals, for example. Note, however, that a few icons, such as Volume, Network, and Power, are members of both groups; that is, you can turn them on or off in either of two places.

To customize the system icons, go to Settings > Personalization > Taskbar. Under the Notification Area heading, click Turn System Icons On Or Off to specify which icons appear. As Figure 3-8 shows, the available items are denoted by icons and switches.

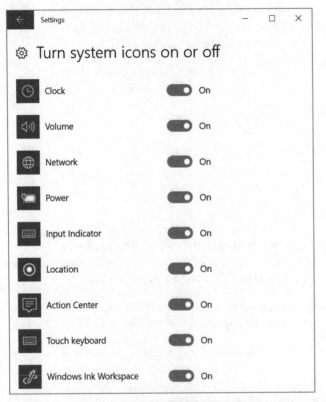

Figure 3-8 Each notification area icon shown here is currently turned on. With a flick of the switch, you can remove any that you don't need or want.

To customize your other taskbar icons, go to Settings > Personalization > Taskbar. Under the Notification Area heading, click Select Which Icons Appear On The Taskbar. You'll probably see a long list, comparable to the one shown in Figure 3-9.

You can use the On-Off switches to add or remove items. In case you want them all, Windows provides a master switch at the top of the list.

Figure 3-9 Some icons in this list provide status messages. Others are shortcuts to associated programs.

Using and customizing Action Center

Action Center is the formal name of the pane that appears at the right side of your screen when you swipe in from the right (on a touchscreen), press Windows key+A, or click the small button just to the right of the clock on your taskbar. It serves two important functions. First, it supplies a notification area that can display messages from various apps and system components. These notifications occupy the upper part of Action Center. Second, it provides a panel of

Quick Action buttons for such things as switching in and out of Airplane Mode or Tablet Mode, creating a note in OneNote, selecting and connecting to a Wi-Fi signal, and so on. The action buttons appear as one or more rows of tiles along the lower edge of Action Center. Figure 3-10 shows an example of Action Center with two notifications and 15 Quick Action buttons.

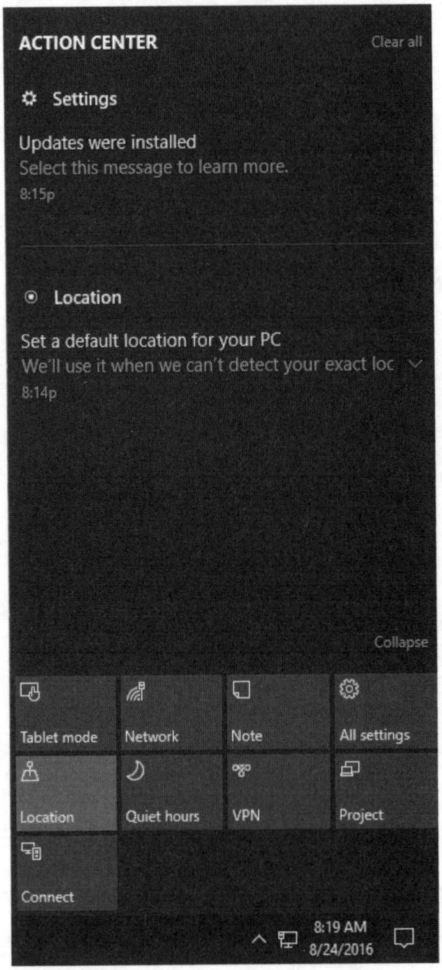

Figure 3-10 Action Center consists of two parts: a set of notifications at the top and one or more rows of Quick Action buttons at the bottom.

You can respond to notifications in various ways. If you hover the mouse pointer over a notification, a Close button appears in its upper right corner, and you can dismiss the notification by clicking there. If you click on the body of the notification, the relevant action occurs. For example, clicking on a news bulletin opens the story in the News app; clicking on a message from

Windows Update telling you that a system restart is pending might open a secondary message with more details and a button for effecting an immediate restart.

Some Quick Action buttons are simple commands. Clicking All Settings, for example, opens Settings; clicking Note launches the OneNote universal app with a new note page. Others, such as Tablet Mode and Wi-Fi, are toggle switches. Action Center uses the current accent color to indicate which switches are currently on.

Customizing the Quick Actions panel

To rearrange the contents of the Quick Actions panel, go to Settings > System > Notifications & Actions. The current Quick Actions layout is shown near the top of the page:

You can change the order in which your Quick Actions are displayed by dragging with the mouse or other pointer. On a touchscreen, press and hold a button to select it, and then drag. Note that you do not have to have an empty space in the panel to do the rearranging; Windows adjusts button positions as you drag.

The arrangement of the Quick Actions panel matters in one way. With the Collapse button that appears directly above the panel in Action Center (shown in Figure 3-10), you can reduce the panel to a single row of four. The row that appears then is the top row shown in Settings > System > Notifications & Actions. You can think of this row as the quickest of your Quick Actions. If you want to get in and out of Airplane Mode effortlessly, for example, you can put that button in the top row, collapse the panel in Action Center, and then swipe in from the right when you board the plane. Your Airplane Mode Quick Action button will be right there, more or less under your thumb.

To change the content of the Quick Actions panel, click Add Or Remove Quick Actions. (See the previous illustration.) The list of choices that appears is appropriate for your hardware. Figure 3-11, for example, shows the Quick Actions available on a Surface Pro 3. Some of these, such as Battery Saver and Rotation Lock, would not appear on a desktop computer.

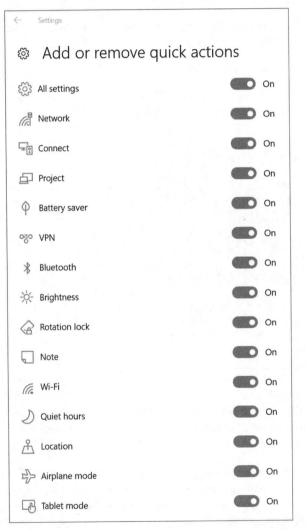

Figure 3-11 The list of available Quick Actions is appropriate for your hardware. On a portable PC like this Surface Pro 3, the list includes Battery Saver, Brightness, and Rotation Lock.

Customizing notifications

The options for controlling which "senders" can deliver messages to the notification area of Action Center are also located at Settings > System > Notifications & Actions, just below those for Quick Actions. Switches here also control whether or not messages are displayed on your lock screen. The following illustration shows the options governing general notification behavior:

Notifications

Get notifications from apps and other senders
On

Show notifications on the lock screen
On

Show alarms, reminders, and incoming VoIP calls on the lock screen
On

Hide notifications when I'm duplicating my screen
Off

Get tips, tricks, and suggestions as you use Windows
On

If you don't want any notifications in Action Center or on the lock screen, you can turn them off using the first two of these switches.

Scroll down from these general switches, and you'll come to switches for individual senders. You can use the switches to squelch or permit notifications from particular senders. Clicking on the sender takes you to a more granular set of controls, shown next.

CHAPTER 3

You can use this set of controls for such things as determining whether a sender provides a notification banner (a pop-up that appears briefly when a notification arrives), whether a sound is played, the maximum number of notifications that will be displayed at one time in Action Center (you can use an Expand button to see the remainder), and the priority given to the sender's notifications. For example, if you want your Calendar notifications always to show up at the top of Action Center, you can select Top.

Switching tasks

As in previous Windows versions, you can switch to a different program by clicking its taskbar button. And if you're not sure which icon your document is hidden under, hover the mouse pointer over a taskbar button to display a thumbnail image of the window above the button. If a taskbar button combines more than one window (representing multiple Microsoft Excel spreadsheets, for example), hovering the mouse pointer over the taskbar button displays a preview of each window.

If the live thumbnail isn't enough to help you select the correct window, hover the mouse pointer over one of the preview images. Windows brings that window to the forefront, temporarily masking out the contents of all other open windows.

The alternative to this manual hunt-and-click technique is a new feature in Windows 10 called Task View, which displays large, live thumbnails of running programs on the screen so that you can switch with confidence.

To begin, click the Task View button or use the Windows key+Tab shortcut. On a touchscreen-equipped device, you can swipe in from the left edge. Figure 3-12 shows the results on a system with six running programs.

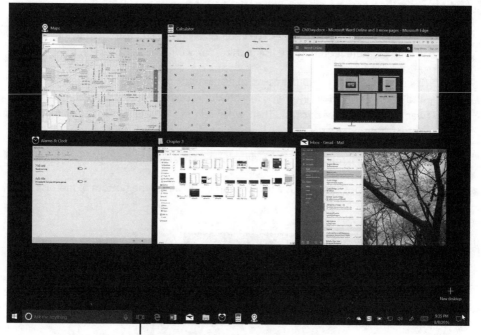

Task View button

Figure 3-12 Opening Task View shows running programs using their windowed dimensions. Clicking or tapping any thumbnail opens it in its current position.

Those thumbnails remain open until you do something, usually by clicking or tapping a thumbnail to switch to that window or by pressing Esc to return to the current window.

If there are too many open windows to fit as thumbnails on the display, use the up and down arrows at the bottom of the screen to scroll through the full list.

CHAPTER 3

The old-fashioned Alt+Tab task switcher, familiar to every Windows user of a certain age, is still available as well. The concept is similar, but the thumbnails appear only as long as you continue to hold down the Alt key. Hold down Alt and tap the Tab key to cycle (left to right, top to bottom) through all open windows. When you've highlighted the window you want to bring to the fore, release the Alt and Tab keys.

When using Task View, you also have the option of closing a window by clicking the red X in the upper right corner of the preview or, if your mouse scroll wheel supports clicking, by middle-clicking anywhere in the preview image. Other basic window tasks are available on the shortcut menu that appears when you right-click the preview image.

Switching between virtual desktops

Virtual desktops have been reserved exclusively for power users in previous Windows versions, with the feature requiring the use of third-party utilities.

The idea is straightforward: Instead of just a single desktop, you create a second, third, fourth, and so on. On each desktop, you arrange individual programs or combinations of apps you want to use for a specific task. Then, when it's time to tackle one of those tasks, you switch to the virtual desktop and get right to work.

To create a desktop, click New Desktop in the lower right corner of the Task View window.

Virtual desktops show up as a row of thumbnails along the bottom of the Task View window, like this:

The system depicted here has three virtual desktops, of which the second is currently active. You can switch from one virtual desktop to another by clicking its thumbnail. You'll notice that your taskbar changes to reflect the makeup of the current desktop.

Managing and arranging windows

Windows 10 includes a host of keyboard shortcuts and mouse gestures that greatly simplify the everyday tasks of resizing, moving, minimizing, arranging, and otherwise managing windows. The most useful trick is a collection of "snap" techniques. These have been around for several

Windows versions, but Windows 10 adds some extremely useful new tricks to the old familiar methods.

The simplest window-snapping scenario is a PC with a single display, where you want to arrange two windows side by side. You might want to compare two Word documents, move files between the Documents folder and an archive, or do financial research in a web browser and plug the numbers into an Excel spreadsheet.

Drag a window title bar to the left or right edge of the screen, and it snaps to fill that half of the display. As soon as you let go of the title bar, the window snaps into its position and Windows helpfully offers thumbnails for all other open windows to help you choose what to run alongside your first snapped window.

In Figure 3-13, for example, we've just snapped a File Explorer window to the right side of the screen and now have a choice of three other running windows to snap opposite it. (If you don't feel like snapping a second window, just press Esc or click anywhere except on one of those thumbnails. They vanish immediately.)

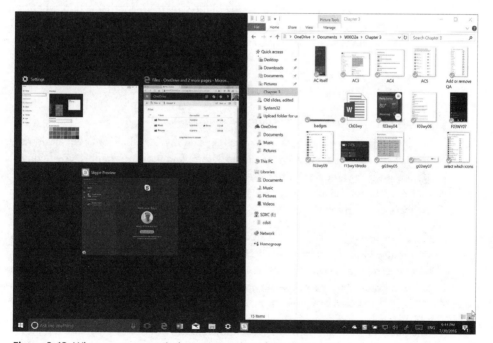

Figure 3-13 When you snap a window to one edge of the display, Windows shows other open windows in thumbnails alongside the snapped window for easy side-by-side arrangement.

Note that the window resizes when the mouse pointer hits the edge of the screen. To use this feature with minimal mouse movement, start your drag action by pointing at the title bar near the edge you're going to snap to.

As soon as you begin dragging a snapped window away from the edge of the screen, it returns to its previous size and position.

Here are a few ways you can snap windows in Windows 10 by using a mouse or by dragging directly on a touchscreen:

- Drag the title bar to the top of the screen to maximize the window, or drag the title bar away from the top edge to restore it to its previous window size.

- Drag a window title bar to any corner of the screen, and it snaps to fill that quadrant of the display. This capability is new in Windows 10 and is most useful on large, high-resolution desktop displays.

- Drag the top window border (not the title bar) to the top edge of the screen, or drag the bottom border to the bottom edge of the screen. With either action, when you reach the edge, the window snaps to full height without changing its width. When you drag the border away from the window edge, the opposite border snaps to its previous position.

Inside OUT

Snap side-by-side windows at different widths

Although Windows automatically arranges side-by-side windows at equal widths, you don't have to settle for symmetry. On a large desktop monitor, for example, you might want to arrange a news feed or Twitter stream along the right side of your display, using a third or less of the total display width and leaving room for Word or Excel to have a much larger share of the screen real estate.

The secret is to snap the first window and immediately drag its inside edge to adjust the window to your preferred width. Now grab the title bar of the window you want to see alongside it, and snap it to the opposite edge of the display. The newly snapped window expands to fill the space remaining after you adjusted the width of the first window.

The rules work the same with multimonitor setups. With two side-by-side monitors, for example, you can drag the mouse to the inside edge of a display and snap a window there, allowing for four equal-size windows lined up from left to right. By dragging the title bar, you also can move a maximized window from one screen to another on a multimonitor system.

Inside OUT

Shake to minimize distractions

An ancient Windows feature called Aero Shake, first introduced with Windows Vista, survives into Windows 10. Grab the window's title bar with the mouse or a finger and quickly move it back and forth a few times. Suddenly, all windows retreat to the taskbar except the one whose title bar you just shook. This move takes a bit of practice, but it's worth mastering. It requires only three smooth "shakes"—a left, right, left motion is best—not maniacal shaking.

Windows 10 includes keyboard shortcuts that correspond with the preceding mouse gestures. These (and a few extras) are shown in Table 3-1.

Table 3-1 Keyboard shortcuts and gestures for resizing and moving windows

Task	Keyboard shortcut	Gesture
Maximize window	Windows key+ Up Arrow	Drag title bar to top of screen
Resize window to full screen height without changing its width	Shift+Windows key+ Up Arrow	Drag top or bottom border to edge of screen
Restore a maximized or full-height window	Windows key+ Down Arrow	Drag title bar or border away from screen edge
Minimize a restored window	Windows key+ Down Arrow	Click the Minimize button
Snap to the left half of the screen	Windows key+ Left Arrow*	Drag title bar to left edge
Snap to the right half of the screen	Windows key+ Right Arrow*	Drag title bar to right edge
Move to the next virtual desktop	Ctrl+Windows key+ Left/Right Arrow	Three-finger swipe on precision touchpad; none for mouse
Move to the next monitor	Shift+Windows key+ Left/Right Arrow	Drag title bar
Minimize all windows except the active window (press again to restore windows previously minimized with this shortcut)	Windows key+ Home	"Shake" the title bar
Minimize all windows	Windows key+M	
Restore windows after minimizing	Shift+Windows key+M	

* Pressing this key repeatedly cycles through the left, right, and restored positions. If you have more than one monitor, it cycles these positions on each monitor in turn.

CHAPTER 3

The Windows 10 taskbar also exposes some traditional window-management menus. The secret? Hold the Shift key as you right-click a taskbar button. For a button that represents a single window, the menu includes commands to Restore, Move, Size, Minimize, Maximize, and Close the window. For a grouped taskbar button, Shift+right-click displays commands to arrange, restore, minimize, or close all windows in the group.

If you find it disconcerting to have windows snap to a certain size and position when you drag their title bars, you can disable Snap. The options controlling Snap are at Settings > System > Multitasking.

Using a keyboard and mouse in Windows 10

As of the Anniversary Edition of Windows 10, version 1607, the options for customizing a key-board had not yet made the transition from Control Panel to Settings. To find these options, type **keyboard** in the Search box. The options are few, but they might affect your typing com-fort level:

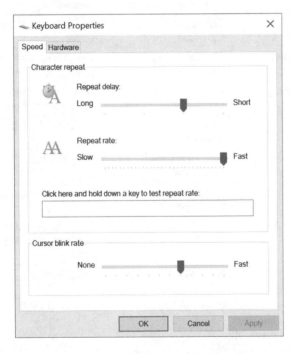

The repeat delay—the amount of time Windows waits as you hold down a key before repeat-ing that key—is set, by default, a bit long for the tastes of some proficient typists. You can make it shorter by dragging the slider to the right. On the other hand, if you sometimes find that

Windows gives you an unwanted string of repeated characters, you can drag the slider leftward. You might also then want to reduce the repeat rate as well.

Inside OUT

Reconfigure the Caps Lock key to avoid shouting

If you occasionally find yourself accidentally stuck in Caps Lock mode so that your emails are shouting or your text documents look like a demand letter from a creditor, consider the following tweak.

On a standard 101-key desktop keyboard, you can disable the Caps Lock key so that it does nothing whatsoever: Open Registry Editor and navigate to HKLM\System\CurrentControl-Set\Control\Keyboard Layout. Add a Binary value called Scancode Map. Set the data for this key to

00000000 00000000 02000000 00003A00 00000000

Close Registry Editor, restart, and you'll never be stuck in Caps Lock again.

Alternatively, you can use SharpKeys (a free download from *https://sharpkeys.codeplex.com*) to remap the Caps Lock key to anything you might find more useful—a second Windows key, for example.

CHAPTER 3

Mastering keyboard shortcuts

Windows 10 offers so many keyboard shortcuts that mastering them all would be a remarkable feat, a bit like memorizing 80 digits of pi. Learning a handful or several handfuls, on the other hand, can definitely improve your productivity.

Table 3-1, earlier in this chapter, offered a list of keyboard shortcuts having to do with window management. Table 3-2 presents an idiosyncratic selection of everyday shortcuts—the ones that we use most often and would have trouble living without. Because your own needs probably differ from ours, however, you might want to peruse the exhaustive list that appears at *https://aka.ms/keyboard-shortcuts*.

Table 3-2 A short list of general-purpose keyboard shortcuts

Shortcut	Effect
Ctrl+C	Copy selection
Ctrl+X	Cut selection
Ctrl+V	Paste Clipboard contents

Shortcut	Effect
Ctrl+Z	Undo
Ctrl+Y	Redo
Ctrl+N	Open new window (in many apps)
Ctrl+S	Save
Ctrl+W	Close current window (in many apps)
Ctrl+P	Print (in many apps)
Ctrl+A	Select all
Ctrl+Shift+Esc	Open Task Manager
F2	Rename (in File Explorer)
F3	Search (File Explorer and many browsers)
F5	Refresh (File Explorer and many browsers)
Alt+F4	Close current window
Alt+Enter	Display properties dialog box
Windows key	Display Start
Windows key+E	Open new File Explorer window
Windows key+I	Open Settings
Windows key+R	Open the Run command
Windows key+X	Open the Quick Link menu

Using alternative keyboard layouts

At the release of the Anniversary Edition, Windows 10 offered keyboard support for 140 languages (including English but not including Dvorak). Most of these languages are available as extra-cost language packs, and installing a language pack changes the entire Windows user interface—menus, dialog boxes, and all—to the selected language. But you can install a keyboard layout for another language for free and without changing the user interface. This might prove handy if you work in an international environment and occasionally need to dash off an email to, say, a Russian-speaking colleague or customer.

To install another keyboard, go to Settings > Time & Language > Region & Language. When you click on Add A Language, the entire set of available languages appears, and you can make your choice. When the keyboard is installed, it becomes available through the Input Indicator system icon, which typically lives on the taskbar, adjacent to the clock. Clicking there pops up a menu of available keyboards, along with a Language Preferences command:

Clicking Language Preferences takes you back to Settings > Time & Language > Region & Language.

To remove a language, make it the default, or set options relating to the language, return to Settings > Time & Language > Region & Language and then click on the language.

Inside OUT

For emojis, accented characters, and language assistance, use the Touch keyboard

The primary purpose of the Touch keyboard, as its name suggests, is to facilitate input on a touch-enabled device. We discuss and illustrate it, therefore, later in this chapter. (See "Using Windows 10 on a touchscreen device.") But it's invaluable for certain kinds of input on any computer—which is why it's included on non-touch machines as well as tablets.

To enter an emoji—one of the whimsical characters available on all mobile platforms and on Windows 10—click on the smiley-face icon on the bottom row of the keyboard. To enter a character with a diacritical mark, click and hold the unadorned character; your choices will appear in a pop-up window. Hold the *n*, for example, and the option to type ñ will appear. Hold the *o* and you'll have the opportunity to enter variants like ò, ö, ô, and even œ. If you've ever labored to memorize ANSI codes or wandered through Character Map in search of the accent you need, you'll certainly appreciate this feature.

As for language assistance, suppose you're a whiz touch typist in English but you hunt and peck in Russian. When you select Russian as your input source, the touch keyboard will turn to Cyrillic. You can use it as a visual layout guide while you type with your standard keyboard. Or you can use the touch keyboard to do the pecking as well as the hunting.

CHAPTER 3

Taming your mouse or other pointing device

To teach your mouse new tricks, go to Settings > Devices > Mouse & Touchpad. With settings here under Mouse, you can swap the functions of your left and right mouse buttons (great for left-handed folks) and control how much to scroll each time you roll the mouse wheel. You'll find other mouse settings by scrolling to the bottom of the Mouse & Touchpad page and clicking Additional Mouse Options. Doing so opens the Mouse Properties dialog box:

Mouse Properties has settings that define a double-click (that is, how quickly you must twice press the mouse button for it to be detected as a double-click instead of two clicks), change pointer shapes, configure other pointer options, and more. Depending on the mouse you have, you might find additional options in Mouse Properties or in a separate app.

If your computer has a precision touchpad, the Mouse & Touchpad page in Settings > Devices has a lot to offer, as shown in Figure 3-14.

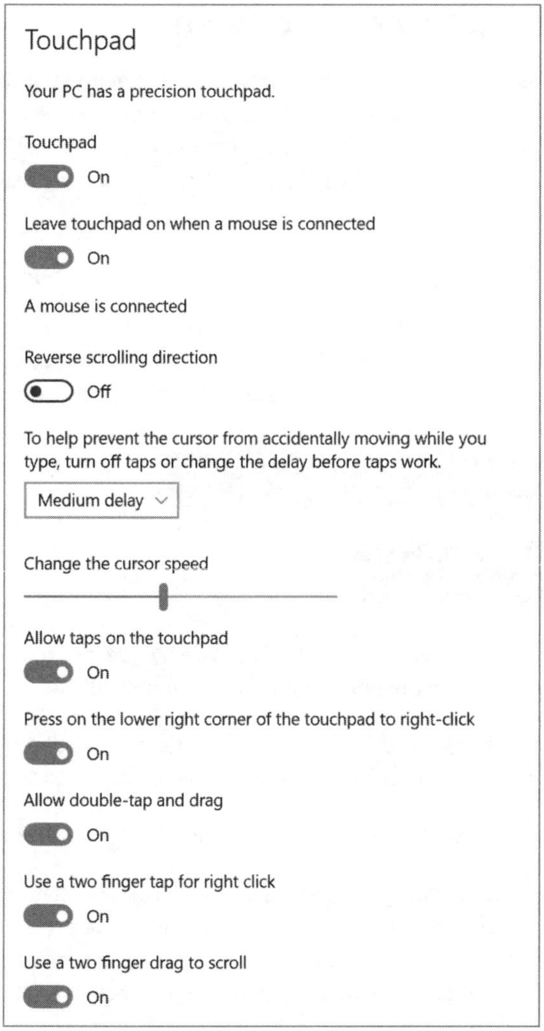

Touchpad

Your PC has a precision touchpad.

Touchpad

On

Leave touchpad on when a mouse is connected

On

A mouse is connected

Reverse scrolling direction

Off

To help prevent the cursor from accidentally moving while you
type, turn off taps or change the delay before taps work.

Medium delay ∨

Change the cursor speed

Allow taps on the touchpad

On

Press on the lower right corner of the touchpad to right-click

On

Allow double-tap and drag

On

Use a two finger tap for right click

On

Use a two finger drag to scroll

On

Figure 3-14 Touchpad users are richly rewarded by visiting Settings > Devices > Mouse & Touchpad
and scrolling down to the settings under Touchpad.

You can use options here to turn off the touchpad when you have a mouse attached or disable
it altogether. Those who've been annoyed when the pointer suddenly hops to a new location
while they type (usually because a thumb lightly grazed the touchpad) will shout hosannas
about the setting that delays cursor moves. Other settings determine what various gestures
(tapping, double-tapping, tapping with two or three fingers, dragging with two or three fingers,
and so on) will do.

CHAPTER 3

Using Windows 10 on a touchscreen device

Tablet Mode was specifically designed for sustained use with a touchscreen-equipped device such as a tablet or hybrid PC. We already discussed the Windows user experience with a conventional PC. Tablet Mode introduces a series of significant changes—automatically if it detects you're using a touchscreen device without a keyboard attached, or manually if you want to treat a touchscreen-equipped laptop as if it were a tablet.

Turning on Tablet Mode makes the following changes in the Windows 10 user experience:

- Reconfigures the taskbar, bumping up button sizes, adding a back button, replacing the search box with a search button, and hiding all taskbar buttons. The following comparison shows the normal taskbar on top and the same area in Tablet Mode below it:

- All apps run in full screen. It's possible to snap two apps side by side, but they have a thick sizing bar between them, similar to the one introduced in Windows 8.

- Start opens in full screen, with the left column hidden by default and accessible only by tapping the hamburger menu in the upper left corner of the display.

- Swiping from the left and right enables Task View and Action Center, respectively.

Windows 10 makes some assumptions about your preferences based on your hardware. On conventional PCs with a keyboard and mouse, Tablet Mode is off. On dedicated tablets, this mode is on by default. You can adjust these preferences at Settings > System > Tablet Mode. On a hybrid device with a relatively small touchscreen, you might prefer to have Tablet Mode on full time, for example.

The other essential feature of a touchscreen-equipped device, especially one without a keyboard, is the presence of the extremely versatile Windows 10 Touch Keyboard. It allows text entry into dialog boxes, web forms, your browser's address bar, documents, the search box—anywhere you would normally need a physical keyboard to provide input.

Figure 3-15 shows the standard Touch Keyboard layout.

The Touch Keyboard should appear automatically when you tap to position the insertion point in a place that accepts text entry. On touchscreen-equipped devices, you can make the Touch Keyboard appear by tapping its button, which appears in the notification area on the right of the taskbar. (If this button is hidden, right-click or do a long press on the taskbar and then select the Show Touch Keyboard Button option.)

Figure 3-15 This is the standard Touch Keyboard; use the controls in the upper right to move, dock, or close the keyboard. Use the &123 key to switch to other layouts.

The limited screen space available for the Touch Keyboard means you have to switch layouts to enter symbols and numbers. Tap the &123 key in the lower left corner to switch between the standard QWERTY layout and the first of two symbol layouts, as shown in Figure 3-16. Note that the layout includes a dedicated number pad, which is extremely handy for working with spreadsheets and performing other data-entry tasks.

Click to see additional symbol layouts

Figure 3-16 Tap the &123 key in the lower left corner to switch between the standard QWERTY keys and this alternate view of symbols and numbers.

In some respects, the Touch Keyboard is more versatile than its physical counterparts. Entering typographic symbols like the interrobang or emoji doesn't require the use of ANSI codes. Instead, you can enter characters directly. To show the first of more than 30 emoji keyboard layouts, each containing 30 symbols, click the "happy face" button on the bottom row.

CHAPTER 3

With the emoji keyboard layout visible, the bottom row displays keys you can use to switch between different categories, several of which have multiple layouts, accessible via the left and right arrows below the Tab key. Figure 3-17 shows an example.

Figure 3-17 Windows 10 supports hundreds of emoji characters. Pick a category from the bottom row and use the arrow keys to scroll through different character sets, 30 at a time.

NOTE

For a full list of officially supported Windows-compatible emoji characters, see *http://emojipedia.org/microsoft-emoji-list/*.

In addition to the conventional QWERTY layout, the Touch Keyboard comes in some variations, which are accessible by tapping the Switch key in the lower right corner, as shown in Figure 3-18.

Figure 3-18 Tap the Switch key in the lower right corner of any keyboard layout to change to a different arrangement or adjust language preferences.

The Handwriting panel, shown in Figure 3-19, is most useful with devices that support pen input, such as Microsoft's line of Surface and Surface Pro devices. Text you enter in the input box is automatically translated into characters for entry at the current insertion point.

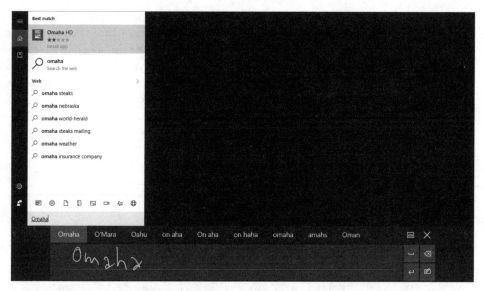

Figure 3-19 The handwriting input box does a frankly remarkable job at translating even sloppy penmanship into readable results.

Handwriting recognition is excellent, even for casual entry. As Figure 3-19 shows, you also have autocorrect options if the recognition engine guesses wrong.

The Split Keyboard divides the keyboard into halves, moving the left half to the left edge of the display and the right to the right edge. With the split layout, you can grip a tablet in portrait or landscape mode and use your thumbs for typing. It takes some practice, but anyone who ever used an old-school BlackBerry phone can confirm that with practice you can achieve startling typing speed.

By default, the Touch Keyboard appears at the bottom of the screen, pushing the contents of the page above it for unobstructed text entry. An X in the upper right corner lets you close any keyboard layout, a second button allows you to lock the keyboard into position, and the four-headed button lets you move a floating keyboard to a more comfortable position on a larger display.

Using the Windows Ink workspace

The Windows Ink workspace, shown in Figure 3-20, is a new feature in version 1607 that gathers pen-enabled apps into a pane that appears on the right side of your screen when you tap (or click) the Windows Ink Workspace taskbar button. (If you don't see that button, right-click the taskbar and click or tap the Show Windows Ink Workspace button.)

The three apps shown in the figure are Sticky Notes, Sketchpad, and Screen Sketch. Sticky Notes has been around for many iterations of Windows. In the—perhaps near—future, the app will let you dash off a reminder to yourself and have Cortana pick up that reminder. Sketchpad is a blank canvas for freehand drawing, and Screen Sketch offers an image of the desktop for drawing. Much as you use the Web Note feature in Microsoft Edge to annotate the current webpage, Screen Sketch gives you a way to mark up whatever is on your desktop. An editing toolbar atop both Screen Sketch and Sketchpad provides basic drawing tools, a ruler for drawing straight lines, and commands to copy, save, share, and delete your work.

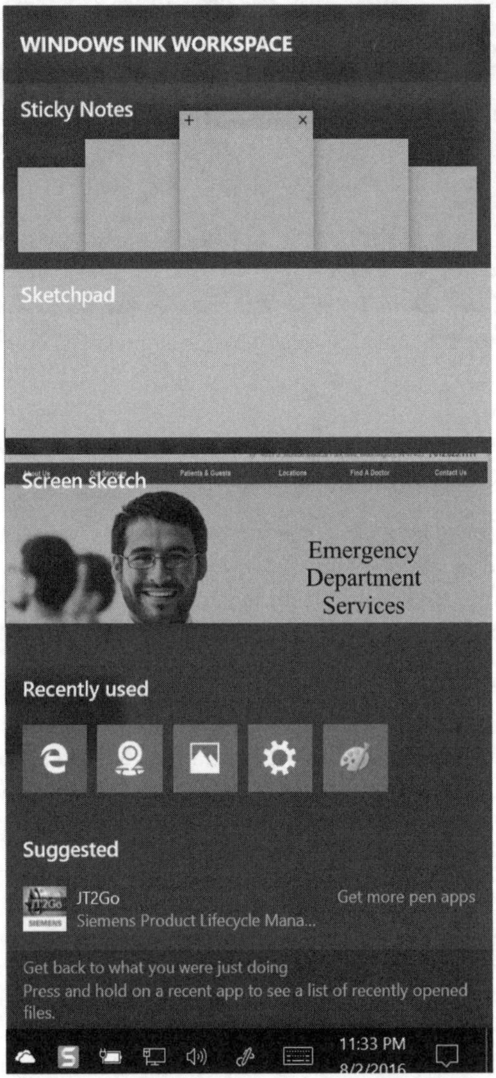

Figure 3-20 The Windows Ink workspace offers a menu of pen-enabled applications, along with links to recently used apps of any kind and links to items you might want to pick up at the Windows Store.

The apps in the Windows Ink workspace, of course, are intended to give you a taste of what you can do with the pen. Much more elaborate pen-friendly programs exist, and you can use them to perform some remarkable feats. Using Microsoft Word, for instance, you can insert handwritten comments and annotations into a document. Another member of the Office family, OneNote, goes even further, indexing your handwritten notes and allowing you to search through an entire notebook for a word or phrase.

Setting pen options

Options relating to your pen are located at Settings > Devices > Pen & Windows Ink. In the lower portion of that settings page, you'll find a set of options for configuring pen shortcuts. (See Figure 3-21.) These options, which require a pen with a shortcut button, govern what happens when you press that button once, press it twice in quick succession, and press and hold.

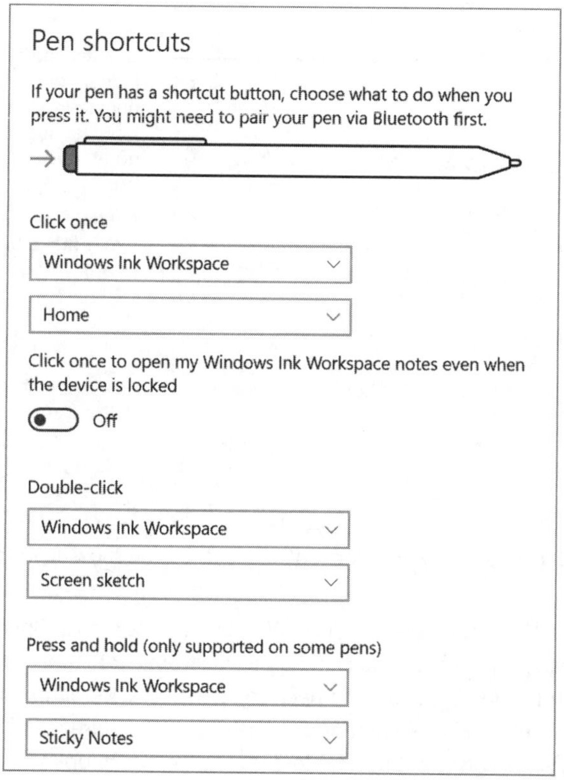

Pen shortcuts

If your pen has a shortcut button, choose what to do when you press it. You might need to pair your pen via Bluetooth first.

Click once

| Windows Ink Workspace ⌄ |

| Home ⌄ |

Click once to open my Windows Ink Workspace notes even when the device is locked

Off

Double-click

| Windows Ink Workspace ⌄ |

| Screen sketch ⌄ |

Press and hold (only supported on some pens)

| Windows Ink Workspace ⌄ |

| Sticky Notes ⌄ |

Figure 3-21 With the single-click, double-click, and hold settings, you can train your pen to launch a program, perform a screen capture, summon Cortana, or simply open the Windows Ink workspace.

Within the three sets of drop-downs, you'll find options to launch programs, capture screens, open Cortana, and more.

Working with fonts

The days when your choice of fonts ended just beyond Arial and Times New Roman are long gone; if you include all the language variants and style variants (bold, italic, and so on), Windows 10 comes with hundreds of fonts.

The headquarters for font management is Fonts in Control Panel, which is shown in Figure 3-22. From this list of fonts, you can select a font (or a font family, which appears as a stack) and then click Preview to open a window that shows the font's characters in sizes ranging from 12 point to 72 point. (A point is a printer's measurement that is still used in modern digital typography. There are 72 points to an inch.)

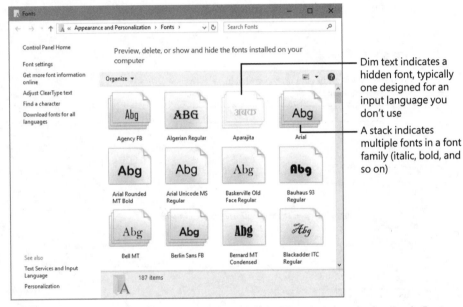

Dim text indicates a hidden font, typically one designed for an input language you don't use

A stack indicates multiple fonts in a font family (italic, bold, and so on)

Figure 3-22 Hidden fonts don't appear in application font lists, but they do show up in Fonts.

The primary font format used by Windows is TrueType. Windows also supports OpenType and PostScript Type 1 fonts. To install a new font, you can drag its file from a folder or compressed .zip archive to Fonts in Control Panel. But you don't need to open Fonts; the simplest way to install a font is to right-click its file in File Explorer and choose Install. Because font file names are often somewhat cryptic, you might want to double-click the file, which opens the font preview window, to see what you're getting. If it's a font you want, click the Install button.

NOTE

PostScript Type 1 fonts normally consist of two or three files. The one you use to install the font—regardless of which method you use—is the .pfm file, whose file type is shown in File Explorer as Type 1 Font File.

Making text easier to read

If you like to work at high screen resolutions but find yourself straining to read the text, you can try the following:

- Look for scaling ("zoom") commands in the text-centric programs you use. Many programs, including most modern word processors, include these scaling features. Scaling text up to a readable size is a good solution for particular programs, but it doesn't change the size of icon text, system menus (such as Start), or system dialog boxes.

- To enlarge part of the screen, use the Magnifier tool. (For more information, see "Overcoming challenges" in Chapter 4.)

- Use the scaling options in Display settings. Adjusting the scaling to a higher level enables you to have readable text at higher screen resolutions.

To adjust display scaling, go to Settings > System > Display. Adjust the slider below Change The Size Of Text, Apps, And Other Items, as shown in Figure 3-23. The slider for adjusting display sizes has only three or four (depending on your display hardware) predefined settings; it's not continuously adjustable as a slider control might imply.

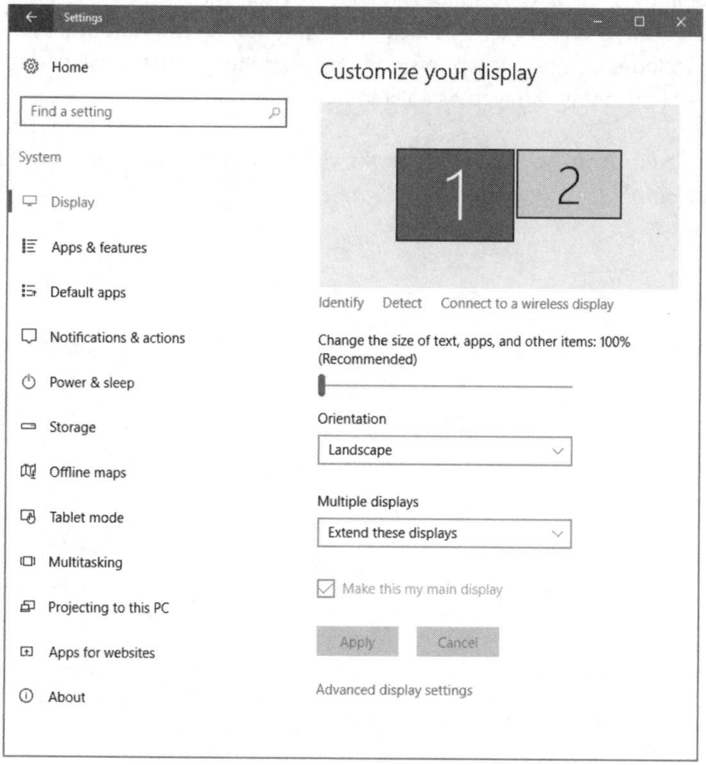

Figure 3-23 By moving the slider to the right, you can magnify the size of text throughout Windows.

➤ For information about screen resolution and other display configuration tasks, see "Configuring displays" in Chapter 13.

Using font smoothing to make text easier on the eyes

ClearType is a font-smoothing technology that reduces jagged edges of characters, thus easing eye strain.

To check or change your font-smoothing settings, type **cleartype** in the search box and then click Adjust ClearType Text. Doing so opens the ClearType Text Tuner, which, in its first screen, has a check box that turns ClearType on when it's selected. The ensuing screens that appear each time you click Next offer optometrist-style choices ("Which is better, number 1 or number 2?") to help you reach ClearType perfection. If you have more than one monitor attached, the ClearType Text Tuner goes through this exercise for each one.

Windows includes seven fonts that are optimized for ClearType. The names of six of these—Constantia, Cambria, Corbel, Calibri, Candara, and Consolas—begin with the letter c—just to help cement the connection with ClearType. If you're particularly prone to eye fatigue, you might want to consider favoring these fonts in documents you create. (Constantia and Cambria are serif fonts, considered particularly suitable for longer documents and reports. The other four are sans serif fonts, good for headlines and advertising.) The seventh ClearType-optimized font, Segoe UI, is the typeface used for text elements throughout the Windows user interface. (Windows also includes a ClearType-optimized font called Meiryo that's designed to improve the readability of horizontally arrayed Asian languages.)

➤ For information about how ClearType works, visit Microsoft's ClearType site at *https://bit.ly/ ClearTypeInfo*.

Personalizing Windows 10

One could argue that color schemes, desktop backgrounds, and lock screens that feature your kids or your favorite sports team are just eye candy, unrelated to personal productivity.

We beg to differ.

Those seemingly small changes might not affect your productivity directly, the way that, say, pinning shortcuts to the taskbar does. But creating a visually pleasing workspace makes you more comfortable with your PC. And when you're more comfortable, you're more productive.

With that goal in mind, we introduce the extensive lineup of personalization features in Microsoft Windows 10. It's your PC; make it reflect your preferences, your needs, your style. Make it work for you.

Many of the features we discuss in this chapter will be familiar from earlier Windows versions, but a few are genuinely new, including the capability to use the same image on both the sign-in screen and the lock screen.

We start with a quick review of what you'll find on the Personalization page in Settings.

Settings vs. Control Panel

As we've noted elsewhere in this book, the engineers and designers who build Windows have been steadily migrating settings from the old Control Panel to the modern Settings app. The Settings app made its first appearance in Windows 8, beginning the transition of personalization and other settings from Control Panel, the desktop app that has served this function since the beginning of Windows back in 1985. In the Windows 10 Anniversary Update, released in the summer of 2016, you'll find that transition has made impressive progress.

Although you'll find Personalization options in both Settings and Control Panel, the latter contains mostly legacy settings. The far more complete selection is in Settings, where Personalization is one of the nine top-level categories.

You'll find a shortcut to Settings just above the Power button when you open Start. Alternatively, you can launch it with a keyboard shortcut: Windows key+I. (That's a capital "eye," not a lowercase "ell.") To open Control Panel, right-click or long-tap the Start button (or press Windows key+X), and then click or tap Control Panel. Of course, using the search box, you can find and launch either one, as well as find and launch the page or app for individual settings.

In this chapter, we guide you to the most effective way to make a specific setting, be it via Settings or Control Panel. But there's no need to memorize a particular pathway. Use the search box in Settings; the results include matches from Settings *and* Control Panel. (The corresponding search box in Control Panel searches only within Control Panel.) In Figure 4-1, for example, you can see the two options from the classic Control Panel beneath the top three options from Settings.

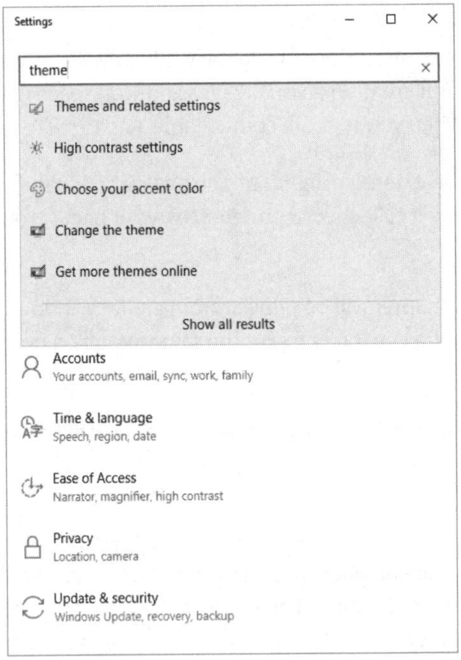

Figure 4-1 When you search from the modern Settings app, the results include options from Control Panel as well.

Customizing the visual appearance

The most obvious way to personalize your Windows experience is to customize its visual appearance—the desktop background, lock screen picture, accent colors, and so on. These options are neatly arranged under the Personalization heading in Settings.

Selecting the desktop background

You can perk up any desktop with a background image. Your background can be supplied by a graphics file in any of several common formats: BMP, GIF (static only, not animated), JPEG, PNG, and TIFF. If you can't settle on a single image, set up a slide show of images instead. And if you find pictures too distracting, just pick a background color. (That last option is especially useful if you use the desktop as a place to store files and program shortcuts.)

To select any of these options, go to Settings > Personalization > Background. The Background drop-down list offers the three options shown in Figure 4-2.

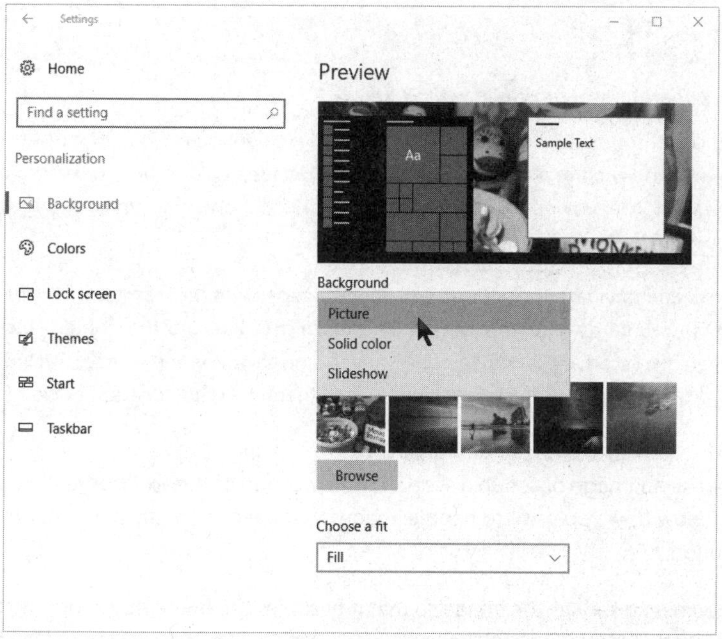

Figure 4-2 The options on the Background page change, depending on which of these three options you select.

CHAPTER 4

Here's what you can do with each of the options in this list:

- **Picture** displays a single image of your choice, scaled to fit the resolution of your display. Windows 10 includes a default selection of images, and PC makers often include an additional selection of their own. Click Browse to choose one of your own pictures.

- **Solid Color** covers the background with a color you select from a palette of two dozen shades.

- **Slideshow** is like the Picture option, but with a twist: At an interval you select (at one of six preconfigured intervals ranging from 1 minute to 1 day), Windows changes the desktop background to a new picture from the folder you specify. Unless you specify otherwise, Windows uses the Pictures library (which includes the Pictures folder in your user profile and its counterpart on OneDrive) as sources for the slide show. For best results, we recommend that you select a group of properly sized images, copy them to their own folder, and then click Browse to replace the default choice with your custom folder.

Inside OUT

Restore the photographs furnished with Windows

When you click Browse and select a new picture, your selection replaces the rightmost one of the five existing picture choices. But what if you decide you'd rather go back to one of those terrific photos provided with Windows? Getting any one of them back is simple, but not obvious.

Click Browse and navigate to %Windir%\Web\Wallpaper. (On most systems, %Windir% is C:\Windows.) You'll find a handful of nice pictures in subfolders of that folder—including the ones you displaced. If you downloaded any themes from online sources, including those offered by Microsoft, you'll find pictures for those themes in that location as well.

After you choose an image or set up a slide show, select one of the six Choose A Fit options to let Windows know how you want to handle images that are not exactly the same size as your screen resolution:

- **Fill** stretches or shrinks the image so that it occupies the full screen, cropping the image in one or both dimensions so that no blank space remains on the sides or the top and bottom.

- **Fit** reduces or enlarges the image to exactly the width or height of the display, without changing its aspect ratio or cropping the image; this option might result in letterbox bars (using the current background color) on either side or above and below the image.

CHAPTER 4

Inside OUT

Assign separate images to multiple monitors

Of the six fit options we describe here, only Span is specifically intended for use with systems that have additional monitors attached. For the remaining five options, the image you select and the fit options are repeated on each display, and there's no obvious way in Settings to assign a different image to each monitor.

Even though it's not obvious, there's a secret menu that allows you to specify that you want to use an image with a specific monitor. The images you want to use must be available in the list of five thumbnails on the Background page in Settings. Right-click each thumbnail in turn to display a message like the one shown here, with options for each available monitor:

Alas, these settings aren't saved when you switch between single and multiple monitors, as you might with a laptop that occasionally connects to a docking station. If that feature means a lot to you, try the third-party utility DisplayFusion (*https://displayfusion.com*). The software is available in a free version that supports per-monitor background images; a paid Pro version is also available.

- **Stretch** reduces or enlarges the image so that it fits both dimensions, distorting the image if necessary. If there's a significant mismatch between the aspect ratios of the image and the display, the effect can be unpleasant.

- **Tile** repeats the image at its original size to fill all monitors. This option is most effective for abstract backgrounds or for simple, small images where the repeated design looks like a pattern.

CHAPTER 4

- **Center** displays the image at its original size in the center of the screen, without stretching. If the image is smaller than the display resolution, this can leave blank space on the sides or at the top and bottom; if the image is larger than the display, some parts of the image might be cropped away to fit.

- **Span** works like Fill to display a single image across multiple monitors. On a single-monitor PC, this option is the same as Fill.

Here are some other ways to change the desktop background:

- Right-click an image file in File Explorer, and choose Set As Desktop Background.

- Right-click an image in Internet Explorer, and choose Set As Background.

- Open any image file in Paint, open the File menu, and choose Set As Desktop Background. A submenu lets you choose the Fill, Tile, or Center picture position.

- Use the Photos app to open an image file, click or tap the ellipsis at the right side of the menu bar, and then click or tap Set As Background.

In fact, the Photos app contains a secret feature you can use to crop and resize images so that they're a perfect fit with your display. Here's how:

1. Open the image in the Photos app, and click Edit > Crop.

2. Click Aspect Ratio > Lock Screen to display crop controls on the image, as shown in Figure 4-3.

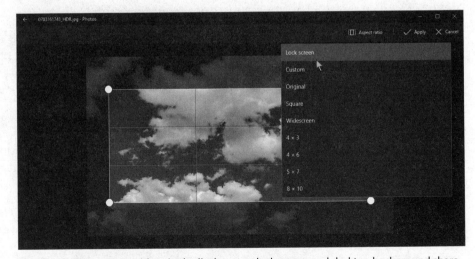

Figure 4-3 On a system with a single display, your lock screen and desktop background share the same aspect ratio. Use the Photos app to crop an image so that it's a perfect fit in either place.

3. Move any of the four crop controls to expand or shrink the crop area, preserving the aspect ratio. Move the image under the crop area to select the portion you want in the final file.

4. When you're finished, click Apply, and then click Save A Copy.

    That option doesn't allow you to specify a location or file name for the saved file; it simply creates a copy with a number appended to the end of the file name, in the same folder as the original image. To make that custom background image easier to find, go through one more step, immediately after you finish saving the cropped image.

5. Right-click the image in the Photos app, and click Open Folder from the shortcut menu. That opens File Explorer with the newly saved file already selected.

6. Press Ctrl+X to cut the file, and then paste it in a folder of your choosing.

If you use this procedure to customize your favorite images, we recommend creating a Desktop Backgrounds subfolder in the Pictures folder or in OneDrive to ensure that your collection stays together.

Selecting colors

With a beautiful desktop background in place, your next personalization step might be to select a complementary accent color and specify where and how to use it. If you're coming to Windows 10 directly from Windows 7, this group of settings represents a major change. In Windows 7, you can assign separate colors to dozens of different pieces of the Windows interface. In Windows 10, you choose one systemwide accent color from a palette of 48 solid colors, or allow Windows to choose a color that matches your desktop background, as shown in Figure 4-4. Sliders beneath the Accent Color palette provide limited control over where that color appears.

The Automatically Pick An Accent Color From My Background option is the best choice if you configured a slide show for the desktop background. With this setting on, the accent color changes each time the background picture changes, minimizing the chances that a particular image will represent a poor contrast with a background color you choose manually. On the other hand, be prepared to see shades of purple, pink, and yellow, depending on the image.

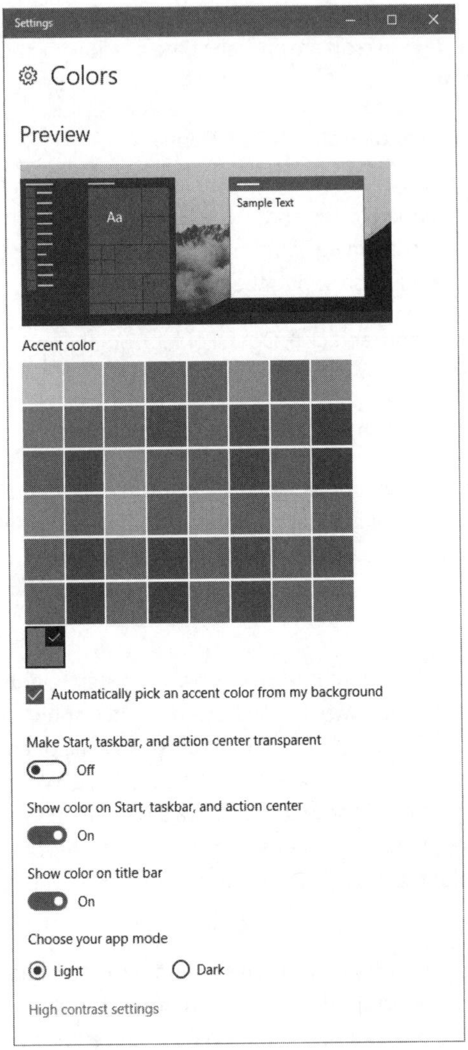

Figure 4-4 Use the check box just below the color palette to specify that you want Windows to match the accent color to your background automatically.

The accent color you choose appears in some places automatically—the background of tiles that don't assign a custom color, text links in universal apps, and on the desktop when a background image doesn't fill the display fully. Use the sliders beneath the palette to apply your accent color (with or without transparency) to other parts of Windows 10.

Turning on the Show Color On Start, Taskbar, And Action Center option applies the accent color as a background to the taskbar and to Start and Action Center, when they're visible. With this option turned off, those areas have a dark background. A separate Show Color On Title Bar switch toggles color on or off for the title bars in desktop programs and universal apps that don't specify a custom color.

If you're expecting the Make Start, Taskbar, And Action Center Transparent option to resemble the older Aero Glass effect, you'll be disappointed. The effect is not "transparent" as in clear glass; rather, it's more like darkly tinted glass, which allows you to see through each of these elements to a faint shadow of the underlying desktop and any windows that might be open on it. To some, transparency is a cool effect; others find it distracting.

Choose Your App Mode is a new option with the Anniversary Update, giving you a choice of light and dark backgrounds for modern apps, including Settings. On some portable devices, you might prefer a dark background as a power-saving measure.

The final option on the Colors tab is High Contrast Settings. That option is intended to help users with visual impairments. For more information, see "Overcoming challenges" later in this chapter.

TROUBLESHOOTING

The automatic color option doesn't change the color

Suppose you turn off the first option and select a color, and then later decide you'd rather go back to the automatic color. So you turn on the option to automatically select an accent color and . . . nothing happens. When you turn it on, the automatic option doesn't take effect until the *next time* the background changes. If you want to use the automatic color associated with the current background, return to the background page and select the same background again; that triggers Windows to "automatically" select an accent color.

Customizing the lock screen and sign-in screen

The lock screen is a security precaution that prevents someone from accessing your account when you step away from the computer while you're signed in. To display the lock screen, click Start, and then click your account picture, where you'll find Lock on the menu of available options. Of course, the much faster way to lock the screen is with a keyboard shortcut—Windows key+L.

Just as you can customize the desktop background, you can change the lock screen to your liking by adding custom images and specifying which notifications appear on the lock screen when you're away. Go to Settings > Personalization > Lock Screen to see your options, as shown in Figure 4-5.

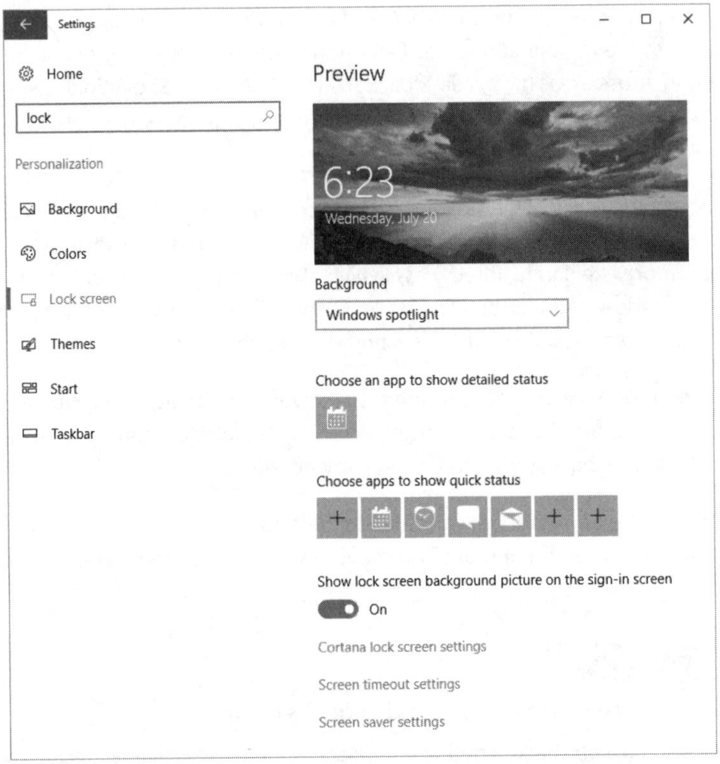

Figure 4-5 The Windows Spotlight option changes the lock screen background at regular intervals, using visually compelling images from Microsoft's vast collection.

These settings closely resemble those for the desktop background. In fact, under the Background menu, you'll find Picture and Slideshow options that work exactly like those under the Background headings, so we won't repeat the detailed instructions here.

The Windows Spotlight option supplies a continually changing assortment of background images along with occasional helpful tips and the option to indicate whether you like or dislike a particular image—that feedback goes into the algorithm that serves future images to you.

New in the Anniversary Update is the Show Lock Screen Background Picture On The Sign-In Screen option. After you slide this switch to On, you can clear the lock screen—by clicking, swiping, or tapping any key—and see the box to enter your credentials with the same image behind it.

NOTE

Windows uses the custom lock screen image for the user who last signed in. On a PC with multiple user accounts and different lock-screen settings, this might result in you seeing a lock screen image configured by another user. If you sign out completely and then restart, Windows might display the default sign-in screen instead.

You can allow one or more apps to display their current status—such as the number of new email messages, upcoming appointments, and so on—on the lock screen. You can also see alarms and reminders here. Depending on your personal preferences, these notifications are either a convenience or a potential privacy issue; if you don't want anyone who passes by your desk to see any notifications, go to Settings > System > Notifications & Actions. Under Notifications, turn off Show Notifications On The Lock Screen and Show Alarms, Reminders, And Incoming VOIP Calls On The Lock Screen.

If you choose to use lock-screen notifications, you can configure a single app to display detailed status (the time, title, and location of your next appointment, for example) and up to seven additional apps to show quick status information. Status icons appear in the order you specify here.

Tap one of the app icons to change the app assigned to that position, or tap a plus sign to add a new notification to that position. In either case, you'll see a list of apps that support status notifications, as shown here.

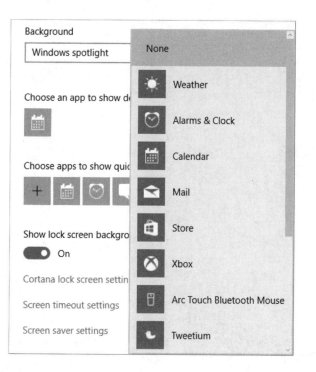

Fine-tuning visual options

Windows 10 contains a handful of legacy customization options that give you fine-grained control over small aspects of the user experience. Most of the options we discuss in this section are in the classic Control Panel, and there's a strong likelihood that some will not survive the transition to the newer Settings app in a future upgrade. So enjoy the following features while they last.

Customizing mouse pointers

As we noted at the beginning of this chapter, personalization options have been moving from the classic Control Panel to the new Settings app over time. Options to change the appearance of the mouse pointer offer a particularly good example of where this transition is not yet complete.

For example, you might want to change the size and color of the mouse pointer to make it easier to see, especially on a large, high-resolution display where the default white pointer is so small you can find it hard to make out against light backgrounds.

To quickly change the pointer size and color, go to Settings > Ease Of Access > Mouse, where you'll see the options shown in Figure 4-6.

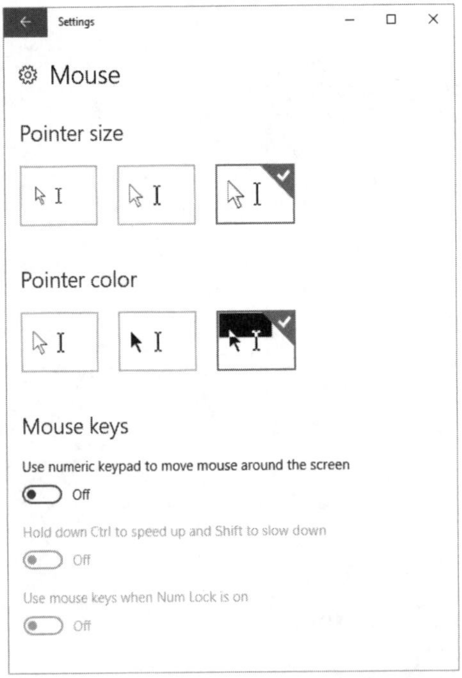

Figure 4-6 A larger pointer, especially one that shifts between dark and light depending on the background, can be easier to pick out on a large display.

Meanwhile, you can find a completely separate entry point to a closely related group of options by going to Control Panel > Ease Of Access > Ease Of Access Center > Make The Mouse Easier To Use. Figure 4-7 shows the resulting options.

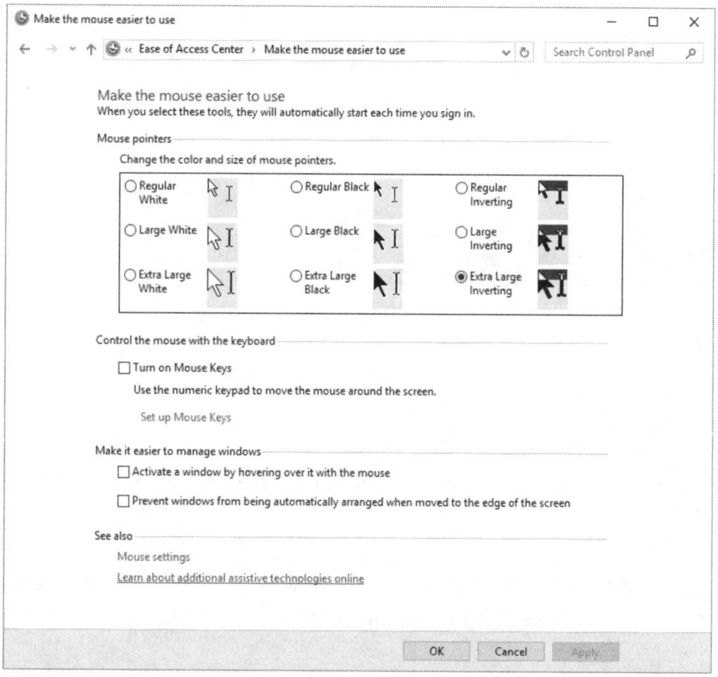

Figure 4-7 The options at the top of this dialog box are an alternative entry point to the same options in the Settings app.

The one unique option here, which isn't in the modern Settings app, is the check box next to Activate A Window By Hovering Over It With The Mouse. This behavior, sometimes known as "focus follows mouse," will be familiar to those who've used Linux-based operating systems. It definitely takes some getting used to.

Elsewhere in Control Panel, some old-style mouse pointer options are still available—at least for now.

If you think an hourglass depicts the passage of time more unambiguously than a rolling doughnut, you can easily bring back the Windows XP–era shape. You can customize the entire array of pointer shapes your system uses by going to Settings > Personalization > Themes > Mouse Pointer Settings, which opens a dialog box like the one shown in Figure 4-8. (If you find yourself on the Mouse & Touchpad page in Settings, scroll down to the bottom. Under Related Settings, click Additional Mouse Options to open the Mouse Properties dialog box.)

CHAPTER 4

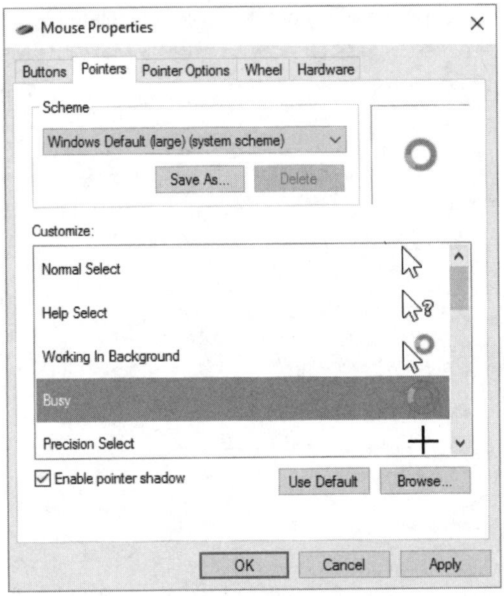

Figure 4-8 Use the options at the bottom of this dialog box to customize the predefined mouse pointer schemes.

On the Pointers tab of the Mouse Properties dialog box, you can select a Scheme from the list at the top. For those who are keeping score, this is a third way to set the size and color of the pointer.

What makes this entry point different is the list of options at the bottom, where you can change the pointer associated with specific actions, such as resizing and selecting. Windows wraps up a gamut of pointer shapes as a mouse-pointer scheme. The system comes with an assortment of predefined schemes, making it easy for you to switch from one set of pointers to another as needs or whims suggest.

Pick a pointer from the Customize box and then click Browse to select an alternative pointer shape. (The Browse button takes you to %Windir%\Cursors and displays files with the extensions .cur and .ani. The latter are animated cursors.)

The pointers included with Windows won't win any cutting-edge design awards; some of them date back to an era when an hourglass actually *was* used for keeping time. If you're inclined to roll your own mouse scheme (by using the Browse button to assign cursor files to pointer types), be sure to use the Save As command and give your work a name. That way you'll be able to switch away from it and back to it again at will.

CHAPTER 4

A few additional settings of interest are available on the Pointer Options tab, shown in Figure 4-9.

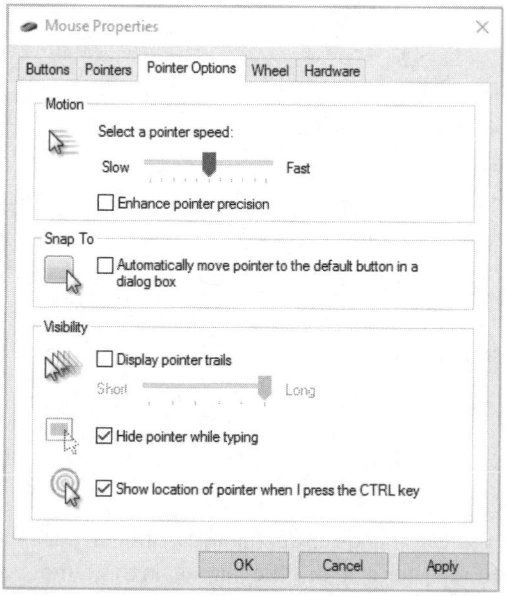

Figure 4-9 Use these pointer options to ease eyestrain by making the mouse pointer easier to spot as it moves.

If you sometimes struggle to find the mouse even after you've moved it slightly, consider turning on the Display Pointer Trails option. The last option on the page, Show Location Of Pointer When I Press The CTRL Key, provides a clever shortcut when you find yourself involuntarily playing "Where's the pointer?" Tap Ctrl to see a series of concentric circles where the mouse pointer is currently hiding.

Configuring desktop icons

A fresh, cleanly installed Windows 10 desktop (as opposed to one generated by an upgrade installation) includes a single lonely icon—Recycle Bin. If you want to display other system icons, go to Settings > Personalization > Themes > Desktop Icon Settings. The resulting dialog box, shown next, provides check boxes for five system folders—Computer, User's Files (the root folder of your own profile), Network, Recycle Bin, and Control Panel.

If you're really into customization, you can change any of the five icons that appear in the large box in the center. Note that the Control Panel icon does not appear in this center box even if you select its check box; Windows doesn't provide a way to change it.

To change an icon, select it in the center box and click Change Icon. By default, the Browse button displays the selection of alternative icons from the file %Windir%\System32\Imageres.dll. (Be sure to use the horizontal scroll bar to see them all.) If none of these suit you, try browsing to %Windir%\System32\Shell32.dll.

After you populate your desktop with icons, you might want to control their arrangement. If you right-click the desktop, you'll find two commands at the top of the shortcut menu that can help in this endeavor. To make your icons rearrange themselves when you delete one of their brethren, click View > Auto Arrange Icons. To ensure that each icon keeps a respectable distance from each of its neighbors (and that the whole gang stays together at the left side of your screen), click View > Align Icons To Grid. And if you don't want desktop icons to get in the way of your gorgeous desktop background image, click View and then clear the check mark to the left of Show Desktop Icons. (Return to this option if you decide you miss those desktop icons.)

To change the sort order of desktop icons, right-click the desktop and click Sort By. You can sort on any of four attributes: Name, Size, Item Type, or Date Modified. Sorting a second time on any attribute changes the sort order from ascending to descending (or vice versa).

Making other small visual tweaks

Windows is alive with little animations, such as when you open or close a window. Along with other effects, these can help to direct your focus to the current window or activity. But some folks find them annoying, and an argument can be made that they do take a small bite out of your computer's performance. So if you don't like them, turn them off!

In the search box of Settings or Control Panel, type **performance** and then choose Adjust The Appearance And Performance Of Windows. Alternatively, you can tap your way through this lengthy sequence: Control Panel > System And Security > System > Advanced System Settings, and then click the Settings button under Performance. The Performance Options dialog box looks like the one shown next, and you can use it to control animations and other effects on a granular level.

On modern hardware with even a moderate graphics processor, these options make little or no difference in actual performance. The loss of animation can be disconcerting in fact, as you wonder where a particular item went when you minimized it. These options offer the most pay-off on older devices with underpowered graphics hardware.

Selecting sounds for events

To specify the sounds that Windows plays as it goes through its paces, go to Settings > Personalization >Themes > Advanced Sound Settings. Custom sound schemes were extremely popular in the early days of Windows, with collections of beeps, gurgles, and chirps that Windows and various apps play in response to various system and application events. Whimsical sounds were typically included in packaged themes that also set up desktop backgrounds and animated cursors. Those sound schemes have gone the way of Pet Rocks, Beanie Babies, and other once-popular fads, but they live on in the Sound dialog box shown here:

A new installation of Windows comes with only a single scheme, called Windows Default. If you can find and install a custom sound scheme, you can choose it from the Sound Scheme list, or you can customize the current sound scheme to match your preferences.

To see which sounds are currently mapped to events, scroll through the Program Events list. If an event has a sound associated with it, its name is preceded by a speaker icon, and you can click Test to hear it. To switch to a different sound, scroll through the Sounds list or click Browse. The list displays .wav files in %Windir%\Media, but any .wav file is eligible. To silence an event, select None, the item at the top of the Sounds list.

If you rearrange the mapping of sounds to events, consider saving the new arrangement as a sound scheme. (Click Save As and supply a name.) That way, you can experiment further and still return to the saved configuration.

Inside OUT

Mute your computer

If you like event sounds in general but occasionally need complete silence from your computer, choose No Sounds in the Sound Scheme list when you want the machine to shut up. (Be sure to clear the Play Windows Startup Sound check box as well.) When sound is welcome again, you can return to the Windows Default scheme—or to any other scheme you have set up. Switching to the No Sounds scheme won't render your system mute (you'll still be able to play music when you want to hear it), but it will turn off the announcement of incoming mail and other events.

If you want to control sound levels on a more granular level—perhaps muting some applications altogether and adjusting volume levels on others—right-click the volume icon in the notification area and choose Open Volume Mixer. Volume Mixer provides a volume slider (and a mute button) for each output device and each desktop program that emits sounds.

A third option is to click the Quiet Hours button in the Quick Actions pane at the bottom of Action Center. By default, Quiet Hours are from midnight until 6 A.M., and (at least for now) there's no way to customize those hours.

Choosing a screen saver

Screen savers don't save screens, and they certainly don't save energy compared to simply blanking the display.

In the distant past, when screens were invariably CRTs and many offices displayed the same application at all hours of the working day, having an image move about during idle times probably did extend the service life of some displays. Today, this legacy feature is strictly for nostalgia buffs who want to compute like it's 1999.

By default, Windows 10 does not configure a screen saver, although it includes a handful of old favorites. To see what's available, click in the search box, type **screen saver**, and then click Change Screen Saver.

In the Screen Saver Settings dialog box (shown next), select an option under Screen Saver. Some screen savers have additional configuration options; click Settings to review your choices.

Setting date and time, currency, and other regional options

A personalized experience requires Windows to know some things about you. Not just how to read your handwriting, or your dining preferences, but some basic information about how other people in your part of the world display the date and time, currency symbols, and preferred number formats, such as whether to use a comma or a period as a separator.

In Windows 10, some language options are determined by the base Windows version. Windows configures additional regional settings using your location (with your permission) as well as settings you specify for Cortana.

In most cases, Windows 10 picks the right regional settings. You might need to customize some of these options if you prefer settings from one region (your home, typically) but Windows insists on applying settings for a different region, such as one you're visiting. Your first stop is the Time & Language section in Settings, where you can change time zones and make other time-related settings, as shown in Figure 4-10.

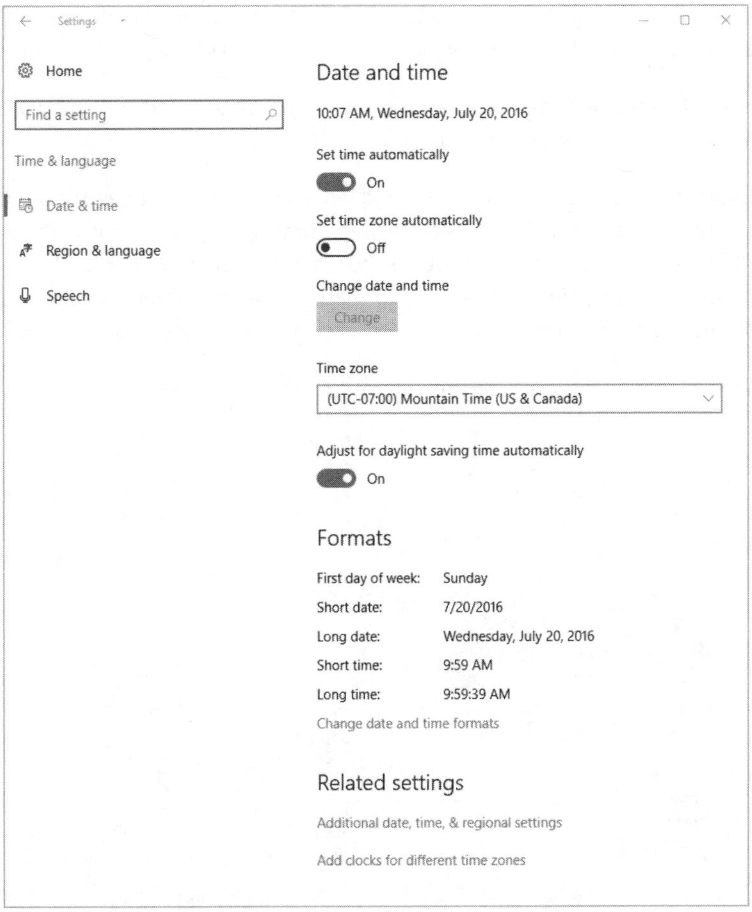

Figure 4-10 The two automatic options at the top of this Settings page usually get the time and date right. Slide either option to Off if you need to make adjustments.

If you have an always-on internet connection, we recommend leaving the top two options enabled. Windows 10 periodically synchronizes your computer's clock to an internet-based time server, fixing any "drift" if your PC's clock isn't working correctly. You can also manually set the PC's time zone here if it's not detected properly. (On a domain-based network, this setting is controlled by the domain server.)

Windows uses your country/region and language settings to provide some personalized content and for regional formats such as the way dates, times, and numbers are displayed and which measurement system is preferred. You can review the current formats by looking at the samples under Formats. Windows uses the formats you set here for displaying dates and times in the taskbar. Initially, these are set based on the country/region you specify during Windows setup, but you can easily change any or all of them by clicking Change Date And Time Formats.

On the Region & Language page, you can set a country or region and add language packs if your edition of Windows supports them.

For even more fine-grained control over the full range of settings, you need to go deep into legacy Control Panel options. Click Additional Date, Time, & Regional Settings at the bottom of the Date & Time page in Settings. That opens the Clock, Language, And Region page in Control Panel. Click Change Date, Time, Or Number Formats to open the Region dialog box, with its handful of settings; to display the full collection, click Additional Settings.

After all that clicking, you should see the options shown in Figure 4-11.

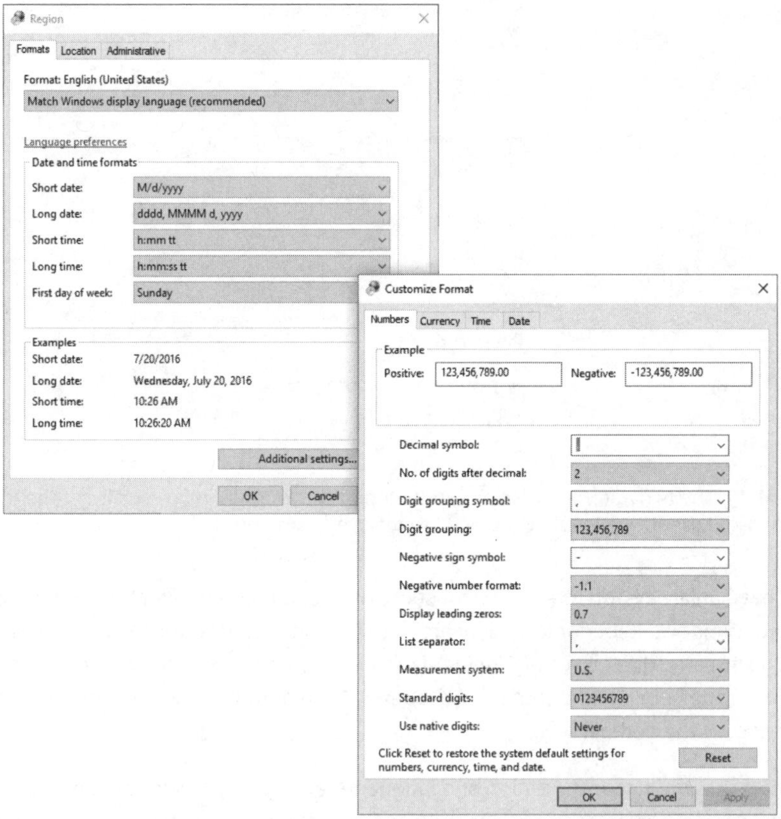

Figure 4-11 For fine-grained control over number formats, you need to dive deep into Control Panel.

If you frequently communicate with people in other time zones, you might want to scroll down to the bottom of the Date & Time page in Settings and click Add Clocks For Different Time Zones. This opens a dialog box in which you can add one or two clocks to the top of the calendar that appears when you click or tap the clock in the notification area, as shown next.

Current local time

Click to return to today's date

Optional clocks for other time zones

Click to display calendar for another month, year, or decade

Agenda shows appointments from all connected accounts

The agenda section at the bottom of that calendar displays appointments from any account you connected to the Windows Calendar app as well as reminders you set using Cortana.

CHAPTER 4

Syncing your settings between computers

When you sign in using a Microsoft account or an Azure Active Directory (Azure AD) account, Windows 10 offers the capability to synchronize settings between computers you use. When you sign in on a new PC using that account, Windows retrieves those personalized options from Microsoft OneDrive and applies them to the new device.

To manage synchronization options, go to Settings > Accounts > Sync Your Settings. Figure 4-12 shows the window that appears.

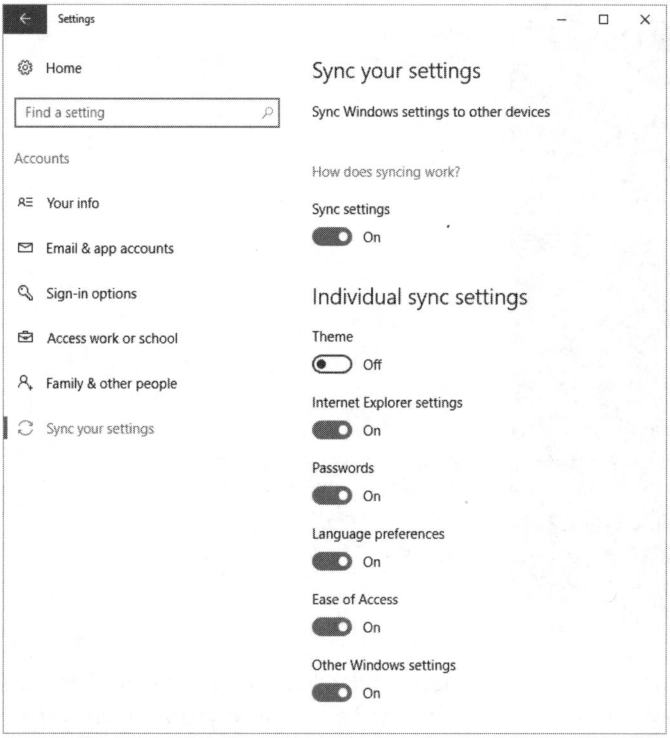

Figure 4-12 You can enable or disable all sync settings with a single setting, or control settings individually. By not syncing themes, for example, each of your PCs can have a unique visual identity.

The settings available for synchronization include the following:

- **Theme**   This group of settings includes the desktop background, accent color, sound scheme, screen saver, desktop icons, and mouse pointers.

- **Internet Explorer Settings** Custom options you set using the Internet Options command in Internet Explorer are synced. Because Microsoft Edge is a universal app, its settings are synced separately.

- **Passwords** This group includes passwords you saved for access to secure websites and other network computers.

- **Language Preferences** These settings are from the Time & Language page in the Settings app.

- **Ease Of Access** Any accessibility options you set using the Ease Of Access group in the Settings app are in this group. (For details, see the next section, "Overcoming challenges.")

- **Other Windows Settings** This group includes settings that don't fit into other categories, including printers, mouse options, File Explorer settings, notification preferences, and more.

Note that settings are synced on a per-user basis. Settings that apply to all users at your computer, such as screen resolution, are not included in the current theme or other synchronized settings. Also, settings associated with a local user account are not synchronized with other computers.

Windows 10 also supports the legacy theme formatting options, which are available in the classic Control Panel. (The short route is Settings > Personalization > Themes > Theme Settings.) The dialog box shown in Figure 4-13 shows predefined themes as well as those that are saved and synced with the current user account.

You can save themes for your own later reuse; these settings are saved as a .theme file in your %LocalAppData%\Microsoft\Windows\Themes folder. (A .theme file is a standard text file that describes all the theme settings. For complete details about .theme files, see "Theme File Format" at *https://msdn.microsoft.com/en-us/library/bb773190.aspx*.) You can also delete unwanted items from the My Themes list; simply right-click the item you no longer want and choose Delete Theme. Note that you can't delete the theme that's currently in use.

CHAPTER 4

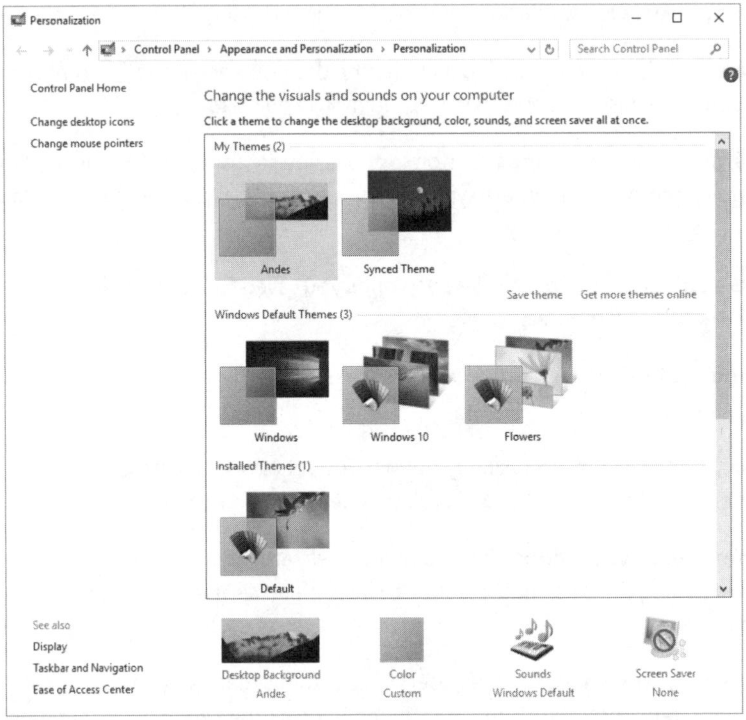

Figure 4-13 After making a set of customizations, you can save your changes as a theme for reuse later.

Inside OUT

Share themes with friends or from a local user account

Syncing themes among your devices is effortless when you sign in with a Microsoft account. But even if you use a local account, you still might want to use a theme on your other computers or share it with other users. Because a .theme file is just a text file, it doesn't contain the graphics images that make up your desktop background, the sound files you use for various events, or other necessary files that make up the entire theme experience. For the purpose of sharing themes, Windows uses a .deskthemepack file, which includes the .theme file as well as all other nonstandard theme elements. A .deskthemepack file uses the standard compressed folder (ZIP archive) format to envelop its component files. To create a .deskthemepack file from an item in My Themes, right-click it and choose Save Theme For Sharing. Unless you specify otherwise, Windows saves the .deskthemepack file in the default save location of your Documents library.

Because themes are so easily portable, you can find many compelling Windows themes online. Start your quest by clicking Get More Themes Online (under My Themes in Personalization), where Microsoft offers a nice selection.

Overcoming challenges

Microsoft has a longstanding commitment to making computing accessible and easier to use for persons with vision, hearing, or mobility impairments. Windows 10 groups these options into the Ease Of Access section of Settings. (Alternatively, you can press Windows key+U to open this page directly.) Additional options are available in the Ease Of Access Center in Control Panel.

NOTE

Because continuing development in accessibility features makes newer versions of Windows more usable than older ones, Microsoft offers free upgrades to Windows 10 for anyone who uses assistive technology products, such as screen readers, which are intended for people with significant vision, hearing, dexterity, language or learning needs. For more details, see *https://www.microsoft.com/en-us/accessibility/ windows10upgrade.*

Ease Of Access in Settings provides a prominent link to each of the following settings, which can be used alone or in combination:

- **Narrator.** This tool converts on-screen text to speech and sends it to your computer's speakers. This option allows people who are blind or have severe vision impairments to use Windows.

- **Magnifier.** This tool enlarges part of the screen, making it easier for persons with vision impairments to see objects and read text. (You can also launch Magnifier with a keyboard shortcut: Press Windows key+plus sign to launch it and zoom in. Press again to zoom in more, or press Windows key+minus sign to zoom out.)

- **High Contrast.** This tool configures Windows to use a high-contrast color scheme (by default, white text on a black background) that makes it easier for visually impaired users to read the screen.

- **Closed Captions.** This tool lets you set the appearance of closed captioning in videos for apps that support closed captioning.

- **Keyboard.** This collection of tools includes an alternate means for Windows users with impaired mobility to enter text using a pointing device. Options that appear when you click Options in On-Screen Keyboard let you control how it works—you can choose whether to select a letter by clicking, for example, or by allowing the pointer to pause

CHAPTER 4

over a key for a specific amount of time. Other tools on the Keyboard page allow users with impaired mobility to more easily deal with key combinations and repeated keystrokes.

- **Mouse.** This page includes tools that make the mouse pointer easier to see for visually impaired users. Another tool enables the numeric keypad to move the mouse pointer instead of by using a mouse.

- **Other Options.** This page includes a smattering of appearance-related options to assist those with visual or hearing impairments.

The easiest way to configure your computer for adaptive needs in one fell swoop is to open Ease Of Access Center in Control Panel and then click Get Recommendations To Make Your Computer Easier To Use, a link near the center of the page. The link launches a wizard, shown here, that walks you through the process of configuring accessibility options:

If you want accessibility options to be available at all times, even before signing in to the computer, click the Change Sign-In Settings link in the left pane of Ease Of Access Center in Control Panel. This option (shown next) applies any changes you make to the sign-in desktop. If you choose not to enable this option, you can still turn accessibility features on or off at the sign-in screen; click the small Ease Of Access icon in the lower right corner of the sign-in screen to display a list of available settings, as shown next. Press the Spacebar to enable each one.

Change sign-in settings

You can have assistive technologies start automatically when you sign in, after you sign in, or both. Select the check boxes for each option you'd like to use.

Assistive Technology	At sign-in	After sign-in
Hear text on screen read aloud (Narrator)	☐	☐
Make items on the screen larger (Magnifier)	☐	☐
Type without the keyboard (On-Screen Keyboard)	☐	☐
Press keyboard shortcuts one key at a time (Sticky Keys)	☐	☐
If I press keys repeatedly, ignore extra presses (Filter Keys)	☐	☐
Use the numeric keypad to move the mouse around the screen (Mouse Keys)	☐	☐
Hear a tone when you press CAPS LOCK, NUM LOCK, or SCROLL LOCK (Toggle Keys)	☐	☐

Touch and tablets

Pressing the Windows button and Volume Up button together on your tablet can start an accessibility tool. To change which tool launches when you press these buttons after you've signed in, go to the Make touch and tablets easier to use page.

☐ Launch this tool from the sign-in screen

See also

🛡Create a restore point for backup

CHAPTER 4

Networking essentials

Modern computing is defined by our ability to communicate and share with one another by using devices of all shapes and sizes. These days, most of that activity happens over the world's largest global network, the internet, using a variety of widely accepted hardware and software standards. The internet is also the driving force behind cloud-based services, which are transforming the way we work and play.

The same network standards that allow connections to the internet can also be used to create a local area network (LAN), which makes it possible to share files, printers, and other resources in a home or an office.

In the not-so-distant past, setting up a network connection was a painful process, one that often required professional help. Today, network hardware is ubiquitous, and setting up a network connection in Microsoft Windows 10 requires little or no technical knowledge. That doesn't mean the process is entirely pain free; troubleshooting network problems can be maddeningly frustrating, and understanding the basics of networking is tremendously helpful in isolating and fixing problems.

In this chapter, we cover the essentials of connecting a Windows 10 device to wired and wireless networks in a home or small office. We also explain how to share resources securely and how to check the status of your network connection to confirm that it's working properly.

> ➤ We cover other methods of managing and sharing network resources in Chapter 20, "Advanced networking."

Getting started with Windows 10 networking

Before you can connect to the internet or to a local area network, your Windows 10 device needs a network adapter, properly installed with working drivers.

Since the release of Windows 7, Microsoft's hardware certification requirements have mandated that every desktop PC, laptop, all-in-one, and portable device include a certified Ethernet or Wi-Fi adapter.

You'll typically find wired Ethernet adapters in desktop PCs and all-in-ones, where a permanent wired network connection is appropriate. These adapters can be integrated into the motherboard or installed in an expansion slot and accept RJ45 plugs at either end of shielded network cables.

Most modern wired adapters support either the Fast Ethernet standard (also known as *100Base-T*), which transfers data at 100 megabits per second, or the more modern Gigabit Ethernet standard, which allows data transfers at 1 gigabit (1,000 megabits) per second. In an office or a home that is wired for Ethernet, you can plug your network adapter into a wall jack that connects to a router, hub, or switch at a central location called a *patch panel*. In a home or an office without structured wiring, you need to plug directly into a network device.

Inside OUT

Connect to a wired network using a USB port

If you crave the consistent connection speed and reliability of a wired network but have a portable PC or mobile device that lacks a built-in Ethernet connection, consider investing in a USB network adapter. A USB 2.0 port will support Fast Ethernet speeds, whereas a modern device with a USB 3.0 or USB Type-C port should be capable of Gigabit Ethernet speeds. Some network docking stations and USB hubs include an Ethernet adapter; this option allows you to use a single USB connection for instant access to a wired network and other expansion devices while you're at your desk, using Wi-Fi when you're on the go.

In recent years, wireless networking technology has enjoyed an explosion in popularity. Wireless access points are a standard feature in most home routers and cable modems, and Wi-Fi connections are practically ubiquitous. You can connect to Wi-Fi, often for free, in hotels, trains, buses, ferries, and airplanes in addition to the more traditional hotspot locations such as cafés and libraries.

All laptops and mobile devices designed for Windows 10 include a Wi-Fi adapter, which consists of a transceiver and an antenna capable of communicating with a wireless access point. Wireless adapters are also increasingly common in desktop and all-in-one computer designs, allowing them to be used in homes and offices where it is impractical or physically impossible to run network cables.

Ethernet and Wi-Fi are the dominant networking technologies in homes and offices. Alternatives include phone-line networks, which plug into telephone jacks in older homes, and powerline technology, which communicates using adapters that plug into the same AC receptacles you use for power. The availability of inexpensive wireless network gear has relegated phone-line and power-line technologies to niche status; they're most attractive in older homes and offices, where adding network cable is impractical and wireless networks are unreliable because of distance, building materials, or interference. (A hybrid approach, useful in some environments, allows you to plug a Wi-Fi extender into an existing power line to increase signal strength in a remote location.)

You don't need to rely exclusively on one type of network. If your cable modem includes a router and a wireless access point, you can plug network cables into it and use its wireless signal for mobile devices or for computers located in areas where a network jack isn't available.

When you upgrade to Windows 10, the setup program preserves your existing network connection. If you perform a clean setup of Windows 10, your wired internet connection should be detected automatically; you're prompted to enter the access key for a wireless connection during the setup process.

> ### NOTE
> In this chapter, we assume you have an always-on broadband connection in your home or office or that you're connecting to the internet through a public or private Wi-Fi connection with internet access. Although Windows 10 supports dial-up connections, we do not cover this option.

Checking your network's status

As we noted earlier, most network connections in Windows 10 should configure themselves automatically during setup. Three tools included with Windows 10 allow you to inspect the status of the current connection and either make changes or troubleshoot problems.

Using the network icon and flyout

The most easily accessible network tool is the status icon that appears by default in the notification area at the right side of the taskbar. Its icon indicates the current network type (wired or wireless) and the status of the network. Click that icon to display the network flyout, which displays options relevant to your type of network connection.

> ### NOTE
> A portable computer with no physical Ethernet adapter sometimes shows the icon for a wired connection rather than wireless. That can occur when you have a virtual network adapter set up for virtual machines as well as when you have a USB Ethernet adapter. (For details about virtual network adapters, see Chapter 22, "Running virtual machines with Hyper-V.")

Figure 5-1 shows the network flyout for a tablet with a USB Ethernet adapter connected to a wired network and a Wi-Fi connection to the Lmsint access point. Both networks appear to be

CHAPTER 5

operating properly. (As we explain later, a status of Limited indicates problems with the network's ability to connect to the internet.)

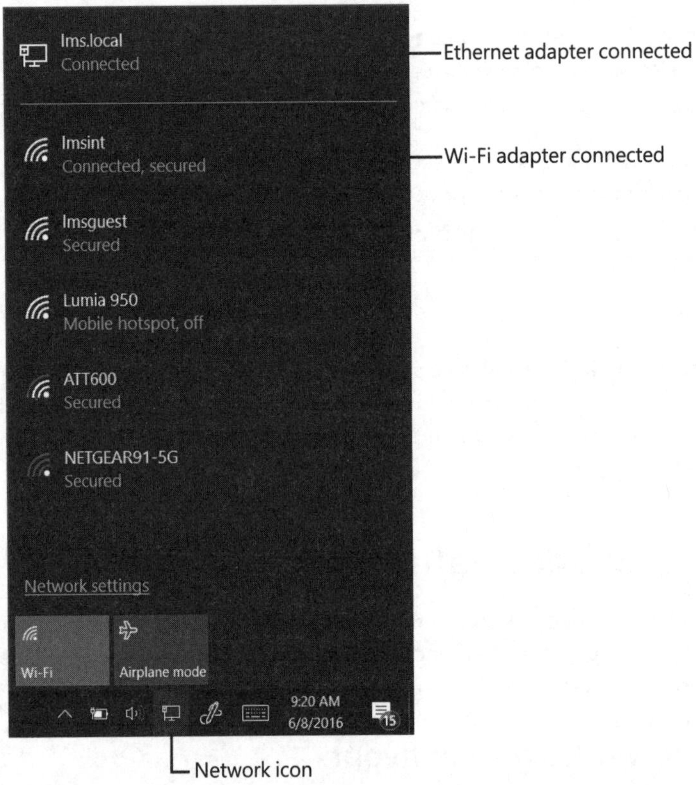

Figure 5-1 The network icon in the notification area shown here indicates that the wired connection is the primary connection. The list above shows that the system is also connected to a Wi-Fi connection.

Every available network is shown on this list, including wired connections and wireless access points that are broadcasting their names. In Figure 5-1, the PC is connected to both a wired network and a wireless access point. Because the wired connection is faster, it gets priority, sitting at the top of the list with a line separating it from the wireless networks.

The icon for each access point indicates its signal strength, with the better signals rising to the top of the list.

Two buttons at the bottom of the network flyout are available on laptops and mobile devices. Click or tap Wi-Fi to temporarily disable Wi-Fi connections; tap again to reconnect to a wireless network. Clicking or tapping Airplane Mode shuts down all wireless communications, including

Wi-Fi, Bluetooth, cellular, GPS, and near field communication (NFC). (You can selectively enable wireless devices by opening Settings > Network & Internet > Airplane Mode.)

A red X or yellow triangle over the network icon means your connection is not working properly. In Figure 5-2, for example, the yellow triangle with an exclamation point is Windows 10's way of warning that something's wrong with that connection. The network flyout shows that the wireless adapter is connected to an access point but isn't able to reach the internet.

└ Yellow icon indicates a problem

Figure 5-2 The warning icon over the wireless icon means there's a problem with the connection. The flyout provides more details: The connection has no internet access.

➤ **For help with troubleshooting network problems (wired and wireless), see Chapter 20.**

The Network Settings link at the bottom of the network flyout leads to Network & Internet in Settings, with details for the current network shown by default. On a tablet with a wireless connection, that page looks something like the one shown in Figure 5-3.

CHAPTER 5

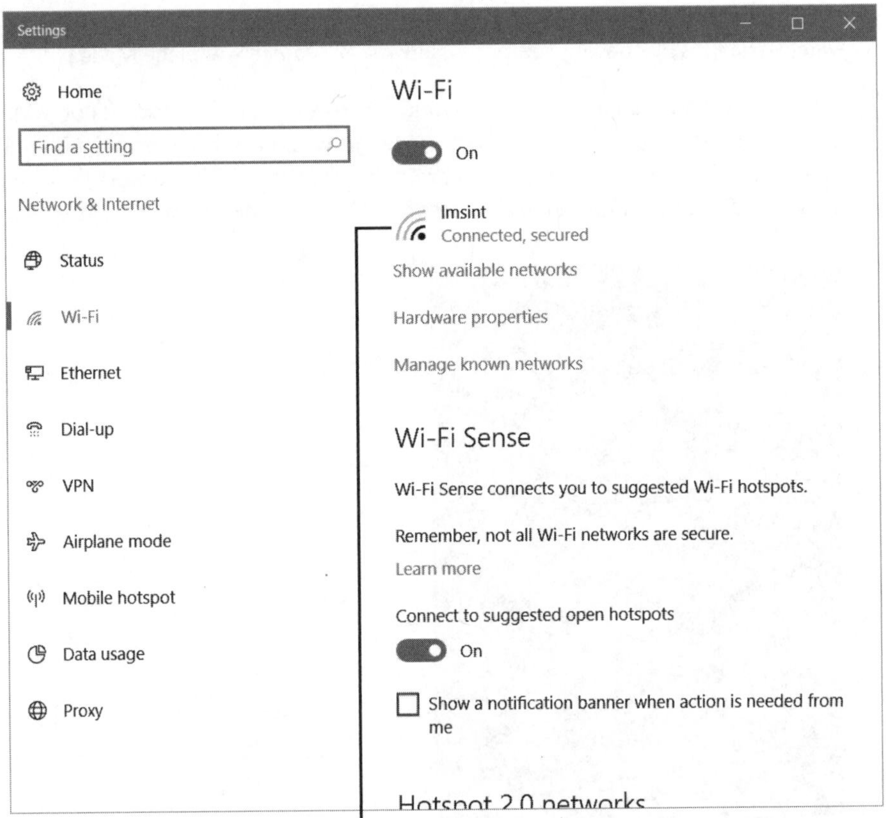

Click to view connection properties

Figure 5-3 Scrolling down to the bottom of this page displays a number of options under Related Settings (not shown here); these links lead to the classic desktop Control Panel.

Inside OUT

Mobile hotspots and other metered connections

Some devices with data connections on a cellular network allow you to turn the device into a mobile Wi-Fi hotspot, sometimes referred to as *tethering*. This capability is invaluable when you need to get some work done on a portable PC and an affordable, reliable Wi-Fi connection isn't available. The list of available network connections in Figure 5-1, for example, includes a phone running Windows 10 Mobile (the one called *Lumia 950*), which is capable of acting as a hotspot once the option is turned on. Most modern smartphones, including iPhones and Android devices, are capable of acting as a hotspot as well, although the cellular data provider must allow this capability.

The downside of using a mobile hotspot where you pay by the megabyte or gigabyte is potentially higher costs (especially if you're roaming outside your home network) or the risk that you'll hit your data limit and have your connection throttled or stopped completely. To avoid that possibility, Windows 10 identifies mobile hotspots as metered connections and automatically limits certain types of background activity. By default, the list of restricted activities includes downloads from Windows Update and always-on connections to an Exchange Server implementation in Microsoft Outlook. You can use the Data Usage option in Settings > Network & Internet to see how much data a specific network connection has used in the past 30 days.

If Windows 10 doesn't realize that a specific network is on a pay-as-you-go connection, open Settings > Network & Internet > Wi-Fi, and click or tap Manage Known Networks. In the list of networks that appears, tap the one you want to mark as metered, and then tap Properties. Slide the Set As Metered Connection switch to the On position, as shown here:

Clicking the icon for a wired connection in the flyout displays details about that connection: its IP addresses, Domain Name System (DNS) settings, and network adapter (including manufacturer name and current driver version). You can get to the equivalent information for a wireless connection by clicking the icon in the flyout and then clicking or tapping Properties. For either type of connection, you can reach the same details by clicking the network's icon in Settings > Network & Internet, as shown in Figure 5-3.

Figure 5-4 shows the properties for a wireless network connection, which includes details about the wireless network and the network adapter.

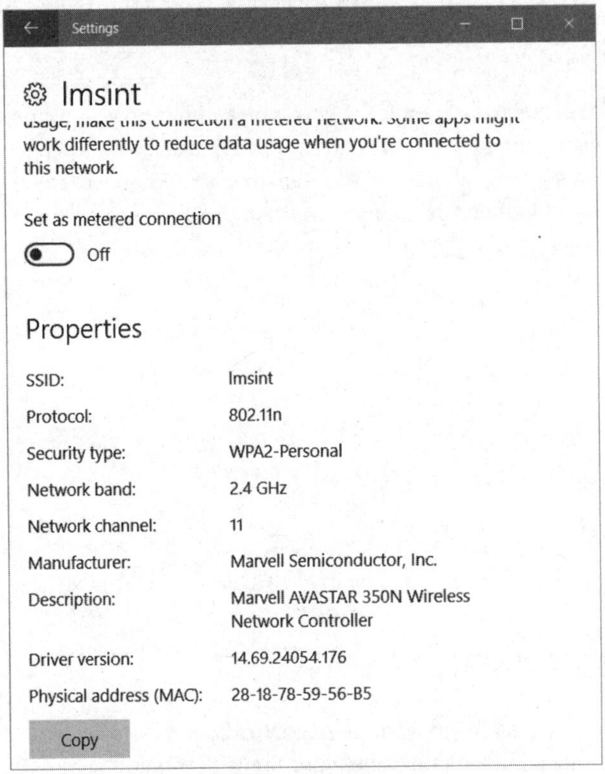

Figure 5-4 These details for a network connection are essential for troubleshooting networking problems. Click Copy to save the settings to the Clipboard to paste into a help desk ticket or an email message.

On the Network & Internet Settings page (shown earlier in Figure 5-3), each item in the list under the Related Settings heading leads to an option in the classic desktop Control Panel. (You might need to scroll down to see the heading and the links below it.)

> ➤ We cover Change Adapter Options and Change Advanced Sharing Options more fully in Chapter 20. For information about Windows Firewall, see Chapter 7, "Securing Windows 10 devices."

Network And Sharing Center

If you've managed a network in Windows 7, you're probably already familiar with Network And Sharing Center, which was the hub of almost all networking activities. You can get to the Windows 10 version of Network And Sharing Center in any of the following ways:

- In the notification area, right-click the Network icon and then click Open Network And Sharing Center.

- In the search box, begin typing **network** until the Network And Sharing Center item appears at the top of the menu; click it.

- In Settings, click or tap Network & Internet and then click or tap Network And Sharing Center. You can find it near the bottom of the Status page or the page for any network adapter (that is, Wi-Fi, Ethernet, Dial-up, and so on).

- In Control Panel, click Network And Internet, and then click Network And Sharing Center.

- In File Explorer, select the Network folder, open the Network tab on the ribbon, and then click the Network And Sharing Center button.

As you can see in Figure 5-5, this iteration of Network And Sharing Center is a bit tidier than its predecessors but still strongly rooted in the desktop Control Panel, offering access to most of the same information and functions.

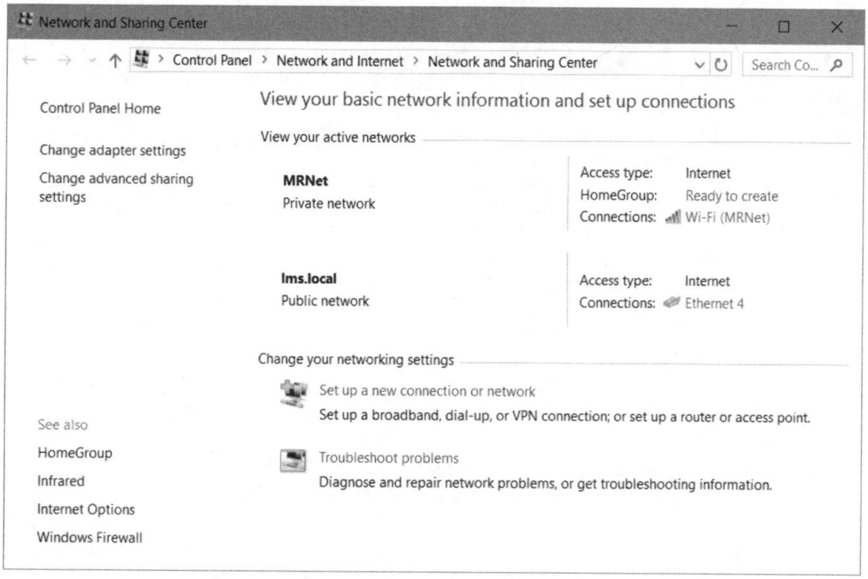

Figure 5-5 Network And Sharing Center provides a snapshot of the active network (or networks, as shown here) and includes links to nearly every relevant related task or setting.

The block of options along the left side is essentially the same as the choices under the Related Settings heading on the connection pages in Settings > Network & Internet. The most useful information in Network And Sharing Center appears in the center, under the heading View Your Active Networks.

In Figure 5-5, you can see that this computer is connected to two networks. One is a wireless connection that is configured to be private, allowing other PCs and devices on the same network to view shared resources. The Ethernet connection is currently set up as a public network, such as one in a public location like an airport or hotel. (We explain how and why to choose between public and private networks later in this chapter in "Setting network locations.")

Clicking the name of an active connection—in this example, Ethernet 4—leads to a status dialog box, where a Details button leads to additional information. The list of network details is a bit longer than its counterpart in the Settings app, as Figure 5-6 illustrates.

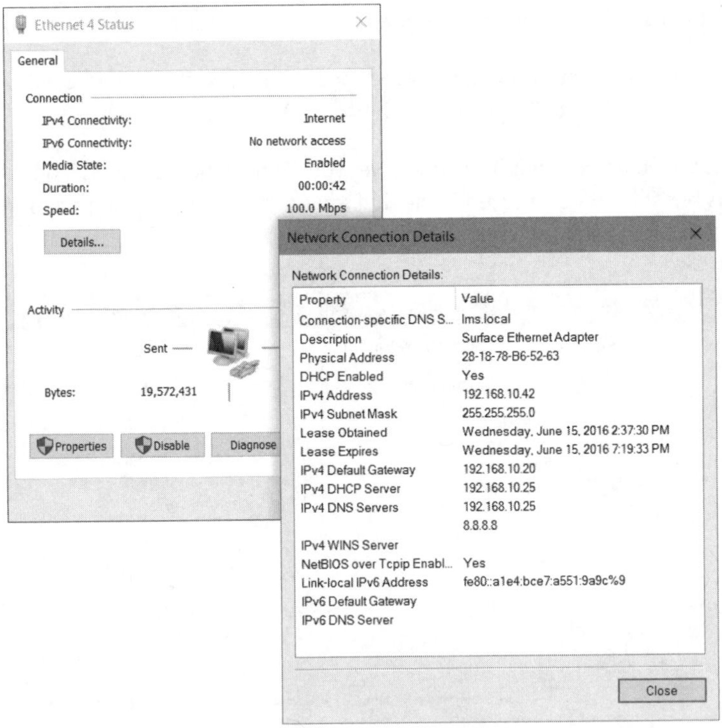

Figure 5-6 Click the Details button in the status dialog box for a connection (left) to open an information-dense listing of IP addresses and other details (right).

NOTE

Many tasks related to configuring networks require elevation to administrator privileges, as indicated by the shield icon next to commands and on command buttons.

Network And Sharing Center in Control Panel?! What about Settings?

The Windows 10 Anniversary update marks the debut appearance of Settings, Network & Internet, Status—another step in the move away from the old Control Panel settings. You might find this page, shown here, to be more convenient than using Network And Sharing Center.

The Network Status page offers much of the same information and links to additional tools such as Network And Sharing Center—indeed, the links go to the same old Control Panel destinations. It even has a link (not shown in the figure) directly to Network And Sharing Center, which is kind of handy because the latter shows more information about your network, which is why we still prefer it.

The Network Status page does have one neat trick you won't find in Network And Sharing Center: a link (also not visible in the figure) to Network Reset. If you're unable to resolve networking problems using the network troubleshooter, click Network Reset to remove your network adapters, reinstall them, set other networking components to their default settings, and restart your computer.

Although there's no obvious way to copy information from the Network Connections Details dialog box (to share with a support engineer, for example, or to paste into a post on a community support forum), it is possible to do so. Use your mouse to select a single row, or hold down Ctrl or Shift and click to select multiple rows, and then press Ctrl+C to copy the selection to the Clipboard.

Monitoring network performance in Task Manager

Sometimes it's useful to know not just whether a network connection is working but how well it's handling its primary job of transmitting and receiving packets of data. For a real-time graph of network throughput, open Task Manager, click the Performance tab, and then select a connection name from the list on the left. Figure 5-7 shows a file download in progress on a Wi-Fi connection.

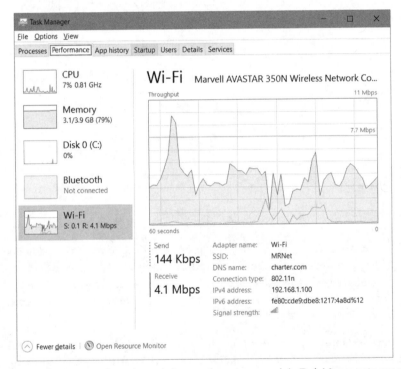

Figure 5-7 You can use the real-time performance graph in Task Manager to see not just whether your network connection is working but also how well.

The scale of the real-time performance graph adjusts dynamically so that you can see relative differences easily. In Figure 5-7, for example, the speedy download rate averaging 7.7 megabits per second is displayed on a scale that reaches 11 megabits per second rather than the theo-retical maximum speed of an 802.11n Wi-Fi adapter. (Some 802.11n implementations have a theoretical maximum speed of up to 600 megabits per second.) With a scale of 11 megabits per second, both the send and receive graphs are capable of telling the story of whether the con-nection is working as expected.

➤ For more information on basic techniques for identifying problems on Windows networks, see "Troubleshooting network problems" in Chapter 20.

Inside OUT

IPv6 and Windows 10

The longer you've worked with Windows, the more likely you are to be familiar with the granddaddy of Windows networking, Internet Protocol version 4, also known as IPv4. A default network connection in Windows 10, wired or wireless, uses IPv4 but also enables the newer IP version 6. IPv6 is on by default and has been the preferred protocol in all desktop and server versions of Windows for nearly a decade, since the release of Windows Vista.

Without getting into the minutiae of network addressing, suffice it to say that IPv4, with its addresses based on four groups of numbers from 0 to 255, has a big problem. When the internet was young, that address space, consisting of 4.3 billion unique combinations of dotted addresses, like 192.168.1.108 or 10.0.0.242, seemed huge. Unfortunately, nobody anticipated just how big the internet would become, and the authorities who assign IP addresses on the internet have literally run out of IPv4 addresses.

The solution is IPv6, which uses 128-bit addresses and therefore has a maximum address space of 3.4×10^{38} addresses, which we are confident is enough to last for the next few gen-erations of internet users. IPv6 is slowly but surely taking over large swaths of the internet. The giant American internet and cable provider Comcast has fully enabled its network for IPv6, with most of its competition not far behind. Major mobile carriers are also providing the majority of traffic on native IPv6 connections.

Major content providers are enabled for IPv6 as well. You can read about Microsoft's IPv6 efforts at *https://bit.ly/ms-ipv6*. Almost all of Google's services now work over IPv4 and IPv6, as does Yahoo. Facebook's giant data centers now run IPv6 exclusively, and Netflix has supported IPv6 for years.

Windows veterans might be tempted to shy away from IPv6, preferring the more familiar IPv4. In our experience, that's a mistake. IPv6 is here to stay. Learn about it and embrace it. For more information, see Chapter 20.

Setting network locations

A desktop PC connected to a wired home or small office network typically remains in a single location. In contrast, mobile devices running Windows 10 can connect to different types of networks—a corporate domain, a wireless hotspot at a coffee shop, or a private home network. Each type of network has its own security requirements. Windows uses network locations to categorize each network and then applies appropriate security settings. When you connect to a new network, Windows applies one of three security settings:

- **Public.** This is the default setting for any new, untrusted network connection. Network discovery is turned off for public networks, making it impossible for other people on the same access point to connect to your computer. This option is appropriate for networks in public places, such as wireless hotspots in coffee shops, hotels, airports, and libraries. It's also the correct choice if your desktop or laptop PC is directly connected to a cable modem or other broadband connection without the protection of a router and hardware firewall.

- **Private.** This option is appropriate when you're connecting to a trusted network, such as your own network at home—if and only if that network is protected by a router or residential gateway (a consumer device that combines a cable modem, router, and wireless access point in a single box) or comparable internet defense. When you make this choice, Windows enables network discovery and allows you to enable the HomeGroup feature for sharing with other users on the network.

- **Domain.** This option is applied automatically when you sign in to Windows using a computer that's joined to a Windows domain, such as your company network. In this scenario, network discovery is enabled, allowing you to see other computers and servers on the network by using accounts and permissions controlled by a network administrator.

> ➤ If you have a mobile computer that connects to multiple networks, keep in mind that the Windows Firewall maintains separate network security profiles for private (home or work), public, and domain-based networks. For more information about Windows Firewall, see "Blocking intruders with Windows Firewall" in Chapter 7.

The location of the current network is shown in Network And Sharing Center, below the name of the network. (See Figure 5-5 earlier in this chapter.)

To change a public network to a private one, or vice versa, open Settings > Network & Internet, and then tap or click the Wi-Fi or Ethernet heading in the list on the left. Click or tap the icon for the connection to open the properties dialog box for the active connection, shown in Figure 5-8. When Make This PC Discoverable is Off, the network is public. Slide the switch to On to make the network private.

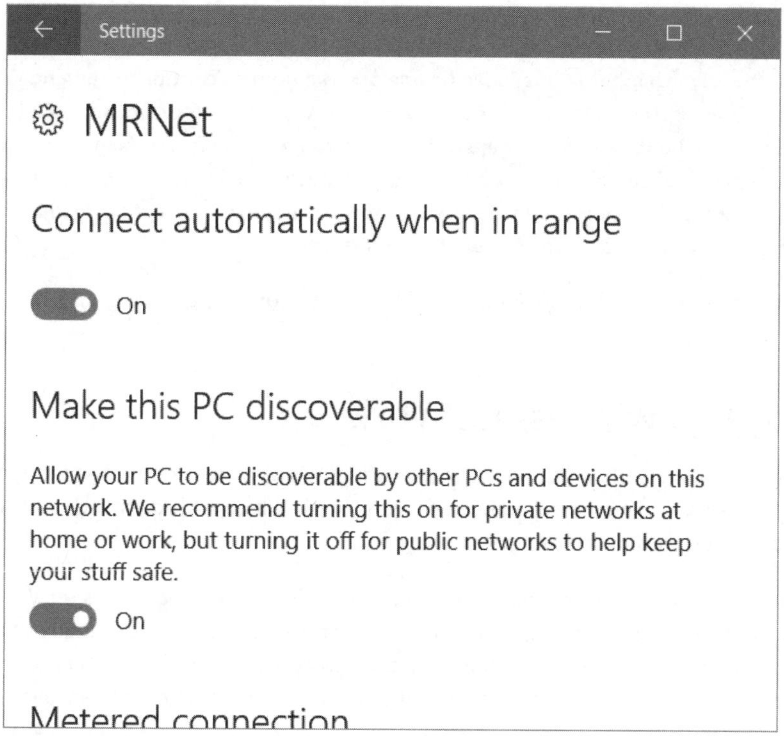

Settings   —   □   ✕

⚙ MRNet

Connect automatically when in range

 On

Make this PC discoverable

Allow your PC to be discoverable by other PCs and devices on this network. We recommend turning this on for private networks at home or work, but turning it off for public networks to help keep your stuff safe.

 On

Metered connection

Figure 5-8 Making a PC discoverable tells Windows that it's a private network and it's safe for other PCs and network devices to connect to this computer. In the Off position, the network location is set to Public and outside access is blocked.

Inside OUT

Workgroups vs. domains

Computers on a network can be part of a workgroup or a domain.

In a workgroup, the security database for each computer (including, most significantly, the list of user accounts and the privileges granted to each one) resides on that computer. When you sign in to a computer in a workgroup, Windows checks its local security database to see whether you provided a user name and password that matches one in the database. Similarly, when network users attempt to connect to your computer, Windows again consults the local security database. All computers in a workgroup must be on the same subnet. A workgroup is sometimes called a *peer-to-peer network*.

CHAPTER 5

By contrast, a domain consists of computers that share a security infrastructure, Active Directory, which in turn is managed on one or more domain controllers running Windows Server. Microsoft's cloud-based alternative, Azure Active Directory, provides similar infrastructure without requiring IT departments to manage local servers. Active Directory and Azure Active Directory can be combined to create effective hybrid environments. When you sign in using a domain account, Windows authenticates your credentials against the security database defined by your network administrator.

In this chapter (and throughout this book), we focus primarily on workgroup networks.

Connecting to a wireless network

In this section, we assume you have already configured a wireless access point (often included as a feature in cable modems and DSL adapters supplied by your broadband provider) and confirmed that it is working correctly.

Whenever your computer's wireless network adapter is installed and turned on, Windows scans for available wireless access points. If it finds at least one (and you're not already connected to a wireless network), it alerts you via the wireless network icon, which looks a bit like an antenna. If you see a bright dot at the end of an otherwise gray antenna, connections are available.

Unless you're out in the country, far from civilization, you're likely to see lots of access points available for connection, most of them owned by your neighbors or nearby visitors. Assuming those networks are adequately secured with a network security key you don't know and can't guess, you'd have no luck connecting to them.

Clicking or tapping the entry for a secured access point reveals a box in which you're expected to enter a passphrase, as in Figure 5-9. If what you enter matches what's stored in the access point's configuration, you're in. Getting in is easy on a network you control, where you set the network security key. For a secured access point controlled by someone else—a doctor's waiting room, a coffee shop, a friend's office—you need to ask the network owner for the passphrase or key.

Before you reach that security prompt, you're asked whether you want to connect automatically to that network in the future. If this is a place you expect to visit again (or in the case of a coffee shop, again and again and again . . .), say yes to save the credentials. Note that saved Wi-Fi network security keys are synced between devices when you sign in with a Microsoft account, so you might find that a brand-new device, one you've never used before, automatically connects to your home or office Wi-Fi without having to ask you.

A router that supports Wi-Fi Protected Setup (WPS) offers a way to connect without entering a security key

Figure 5-9 Connecting to a secure network for the first time requires that you correctly enter a pass-phrase or security key.

To disconnect from a Wi-Fi access point, click or tap its entry in the network flyout and then tap Disconnect. Doing so automatically turns off the option to connect automatically to that network in the future.

Windows 10 saves credentials for every Wi-Fi access point you connect to, giving you the option to connect with a tap when you revisit. If that thought makes you uncomfortable, you can see and manage the full list of networks by opening Settings > Network & Internet > Wi-Fi and clicking Manage Known Networks. That list can be startling, especially if you're a frequent traveler. Tap any name in the list, and you'll see two buttons, as in Figure 5-10.

Tapping Properties shows information about the network, as shown earlier in Figures 5-4 and 5-8. Tapping the Forget button deletes any saved security information and removes the network name from the list.

CHAPTER 5

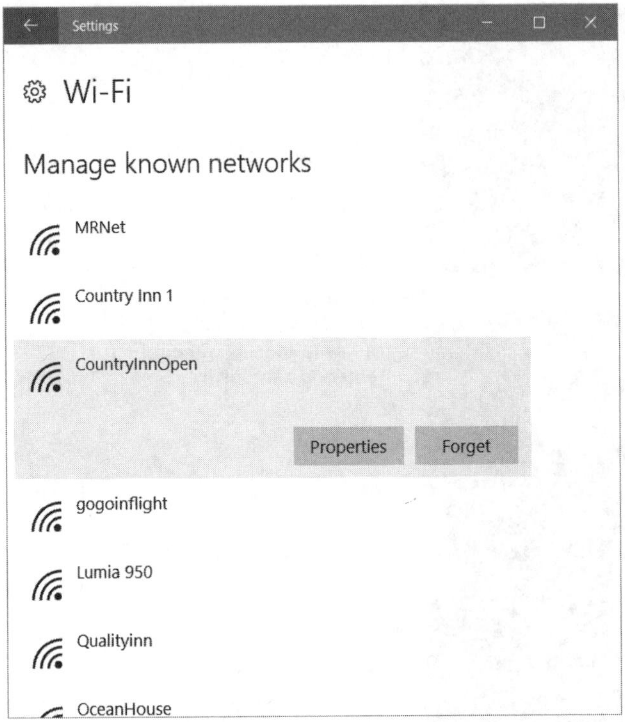

Figure 5-10 Wireless networks you connect to are saved in this list. Tap Forget to delete the saved security key and remove the network from the list.

Inside OUT

Decoding Wi-Fi standards

The most popular wireless networks use one of several variants of the IEEE (Institute of Electrical and Electronics Engineers) 802.11 standard, also known as Wi-Fi. On modern Wi-Fi networks, you're likely to encounter one of the following three standards (going from oldest to newest):

- **802.11g.** This standard was current up until 2009, just before the release of Windows 7. It's still in wide use on older PCs and wireless access points. It can transfer data at a maximum rate of 54 megabits per second using radio frequencies in the 2.4-GHz range. (Some manufacturers of wireless networking equipment have pushed the standard with proprietary variations that approximately double the speed.) 802.11g-based networks largely supplanted those based on an earlier standard, 802.11b, which offers a maximum speed of 11 megabits per second.

- **802.11n.** Using this standard, adopted in 2009, you can expect to see dramatic improvements in speed (600 megabits per second) as well as significantly greater range. Unlike the earlier standards, the 802.11n standard allows use of the 5-Ghz frequency range as well as 2.4 GHz. However, not all 802.11n hardware supports both bands.

- **802.11ac.** This standard, finalized in 2014, builds on the 802.11n specification and allows multiple links at both ends of the wireless connection, advertising throughput rates of 500 megabits per second per link, with a theoretical maximum speed of up to 2,600 megabits per second.

Although the newer Wi-Fi standards are backward compatible with hardware that uses the older, slower standards, be aware that all traffic on your network runs at the speed of the slowest wireless standard in use; if you just bought an 802.11ac router, you'll see the faster speed only if you replace your old network adapters.

For the maximum throughput, use 5-Ghz 802.11ac devices throughout your network. The 5-Ghz band is subject to less radio interference than 2.4 Ghz and is capable of a higher maximum theoretical data rate. If you must maintain compatibility with older 2.4-Ghz devices, the ideal solution is to use a dual-band wireless access point.

Connecting to a hidden network

Every wireless network has a name, formally known as a *service set identifier* but typically referred to as an *SSID*. Some wireless networks are set up so that they don't broadcast their SSID. Connecting to such a hidden network is a bit more challenging because its name doesn't appear in the list of available networks on the network flyout or in Network & Internet Settings. Making such a connection is possible, however, as long as you know the network name and its security settings.

NOTE

Configuring a router so that it doesn't advertise its name has been incorrectly promoted by some as a security measure. Although it does make the network less accessible to casual snoops, lack of a broadcast SSID is no deterrent to a knowledgeable attacker. Furthermore, attackers can learn the SSID even when they're not near your wireless access point because it's periodically broadcast from your computer, wherever it happens to be. We provide these steps to help you connect to a hidden network managed by someone else; we don't recommend that you configure your home or office network in this fashion.

CHAPTER 5

If one or more nearby networks aren't broadcasting their SSID, you'll see Hidden Network in the list of available networks. Click or tap that entry, and then you'll need to enter the correct SSID before you're allowed to take the real security test, entering your passphrase or security key.

After you jump through that one extra hoop, the process is no different from connecting to a network that broadcasts its name.

To set up your computer so that it connects to a particular nonbroadcasting wireless network whenever you're in range, follow these steps:

1. Open Network And Sharing Center, and click Set Up A New Connection Or Network.

2. In the Set Up A Connection Or Network dialog box, select Manually Connect To A Wireless Network and click Next.

3. Specify the network name (SSID), the type of security used by the network, the encryption type if the network uses WPA or WPA2 security, and the security key or passphrase, as shown in Figure 5-11. Select Connect Even If The Network Is Not Broadcasting. (What is the privacy risk mentioned in the dialog box? When this option is turned on, your computer sends out probe requests to locate the wireless network; an attacker can detect

these probe requests and use them to determine the network's SSID. Your computer continues to send these requests even when you're away from your network's access point.) Click Next.

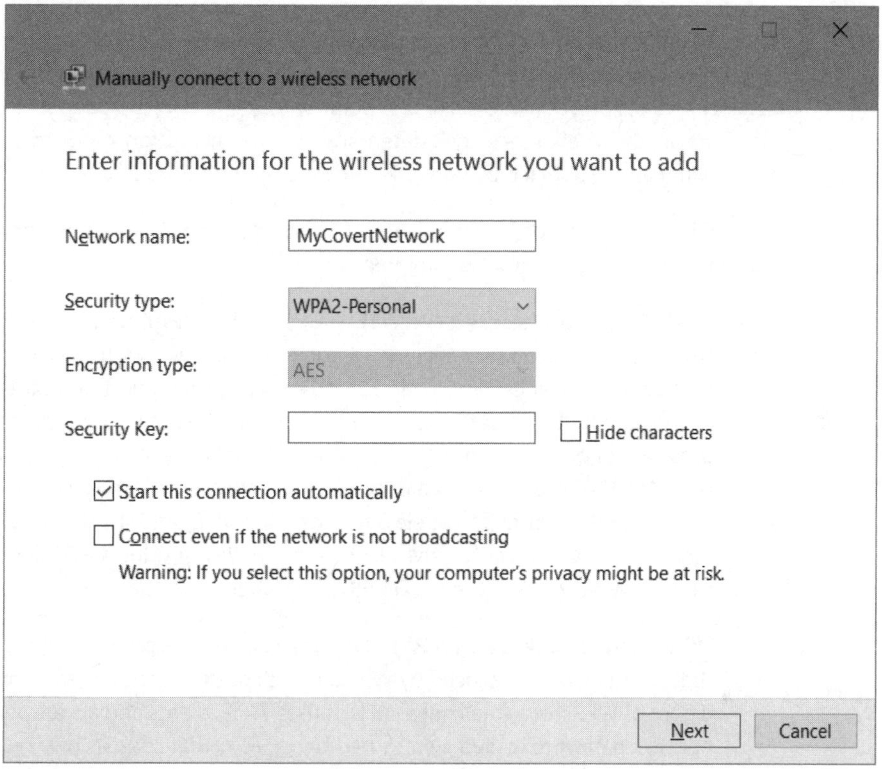

Figure 5-11 Use this well-hidden dialog box to configure a hidden network so that it's always available to connect to automatically.

4. Click Next, and then click Close.

Wireless security

On a conventional wired network, especially in a private home or office, physical security is reasonably easy to maintain: If someone plugs a computer into a network jack or a switch, you can trace the physical wire back to the intruder's computer. On wireless networks, however, anyone who comes into range of your wireless access point can tap into your network and intercept signals from it.

If you run a small business, you might want to allow internet access to your customers by using an open internet connection. Some internet service providers create secure guest accounts on their customers' cable modems that allow other customers of that service to connect using their network credentials.

Other than those scenarios, however, you probably want to secure your network so that the only people who can connect to it are those you specifically authorize. Doing that means configuring security settings on your wireless access point or router. When you connect to a network, known or unknown, the level of security is determined by the encryption standard chosen by the network owner and supported by network hardware on both sides of the connection.

Depending on the age of your hardware, you should have a choice of one or more of the following options, listed in order of preference:

- **Wi-Fi Protected Access 2 (WPA2).** Based on the 802.11i standard, WPA2 provides the strongest protection for consumer-grade wireless networks. It uses 802.1x-based authentication and Advanced Encryption Standard (AES) encryption; combined, these technologies ensure that only authorized users can access the network and that any intercepted data cannot be deciphered. WPA2 comes in two flavors: WPA2-Personal and WPA2-Enterprise. *WPA2-Personal* uses a passphrase to create its encryption keys and is currently the best available security for wireless networks in homes and small offices. *WPA2-Enterprise* requires a server to verify network users. All wireless products sold since early 2006 must support WPA2 to bear the Wi-Fi CERTIFIED label.

- **Wi-Fi Protected Access (WPA).** WPA is an earlier version of the encryption scheme that has since been replaced by WPA2. It was specifically designed to overcome weaknesses of WEP. On a small network that uses WPA, clients and access points use a shared network password (called a *preshared key*, or *PSK*) that consists of a 256-bit number or a passphrase that is from 8 to 63 bytes long. (A longer passphrase produces a stronger key.) With a sufficiently strong key based on a truly random sequence, the likelihood of a successful outside attack is slim. Most modern network hardware supports WPA only for backward compatibility.

- **Wired Equivalent Privacy (WEP).** WEP is a first-generation scheme that dates back before the turn of the century. It suffers from serious security flaws that make it inappropriate for use on any network that contains sensitive data. Most modern Wi-Fi equipment supports WEP for backward compatibility with older hardware, but we strongly advise against using it unless no other options are available.

You might see other encryption options, but those are typically designed for use on enterprise networks and are beyond the scope of this book.

Inside OUT

Beef up security at the access point

If your data is sensitive and your network is in an apartment building or an office complex where you can reasonably expect other people to wander into range with wireless adapters, you should take extra security precautions in addition to enabling WPA. Consider any or all of the following measures to protect your wireless access point from intruders:

- Change the network name (SSID) of your access point to one that doesn't match the hardware defaults and doesn't give away any information about you or your business.

- Disable remote administration of the access point; if you need to change settings, you can do so directly, using a wired connection.

- Whether you decide to allow remote administration of the access point or not, set a strong password so that a visitor can't tamper with your network settings.

- Check the firmware and drivers for wireless hardware (access points and adapters) at regular intervals and install the most recent versions, which might incorporate security fixes.

- Consider using a virtual private network (VPN) for wireless connections. A VPN sends all wireless traffic over an encrypted connection, making it impossible for others to snoop on your wireless traffic. Corporate network administrators can help set up a VPN using your company's security infrastructure. For unmanaged Windows 10 devices, VPN software and services are available.

When setting up a wireless access point for a home or small office, choose a strong passphrase. A passphrase for WPA or WPA2 can be up to 63 characters long and can contain letters (case-sensitive), numbers, and spaces (no spaces at the beginning or end, however). Many devices generate a random alphanumeric key, but you might prefer to use a memorable phrase instead of random characters. If you do, choose a phrase that's not easily guessed and make it long. Also consider incorporating letter substitution or misspellings to thwart attackers. Because the phrase can be saved and synced between devices, you shouldn't need to enter it often.

You must use the same encryption option on all wireless devices on your network—access points, routers, network adapters, print servers, cameras, and so on—so choose the best option that's supported by all your devices. If you have an older device that supports only WEP (and it can't be upgraded with a firmware update), consider retiring or replacing that device.

CHAPTER 5

TROUBLESHOOTING

You can't connect to other computers

If you're connecting to a network in your home or office (as opposed to a public hotspot, such as at an internet café), be sure the network is defined as a private network (either home or work). By default, Windows errs on the side of security, setting the location of all new networks as public, and thus not open to connections from other devices on the same network. That's safe, but it also means you won't be able to see other local computers you trust. To see whether this is the problem, open Network And Sharing Center. If Public Network appears beneath the name of your network, there's an easy fix. You can, of course, make the computer discoverable. (See "Setting network locations," earlier in this chapter.)

Alternatively, open File Explorer and click or tap Network in the list on the left. A yellow banner appears at the top of the list noting that network discovery and file sharing are turned off. Click that banner, and then click Turn On Network Discovery And File Sharing in the resulting menu, as shown in Figure 5-12.

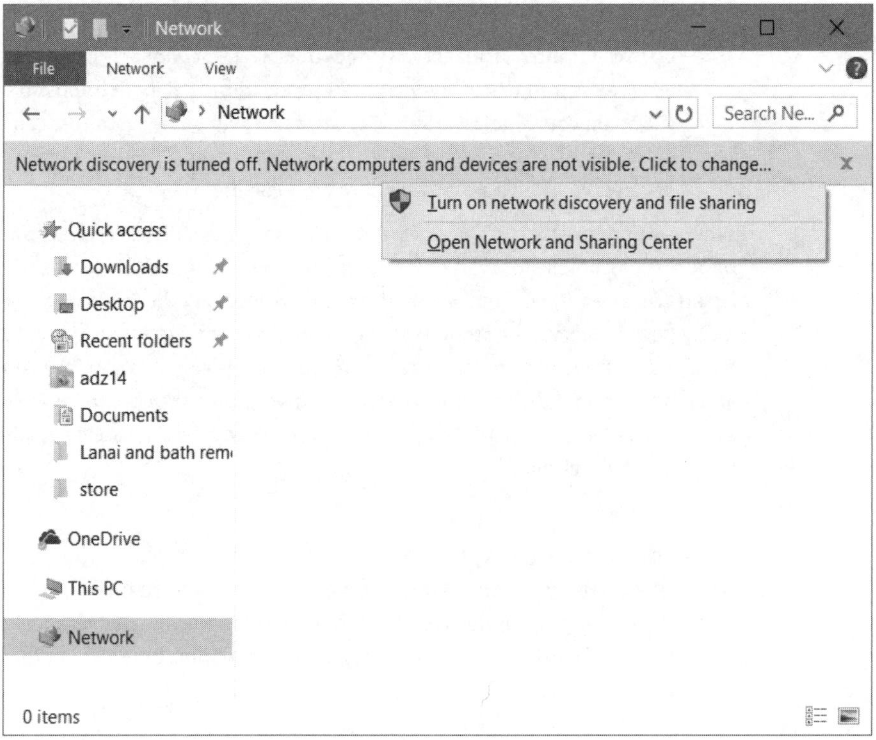

Figure 5-12 If your network location is set to Public, you'll see this banner when you select the Network folder; click it to make the network private and see other devices on the local network.

Windows then offers a choice: you can change the network to a private network, or you can turn on network discovery for public networks. Click the first option to toggle the network location from public to private, which should allow you to see the rest of the network (and vice versa). Do this only if you're certain the other devices connected to this network can be trusted.

Connecting to other wireless networks

Aside from connecting to your own wireless network at home or work, a Wi-Fi–enabled PC gives you the freedom to travel nearly anywhere and still connect to the internet. Nowadays, wireless hotspots are nearly ubiquitous at airports, hotels, coffee shops, fast-food restaurants, and many other places. In most cases, you use the same procedure to connect to one of these networks as you do to connect to your own Wi-Fi network.

Windows 10 also includes support for easier wireless connections. Using these tools can provide internet access in additional locations, and they often can be more convenient (and sometimes less expensive) to use than the public Wi-Fi hotspots you'll find at airports, hotels, and so on.

In the following sections, we discuss three Windows 10–supported alternative wireless connections:

- Wi-Fi Sense

- Hotspot 2.0

- Paid Wi-Fi

Using Wi-Fi Sense

Windows 10 includes a feature called Wi-Fi Sense that makes it easier to find and connect to open Wi-Fi hotspots. When enabled, Wi-Fi Sense automatically connects you to an open Wi-Fi hotspot listed in a crowd-sourced database when you're nearby.

NOTE
The original version of Windows 10 had a related feature—also called Wi-Fi Sense—that you could use to share your Wi-Fi network with your Facebook friends, Outlook.com contacts, and Skype contacts. When enabled, trusted users could connect to your Wi-Fi access point without entering a network security key. Beginning with Windows 10 Anniversary Update, this feature is no longer part of Windows.

To configure Wi-Fi Sense, open Settings > Network & Internet > Wi-Fi. Under the Wi-Fi Sense heading, shown earlier in Figure 5-3, turn Connect To Suggested Open Hotspots on or off.

So what is a "suggested" open hotspot? Microsoft manages a database of open hotspots by collecting information about each open Wi-Fi network to which you—and millions of other Windows users—connect. Information collected includes the quality of the internet connection. When you're in range of more than one open hotspot, Wi-Fi Sense selects the best one based on several factors, including the internet quality, whether other Wi-Fi Sense users have connected to it, whether you previously connected to it, and signal strength.

Keep in mind that these are *open* hotspots—ones that are not secured with a security protocol such as WPA2. The advantage is that no password or security key is required; the risk is that anybody can connect to it and other users might be able to see information you send over the network. When you're browsing the web, streaming videos or music, reading news, or performing other network tasks that transmit little or no personal data, a snoop can get nothing of value.

However, if you're shopping online or visiting your banking or brokerage accounts, it's essential that your connection to the site uses HTTPS. A secured HTTPS connection encrypts all data transmitted between your computer and the web server. You'll know you're using HTTPS when a lock icon appears in your browser's address bar.

➤ For more information about Wi-Fi Sense, visit *https://bit.ly/about-wifi-sense*.

Inside OUT

Keep your open network out of the Wi-Fi Sense database

If you have an open hotspot at your home or business and you want to prevent Wi-Fi Sense users from connecting to it, you can do so. (First, however, you should ask yourself why you have an open hotspot. If you truly want to provide an open connection for others to use, allowing Wi-Fi Sense merely makes it more convenient for users. If you do *not* want others using your Wi-Fi network, you should secure your network using one of the security protocols described earlier in this chapter under "Wireless security.")

To prevent Wi-Fi Sense connections to your open hotspot, append "_optout" to the name of your network. For example, you can change the SSID to OpenNet_optout.

Using Hotspot 2.0

Hotspot 2.0 (which also goes by the names *HS2* and *Wi-Fi Certified Passport*) is designed to make Wi-Fi connection effortless *and* secure. Based on the 802.11u Wi-Fi standard, all Hotspot 2.0 networks use WPA2-Enterprise security. Once you enroll in Hotspot 2.0 and download a profile, your computer automatically connects to a secure Wi-Fi hotspot when you're in range.

To use Hotspot 2.0, your device must support it. To confirm that it does, open a command prompt window and type

```
netsh wlan show wirelesscapabilities
```

If ANQP Service Information Discovery is shown as Supported, you're good to go.

Next, you need to set up an account with a Hotspot 2.0 provider and download the profile. Start by going to Settings > Network & Internet > Wi-Fi, and turn on Let Me Use Online Sign-Up To Get Connected (below the Hotspot 2.0 Networks heading). When you're in range of a Hotspot 2.0 network, Windows displays a list of providers for online sign-up. Follow the provider's instructions for creating an account and installing the profile.

Thereafter, whenever you're near a Hotspot 2.0 access point, your device automatically and seamlessly connects to the network. Because Hotspot 2.0 uses a certificate installed as part of the profile as your login credential, you won't need to enter a user name or password to get online securely.

Using paid Wi-Fi

If you scroll further down on the Settings > Network & Internet > Wi-Fi page, you'll come across a Paid Wi-Fi Services heading. Turning this option on enables the use of Microsoft Wi-Fi, a paid service that provides internet connectivity at locations such as hotels, airports, and cafes. Using the payment method associated with your Microsoft account, you can easily purchase a block of Wi-Fi access time.

After you turn on paid Wi-Fi services, when you're near a Microsoft Wi-Fi hotspot, its name appears in the list of available networks on the network flyout. Select the network and then click or tap View Plans to see and purchase a prepaid plan. You can use the plan at that location or at other Microsoft Wi-Fi hotspots as long as time remains on your plan; while your plan is active, your computer automatically connects to other Microsoft Wi-Fi hotspots when you come into range. To see the time remaining, click the network icon in the notification area.

At the time we wrote this book, Microsoft Wi-Fi was available in a small number of countries and regions—mostly in Europe, Australia, and New Zealand. Microsoft intends to expand the service globally, however, so by the time you read this it could be in your area. For more information, visit *https://www.microsoftwifi.com*.

Sharing files, digital media, and printers in a homegroup

The HomeGroup feature, originally introduced as part of Windows 7 and maintained through Windows 10, allows Windows devices to share resources on a home network. The list of shareable things includes USB-connected printers as well as files from the default libraries: Documents, Music, Pictures, and Videos. You can print a boarding pass, concert tickets delivered via email, or a Microsoft Word document from your PC, with the documents emerging from a printer attached to a different PC on the same network. You also can use the HomeGroup feature to search across all computers in a homegroup to find pictures from a recent event. Files on other devices are almost as easily accessible as if they were on your own computer.

(Oh, and if you're confused by the capitalization of the term, you're not alone. Microsoft hasn't budged from the conventions it adopted when this feature appeared in Windows 7. The correct spelling is HomeGroup when the term refers to the feature and the associated Control Panel option where you configure it. The collection of Windows computers joined together this way is called a homegroup, with no capitalization. In File Explorer, in dialog boxes and menus, and in this book, the term might be capitalized to indicate that it is part of the name of an option. We apologize profusely for the confusion.)

> **NOTE**
>
> The HomeGroup feature works only with computers running a desktop version of Windows 7 or later. To share files with computers running other operating systems (including earlier versions of Windows), or to enable users of those computers to access files on your Windows 10 computer, you must use network-sharing methods compatible with those older versions. For details, see "Sharing resources with other users" in Chapter 20.

The HomeGroup feature is specifically designed for environments where the connected computers are in a physically secure location (a private home or an office) with users who are fully trusted. Traditional network sharing requires matching account credentials on every device and will not work with devices for which the user has a blank password. HomeGroup is designed to work well regardless of whether computers and user accounts have passwords. Sharing is accomplished through the use of a special password-protected user account. If you're interested in the technical workings, see the "How HomeGroup works" sidebar.

The requirements to implement and use HomeGroup are few:

- At least one computer running Windows 7 Home Premium or above or any edition of Windows 8, Windows 8.1, or Windows 10 to create the homegroup

- All computers in the homegroup running Windows 7 or newer

- The network location for all computers must be set to Private. Although domain-joined PCs were able to access homegroup resources in earlier versions, that capability is not available in Windows 10.

How HomeGroup works

The simplicity of setting up and using HomeGroup belies its complexity. The basic sharing mechanism uses standard sharing protocols that have been part of Windows for many years. Here's the short version: HomeGroup grants share permissions and applies an access control entry (ACE) to each shared object, allowing access to a group called HomeUsers. A hidden, password-protected account (which is required for accessing shared objects over a network connection) named HomeGroupUser$ is a member of HomeUsers and acts as your proxy in accessing shared network resources. (In fact, even if your user account is password protected, HomeGroup still uses the HomeGroupUser$ account instead of your account to connect to a remote computer.) You can work around this setting by selecting the Use User Accounts And Passwords To Connect To Other Computers option in Advanced Sharing Settings. For more information about this setting, see "Configuring your network for sharing" in Chapter 20.

CAUTION

Do not change the password for the HomeGroupUser$ account; doing so is a recipe for disaster. (Note that the *account* password is *not* the same as the *homegroup* password.)

But there's much more going on with HomeGroup. Creating or joining a workgroup creates the HomeGroupUser$ account and the HomeUsers group, and it adds all local accounts to the group. HomeGroup setup also configures Windows Firewall. (Specifically, it enables certain rules in the Core Networking, Network Discovery, and HomeGroup groups. And for computers that are not joined to a domain, it enables rules in the File And Printer Sharing, Windows Media Player, and Windows Media Player Network Sharing Service groups.) In addition, it configures the HomeGroup Provider and HomeGroup Listener services. (HomeGroup also relies on Function Discovery and several other networking services.)

For users, setting up HomeGroup is a straightforward process. On one computer—it doesn't matter which one because HomeGroup is a true peer-to-peer networking system without a designated server/controller—you create a homegroup. Then, on other computers, you join the homegroup.

CHAPTER 5

Creating a homegroup

The current HomeGroup status is visible with the details of any active network in Network And Sharing Center. (See Figure 5-5, earlier in this chapter.) If no homegroup exists, click Ready To Create to begin the setup process. You also can set up the HomeGroup feature at a later time; open Settings > Network & Internet > Status and click or tap Homegroup. Alternatively, type **homegroup** in the taskbar or Control Panel search box, and then click HomeGroup in the list of search results.

If no homegroup currently exists on your network, the HomeGroup page in Control Panel informs you of that fact, as in Figure 5-13. Click Create A Homegroup to open a wizard that walks you through the process.

Figure 5-13 You'll see this Control Panel page only once. After your homegroup is created, this page offers options for you to change, join, or leave the homegroup.

In the first step, you select which default libraries on your own computer should be shared with other homegroup members and which should remain out of bounds. As the example in Figure 5-14 shows, the Documents folder is excluded from sharing by default, whereas Pictures, Videos, Music, and printers and other shareable devices are included. You can change any of these settings now or later.

Click Next, and the wizard generates a password for your homegroup, as shown in Figure 5-15. (Behind the scenes, the wizard also sets up the requisite user accounts and security groups, services, firewall rules, and shares.) Click Finish, and you're done.

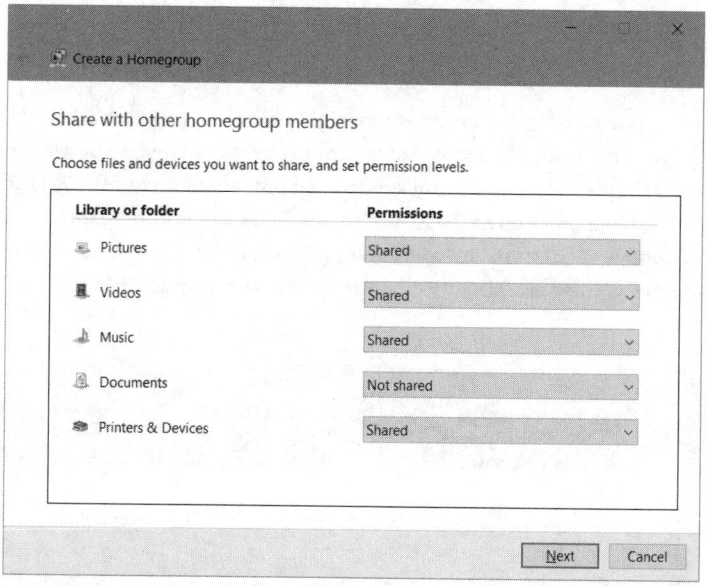

Figure 5-14 The first step in setting up a homegroup is to specify which of your default libraries you want to share as well as whether to share printers.

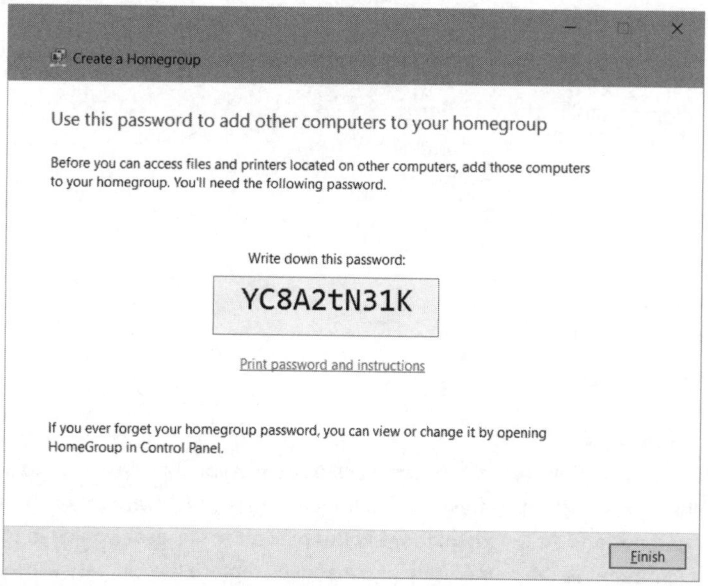

Figure 5-15 You'll use this same (shared) password to join other computers to the homegroup.

CHAPTER 5

Inside OUT

Go ahead, change the homegroup password

The homegroup password isn't intended to be highly secure. The only machines that can connect to your homegroup are those that are connected to your wired or wireless network, so even a simple password is sufficient to keep out uninvited guests. To change the randomly generated alphanumeric password to one that's easier to remember, visit the HomeGroup Control Panel from any computer that's already joined the homegroup. Using an administrator's credentials, click the Change The Password option (shown here) and follow the prompts.

In the dialog box that follows, you can enter any password you like. (We suggest a memorable passphrase.) Or click the refresh button until you're satisfied with one of the automatically generated options. As the instructions in this process make clear, you need to visit every other computer in the homegroup and manually replace the old password with the new one you just created.

Joining a homegroup

After a homegroup has been created, other computers on the network can join it by using a similarly brief process. Open HomeGroup in Control Panel and click Join Now to reach a wizard that informs you that a homegroup already exists and gives you the opportunity to join it.

Click Next, and the wizard asks you to choose the resources you want to share with other devices that are part of the same homegroup. Click Next again to enter the homegroup password. Enter the password and click Next, and you're ready to view resources from other computers in the homegroup.

To do that, open File Explorer. In the left pane, expand Homegroup to see a subfolder for each user account. Continue expanding, and you'll see a subfolder for each of that user's computers in the homegroup. Below that in the hierarchy, you'll find the shared folders on each computer, as shown in Figure 5-16.

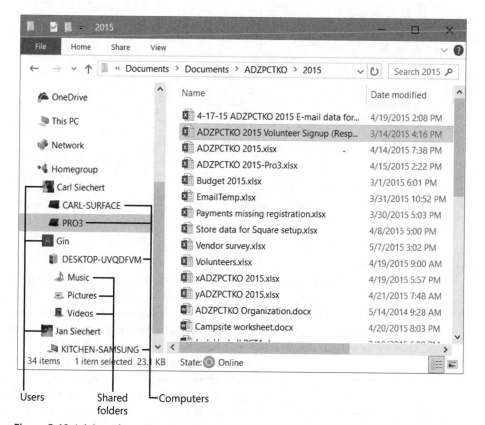

Figure 5-16 Joining a homegroup enables access to libraries on other computers.

CHAPTER 5

By default, every homegroup user has View (read-only) access to the shared personal libraries and folders on other computers in the homegroup.

Fortunately, you're not limited to sharing only the content of the Documents, Music, Pictures, or Videos libraries. If you would like to share other folders or files with users of other computers in your homegroup, you can add the folder (or folders) to an existing library or create a new custom library. (For instructions on working with libraries, see "Using libraries" in Chapter 12, "Managing files on PCs and in the cloud.")

To share a folder that's not in a library, locate that folder in File Explorer, right-click and click Share With, and then choose Homegroup (View) or Homegroup (View And Edit), as shown in Figure 5-17. (The same commands are also available on the Share tab of the File Explorer ribbon.)

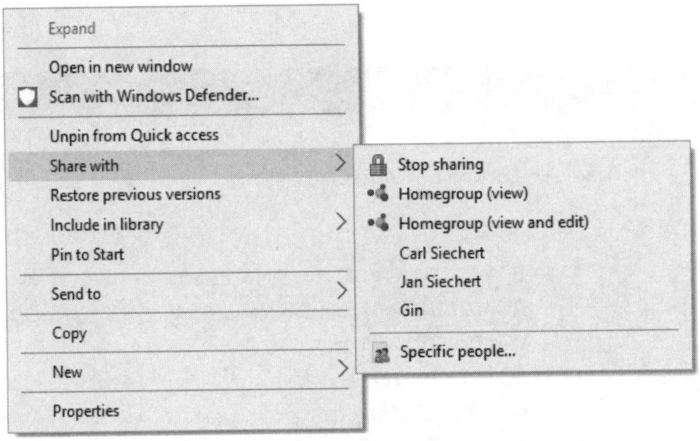

Expand
Open in new window
Scan with Windows Defender...
Unpin from Quick access
Share with
Restore previous versions
Include in library
Pin to Start
Send to
Copy
New
Properties

Stop sharing
Homegroup (view)
Homegroup (view and edit)
Carl Siechert
Jan Siechert
Gin
Specific people...

Figure 5-17 In a homegroup, you can choose to share individual folders using this well-hidden option.

CAUTION

Don't share the root folder of a drive (for example, D:\). Although sharing the root folder has long been common practice, we recommend against doing so. Because of the way permissions are inherited, changing permissions on the root folder can cause various access problems. A better solution is to create a subfolder within that root folder to hold the files and subfolders you want to share, and then share the subfolder.

Which command you select, of course, determines whether a homegroup user on another computer can create, modify, and delete folders and files within the shared folder. Both options share the selected item with your entire homegroup.

To share with only certain individuals, choose Share With > Specific People. Doing so opens the File Sharing dialog box shown in Figure 5-18.

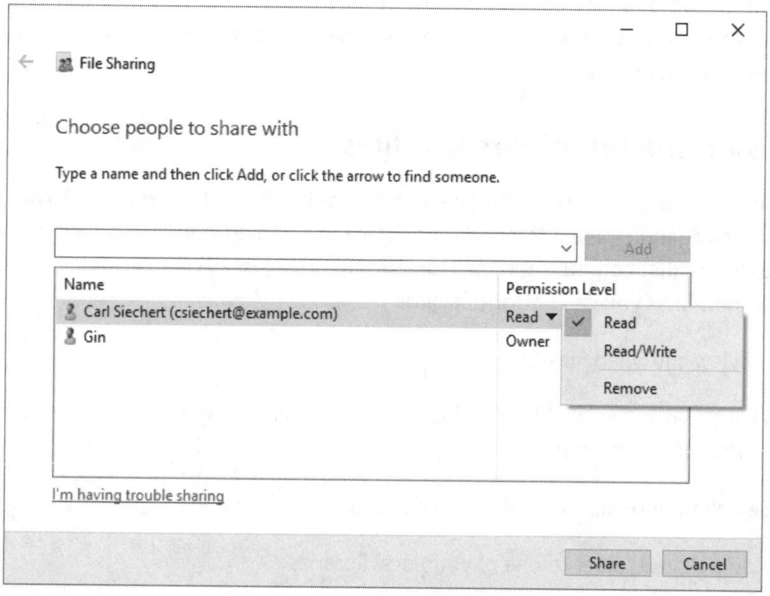

Figure 5-18 Clicking the arrow in the top box displays a list of local user accounts as well as homegroup users who have signed in using a Microsoft account.

You can use this feature with homegroups to set per-user permissions that override homegroup permissions. So if you allow homegroup users View access, you can allow specific individuals Read/Write access. The time-honored Windows technique to implement this level of sharing is to set up user accounts with matching names and passwords on different PCs. That can lead to management hassles and messy logon screens.

> **NOTE**
>
> The File Sharing dialog box describes its two permission levels as Read and Read/Write. In File Explorer's Share With menu, the homegroup options are View and View And Edit. They are, for all practical purposes, the same set of permissions described differently.

You also use the Share With command on the ribbon or the shortcut menu to prevent sharing of a particular folder or file within a shared library or folder. Select the items, click Share With, and then click Stop Sharing.

Similarly, you can override the default sharing settings for private folder profiles within a library—normally, these are shared with View access—by selecting a folder or file within the shared library or folder and clicking Share With.

CHAPTER 5

NOTE
A computer joins a homegroup and, therefore, all users on that computer have access to the homegroup's shared resources. However, sharing options are maintained on a per-user basis; on a computer with more than one user account, each user decides which of his or her libraries to share.

Browsing shared folders and files

If your network location is set as Private, you probably noticed the Homegroup node in File Explorer's navigation pane. After adding a device to a homegroup, you can work with folders and files from other computers in the Homegroup node just as you use folders and files in your own libraries. Tasks you can perform include these:

- Preview and open files

- Play music or view pictures or video (in a folder filled with music files, look for the Play All button on the toolbar)

- Search through all files within a folder, a library, a user node, or the entire homegroup

- Add a shared folder to one of your local libraries

- Add, modify, and delete files (only in libraries or folders shared with Read/Write access)

The Homegroup node also responds politely to right-clicks, displaying a convenient menu you use to change settings for the homegroup, view the homegroup password, or start a trouble-shooter to figure out why sharing isn't working properly.

Sharing a printer

Printer sharing isn't as big a deal today as it was when the HomeGroup feature debuted many years ago.

Today, we carry boarding passes and concert tickets on our smartphones. And for the rare pages we do need to commit to paper, it's often easiest to save a file to the cloud and then retrieve that file using the PC that has a printer attached.

Still, there's nothing quite like the convenience of sitting on the couch with a Windows 10 tablet and printing out a document to a printer in your home office.

If a homegroup member computer has a printer connected to one of its USB ports, and if the computer's user has chosen to share its printers (by selecting the Printers And Devices check box in HomeGroup), all homegroup users have access to that printer.

If the printer has been certified by the Windows Logo Program, it shows up automatically in Control Panel's Devices And Printers folder for all homegroup users. HomeGroup obtains the driver files from the host computer whenever possible or downloads them from the internet if necessary (for example, if the host computer runs 32-bit Windows and your computer has 64-bit Windows installed), and then it installs the driver without requiring any user intervention. (Note that it might take a few minutes after joining or connecting to a homegroup for Home-Group to discover the shared printer and install the driver.)

If the shared printer is connected to a desktop computer (but not a laptop) that's in sleep mode, sending a print request to the printer uses Wake On LAN to awaken the computer so that it can perform the print job. After completing the print job, the computer returns to sleep.

Leaving a homegroup

If you decide that HomeGroup isn't for you (or, perhaps, you want to join a different home-group), you can leave a homegroup. Open HomeGroup in Control Panel and click Leave The Homegroup. Because HomeGroup is a true peer-to-peer network, when any computer leaves the homegroup, the homegroup remains intact and all other members are unaffected (except they'll no longer be able to see your computer's resources, of course).

Note, however, that the Homegroup icon remains in File Explorer even after you leave the homegroup. Selecting the icon displays a message that includes an option to join a homegroup (if one is detected) or create one.

CHAPTER 5

Managing user accounts, passwords, and credentials

Before you can begin working with a device running Microsoft Windows 10, you must sign in with the credentials for a user account that is authorized to use that device. User accounts are an essential cornerstone of Windows security and are key to providing a personalized user experience. As an administrator, you determine which user accounts are allowed to sign in to a specific device. In addition, you can configure user accounts on a Windows 10 device to accomplish the following goals:

- Control access to files and other resources.

- Audit system events, such as sign-ins and the use of files and other resources.

- Sync files and settings between different computers when signing in with the same account.

- Require each user to provide additional proof of their identity when signing in for the first time on a new device.

The credentials associated with a user account consist of a user name and password that serve as identification and, in theory, ensure that no one can use the computer or view files, email messages, and other personal data associated with a user account unless they're authorized to do so.

If your computer is in a seemingly secure location where only people you trust have physical access to it, you might be tempted to allow family members or co-workers to share your user account. We strongly caution against using that configuration and instead recommend that you create a user account for each person who uses the computer. Doing so allows each account to access its own user profile and store personal files and user preferences within that profile. With fast user switching, a feature described in this chapter, you can switch between user accounts with only a few clicks.

Working with user accounts

When you install Windows 10 on a new computer, the setup program creates a profile for one user account, which is an administrator account. (An *administrator account* is one that has full control over the computer. For details, see "User accounts and security groups" at the end of this chapter.) Depending on what type of account you select during setup, that initial account can be a Microsoft account, an Azure Active Directory (Azure AD) account, or a local user account. A fourth user account type—an account on a local Active Directory domain—is available only on a managed network after this initial account is created and you join the machine to the domain. (For information about the differences between these account types, see the next section, "Choosing an account type.")

If you upgrade to Windows 10 from Windows 7 or Windows 8.1 and you had local accounts set up in your previous operating system, Windows migrates those accounts to your Windows 10 installation. These migrated accounts maintain their group memberships and passwords.

After signing in for the first time, you can go to Settings > Accounts to create new user accounts and make routine changes to existing accounts. The Your Info page provides an overview of your account, similar to the one shown in Figure 6-1.

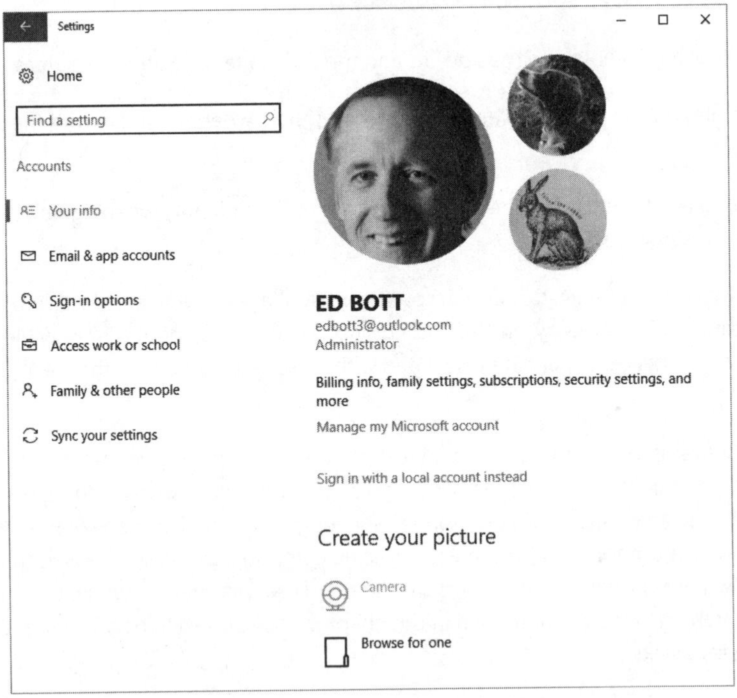

Figure 6-1 The Your Info page offers an overview of your user account along with tools administrators can use to manage all accounts associated with the current device.

Inside OUT

Quickly change your user account picture

Using a new feature in the Windows 10 Anniversary Update, version 1607, the Your Info page keeps track of the three account pictures you've used most recently. Under the Create Your Picture heading, use the Camera link to snap a selfie using a webcam or other connected camera, or click Browse For One to select a picture you saved previously. After you select a picture, the one you were using previously moves to one of the two smaller circles on the right. Click any of the three saved pictures to make it the primary one that appears on the sign-in page.

You'll find different options and settings in Accounts depending on the type of account you use (Microsoft account or local account), whether your account is a member of the Administrators group, and—if your computer is joined to a domain—group policies in effect. On a computer joined to an Active Directory domain, all management of user accounts beyond basic tasks such as selecting a picture is normally handled at the domain level.

You'll find some account-related settings under the User Accounts heading in the old-school Control Panel, which is shown in Figure 6-2. Several of these settings duplicate functions that are available in Settings > Accounts.

Figure 6-2 Visiting this old-school Control Panel page is rarely necessary, as most options for creating and managing accounts are available in the modern Settings app.

You can add a new account only from the Accounts page in Settings. You can remove an account or change its type from that location or its Control Panel counterpart. All the esoteric options along the left side of the User Accounts page, as well as the Change User Account Control Settings option, are available only in Control Panel.

CHAPTER 6

Choosing an account type

As we mentioned earlier, Windows 10 supports four different account types.

Microsoft account

When you go through the Out of Box Experience on a new PC (or a fresh installation of
Windows 10), the default options strongly encourage you to sign in using a Microsoft account.
If you click Learn More during that initial setup process, you see this explanation.

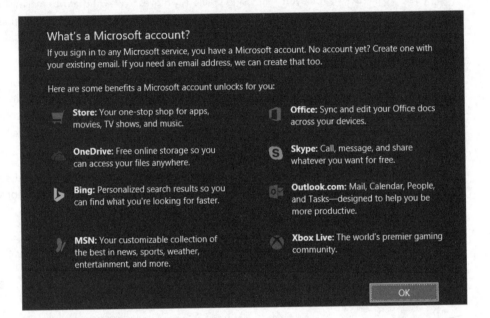

You've probably used Microsoft accounts for years, perhaps without even knowing it. If you've
signed up for a Microsoft service, including Outlook.com (or its predecessor, Hotmail), Office
365 Home or Personal, or Xbox Live, you already have a Microsoft account. Every email address
that ends with msn.com, hotmail.com, live.com, or outlook.com is, by definition, a Microsoft
account.

During setup, you can enter the email address associated with an existing Microsoft account,
or you can create a new email address in the outlook.com domain. However, you do not need
a Microsoft address to create a Microsoft account; you can set up a Microsoft account using an
existing email address from any domain and any email provider.

Inside OUT

Avoid using an Office 365 business email address as a Microsoft account

As we noted earlier in this section, you can use any email address as a Microsoft account. That includes free Gmail and Yahoo Mail accounts as well as accounts supplied by an internet service provider or a web hosting company.

If you have an email address on a custom domain as part of an Office 365 Business or Enterprise subscription, however, we strongly recommend against using that address as a Microsoft account. Although it's technically possible to do so, the result is an extra step every time you try to sign in to either service, because Windows 10 asks you whether you meant to use your Microsoft account or your work or school account.

The biggest advantage of signing in with a Microsoft account is synchronizing PC settings between multiple computers. If you use more than one PC—say, a desktop PC at work, a different desktop at home, a laptop for travel, and a tablet around the house—signing in with a Microsoft account lets you effortlessly use the same desktop colors and background, stored passwords, browser favorites and history, account picture, accessibility configuration, and so on. The synchronization happens automatically and nearly instantly.

> ➤ For more details on how to configure synchronization options, see "Syncing your settings between computers," in Chapter 4, "Personalizing Windows 10."

Some features in Windows 10 require the use of a Microsoft account. The best example is Cortana, the personal assistant included as part of Windows 10; Cortana's services are available only when you sign in with a Microsoft account.

It's possible to use OneDrive and other universal apps that depend on a Microsoft account even if you sign in to Windows with a local account. However, you must sign in to each app individually, and some features might be unavailable or less convenient to use. (For more information about OneDrive, see Chapter 12, "Managing files on PCs and in the cloud.")

Inside OUT

For extra security, turn on two-factor authentication

The single greatest advantage of a Microsoft account, as far as we're concerned, is its support for two-factor authentication, which provides security for your PC and its data. This feature requires that you prove your identity when signing in on a new device for the first time by supplying a code from a previously verified device, such as your smartphone. If an attacker manages to steal your Microsoft Account password, he won't be able to do any damage because he doesn't have access to your device and thus can't provide the additional verification required.

To turn on this feature, go to *https://account.live.com/proofs* and sign in using your Microsoft account. There, you can add approved contact info for receiving security requests and turn on two-step verification. You can also set up identity verification by installing the Microsoft Authenticator app, which is available on Android, iOS, and Windows 10 Mobile devices. This new app, released in August 2016, replaces the Azure Authenticator app on all platforms and also supersedes the Microsoft Account app on Android devices. It supports fingerprint-based approvals on compatible hardware and also works with several types of smart watches.

Local account

A *local account* is one that stores its sign-in credentials and other account data on your PC. A local account works only on a single computer. It doesn't require an email address as the user name, nor does it communicate with an external server to verify credentials.

This type of account was the standard in Windows for decades. Beginning with Windows 8 and continuing in Windows 10, Microsoft recommends the use of a Microsoft account rather than a local user account for PCs that aren't part of a managed business network. But using a Microsoft account is not a requirement; local accounts are still fully supported.

You might prefer a local account if your home or small business network includes computers running Windows 7 or earlier (that is, versions that do not support the use of Microsoft accounts). For details, see "Sharing resources with other users" in Chapter 20, "Advanced networking."

In addition, some folks have privacy and data security concerns about storing personal information on the servers of a large corporation, whether it is Microsoft, Google, Apple, Amazon, or others. Signing in with a local account minimizes the amount of information your PC exchanges with Microsoft's servers.

You can switch between using a Microsoft account and a local account by going to Settings, Accounts. On the Your Info page (shown earlier in Figure 6-1), click Sign In With A Local Account Instead. Windows leads you through a few simple steps to create a local account, which you'll then use for signing in.

If you're currently signed in using a local account, the link on that page reads Sign In With A Microsoft Account Instead. As an alternative, you can use the Add A Microsoft Account option, available when you go to Settings > Update & Security > Activation, as shown in Figure 6-3.

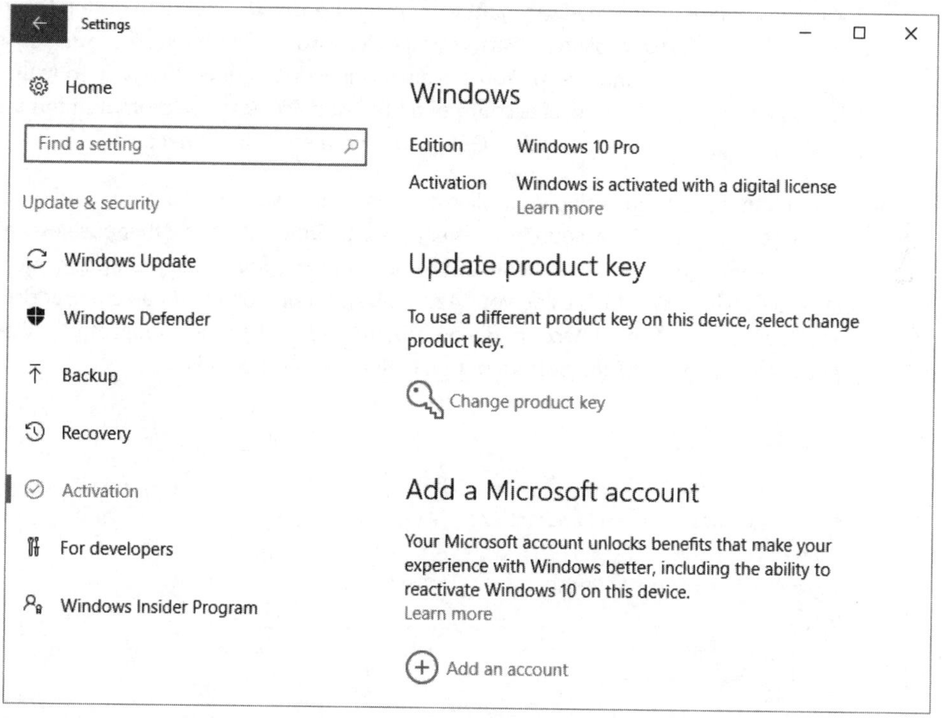

Figure 6-3 Switching from a local account to a Microsoft account preserves your digital license details online, making activation easier if you need to reinstall Windows later.

As part of making the switch, you need to enter your local password one more time. A few screens later, you're connected to an existing Microsoft account or a new one you create. From that time forward, you sign in using your Microsoft account.

Azure Active Directory account

The third type of account, available during initial setup of Windows 10 Pro, Enterprise, or Education, is a work or school account using Azure Active Directory. Azure AD offers some of the advantages of a Microsoft account, including support for two-factor authentication and single sign-on to online services, balanced by the capability of network administrators to impose restrictions using management software. These accounts are most common in medium-size and large businesses and schools.

Organizations that subscribe to Microsoft's business-focused online services—including Business or Enterprise editions of Office 365, Microsoft Intune, and Microsoft Dynamics CRM Online—automatically have Azure Active Directory services as part of their subscription. Every user account in that service automatically has a corresponding Azure AD directory entry.

You can connect an Azure AD account to a new Windows 10 installation during the initial setup of Windows 10, as we explain in "Performing a clean install," in Chapter 2, "Installing, configuring, and deploying Windows 10." You can also connect a Windows 10 device to Azure AD after it has been set up using a local account or a Microsoft account. To accomplish this task, go to Settings > Accounts > Access Work Or School, and then click Connect.

If you want to continue using your Microsoft account or your local account and only want to connect your Azure AD account for easier access to Office 365 and other business services, enter the email address associated with that account and follow the prompts. If you want to be able to sign in to Windows using your Azure AD account, don't enter an email address in the Set Up A Work Or School Account dialog box; instead, click the small Join This Device To Azure Active Directory link at the bottom of that dialog box, as shown here:

That option opens the dialog box shown in Figure 6-4. After you sign in using your Azure AD credentials, you have one final chance to confirm that you want to sign in with your organization's credentials and allow administrators to apply policies to your device.

Figure 6-4 Enter credentials from an Azure Active Directory account, such as an Office 365 Enterprise subscription, to join the device to that directory.

After connecting a Windows 10 PC to Azure AD, you can view and edit your user profile by going to Settings > Accounts > Your Info and clicking Manage My Account. You can use the options on the Profile page to request a password reset and manage multifactor authentication settings. The Applications tab includes any apps that have been set up by your administrator for single sign-on.

Active Directory domain account

In organizations with Windows domains running Active Directory services, administrators can join a PC to the domain, creating a domain machine account. (This option is available only with Windows 10 Pro, Enterprise, or Education editions.) After this step is complete, any user with a domain user account can sign in to the PC and access local and domain-based resources. We cover this account type more fully in Chapter 21, "Managing Windows 10 in business."

Changing account settings

With options in Settings and Control Panel, you can make changes to your own account or another user's account.

To change your own account, go to Settings > Accounts > Your Info, shown earlier in Figure 6-1. Even quicker: Open Start, click or tap your account picture at the top of the column of icons on the left, and then choose Change Account Settings.

Here, you can change your account picture, either by browsing for a picture file or by using your computer's built-in camera to take a picture. If you sign in with a Microsoft account, the Manage My Microsoft Account link opens your default web browser and loads your account page at *https://account.microsoft.com*. On that page, you can change your password or edit the name associated with your Microsoft account. Click other links along the top of the page to review your subscriptions and Store purchases, change your payment options, and get information about other devices associated with your Microsoft account. You can also set security and privacy options, which we discuss in more detail later in this chapter.

If you have added one or more users to your computer, you (as a computer administrator) can make changes to the account of each of those users. (For information about adding users, see "Adding a user to your computer" later in this chapter.)

To change a user's account type, go to Settings > Accounts > Family & Other People. Click the name of the account you want to change, and click Change Account Type. (Your choices are Standard User or Administrator. For details, see "User accounts and security groups" later in this chapter.)

If the person signs in with a Microsoft account, there are no other changes you can make. (You can't make changes to someone else's Microsoft account at *https://account.microsoft.com*.) For users who sign in with a local user account, you can make a few additional changes, but you must start from User Accounts in Control Panel (shown earlier in Figure 6-2). Click Manage Another Account, and then click the name of the account you want to change. You can make the following changes:

- **Account Name.** The name you're changing here is the full name, which is the one that appears on the sign-in screen, on the Start menu, and in User Accounts.

- **Password.** You can create a password and store a hint that provides a reminder for a forgotten password. If the account is already password protected, you can use User Accounts to change the password or remove the password. For more information about passwords, see "Setting or changing a password" later in this chapter.

- **Account Type.** Your choices here are the same as in Settings > Accounts: Administrator (which adds the account to the Administrators group) or Standard User (which adds the account to the Users group).

If you sign in with a local user account, you can make the following additional changes to your own account (that is, the one with which you're currently signed in) by clicking links in the left pane:

- **Manage Your Credentials.** This link opens Credential Manager, where you can manage stored credentials that you use to access network resources and websites.

- **Create A Password Reset Disk.** This link, available only when you are signed in with a local account, launches the Forgotten Password Wizard, from which you can create a password reset tool on removable media.

- **Manage Your File Encryption Certificates.** This link opens a wizard you can use to create and manage certificates that enable the use of Encrypting File System (EFS). EFS, which is available only in Pro and Enterprise editions of Windows 10, is a method of encrypting folders and files so that they can be used only by someone who has the appropriate credentials. For more information, see "Encrypting information" in Chapter 7, "Securing Windows 10 devices."

- **Configure Advanced User Profile Properties.** This link is used to switch your profile between a local profile (one that is stored on the local computer) and a roaming profile (one that is stored on a network server in a domain environment). With a local profile, you end up with a different profile on each computer you use, whereas a roaming profile is the same regardless of which computer you use to sign in to the network. Roaming profiles require a domain network running Windows Server Active Directory services.

- **Change My Environment Variables.** Of interest primarily to programmers, this link opens a dialog box in which you can create and edit environment variables that are available only to your user account; in addition, you can view system environment variables, which are available to all accounts.

Deleting an account

As a local administrator, you can delete any local account or Microsoft account set up on a Windows 10 PC, unless that account is currently signed in. To delete an account, go to Settings > Accounts > Family & Other People (the Family option is unavailable and this category is called simply Other People if you're signed in using an Azure AD account), and click the name of the account you want to delete. Then click Remove. Windows then warns about the consequences of deleting an account, as shown in Figure 6-5.

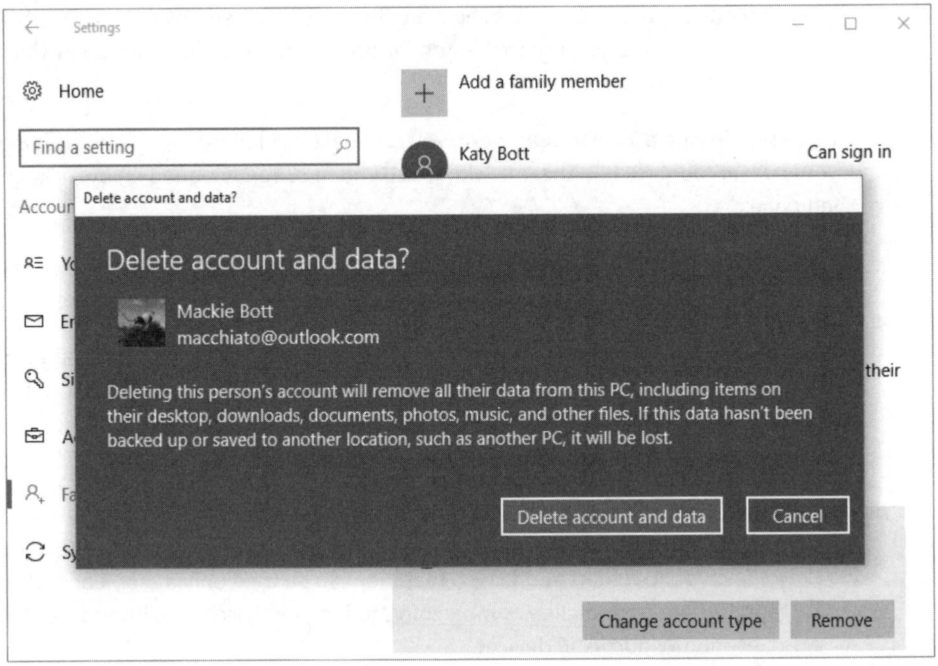

Figure 6-5 Before you click Delete Account And Data, be sure you have saved any local data you don't want to lose.

NOTE

Windows won't let you delete the last local account on the computer, even if you signed in using the built-in account named Administrator. This limitation helps to enforce the sound security practice of using an account other than Administrator for your everyday computing.

After you delete an account, of course, that user can no longer sign in. Deleting an account also has another effect you should be aware of: You cannot restore access to resources that are currently shared with the user simply by re-creating the account. This includes files shared with the user and the user's encrypted files, personal certificates, and stored passwords for websites and network resources. That's because those permissions are linked to the user's original security identifier (SID)—not the user name. Even if you create a new account with the same name, password, and so on, it will have a new SID, which will not gain access to anything that was restricted to the original user account. (For more information about security identifiers, see "Introducing access control in Windows" later in this chapter.)

Inside OUT

Delete an account without deleting its data

Earlier versions of Windows included an option for preserving an account's data files—documents, photos, music, downloads, and so on stored in the user's profile—when you delete the user account. Windows 10 offers that option too, but you won't find it in Settings. Instead, open User Accounts in Control Panel. Click Manage Another Account, select the account you want to remove, and then click Delete The Account.

User Accounts gives you a choice about what to do with the account's files:

- **Delete Files.** After you select Delete Files and confirm your intention in the next window, Windows deletes the account, its user profile, and all files in that account's user profile.

- **Keep Files.** Windows copies certain parts of the user's profile—specifically, files and folders stored on the desktop and in the Documents, Favorites, Music, Pictures, and Videos folders—to a folder on your desktop, where they become part of your profile and remain under your control. The rest of the user profile is deleted after you confirm your intention in the next window that appears; the deleted content includes email messages and other data stored in the AppData folder; files stored in the Contacts, Downloads, Saved Games, and Searches folders; and settings stored in the registry.

Managing the sign-in process

Users of Windows (as well as most other operating systems) are familiar with the time-honored sign-in method: At the sign-in screen, select your name (if it's not already selected) and then enter a password. This continues to be a valid technique in Windows 10.

NOTE

When you first turn on your computer or return to it after signing out, the *lock screen* is displayed. The lock screen normally shows a snazzy picture, the current time and date, and alerts from selected apps. (You can select your own lock screen picture and specify what information you want displayed on the lock screen. For details, see "Customizing the lock screen and sign-in screen" in Chapter 4.) To get from the lock screen to the sign-in screen, click anywhere, press any key, or (if you have a touchscreen) swipe up.

Inside OUT

Press Ctrl+Alt+Delete without a keyboard

Some network administrators enable a policy that requires you to press Ctrl+Alt+Delete to switch from the lock screen to the sign-in screen. That's tough to do on a tablet with no keyboard—until you know the trick: Press the Windows button (usually on the bezel along the right or bottom edge of the screen) and the power button. If you're using a tablet that has no dedicated Windows button, such as the Surface Book, press and hold the power button, and then press Volume Down.

Windows 10 has other sign-in options that add security as well as convenience:

- You can enter a numeric PIN.

- You can trace a pattern of gestures on a picture.

- With appropriate hardware, you can use Windows Hello—a biometric sign-in method that scans your fingerprint, your face, or your iris.

These three methods each provide a form of *two-factor authentication*, a means of identifying yourself with multiple proofs. In the case of Windows sign-ins, the components include two of the following: something you know (such as a PIN or the gesture pattern), something you have (the device itself, which is registered with the Microsoft account servers), and something that's inseparable from you (your fingerprint, face, or iris).

The device you sign in on acts as an authentication component because your information (the PIN or your biometric data) is stored, in encrypted form, on the device—not on a remote server. So, for example, if someone learns your PIN, that person can use it only on that device; he can't

CHAPTER 6

use it to sign in to your account on any other device. If someone steals your computer, that person can't sign in unless she knows your PIN.

In the following sections, we explain how to set up each of these sign-in methods: password, PIN, picture password, and biometric. You configure each of these variations on the Sign-In Options page in Settings, Accounts, as shown in Figure 6-6.

← Settings	← Settings
⚙ **Sign-in options**	⚙ **Sign-in options**
Require sign-in	⠿ **PIN**
If you've been away, when should Windows require you to sign in again?	You can use this PIN to sign in to Windows, apps, and services.
[Never ∨]	[Change] [Remove]
☺ **Windows Hello**	I forgot my PIN
	Sorry, this PIN isn't working for your organization's resources.
Sign in to Windows, apps and services by teaching Windows to recognize you.	Tap or click here to fix it.
Learn more about Windows Hello	⊠ **Picture password**
Fingerprint	For best results, set up picture password on the display you use to sign in to your PC
[Add another] [Remove]	[Add]
⚷ **Password**	**Privacy**
	Show account details (e.g. email address) on sign-in screen
Change your account password	(●) Off
[Change]	

Figure 6-6 Choices on the Sign-In Options page in Settings depend on your computer's hardware. For example, Windows Hello options are available only if you have a compatible fingerprint reader or camera.

If you set up more than one option for signing in, you can choose a method other than the default by clicking Sign-In Options on the sign-in screen. This ability might come in handy, for example, if the fingerprint reader fails to recognize your grubby mitt. Icons for each of the options you set up then appear as shown next; click or tap one to switch methods.

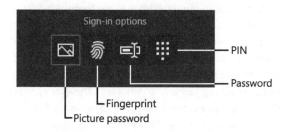

Note that these alternative sign-in options also work for some applications, including the Store.

Setting or changing a password

When you create a Microsoft account, you're required to create a password. Similarly, if you add a local user account to your computer, Windows 10 requires you to specify a password. Earlier versions of Windows did not have this requirement, however, so if you upgrade from an earlier version, you might need to add passwords for existing local accounts.

NOTE

If you sign in with a local account, you must add a password before you can use a PIN, picture password, or Windows Hello.

To set or change your own password, go to Settings > Accounts > Sign-in Options. Click or tap Change under Password. If Windows Hello is set up, you first need to enter your PIN or supply biometric authentication. Next, you must enter your existing password to confirm your identity. Windows then asks you to enter your new password twice. For a local account, you must specify a password hint. The password hint appears after you click your name on the sign-in screen and type your password incorrectly. Be sure your hint is only a subtle reminder, because any user can click your name and then view the hint. (Windows will not allow you to create a password hint that contains your password.)

NOTE

If you sign in with a local account, you can use a quicker alternative: Press Ctrl+Alt+Delete, and click Change A Password. This method does not include the option to enter a password hint.

You can also set or change the password for the local account of another user on your computer. To do so, open User Accounts in Control Panel, click Manage Another Account, and click the name of the user whose password you want to change. Then click Change The Password or (if the account doesn't currently have a password) Create A Password.

CAUTION

If another user has files encrypted with EFS, do not create a password for that user; instead, show the user how to create a password for his own account. Similarly, do not remove or change another user's password unless the user has forgotten the password and has absolutely no other way to access the account. (For more information, see the sidebar "Recovering from a lost password.") If you create, change, or remove another user's password, that user loses all personal certificates and stored passwords for websites and network resources. Without the personal certificates, the user loses access to all of his encrypted files and all email messages encrypted with the user's private key. Windows deletes the certificates and passwords to prevent the administrator who makes a password change from gaining access to them—but this security comes at a cost!

Recovering from a lost password

It's bound to happen: Someday when you try to sign in to your computer and are faced with the password prompt, you will draw a blank.

For a Microsoft account, use another computer or a mobile device to go to *https://account. live.com/password/reset*. Answer a series of questions there and you'll be able to send a code to one of the alternative verification methods on your account—a text message to your mobile device or an email message to an account you control. Enter the code to prove your identity and you can reset your password.

For a local account, if the password hint doesn't jog your memory, your only supported option is to use a password reset disk, which you presumably created before you needed it and then stashed in a safe place. To create a password reset disk, you need removable media, such as a USB flash drive, external hard drive, or memory card. After signing in to your account, open Control Panel > User Accounts and click Create A Password Reset Disk. Follow the Forgotten Password Wizard's instructions.

You can have only one password reset disk for each local user account. If you make a new one, the old one is no longer usable.

To use the reset disk when password amnesia sets in, take your best guess at a password. If you're wrong, Windows informs you that the password is incorrect and offers both a hint and a Reset Password link, which opens the Password Reset Wizard. That wizard asks for the location of the password reset disk, reads the encrypted key, and then asks you to set a new password, which it then uses to sign you in. Your password reset disk remains usable in case you forget the new password; you don't need to make a new one.

If you can't remember the password and you don't have a password reset disk, you're out of luck. A local administrator can sign in and change or remove your password for you, but you'll lose access to your encrypted files and email messages and your stored credentials. If that prospect gives you chills, perhaps you should consider switching to a Microsoft account.

Using a PIN

To set up a PIN for signing in to your computer, go to the Sign-In Options page (shown in Figure 6-7) and click Add under PIN. After entering your password to confirm your identity, you enter numbers in a dialog box like the one shown here. The minimum length is four digits (0–9 only; no letters or special characters allowed), but your PIN can be as long as you want.

To sign in using a PIN, you can type the numbers on your keyboard. If your computer doesn't have a keyboard, a numeric pad appears on the screen so that you can tap your PIN. (If the numeric pad does not appear, tap in the PIN-entry box.)

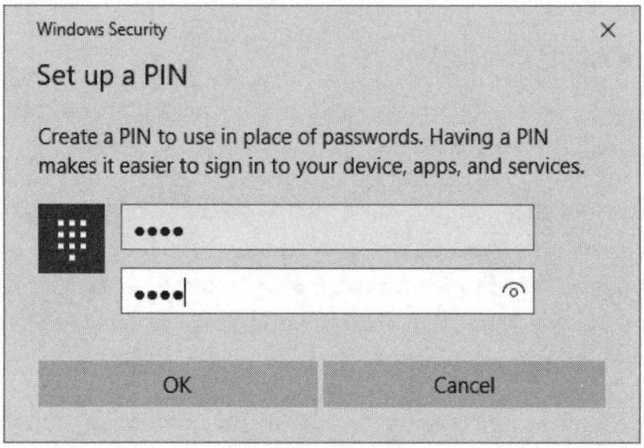

Figure 6-7 A PIN serves as a convenient alternative for signing in to Windows and verifying your identity in apps and services. You can choose a PIN that's longer than the minimum of four characters.

Inside OUT

Make your PIN even stronger

You might be worried that a four-digit numeric PIN is too easy to guess. You'll probably rest a little easier knowing that Windows 10 offers only five incorrect tries before locking you out. After four incorrect attempts, you're required to enter a challenge phrase (which incidentally confirms that your keyboard is working correctly). After the fifth incorrect attempt, a would-be intruder is locked out. At that point, Windows requires you to either enter the password or restart the device and try signing in again. After a handful of failed tries, Windows stops accepting new guesses and requires you to enter your password.

And imagine their surprise when they learn that a PIN can be more than four digits long. When you set up your PIN, make it six digits instead of four, allowing up to 1 million possible numeric combinations and trying the patience of even the most persistent attacker. Even an eight-digit PIN (100 million numeric combinations) is still easier to enter than a complex password.

If you sign in to an Active Directory domain or Azure AD, a network administrator can use Group Policy on Windows 10 Pro or Enterprise to mandate a minimum PIN length and to force the use of letters and numbers, making the PIN practically unguessable. These settings are in the Group Policy Editor under Computer Configuration > Administrative Templates > System > Windows Components > Windows Hello For Business.

Using a picture password

With a picture password, you can sign in on a touchscreen using a combination of gestures (specifically, circles, straight lines, and taps) that you make on a picture displayed on the sign-in screen. The easiest way to get comfortable with a picture password is to go ahead and create one.

To get started, go to Settings > Accounts > Sign-In Options. Under Picture Password, click Add. Verify your identity by entering your password to display an introductory screen where you can choose a picture. You then get to select one of your own pictures to appear on the sign-in screen. When you're satisfied with your selection, click Use This Picture.

On the next screen that appears, you specify the three gestures you'll use to sign in. These gestures can consist of circles, straight lines, and taps. After repeating the series of gestures to confirm your new "password," click Finish.

To sign in with a picture password, on the sign-in screen you must perform the same three gestures, in the same order, using the same locations, and in the same direction. You don't need to be *that* precise; Windows allows minor variations in location.

Using Windows Hello for biometric sign-ins

With the proper hardware, you can sign in simply by swiping your fingerprint or, even easier, showing your face in front of your computer's camera. (Some Windows 10 Mobile devices also support iris recognition.) You might also be asked to verify your identity when making a purchase or accessing a secure service. When Windows Hello recognizes a fingerprint, face, or iris, it greets you by briefly displaying your name and a smiley face on the sign-in screen before going to your desktop, as shown in Figure 6-8.

To use Windows Hello for biometric sign-ins on a PC, you need one of the following:

- A fingerprint reader that supports the Windows Biometric Framework; if this hardware isn't built in, you can add a USB-based fingerprint reader.

- An illuminated 3-D infrared camera such as those found on the Surface Pro 4, Surface Book, and other advanced devices; note that a standard webcam will not work.

NOTE
You must add a PIN as described earlier in this chapter before you can use Windows Hello.

CHAPTER 6

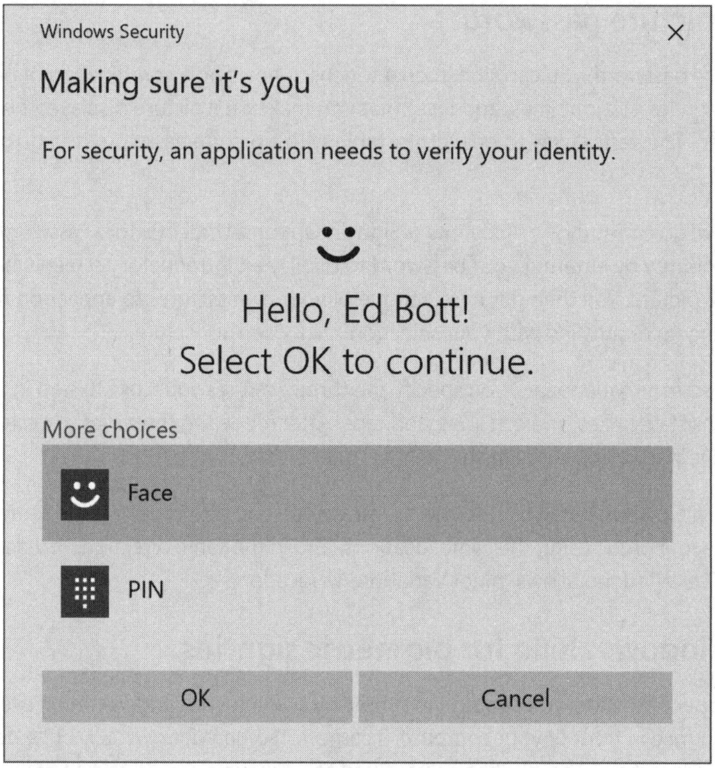

Figure 6-8 After you set up facial recognition (or a fingerprint reader), Windows Hello uses biometric hardware to identify you when you sign in or access apps and services that need verification.

To set up Windows Hello, go to the Sign-In Options page in Settings, Accounts. Under Windows Hello, click Set Up for the biometric device you want to use. Windows asks you to enter your PIN to verify your identity. After that, you need to enter your biometric data. With face recognition, that involves staring into the camera; to set up a fingerprint reader, follow the prompts (as shown in Figure 6-9) to swipe your fingerprint several times, until Windows Hello has recorded the data it needs.

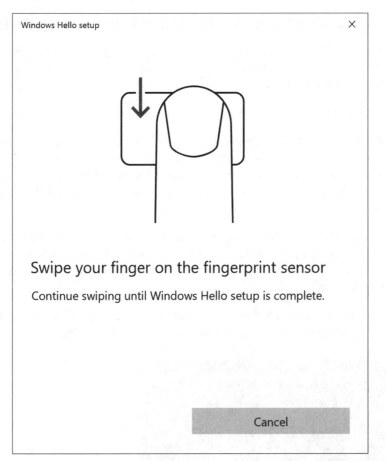

Windows Hello setup   ✕

Swipe your finger on the fingerprint sensor

Continue swiping until Windows Hello setup is complete.

Cancel

Figure 6-9 Setup for Windows Hello guides you through the brief process of scanning and storing your biometric data.

If you're setting up fingerprint scanning, you can enroll additional fingers (so that you don't have to be particular about using the same finger all the time) by clicking Add Another after you complete registration for a fingerprint. (To add another fingerprint later, return to Settings > Accounts > Sign-In Options and click Add Another.) You can also associate an additional fingerprint with a different user account on the same device. Sign in to the alternate account, and set up the second fingerprint there. When you restart, you can choose your account by choosing the fingerprint associated with that account.

Signing out, switching accounts, or locking your computer

When you're finished using your computer, you want to be sure you don't leave it in a condition in which others can use your credentials to access your files. To do that, you need to sign out, switch accounts, or lock your computer:

- **Sign Out.** With this option, all your programs close and the lock screen appears.

- **Switch Account.** With this option, also known as fast user switching, your programs continue to run. The sign-in screen appears, ready for the sign-in credentials of the person you select. Your account is still signed in, but only you can return to your own session, which you can do when the user you switch to chooses to sign out, switch accounts, or lock the computer.

- **Lock.** With this option, your programs continue to run, but the lock screen appears so that no one can see your desktop or use the computer. Only you can unlock the computer to return to your session; however, other users can sign in to their own sessions without disturbing yours.

To sign out, switch accounts, or lock your computer, open the Start menu and click or tap your name at the top of the menu to display a menu like the one shown in Figure 6-10.

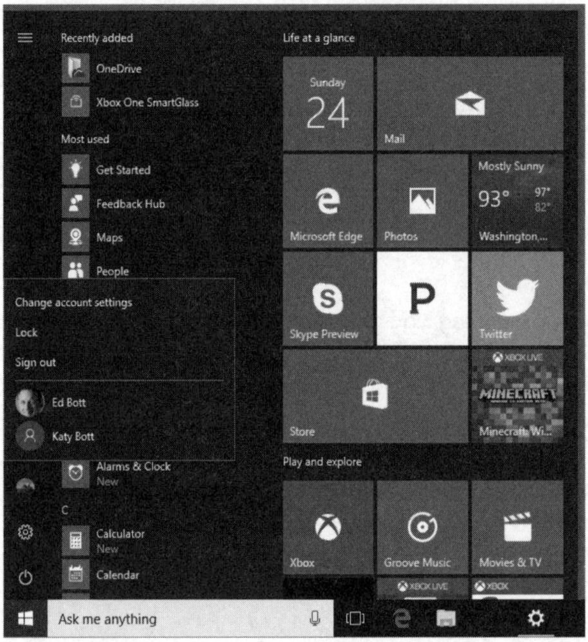

Figure 6-10 On a computer that's joined to a domain, Switch Account appears instead of individual account names. You can then enter an account name on the sign-in screen.

Inside OUT

Use keyboard shortcuts

To lock your computer, press Windows key+L. (You might also find it more convenient to use this shortcut for switching accounts; the only difference is that it takes you to the lock screen instead of to the sign-in screen.)

For any of these actions—sign out, switch accounts, or lock—you can start by pressing Ctrl+Alt+Delete, which displays a menu that includes all three options.

Configuring privacy options

These days, you don't need to be a conspiracy theorist to be concerned about privacy. Some companies abuse your trust by taking your information—often without your knowledge or consent—and sharing it with others who hope to profit from that information.

Because Windows 10 is tightly integrated with cloud services, some of your information is stored, with your permission, on Microsoft-owned servers. Likewise, Microsoft acknowledges using some of your information to provide personalized suggestions; for example, opting in to the Cortana service allows the use of location data from your device and appointments from your calendar to give you reminders about when you need to leave for a meeting. In addition, Windows 10 shares what Microsoft calls *telemetry* data for the purpose of improving the reliability of the operating system.

Telemetry data includes information about the device and how it's configured (including hardware attributes such as CPU, installed memory, and storage), as well as quality-related information such as uptime and sleep details and the number of crashes or hangs. Additional basic information includes a list of installed apps and drivers. For systems where the telemetry is set to a level higher than Basic, the information collected includes events that analyze interaction between the user and the operating system and apps.

Microsoft insists that its telemetry system is designed to prevent any privacy issues. "We collect a limited amount of information to help us provide a secure and reliable experience," the company says. "This includes data like an anonymous device ID and device type. . . . This doesn't include any of your content or files, and we take several steps to avoid collecting any information that directly identifies you, such as your name, email address or account ID."

NOTE

For a full discussion of how Windows 10 telemetry works, with an emphasis on how to manage telemetry settings in an organization, see *https://bit.ly/configure-telemetry*.

CHAPTER 6

Some of your personal information is used to provide more relevant advertising in apps. If you opt to turn off that personalization, you'll still see ads, but those ads will not be based on your browsing history or other information about you. Regardless of your privacy settings, Microsoft does not use your email, chat, files, or other personal content to target ads.

A single privacy statement covers most of Microsoft's consumer products and services, including Windows 10 and related services. For information about the privacy policy and to make choices about how Microsoft uses your data, visit *https://privacy.microsoft.com*. (A link to detailed information is also available when you go to Settings > System > About.)

More important still, Windows includes a raft of options for controlling your privacy. You'll find them under the Privacy heading in Settings, where you can specify which apps are allowed to use each of your computer's many devices, whether to disclose your location, whether to let Cortana better know your voice and word pronunciations, and so on.

For each privacy option, you'll find a link to the Microsoft privacy statement and links to additional information as well as the controls for making settings. The privacy statement is detailed yet clearly written, and it's an important aid for deciding which options to enable. You should examine each of these options carefully and decide for yourself where the proper balance is between your personal privacy and convenience.

To minimize the collection of telemetry information, for example, go to Settings > Privacy > Feedback & Diagnostics. Under the Diagnostic And Usage Data heading, change the default setting (Full on Windows 10 Home or Pro, Enhanced on Windows 10 Enterprise) to Basic, as shown here:

In organizations that use Windows 10 Enterprise edition, a fourth level, Security, is available via Group Policy and device management software. Note that this setting also disables Windows Update and should thus be used only when an alternative update mechanism is available.

Devices that are enrolled in the Windows Insider Program and are receiving preview builds have some privacy settings that can't be changed. For example, the Diagnostic And Usage Data setting is locked on Full; other options are unavailable. For more information, see Chapter 23, "What's next for Windows 10?"

Sharing your PC with other users

Personal computers are usually just that—personal. But there are situations in which it makes sense for a single PC to be shared by multiple users. In those circumstances, it's prudent to configure the shared device securely. Doing so helps to protect each user's data from inadvertent deletions and changes as well as malicious damage and theft.

> NOTE
> In this section, we offer advice for configuring a PC with Microsoft accounts and local accounts. Azure AD and domain accounts are administered centrally.

When you set up your computer, consider these suggestions:

- **Control who can sign in.** Create accounts only for users who need to use your computer's resources, either by signing in locally or over a network. If an account you created is no longer needed, delete or disable it.

- **Use standard accounts for additional users.** During setup, Windows sets up one local administrative account for installing programs, creating and managing accounts, and so on. All other accounts can and should run with standard privileges.

- **Be sure that all accounts are protected by a strong password.** This is especially important for administrator accounts and for other accounts whose profiles contain important or sensitive documents. Windows 10 requires a password on all local accounts. If you have local accounts that were migrated from Windows 7, make sure they're all password-protected.

- **Restrict sign-in times.** You might want to limit the computing hours for some users, especially children. The easiest way for home users to do this is by setting up family accounts; for details, see "Controlling your family's computer access" later in this chapter.

- **Restrict access to certain files.** You'll want to be sure that some files are available to all users, whereas other files are available only to the person who created them. The Public folder and a user's personal folders provide a general framework for this protection. You can further refine your file-protection scheme by selectively applying permissions to varying combinations of files, folders, and users.

Adding a user to your computer

To allow another user to sign in on your computer, you as administrator must add that user's account. Go to Settings > Accounts > Family & Other People, shown in Figure 6-11. There, you'll find two separate sets of controls: one for adding members of your family and the second for adding "other people." Accounts you add as family members are subject to restrictions that an adult member of the family can manage using a web-based interface (for details, see the next section, "Controlling your family's computer access"). Accounts you create under the Other People heading have all the rights and privileges associated with their account type, administrator or standard.

> **NOTE**
> The Family & Other People page is available only when you sign in with an administrator account.

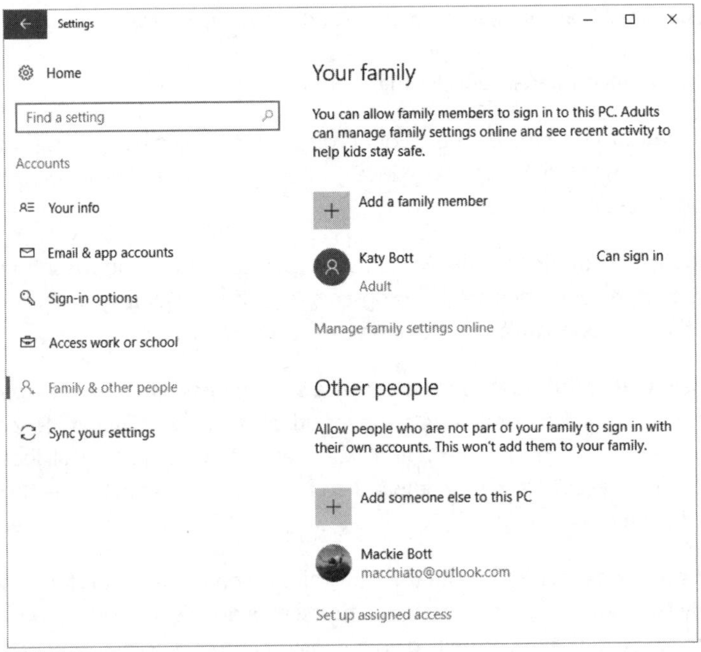

Figure 6-11 Under Other Users, you can add a local account or a Microsoft account. Family members must have a Microsoft account.

To add a user who's not a family member, under Other Users click Add Someone Else To This PC. Windows then asks for the email address of the new user. If the email address is already associated with a Microsoft account, all you need to do is click Next and the new user is ready to go. (The first time the new user signs in, the computer must be connected to the internet.) If the email address you provide is not associated with a Microsoft account, Windows provides a link to sign up for a new Microsoft account.

What if you want to add a local account? At the first screen—when Windows asks for an email address—instead click the link near the bottom: I Don't Have This Person's Sign-in Information. In the next dialog box, shown in Figure 6-12, ignore the offer to set up a new Microsoft account and instead click Add A User Without A Microsoft Account.

Click here to create a local account

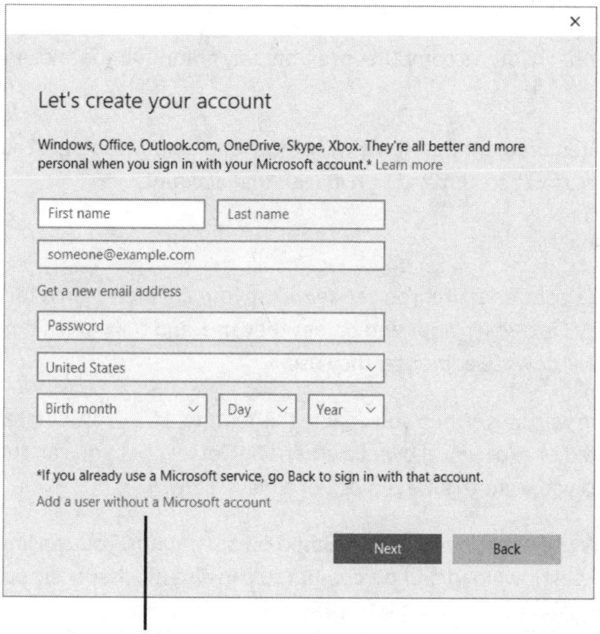

Figure 6-12 Microsoft really, really wants you to set up a Microsoft account. To refuse the offer and set up a local account instead, click the Add A User Without A Microsoft Account option at the bottom of this dialog box.

That option opens a different dialog box where you can specify a user name and password for the new user. (If your computer has only local accounts set up, you go directly to this final dialog box, skipping the two that guide you toward a Microsoft account.) Click Next, and your work is done.

CHAPTER 6

Controlling your family's computer access

Previous versions of Windows had a feature called Parental Controls (Windows Vista and Windows 7) or Family Safety (Windows 8), which allowed parents to restrict and monitor their children's computer use. Windows 10 offers similar capabilities, but the implementation is completely different. Those earlier versions stored their settings on your PC, but in Windows 10 family settings are now stored and managed as part of your Microsoft account.

This architectural change has some obvious benefits:

- You don't need to make settings for each child on each computer. After you add a family member on one PC, you manage the settings for each child in the cloud, and those settings apply to all the family PCs where they sign in.

- You can manage your children's computer use from any computer that's connected to the internet.

Family settings have one requirement that some will perceive as a disadvantage: Each family member must have a Microsoft account and sign in with that account.

What can you do with family settings?

- Monitor each child's computer use. You can see what your children search for on the web and which sites they visit, which apps and games they use, and how much time they're signed in to each Windows 10 computer they use.

- Block inappropriate websites. When you enable this feature, Microsoft-curated lists of sites that are blocked or explicitly allowed are used by default, but you can supplement these lists with sites you want to always block or always allow.

- Control each child's use of apps and games. Based on age ratings, you can limit the apps and games a child can download and purchase. You can also block specific apps and games from running.

- Set spending limits for Store purchases. You can add money to a child's account and remove other purchase options.

- Restrict when your children can use the computer, and for how long.

You can add a family member using the online management interface or from within Windows 10; go to Settings > Accounts > Family & Other People, and click Add A Family Member. Windows asks whether you want to add an account for an adult or a child; the difference is that an adult can manage family settings, whereas a child is controlled by family settings.

You then enter the family member's email address; if a Microsoft account is not associated with that address, Windows gathers the needed information to set one up. Because all family settings are managed online using Microsoft accounts, there is no option to use a local account.

NOTE
If you don't see the Family & Other People page, confirm that you're signed in with a Microsoft account and that your account type is administrator.

All other management tasks occur online. Click the Manage Family Settings Online link under the Your Family heading or visit *https://account.microsoft.com/family* to get started. Figure 6-13 shows a portion of the interface for setting up both daily limits and the times during which a child can use a Windows 10 PC.

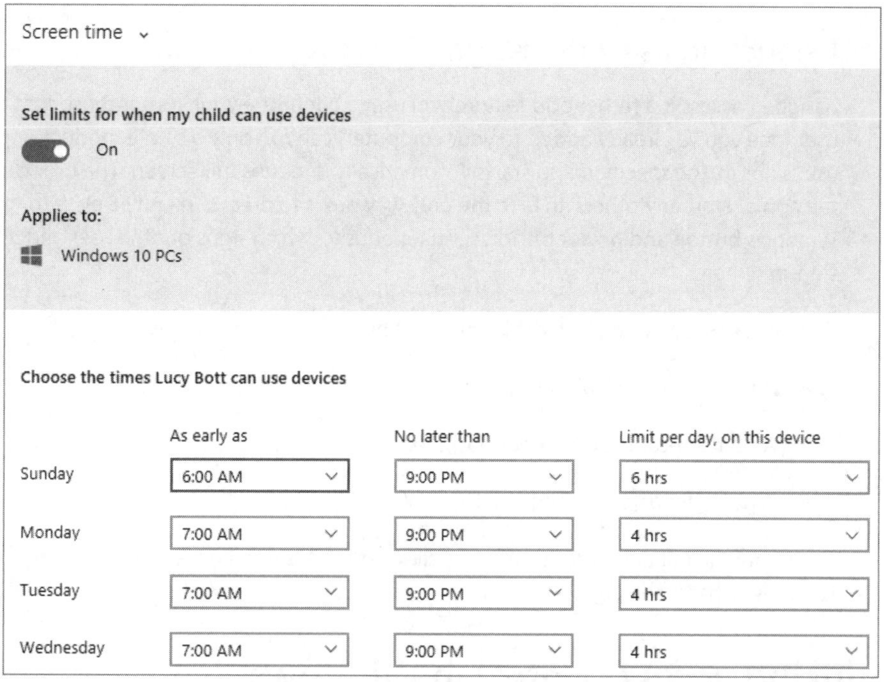

Figure 6-13 With Screen Time settings, for each day of the week you specify an allowable range of times for a child's computer use, plus an optional overall daily limit.

After you select a Microsoft account for the new family member, Microsoft Family sends an email invitation to that person. (If you use the web-based interface to add a child's account, you can sign in on the child's behalf using his credentials.) A new family member can sign in to your computer right away, but family settings take effect only after that family member opens the email message and clicks the Accept Invitation button. (Until that happens, the word *Pending* appears next to the family member's name on the Family & Other Users page.)

CHAPTER 6

The email invitation never arrives

Despite repeated attempts on your part to use the Family & Other People page, some-times the invitation isn't sent. To get around this, click Manage Family Settings Online. (Alternatively, browse to *https://account.microsoft.com/family*.) On the webpage that appears, click the Add button for a child or an adult.

Note that when you sign in to one of your other computers, your family's accounts are already in place; you don't need to add family members on each device. However, by default the other family members cannot sign in to these other devices. To enable access, click the name of the family member and then click Allow. To disable access for a family member on a specific device, click Block.

Restricting use with assigned access

Assigned access is a rather odd feature you use to configure your computer so that a certain user (one you've already added to your computer) can run only a single modern app. When that user signs in, the specified app starts automatically and runs full-screen. The user can't close the app or start any others. In fact, the only way out is to press Ctrl+Alt+Delete (or press the Windows button and power button simultaneously), which signs out the user and returns to the sign-in screen.

The use cases for this feature are limited, but here are a few examples:

- A kiosk app for public use

- A point-of-sale app for your business

- A game for a very young child

If you can think of a use for this feature, click Set Up Assigned Access, at the bottom of the Family & Other Users page.

Introducing access control in Windows

We've saved this fairly technical section for last. Most Windows users never need to deal with the nuts and bolts of the Windows security model. But developers, network administrators, and anyone who aspires to the label "power user" should have at least a basic understanding of what happens when you create accounts, share files, install software drivers, and perform other tasks that have security implications.

The Windows approach to security is discretionary: Each securable system resource—each file or printer, for example—has an owner. That owner, in turn, has discretion over who can and cannot access the resource. Usually, a resource is owned by the user who creates it. If you create a file, for example, you are the file's owner under ordinary circumstances. (Computer administrators, however, can take ownership of resources they didn't create.)

NOTE

To exercise full discretionary control over individual files, you must store those files on an NTFS volume. For the sake of compatibility, Windows 10 supports the FAT and FAT32 file systems used by early Windows versions and many USB flash drives, as well as the exFAT file system used on some removable drives. However, none of the FAT-based file systems support file permissions. To enjoy the full benefits of Windows security, you must use NTFS. For more information about file systems, see "Choosing a file system" in Chapter 14, "Managing disks and drives."

What are security identifiers?

Windows security relies on the use of a security identifier (SID) to identify a user. When you create a user account on your computer, Windows assigns a unique SID to that account. The SID remains uniquely associated with that user account until the account is deleted, whereupon the SID is never used again—for that user or any other user. Even if you recreate an account with identical information, a new SID is created.

A SID is a variable-length value that contains a revision level, a 48-bit identifier authority value, and a number of 32-bit subauthority values. The SID takes the form S-1-x-y1-y2- . . . . S-1 identifies it as a revision 1 SID; x is the value for the identifier authority; and y1, y2, and so on are values for subauthorities.

You'll sometimes see a SID in a security dialog box (for example, on the Security tab of a file's properties dialog box) before Windows has had time to look up the user account name. You'll also spot SIDs in the hidden and protected $RECYCLE.BIN folder (each SID you see in this folder represents the Recycle Bin for a particular user) and in the registry (the HKEY_USERS hive contains a key, identified by SID, for each user account on the computer), among other places. The easiest way to determine your own SID is with the Whoami command-line utility. For details, see the following tip.

Not all SIDs are unique (although the SID assigned to your user account is always unique). A number of commonly used SIDs are constant among all Windows installations. For example, S-1-5-18 is the SID for the built-in Local System account, a hidden member of the Administrators group that is used by the operating system and by services that sign in using the Local System account. You can find a complete list of such SIDs in the Microsoft Knowledge Base article "Well-known security identifiers in Windows operating systems" (*https://support.microsoft.com/kb/243330*).

To control which users have access to a resource, Windows uses the security identifier (SID) assigned to each user account. Your SID (a gigantic number guaranteed to be unique) follows you around wherever you go in Windows. When you sign in, the operating system first validates your user name and password. Then it creates a security access token. You can think of this as the electronic equivalent of an ID badge. It includes your user name and SID, plus information about any security groups to which your account belongs. (Security groups are described later in this chapter.) Any program you start gets a copy of your security access token.

Inside OUT

Learn about your own account with Whoami

Windows includes a command-line utility called Whoami (Who Am I?). You can use Whoami to find out the name of the account that's currently signed in, its SID, the names of the security groups of which it's a member, and its privileges. To use Whoami, start by opening a Command Prompt window. (You don't need elevated privileges.)

Then, to learn the name of the signed-in user, type **whoami**. (This is particularly useful if you're signed in as a standard user but running an elevated Command Prompt window—when it might not be obvious which account is currently "you.") If you're curious about your SID, type **whoami /user**. For a complete list of Whoami parameters, type **whoami /?**

With User Account Control (UAC) turned on, administrators who sign in get two security access tokens—one that has the privileges of a standard user and one that has the full privileges of an administrator.

Whenever you attempt to walk through a controlled "door" in Windows (for example, when you connect to a shared printer), or any time a program attempts to do so on your behalf, the operating system examines your security access token and decides whether to let you pass. If access is permitted, you notice nothing. If access is denied, you get to hear a beep and read a refusal message.

In determining whom to let pass and whom to block, Windows consults the resource's access control list (ACL). This is simply a list of SIDs and the access privileges associated with each one. Every resource subject to access control has an ACL. This manner of allowing and blocking access to resources such as files and printers is essentially unchanged since Windows NT.

CHAPTER 6

What are ACLs?

Each folder and each file on an NTFS-formatted volume has an ACL (also known as DACL, for discretionary access control list, and commonly called NTFS permissions). An ACL comprises an access control entry (ACE) for each user who is allowed access to the folder or file. With NTFS permissions, you can control access to any file or folder, allowing different types of access for different users or groups of users.

To view and edit NTFS permissions for a file or folder, right-click its icon and choose Properties. The Security tab lists all the groups and users with permissions set for the selected object, as shown here. Different permissions can be set for each user, as you can see by selecting each one.

To make changes to the settings for any user or group in the list, or to add or remove a user or group in the list, click Edit. (Use caution. Setting NTFS permissions without understanding the full consequences can lead to unexpected and unwelcome results, including a complete loss of access to files and folders. Before you delve into the inner workings of NTFS permissions on the Security tab, be sure to try the safer and less complicated homegroup sharing or the Share With command. For details, see "Sharing files, digital media, and printers in a homegroup" in Chapter 5, "Networking essentials," and "Sharing files and folders from any folder" in Chapter 20.)

CHAPTER 6

The access granted by each permission type is as follows:

- **Full Control.** Users with Full Control can list contents of a folder, read and open files, create new files, delete files and subfolders, change permissions on files and subfolders, and take ownership of files.

- **Modify.** Allows the user to read, change, create, and delete files but not to change permissions or take ownership of files.

- **Read & Execute.** Allows the user to view files and execute programs.

- **List Folder Contents.** Provides the same permissions as Read & Execute, but can be applied only to folders.

- **Read.** Allows the user to list the contents of a folder, read file attributes, read permissions, and synchronize files.

- **Write.** Allows the user to create files, write data, read attributes and permissions, and synchronize files.

- **Special Permissions.** The assigned permissions don't match any of the preceding permission descriptions. To see precisely which permissions are granted, click Advanced.

UAC, which was introduced in Windows Vista, adds another layer of restrictions based on user accounts. With UAC turned on, applications are normally launched using an administrator's standard user token. (Standard users, of course, have only a standard user token.) If an application requires administrator privileges, UAC asks for your consent (if you're signed in as an administrator) or the credentials of an administrator (if you're signed in as a standard user) before letting the application run. With UAC turned off, Windows works in the same (rather dangerous) manner as pre–Windows Vista versions: Administrator accounts can do just about anything (sometimes getting those users in trouble), and standard accounts don't have the privileges needed to run many older programs.

➤ For more information about UAC, see "Preventing unsafe actions with User Account Control" in Chapter 7.

Permissions and rights

Windows distinguishes two types of access privileges: permissions and rights. A permission is the ability to access a particular object in some defined manner—for example, to write to an NTFS file or to modify a printer queue. A right is the ability to perform a particular system-wide action, such as signing in or resetting the clock.

The owner of a resource (or an administrator) assigns permissions to the resource via its properties dialog box. For example, if you're the printer owner or have administrative privileges, you can restrict someone from using a particular printer by visiting the properties dialog box for that printer. Administrators set rights via the Local Security Policy console. For example, an administrator could grant someone the right to install a device driver. (The Local Security Policy console is available only in the Pro and Enterprise editions of Windows 10. In the Home edition, rights for various security groups are predefined and unchangeable.)

NOTE
In this book, as in many of the Windows messages and dialog boxes, *privileges* serves as an informal term encompassing both permissions and rights.

User accounts and security groups

The backbone of Windows security is the ability to uniquely identify each user. While setting up a computer—or at any later time—an administrator creates a user account for each user. The user account is identified by a user name and is normally secured by a password, which the user provides when signing in to the system. Windows then controls, monitors, and restricts access to system resources on the basis of the permissions and rights associated with each user account by the resource owners and the system administrator.

Account type is a simplified way of describing membership in a security group, which is a collection of user accounts. Windows classifies each user account as one of two account types:

- **Administrator.** Members of the Administrators group are classified as administrator accounts. By default, the Administrators group includes the first account you create when you set up the computer and an account named Administrator that is disabled and hidden by default. Unlike other account types, administrators have full control over the system. Among the tasks that only administrators can perform are the following:
    - Create, change, and delete user accounts and groups
    - Install and uninstall desktop programs
    - Configure automatic updating with Windows Update
    - Install an ActiveX control
    - Install or remove hardware device drivers
    - Share folders
    - Set permissions
    - Access all files, including those in another user's folder
    - Take ownership of files

- Copy or move files into the %ProgramFiles% or %SystemRoot% folders
- Restore backed-up system files
- Grant rights to other user accounts and to themselves
- Configure Windows Firewall

- **Standard user.** Members of the Users group are classified as standard user accounts. A partial list of tasks available to standard user accounts includes

  - Change the password and picture for their own user account
  - Use desktop programs that have been installed on the computer
  - Install system and driver updates using Windows Update
  - Install and run apps from the Windows Store
  - Install approved ActiveX controls
  - Configure a secure Wi-Fi connection
  - Refresh a network adapter and the system's IP address
  - View permissions
  - Create, change, and delete files in their document folders and in shared document folders
  - Restore their own backed-up files
  - View the system clock and calendar, and change the time zone
  - Set personalization options, such as themes, desktop background, and so on
  - Select a display dots-per-inch (DPI) setting to adjust text size
  - Configure power options
  - Sign in in Safe Mode
  - View Windows Firewall settings

Assigning an appropriate account type to the people who use your computer is straightforward. At least one user must be an administrator; naturally, that should be the person who manages the computer's use and maintenance. All other regular users should each have a standard user account.

What happened to the Administrator account?

Every computer running Windows has a special account named Administrator. In versions of Windows before Windows 7, Administrator was the primary account for managing the computer. Like other administrator accounts, the Administrator account has full rights over the entire computer. But in Windows 10, the Administrator account is disabled by default.

In Windows 10, there's seldom a need to use the Administrator account instead of another administrator account. With default settings in Windows, the Administrator account does have one unique capability: It's not subject to UAC, even when UAC is turned on for all other users. All other administrator accounts (which are sometimes called Protected Administrator accounts) run with standard-user privileges unless the user consents to elevation. The Administrator account runs with full administrative privileges at all times and never needs your consent for elevation. (For this reason, of course, it's rather risky. Any application that runs as Administrator has full control of the computer—which means applications written by malicious or incompetent programmers can do significant damage to your system.)

Inside OUT

And the Guest account?

Historically, the built-in Guest account provided a way to offer limited access to occasional users. Not so in Windows 10. Although this account still exists, it's disabled by default, and the supported tools for enabling it (the Local Users And Groups console, for example) do not work as expected. In our experience, trying to trick Windows 10 into enabling this capability is almost certain to end in frustration. In the cloud-centric world of Windows 10, the Guest account no longer works as it used to and enabling it can cause a variety of problems. A better solution (if your guests don't have their own device that can connect to your wireless network) is to set up a standard account for guest use.

Security groups allow a system administrator to create classes of users who share common privileges. For example, if everyone in the accounting department needs access to the Payables folder, the administrator can create a group called Accounting and grant the entire group access to that folder. If the administrator then adds all user accounts belonging to employees in the accounting department to the Accounting group, these users will automatically have access to the Payables folder. A user account can belong to one group, more than one group, or no group at all.

In large networks based on Active Directory domains, groups can be a valuable administrative tool. They simplify the job of ensuring that all members with common access needs have an identical set of privileges. We don't recommend creating or using groups other than the built-in Administrators and Users groups on standalone and workgroup-based computers, however.

Permissions and rights for group members are cumulative. That means that if a user account belongs to more than one group, the user enjoys all the privileges accorded to all groups of which the user account is a member.

Securing Windows 10 devices

We don't mean to be scaremongers, but they *are* out to get you. Computer attacks continue to increase in number and severity each year. And while the big data breaches—the loss of millions of credit card numbers from a major retailer or the loss of millions of personnel records from the U.S. government—command the most media attention, don't think that the bad guys wouldn't like to get into your computer too. Whether it's to steal your valuable personal data or hold it for ransom, appropriate your computing resources and bandwidth, or use your PC as a pathway into a bigger target with whom you do business, there are plenty of actors with bad intent.

According to Symantec's latest Internet Security Threat Report, 43 percent of all targeted attacks in 2015 struck small businesses. Like individuals, these organizations often don't have the resources to invest in security—making them juicy targets. Employees at large organizations are vulnerable to being targeted with "spear phishing" campaigns that allow outside access into otherwise secure networks.

In this chapter, we examine the types of threats you're likely to face at home and at your office. More importantly, we describe some of the more significant security improvements made in Microsoft Windows 10—many of which are in layers you can't see, such as hardware-based protection that operates before Windows loads. Then we explain how to use the more visible security features, including Windows Firewall, User Account Control, BitLocker, and Windows Defender.

Understanding security threats

A decade ago, the threat landscape for Windows users was dominated by viruses and worms. Ah, for the good old days! The modern threat landscape is much more complex and, unfortunately, more insidious. Today, an attacker is likely to be part of an organized crime ring or even acting on behalf of a state-sponsored organization, and attacks are typically designed to go unnoticed for as long as possible.

A rogue program, installed without your knowledge and running without your awareness, can perform malicious tasks and transfer data without your consent. This category of software is often referred to as *malware*.

The goal of the bad guys is to get you to run their software. They might, for example, convince you to install a *Trojan*—a program that appears legitimate but actually performs malicious actions when it's installed. This category of malware doesn't spread on its own but instead uses social engineering (often using popular social networking sites such as Facebook and Twitter) to convince its victims to cooperate in the installation process. As part of its payload, a Trojan can include a downloader that installs additional malicious and unwanted programs. Some Trojans install a "back door" that allows an outside attacker to remotely control the infected computer.

What's in it for the bad guys? Money, mostly, gathered in various ways, depending on how the attackers got through your defenses. Here are just a few examples:

- A *password stealer* runs in the background, gathers user names and passwords, and forwards them to an outside attacker. The stolen credentials can then be used to make purchases, clean out bank accounts, or commit identity theft.

- Bad guys prey on fear with rogue security software (also known as *scareware*), which mimics the actions and appearance of legitimate antivirus software. If you install one of these programs, it inevitably reports the presence of a (nonexistent) virus and offers to remove the alleged malware—for a fee, of course.

- In 2016, the fastest rising star in the malware hall of shame continues to be *ransomware*, a form of digital blackmail in which a program encrypts all your data files and offers to unlock them only upon payment of a ransom.

- *Phishing attacks*, which use social engineering to convince visitors to give away their sign-in credentials, are a separate but potentially devastating avenue to identity theft that can strike in any browser using any operating system.

You can review lists of current malware threats, along with links to details about each one, at the Microsoft Malware Protection Center, *https://bit.ly/malware-encyclopedia*. For a more comprehensive view of the changing threat landscape, the Microsoft Malware Protection Center issues a twice-yearly report, using data from hundreds of millions of Windows users and other sources. You'll find the latest Microsoft Security Intelligence Report at *https://microsoft.com/security/sir*.

Securing your computer: A defense-in-depth strategy

A multidimensional threat landscape requires a multilayered approach to protecting your PC and your network. The big-picture goal is to secure your device, secure your data, secure your identity, and block malware. On a home or small business network, those layers of security include the following:

- **Use a hardware router to protect your broadband connection.** This is an essential part of physical security, even if your network consists of a single PC. We provide an overview of the technology in "Getting started with Windows 10 networking" in Chapter 5, "Networking essentials."

- **Enable a software firewall, and keep it turned on.** You can use Windows Firewall, which is included with Windows 10, or a third-party firewall such as those included with security suites. To learn more, see "Blocking intruders with Windows Firewall" later in this chapter.

- **Use biometric sign-in.** Biometric sign-in using a fingerprint reader or facial recognition with Windows Hello offers much more than convenience. Because biometric sign-in is linked to a specific device, it provides effective two-factor authentication. If you don't have the necessary hardware, use a PIN or picture password for sign-in—both of which can be more secure than a traditional password. For more information, see "Managing the sign-in process" in Chapter 6, "Managing user accounts, passwords, and credentials."

- **Set up standard user accounts, and keep User Account Control enabled.** Standard accounts help to prevent (or at least minimize) the damage that an untrained user can do by installing untrusted programs. User Account Control (UAC) helps in this regard by restricting access to administrative tasks and virtualizing registry and file-system changes. For details, see "Introducing access control in Windows" in Chapter 6 and "Preventing unsafe actions with User Account Control" later in this chapter.

- **Keep Windows and vulnerable programs up to date.** Windows Update handles this chore for Windows, Office, and other Microsoft programs. You're on your own for third-party programs. We provide an overview of security updates in "Staying on top of security updates" later in this chapter.

- **Use an antimalware program, and keep it up to date.** Windows Defender, which is included with Windows 10, provides antimalware protection, but many third-party solutions are also available. For details, see "Using Windows Defender to block malware" later in this chapter.

- **Protect yourself from threats in email messages.** At a minimum, your email solution should block or quarantine executable files and other potentially dangerous attachments. In addition, effective antispam features can block scripts and prevent phishing attempts.

- **Use parental controls to keep kids safe.** If you have children who use your computer, family safety features in Windows can help you keep them away from security threats and keep them from wandering into unsafe territory online by restricting their computer activities in other ways. For details, see "Controlling your family's computer access" in Chapter 6.

Security And Maintenance, included in Control Panel, monitors many of these areas to be sure you're protected, and it displays an alert if something needs attention. For details, see "Monitoring your computer's security" later in this chapter.

The most important protective layer—and the one that's most easily overlooked—is user education and self-control. Everyone who uses a computer must have the discipline to read and evaluate security warnings when they're presented and to allow the installation only of software that is known to be safe. (Although a user with a standard account can't install or run a program that wipes out the entire computer, he can still inflict enough damage on his own user profile to cause considerable inconvenience.) Countless successful malware attacks worldwide have proven that many users do not have adequate awareness of safe computing methods.

New security features in Windows 10

Because the bad guys are always upping their game, a hallmark of each new version of Windows is a number of new and improved security features. Windows 10 is no exception. Here we enumerate changes available in Windows 10 Home and Windows 10 Pro; several additional features are included with Windows 10 Enterprise on a managed network.

Securing devices

Security features in Windows 10 begin with support for modern hardware designs. Although Windows 10 continues to support legacy hardware, some security features require two elements built in to most newer computers:

- **Unified Extensible Firmware Interface (UEFI).** UEFI is a firmware interface that replaces the BIOS, which has been a part of every PC since the beginning of personal computing. Among other improvements, UEFI enables Secure Boot and Device Encryption, features that are described in the following pages. PCs designed for Windows 8 and later must use UEFI.

- **Trusted Platform Module (TPM).** A TPM is a hardware chip that facilitates encryption and prevents altering or exporting encryption keys and certificates. The presence of a TPM makes it easy to turn on BitLocker Drive Encryption (described later in this chapter). Other security features in Windows 10, such as Measured Boot and Device Guard, require the presence of a TPM.

With UEFI and TPM in place, Windows 10 is able to secure the boot process. (Many recent malware attacks take control of the system early in the boot process, before Windows is fully running and before antimalware programs spring into action. This type of malware is called a *rootkit*.) The Windows 10 boot process steps through the following features:

- **Secure Boot.** Secure Boot, a basic feature of UEFI, prevents the use of any alternative operating system loader. Only an operating system loader that's digitally signed using a certificate stored by UEFI is allowed to run. (A conventional BIOS allows interruption of the boot process to use any operating system loader, including one that's been corrupted or compromised.)

- **Early Launch Antimalware (ELAM).** Antimalware software—including compatible third-party programs as well as Windows Defender—that has been certified and signed by Microsoft loads its drivers before any other third-party drivers or programs. This sequence of events allows the antimalware software to detect and block attempts to load malicious code.

- **Measured Boot.** With this feature, measurements of the UEFI firmware and each Windows component are taken as they load. The measurements are then digitally signed and stored in the TPM, where they can't be changed. During subsequent boots, measurements are compared against the stored measurements.

Securing data

The increased mobility of PCs also increases the risk of theft. Losing a computer is bad enough, but handing over all the data you've stored on the computer is by far the greater loss. Windows 10 includes new features to ensure the thief can't get your data.

- **Device encryption.** On devices that support InstantGo, data on the operating system volume is encrypted by default. (Formerly called Connected Standby, InstantGo is a Microsoft hardware specification that enables advanced power-management capabilities. Among other requirements, InstantGo devices must boot from a solid state drive.) The encryption initially uses a clear key, but when a local administrator first signs in with a Microsoft account, the volume is automatically encrypted. A recovery key is available when you sign in using that Microsoft account at *https://onedrive.com/recoverykey*; you'll need the key if you reinstall the operating system or move the drive to a new PC.

- **BitLocker Drive Encryption.** BitLocker Drive Encryption offers similar (but stronger) whole-volume encryption, and on corporate networks it allows centralized management. In Windows 10, BitLocker encrypts drives more quickly than in previous Windows versions; additional speed comes from the new ability to encrypt only the part of a volume in use. For more information, see "Encrypting with BitLocker and BitLocker To Go" later in this chapter.

Securing identities

It seems like every week we hear about another data breach where millions of user names and passwords have been stolen. There's a thriving market for this type of information because it enables the thieves to sign in anywhere using your credentials. Furthermore, because many people use the same password for different accounts, criminals can often use the stolen information to gain unauthorized access into a theft victim's other accounts. Windows 10 marks the beginning of the end of passwords.

With Windows 10, enterprise-grade two-factor authentication is built in. After enrolling a device with an authentication service, the device itself becomes one factor; the second factor is a PIN or a biometric, such as a fingerprint, facial recognition, or an iris scan.

After Windows Hello signs you in, it enables sign-in to networks and web services. Windows Hello supports Microsoft accounts, Active Directory and Azure Active Directory (Azure AD) accounts, and any identity provider that supports the Fast ID Online (FIDO) v2.0 standard. Your biometric data remains securely stored in your computer's TPM; it's not sent over the network. (In the initial release of Windows 10, this secure sign-in feature was called Microsoft Passport. Effective with the Anniversary Update, the feature is considered a part of Windows Hello.)

With this combination of authentication methods, an attacker who has a trove of user names and passwords is stymied. To unlock your encrypted information (and, by extension, gain the ability to sign in to your web services), he needs the enrolled device. And a thief who steals your computer needs your PIN or biometric data. Active Directory, Azure Active Directory, and Microsoft accounts support this new form of credentials; other services are sure to follow.

➤ For more information about Windows Hello, see "Managing the sign-in process" in Chapter 6.

Blocking malware

Since the days of Windows 7, several features that block malicious software have been beefed up:

- **Address Space Layout Randomization (ASLR).** ASLR is a feature that randomizes the location of program code and other data in memory, making it difficult for malware to carry out attacks that write directly to system memory because the malware can't find the memory location it needs. In Windows 10, memory locations are scrambled even more. And because the randomization is unique to each device, a successful attack on one device won't work on another.

- **Data Execution Prevention (DEP).** DEP is a hardware feature that marks blocks of memory so that they can store data but not execute program instructions. Windows 10 can't be installed on a system that doesn't support DEP.

- **Windows Defender.** In Windows 7, Windows Defender is a lightweight antispyware program. But starting with Windows 8 and continuing in Windows 10, Windows Defender includes the well-regarded antimalware capabilities of Windows Security Essentials, a free add-on for Windows 7. Windows Defender supports ELAM, described earlier in this chapter, which means that it can defend against rootkits that attempt to co-opt the boot process. For more information, see "Using Windows Defender to block malware" later in this chapter.

- **SmartScreen.** The goal of SmartScreen is similar to that of Windows Defender: Stop malicious code from running, thus avoiding the headache of cleaning up damage after a successful attack. But SmartScreen takes a completely different approach: Instead of looking for signatures of known bad programs, it checks a hash of each executable downloaded from an online source against Microsoft's application-reputation database. Files that have established a positive reputation are deemed safe and are allowed to run, whereas files with a negative reputation (or those that are unknown and potentially dangerous) are blocked.

  When SmartScreen was introduced in Windows 7, it was a feature of Internet Explorer. Beginning with Windows 8, SmartScreen is an integral part of Windows (and continues to be a feature of Internet Explorer and, in Windows 10, Microsoft Edge). Therefore, it prevents all unknown programs that originated from an online source—including those downloaded with a non-Microsoft browser—from running. SmartScreen works not just as you download a program in a browser but any time you attempt to run such a program.

CHAPTER 7

Monitoring your computer's security

In Windows 10, security-related options are available in one location when you go to Control Panel > System And Security > Security And Maintenance, shown in Figure 7-1. (Veteran users of Windows 7 and Windows 8 will recognize this as the new name for what was called Action Center in those earlier operating systems. In Windows 10, *Action Center* refers to the list of notifications and buttons that can appear on the right side of the screen.) You can open Security And Maintenance from Control Panel or Settings: In the search box of either app, type **security** and then click Security And Maintenance.

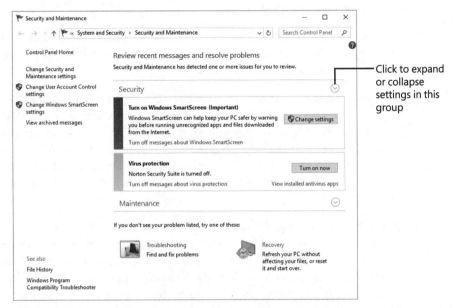

Figure 7-1 The Security section in Security And Maintenance highlights potential issues with bright red or yellow bands and offers access to other settings in a single window.

The Security section in Security And Maintenance provides at-a-glance information about your security settings. Items that need your attention have a red or yellow bar, as shown in Figure 7-1. A red bar identifies important items that need immediate attention, such as detection of a virus or spyware or that no firewall is enabled. A yellow bar denotes informational messages about suboptimal, but less critical, settings or status. Next to the bar appear explanatory text and buttons you can use to correct the problem (or configure Security And Maintenance so that it won't bother you).

If all is well, the Security category is collapsed and you see nothing in that category when you open Security And Maintenance. Click the arrow to expand the category, and you'll see all the security-related items that Security And Maintenance monitors.

Security And Maintenance is designed to work with third-party firewall, antivirus, and anti-spyware programs, as well as with the programs built in to Windows (Windows Firewall and Windows Defender). Systems with more than one program installed in any of these categories include a link to show a list of such programs. The dialog box that appears when you click the link to view installed programs can be used to turn on any installed program that is currently turned off, as shown here:

If you don't want to be bothered with alerts from Security And Maintenance about one or more security features, click Change Security And Maintenance Settings. After clearing the check boxes for items you don't want monitored in the dialog box shown in Figure 7-2, you won't receive any further alerts, and thereafter Security And Maintenance passively indicates the status as Currently Not Monitored.

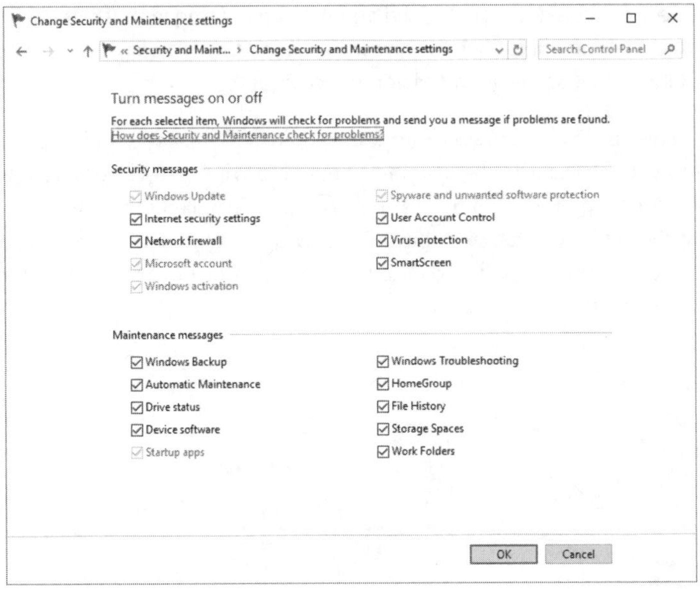

Figure 7-2 You can selectively disable and enable Security And Maintenance monitoring here, or you can manage monitored items individually by clicking links in the main Security And Maintenance window.

Staying on top of security updates

As we noted earlier in this chapter, Microsoft continues to beef up security in Windows. But as new threats emerge, the task is never done, so perhaps the most important step in keeping your system secure is to be sure you stay current with updates to Windows and other programs. Microsoft issues frequent updates that provide replacements for installed device drivers as well as fixes to code that has been found to be faulty. Some updates provide new features or enhanced performance, while others patch security holes.

To install updates automatically, Windows uses Windows Update, accessible via Settings > Update & Security > Windows Update. For more information about Windows Update, see "Keeping Windows up to date" in Chapter 15, "System maintenance and performance."

You might be interested in knowing more about current security threats, including those addressed by Windows Update: What, exactly, is the threat? How serious is it? What work-arounds are available? The Microsoft Security Response Center publishes detailed information, in the form of *security bulletins*, about the threat and the response.

Each cumulative update has its own Knowledge Base (KB) article, identified by a seven-digit KB number. To see the KB number for an installed update, click Update History. Click the installation link below any item for a brief description of it, and then click More Info to go to the associated KB article.

⚙ Update history

Uninstall updates

Recovery options

Update history

Cumulative Update for Windows 10 Version 1607 for x64-based Systems (KB3176927)

Successfully installed on 7/26/2016

Cumulative Update for Windows 10 Version 1607 for x64-based ⧸ystems (KB3176925) Systems (KB3176927)

Install this update to resolve issues in Windows. For a complete listing of the issues that are included in this update, see the associated Microsoft Knowledge Base article for more information. After you install this item, you may have to restart your computer.

More info

That KB article, in turn, might contain a list of security updates and other fixes that are new in that cumulative update, each of which has its own KB article for additional information. You can open any KB article directly by using the URL format https://support.microsoft.com/kb/ *nnnnnnn/* and replacing *nnnnnnn* with the seven-digit number following "KB."

For a chronological list of security bulletins, visit the Security Advisories And Bulletins page (*https://bit.ly/security-advisories*). Here you'll find links to chronologically ordered information (most recent first) in the following formats:

- **Security bulletin summaries.** A single document is published each month containing a complete list of security bulletins published during that month. For each bulletin in the list, you'll find a title and an executive summary, a severity rating (which you can learn more about on the following page), a list of affected software, and a link to the bulletin.

    You can go directly to a monthly security bulletin summary by using the URL format https://technet.microsoft.com/library/security/ms*yy-mmm*/ and replacing *yy* with the last two digits of the year (for example, use 16 for 2016) and *mmm* with the standard three-letter abbreviation for the month (for example, use "nov" for November).

- **Security bulletins.** Each bulletin contains detailed information about the issue, including a complete list—with version numbers—of software affected by the threat and, for each affected version, an assessment of the severity. Each security bulletin is assigned a name in the following format: MS*yy-nnn*, where *yy* is the last two digits of the year and *nnn* is a consecutive number that starts with 001 each year. For example, the twenty-seventh security bulletin of 2015 is called MS15-027.

  You can go directly to a security bulletin by appending the bulletin number to this URL: *https://technet.microsoft.com/library/security/*.

- **Security advisories.** Advisories describe security issues that might not require a security bulletin (and with it, a security update) but that can still affect your computer's security.

Each security bulletin includes a rating of the threat's severity. These are the four ratings that are used, listed in order of severity (with the most severe first):

- **Critical.** A critical vulnerability can lead to code execution with no user interaction.

- **Important.** An important vulnerability is one that can be exploited to compromise the confidentiality or integrity of your data or to cause a denial-of-service attack.

- **Moderate.** A moderate vulnerability is one that's usually mitigated by default settings and authentication requirements. In other words, you'd have to go a bit out of your way for one of these to damage your system or your data.

- **Low.** A vulnerability identified as low usually requires extensive interaction or an unusual configuration to cause damage.

For more information about these ratings, see "Security Bulletin Severity Rating System" at *https://bit.ly/severity-ratings*.

Blocking intruders with Windows Firewall

Typically, the first line of defense in securing your computer is to protect it from attacks by outsiders. Once your computer is connected to the internet, it becomes just another node on a huge global network. A firewall provides a barrier between your computer and the network to which it's connected by preventing the entry of unwanted traffic while allowing transparent passage to authorized connections.

Using a firewall is simple, essential, and often overlooked. You'll want to be sure that all network connections are protected by a firewall. You might be comforted by the knowledge that your portable computer is protected by a corporate firewall when you're at work and that you use a firewalled broadband connection at home. But what about the public hotspots you use when you travel?

And it makes sense to run a firewall on your computer even when you're behind a residential router or corporate firewall. Other people on your network might not be as vigilant as you are about defending against viruses, so if someone brings in a portable computer infected with a worm and connects it to the network, you're toast—unless your network connection has its own firewall protection.

Windows includes a two-way, stateful-inspection, packet-filtering firewall called, cleverly enough, Windows Firewall. Windows Firewall is enabled by default for all connections, and it begins protecting your computer as it boots. The following actions take place by default:

- The firewall blocks all inbound traffic, with the exception of traffic sent in response to a request sent by your computer and unsolicited traffic that has been explicitly allowed by creating a rule.

- All outgoing traffic is allowed unless it matches a configured rule.

You notice nothing if a packet is dropped, but you can (at your option) create a log of all such events.

Using Windows Firewall with different network types

Windows Firewall maintains a separate profile (that is, a complete collection of settings, including rules for various programs, services, and ports) for each of three network types:

- **Domain.** Used when your computer is joined to an Active Directory domain. In this environment, firewall settings are typically (but not necessarily) controlled by a network administrator.

- **Private.** Used when your computer is connected to a home or work network in a workgroup configuration.

- **Guest or public.** Used when your computer is connected to a network in a public location, such as an airport or a library. It's common—indeed, recommended—to have fewer allowed programs and more restrictions when you use a public network.

If you're simultaneously connected to more than one network (for example, if you have a Wi-Fi connection to your home network while you're connected to your work domain through a virtual private network, or VPN, connection), Windows uses the appropriate profile for each connection with a feature called multiple active firewall profiles (MAFP).

You make settings in Windows Firewall independently for each network profile. The settings in a profile apply to all networks of the particular type to which you connect. (For example, if you allow a program through the firewall while connected to a public network, that program rule is then enabled whenever you connect to any other public network. It's not enabled when you're connected to a domain or private network unless you allow the program in those profiles.)

➤ For more information about network types, see "Setting network locations" in Chapter 5.

Managing Windows Firewall

Windows Firewall is a Control Panel application that provides a simple interface for monitoring firewall status and performing routine tasks, such as allowing a program through the firewall or blocking all incoming connections. To open Windows Firewall, type **firewall** in the search box or in Control Panel. Click Windows Firewall to display a window similar to the one shown in Figure 7-3.

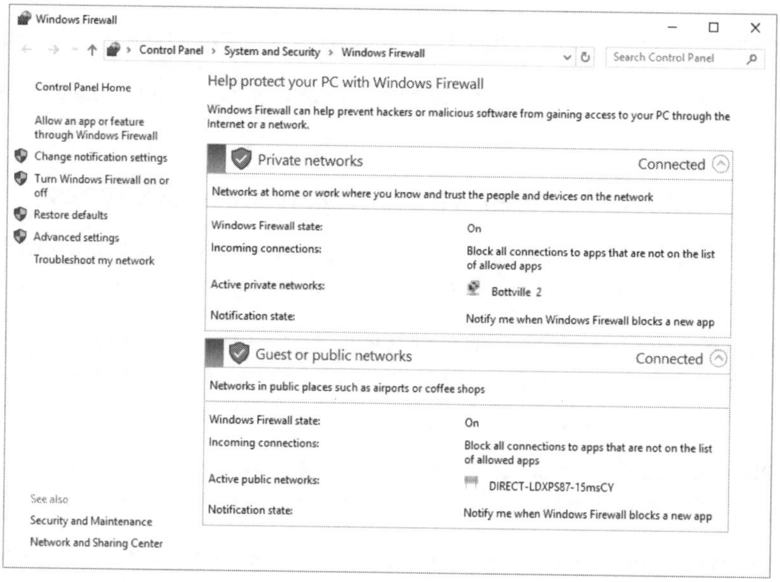

Figure 7-3 Windows Firewall shows status and settings for each currently connected network. The Domain Networks profile appears only on computers that have been joined to a domain.

Enabling or disabling Windows Firewall

The main Windows Firewall application, shown in Figure 7-3, is little more than a status window and launch pad for making various firewall settings. The first setting of interest is to enable or disable Windows Firewall. To do that, click Turn Windows Firewall On Or Off to open the screen shown next. From here, you can enable (turn on) or disable (turn off) Windows Firewall for each network type. In general, the only reason to turn off Windows Firewall is for brief (and extremely cautious) troubleshooting purposes, or if you have installed a third-party firewall that you plan to use instead of Windows Firewall. Most compatible third-party programs perform this task as part of their installation.

As you'll discover throughout Windows Firewall, domain network settings are available only on computers that are joined to a domain. You can make settings for all network types—even those to which you're not currently connected. Settings for the domain profile, however, are often locked down by the network administrator using Group Policy.

The Block All Incoming Connections check box in Customize Settings provides additional safety. When it's selected, Windows Firewall rejects all unsolicited incoming traffic—even traffic from allowed programs that would ordinarily be permitted by a rule. (For information about firewall rules, see the next section, "Allowing connections through the firewall.") Invoke this mode when extra security against outside attack is needed. For example, you might block all connections when you're using a public wireless hotspot or when you know that your computer is actively under attack by others.

NOTE

Selecting Block All Incoming Connections does not disconnect your computer from the internet. Even in this mode, you can still use your browser to connect to the internet. Similarly, other outbound connections—whether they're legitimate services or some sort of spyware—continue unabated. If you really want to sever your ties to the outside world, open Network And Sharing Center and disable each network connection. (Alternatively, use brute force: physically disconnect wired network connections and turn off wireless adapters or access points.)

Allowing connections through the firewall

In some situations, you want to allow other computers to initiate a connection to your computer. For example, you might use Remote Desktop, play multiplayer games, or chat via an instant messaging program; these types of programs typically require inbound connections so that others can contact you.

The simplest way to allow a connection for a program that does not create its own firewall rules is to click Allow An App Or Feature Through Windows Firewall, a link in the left pane of the main Windows Firewall window. The list of programs and features that initially appears in Allowed Apps, shown in Figure 7-4, depends on which programs and services are installed on your computer; you can add others, as described in the following sections. In addition, program rules are created (but not enabled) when a program tries to set up an incoming connection. To allow connections for a program or service that has already been defined, simply select its check box for each network type on which you want to allow the program. (You need to click Change Settings before you can make changes.)

In each of these cases, you enable a rule in Windows Firewall that pokes a small hole in the firewall and allows a certain type of traffic to pass through it. Each rule of this type increases your security risk to some degree, so you should clear the check box for all programs you don't need. If you're confident you won't ever need a particular program, you can select it and then click Remove. (Many items on this list that represent apps or services included with Windows don't allow deletion, but as long as their check boxes are not selected, these apps present no danger.)

The first time you run a program that tries to set up an incoming connection, Windows Firewall asks for your permission by displaying a dialog box. You can add the program to the allowed programs list by clicking Allow Access.

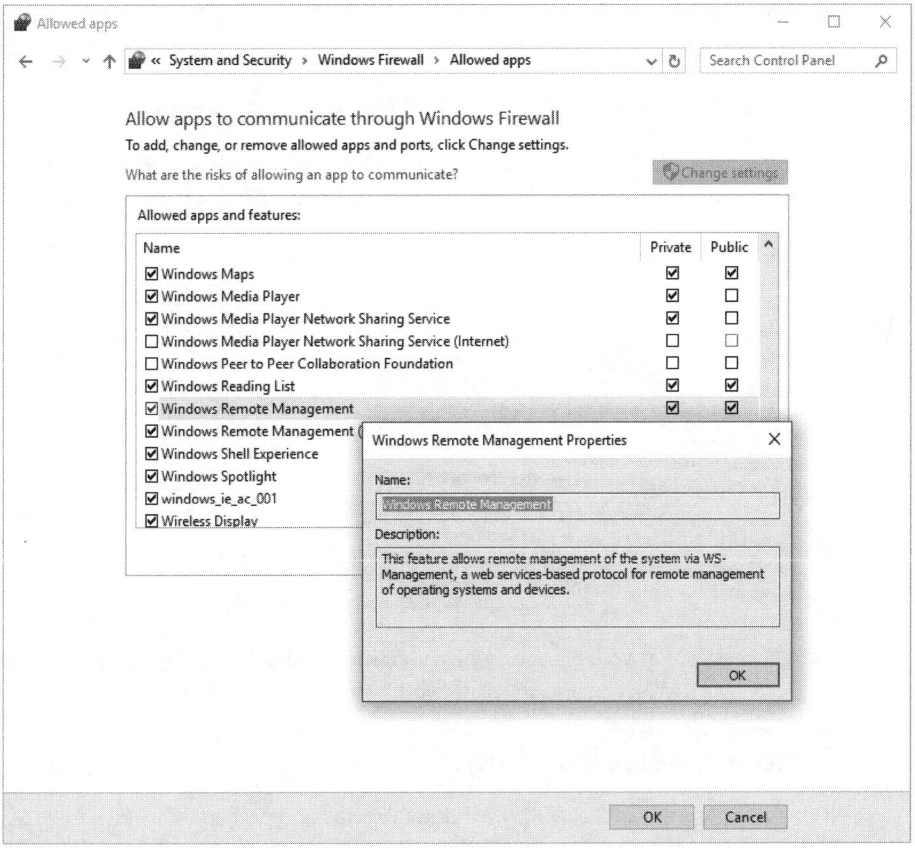

Figure 7-4 Selecting an item and clicking Details displays a description of the program or service.

When such a dialog box appears, read it carefully:

- Is the program one that you knowingly installed and ran?

- Is it reasonable for the program to require acceptance of incoming connections?

- Are you currently using a network type where it's OK for this program to accept incoming connections?

If the answer to any of these questions is no—or if you're unsure—click Cancel. If you later find that a needed program isn't working properly, you can open the allowed apps list in Windows Firewall and enable the rule.

Alternatively, you can set up the program from the Allowed Apps window shown in Figure 7-4 without waiting for a Windows Security Alert dialog box to appear. Follow these steps:

1. Click Allow Another App. The Add An App dialog box appears.

2. In Add An App, select the program for which you want to allow incoming connections. Or click Browse and navigate to the program's executable file if it isn't shown in the Apps list.

3. Click Network Types.

4. Select the network types on which you want to allow the program, click OK, and then click Add. (You can also select network types in Allowed Apps after you add the program.)

Restoring default settings

If you've played around a bit with Windows Firewall and perhaps allowed connections that you should not have, you can get back to a known secure state by clicking Restore Defaults in Windows Firewall. Be aware that doing so removes all rules you've added for all programs. Although this gives you a secure setup, you might find that some of your network-connected programs no longer work properly. As that occurs, you can add again each legitimate program that needs to be allowed, as described on the previous pages.

Advanced tools for managing Windows Firewall

If you have any experience at all configuring firewalls, you'll quickly realize that the Windows Firewall application in Control Panel covers only the most basic tasks. Don't take that as an indication that Windows Firewall is underpowered. To the contrary, you can configure all manner of firewall rules, allowing or blocking traffic based on program, port, protocol, IP address, and so on. In addition, you can enable, disable, and monitor rules; configure logging; and much more. With advanced tools, you can also configure Windows Firewall on remote workstations. Because the interface to these advanced features is rather daunting, Windows Firewall provides the simplified interface described earlier. It's adequate not only for less experienced users, but also for performing the routine firewall tasks needed by information technology (IT) professionals and others.

Nonetheless, our tour of security essentials would not be complete without a visit to Windows Firewall With Advanced Security, a snap-in and predefined console for Microsoft Management Console (MMC) that offers granular control over rules, exceptions, and profiles. From Windows Firewall, click Advanced Settings to open Windows Firewall With Advanced Security, as shown in Figure 7-5.

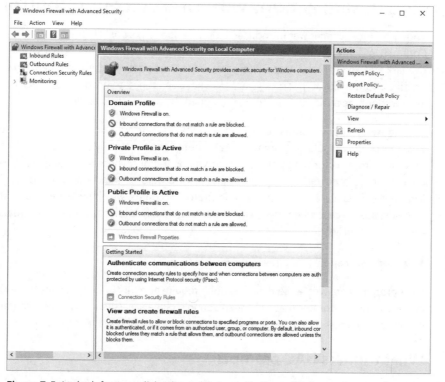

Figure 7-5 In the left pane, click Inbound Rules or Outbound Rules to view, configure, create, and delete firewall rules. The Domain Profile appears even on a computer that's not part of a Windows domain.

The initial view presents information similar to that shown in Windows Firewall. Go just a few steps farther into the cave, however, and you could be lost in no time. The "Windows Firewall with Advanced Security Getting Started Guide" can brighten your path; view it at *https://aka. ms/firewall*.

CHAPTER 7

Inside OUT

Open Windows Firewall With Advanced Security directly

You don't need to open Windows Firewall to get to Windows Firewall With Advanced Security. In the search box, type **wf.msc** and press Ctrl+Shift+Enter to run it as an administrator.

Preventing unsafe actions with User Account Control

Widely scorned when it was introduced a decade ago as part of Windows Vista, User Account Control (UAC) intercedes whenever a user or program attempts to perform a system administrative task and asks for the consent of a computer administrator before commencing what could be risky business. Since that rocky start, UAC has been tuned to become an effective security aid—without the annoyance factor that plagued the original implementation.

In Windows 10, user accounts you set up after the first one are standard (nonadministrator) accounts by default; although they can carry out all the usual daily computing tasks, they're prevented from performing potentially harmful operations. These restrictions apply not just to the user; more importantly, they also apply to any programs launched by the user. Even administrator accounts run as "protected administrator" accounts, which are allowed only standard-user privileges except when they need to perform administrative tasks. (This is sometimes called Admin Approval Mode.)

➤ For information about user accounts, see Chapter 6.

Most programs are written so that they don't require administrator privileges for performing everyday tasks. Programs that truly need administrative access (such as utility programs that change computer settings) request elevation—and that's where UAC comes in.

What triggers UAC prompts

The types of actions that require elevation to administrator status (and therefore display a UAC elevation prompt) include those that make changes to system-wide settings or to files in %SystemRoot% or %ProgramFiles%. (On a default Windows installation, these environment variables represent C:\Windows and C:\Program Files, respectively.) Among the actions that require elevation are the following:

- Installing and uninstalling most desktop applications

- Installing device drivers that are not included in Windows or provided through Windows Update

- Installing ActiveX controls

- Changing settings for Windows Firewall

- Changing UAC settings

- Configuring Windows Update

- Adding or removing user accounts

- Changing a user's account type

- Running Task Scheduler

- Editing the registry

- Restoring backed-up system files

- Viewing or changing another user's folders and files

Within Windows, you can identify in advance many actions that require elevation. A shield icon next to a button or link indicates that a UAC prompt will appear if you're using a standard account.

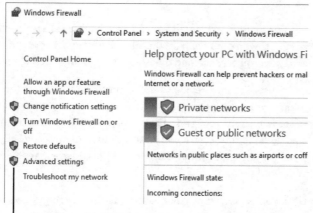

Shield icons identify actions that require UAC elevation

If you sign in with an administrator account (and if you don't change the default UAC settings), you'll see fewer consent prompts than if you use a standard account. That's because the default setting prompts only when a program tries to install software or make other changes to the computer, but not when you make changes to Windows settings—even those that would trigger a prompt for a standard user with default UAC settings. Windows uses autoelevation to elevate without prompting certain programs that are part of Windows. Programs that are elevated automatically are from a predefined list; they must be digitally signed by the Windows publisher, and they must be stored in certain secure folders.

Limitations of User Account Control

User Account Control isn't a security silver bullet. It's one layer of a defense-in-depth strategy.

Some Windows users assume that UAC consent dialog boxes represent a security boundary. They don't. They simply represent a place for an administrator to make a trust decision. If a bad guy uses social engineering to convince you that you need his program, you've already made a trust decision. You'll click at least a half-dozen times to download, save, and launch the bad guy's program. A UAC consent request is perfectly normal in this sequence, so why wouldn't you click one more time?

If this scenario bothers you, the obvious solution is to adjust UAC to its highest level. Among other changes, this setting disables the autoelevation behavior. (For details on how to do this, see "Modifying UAC settings" later in this chapter.) If a program tries to use this subterfuge to sneak system changes past you, you'll see an unexpected consent dialog box from the system. But as soon as you provide those elevated credentials, the code can do anything it wants.

A better alternative is to sign in using a standard account, which provides a real security boundary. A standard user who does not have the administrator password can make changes only in her own user profile, protecting the system from unintended tampering.

Even running as a standard user doesn't provide complete protection. Malware can be installed in your user profile without triggering any system alarms. It can log your keystrokes, steal your passwords, encrypt your personal data files and hold them for ransom, and send out email using your identity. Even if you reset UAC to its highest level, you could fall victim to malware that lies in wait for you to elevate your privileges and then does its own dirty work alongside you.

As we said, enabling UAC is only one part of a multilayered security strategy. It works best when supplemented by a healthy skepticism and up-to-date antimalware software.

Dealing with UAC prompts

At sign-in, Windows creates a token that's used to identify the privilege levels of your account. Standard users get a standard token, but administrators actually get two: a standard token and an administrator token. The standard token is used to open Explorer.exe (the Windows shell), from which all subsequent programs are launched. Child processes inherit the token of the process that launches them, so by default all applications run as a standard user—even when you're signed in with an administrator account. Certain programs request elevation to administrator privileges; that's when the UAC prompt is displayed. If you provide administrator credentials, Windows then uses the administrator token to open the program. Note that any process that the successfully elevated program opens also runs as an administrator.

As an elevation-requesting application attempts to open, UAC evaluates the application and the request and then displays an appropriate prompt. As an administrator, the most common prompt you're likely to see is the consent prompt, which is shown in Figure 7-6. (And no, it's not your imagination. The design of this dialog box is new in Windows 10 version 1607; it looks significantly different from the design in earlier Windows versions.) Check the name of the program and the publisher, click Yes if you're confident that it's safe to proceed, and carry on.

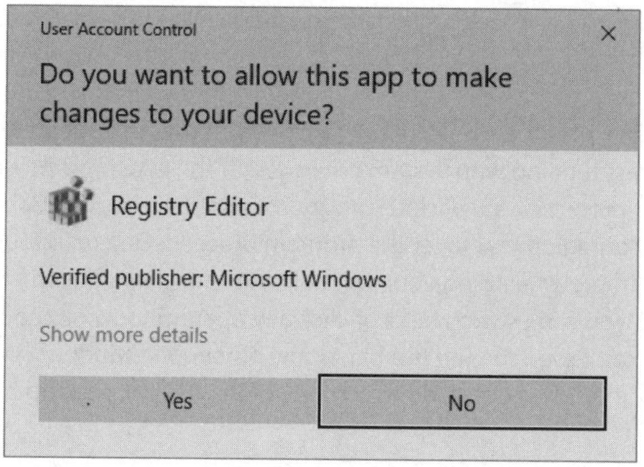

Figure 7-6 For a program that's digitally signed, clicking Show More Details displays a link to the associated certificate.

If you use a standard account, any attempt to run a program that requires elevation displays the credentials prompt, which is shown in Figure 7-7. If the user is able to provide the credentials of an administrator (that is, user name and password, smart card, or biometric authentication, depending on how sign-in options are configured on the computer), the application opens using the administrator's access token.

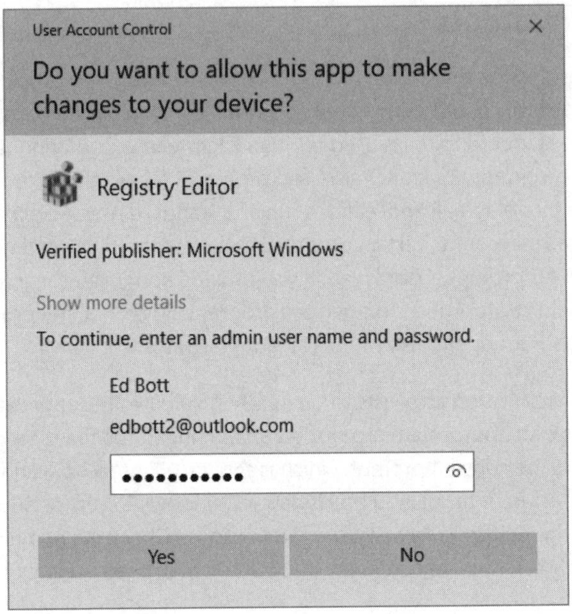

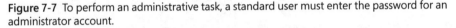

Figure 7-7 To perform an administrative task, a standard user must enter the password for an administrator account.

By default, the UAC dialog box sits atop the secure desktop, which runs in a separate session that requires a trusted process running with System privileges. (If the UAC prompt were to run in the same session as other processes, a malicious program could disguise the UAC dialog box, perhaps with a message encouraging you to let the program proceed. Or a malicious program could grab your keystrokes, thereby learning your administrator sign-in password.) When the secure desktop is displayed, you can't switch tasks or click any open window on the desktop. (In fact, in Windows 10 you can't even see the taskbar or any other open windows. When UAC invokes the secure desktop, it displays only a dimmed copy of the current desktop background behind the UAC dialog box.)

TROUBLESHOOTING

There's a delay before the secure desktop appears

On some systems, you have to wait a few seconds before the screen darkens and the UAC prompt appears on the secure desktop. There's no easy way to solve the slowdown, but you can easily work around it. In User Account Control Settings (described in the next section, "Modifying UAC settings"), you can take the protection level down a notch. The setting below the default provides the same level of UAC protection (albeit with a slight risk that malware could hijack the desktop), except that it does not dim the desktop.

NOTE

If an application other than the foreground application requests elevation, instead of interrupting your work (the foreground task) with a prompt, UAC signals its request with a flashing taskbar button. Click the taskbar button to see the prompt.

It becomes natural to click through dialog boxes without reading them or giving them a second thought. But it's important to recognize that security risks to your computer are real and that actions that trigger a UAC prompt are potentially dangerous. Clearly, if you know what you're doing and you click a button to, say, change Windows Update settings, you can blow past that security dialog box with no more than a quick glance to be sure it was raised by the expected application. But if a UAC prompt appears when you're not expecting it—stop, read it carefully, and think before you click.

Modifying UAC settings

To review your User Account Control options and make changes to the way it works, search for **uac** and then click Change User Account Control Settings. A window similar to the one shown in Figure 7-8 appears.

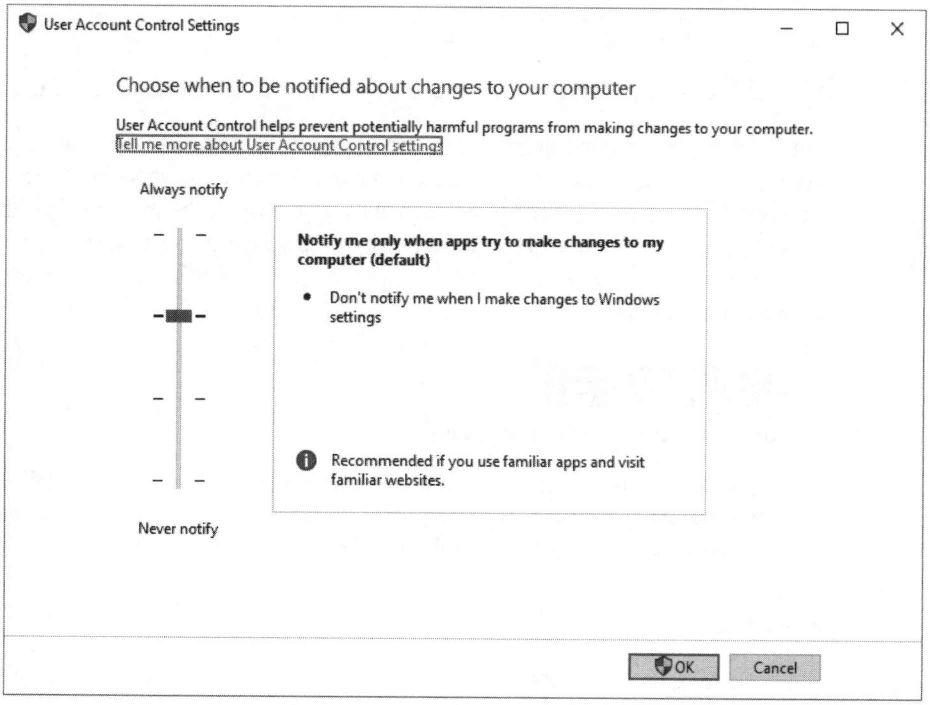

Figure 7-8 We don't recommend changing the default UAC settings unless you fully understand the consequences.

Your choices in this window vary slightly depending on whether you use an administrator account or a standard account. For standard accounts, the top setting is the default; for administrator accounts, the second setting from the top is the default. Table 7-1 summarizes the available options.

Table 7-1 User Account Control settings

Slider position	Prompts when a program tries to install software or make changes to the computer	Prompts when you make changes to Windows settings	Displays prompts on a secure desktop
Standard user account			
Top (default)	✔	✔	✔
Second	✔	✔	
Third	✔		
Bottom (off)			
Administrator account			
Top	✔	✔	✔
Second (default)	✔		✔
Third	✔		
Bottom (off)			

To make changes, move the slider to the position you want. Be sure to take note of the advisory message in the bottom of the box as you move the slider. Click OK when you're done—and then respond to the UAC prompt that appears! Note that when you're signed in with a standard account, you can't select one of the bottom two options, even if you have the password for an administrator account. To select one of those options, you must sign in as an administrator and then make the change.

TROUBLESHOOTING

User Account Control settings don't stick

If you find that nothing happens when you make a change to User Account Control settings, be sure you're the only one signed in to your computer. Simultaneous sign-ins that use Fast User Switching can cause this problem.

Inside OUT

Use Local Security Policy to customize UAC behavior

Users of the Pro and Enterprise editions of Windows 10 can use the Local Security Policy console to modify the behavior of UAC. Start Local Security Policy (Secpol.msc), and open Security Settings\Local Policies\Security Options. In the details pane, scroll down to the policies whose names begin with "User Account Control." For each policy, double-click it and then click the Explain tab for information before you decide on a setting. With these policies, you can make several refinements in the way UAC works—including some that are not possible in the User Account Control Settings window. (Administrators on Windows-based enterprise networks can also configure these options using Group Policy management tools.) For details about each of these policies, see "UAC Group Policy Settings" at *https://bit.ly/uac-gpo.*

Regardless of your UAC setting, the shield icons still appear throughout Control Panel, but you won't see UAC prompts if you've lowered the UAC protection level. Clicking a button or link identified with a shield immediately begins the action. Administrators run with full administrator privileges; standard users, of course, still have only standard privileges.

CAUTION

Don't forget that UAC is more than annoying prompts. Only when UAC is enabled does an administrator run with a standard token. Only when UAC is enabled does Internet Explorer run in a low-privilege Protected Mode. Only when UAC is enabled does it warn you when a rogue application attempts to perform a task with system-wide impact. And, of course, disabling UAC also disables file and registry virtualization, which can cause compatibility problems with applications that use fixes provided by the UAC feature. For these reasons, we urge you not to select the bottom option in User Account Control Settings, which turns off UAC completely.

Encrypting information

Windows provides the following encryption tools for preventing the loss of confidential data:

- Encrypting File System (EFS) encodes your files so that even if someone is able to obtain the files, that person won't be able to read them. The files are readable only when you sign in to the computer using your user account.

- BitLocker Drive Encryption provides another layer of protection by encrypting entire hard-disk volumes. By linking this encryption to a key stored in a Trusted Platform Module (TPM), BitLocker reduces the risk of data being lost when a computer is stolen or when a hard disk is stolen and placed in another computer. A thief's standard approach in these situations is to boot into an alternate operating system and then try to retrieve data from the stolen computer or drive. With BitLocker, that type of offline attack is effectively neutered.

- BitLocker To Go extends BitLocker encryption to removable media, such as USB flash drives.

NOTE

Encrypting File System and BitLocker Drive Encryption are not available in Windows 10 Home. Encrypting a removable drive with BitLocker To Go requires that you be running Windows 10 Pro, Enterprise, or Education; the resulting encrypted drive can be opened and used on a device running Windows 10 Home (or, for that matter, any edition of Windows 7 or later).

Using the Encrypting File System

EFS provides a secure way to store your sensitive data. Windows creates a randomly generated file encryption key (FEK) and then transparently encrypts the data, using this FEK, as the data is being written to disk. Windows then encrypts the FEK using your public key. (Windows creates a personal encryption certificate with a public/private key pair for you the first time you use EFS.) The FEK, and therefore the data it encrypts, can be decrypted only with your certificate and its associated private key, which are available only when you sign in with your user account. (Designated data-recovery agents can also decrypt your data.) Other users who attempt to use your encrypted files receive an "access denied" message. Even administrators and others who have permission to take ownership of files are unable to open your encrypted files.

You can encrypt individual files, folders, or entire drives. (You cannot, however, use EFS to encrypt the boot volume—the one with the Windows operating system files. For that, you must use BitLocker.) We recommend you encrypt folders or drives instead of individual files. When you encrypt a folder or drive, the files it contains are encrypted, and new files you create in or copy to that folder or drive are encrypted automatically.

To encrypt a folder, follow these steps:

1. In File Explorer, right-click the folder, choose Properties, click the General tab, and then click Advanced, which displays the dialog box shown next. (If the properties dialog box doesn't have an Advanced button, the folder is not on an NTFS-formatted volume and you can't use EFS.)

Advanced Attributes   ✕

Choose the settings you want for this folder.

When you click OK or Apply on the Properties dialog, you will be asked if you want the changes to affect all subfolders and files as well.

Archive and Index attributes

☐ Folder is ready for archiving

☑ Allow files in this folder to have contents indexed in addition to file properties

Compress or Encrypt attributes

☐ Compress contents to save disk space

☐ Encrypt contents to secure data   Details

OK   Cancel

2. Select Encrypt Contents To Secure Data. (Note that you can't encrypt compressed files. If the files are already compressed, Windows clears the compressed attribute.)

3. Click OK twice. If the folder contains any files or subfolders, Windows then displays a confirmation message:

Confirm Attribute Changes   ✕

You have chosen to make the following attribute changes:

encrypt

Do you want to apply this change to this folder only, or do you want to apply it to all subfolders and files as well?

○ Apply changes to this folder only

⦿ Apply changes to this folder, subfolders and files

OK   Cancel

NOTE

If you select Apply Changes To This Folder Only, Windows doesn't encrypt any of the files currently in the folder. Any new files you create in the folder, however, including files you copy or move to the folder, will be encrypted.

After a file or folder has been encrypted, File Explorer displays its name in green. This minor cosmetic detail is the only change you're likely to notice. Windows decrypts your files on the fly as you use them and reencrypts them when you save.

CAUTION

Before you encrypt anything important, you should back up your file-recovery certificate and your personal encryption certificate (with their associated private keys), as well
as the data-recovery-agent certificate, to a USB flash drive or to your OneDrive. Store
the flash drive in a secure location. To do this, open User Accounts in Control Panel, and
then click Manage Your File Encryption Certificates.

If you ever lose the certificate stored on your hard drive (because of a disk failure, for
example), you can restore the backup copy and regain access to your files. If you lose
all copies of your certificate (and no data-recovery-agent certificates exist), you won't
be able to use your encrypted files. To the best of our knowledge, there's no practical
way for anyone to access these encrypted files without the certificate. (If there were, it
wouldn't be very good encryption.)

To encrypt one or more files, follow the same procedure as for folders. You'll see a different
confirmation message to remind you that the file's folder is not encrypted and to give you
an opportunity to encrypt it. You generally don't want to encrypt individual files because the
information you intend to protect can too easily become decrypted without your knowledge.
For example, with some applications, when you open a document for editing, the application
creates a copy of the original document. When you save the document after editing, the application saves the copy—which is not encrypted—and deletes the original encrypted document.
Static files that you use for reference only—but never for editing—can safely be encrypted
without encrypting the parent folder. Even in that situation, however, you'll probably find it simpler to encrypt the whole folder.

Encrypting with BitLocker and BitLocker To Go

BitLocker Drive Encryption can be used to encrypt entire NTFS volumes, which provides excellent protection against data theft. BitLocker can secure a drive against attacks that involve
circumventing the operating system or removing the drive and placing it in another computer.
BitLocker provides the greatest protection on a computer that has TPM version 1.2 or later; on
these systems, the TPM stores the key and ensures that a computer has not been tampered with
while offline. If your computer does not have a TPM, you can still use BitLocker on your operating system volume, but an administrator must first turn on the Group Policy option "Allow
BitLocker without a compatible TPM." In that configuration, you must supply the encryption key
on a USB flash drive each time you start the computer or resume from hibernation. Non-TPM
systems do not get the system integrity check at startup.

With BitLocker To Go, a feature introduced in Windows 7, you can encrypt the entire contents
of a USB flash drive or other removable device. If it's lost or stolen, the thief will be unable to
access the data without the password.

To apply BitLocker Drive Encryption or BitLocker To Go, right-click the drive in File Explorer and
then click Turn On BitLocker. BitLocker asks how you want to unlock the encrypted drive—with

a password, a smart card, or both. After you have made your selections and confirmed your intentions, the software gives you the opportunity to save and print your recovery key, as shown in Figure 7-9. (Note that in some configurations you might see a fourth option, to save the recovery key to a USB flash drive.)

Your recovery key is a system-generated, 48-character, numeric backup password. If you lose the password you assign to the encrypted disk, you can recover your data with the recovery key. BitLocker offers to save that key in a plain text file; you should accept the offer and store the file in a secure location.

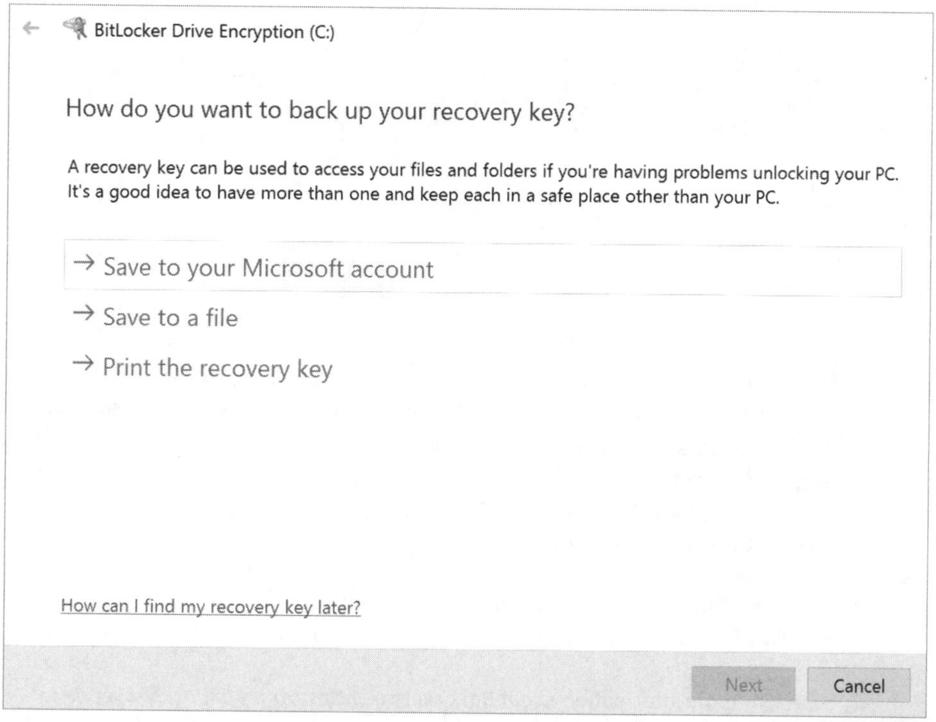

← ⬝ BitLocker Drive Encryption (C:)

How do you want to back up your recovery key?

A recovery key can be used to access your files and folders if you're having problems unlocking your PC. It's a good idea to have more than one and keep each in a safe place other than your PC.

→ Save to your Microsoft account

→ Save to a file

→ Print the recovery key

How can I find my recovery key later?

Next   Cancel

Figure 7-9 The option of saving the recovery key to your Microsoft account is new with Windows 10.

Inside OUT

Store your recovery keys on OneDrive

Clicking Save To Your Microsoft Account saves the recovery key on OneDrive, making it possible to recover from an encryption problem from anywhere, provided that you have an internet connection. To retrieve that key, go to *https://onedrive.com/recoverykey*.

With all preliminaries out of the way, BitLocker begins encrypting your media. This process takes a few minutes, even if the disk is freshly formatted. However, if you're in a hurry, you can opt to encrypt only the used space on the drive. This choice can save you a considerable amount of time if your disk contains only a small number of files.

To read a BitLocker-encrypted removable disk, you need to unlock it by using whatever method you stipulated. If you're prompted for a password you have lost or forgotten, click More Options and then click Enter Recovery Key. In case you have several recovery-key text files, BitLocker To Go gives you the key's identification code:

BitLocker (G:)

Enter the 48-digit recovery key to unlock this drive.
(Key ID: E5844976)

Unlock

Find the entry on OneDrive (*https://onedrive.com/recoverykey*) or the text file whose name matches the identification code, and then enter the recovery key in the BitLocker dialog box. You'll be granted temporary access to the files, which is good until you remove the disk or restart the computer. At this point, you might want to change the password; go to Control Panel > System And Security > BitLocker Drive Encryption. Select the encrypted removable drive and then click Change Password.

To remove BitLocker encryption from a disk, open BitLocker Drive Encryption in Control Panel and click Turn Off BitLocker. The software will decrypt the disk; allow some time for this process.

➤ **For more information about BitLocker, see** *https://bit.ly/bitlocker-overview*.

Using Windows Defender to block malware

The best way to fight unwanted and malicious software is to keep it from being installed on any PC that's part of your network. Over the years, malicious hackers have found various ways to install malware: floppy disks, document files, email attachments, instant messaging attachments, AutoPlay on USB flash drives, scripts, browser add-ons . . . and the list goes on. Many of these transmission methods rely on social-engineering techniques designed to lure inattentive or unsophisticated users into opening an infected attachment, visiting an infected website, or otherwise falling into a trap. Not satisfied with being able to pick off the inattentive and gullible, authors of hostile software are always on the lookout for techniques they can use to spread infections automatically.

Any program that tries to sneak onto your PC without your full knowledge and consent should be blocked. An important layer in a basic PC protection strategy, therefore, is to use up-to-date antimalware software. Into the breach steps Windows Defender, the antimalware program included in Windows 10.

Windows Defender runs as a system service and uses a scanning engine to compare files against a database of virus and spyware definitions. It also uses heuristic analysis of the behavior of programs to flag suspicious activity from a file that isn't included in the list of known threats. It scans each file you access in any way, including downloads from the internet and email attachments you receive. (This feature is called *real-time protection*—not to be confused with scheduled *scans*, which periodically inspect all files stored on your computer to root out malware.)

Using Windows Defender

In general, you don't need to "use" Windows Defender at all. As a system service, it works quietly in the background. The only time you'll know it's there is if it finds an infected file; one or more notifications will pop up to alert you to the fact.

Nonetheless, you might want to poke around a bit. To start, go to Settings > Update & Security > Windows Defender, where you'll find the most common options. Slide the Real-Time Protection switch to Off to temporarily disable protection (an option you should use only for short periods and only if you're certain you're not allowing malware to sneak onto your PC as a result of actions that would otherwise be blocked).

Two advanced options on this page are worth mentioning as well:

- In the Exclusions section, you can specify files, folders, file types (by extension), or processes you want Windows Defender to ignore. This option is especially useful for developers working with files that might otherwise trigger Windows Defender's alarms.

- Click Windows Defender Offline, an option that's new in Windows 10 version 1607, to restart the computer and run the offline version of Windows Defender. This technique is useful for removing persistent infections that are able to evade real-time detection and removal.

For details about what Windows Defender has been doing recently, click Open Windows Defender, which runs the Windows Defender console, shown in Figure 7-10. The Home tab shows the current status and the results of the most recent scan. This tab also tells you whether real-time protection is enabled.

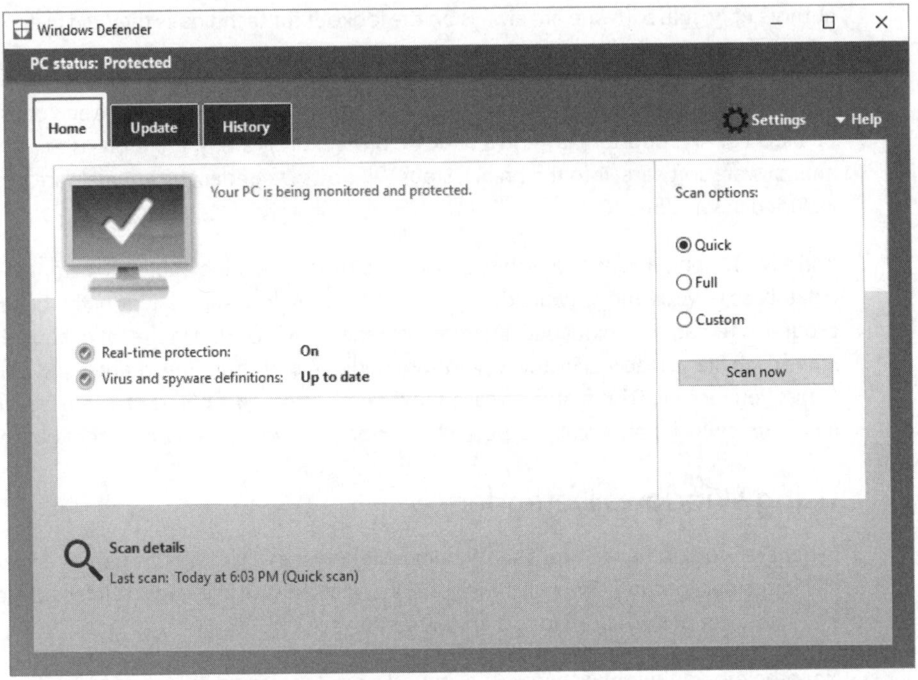

Figure 7-10 The Home tab provides an overview of Windows Defender. If any threats demand your attention, the background changes color to yellow or red.

Manually scanning for malware

The combination of real-time protection and periodic scheduled scanning is normally sufficient for identifying and resolving problems with malware and spyware. However, if you suspect you've been infected, you can initiate a scan on demand. To immediately scan for problems, on the Home tab (shown in Figure 7-10) under Scan Options, select the type of scan you want to perform and click Scan Now.

The Quick option kicks off a scan that checks only the places on your computer that malware and spyware are most likely to infect, and it's the recommended setting for frequent regular scans. Choose Full if you suspect infection (or you just want reassurance that your system is clean) and want to inspect all running programs and the complete contents of all local volumes. Click Custom if you want to restrict the scan to any combination of drives, folders, and files.

Inside OUT

Run a scan from a script or a scheduled task

Windows Defender includes a command-line utility you can use to automate scans with a script or a scheduled task. You'll find MpCmdRun.exe in %ProgramFiles%\Windows Defender. For details about using the utility, open an elevated Command Prompt window and run the program with no parameters.

Dealing with detected threats

If Windows Defender detects the presence of malware or spyware as part of its real-time protection, it displays a banner and a notification in Action Center and, in most cases, resolves the problem without you lifting a finger.

To learn more about its findings, open Windows Defender and click the History tab. Select Quarantined Items, and then click View Details. As Figure 7-11 shows, Windows Defender shows the name, alert level, and detection date of the quarantined item or items. In this case, the detected threats all arrived as attachments in email messages and had been shunted to the Junk folder, where the malicious code was blocked from execution.

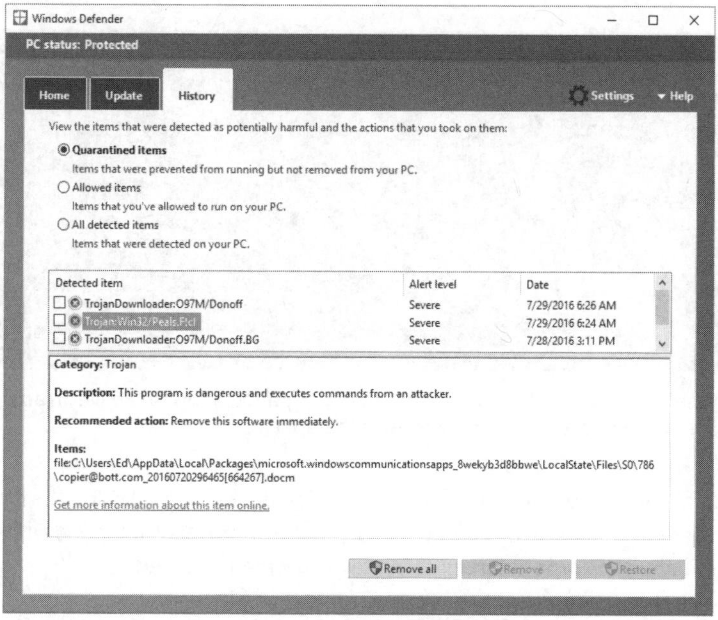

Figure 7-11 The box below the list shows details about the selected item; the link at the bottom of that box leads to online information about the particular threat.

Detected items are moved to a restricted folder (%ProgramData%\Microsoft\Windows Defender\Quarantine) whose permissions include a Deny access control entry that locks out the built-in Users and Everyone groups. Executable files in this folder cannot be run, nor can the folder's contents be accessed from File Explorer. Items moved here can be managed only from the Windows Defender console (preferred) or an elevated Command Prompt window.

Stopping unknown or malicious programs with SmartScreen

SmartScreen, which began as a feature in Internet Explorer in Windows 7, is used to identify programs that other users have run safely. It does so by comparing a hash of a downloaded program with Microsoft's application-reputation database. (It also checks web content used by Windows Store apps.)

This reputation check occurs when you download a program using Microsoft Edge or Internet Explorer. SmartScreen also kicks in when you attempt to run a program you downloaded from the internet—regardless of what browser you use.

Programs with a positive reputation run without any fuss. Programs that are known to be bad or that have not yet developed a reputation are blocked. A message similar to the one shown in Figure 7-12 appears.

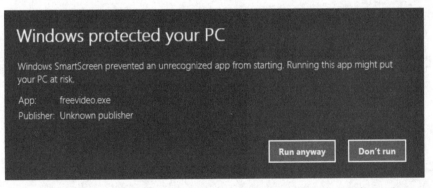

Figure 7-12 When you attempt to run a downloaded program that doesn't have an acceptable reputation in the SmartScreen database, a message like this appears.

If you're certain that a program is safe, you can override the block by clicking the Run Anyway button. With default settings in place, you then need the approval of someone with an administrator account before the program runs. Don't say you weren't warned.

You can turn SmartScreen protection off by going to Security And Maintenance (shown in Figure 7-1 earlier in this chapter) and clicking Change Windows SmartScreen Settings.

Using and managing apps and desktop programs

As the title of this chapter suggests, the programs you can run on Microsoft Windows 10 fall into two broad categories. One category consists of so-called *desktop applications*. These are the programs you might have and could have run under Windows 7 and earlier versions. Windows 10 continues to support such programs. (You might also see these programs described as *Win32 applications*.) These traditional applications are designed, for the most part, for use with a keyboard and a mouse, and many of them first came into being during the era when desktop machines dominated the computing landscape.

The other category consists of programs delivered through the Windows Store. These programs, optimized for touch, ink, and mobile use (although equally usable on desktop systems with traditional input devices) are variously called *modern apps, trusted Windows Store apps,* or *UWP apps*. Windows favors the term *Trusted Windows Store app*. If you enter the name of one of these programs in the search box on your taskbar, you see something like the following:

Maps
Trusted Windows Store app

In this book, for the sake of simplicity, we use the designation *modern app*, but Windows opts for the wordier handle for good reason. These apps, available only through the Windows Store, have passed a stringent vetting process and can be trusted to be free of malware. They are also "sandboxed," which means they run in secure isolation, free from potentially hazardous interactions with other running processes.

The current name for the development platform is *Universal Windows Platform*, or *UWP*. The keyword here is *universal*. The platform offers a core application programming interface (API) developers can use to create a single app package that can be installed on devices with a wide range of sizes and modalities, with adaptive controls that tailor the app to the size and feature set of the target machine. In short, a program you download from the Windows Store to your tablet is likely to work as well on your traditional desktop machine, your all-in-one device, your Xbox console, your phone, and your notebook PC.

Evolution of modern apps

UWP apps are the latest step in a years-long progression toward creating a development platform that simplifies work for software developers, makes finding and purchasing apps easier for consumers, and provides a consistent user experience across a range of devices. The efforts started with the release of Windows 8 and the Windows Runtime (WinRT), a common application architecture. With the move to Windows 8.1 and Windows Phone 8.1, developers could create *universal Windows 8 apps*. Although developers could then use a common codebase for Windows and Windows Phone, they still had to create a separate app package for each of the two operating systems, with each offered in a separate Windows Store.

Windows 10 advanced the marker with the further development of the Windows Runtime model, now dubbed Universal Windows Platform. UWP provides a common app platform that is available on every device that runs Windows 10—IoT (Internet of Things) devices, mobile devices, PCs, Xbox, and so on. In addition to using the WinRT application programming interfaces (APIs) that are common to all devices, programmers can call on APIs that are specific to a particular device family, such as Windows Phone. They can then create a single app package that can be installed on any Windows 10 device and offered in a single, unified Windows Store.

What's in a modern app

Here are some important characteristics of modern apps:

- **Tiles.** Each app gets a tile, which can be displayed on Start or not, as you choose. To add an app to Start, press the Windows key, scroll through the list of apps until you find the one you want, right-click the name of the app, and choose Pin To Start. (You can use similar steps to pin an app to the taskbar or to unpin an app from either location; when you right-click the app, click More to see these options.)

- **Live tiles.** Tiles can be programmed to update dynamically when they're displayed on Start—that is, they can become *live tiles*. Live tiles, for example, can display news headlines, cycle through a set of photos, show calendar information, and so on. If you find a tile to be livelier than you would like, you can render it inanimate by right-clicking it. Then click the ellipsis (...), click More, and finally click Turn Live Tile Off.

- **Notifications and alerts.** Apps can trigger notifications and alerts. To take one example, your calendar app can display appointment information on your lock screen and issue reminders at the appropriate times.

- **Cortana.** Apps can be integrated with Cortana, allowing you to do such things as issue a voice command to send an email.

- **Security and safety.** Modern apps are prevented from accessing system resources. They also don't store their own configuration information in publicly accessible places, such as .ini files.

- **The ability to run without administrative consent.** Because modern apps are certified to be free of potential hazards, you don't need an administrative token to install or run them. You won't find Run As Administrator on the shortcut menus of modern apps; there's no need for it.

- **Power conservation.** By default, an app is suspended within a few seconds if you move away from it. This behavior is particularly valuable on battery-driven systems such as phones and tablets. Apps can be written to run in the background (allowing you, for example, to play music while you work), but this is an exceptional case.

- **Automatic updates.** Modern apps are updated automatically. The Windows Store manages this process for you when an app's publisher makes changes to a program.

- **Per-user installation.** When you install an app, that app is installed only for your user account. Other account holders who want to use the app have to install it as well. Depending on licensing provisions and the number of devices on which you have installed the app in question, other accounts on a system where an app has already been bought and installed might find, on visiting the Windows Store, that the app is identified as "owned." In that case, these users can install the app without going through a payment process. The same is true for other systems you sign in to with the Microsoft account under which you bought the app.

- **Display adaptability.** If you have a modern app running on systems with disparate form factors, such as a phone and a notebook, you can easily see how the app adjusts its user interface to accommodate the different screen sizes. With many apps, you can see the same adaptability simply by adjusting window size. For example, if you display a month view in Calendar on a large display and then narrow the window from either side, you'll note several adjustments, as shown in Figure 8-1.

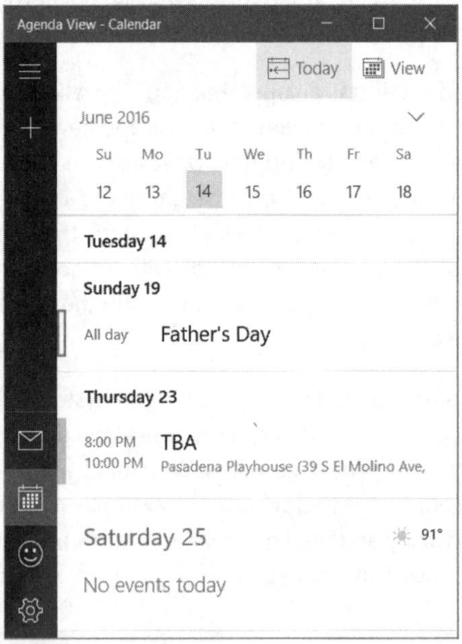

Figure 8-1 As you adjust the width of the Calendar window—or display it on a different type of device—the app hides or shows certain elements and reorients others to fit.

Initially, as you reduce the window's width, Calendar compresses its display but maintains the layout. Eventually, to maintain readability, the program switches to a vertical layout comparable to what you would see on a phone.

> ## Inside OUT
>
> ### Develop modern apps
>
> If you're a software developer who's interested in creating UWP apps, Microsoft offers plenty of resources for more information. First, you might want to dip your toes in the water by converting your existing desktop apps to UWP. For details, check out Project Centennial, the preview version of Desktop App Converter, at *https://aka.ms/converter*. You'll find a description of its use at *https://bit.ly/desktop-bridge*. Then for loads of information about UWP app development, go to the Windows Dev Center at *https://bit.ly/develop-uwp-apps*.

Browsing the Windows Store

The Windows Store (shown in Figure 8-2), much improved and expanded since its debut with Windows 8, is your emporium for games, music, movies, and TV shows, as well as modern Windows apps. Using the menu across the top of the Windows Store page, you can switch between these various kinds of offerings. Below the display ad, you'll find some items the Windows Store thinks you might be interested in, based on what you downloaded earlier. Farther down is a sort of categorized bestseller list—top free games, games that have received stellar ratings from other users, "new and rising" items, and so on.

If you know more or less what you're looking for, you can use the search box to find it. You can search by name or publisher, and the search results will include entertainment offerings (albums and songs, for example), as well as apps.

> ➤ **For information about using the Windows Store to purchase music, movies, and TV shows, see Chapter 11, "Music, photos, movies, and games."**

Figure 8-2 The Windows Store offers items it thinks you might want to download given the items you chose previously.

If you just want to browse, you can start by clicking Apps. Scroll to the bottom of the page to see an alphabetized list of categories. When you find something of interest, click it to see details. Figure 8-3 shows a sample of details you might find. Be sure to scroll down to the rating details and reviews.

You might notice that the price for some apps is adorned with an asterisk and the notation that the app comes with "in-app products." This is a delicate way of alerting you that the app, once installed, will give you the opportunity to buy extra goodies. Some apps are quite low-key about this; others have been known to be nearly useless without at least some of the extra items. A quick check of the reviews might help you spot an app whose effective price is not what it seems. As Figure 8-4 shows, the details page should also enumerate the extra offerings.

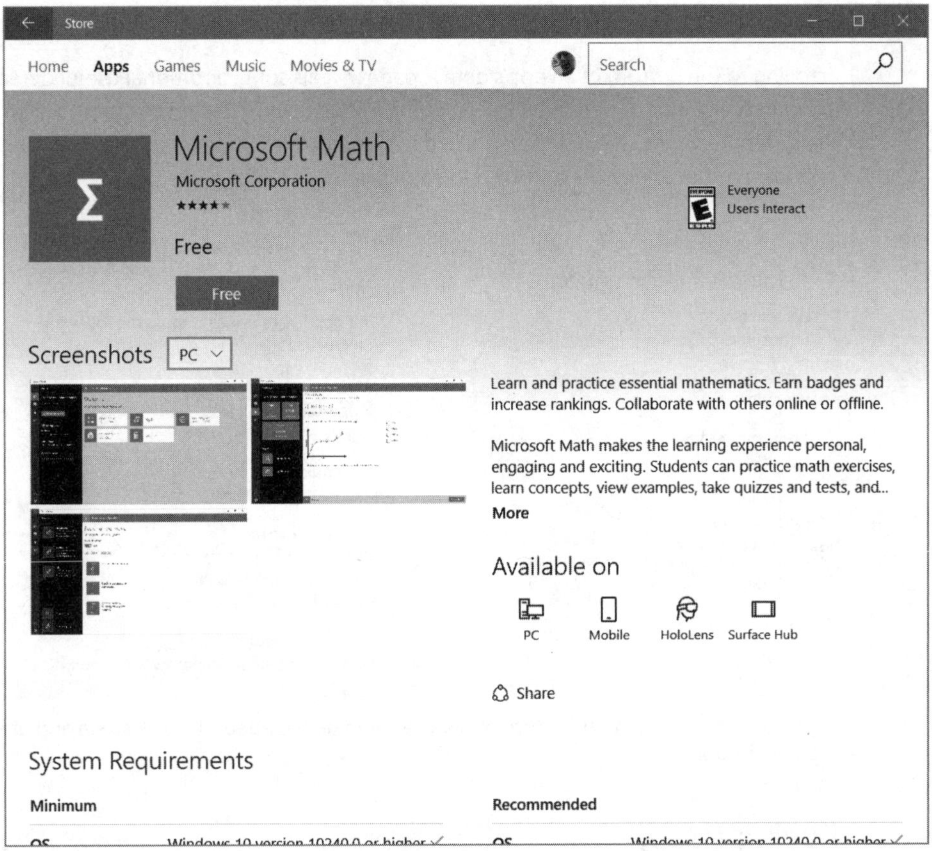

Figure 8-3 The details page for an app shows screenshots, reviews and ratings, and suggestions of what else you might like.

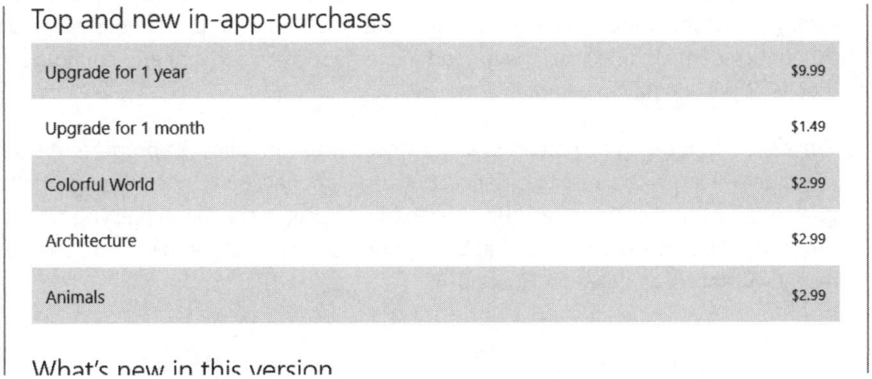

Figure 8-4 The details page for Microsoft Jigsaw lists its in-app purchase offerings.

Finding additional information

Scrolling to the bottom of an app's details page reveals some additional useful details, as shown in Figure 8-5. Items of particular interest here might include the approximate size of the app, the system resources the app is permitted to use (in the example here, the internet connection), and the number of devices on which the app can be installed.

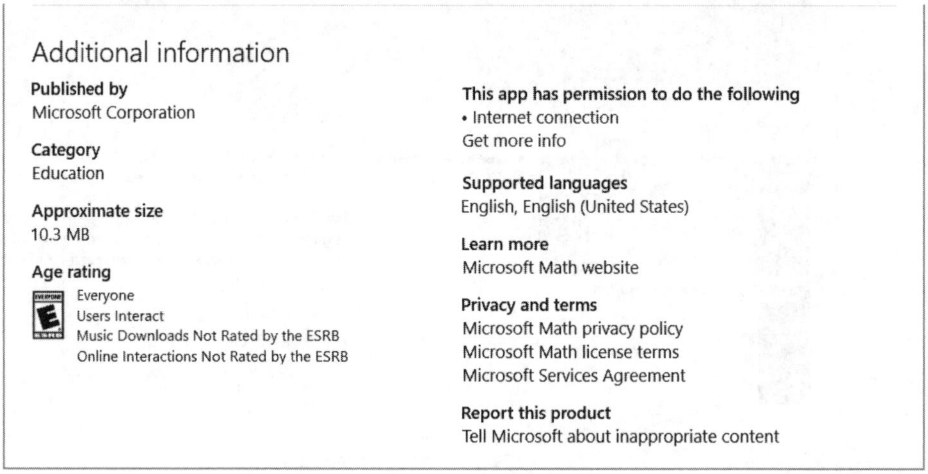

Additional information

Published by
Microsoft Corporation

Category
Education

Approximate size
10.3 MB

Age rating

Everyone
Users Interact
Music Downloads Not Rated by the ESRB
Online Interactions Not Rated by the ESRB

This app has permission to do the following
• Internet connection
Get more info

Supported languages
English, English (United States)

Learn more
Microsoft Math website

Privacy and terms
Microsoft Math privacy policy
Microsoft Math license terms
Microsoft Services Agreement

Report this product
Tell Microsoft about inappropriate content

Figure 8-5 Under Additional Information, you'll find details about the disk space and other resources used by the app.

Buying an app

To begin the process of installing a new app, simply click its price. If the app is free (many are), the download and installation process begins at once. If money is required, the payment process is managed through your Microsoft account. (If your Windows 10 user account signs in locally, rather than through a Microsoft account, you'll be prompted at this point for Microsoft account credentials, and you'll be guided to create such an account and configure a payment mechanism if you haven't already done so.)

While the app is being downloaded and installed, you can follow its progress. A status message—along with Pause and Cancel buttons—appears on the details page in place of the purchase button. Or, if you click the download indicator in the menu bar, you can view the progress of this installation as well as others you queued for download and apps that have been recently installed, as shown in Figure 8-6.

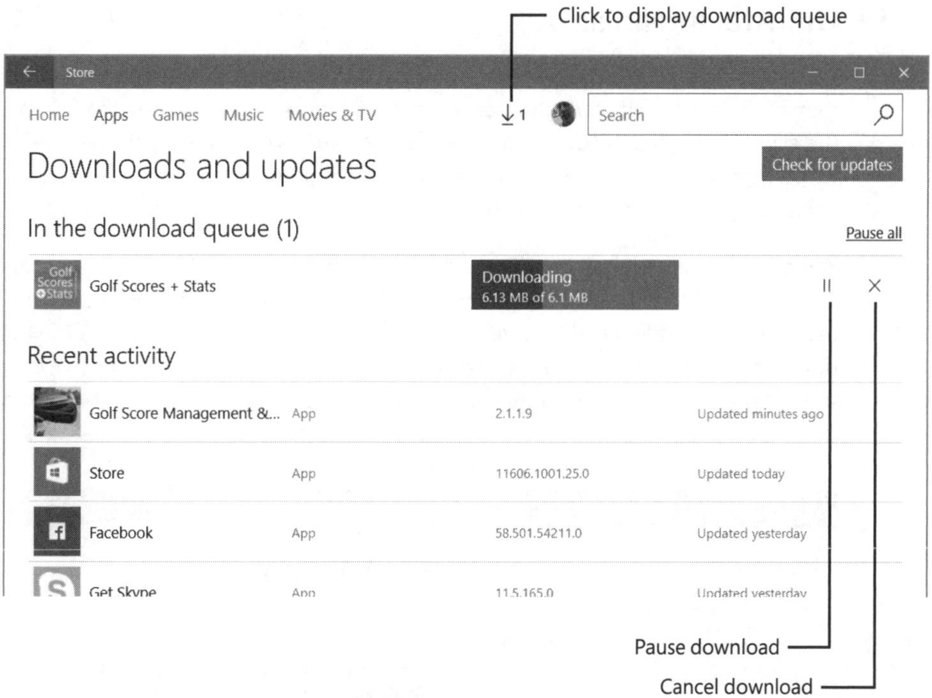

Click to display download queue

Pause download

Cancel download

Figure 8-6 While one or more downloads are in progress, an indicator appears in the menu bar. Clicking that indicator displays this list of current and recent downloads.

Next to the progress indicator—either on the details page or the Downloads And Updates page—you can also pause or cancel a download. You might want to pause if you have several lengthy downloads going at once and want to prioritize them.

Inside OUT

Get updates and more information about Windows Store apps

On the Downloads And Updates page (shown in Figure 8-6), clicking or tapping the name of any app takes you directly to the details page for that app in the Windows Store. A button in the upper right corner lets you check for updates to Windows Store apps at any time. (In theory, checking for updates shouldn't be necessary because Windows Store apps periodically check for and install updates automatically. But if your computer has been offline for an extended time, you might want to oversee the updating process.)

You can display the Downloads And Updates page at any time—even when the download indicator shown in Figure 8-6 is not displayed. Simply click or tap your picture (next to the search box) and choose Downloads And Updates.

Uninstalling an app

The easiest way to uninstall an app—either modern or desktop—is to right-click it on Start and then click Uninstall. (If you right-click a pinned tile rather than an app in the list, you must click the ellipsis [...] to see the Uninstall command.) Because an app is installed per user, uninstalling works that way as well; if you want to be rid of a program everywhere it has been installed, you need to repeat the procedure to uninstall it.

You can also uninstall both modern and desktop apps by opening Settings > System > Apps & Features. The list of installed programs that appears provides useful information about when each app was installed and how much disk space it is using. (See Figure 8-7.) The list includes both modern and desktop apps and can be sorted by size, name, or installation date. Note that the size given for an app includes executable files and resources required for the program. It does not include data files such as music and photo collections or email messages.

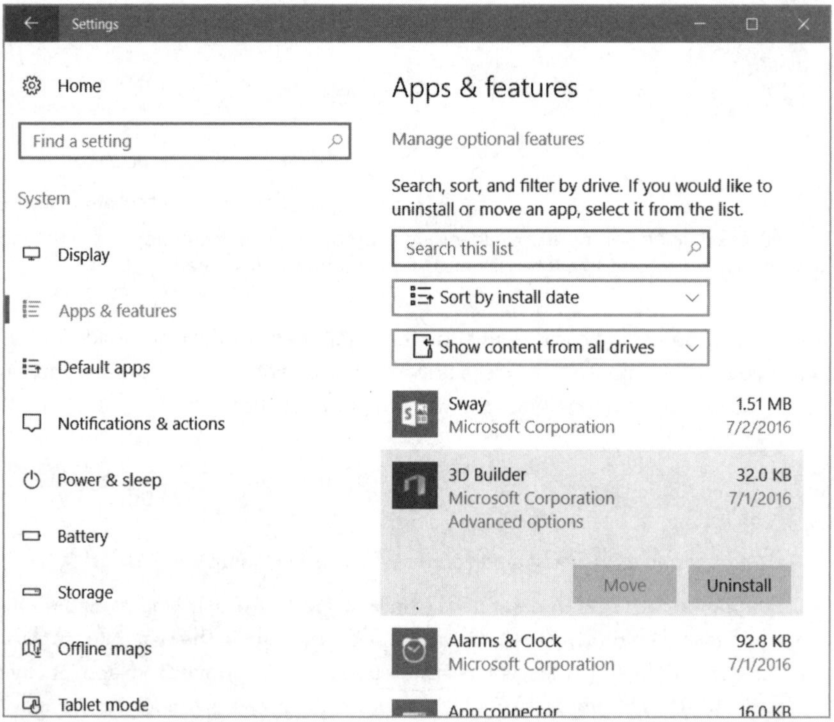

Figure 8-7 The Apps & Features section of Settings provides a way to uninstall both modern and desktop apps. If your computer has more than one drive, the Move button for some apps allows you to move the app to a different drive. Other apps display a Modify button, which you can use to add or remove optional features.

To uninstall an app from the Apps & Features list, click its name and then click the Uninstall button that appears.

Inside OUT

Find the version number of an app

You'll sometimes need to know the version number of an installed app. Having that number might help, for example, when you're troubleshooting a problem and a support article says something like "this problem has been fixed in version 8.0.20623.2."

Different methods for modern apps and desktop programs reveal the version number.

For a modern app, open Windows Store, click your picture, and click Downloads And Updates to display a screen similar to the one shown earlier in Figure 8-6. The version number is displayed next to the name of each app.

For desktop programs, open Programs And Features, the Control Panel app that has been replaced by Apps & Features in Settings. (In addition to the usual search methods, you'll find a link to Programs And Features at the bottom of the Apps & Features page.) You'll see the version number for each installed desktop program in a column at the right side of the window. The version number for a particular program also appears at the bottom of the window when you select that program in the list.

TROUBLESHOOTING

Modern apps won't uninstall

If the normal uninstall routine for a modern app doesn't seem to work, you can remove the troublesome item by using Windows PowerShell. (See Chapter 19, "Automating tasks and activities," for information about PowerShell.) Use the Get-AppxPackage cmdlet to obtain a list of packages installed on your system. Find the one you want to remove, and note its *PackageFullName* property. Then supply this property as a parameter to the Remove-AppxPackage cmdlet. Note that you must be working in a PowerShell session with administrative privileges.

Resetting an app

For a variety of reasons, sometimes an app stops working properly. In times past, often the suggested solution was to uninstall and reinstall an app in the hopes that would produce a clean installation with default settings. Unfortunately, this approach didn't always work because some settings and data weren't deleted as part of the uninstall process.

CHAPTER 8

With modern apps in Windows 10 Anniversary Update, there's a better way to repair a trouble-some app: reset it. Follow these steps:

1. Open Settings > System > Apps & Features.

2. Select the app you want to reset, and then click Advanced Options.

3. Click Reset, and then (after reading the warning) click Reset again.

Note that resetting an app permanently deletes the app's data and settings. After resetting an app, you need to sign in again (if the app requires it) and re-create your preferences.

Managing line-of-business apps

Enterprises can develop line-of-business (LOB) apps for use within their organizations. Such apps can be deployed either through a private Business Store—managed and deployed by the Windows Store—or through a process called *sideloading*.

The process of distributing a Windows 10 app through a private Business Store requires that an enterprise have Azure Active Directory accounts for each user in the organization. (These accounts are used instead of Microsoft accounts.) Installation files are managed and deployed by the Windows Store, which also tracks license usage. Updates are delivered via normal update channels—Windows Update or Windows Server Update Services (WSUS).

LOB apps distributed within an organization without using the Windows Store don't need to be signed by Microsoft and don't require Azure Active Directory accounts. They do need to be signed with a certificate that's trusted by one of the trusted root authorities on the system. Using a sideloaded app requires three steps:

1. **Turn on sideloading.** In a domain environment, this can be done with Group Policy. For an unmanaged computer, go to Settings > Update & Security > For Developers. Then select Sideload Apps.

2. **Trust the app.** Open the security certificate provided for the app package, and choose Install Certificate. In the Certificate Import wizard, select Local Machine and import the certificate to the Trusted Root Certification Authorities folder.

3. **Install the app.** Open PowerShell in the folder with the app package and then run the Add-AppxPackage cmdlet.

In addition to creating and deploying apps, administrators can also use Group Policy to control the use of all apps, including those that are supplied by Windows itself. For example, an organi-zation might choose to remove the Movies & TV app or prohibit it from running.

Apps included with Windows 10

If you click through the Apps & Features list in Settings (shown in Figure 8-7), you'll find that for some items the Uninstall button is not available. These are apps that are supplied with a default installation of Windows 10, and Windows intends for you to keep them. (You'll find a few other apps in the All Apps section of Start that can't be uninstalled.) In Windows 10 version 1607, the list of built-in programs includes the following, among others:

- **3D Builder** designs objects and prints to a 3-D printer.

- **Alarms & Clock** shows world time and acts as an alarm, stopwatch, and timer; for more information, see "Using Alarms & Clock" in Chapter 10, "Productivity and communication tools."

- **Calculator** includes a programmer mode (specialized for bitwise operations on binary, octal, and hexadecimal values) along with the more common standard and scientific modes, and it can serve as a handy converter for measurements of volume, length, angles, time, and so on.

- **Calendar** keeps track of appointments and other events; for details, see "Mail, Calendar, and People" in Chapter 10.

- **Camera** captures still images and video.

- **Connect** allows you to use your computer as an extended screen from your phone or other device; when using Windows 10 mobile, this feature is sometimes referred to as *Continuum*.

- **Contact Support** provides a connection to technical support, warranty details, account settings, and subscription billing information.

- **Cortana** is a digital personal assistant; for details, see Chapter 9, "Cortana and the web."

- **Get Started** provides videos and other instructional information about Windows 10.

- **Groove Music** is a music player and streaming music service; for more information, see "Music" in Chapter 11.

- **Mail** creates, sends, receives, and manages email; for details, see "Mail, Calendar, and People" in Chapter 10.

- **Maps** displays maps and aerial photos along with directions between points; for details, see "Using Maps" in Chapter 10.

- **Microsoft Edge** is the new web browser in Windows 10; for details, see Chapter 9.

- **Movies & TV** plays videos that you create, purchase, or rent; for more information, see "Watching movies, recorded TV shows, and video clips" in Chapter 11.

- **OneDrive** is a synced connection to your OneDrive cloud storage; for details, see Chapter 12, "Managing files on PCs and in the cloud."

- **OneNote** is a place for creating, storing, and managing notes of all kinds; for more information, see "Using the mobile and desktop versions of OneNote" in Chapter 10.

- **Paid Wi-Fi & Cellular** provides connection to Wi-Fi hotspots in popular locations; for more information, see "Using paid Wi-Fi" in Chapter 5, "Networking essentials."

- **People** keeps track of contact information; for details, see "Mail, Calendar, and People" in Chapter 10.

- **Photos** stores, organizes, and displays your collection of pictures; for more information, see "Managing photos and digital images" in Chapter 11.

- **Skype** is an app for communicating with others via text message or video conferencing.

- **Sticky Notes** provides a place to jot notes—notes that can be enhanced with information from Cortana, turned into a pop-up reminder, and more.

- **Store** is the place to obtain modern apps of all kinds; see "Browsing the Windows Store" earlier in this chapter.

- **Voice Recorder** captures notes in audible form.

- **Weather** displays current conditions and detailed forecasts for locations around the world.

- **Xbox** connects you to the world of computer gaming in genres ranging from card games to shoot-em-ups; for more information, see "Xbox and other forms of online entertainment" in Chapter 11.

Windows 10 also includes the full complement of small programs that have been part of Windows for decades: Notepad, Paint, Character Map, WordPad, and the like. You can find these programs under Windows Accessories in the list of apps on Start.

Installing, running, and managing desktop applications

Windows 10 supports virtually all desktop applications that are compatible with Windows 7. If you upgraded from Windows 7 (or from a Windows 8.1 system that itself was upgraded from Windows 7), all your desktop applications from the earlier environment should be happy and ready to go. Desktop programs can be installed anew in the usual ways, from installation media or by download from the internet.

Desktop programs appear in the apps list on Start (or on Start tiles if you put them there) alongside modern apps. Indeed, since the not-so-glorious days of Windows 8 in which switching between modern and desktop apps was a jarring change that made it appear that you were using two completely different operating systems, it's increasingly difficult to differentiate between the two types of apps. They both run in resizable windows on the desktop, and they share many similar features.

You might notice a few differences on Start: Pinned desktop applications do not have a live tile (but then, not all modern apps do either). And as shown in Figure 8-8, the shortcut menu that appears if you right-click is a bit different.

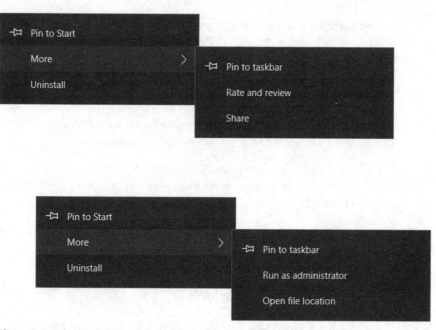

Figure 8-8 When you right-click an app on Start, the menu that appears is slightly different for a modern app (top) than for a desktop application (bottom).

The Run As Administrator and Open File Location commands do not appear on this menu for modern apps. Running modern apps with administrative privileges is never required because such apps don't have the ability to mess with system files. Open File Location is absent from modern app shortcut menus because, as mentioned earlier, modern apps are defined by *package* data structures (in %LocalAppData%\Packages), and Windows assumes you have no need to inspect these structures.

The file locations for desktop apps (usually in a subfolder of %ProgramData%) are useful if you like to create shortcuts to your programs. For example, if you were accustomed to having shortcuts on your desktop to the programs you most frequently use, there's no reason not to populate your Windows 10 desktop the same way. Use Start's shortcut menu to go to a program's file location. (That actually takes you to the shortcut's location in the Start Menu folder; if you do want to go to the folder where the program's files are stored, right-click the shortcut and once again choose Open File Location.) Then right-click the item in the Start Menu folder and click Create Shortcut. Windows informs you that you can't create a shortcut in that location, but it offers to create a shortcut on the desktop—which is just what you set out to do.

Inside OUT

Another difference for modern apps: file location

The executable file (along with supporting files) for a desktop application is normally stored in a subfolder of %ProgramFiles% or %ProgramFiles(x86)%. By contrast, modern apps are stored in a hidden folder called %ProgramFiles%\WindowsApps. This folder is locked so that only Windows Store or the Windows system itself can view, run, or modify its contents. Although that might frustrate folks who like to crawl through every hidden nook and cranny of their hard drive, there's a good reason for the high security: Unlike most desktop applications, the executable file for most modern apps is not digitally signed. Because users or other apps are prevented from making changes, the app files are safe.

If you're intent on seeing what's in the WindowsApps folder, there is a backdoor. (Don't worry: Although you can view the folder directories, you can't make any changes.) The following steps will get you there:

1. Open Task Manager. (For details, see "Managing programs and processes with Task Manager" later in this chapter.)

2. On the Processes tab, right-click the name of a modern app of interest.

3. In the menu that appears, click Go To Details, which highlights the app's executable on the Details tab of Task Manager.

4. Right-click, choose Open File Location, and you're in. Just don't try to make any changes.

Note that built-in apps, including Microsoft Edge, are stored in a different location: C:\Windows\SystemApps.

Running desktop applications as an administrator or another user

As in Windows 7, some desktop applications must be run with an administrative token. If you want to edit the registry, for example, you need to run Registry Editor (regedit.exe) as an administrator. You can run a program as an administrator by right-clicking the executable file or any shortcut for the program (on Start or elsewhere), choosing Run As Administrator, and satisfying the User Account Control (UAC) prompt with either consent or credentials. Here are two additional ways to do it:

- Start a Command Prompt session as Administrator: Press Windows key+X and then choose Command Prompt (Admin). Then, in the Command Prompt window, type the name of the executable file for whichever program you want to run as an administrator.

  To run Registry Editor, for example, type **regedit**. Because you already passed UAC inspection for the Command Prompt session, and because whatever you run from Command Prompt is a child process of Command Prompt, you don't have to deal with any further UAC prompts. This method is excellent for situations where you need to run a sequence of programs as an administrator. Keep one administrative-level Command Prompt window open, and run your programs from the command line.

- Type the name of the program you want to run in the taskbar search box, and then press Ctrl+Shift+Enter.

To run a program under a different user account, you can use the Runas command. You can do this from Command Prompt. The syntax is

```
Runas /user:username programname
```

Inside OUT

Use Steps Recorder to troubleshoot misbehaving software

When you need to report details about a software problem to a tech support person, the Steps Recorder tool can prove valuable. Run this program by typing **steps** in the taskbar search box and then clicking the Steps Recorder item that appears. Click Start Record, retrace your steps through the problematic program, and then click Stop Record.

Steps Recorder takes a screenshot and time stamp at each crucial juncture (each mouse click or command), and then appends a verbal description of each step. You can add your own comments along the way. After you stop and save your recording, you can share it with tech support. (Steps Recorder is also an excellent tool for creating documentation to be used by others in your organization.)

CHAPTER 8

After you issue the command, you're prompted to enter the password for the specified user account. Note that the Runas command does not work with File Explorer or with Microsoft Management Console (MMC) snap-ins.

Dealing with compatibility issues

As mentioned, programs that run without problems on Windows 7 should run equally well on Windows 10. Certain older desktop applications might create problems, however. Windows attempts to flag potential compatibility problems when you first run such a program. The Program Compatibility Assistant that appears offers you the alternatives of checking online for solutions (such as downloading a more recent version) or going ahead and running the program.

If you install a program and subsequently run into compatibility issues, a program compatibility troubleshooter might appear. Alternatively, you can run the troubleshooter yourself from Control Panel. You can find it by typing **compatibility** in the Control Panel search box. Under the heading Programs And Features, you'll find the link Run Programs Made For Previous Versions Of Windows. Click this link to launch the troubleshooter, and then click past the opening screen.

The troubleshooter begins by scanning for problems it can detect automatically. If it finds none, it presents a list of applications installed on your system from which you can select the one that's giving you difficulty. Select the offending program, and follow the prompts to try to resolve your problem.

Managing programs and processes with Task Manager

Task Manager is a tool that serves two essential purposes. You can use it to track aspects of your system's performance and to see what programs and processes are running, and you can use it to terminate items when the normal shutdown methods aren't working.

➤ **For information about using Task Manager to monitor system performance, see Chapter 15, "System maintenance and performance."**

The easiest way to run Task Manager is by means of its keyboard shortcut, Ctrl+Shift+Esc. Without a keyboard, right-click or long-tap the taskbar and choose Task Manager. Figure 8-9 shows the Processes tab of Task Manager. If you don't see a tabular layout similar to that shown in Figure 8-9, click More Details at the bottom of the window.

By default, the items listed on the Processes tab are grouped by type—apps at the top, followed by background processes, Windows processes, and so on. Grouping is optional; clear Group By Type on the View menu if you want a single list.

Note that some items in the Apps list have outline controls. You can expand these to see what files or documents are open. In Figure 8-9, for example, the Microsoft Outlook entry has been expanded to reveal the name of the message that's currently open. The lists are initially sorted in ascending alphabetical order. Click a heading to reverse the sort. You can also click one of the performance headings to see which processes are using resources on your system. Clicking CPU, for example, gives you a constantly updating readout of how your apps and background processes are taxing the CPU.

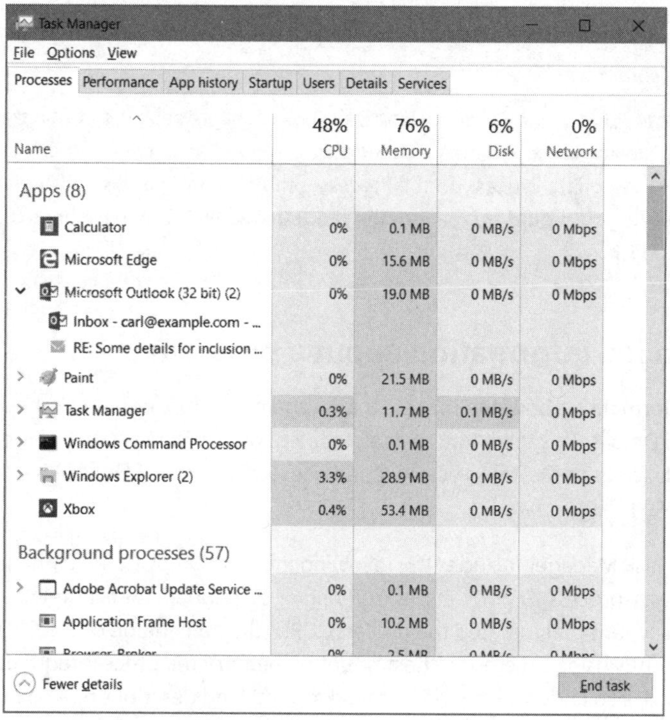

Figure 8-9 Task Manager is useful for terminating recalcitrant applications and processes, as well as for monitoring system performance.

Terminating a program with Task Manager

The Processes tab also includes a Status column. (If it's not visible, right-click a column heading and choose Status.) Most of the time, the entries in this column will be blank, indicating that everything is humming along. If an app hangs for any reason, you'll see the words *Not Responding* in this column. In that case, you can attempt to shut down the miscreant by right-clicking its name and clicking End Task. Don't be too quick on the trigger, however; Not Responding doesn't necessarily mean permanently out to lunch. If the program is using every bit of resources to handle a different task, it might simply be too busy to communicate with Task Manager.

CHAPTER 8

Before you decide to end the program, give it a chance to finish whatever it's doing. How long should you wait? That depends on the task. If the operation involves a large data set (performing a global search-and-replace in a large Microsoft Access database, for instance), it's appropriate to wait several minutes, especially if you can hear the hard disk chattering or see the disk-activity light flickering. But if the task in question normally completes in a few seconds, you needn't wait that long.

Inside OUT

Be smart about shutdowns

When you shut down an app by clicking End Task, Task Manager zaps the item immediately and irrevocably, closing any open files without giving you a chance to save them. (This is equivalent to choosing End Process on the Processes tab of the Windows 7 Task Manager.) Whenever possible, you should try to close the program by the normal methods before resorting to End Task.

Finding detailed information about a program

To see detailed information about the process that's running an app, right-click the app and choose Go To Details. This takes you to a related item on the Details tab. Right-clicking Microsoft Outlook, for example, takes you to Outlook.exe, the name of Outlook's executable file. (See Figure 8-10.)

For each process, Task Manager includes the following information by default: image name (the name of the process), process ID (PID), status (running or suspended, for example), user name (the name of the account that initiated the process), CPU (the percentage of the CPU's capacity the process is currently using), memory (the amount of memory the process requires to perform its regular functions, also known as the private working set), and description (a text field identifying the process). To display additional information for each process, right-click one of the headings and choose Select Columns.

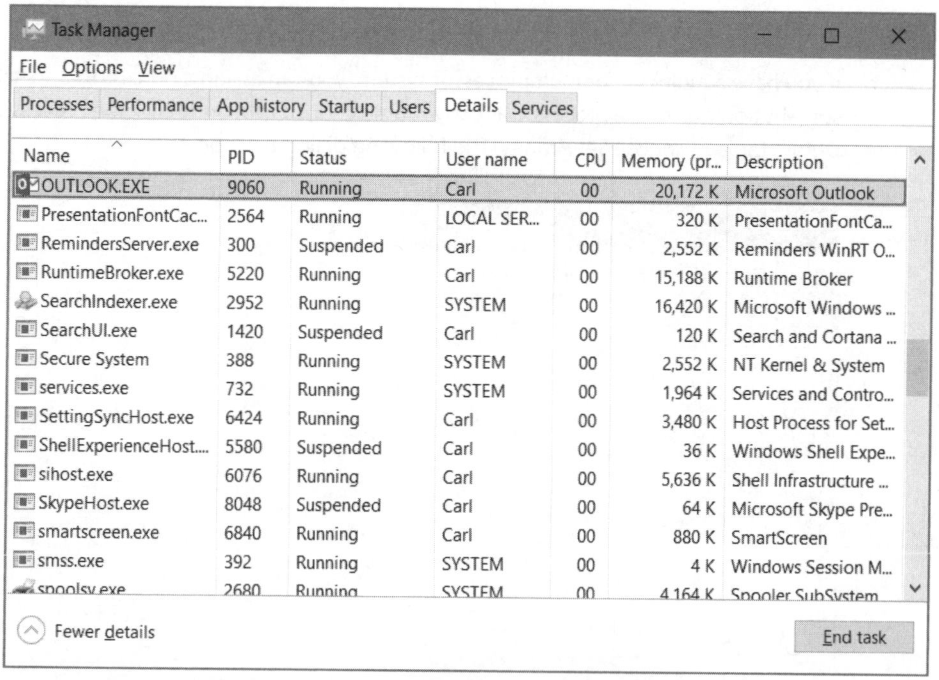
Task Manager
File Options View
Processes Performance App history Startup Users Details Services
Name PID Status User name CPU Memory (pr... Description
OUTLOOK.EXE 9060 Running Carl 00 20,172 K Microsoft Outlook
PresentationFontCac... 2564 Running LOCAL SER... 00 320 K PresentationFontCa...
RemindersServer.exe 300 Suspended Carl 00 2,552 K Reminders WinRT O...
RuntimeBroker.exe 5220 Running Carl 00 15,188 K Runtime Broker
SearchIndexer.exe 2952 Running SYSTEM 00 16,420 K Microsoft Windows ...
SearchUI.exe 1420 Suspended Carl 00 120 K Search and Cortana ...
Secure System 388 Running SYSTEM 00 2,552 K NT Kernel & System
services.exe 732 Running SYSTEM 00 1,964 K Services and Contro...
SettingSyncHost.exe 6424 Running Carl 00 3,480 K Host Process for Set...
ShellExperienceHost.... 5580 Suspended Carl 00 36 K Windows Shell Expe...
sihost.exe 6076 Running Carl 00 5,636 K Shell Infrastructure ...
SkypeHost.exe 8048 Suspended Carl 00 64 K Microsoft Skype Pre...
smartscreen.exe 6840 Running Carl 00 880 K SmartScreen
smss.exe 392 Running SYSTEM 00 4 K Windows Session M...
spoolsv.exe 2680 Running SYSTEM 00 4,164 K Spooler SubSystem
Fewer details
End task

Figure 8-10 Right-clicking an item on the Processes tab takes you straight to the related item on the Details tab.

Inside OUT

Go online to read about programs and processes

Task Manager makes it easy to learn more about items on the Processes or Details tab. Simply right-click an item and choose Search Online. Task Manager opens a browser window and funnels the name of the app and the name of its process to your default search engine. There you'll typically find numerous links to official and unofficial information. If you're suspicious about the legitimacy of anything that shows up in Task Manager, by all means use this tool as a starting point to find out what others are saying.

Assigning a program to a specific processor

If you have a multicore or multiprocessor system, you can assign a process to a specific processor—but only after the process is already running. To do this, right-click the process on the Details tab and choose Set Affinity. The following dialog box appears:

Processor affinity   ✕

Which processors are allowed to run "OUTLOOK.EXE"?

☑ <All Processors>
☑ CPU 0
☑ CPU 1
☑ CPU 2
☑ CPU 3

OK   Cancel

To assign a process to a particular CPU, clear the check boxes for the other entries in this dialog box.

Reviewing history

The App History tab, like the Processes tab, provides information about how programs are using system resources. But App History, shown in Figure 8-11, knows only about modern apps; you won't find your desktop applications listed here. App History accumulates its information over some range of time, giving you an approximate idea of how you have been using your computer. If you never clear and restart the history, it will record everything going back to your installation of Windows 10. You can start fresh by clicking Delete Usage History.

As on other Task Manager tabs, you can sort information on the App History tab by clicking column headings. Clicking CPU Time, for example, brings the heavy hitters to the top of the list. Note, however, that Task Manager already calls your attention to the biggest consumers by means of color mapping, with the darkest colors assigned to the largest numbers.

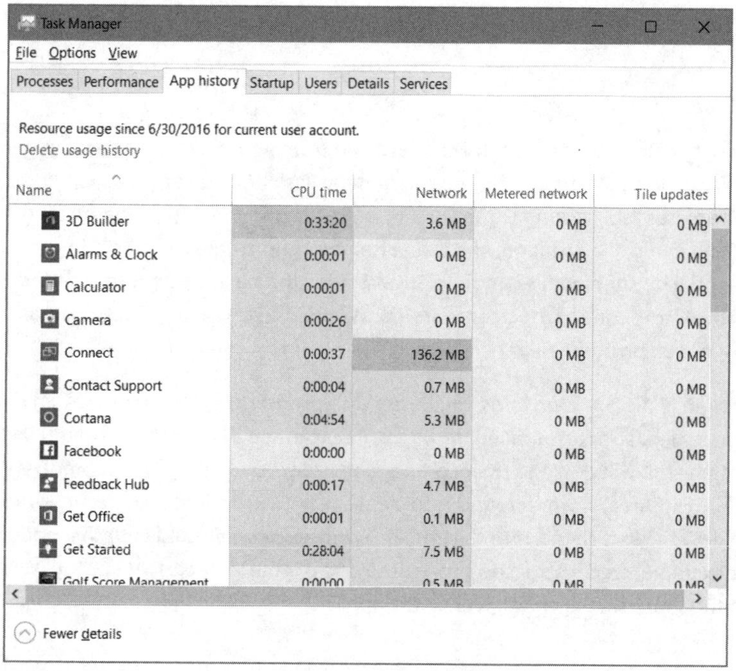

Figure 8-11 The App History tab tells you how much CPU time and other resources each modern app has used over a period of time.

History is interesting, but you might also find the App History tab useful as a program launcher. Right-click any item in any column, and you'll find a Switch To command. If the program is running, this command brings it front and center. If it's not running, Task Manager launches it.

Managing startup programs

Setting up a desktop application to run automatically when you start Windows is easy. If the program's installer doesn't offer to do this for you (many do) and you want the program to run every time you begin a Windows session, create a shortcut for the program in the Startup folder. Here's one way to do it:

1. On Start, right-click the program you want to run at startup and choose Open File Location. You'll find a shortcut for the program in the File Explorer window that appears.

2. Open a second File Explorer window, and type **shell:startup** in the address bar to navigate to %AppData%\Microsoft\Windows\Start Menu\Programs\Startup.

3. Copy the program's shortcut from the first File Explorer window to the second.

Inside OUT

Run a modern app at startup

You'll find it challenging to launch a modern app from your Startup folder. If you find the app's executable by starting the program, running Task Manager, right-clicking the program on the Processes tab, clicking Go To Details, right-clicking the process name on the Details tab, clicking Open File Location, and then attempting to create a shortcut in your Startup folder—you'll be stymied by Windows SmartScreen the next time you start Windows. Even if you ignore the SmartScreen warning, Windows still won't run the program, instead throwing out an error message.

The problem is that modern apps, unlike desktop programs, must be run within the context of elaborate data structures called *packages*. (You can see a list of the packages installed on your system and drill down to their component folders by visiting %LocalAppData%\Packages in File Explorer.) A workaround is to create your Startup folder shortcut not to the app but to a data file associated with the app. If .jpg files are associated with the modern Photos app, for example, create a startup shortcut to one of your .jpg files. At startup, Windows will execute the shortcut, which will launch the app.

Suspending or removing startup items

The problem many users have with startup programs is not with creating them (that's easy, and in many cases it happens without your explicit consent when the program is installed) but getting rid of them. Having too many startup programs not only makes your system take longer to start, it also has the potential to waste memory. If you don't require a program at startup, you should get it out of your startup path.

If you created the startup item in the first place by the method described in the previous section, you can remove it by revisiting the Startup folder and pressing the Delete key. Often, the situation is not so simple, however, because—as you'll see next—there are many other ways by which a program can be made to run at startup.

You can see a list of startup processes on the Startup tab of Task Manager. As Figure 8-12 shows, the Startup tab identifies each item by its estimated impact on the time required to start your Windows environment.

You can't remove a startup item from this list, but you can disable it so that the item will not run automatically at your next startup. To do this, right-click the item and then click Disable.

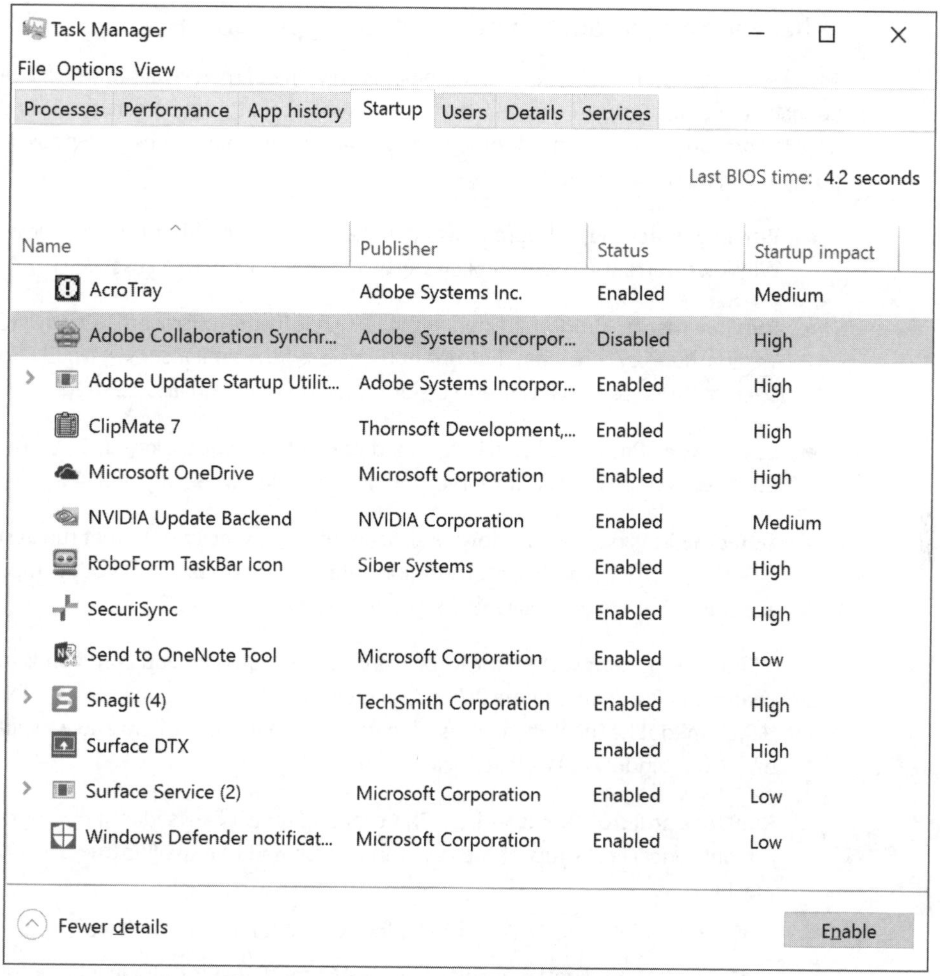

Task Manager			— □ ×

File Options View

Processes Performance App history **Startup** Users Details Services

Last BIOS time: 4.2 seconds

Name	Publisher	Status	Startup impact
AcroTray	Adobe Systems Inc.	Enabled	Medium
Adobe Collaboration Synchr...	Adobe Systems Incorpor...	Disabled	High
> Adobe Updater Startup Utilit...	Adobe Systems Incorpor...	Enabled	High
ClipMate 7	Thornsoft Development,...	Enabled	High
Microsoft OneDrive	Microsoft Corporation	Enabled	High
NVIDIA Update Backend	NVIDIA Corporation	Enabled	Medium
RoboForm TaskBar Icon	Siber Systems	Enabled	High
SecuriSync		Enabled	High
Send to OneNote Tool	Microsoft Corporation	Enabled	Low
> Snagit (4)	TechSmith Corporation	Enabled	High
Surface DTX		Enabled	High
> Surface Service (2)	Microsoft Corporation	Enabled	Low
Windows Defender notificat...	Microsoft Corporation	Enabled	Low

⌃ Fewer details   Enable

Figure 8-12 The Startup tab in Task Manager shows you which startup programs are enabled and how much impact each is estimated to have on your startup time.

If you're not sure whether an item on the Startup tab is justifying its existence there, try disabling it and restarting. Alternatively, or additionally, you can right-click the item and use the handy Search Online command to learn more about it.

CHAPTER 8

Other ways a program can be made to run at startup

As mentioned, a shortcut in the Startup folder is only one of many ways in which a program can be made to run at startup. Programs that set themselves up to run automatically and administrators who configure systems for others to use have a great many other methods at their disposal, including the following:

- **Run key (machine).** Programs listed in the registry's HKLM\Software\Microsoft\ Windows\CurrentVersion\Run key are available at startup to all users.

- **Run key (user).** Programs listed in the HKCU\Software\Microsoft\Windows\Current-Version\Run key run when the current user signs in. A similar subkey, HKCU\Software\ Microsoft\Windows NT\CurrentVersion\Windows\Run, can also be used.

- **Load value.** Programs listed in the Load value of the registry key HKCU\Software\ Microsoft\Windows NT\CurrentVersion\Windows run when any user signs in.

- **Scheduled tasks.** The Windows Task Scheduler can specify tasks that run at startup. (See Chapter 19.) In addition, an administrator can set up tasks for your computer to run at startup that are not available for you to change or delete.

- **Win.ini.** Programs written for 16-bit Windows versions can add commands to the Load= and Run= lines in the [Windows] section of this startup file, which is located in %SystemRoot%. The Win.ini file is a legacy of the Windows 3.1 era and is available only on 32-bit Windows 10 installations.

- **RunOnce and RunOnceEx keys.** This group of registry keys identifies programs that run only once, at startup. These keys can be assigned to a specific user account or to the machine:

  - HKLM\Software\Microsoft\Windows\CurrentVersion\RunOnce
  - HKLM\Software\Microsoft\Windows\CurrentVersion\RunOnceEx
  - HKCU\Software\Microsoft\Windows\CurrentVersion\RunOnce
  - HKCU\Software\Microsoft\Windows\CurrentVersion\RunOnceEx

- **RunServices and RunServicesOnce keys.** As their names suggest, these rarely used keys can control the automatic startup of services. They can be assigned to a specific user account or to a computer.

- **Winlogon key.** The Winlogon key controls actions that occur when you sign in to a computer running Windows. Most of these actions are under the control of the operating system, but you can also add custom actions here. The HKLM\Software\Microsoft\Windows NT\CurrentVersion\Winlogon\Userinit and HKLM\Software\Microsoft\Windows NT\CurrentVersion\Winlogon\Shell subkeys can automatically launch programs.

- **Group Policy.** The Group Policy console includes two policies (one in Computer Configuration > Administrative Templates > System > Logon and one in the comparable User Configuration folder) called Run These Programs At User Logon that specify a list of programs to be run whenever any user signs in.

- **Policies\Explorer\Run keys.** Using policy settings to specify startup programs, as described in the previous paragraph, creates corresponding values in either of two registry keys: HKLM\Software\Microsoft\Windows\CurrentVersion\Policies\Explorer\Run or HKCU\Software\Microsoft\Windows\CurrentVersion\Policies\Explorer\Run.

- **Logon scripts.** Logon scripts, which run automatically at startup, can open other programs. Logon scripts are specified in Group Policy in Computer Configuration > Windows Settings > Scripts (Startup/Shutdown) and User Configuration > Windows Settings > Scripts (Logon/Logoff).

The Startup tab in Task Manager is a fine way to disable startup behavior established by registry keys. Note, however, that Task Manager might not list every startup item; in particular, the list does not include items established by Group Policy or Task Scheduler. For a somewhat more complete list, run System Information. (Type **system information** in the taskbar search box; the utility should appear at or near the top of the search results.)

In System Information, expand Software Environment and select Startup Programs. Unlike Task Manager, System Information includes items in the All Users startup folder (%ProgramData%\Microsoft\Windows\Start Menu\Programs\Startup) as well as those in the startup folder for your own account. It also tells you *which* registry keys are responsible for a program's startup status, instead of simply indicating "Registry." Unfortunately, System Information, like Task Manager, also omits Group Policy and Task Scheduler items.

To get the most comprehensive listing of items that run at startup, as well as a handy tool to prevent certain programs from starting, we recommend using Autoruns, a free utility from Windows Sysinternals. Autoruns, which you can download from *https://bit.ly/autoruns*, shows all the registry keys and startup locations listed earlier, and it also shows Explorer shell extensions, services, browser helper objects, and more. Autoruns is particularly useful for finding processes that don't belong (such as a Trojan horse or other malware) or that you suspect of causing problems. You can then disable these items without removing them while you test your theory, or you can delete their autorun command altogether.

Select an item, and its details appear at the bottom of the screen, as shown next. Disable an item by clearing the check box next to its name; you can later reenable it by selecting the check box. To clear an item from the autorun list, select it and click Entry, Delete. (Note that deleting removes only the entry in the registry or other location that causes the item to run; it does not delete the program.)

CHAPTER 8

Although the tabs at the top of the Autoruns window filter the list of autorun items into various categories, the number of items can still be daunting. One nice feature of Autoruns is its ability to filter out components that are part of Windows or are digitally signed by Microsoft, because these are presumably safe to run. Commands on the Options menu control the appearance of these items.

You can also use the Compare feature in Autoruns to compare before and after snapshots of the data the program finds. Run Autoruns before you install a new program, save the data, run Autoruns again after you install the program, and compare the results to see what changes to autorun behavior were made by the program's installation.

Setting default programs and file-type associations

Most programs you use in Windows are associated with particular file types and protocols. These associations are what enable you, for example, to open an MP3 file in File Explorer and have your favorite audio program play the file, or click a hyperlink in a document or an email message and have your preferred browser take you to the appropriate website. Some of these associations were probably established by the operating system when you performed a clean install or an upgrade from an earlier version of Windows. (The Windows setup program gives you choices in this matter during the installation process, allowing you, for example, to accept the associations that Windows proposes or keep the ones you established before upgrading.) Regardless of how the associations between programs and file types and protocols are currently set, Windows allows you to see and modify the settings.

Most parts of the user interface used for managing file-type associations and default programs have been migrated to the Windows 10 Settings app, while a few parts remain in the old-style Control Panel. Microsoft has indicated that, over time, all of these configuration settings will be available in the Settings app. But as of the Windows 10 Anniversary Update, version 1607, this work was still incomplete. You might find yourself using both Settings and Control Panel to get everything set up the way you want it.

For a quick and easy way to set the default app for certain kinds of documents, go to Settings > System > Default Apps. Figure 8-13 shows an example of what you're likely to see.

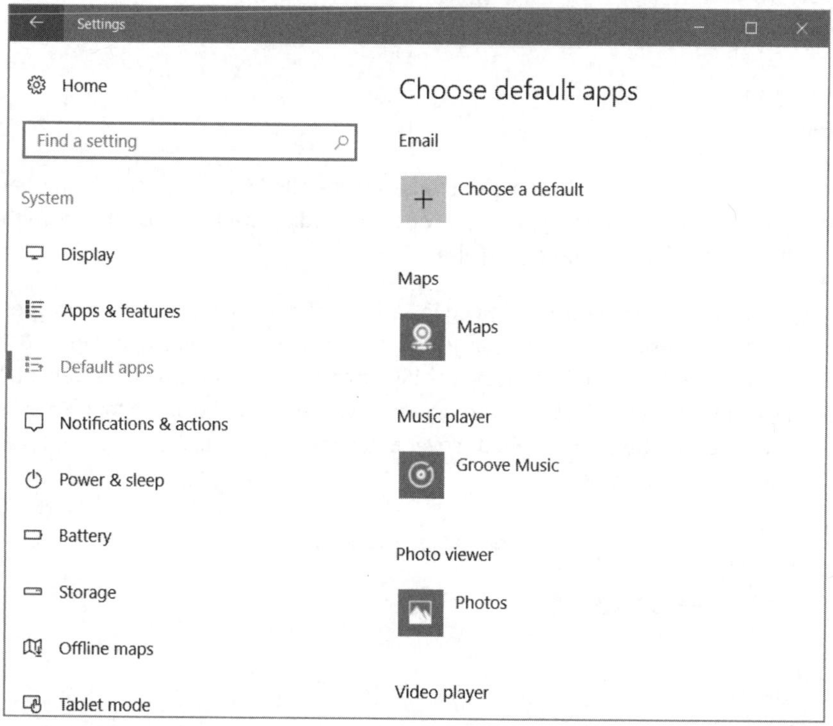

Figure 8-13 The Default Apps page in Settings provides a quick way to change the program associated with certain types of documents.

In the figure, you can see that, for example, Groove Music is the default handler for music files. To change that, click the Groove Music icon:

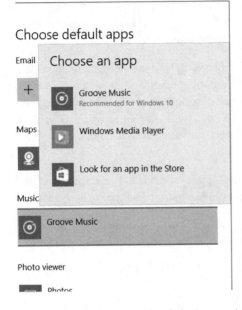

Here, two programs capable of playing music are installed on the system: the modern Groove Music app and the desktop application Windows Media Player. You could select either one or visit the Store to look for something else.

But just because a program is identified in Settings as the default for a file type does not mean that program is assigned to open *every* file type it can open. For example, Figure 8-13 shows Groove Music as the default music player. If you scroll to the bottom of the Default Apps list in Settings and click Set Defaults By App, however, you arrive in the Set Default Programs section of Control Panel, where you might discover that Groove Music is the designated player for only 10 of 15 possible file types:

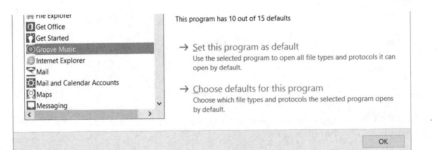

To see which file types Groove Music is assigned to handle and which ones it is not, click Choose Defaults For This Program. A quick glance at the file-type list that appears shows that Windows Media Player is the default for .wav and .wma files, while the rest of the file types are assigned to Groove Music, as shown in Figure 8-14.

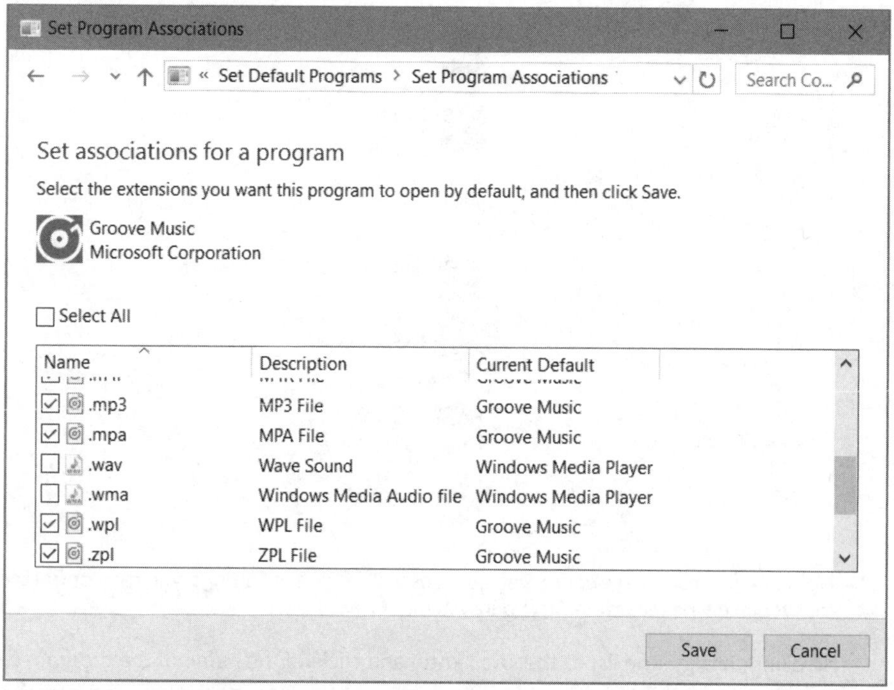

Figure 8-14 You can select types currently assigned to a different program—such as .wav and .wma in this example—and change their default to the program you selected on the previous screen.

Clicking Select All (or selecting the individual check boxes for .wav and .wma) puts everything in the Groove Music camp.

What if, for some reason, you want to assign a file type in this list—say, .mp3—to an altogether different program, perhaps an app you intend to download from the Windows Store? To do this, return to the Default Apps page in Settings and click Choose Default Apps By File Type. As Figure 8-15 shows, Windows responds with a long alphabetized list of all the file types known to your system.

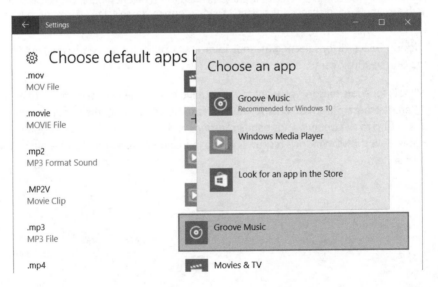

Figure 8-15 By clicking Choose Default Apps By File Type in Settings, you can control the associations for every file type recognized by your system.

Scrolling through the list to the .mp3 entry and clicking the name of the program currently associated with this type allows you to choose a different installed program or visit the Store:

Using a nondefault program on a case-by-case basis

If you just want to open a file occasionally in an application that's not the default for that file type, there's no need to go through all the business of changing the default application. Right-click the file in File Explorer and choose Open With. Windows displays a menu offering the various applications that can open the selected file type. If you don't find the one you want, click Choose Another App. This time a menu similar to the one shown in Figure 8-16 appears.

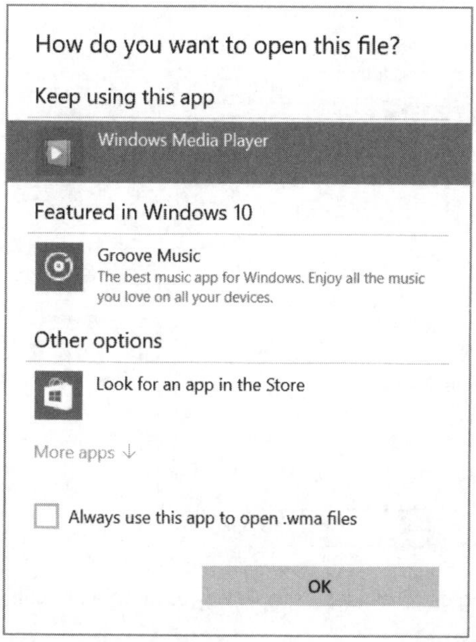

Figure 8-16 Right-clicking a file in File Explorer and choosing Open With > Choose Another App leads to a menu like this.

You can do two things in this menu. You can change the default for the selected file type (by selecting one of the listed apps and then clicking Always Use This App), or you can go for something altogether different by clicking More Apps. Doing this brings up a list of programs, many if not most of which will be completely unsuitable for the selected file type. Select one of these if you're curious to see what will happen. But don't click Always Use This App unless you're quite sure. If the program isn't what you want, it will simply make a nuisance of itself, and you'll have to go to the trouble of making something else the default.

Turning Windows features on or off

If you want to disable or enable certain default Windows features, open Settings and type **turn windows features on or off** in the search box. The dialog box shown in Figure 8-17 appears.

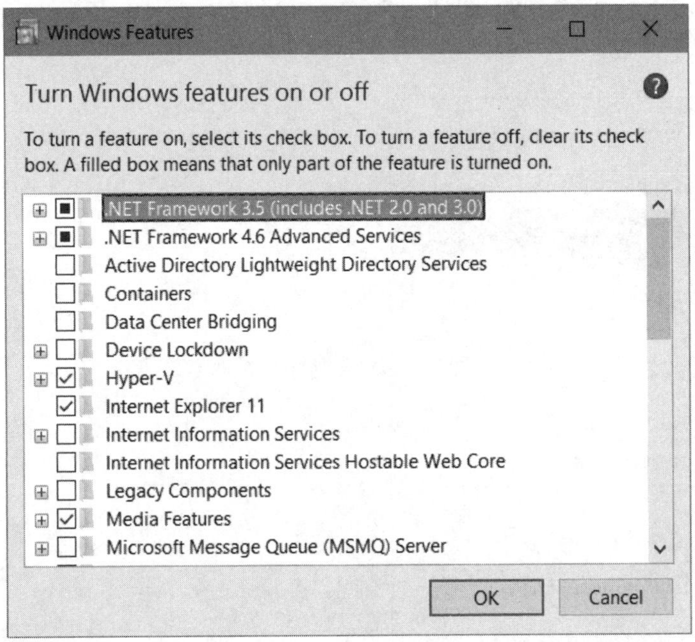

Figure 8-17 The Windows Features dialog box provides a simple way to disable or enable selected programs.

Here you can enable Hyper-V Management Tools (if they're not already enabled), disable Internet Explorer 11 if you have no further need for it, and so on. Note that some items in the list have subentries. Those marked by a filled check box have some components enabled and some not.

Setting AutoPlay options

AutoPlay is the feature that enables Windows to take appropriate action when you insert a removable device such as a CD, DVD, or memory card into a drive. The operating system detects the kind of disc or media you inserted and takes the action you requested for that type of media. If you have not already made a decision about what the operating system should do, a window similar to this one appears:

(E:)
Select to choose what happens with removable drives.

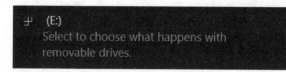

If you don't want Windows to take any action, you can simply ignore the message; it disappears after a few seconds. Otherwise, clicking or tapping the message brings you to the screen shown in Figure 8-18.

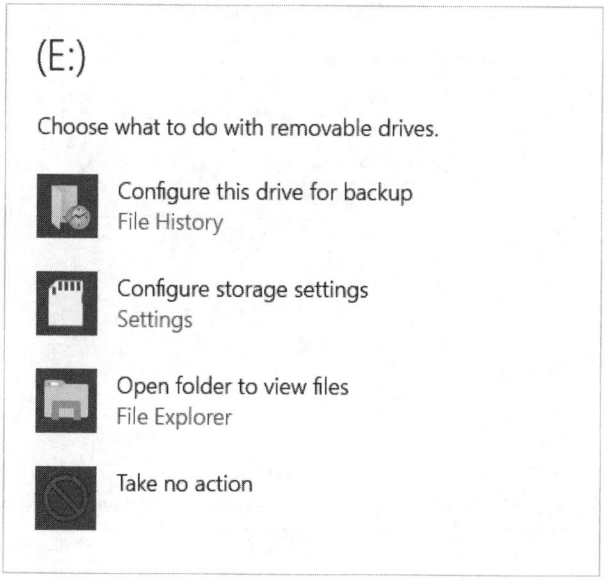

(E:)
Choose what to do with removable drives.
Configure this drive for backup
File History
Configure storage settings
Settings
Open folder to view files
File Explorer
Take no action

Figure 8-18 If you click the message that appears when you insert a removable device, Windows asks what you'd like to do with the device.

Notice that your choices here are limited to ones that are appropriate for the device type and Take No Action. (For example, if you insert an audio CD, your only choices are the default app for playing audio CDs and Take No Action.) If you don't want to commit to any of the options on this menu, press Esc.

In any case, if you set a default action for a particular media type and subsequently change your mind and want a different default, you can open Settings > Devices > AutoPlay. Shown in Figure 8-19, AutoPlay in Settings gives you options for configuring some types of media but not others. You might need to search for AutoPlay in Control Panel to see the rest.

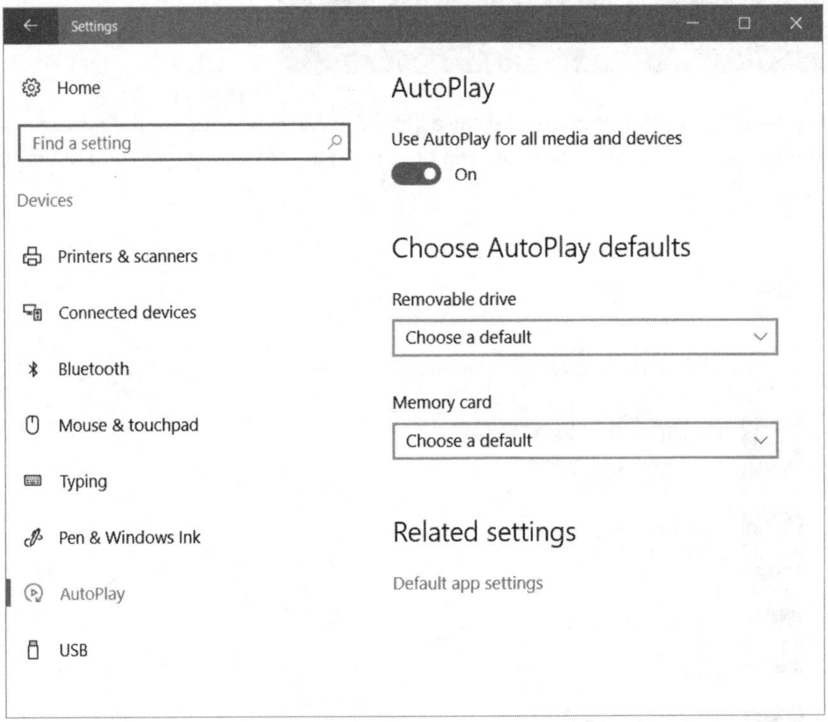

Figure 8-19 The AutoPlay page in Settings lets you configure AutoPlay behavior for some types of media. You might need to visit Control Panel to configure other types.

In the Control Panel counterpart for this corner of Settings, you'll see a dialog box comparable to the one shown in Figure 8-20.

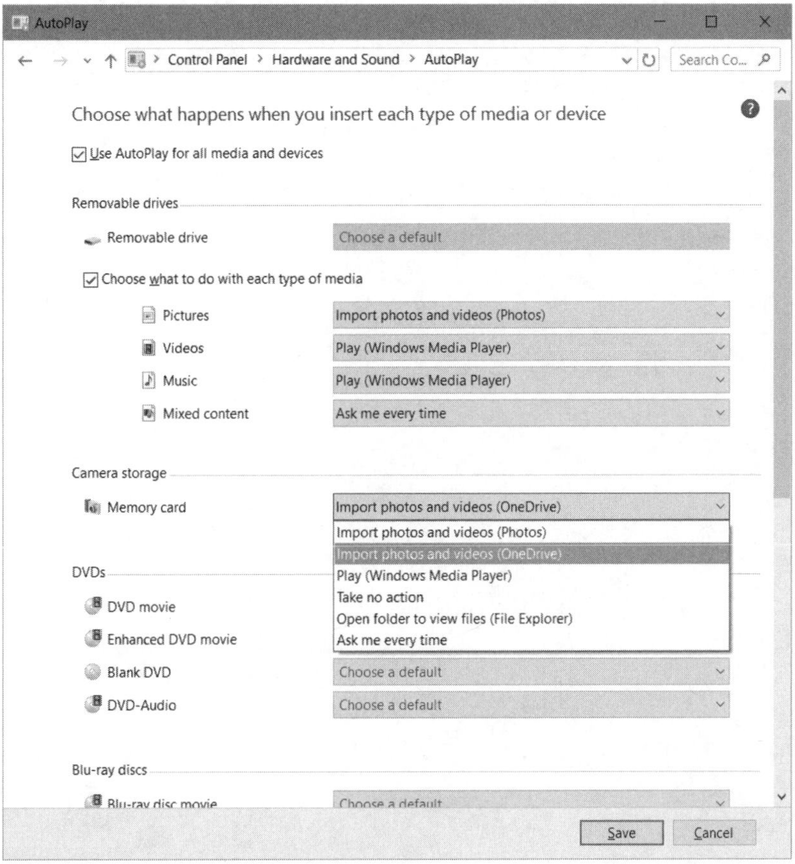

Figure 8-20 For each media type, Windows displays a list of appropriate possibilities you can choose from.

Inside OUT

You don't want a default action?

To have no default action for a given media type, choose Ask Me Every Time as the option for that media type. To suppress the AutoPlay dialog box completely, choose Take No Action.

Cortana and the web

Microsoft founder Bill Gates first articulated his vision of "information at your fingertips" back in 1994, at the dawn of the internet era. Two decades later, we're almost there.

With a Windows 10 PC, you really can get the answer to just about any question. You could ask the old-fashioned way, by opening a web browser and typing a query into your favorite search engine. Or you could skip the browser and the typing and just say "Hey Cortana" to invoke Microsoft's web-connected intelligent personal assistant.

In Windows 10, Cortana neatly ties together all the ways you might want to search for answers. You can quickly open apps and jump to a system setting, find local files and folders, search through your music collection, and track down a picture. You can also extend your search to the web and connect Cortana to cloud services to get personalized answers to questions like "What's on my calendar next week?"

In this chapter, we cover the many ways you can get your hands on useful information with the help of Windows 10. That includes, naturally, the two web browsers included by default: Microsoft Edge and Internet Explorer. But we begin with the unified search capability that sets Windows 10 apart from its predecessors.

Using Cortana for search and more

Search, as a Windows 10 feature and as an online service, is evolving at breathtaking speed. The results that show up in the search box are powered in large part by online services that are constantly improving, as are the Windows features you use to make those requests.

In the initial release of Windows 10, Cortana was a feature layered over traditional Windows search capabilities. If you didn't want the help of an occasionally sassy assistant, you could turn off Cortana with a simple switch.

Beginning with version 1607, that on-off switch is gone (although, as we explain later in this section, you can accomplish the same goal with Group Policy). Cortana is now neatly integrated with other search capabilities in Windows 10. You still have full control over what personal information is available to Cortana, and you have extensive customization capabilities as well.

Search is built into Windows 10 as an integral feature that gets prime real estate, just to the right of the Start button.

By default, on desktop and laptop PCs, you'll find a search box here. In Tablet Mode (or if you change the default setting), a search button appears, which expands to reveal a box when you tap or click it. And if even that icon is too much, you can hide it completely.

For most simple tasks, such as searching for an app or a setting, using the search box is as simple as tapping the Windows key and typing a few characters. The results, as shown in Figure 9-1, are businesslike and efficient, with no personality. As this example demonstrates, Windows Search is great at finding settings and apps.

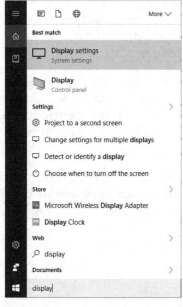

Figure 9-1 Type a word or phrase in the search box, and you get a categorized list of results that match the search term, starting with settings and apps. Use the options at the top to change the search scope.

If your search goal is finding a photo, you can narrow the scope of the search to just that category. After entering your search term, click or tap More to refine the results using any of the categories shown here:

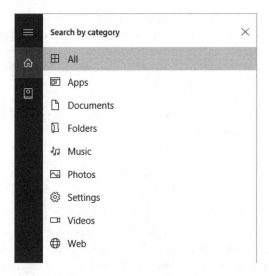

Choosing one of those categories immediately changes the search results list to show only the category you selected. Choosing Photos, for example, results in a display like the one shown in Figure 9-2.

Figure 9-2 Changing the search scope filters the results list to include only the selected category. Note the addition of a category filter before the search term.

CHAPTER 9

Two details are worth noting in Figure 9-2. First, because we customized the taskbar to show only a search icon, the search box is above the taskbar rather than in it. Second, clicking the Photos category inserted the **photos:** prefix in the search box, before the search term. As you might suspect, you can filter by any of the available categories manually, by typing the name of the category followed by a colon, space, and search term.

➤ For more detailed instructions on how to use Windows Search from File Explorer, see "Using Windows Search" in Chapter 12, "Managing files on PCs and in the cloud."

Inside OUT

Don't want Cortana at all? Turn it off with Group Policy or a registry edit

As with most things Windows, you can remove the search button or box completely if you're really convinced you won't use it. Right-click the taskbar and then click Cortana > Hidden. With that option set, you can still access Cortana's full feature set by tapping the Windows key and typing.

To turn off all of Cortana's features, leaving only the ability to search for local apps, files, and settings, you need to make a simple registry edit. On a system running Windows 10 Pro or Enterprise edition, you can use Group Policy to apply this setting across multiple machines; on a single PC, use the local Group Policy Editor, gpedit.msc, to open the policy Computer Configuration > Administrative Templates >Windows Components > Search > Allow Cortana and set it to Disabled.

On a system running Windows 10 Home, you need to make a manual edit to the registry. Find the key HKLM\Software\Policies\Microsoft\Windows\Windows Search (which you might need to create if it doesn't exist), and then create the DWORD value AllowCortana and set it to 0.

In either case, this change applies to all user accounts. Restart the PC and you'll notice that the text in the search box has changed from "Ask me anything" to "Search Windows." Clicking in the search box displays only a simple prompt. In addition, Cortana's Notebook is unavailable and only a few settings are available when you click the gear icon.

So far, none of what we've done using the search box involves Cortana. In the next section, we discuss what Cortana adds to this basic search experience.

What you can do with Cortana

Cortana, the intelligent search assistant built into Windows 10, adds an adult's voice and a (programmed) sense of humor to the core search experience. With your permission, Cortana also has the capability to perform additional tasks, such as adding items to a to-do list and delivering regular updates that match your interests and your schedule, as defined in a notebook full of settings.

In many ways, Cortana today is still like a child prodigy. Despite the pleasant female voice (no additional voice options are available) and the mostly natural intonations, "she" is really a web service, which is constantly learning and adding capabilities.

To get started with Cortana, you have to first agree to some terms, as shown in Figure 9-3. (You can change these and other settings later.)

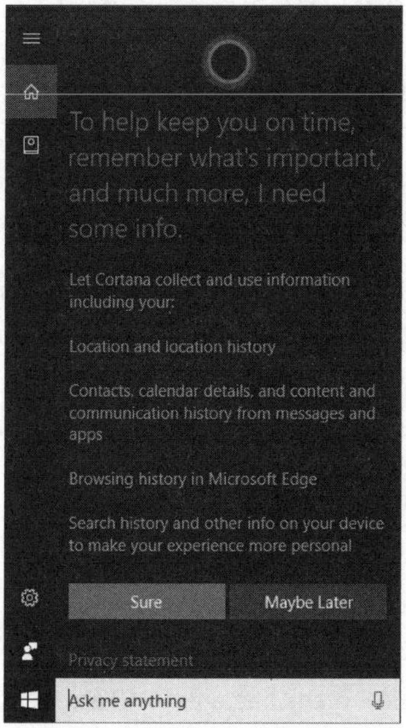

To help keep you on time, remember what's important, and much more, I need some info.

Let Cortana collect and use information including your:

Location and location history

Contacts, calendar details, and content and communication history from messages and apps

Browsing history in Microsoft Edge

Search history and other info on your device to make your experience more personal

Sure   Maybe Later

Privacy statement

Ask me anything

Figure 9-3 Cortana doesn't have access to personal information unless you provide your consent first.

If you agree, you give Cortana permission to search your information on your behalf.

The other feature you might want to turn on now is speech recognition. Click in the search box and then click the gear icon to configure your microphone and, optionally, tell Cortana you want a response when you say "Hey Cortana."

For a lengthy (but still not exhaustive) list of things Cortana can do for you, click the microphone button and just ask: "What can you do?" (If your system doesn't support input via a microphone, click in the search box and type the question.) The resulting list includes the following, which all appear in the Cortana window:

- **Basic facts** Cortana knows the dates of upcoming holidays ("When is Thanksgiving this year?") and biographic details of famous people ("How old is Bill Gates?").

- **Basic math** Enter any valid mathematical format—addition, subtraction, multiplication, division, exponentiation, and more, with support for using parentheses to group operations—and see the answer directly in the results pane. Press Enter or click the result to see a full calculator like the one shown here:

- **Conversions** How many liters in a gallon? How many hectares in 40 acres? How many teaspoons in a tablespoon? Cortana knows.

- **Exchange rates** Look up today's rates and convert any amount in one currency to its equivalent in another.

- **Translation** Using the microphone, say "How do you say good afternoon in French?" and Cortana responds by both showing the translation and pronouncing it for you. Using the keyboard, try typing **translate good afternoon into French**.

- **Definitions** Ask Cortana to define an unfamiliar word and you can view a short definition in the results pane. Click that result to see an expanded definition with an option to hear the word's pronunciation or jump to an online dictionary.

- **Reminders, alarms, and timers** Cortana can keep track of time and pop up an alert when the chosen time arrives. Try saying "Set a timer for 30 minutes."

- **Tracking flights and packages** Say or type **status british 75** to get routes, departure and arrival times, and gate information for British Airways flight 75. Cortana can also track a package by spotting a confirmation number in an incoming email message, or you can enter it manually.

- **Sports scores** You can see scores and standings for your favorite team, even for games that are in progress.

- **Stock prices** If you enter ticker symbols in Cortana's notebook for stocks you're following, just say "show me my stocks" to get the latest prices.

- **Weather** Say "Show me the weather" to get the forecast for your location. Add a city name to see a five-day forecast that can help you decide whether to pack an umbrella or sunscreen for an upcoming trip, as shown here:

And that only scratches the surface.

In addition to taking over search duties for files, folders, settings, music, and so on, Cortana can return results based on information you've given permission to search. Just clicking in the search box opens Cortana's summary of the things you're interested in, a scrolling list of useful information that can include news headlines, stock prices from your watch list, results from your favorite team's latest game, weather forecasts, and reminders on when you need to leave to arrive on time for an appointment.

Other tasks Cortana can complete on your behalf include adding appointments and reminders, creating notes and to-do lists, and checking your calendar for upcoming events. Figure 9-4, for example, shows the response when you ask Cortana to set a reminder. Reminders don't have to be triggered by a time. They can also be attached to a location or to a person.

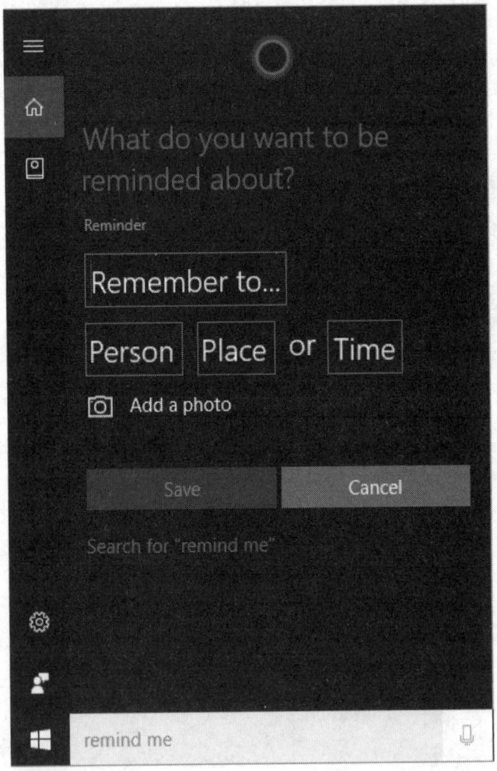

Figure 9-4 If you ask Cortana to set a reminder or create an appointment, you get this crisply efficient form.

Your timers and alarms appear as notifications, and you can ask Cortana to show you your reminders any time.

Configuring Cortana

Cortana learns by observing, but you can take control of that process by filling in the notebook, shown in Figure 9-5, which starts with information about you, such as the name you want to be called and your favorite places. You can connect accounts to Cortana so that calendar items and commitments from email messages make it into your daily agenda. Next, it provides dozens of sections where you can list your preferences—favorite sports teams, preferred cuisines and restaurant budgets, and news topics you want to follow.

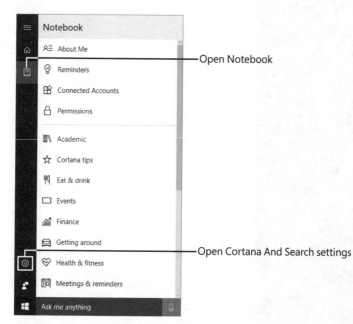

Figure 9-5 Use Cortana's notebook to customize your interests and help make the "Here's what's happening now" summaries more useful.

Click any category to fill in information that can help make for more tailored recommendations and reminders later. If this seems like a tedious process, remember two things: First, you can do this over time. Just pop in every so often and check out a category or two. Second, all of your settings are saved with your Microsoft account and available for you when you use other devices as well. That includes mobile devices running Android and iOS as well.

You have every right to be concerned about privacy when using a service that knows so much about your daily routine. That's why Cortana has options to eliminate your device history and your local search history. To delete personal information saved on Microsoft's servers, open Cortana's Settings, click or tap Change What Cortana Knows About Me In The Cloud, and follow the instructions.

You can read the Cortana privacy policy by following a link at the bottom of the Cortana Settings pane, shown in Figure 9-6.

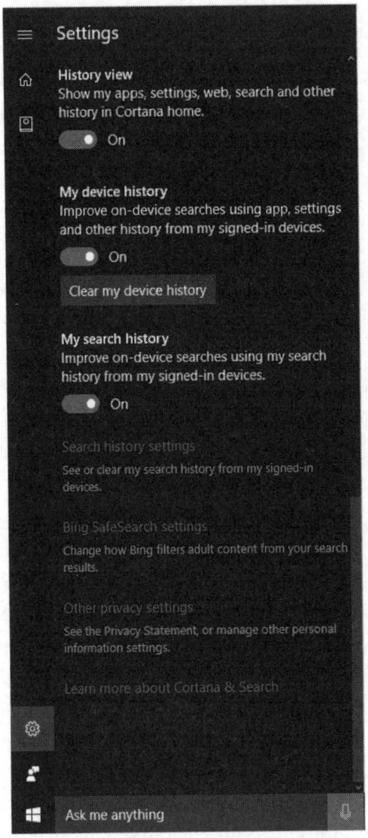

Figure 9-6 The Cortana Settings pane provides you with a link if you want to read the privacy policy, clear local information, or go online and delete all saved information.

Using Cortana in Microsoft Edge

Cortana has a special relationship with Microsoft Edge, the new default browser in Windows 10, which we discuss at length later in this chapter. A search result might pop up in your browser immediately if you type something about which Cortana is particularly knowledgeable. Enter a flight number or the name of a currency, for example, and you'll get status or rate information, exactly as it would appear in the search results pane from Start. Cortana also has a fairly broad knowledge of restaurants.

If Cortana doesn't volunteer the information you need, take matters into your own hands. If you run across an interesting term while viewing a webpage in Microsoft Edge, right-click the word, name, or phrase and then click Ask Cortana. That opens a sidebar like the one shown in Figure 9-7, with additional information drawn from online sources.

-style suite at the Pestana Palace—a fondar

m—I'm torn. Do I go for a dip in the garde

b? I don't often get to soak under a chand

hat has even more frescoes than my room

g the buffet table would be a talking point.

ure a cherub is glaring at me.

ne to Torre de Belém, a dinky fort at the m

ny naval adventures, the structure bears as

I is just as camp. Maritime motifs meet Mo

t architectural mashup known as Manueli

Near the fort's tiny drawbridge, a busker pl

lin.

I've fetched this for you.

See all images

Belém Tower

W Wikipedia

Belém Tower or the Tower of St Vincent is a fortified tower located in the civil parish of Santa Maria de Belém in the municipality of Lisbo... +

Opened: 1519
Architectural style: Manueline

People also search for   See all (20+)

Powered by ᑲ Bing

Figure 9-7 Ask Cortana for information about a person, place, or term while using Microsoft Edge, and the results show up in a sidebar along the right side of the browser window.

Cortana already knows a great many useful facts, and as time goes on, you can expect the breadth of that expertise to expand.

And as long as we're on the subject of browsers, let's look more closely at the latest member of the Microsoft family.

Why the new browser?

Windows 10 includes not one but two web browsers. Microsoft Edge, the new kid on the block, is the default, but the venerable Internet Explorer remains as an alternative. Unlike Windows 8.1, however, which offered dual variants of Internet Explorer, the two browsers in Windows 10 are totally distinct. Microsoft Edge is a modern browser built to support modern standards and

CHAPTER 9

to work well with the web as it exists today; Internet Explorer is, by the standards of the World Wide Web, downright ancient and encumbered by the need to maintain compatibility with obsolete web-design practices.

If you're a longtime user of Internet Explorer, we don't need to explain how it works. Its features are locked in place in Windows 10, and they won't change. In this chapter, we focus primarily on Microsoft Edge—with occasional comparisons to the still-present, still-useful Internet Explorer 11.

NOTE

Microsoft Edge, like Windows 10 itself, is a work in progress and receives frequent updates. The first version of Microsoft Edge, which was included with the official launch of Windows 10 in July 2015, was raw and frankly unfinished. For example, the ability to sync favorites between computers using the same Microsoft account was only a promise at launch; a year later, that feature exists. Of the many changes in Microsoft Edge as it appears in Windows 10 version 1607, the addition of a robust extension model, based on JavaScript and HTML technologies, is the most important. We cover the use of extensions later in this chapter.

The history of Internet Explorer, from its inception in 1995 to the present, can be viewed as a struggle to maintain compatibility with the past while trying to adapt to an ever-faster pace of change in web development standards. Worthy competing browsers, such as Mozilla Firefox and Google Chrome, didn't have those compatibility burdens, allowing them to progress much more quickly and outperform Internet Explorer.

With Microsoft Edge, Microsoft has set out to create a clean-slate, modern browser, free of compatibility freight and free of the most egregious security hazards. The focus is on support for current and forthcoming web standards and interoperability, so that sites developed for other modern browsers will run with minimal or no modifications on Microsoft Edge.

After 20 years of service, the Trident rendering engine of Internet Explorer, Mshtml.dll, has been replaced with the new Microsoft Edge rendering engine, Edgehtml.dll. (The *rendering engine* is what translates HTML and other web code into an intelligible, navigable website.) Although the newer engine started with the Trident code as its base, the developers ruthlessly tossed out older features that aren't relevant to the modern web. Among the technologies not included in the new rendering engine are the following:

- ActiveX

- Browser helper objects

- Compatibility view

- Document modes

- Vector Markup Language (VML)

- VBScript

➤ Web developers can get more detailed information about the changes in EdgeHTML from the Microsoft Edge Dev Blog, at *https://blogs.windows.com/msedgedev*. For more information about technologies that are either in development or under consideration for Microsoft Edge, see *https://developer.microsoft.com/microsoft-edge/platform/status/*.

Inside OUT

Microsoft Edge or Internet Explorer?

Internet Explorer 11 is provided with Windows 10 for compatibility reasons, primarily for enterprise environments that require its unique features, such as support for ActiveX controls. Microsoft has pledged to continue to provide technical support and security updates for Internet Explorer, but this legacy browser will not receive any new features. That new development work is reserved exclusively for Microsoft Edge.

Large organizations and other users who rely on older web technologies such as ActiveX for their intranets or line-of-business web applications might have reason to make Internet Explorer the default browser. Most others will prefer Microsoft Edge for its uncluttered design, touch friendliness, new features, speed, and, above all, its enhanced security. By dropping support for technologies like ActiveX and browser helper objects, Microsoft Edge eliminates many of the security hazards that have plagued Internet Explorer over the years.

We know that many of our readers prefer Internet Explorer precisely because of its extensibility options and their longtime familiarity with it. But given its legacy status, we strongly recommend that you have a plan to switch to Microsoft Edge or another modern browser, as we describe in the next section. If you set Microsoft Edge as your default browser, you can still keep Internet Explorer on hand for the occasional website that requires it. Click More > Open With Internet Explorer in Microsoft Edge to reopen the current page using your backup browser.

On managed networks, you can deploy Microsoft Edge as the default browser for all users and then turn on a feature called Enterprise Mode, which uses a custom site list to specify which sites open with Microsoft Edge and which sites must use Internet Explorer. Windows 10 version 1607 includes a new Internet Explorer group policy that restricts Internet Explorer 11 usage to only sites on the Enterprise Mode Site List. We discuss this feature in more detail in "Managing the browsing experience" in Chapter 21, "Managing Windows 10 in business."

Browser and search basics

The two browsers Microsoft includes with Windows 10 have a handful of features in common. In this section, we quickly review these basic tasks and settings.

Specifying your default browser

Microsoft Edge is Microsoft's recommended default browser. To make a different browser your default, go to Settings > System > Default Apps. Under the Web Browser heading, you should see the name of your current default browser. Click that entry to display a menu that lists Microsoft Edge, Internet Explorer, and any third-party browsers you have installed. (You'll also see the option to visit the Store.)

> ➤ For information about fine-tuning your default settings—for example, assigning particular browsers to particular web protocols—see "Setting default programs and file-type associations" in Chapter 8, "Using and managing apps and desktop programs."

Within Microsoft Edge, you can open the current page in Internet Explorer by clicking More (the ellipsis icon at the far right of the toolbar) and then clicking Open With Internet Explorer. If you're working in an environment in which Enterprise Mode has been enabled, clicking any link that leads to a domain on the Enterprise Mode Site List automatically opens that page in Internet Explorer.

Changing your default search provider

On a clean installation of Windows 10, Microsoft Bing, unsurprisingly, is the default search provider for both of Microsoft's browsers. With a few simple steps, you can change the default in either browser. The one gotcha is that to change the search provider in Microsoft Edge, you must first have visited the search provider's website. You don't have to do anything there; if the site you have visited supports the OpenSearch standard, you just have to browse to that page once for the provider to show up on the list of available search engines.

With that excursion completed, open Microsoft Edge and go to More > Settings > View Advanced Settings > Change Search Engine. To make a change, select any entry from the list of search providers:

Change search engine

Choose one

Bing (default)
www.bing.com

Google Search (discovered)
www.google.com

Wikipedia (en) (discovered)
en.wikipedia.org

Yahoo Search (discovered)
www.yahoo.com

Set as default

Remove

After making a selection, click Set As Default to make that site your new default for searches from the address bar, or click Remove to clear that site from the list of available search providers.

To change providers in Internet Explorer, start by clicking Tools > Manage Add-Ons. The Search Providers section of the Manage Add-Ons dialog box displays a list of available search providers.

Not satisfied with the available choices in Internet Explorer? Near the lower left corner of the dialog box, click Find More Search Providers. That takes you to the Internet Explorer Gallery, where you can find a provider and click Add. You can now return to the Manage Add-Ons dialog box and choose the just-added alternative from the Search Providers link.

If you choose not to make the added provider the new default, you can still use the new search engine as an occasional alternative to the current default. When you search in the address bar in Internet Explorer, below the list of suggested sites, you'll find small icons for all your listed search providers. Click one of those icons to perform an ad hoc search with a nondefault provider.

Managing downloads

Downloading documents and programs is straightforward. Both browsers provide options and progress reports in a banner at the bottom of the page, like this one:

> What do you want to do with MediaCreationTool.exe (17.4 MB)? From: download.microsoft.com   **Save**   **Save as**   **Cancel**   ✕

Click Save to begin the download and store the saved file in the Downloads folder of the current user profile. Click Save As to choose a different location for the saved file. For large downloads, Microsoft Edge provides a status message displaying the percentage complete, offering a Pause button to suspend the download temporarily. If you change your mind midstream, you can click Cancel. When the download is complete, another banner in the same location provides additional options: Run, for an executable file, and Open, for a document. Click Open Folder to open a File Explorer window with the downloaded file selected in the folder where you saved it.

Clicking View Downloads in Microsoft Edge (or pressing Ctrl+J) takes you to the Hub and displays a list of current and past downloads, like the one shown in Figure 9-8.

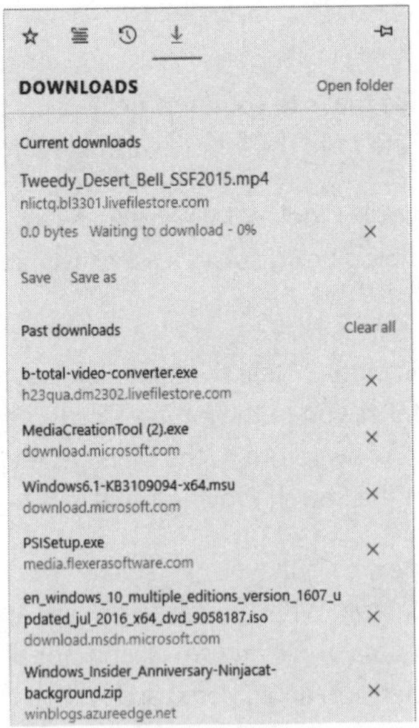

Figure 9-8 Press Ctrl+J to open the Downloads list and view the status of any current downloads. Click any entry under Past Downloads to open that entry.

Click any entry in this list to open a downloaded document or run a downloaded executable—or click Open Folder to browse the contents of your Downloads folder using File Explorer. Clicking the X to the right of any downloaded item removes it from the list; click Clear All to empty the entire download list at once. Note that these actions have no effect on the downloaded files themselves; they simply tidy up the list in the browser.

To get to the comparable set of features in Internet Explorer, click Tools, View Downloads, or use the same Ctrl+J shortcut.

Using tabs

Like all modern browsers, Internet Explorer and Microsoft Edge allow you to keep multiple pages open on separate tabs in the same application window and switch between them quickly. This feature is a tremendous timesaver for anyone doing research or trying to juggle multiple tasks.

In either browser, you can open a new tab in any of several ways:

- To open a new blank tab, press Ctrl+T, or click the New Tab button, just to the right of the current tabs.

- To open a link in a new tab without shifting focus from the current tab, right-click the link and choose Open In New Tab, or hold down Ctrl while you click the link.

- To open a link in a new tab and shift focus to the newly opened tab, hold down Ctrl+Shift and click.

- To duplicate a tab, press Ctrl+K, or right-click the tab and choose Duplicate from the shortcut menu. Note that the duplicated tab also includes the history associated with the original tab.

- To close any open tab, point to its tab heading and click the X at the right side. To close the current tab, press Ctrl+W.

To reposition a tab within an array of tabs, drag the tab you want to move laterally. To peel a tab off from the current browser window and make it appear in a new window, drag the tab away from the tab bar and release it.

If more tabs are open than will fit in the browser window, a scrolling arrow appears to the left of the first tab or to the right of the last (or both). Click the arrow to scroll in the indicated direction. You can also use keyboard shortcuts to cycle between tabs: press Ctrl+Tab to move from left to right or Ctrl+Shift+Tab to go from right to left.

When you have a lot of tabs open, particularly if you're working with more than one browser window, you might prefer to navigate by using thumbnails of each page. In Microsoft Edge, pointing to any inactive tab heading shows an up-to-date thumbnail of that page. For Internet Explorer, point to the program's taskbar icon to display thumbnails for all open tabs, move the mouse pointer over a tab to preview that page, and click to make that the current tab.

CHAPTER 9

Setting tabbed browsing options

If you regularly open large numbers of tabs, you'll probably want to tweak the way your browser handles tabs. To see the options available in Microsoft Edge, click More > Settings > Open New Tabs With. If you prefer your new tabs uncluttered, choose A Blank Page.

If you choose either of the first two options, new tabs will open with one or two rows (depending on screen width) of "top sites." On a clean install, this list contains up to eight suggested sites, chosen based on your regional settings, as shown here:

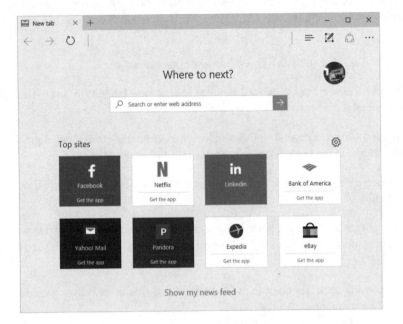

If you find this initial selection arbitrary or irrelevant, you can eliminate any sites you don't want to see by pointing to the thumbnail and clicking the X. After you've used Microsoft Edge for a while, the Top Sites section of the new tab page should reflect your actual browsing history and become a useful navigational tool. You can drag the tile for any site to a different position.

A comparable but slightly different set of options is available in Internet Explorer. To find them, open the Internet Options dialog box and, on the General tab, click Tabs. In the Tabbed Browsing Settings dialog box, open the drop-down list below When A New Tab Is Opened, Open.

Reopening closed tabs

Did you accidentally close a tab before you were quite finished with it? No problem. In either browser, right-click any tab that's currently open and choose Reopen Closed Tab (or use the keyboard shortcut, Ctrl+Shift+Tab). The page you most recently closed reappears in its previous location. You can repeat this procedure for other tabs you might have closed.

Internet Explorer, but not Microsoft Edge, includes a command you can use to reopen a particular closed tab without having to reopen others that were closed later. Right-click a tab and choose Recently Closed Tabs to display a menu from which you can choose the page you want to revisit.

Restoring your last session

When you restart Windows without first closing Microsoft Edge, opening Microsoft Edge in the new session automatically opens all tabs from your previous session. If you want Microsoft Edge to always open all tabs from the previous session, even if you closed Microsoft Edge first, click More > Settings > Open Microsoft Edge With > Previous Pages.

The new tab page in Internet Explorer includes a Reopen Last Session link that reloads every page that was open the last time you closed Internet Explorer. This can spare you some anguish if you accidentally close the browser when you meant to close only the current tab. It can really rescue you if you sit down at your machine and find that your system has been restarted in your absence.

Be aware that if you have two or more Internet Explorer sessions open, each in a separate window, Reopen Last Session revives only the tabs that were open in the session that was closed last.

Customizing your start and home pages

Microsoft Edge distinguishes between a home page and startup pages. Startup pages, of which you can have one or more, appear at the beginning of each new session. The home page, of which you can have but one, arrives only when you click the Home button—which is not displayed by default but can easily be added to your toolbar.

To configure startup pages, click More > Settings > Open Microsoft Edge With. Your options are to open with the default Start page (about:start), the new tab page, all pages that were open when you last closed the browser, or one or more pages of your own choosing.

If you select A Specific Page Or Pages, we recommend that you first open the page and then click in the address bar and press Ctrl+C to copy its URL. Paste that address in the box and save it. Repeat the process, using the Add New Page option, as shown in Figure 9-9.

To use a home page in Microsoft Edge, click More > Settings > View Advanced Settings, and then turn on the Show The Home Button switch. With that option turned on, you can choose where you go when you click the Home button: the Start page, the New Tab page, or a specific page of your choosing—sort of a favorite-favorite shortcut.

CHAPTER 9

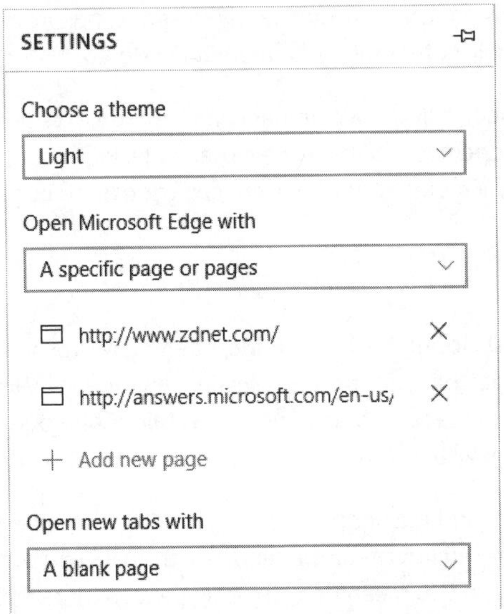

Figure 9-9 You can use the Open Microsoft Edge With option to specify that you always want to begin a new session by opening specific pages.

Internet Explorer offers comparable options. To set multiple home pages, click Tools, Internet Options. On the General tab, under the Home Page heading, enter one or more URLs, each on a separate line.

Note that the Startup section of this dialog box lets you choose whether to open with your home pages or with the tabs that were open in the previous session.

Making text easier to read

Microsoft Edge and Internet Explorer both provide easy ways to make text and graphics on a webpage larger or smaller. If you're working on a touchscreen or on a device with a precision touchpad, you can zoom in and out with the standard touch gestures. Spread two fingers on a page to make the content larger; bring two fingers together to make it smaller.

With a wheel mouse, you can zoom in or out by holding down the Ctrl key as you roll the wheel forward or back. Zooming with the mouse wheel has the advantage of maintaining the position of whatever object you're pointing to when you begin zooming. Suppose, for example, that you're zooming in to get a better look at a graphic element lying near the right edge of the screen. If you use other zooming methods, the element you care about will eventually drift out of the window. But if you zoom in by pointing to it and rolling the wheel, the element retains its position relative to your mouse pointer as it gets larger.

If a mouse is not at hand, hold down Ctrl and press the Plus Sign to increase magnification; hold down Ctrl and press the Minus Sign to zoom back out. To return to normal (100%) magnification, press Ctrl+0.

Should you forget these shortcuts, you can always go to the menu. In Microsoft Edge, click More and then use the plus and minus signs on either side of the Zoom command. In Internet Explorer, click Tools > Zoom.

Using Microsoft Edge

Microsoft Edge continues the trend toward visual simplicity (the minimization of "chrome") that has been characteristic of all modern browsers. Unlike Internet Explorer, Microsoft Edge has no menu bar. The stripped-down interface you see is exactly what you get—with the exception of three possible customizations:

- You can add the Home button to your toolbar by clicking More (the ellipsis icon) > Settings > View Advanced Settings, and then turning on the Show The Home Button switch. From that same location, you can also specify the address of a home page you want to use. On narrow screens, the Home button might push other controls too close together for finger navigation, but otherwise it's a handy item to have on board.

- To display the Favorites bar, click More > Settings > View Favorites Settings > Show The Favorites Bar.

- Make the icon for an extension easier to use by adding it to the toolbar. Click More > Extensions, select an installed extension, and then click Show Button Next To The Address Bar.

Figure 9-10 shows the landmarks in Microsoft Edge, with the Home button displayed. Note that controls in Microsoft Edge are spaced to ease use on touchscreens.

Figure 9-10 The user-interface controls in Microsoft Edge are spaced to accommodate fingers or a stylus.

CHAPTER 9

Many navigation conventions in Microsoft Edge will look familiar from your experience with other browsers. One addition worth pointing out is the Hub, which offers access to favorites, history, and downloads. The reading list feature, also available from the Hub in Microsoft Edge, is a handy alternative to favorites.

Navigating with the Start page and address bar

Unless you configured it to do otherwise, a new instance of Microsoft Edge opens on the Start page, with a large box labeled "Where to next?" near the top of the page. You can enter either an address or a search string here.

If Microsoft Edge can parse your input as a web address, it takes you there directly. Otherwise, it passes the text you entered to your default search provider.

If the Start page is not present (as is the case if you've used about:blank to open a blank page, or if you're already viewing a page), simply type in the address bar, which functions the same way as the Start page's input field. In either place, Microsoft Edge does its best to simplify your typing task. While you type, the browser offers a list of matching sites from your browsing history as well as search suggestions:

The icon that looks like a clock in retrograde motion marks sites derived from your browsing history. The search suggestions that appear below this group are based on your browsing history and, if you've opted in, information gathered by Cortana about your interests and location.

Browsing with favorites

Like every other browser, Microsoft Edge lets you build a repository of favorite sites—sites that you know or suspect you'll want to return to now and then. Once a site has been designated a favorite, you can reopen it with only a few clicks, instead of having to search for it again or pull it up from your browsing history. Your browsing history is available for reuse as well, of course (see "Browsing through history" later in this chapter), but for sites you visit regularly, a well-placed favorite can be more convenient.

The Favorites Bar is a special folder whose contents can be displayed below the address bar in Microsoft Edge. By default, it's hidden. To make it visible, click More > Settings > View Favorites Settings and turn on Show The Favorites Bar, as shown in Figure 9-11.

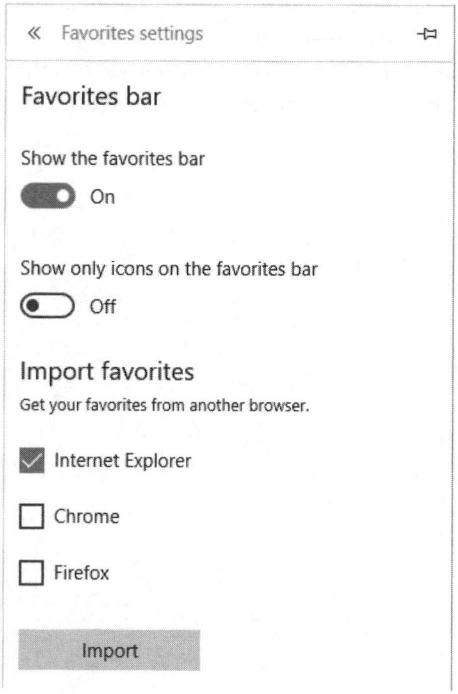

Figure 9-11 You can import favorites into Microsoft Edge from any currently installed browser, but you can't sync favorites between different browsers.

Although Internet Explorer and Microsoft Edge both allow you to save favorites, the two lists are saved in different places and are not shared.

When you switch to Microsoft Edge, you can import favorites you created in Internet Explorer or another browser, using the option at the bottom of the Favorites Settings pane. Select the check boxes for the browsers from which you want to import favorites and then click Import. The newly added favorites appear in Microsoft Edge in a folder called Imported From *Browser*, where *Browser* is the name of the app from which you imported favorites. This is a one-time process. Any subsequent changes you make to the imported favorites are not reflected in the original location, and any new favorites you add in the other browser are exclusive to that browser and not incorporated into Microsoft Edge.

NOTE

The quickest way to add the current page to your favorites is by pressing Ctrl+D. This shortcut works in Internet Explorer (and most third-party browsers) as well.

To add a shortcut for the current page to Favorites or to the Favorites Bar, click the star at the right side of the address bar in Microsoft Edge. As Figure 9-12 shows, that action opens the Add To Favorites Or Reading List dialog box, where you can choose to add the link to your favorites or your reading list. Click Favorites if that's not already selected (as indicated by the underscore and the accent color), edit the name of the saved shortcut if you'd like, choose a location, and click Add.

Figure 9-12 As part of its effort to keep the user interface controls well spaced for touch friendliness, Microsoft Edge combines Add To Favorites and Add To Reading List in a single dialog box, accessed by clicking the star-shaped icon on the right side of the address bar.

To use your favorites, once you have created them, click the Hub icon, just to the right of the separator line next to the Add To Favorites button in the address bar. You can also get to the Hub by pressing Ctrl+I.

Inside OUT

Always rename favorites

Get in the habit of assigning a descriptive name when you save a favorite. Make sure the name you choose contains the words your future self is likely to use as search terms. Steer clear of extra-long file names. Web designers often create outrageously long page titles, packing descriptions and keywords together with the goal of ranking higher on search engines. Shorter, more meaningful names are easier to spot when you're scrolling through a folder full of favorites. And speaking of folders, by all means use them to categorize your favorites. The more favorites you accumulate, the happier you'll be that you have them organized.

As Figure 9-13 shows, the Hub is a multipurpose destination. The four icons at the top take you, from left to right, to Favorites, Reading List, History, and Downloads.

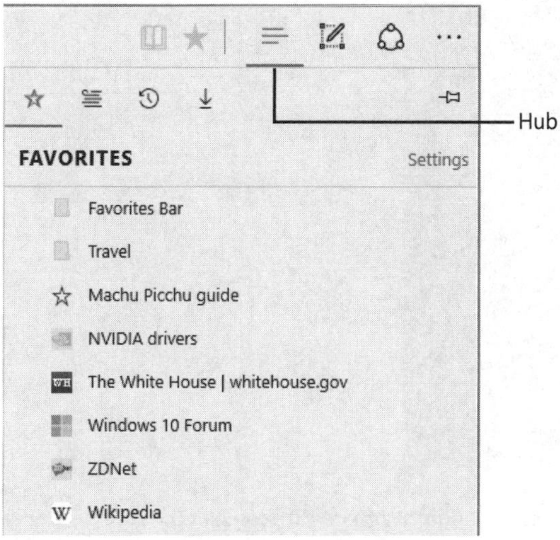

Figure 9-13 Favorites are accessed via the Hub, which also provides entrée to your reading list, history, and downloads.

Click a favorite to launch it in the current tab. To launch it in a new tab, right-click it and then click Open In New Tab. The menu that appears when you right-click also gives you the means to rename or remove a shortcut. Right-click any empty space in the Favorites list to create a new folder on the fly or sort the list by name.

NOTE

If you have enough room on your screen and you expect to be working with several shortcuts, pin the Hub. The pane will remain open until you click the X, which replaces the pin icon in the upper right corner.

Inside OUT

Share or save a page

Given its name, you might expect the Share button on the Microsoft Edge toolbar to be exclusively for sharing a webpage with other people. But clicking the Share button also makes it possible to save a page for your own reference, using any installed app that can act as a share target, as shown here:

The system from which you're sharing might offer a different set of targets—perhaps including Facebook or an RSS reader, for example. If you previously shared pages to Mail, the addresses of your recent recipients appear at the top of the list. The format of the shared content depends on the target, but typically it consists of a hyperlink and a brief summary of the page.

Use an additional, well-hidden option to snap a screenshot of whatever's visible in the current Microsoft Edge tab. At the top of the Share pane, click the down arrow to the right of the page name and choose Screenshot. Click the arrow if you want to share a screenshot of the page (for example, if you're sending a picture rather than text).

CHAPTER 9

TROUBLESHOOTING

You can't find your Microsoft Edge favorites

Internet Explorer saves its favorites in a subfolder of your user profile, %UserProfile%\
Favorites; Microsoft Edge, by contrast, keeps its favorites tucked away in a folder deeply
nested under %LocalAppData%\Packages\Microsoft.MicrosoftEdge_8wekyb3d8bbwe.
We don't recommend you go poking around in search of those favorites; you can't do
anything useful with the File Explorer entries there anyway. If you try to add a favorite by
manually creating a file alongside the others, Microsoft Edge simply ignores it. Use the
Favorites Hub in Microsoft Edge to delete a favorite or rename it.

Using the reading list to save links for later

Favorites are a great way to preserve and categorize websites to which you expect to return
periodically. When you just want to save a link to a page so that you can read it later, when you
have more time, the reading list in Microsoft Edge is a better alternative.

To save the current page to the reading list, click the star at the end of the address bar, just as if
you were saving a favorite, but click Reading List instead. Give the page a name, and click Add.

Microsoft Edge proposes the name of the page as the name of your reading list item, but you
can (and often should) replace that with something easier to recognize. Above the name field,
Microsoft Edge displays an image taken from the page you're saving, assuming that it finds one
near the beginning of the page.

When you finally have some spare time to read your saved items, open the Hub and then click
the Reading List icon. Pages you added to the list are ordered chronologically, with the most
recent on top (as shown in Figure 9-14). Click and read.

When you've finished with an item, right-click it and choose Delete.

> ➤ The reading list that Microsoft Edge maintains is, confusingly, completely unrelated to the
> one created by the Windows Reading List app.

Figure 9-14 Microsoft Edge sorts your reading list in descending chronological order.

Browsing through history

Microsoft Edge and Internet Explorer each maintain separate histories of the sites you visit. If you need to return to a site and you neglected to make it a favorite (or save it to your reading list in Microsoft Edge), you should be able to find it by looking through the history listings.

To inspect your history in Microsoft Edge, click Hub, and then click History. (It's the third icon from the left.) Alternatively, press Ctrl+H. Microsoft Edge presents sites in descending chronological order, using relative dates and times: Last Hour, Earlier Today, Yesterday, Last Week, and so on.

Use the outline controls at the left to expand date categories. As you move the mouse pointer over each item, an X appear to its right, allowing you to quickly clean up pages you don't want or need in your history. As Figure 9-15 shows, each item has its own date and time stamp.

For a more thorough pruning of your history, right-click any entry in the history list and choose the last option on the shortcut menu to delete all visits to that domain. To erase the entire history in Microsoft Edge, click Clear All History at the top of the list.

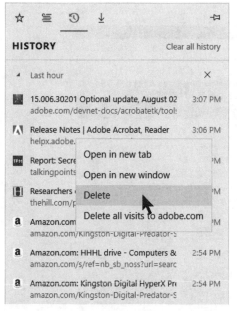

Figure 9-15 Microsoft Edge organizes your browsing history in descending chronological order. Right-click to erase a single entry or remove all visits to a particular domain.

Using Reading View in Microsoft Edge

Zooming in is an excellent way to make small text easier on the eyes. But for more improvement in reading comfort, try Reading View in Microsoft Edge. (This feature is not available in Internet Explorer 11.) Introduced in Windows 8 with the modern app version of Internet Explorer, Reading View removes distracting elements from a webpage and reformats the text so that you can focus on what you're trying to read. Reading View is especially useful on pages that are cluttered with ads and where the designer has used type that's too small or has contrast problems with the background.

To display a page in Reading View, click the Reading View icon, which resembles an open book; it's the first in the set of icons at the right of the address bar. If Reading View is not available (because the page is not suitable for that kind of display), the icon will be dim. (The icon might also be dim for a few seconds while Microsoft Edge analyzes your page to see whether it can be displayed in Reading View.) To switch back to normal view, click the Reading View icon again or click Back.

Figures 9-16 and 9-17 show the same page in normal display and in Reading View.

CHAPTER 9

Figure 9-16 In its normal display, the text you want to read might be surrounded by navigational elements, ads, and other distractions.

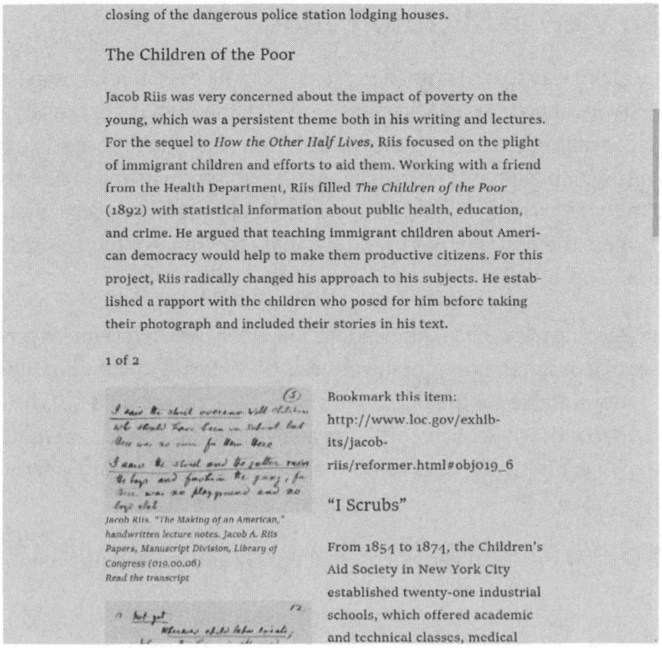

Figure 9-17 In Reading View, the navigational elements have been removed (although hyperlinks are retained), and a generous amount of white space has been added to enhance readability.

In converting a page to Reading View, Microsoft Edge removes such distractions as ads and navigational display elements, while retaining hyperlinks, source information, and graphics that the Reading View algorithm determines are integral to the article. Reading View also makes some intelligent layout decisions—for example, offering multicolumn layouts when the width of the browser window allows it. Generous amounts of white space, a soft sepia background, and a specially designed font further augment readability. (The background and font size can be customized.)

Two customization options for Reading View are available. Click More > Settings, and then adjust the Reading View Style (Light, Medium, Dark, or Default, which matches the browser theme) and Reading View Font Size (Small, Medium, Large, or Extra Large).

Annotating Microsoft Edge pages with web notes

The web note feature in Microsoft Edge lets you draw on, highlight, add text annotations to, and clip sections of webpages you want to call attention to. Microsoft Edge turns your webpage into a static graphic image on which you can draw with your fingers or a pen (on a touchscreen) or use the mouse and keyboard on a conventional display that lacks touch capabilities. After you mark up a page, you can email it, send it to OneNote (or another sharing target), or simply save it to your own favorites or reading list. Figure 9-18 shows an example of a page with a red circle and some yellow highlighting.

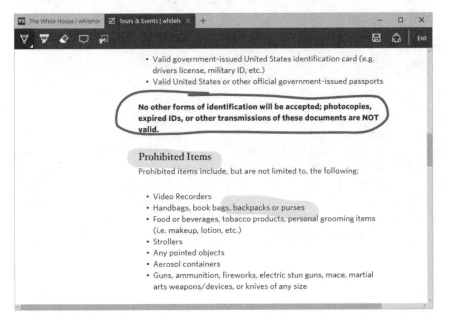

Figure 9-18 The pen and highlighter are two of the tools you can use to create web notes.

To begin creating a web note, click Make A Web Note, the icon to the left of Share on the tool-bar. Microsoft Edge opens a set of drawing tools for your use, shown next:

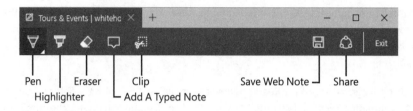

Click the drop-down arrows on the Pen and Highlighter tools to change size and color options. If your stylus or mouse goes astray, use the Eraser tool and try again. To get rid of all the marks you've made, click the drop-down arrow on the Eraser tool and choose Clear All Ink. (Alternatively, you can exit drawing mode and then come back for another go.)

To add a text box to the page, click Add A Typed Note, and then click to indicate where you want the text to go. To copy a snippet to the Clipboard, click the Clip tool, and then select the area you want to copy.

The Save Web Note tool, on the right side of the toolbar, offers OneNote, Favorites, and Reading List as destinations. If you save to your favorites or the reading list, you'll be able to pull the page back up at any time and review your annotations. The Share icon presents a full assortment of sharing options using installed apps that support this functionality.

Inside OUT

Use a web note to freeze a webpage

Website content tends to be ephemeral. If you need to capture the current state of a rapidly changing webpage, grab it with a web note and save it to your reading list, favorites, or OneNote. If you don't care to annotate it, you can simply click Make A Web Note and then click Share. There are many other ways to take screenshots, but this one is right at hand as you browse, and it captures the entire page, not just what you see in the confines of your screen. When you reopen your web note from wherever you put it, you can quickly switch back to the "live" version of the site by means of the Go To Original Page link that appears atop the web note.

Extensions

When Microsoft Edge first arrived in the original release of Windows 10, its single greatest weakness for many was a lack of support for browser extensions. Modern competitors, especially Google Chrome, had built a thriving ecosystem of add-ins that used JavaScript and HTML to extend the capabilities of the browser.

Beginning with Windows 10 version 1607, that's no longer a valid objection to adopting Microsoft Edge. Indeed, you can now peruse the Microsoft Store and find extensions that provide the same functionality available in those competing browsers. Not surprisingly, some of the most useful extensions in the first wave come from Microsoft, including the OneNote Web Clipper and Office Online extensions. Third-party options include LastPass, a popular password manager, and the aptly named AdBlock.

To see all installed extensions, click More > Extensions, which displays a list like the one shown in Figure 9-19. Click Get Extensions From The Store to search for additional extensions.

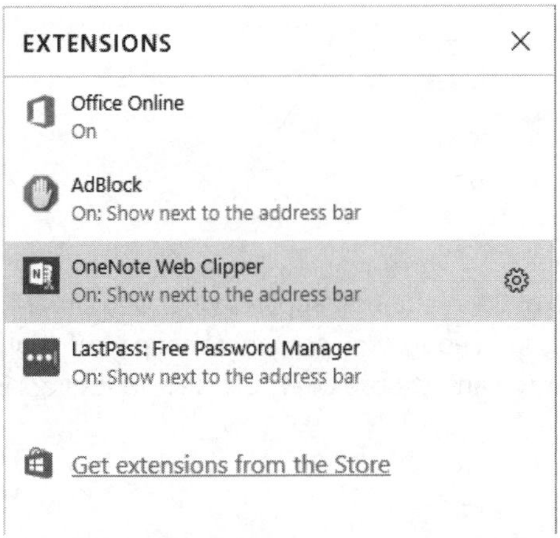

Figure 9-19 Installed extensions show up on this list. Click any extension to see settings, including the option to turn the extension off or uninstall it.

Let the mouse pointer rest over any extension to reveal a gear icon, which is your hint that clicking opens additional options for the extension, including switches for temporarily disabling the extension or uninstalling it if it turns out it doesn't meet your needs, as shown next.

«   OneNote Web Clipper   ×

About

Save anything on the web to OneNote. Clip it to OneNote, organize and edit it, then access it from any device.

Rate and review

Version: 3.1.7.0
Installed: 7/21/2016

This extension is allowed to:

- Read and change content on websites you visit
- Read and change your cookies
- See the websites you visit
- Read and change anything you send or receive from websites
- Store personal browsing data on your device

OneNote Web Clipper

On

Show button next to the address bar

On

Uninstall

Every extension adds an icon at the top of the menu that appears when you click More. For extensions you use infrequently, that's good enough. For those that are part of your regular workflow, feel free to right-click that button and choose the Show Next To Address Bar option.

Privacy and security issues

The beauty of the web is that you can use it to connect instantly to an almost unlimited world of information. The bad news is that some of those destinations are potentially dangerous to your PC's health and to your privacy.

There's no way to make the web perfectly safe, but Windows 10 does include features that help you minimize concerns over security and privacy. We discuss many of those features, including SmartScreen Filter, in Chapter 6, "Managing user accounts, passwords, and credentials," and Chapter 7, "Securing Windows 10 devices."

To make sure that SmartScreen Filter is on in Microsoft Edge, click More > Settings > View Advanced Settings. The switch you're looking for is at the bottom of the Advanced Settings pane.

In Internet Explorer, click Tools > Safety > Turn On SmartScreen Filter. If the link says "Turn Off . . . ," that means the feature is already enabled.

If you care about online security, one smart practice you should adopt for everyday browsing is to prefer secure connections (HTTPS) even on sites that don't traditionally require it. Insecure links to seemingly harmless destinations can leak information about you and can also be used to spoof sites, potentially compromising a machine using a man-in-the-middle attack. In that spirit, we have gone out of our way in this book to use HTTPS links whenever possible. In this section, we focus primarily on features that are unique to web browsing.

Protecting your privacy

Unless you go to extraordinary lengths, simply connecting to a webpage reveals information about your PC, your internet service provider, and your general location. When combined with other details, even a single, seemingly harmless visit to a webpage can become part of your permanent online profile, used by companies and organizations you've never heard of.

You can't completely disappear online, but you can take some common-sense precautions to cover your tracks and avoid disclosing too much about yourself.

Clearing your browser history and other personal information

Your browser keeps a copy of webpages, images, and media you've viewed recently. This cached information is saved to generally inaccessible locations, but even so, it might give another person who has access to your computer more information than you might want him or her to have—especially when combined with cookies, saved form data, saved passwords, and other details.

To wipe away most of your online trail in Microsoft Edge, click More > Settings, and then click Choose What To Clear. These steps take you to the set of check boxes shown in Figure 9-20. (To get to the comparable location in Internet Explorer, click Tools > Safety > Delete Browsing History.)

The most important of these choices are as follows:

- **Browsing History.** This is simply a list of sites you've been to since you last cleared your history, whether you went to them directly or followed another site's hyperlinks. You can also view this list from the History tab of the Hub and right-click any entry to delete that item or all saved addresses from that domain.

- **Cookies And Saved Website Data.** A *cookie* is a small text file that enables a website to store persistent information on your hard disk. Cookies, particularly first-party cookies, are generally benign and useful. Note that removing cookies via this option does not block their arrival in the future. (To do that, see "Blocking cookies and sending Do Not Track requests" later in this chapter.)

- **Cached Data And Files.** These are local copies of pages and media content from sites you visit. The browser saves local copies of this data to speed up its display on subsequent visits.

- **Download History.** This is the list that appears on the Downloads tab of the Hub. Deleting this history here (or clicking Clear All in the Hub—the actions are equivalent) does not remove the downloads themselves, which remain where you put them.

- **Form Data.** Your browser stores some information—for example, your shipping or email address—that you use to fill out forms, simplifying reuse. This option erases all such saved entries.

- **Passwords.** As we discuss later in this chapter (in the "Allowing or not allowing your browser to save sign-in credentials" section), there are pros and cons associated with saving sign-in credentials for websites. If you change your mind after you've allowed the browser to store these credentials, you can erase the data here.

Click Show More to see another half-dozen entries, most of them fairly obscure.

Figure 9-20 Use the options under Clear Browsing Data to specify which elements of your browsing history you want Microsoft Edge to erase.

After making your selections, click Clear. To automatically clear the selected data every time you shut down the browser or sign out, turn on the Always Clear This When I Close The Browser setting.

Squelching history temporarily with InPrivate browsing

If you want to cover your tracks only for a particular browsing session, don't bother fussing with history settings or clearing items after the fact. Instead, open an InPrivate window. In Microsoft Edge, click More > New InPrivate Window. In Internet Explorer, press Ctrl+Shift+P or click Tools > Safety > InPrivate Browsing. When you subsequently close the InPrivate session, the browser deletes any data it stored (session cookies and other temporary files, for example), and no record of the visit is saved in history.

Be aware that browsing privately is not the same as browsing anonymously. Sites you visit can record your IP address, and your network administrator or internet service provider can see which sites you connect to and can capture any unencrypted information you transmit or receive.

During an Internet Explorer InPrivate session, toolbars and extensions are disabled by default. If you want them enabled, click Tools > Internet Options. On the Privacy tab, clear Disable Toolbars And Extensions When InPrivate Browsing Starts.

Blocking cookies and sending Do Not Track requests

Cookies—small bits of information that websites store on your hard disk—come in two flavors. First-party cookies are used by the site you're currently visiting, generally for such purposes as personalizing your experience with the site, storing shopping-cart information, and so on. Third-party cookies are used by a site other than the one you're visiting—such as an advertiser or social media service that has placed an ad or sharing button on the site you're currently visiting.

Cookies do not carry executable code (they're text files), and they can't be used to spread viruses or malware; they can't scurry around your hard disk reading your address book and financial records, for example. A cookie can provide a website only with information you supply while visiting the site. The information a cookie gathers can be read only by pages in the same domain as the one that created the cookie.

Nevertheless, privacy concerns arise when advertisers and web-analytics companies begin to correlate the information from third-party cookies to build a profile of your activities. Because it's not always obvious who's sending you a cookie and what purposes that cookie serves, some people are understandably wary about allowing cookies on their systems.

Both of the Microsoft browsers included with Windows 10 allow you to block either all cookies or third-party cookies. In Microsoft Edge, click More > Settings > View Advanced Settings.

Then open the drop-down list below the Cookies heading. You'll see the following simple set of choices:

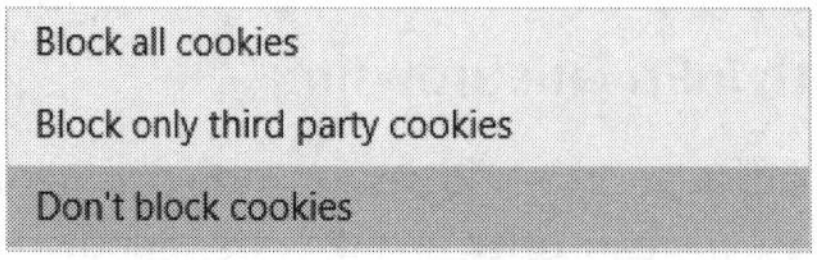

> Block all cookies
>
> Block only third party cookies
>
> Don't block cookies

In Internet Explorer, click Tools > Internet Options. On the Privacy tab, click Advanced to open the Advanced Privacy Settings dialog box, shown in Figure 9-21. There, you can express your preferences separately for first-party and third-party cookies. In addition to accepting or block-ing cookies, you can ask to be prompted each time a first or third party wants to deliver or update a cookie. You're likely to find this choice more trouble than it's worth. In addition, you can also choose to allow all session cookies—cookies that are deleted at the end of your brows-ing session.

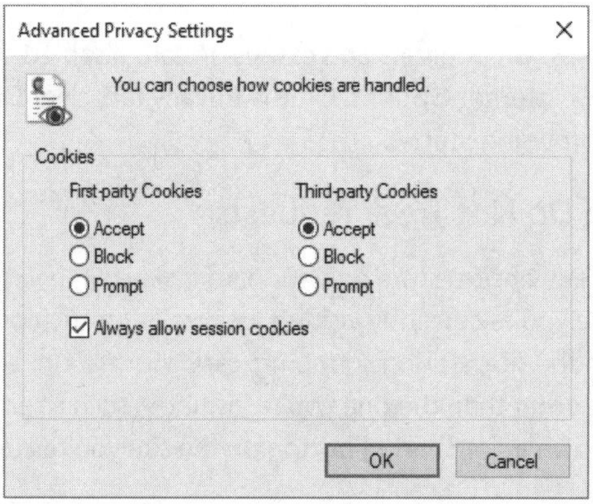

Figure 9-21 It's hard to think of a reason for blocking first-party cookies while allowing cookies from third parties, but Internet Explorer will accept that odd configuration.

In a separate group of settings (which you can access by clicking Sites on the Privacy tab of the Internet Options dialog box), you can block or allow cookies on a per-domain basis.

Sending Do Not Track requests

Some websites use *tracking* capabilities to gather information about your browsing history, information you enter in your browser, and other details of your online life to build a profile that companies can use for targeted advertising and other purposes. If that bothers you, you can ask them to stop.

The Do Not Track (DNT) standard, which is nearing final approval after years of development by a committee of the World Wide Web Consortium (W3C), is now supported by all modern browsers. If DNT is enabled, when you visit a site, the browser sends a DNT=1 header with every request for a new page. Alas, this seemingly straightforward option is not widely accepted, nor is it backed by any technical or legal enforcement mechanisms.

In Windows 8, the option to send Do Not Track requests was turned on by default (included with Internet Explorer's "express settings"). This provoked controversy and resistance from both competing browsers and the advertising industry because the standard, as codified by the W3C, stipulates that DNT requests must result from an active decision by end users. Microsoft reversed its position on the matter, and in both Microsoft Edge and Internet Explorer, DNT is initially turned off. To turn it on in Microsoft Edge, click More > Settings > View Advanced Settings and turn on Send Do Not Track Requests. In Internet Explorer, click Tools > Safety > Turn On Do Not Track Requests.

A far more effective solution for the problem of excessive tracking is ad-blocking software, which has the salutary side effects of speeding page loading times and blocking the most common vectors for serving malware via web exploits. At the time we wrote this chapter, two unrelated extensions, AdBlock and Adblock Plus, were available in the Store as extensions for Microsoft Edge.

Managing and securing your web credentials

When you sign in to a password-protected website using Microsoft Edge or Internet Explorer, you have the option to save your user name and password so that it can enter those credentials for you automatically when you revisit that site. In Microsoft Edge, the prompt looks like this:

| Would you like to save your password for emusic.com? More info | Yes | No | × |

If you click Yes, the user name and password are saved for you. If you click No, the user name is saved but not the password, and you won't be asked to save that password again. Internet Explorer has a similar process for requesting to save credentials.

When you revisit the website, Microsoft Edge (or Internet Explorer) automatically fills in your credentials for you, with the password field masked. (Saved credentials are not filled in automatically when you use InPrivate mode, but the password is filled in when you manually enter the user name.)

If you have multiple credentials saved for a specific site (for example, if you sign in to Microsoft services using more than one Microsoft account), you can position the insertion point in the user name field and press the Down Arrow key to choose from a list of saved credentials.

TROUBLESHOOTING

Windows 10 won't save your user name and password

If your browser doesn't offer to save a specific set of credentials for you, first confirm that the option to save passwords is turned on. Next, check the list of saved credentials (in Microsoft Edge or using Control Panel's Credential Manager). If you see an entry for the uncooperative site, delete it and try again. If that fails, you might be facing a website whose designers have blocked the browser from saving credentials. A third-party password manager might work; otherwise, your only option is entering the password manually.

Windows 10 is responsible for managing web credentials, which are stored in a secure, encrypted vault. Saved credentials are not available directly from any user account but can be accessed by either browser after you're properly authenticated.

Allowing or not allowing your browser to save sign-in credentials

Saving web credentials is an optional feature. It can save you time and trouble when you're revisiting sites—shopping sites, for example—that require you to sign in to an account. It also means anyone who sits down at your unlocked computer can sign in to those same sites without your permission. If you're comfortable typing in your own passwords, or if you use a third-party password manager, you can turn off credential saving in Microsoft Edge. Click More > Settings > View Advanced Settings, and then slide the Offer To Save Passwords switch to the Off position:

Privacy and services

Some features might save data on your device or send it to Microsoft to improve your browsing experience.

Learn more

Offer to save passwords

 Off

Manage my saved passwords

Save form entries

On

Note that disabling the offer to save passwords does not affect any previously saved credentials. To view and manage those credentials, click Manage My Saved Passwords (just below that switch). Rest the mouse pointer over any individual entry in the list of all saved credentials and click the X to remove that item. Right-click to see the option to open that site in a new tab.

If you click a saved password in this list, Microsoft Edge displays the URL, user name, and encrypted password, like this:

You can modify the user name or password in this dialog box and then save your changes, but for your security, Microsoft Edge will not show you (or anyone else using your computer) the current password. (You can, however, inspect passwords using Credential Manager, which we discuss next.)

To reach the comparable setting in Internet Explorer, click Tools (or press Alt+X) and open the Internet Options dialog box. On the Content tab, under the AutoComplete heading, click Settings. The option to save passwords (and to be prompted for approval each time Internet Explorer finds new credentials to save) appears in the AutoComplete Settings dialog box, along with numerous similar options:

Viewing and deleting credentials with Credential Manager

The Manage Passwords button in the AutoComplete Settings dialog box takes you to Credential Manager, a destination you can also reach by searching for Credential Manager in Control Panel. The Web Credentials section of Credential Manager displays a list of user names and passwords saved by either Microsoft Edge or Internet Explorer. Clicking an item reveals details, as shown in Figure 9-22.

The list of credentials here is identical to the one you can see in Microsoft Edge. The Remove option provides a way to clean out credentials you no longer need. Clicking Show allows you to see the saved password for a site, but a casual snoop won't be able to steal that information: For your security, you must first reenter the password you use to sign in to Windows or provide acceptable biometric proof, such as on a device that uses Windows Hello facial recognition.

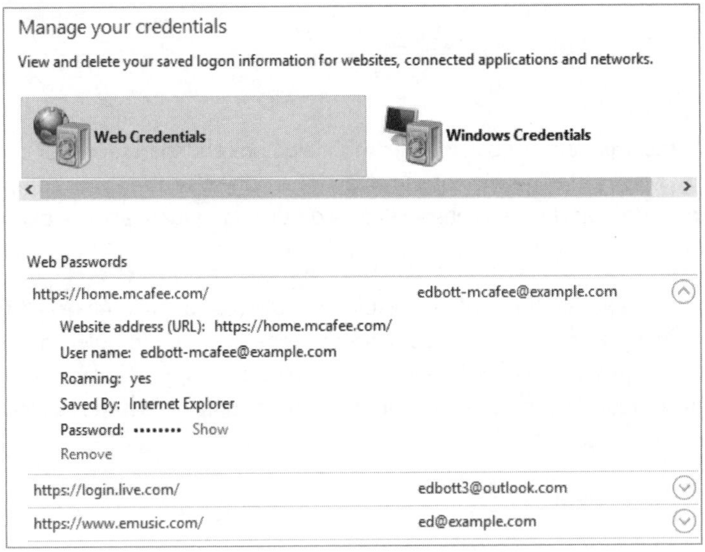

Figure 9-22 Credential Manager, a part of Control Panel, lists all web credentials saved by either browser.

Configuring security zones in Internet Explorer

Internet Explorer uses a system of "security zones" that apply security settings differently for different categories of websites. The zones are called Internet, Local Intranet, Trusted Sites, and Restricted Sites, and you can configure them by going to the Security tab of the Internet

Options dialog box, shown in Figure 9-23. In its quest for a simpler browsing experience, Microsoft Edge does not include any equivalent system.

The four zones are intended to be used as follows. The Restricted Sites zone, designed for sites that you trust the least (or explicitly distrust), has the highest security settings—that is, the maximum in safeguards. The Trusted Sites zone has, by default, a medium level of protection, blocking the download of unsigned ActiveX controls and prompting for permission before downloading other material considered potentially unsafe. The Internet Zone—with medium-high settings—is reserved for all nonintranet sites you have not assigned to the Trusted Sites or Restricted Sites zone. The Intranet Zone, with low security settings, is populated with intranet sites you have not explicitly moved to Trusted Sites or Restricted Sites, sites that bypass your proxy server, and all network servers accessed via a UNC path (*server_name*).

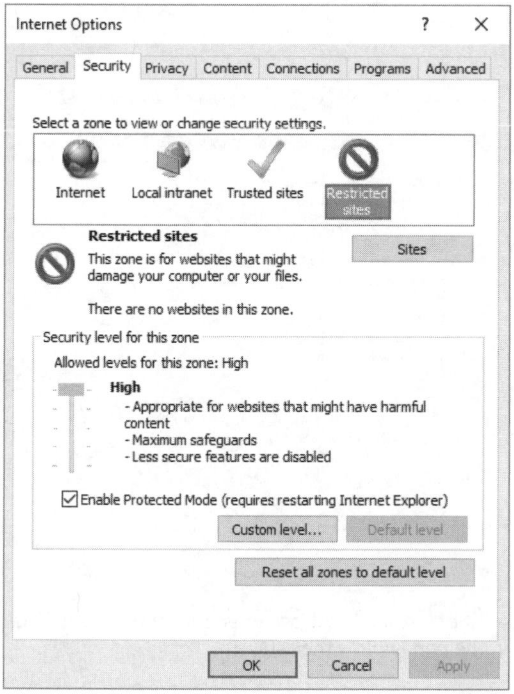

Figure 9-23 Use this dialog box to add sites to specific zones in Internet Explorer or to modify the security settings associated with a zone.

To add sites to a zone, select the zone and click Sites. To change the security settings for a zone, adjust the slider or click Custom Level.

Managing and troubleshooting add-ons in Internet Explorer

One reason Internet Explorer has been relegated to the legacy category is that its add-on model is fundamentally flawed. Through the years, Microsoft's engineers have knocked down some of the most troubling vulnerabilities, but add-ons still remain the weakest link in Internet Explorer.

The Toolbars And Extensions section of the Manage Add-Ons dialog box, shown in Figure 9-24, provides information about whatever ActiveX controls, browser helper objects, and other add-ons you have installed in Internet Explorer. You can inspect version numbers, see how many times an add-on has been used or blocked, and view details of the performance impact of any add-on. More importantly, you can disable an add-on completely, either as a troubleshooting step or as a way to improve the performance and reliability of Internet Explorer.

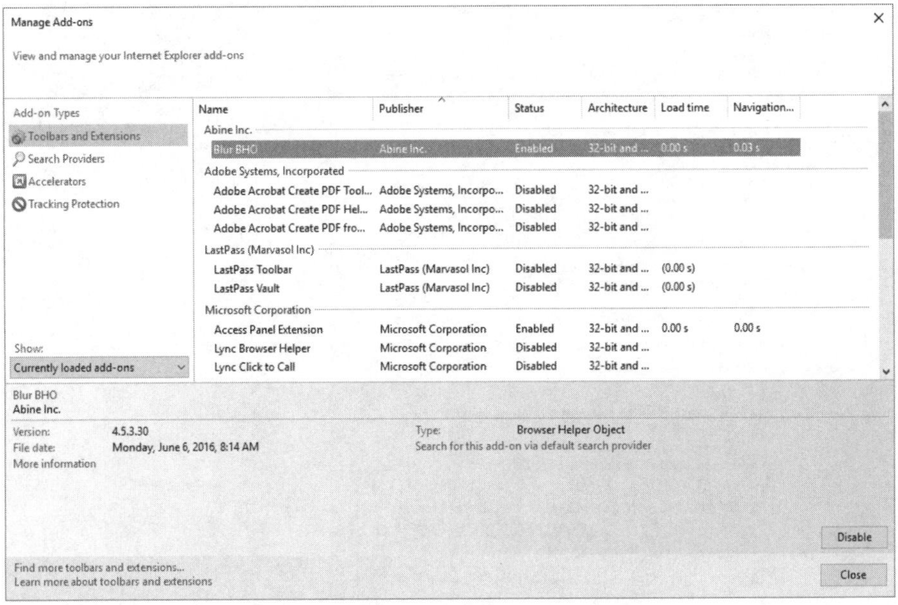

Figure 9-24 Select an item from the list of installed add-ons to enable or disable it. You can view a summary of details about the item in the pane below the list.

When you select an item from the list of add-ons, you can see more details about it in the pane below, including the publisher's name, the version number and file date (if available), and the add-on type. Buttons in the lower right corner let you disable or enable the add-on.

If you're ready to be completely overloaded with information, double-click an add-on's name in the list. If the selected add-on is an ActiveX control, you see an information-rich dialog box like the one shown next:

In the large box here, the asterisk—the wildcard character for "all"—indicates you have approved the add-on to run on all sites. If you're particularly cautious, you might want the option to approve websites on a site-by-site basis. In that case, click the Remove All Sites button. From that point forward, whenever you visit a site that uses that ActiveX control, Internet Explorer will request your permission to run it. If you grant your OK, the domain is added to the list of approved sites.

CHAPTER 10

Productivity and communication tools

In this chapter and Chapter 11, "Music, photos, movies, and games," we discuss specific pro-grams that are included with a default installation of Microsoft Windows 10 or available as free downloads from the Windows Store. We break these programs into two large categories, covering those that serve productive purposes in this chapter and those that entertain in the next. (Although we're well aware that the distinction is fuzzy—one person's amusement might certainly be another's business, and some of us find occasional entertainment in the exploration of mundane workaday programs.)

➤ For information about Microsoft Edge, see Chapter 9, "Cortana and the web."

The list of tools included with Windows grows longer with each iteration, largely because every new version, in addition to introducing new items, must continue to support the work habits developed by users of its predecessors. If you have routinely covered your Windows 7 desktop with color-coded sticky notes, for example, you'll be pleased to know that Sticky Notes—now a modern app—is still with us.

In addition to the obligatory legacy applications, Windows 10 offers a whole set of modern productivity and communication apps, all designed for touch and stylus as well as more tradi-tional input methods. In addition, not installed by default but available without charge from the Store are mobile versions of three Microsoft Office applications: Word, Excel, and PowerPoint. A fourth member of the Office suite, OneNote, is installed by default; you don't have to go to the Store to get it.

NOTE

Because Microsoft regularly delivers feature-enhancing cumulative updates to Windows 10, several apps described in this chapter might have undergone changes—some minor, others significant—by the time you read this. We describe the programs as they appeared as of August 2016, and we'll revisit them with each update to this book.

CHAPTER 10

We begin our survey with a look at the modern communication and productivity apps.

Mail, Calendar, and People

Although they are tightly linked, Mail, Calendar, and People have separate entries in Start. Mail and Calendar, in fact, are two faces of the same unified app package, appearing in Task Manager as Outlook Mail and Outlook Calendar, respectively. You can switch between them by tapping or clicking icons in the lower left corner of the window. And the People app, populated by the accounts you set up in Mail or Calendar, provides a directory of potential addressees when you create Mail messages or invite associates to a meeting. Type the beginning of a contact's name or email address on the To line of a message, and if that name or address is among your contacts in People, the To line will be completed for you.

Inside OUT

Take another look at Mail and Calendar

If you have been using Windows 10 from the start, it's possible you took a cursory look at Mail and Calendar and found them too underpowered for serious use. If that describes you, we urge you to consider a second look. The programs have improved considerably since the initial release of Windows 10—and are likely to continue improving as Microsoft rolls out additional updates to the operating system.

You might find Mail particularly useful if your heavyweight mail client (Outlook 2016, for example) is not available to you on your portable devices. You can stick with the heavyweight on your desktop and use Mail to read and reply while you're on the go.

Setting up and using Mail

The first time you open the Mail app, you'll be asked to set up accounts, as shown next. If you sign on to Windows using a Microsoft account, the email address associated with that account appears at the top of this setup page. If that's the only email account you use, you can move on by clicking Ready To Go. If you log on locally or if you have other accounts, click Add Account. Mail supports Exchange, Outlook.com, Google accounts (Gmail and Google Apps), Yahoo! Mail, and iCloud, as well as generic accounts based on the POP and IMAP standards. The setup process is straightforward, prompting you for your email address and password, as shown next.

Accounts

First things first. Let's add your accounts.

Outlook
dpaschke2016@outlook.com

+ Add account

Ready to go

If your account requires you to enter additional settings, such as the names of your incoming and outgoing servers, scroll to the bottom of the Add An Account list and then click Advanced Setup:

Add an account ✕

Choose an account

Exchange
Exchange, Office 365

Google

Yahoo! Mail

iCloud

Other account
POP, IMAP

Advanced setup

Close

Adding and deleting accounts

To add email accounts subsequently, open Settings by clicking the gear icon in the lower left corner of the Mail window. Click Manage Accounts > Add Account. To delete an existing account, select it in Settings. Note that you cannot delete the address associated with your Microsoft account.

Linking inboxes

If you have two or more email accounts, Mail will create a separate inbox for each. Thus, you'll see all your messages from the first account, followed by all your messages from the second, and so on. You might find it more convenient to link the accounts, thereby creating a unified inbox. To do this, open Settings > Manage Accounts > Link Inboxes. Mail presents a dialog box listing accounts available to be linked:

Link inboxes

When you link inboxes from your different accounts, you'll be able to see all the messages from those accounts in one inbox.

Linked inbox name

Linked inbox

Choose inboxes to link:

☑ Outlook 2 - dpaschke2016@outlook.com

☑ Gmail - paschkedorena@gmail.com

| Save | Cancel |

Supply a name for the combined inbox if you don't like the one that Mail proposes. Then select each account you want to be part of the combine. If you change your mind, you can unlink the accounts by returning to this dialog box and removing check marks.

Setting sync options

To configure sync options for an account, go to Settings > Manage Accounts, select the account you want to configure, and then click Change Mailbox Sync Settings. Note that with a combined inbox, you still configure the component accounts individually. For example, if you have one email account for personal messages and another for business, you can opt to have the one synced every 15 minutes and the other only once every two hours. If you have an account you use primarily as a repository for commercial messages, you might want to set that account up so that only the most recent week's worth of messages appear in Mail.

The default sync settings, shown in Figure 10-1, reflect Mail's intended use as a mail client for users on the go. To save battery and disk space, Mail, by default, bases its sync frequency on your usage patterns. If you use the app with any significant frequency, it will fetch messages at shorter time intervals. In any case, you can override the program's decision making and config-ure a predetermined sync interval by opening the drop-down list at the top of the dialog box.

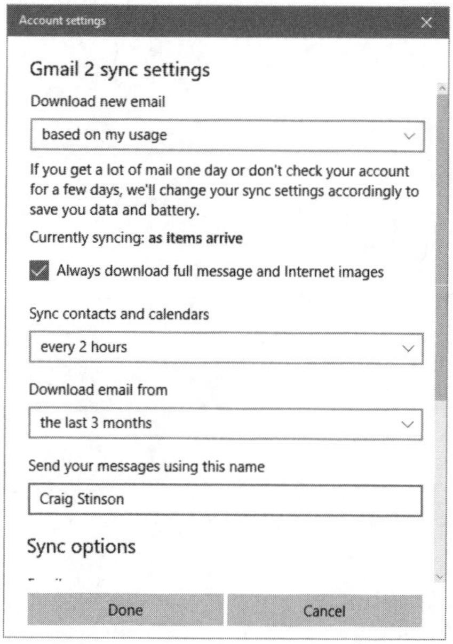

Figure 10-1 By default, the frequency with which Mail syncs messages from your mail server is based on your usage patterns. You can opt to sync more or less frequently.

Because sync settings apply to the device on which they're configured and do not transfer to other devices, you can easily set up different devices for different usage scenarios. Let's say, for example, that you have a desktop computer for use in the office and a tablet for use on the go. You might configure the office PC to download all mail from your server (by opening the Down-load Email From drop-down list and clicking Any Time) but have the traveling machine collect only messages from the last two weeks.

Setting notification options

By default, Mail announces the arrival of new mail by posting a notification to Action Center. You have the option of adding banner and audible notifications. (Banners are pop-up notifications—colloquially known as "toast"—that appear in the lower right corner of your screen.) Of course, you can also dispense with notifications altogether. To make your wishes known, go to Settings > Notifications. Figure 10-2 shows the dialog box.

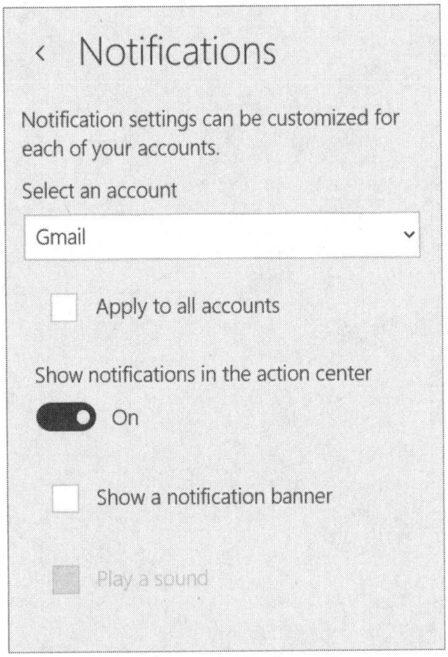

‹ Notifications

Notification settings can be customized for each of your accounts.

Select an account

Gmail ⌄

☐ Apply to all accounts

Show notifications in the action center

⬤ On

☐ Show a notification banner

☐ Play a sound

Figure 10-2 Only Action Center notifications are on by default. If you choose to add banners, an additional option to play a sound becomes available.

Inside OUT

Use Mail for notifications even if you prefer a different mail client

You might already be using a mail client other than Mail and have no need to use Mail for sending and reading messages. If your preferred client does not feed notifications to Action Center, you might still want to set up Mail for that purpose. You can then continue sending and receiving email with the tools you're accustomed to using but rely on Mail to provide Action Center notifications.

Reading and responding to mail

Mail devotes the majority of its screen space to a list of message headers on the left and a reading area on the right. To read a message, tap or click it in the headers pane. To delete a message, click or tap the trash can icon near the upper right corner of the header entry:

The icons to the left and right of the trash can let you archive a message or flag it as important. All three of these functions are also available via a shortcut menu if you right-click a message heading. If you choose to flag important messages, you can also filter the Inbox to show only those flagged messages. Click the drop-down arrow to the right of the current folder heading to see your filtering options:

Creating a new message

To create a new message, click the New Mail icon. Above the To and Subject lines, you'll find a ribbon that provides an elaborate set of editing tools, derived from Microsoft Word. For example, a wealth of styling options is available via the Format tab on the ribbon. Use the arrows on the ribbon to see the full set of options at your disposal:

Format	Insert	Options							Discard	Send
B	*I*	U	⌄	☰	☰	⌄	Heading 1	⌄	Undo	Redo

To attach a file to your message, click the Insert tab. You can use that part of the ribbon to insert tables, pictures, and hyperlinks as well. Alternatively, you can create an attachment by dragging a file into your new message document. Mail also provides a proofreader; click Options and then click Spelling to check the spelling of your messages.

Using folders

The pane to the left of the message headers provides a list of system folders—Inbox, Drafts, Sent Items, and Archive—plus any folders you designated as favorites. (If the Mail window is too narrow, you'll need to click the hamburger icon to see the folder list.) Other folders you have created on your mail server or within Mail are listed in an additional pane that appears if you click More. To create a folder in Mail, click More, and then click Create New Folder (the plus icon), to the right of All Folders or, in a combined inbox, to the right of the account name.

You can add any of your own folders to the Favorites list by right-clicking the folder and then clicking Add To Favorites. Once ensconced in the Favorites list, a folder name makes a convenient drag-and-drop target for received messages. You can also move a message from the headers pane to any folder by right-clicking the header and then clicking Move. Or, if you're working at a touchscreen, you can assign a swipe left or swipe right to the Move command. We discuss Quick Actions momentarily.

Searching for messages

To search for a message, type in the Search box at the top of the message header pane and then click the Search icon. Mail searches the current folder. To search everywhere, click the All Mail link in the Favorites list.

The Search function is, of course, handy for relocating that crucial item of mail that has disappeared in the forest of trivia. But it's also useful when you want to move a collection of messages from your inbox to an appropriate subfolder. For example, if you have a subfolder called Contoso and a few dozen inbox items from Contoso, you can bulk-ship these items to the subfolder quickly and easily by searching for Contoso. When the search results appear, press Ctrl+A to select them all, and then right-click and click Move.

Setting Quick Actions and other options

On a touchscreen PC or tablet, you can make quick work of mail-handling tasks by means of Mail's Quick Actions feature. (See Figure 10-3.) Click or tap Settings > Quick Actions to configure this feature.

You can assign one action to a right swipe and another for swiping left. By default, as shown in the figure, putting your finger or stylus on a message header and whisking it off to the right flags the message as important (or clears the flag if it has already been set). Dragging in the other direction archives the message. Alternatives for either direction include deleting a message, marking it as read or unread, and moving it to a folder. Note that you swipe the header, not the body of the message. In case you accidentally swipe the wrong header, Mail provides an Undo command at the bottom of the message pane.

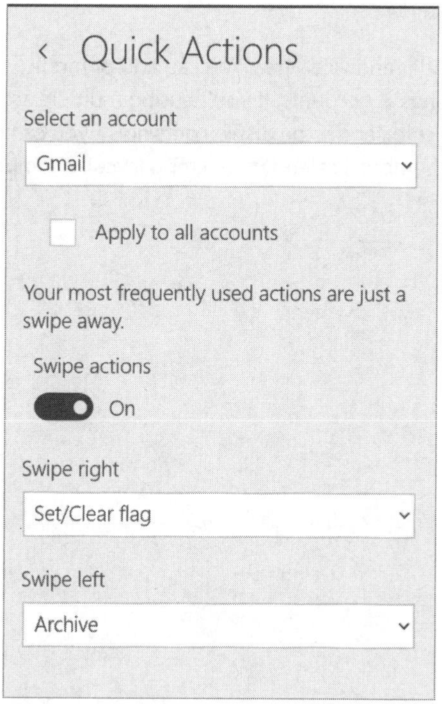

Figure 10-3 The Quick Actions section of the Settings pane lets you configure the way Mail responds to swipes with your finger or a stylus and provides easy ways to manage incoming messages.

If you assign Move to a Quick Action, you get an additional choice:

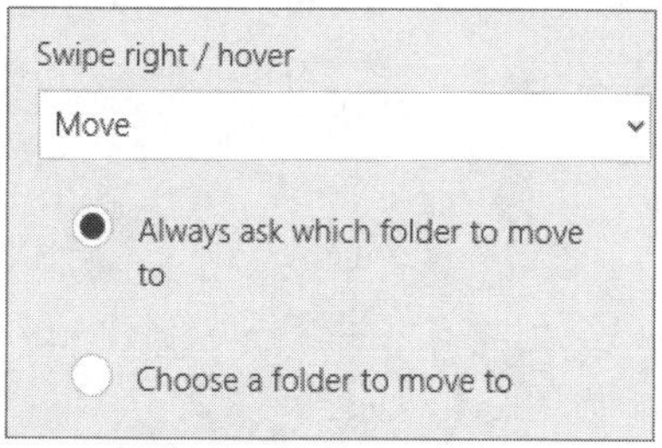

If you find yourself routinely moving a great many messages to the same folder, assign a swipe to the Move command, click Choose A Folder To Move To, and then pick the folder from the list that appears.

Setting up and using Calendar

In both Mail and Calendar, you can use the two icons at the lower left corner to switch from one app to the other. If you're already running Mail, a quick tap takes you straight to Calendar. Alternatively, you can launch Calendar from Start.

Accounts set up in Mail are used in Calendar and vice versa. You can add or modify accounts in Calendar as you would in Mail; click Settings > Accounts. If you're using multiple accounts, your Calendar events will be distinguished by color, and if the display gets noisy, you can use the check boxes in the left pane, below the thumbnail calendar, to filter particular components of your composite calendar:

If you don't see this pane at the left of your screen, click or tap the hamburger icon in the upper left corner. Doing this removes or redisplays the left pane. (You'll find it useful particularly on a small display.)

Adding an event

To add an event to your calendar, either click or tap New Event, or click the calendar itself. If you click New Event, you get the full Details window for the event. If you click a day or an hour on the calendar, you get a smaller version of this window, and you can move to the full view by clicking More Details. In either case, if you have Calendar configured to use more than one account, you'll want to specify which account the new event should belong to.

In the Details view, you can use the Reminder list to specify your preferences regarding alerts. Calendar defaults to a 15-minute heads-up, but you have lots of alternatives, including None. Note that Calendar's live tile (if you have the app pinned to Start) will also alert you to upcoming events. Set the size to wide if you want to see multiple events on the live tile. Depending on your settings, Cortana can offer reminders as well.

Figure 10-4 shows the details of a recurring event. To create such an item, click the circular Repeat icon and specify your parameters. Calendar offers daily, weekly, monthly, and yearly options.

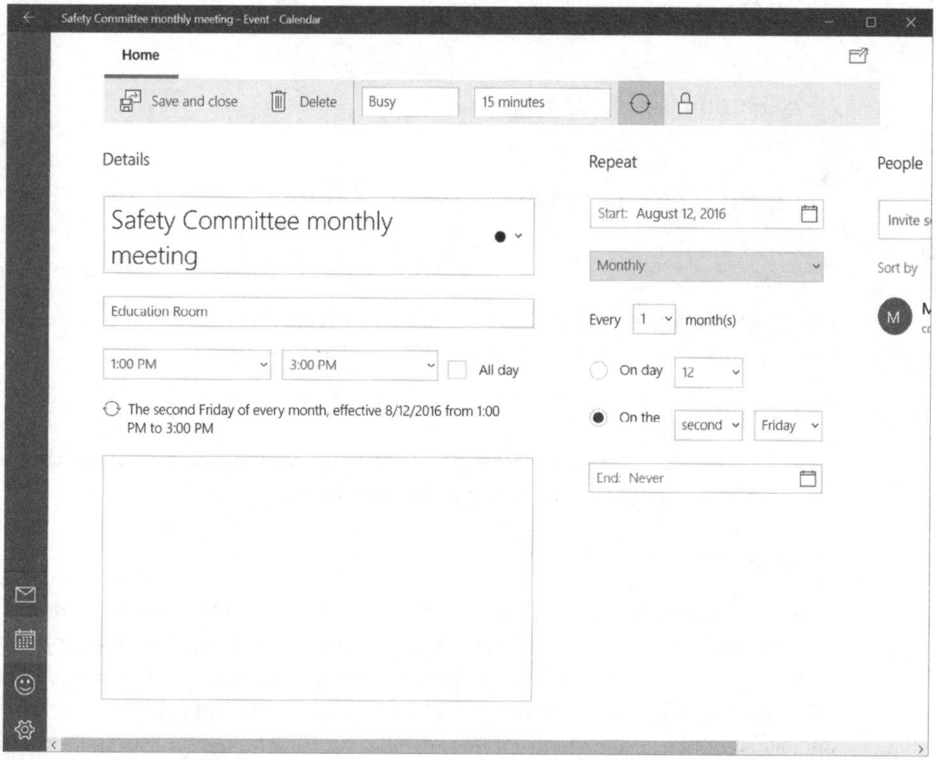

Figure 10-4 Clicking Repeat opens a new set of options, where you can specify yearly, monthly, weekly, or daily parameters for a recurring event.

Inviting others to a meeting

To create a meeting event and invite others to join, add the email addresses of your invitees to the People section of your Details view. Then click Send. Each of the invitees will get an email message allowing him or her to send back a yes-no-maybe response:

CS	**Craig Stinson** 9:28 PM

Campaign kickoff
To: cdstinson@gmail.com

When   Monday, August 15, 2016 8a - 10:30a   View calendar
Where

✓ Accept   ? Tentative ⌄   ✕ Decline ⌄

Edit the response before sending

Send the response now

Don't send email to the organizer

The Accept, Tentative, and Decline links, with associated drop-down options, make it easy for the invitee to respond to the invitation.

CAUTION

Calendar does not currently support time zones. Meeting invitees will all see the meeting time as stated by the person making the invitation.

Setting options

To specify the days of your work week and the hours of your work day, click Settings > Calendar Settings. You can do a few other things as well on the Settings page, such as opting for week numbers and switching to alternative languages and calendars. If you stick with English, the calendar choices include Hijiri, Umm al-Qura, Hebrew Lunar, and Saka Era, in addition to the default Gregorian. Many other options are available for languages other than English.

Printing from Calendar

To print, click Show (the ellipsis icon in the upper right corner of the Calendar window) and then click Print. There you can specify the starting date for your output as well as whether to print the day, week, work week, or month. A preview button gives you the opportunity to check before you commit.

Adding or editing contacts with People

People acts as a repository for contacts derived from the accounts you set up in Mail or Calendar. As the following illustration shows, People lists your contacts, summarizing recent communications and calendar entries for the selected contact in a Timeline pane. In the Timeline pane, you can click an entry to open a message in Mail or Calendar:

You can edit a contact's information by selecting the contact in the left pane and clicking the Edit icon (shaped like a pencil) in the center pane. If you have more than one entry for a contact, you can use the Link icon (to the right of the Edit icon) to consolidate them. Note that a great many fields become available when you click Other on the edit screen:

Using Skype

Skype, Microsoft's internet video telephony and messaging tool, appears in various guises. One is the legacy Skype desktop application, which has been available for years in Windows 7. Given that Windows 7 will be supported until January 2020, you can expect that Microsoft will maintain this desktop app over the next several years. Windows 10 users will also find Skype in a universal app, which was released as a preview in August 2016. In addition to the desktop and modern apps, Skype is available at *https://web.skype.com*.

These three faces of Skype are functionally equivalent and use the same accounts and contact lists. You can log in and use whichever seems most convenient and comfortable on the device you're using.

Microsoft also offers a more richly featured product called Skype for Business (formerly known as Lync), as part of the business and enterprise versions of Office 365. For information about features and pricing of Skype for Business, see *http://skype.com/business*.

Getting started

When you first run Skype, the program prompts you to create an account or sign in to an existing one. You can use your Microsoft account if you don't already have a Skype account.

Before you start making calls, you might want to check your video, microphone, and speaker settings. You can do this by clicking Echo/Sound Test Service in the Contacts pane. Alternatively, open the Tools menu, choose Options, and then click either Audio Settings or Video Settings.

To add contacts, click Search. Type your contact's Skype account name, if you know it, or an email address. You can also type the contact's name, but this approach might produce a long list of Skype users with identical first and last names. When you find the person you want to add, select the name and click Add To Contacts. Your contact will then receive a request message.

Note that if you receive an unwanted contact solicitation and choose to decline, the Decline button provides additional options to block the request or report it as spam.

With your equipment checked out and your contacts list populated, you might then want to flesh out your own profile—the information your contacts will see about you. The profile screen appears when you click your own name in the upper left corner of the window, and here you can add phone information and many other details. (Click Show Full Profile to see the complete list of fields you can change.) If you shot your profile photo with the rear-facing camera by mistake or simply want to transmit a different image, click Change Picture.

Placing or answering an audio or video call

To initiate an internet call, click your contact's name and then choose one of the options that appear on the right side of the screen:

Click More (the ellipsis icon) to add one or more people to the call. The phone icon in the center makes the call audio only. Choose the camera icon on the left to send video as well. You can also switch in and out of video during the call if the need arises—for example, if your internet connection is not strong enough to support video transmission.

Similar buttons appear if someone places a call to you. Before you answer, you'll also get an audio signal to alert you to the call.

Calling people who don't have Skype or aren't online

With Skype, you can also place Voice-over-Internet-Protocol (VoIP) calls to people who don't have Skype accounts or are not online. The calls are charged at per-minute rates that vary by country or region. Before placing a call, you can buy credit by opening the Skype menu and choosing Buy Skype Credit. For users in the United States, credit is available in increments of $10 and $25.

When you're ready to call, click Call Phones. On the dialer that appears, open the Choose Country/Region drop-down list, select the country or region you're calling, click the numbers to dial, and then click the phone icon.

Sending text or video messages, pictures, or files

To send a text message, select a contact name and then type in the text box that appears at the bottom of the window. (You can also send text while you're in an audio or video call.) To send a video message to someone, click the paper-clip icon to the left of the text box and then click Send Video Message. Your camera will come to life, your shining visage will appear on the screen, and you can click the red Record button when you're ready to start. Click the Send button when you're satisfied and ready to transmit.

To send a photo or a file, click the paper-clip icon and choose Send Photo or Send File.

Using OneNote

The full-featured desktop version of OneNote, OneNote 2016, is also available to all Windows 10 users. For those with Office 365 subscriptions or a standalone version of Microsoft Office, OneNote is part of the application package; no separate download is required. A personal version of OneNote 2016 is also available to users without Office. You can download it free from *https://www.onenote.com/download*. The personal version is limited to storing notebooks in OneDrive. All OneNote users with Office 365 subscriptions can store notebooks locally or in OneDrive. Those with Business or Enterprise subscriptions also have access to OneDrive for Business.

With both OneNote 2016 and the universal OneNote app, which should you use? There's no compelling reason to choose one over the other. You can use both, and unless you have turned off the option to sync notebooks automatically, your notebooks will be accessible from either version. The universal app might be ideal when you're on the go or when you're concerned with reading your notes (and those that others have shared with you) and making simple annotations. For more extensive editing and note taking, and for such things as inserting recorded audio or video notes, you'll probably want the much larger feature set provided by OneNote 2016.

A click or a tap on the Note button in Action Center opens your current notebook in the modern app. You can use this whenever a thought or event occurs that you want to record.

If you're new to OneNote, you need to learn these core principles to get started:

- Like the other Office mobile apps (Excel, Word, and PowerPoint), OneNote saves everything you enter immediately and instantly. If your notebook is stored on OneDrive, you have access to it from anywhere.

- Notes are stored in *notebooks*, which are subdivided into *sections*. Each section consists of one or more *pages*. OneNote gives you a notebook to start with, and that notebook contains a single section (called New Section 1) consisting of a single page (called Untitled Page). Sections are identified by tabs arrayed across the top, and pages are listed vertically, on the left (in the mobile version) or the right (in the desktop version). Click the plus signs to add sections or pages.

- OneNote is a free-form editor. You can type or jot anywhere on the page. With drawing tools, you can annotate your annotations.

With the desktop version of OneNote, you can create shared notebooks for collaborative projects. Click File to see a list of your notebooks. To share an existing notebook, click Invite People To This Notebook, below a notebook's name. (The notebook must be stored on OneDrive or OneDrive for Business for this link to be available.) To create a new shared notebook, click File > New. Choose a location, supply a name, and then click Create Notebook. In a moment, the following prompt will appear:

Click Invite People, and then supply email addresses.

To share a notebook, click the Share icon at the upper right corner of the window. Shared notebooks, like all others, are usable in both versions of OneNote.

Using the mobile versions of Word, Excel, and PowerPoint

Microsoft also provides touch-optimized versions of three major Office programs: Word, Excel, and PowerPoint. Comparable to the mobile edition of OneNote described in the previous section, these mobile Office apps are modern apps that are ideal for quick reads and edits on tablets and smartphones. Their large and well-spaced user-interface controls make them easy to manage with fingers and styli.

CHAPTER 10

NOTE

The mobile Office apps are free (you can find them in the Windows Store), but their full functionality requires an Office 365 subscription. Without a subscription, you can open and read Office documents, but you cannot edit or save documents. In any case, you should consider these mobile items as on-the-go complements to their desktop suite-mates. For extensive document generation and editing, you'll want the larger feature set that comes with Office 365 or the standalone Office packages.

Features common to the mobile Office apps

Here are some important features shared by all three mobile Office apps:

- **Autosave.** Changes are saved instantly and automatically. The name under which the current document is being saved appears in the center of the screen, above the ribbon:

You can change the name by clicking it and typing a new one, but you might find it easier to tap the File menu and then tap Save. As Figure 10-5 shows, the Save command serves the function that's assigned to the Save As command in other programs.

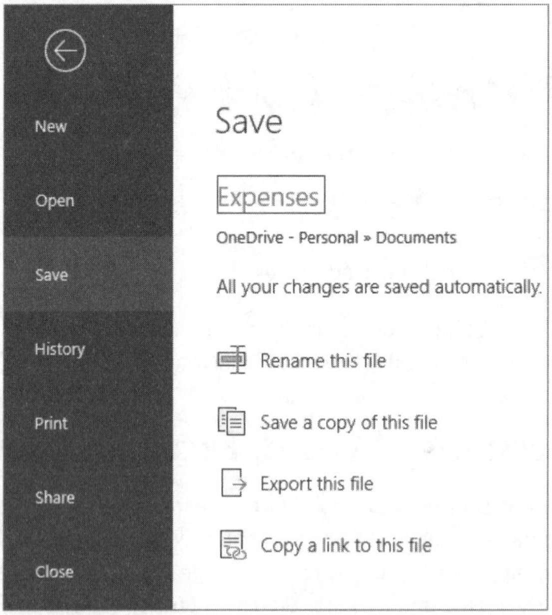

Save

Expenses

OneDrive - Personal » Documents

All your changes are saved automatically.

New
Open
Save
History
Print
Share
Close

Rename this file

Save a copy of this file

Export this file

Copy a link to this file

Figure 10-5 The Save command shows you where and under what name your file is being automatically saved. You can rename or copy the file here.

If you're making tentative edits, or if you're concerned that an errant press of your finger or hand might change the file's content awkwardly, consider working with a copy instead of the original. You can make a copy by visiting the Save command.

● **Sharing.** By clicking the Share icon in the upper right corner of the ribbon, you can extend read or read/write privileges to other people. As Figure 10-6 shows, you can attach a message to your invitation. Below the message appear the names of everyone who already has access to the document.

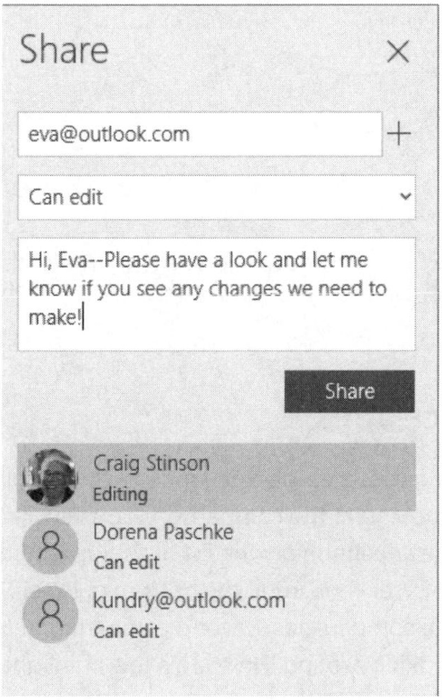

Figure 10-6 By clicking the Share icon, you can send a personalized invitation to a friend or coworker and see who is already on the team.

● **Help.** Near the Share icon on all three apps is a lightbulb icon. This provides access to the "Tell me what you want to do" feature. When you indicate what you want to accomplish here, the program will—if it can—carry out the action you request instead of direct-ing you to an explanation of how to do it. To save you stylus-strokes, a list of commonly requested actions appears, under the heading Try. (See Figure 10-7.) If what you want isn't there, you can type the task. If all else fails—for example, if the program can't understand or carry out your order—you'll be redirected to an internet help source.

CHAPTER 10

Figure 10-7 "Tell me what you want to do" can provide a quicker alternative to traditional Help commands. If it can, the mobile Office app will carry out your instructions directly, without requiring you to do any additional steps.

Exploring the mobile Office apps

If you're familiar with the desktop counterparts of the three mobile Office apps, you might want to start exploring the mobile apps by looking at the comparison topics available via the "Tell me what you want to do" feature. These appear below the list of suggested entries. Figure 10-7, for example, shows the topic Compare Excel Versions at the bottom of Excel Mobile's "Tell me" list. These commands lead you to useful comparisons. Beyond comparing, the best way to learn about these apps is, quite literally, by poking around. Here are a few highlights.

Using Read view in Word Mobile

Word Mobile has a Read view that makes perusing a document on a small screen more comfortable. To get there, tap Read on the View tab or click the Read icon, between the "Tell me" icon and the Share icon, near the upper right edge of the screen. As Figure 10-8 shows, the Read tab offers a number of useful options for sizing, coloring, and spacing text. Read view opens in full-screen mode; to see the Read tab, click the three dots at the upper right side of the window. To get out of Read view, click Edit on the Read tab.

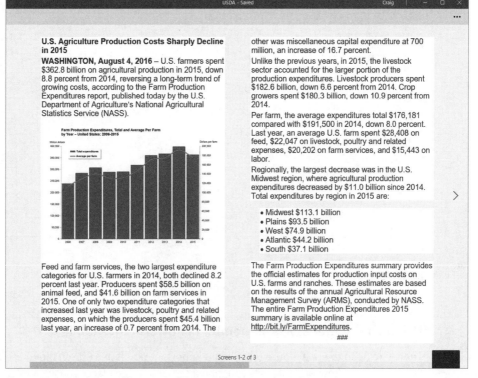

Figure 10-8 Read view offers a set of sizing, coloring, and spacing options to ease your eyes on a small screen.

Simplifying formula entry in Excel Mobile

Options on the Home tab provide quick access to many of Excel Mobile's commonly used commands. You can create sums here, for example, or sort rows in a table, insert rows and columns, and so on. For more complex formula entry, however, click the Formula icon (*fx*) at the left edge, below the ribbon. Using the categorized function list that descends, you can enter the formula you need with a minimum of typing, as shown next.

Using your finger as a laser pointer in PowerPoint Mobile

There's no need to use a mouse to highlight important points in a PowerPoint presentation. Start your slide show, and then use your finger to point to the places you want to underscore. After a pause, your finger press will produce a red dot on the presentation, which you can move as you would a highlighter.

Using Maps

Mapping applications have long been one of the indispensable tools of modern life. Microsoft's modern Maps app should serve you well, whether you want to explore a new city, plot a road trip, find a restaurant or a bank, print a set of turn-by-turn directions to take with you on the road, or just enjoy aerial views of the world or your neighborhood.

On first run, Maps asks for permission to track your location information. If you consent, Maps will plant a marker at your current location. When you start Maps, it always opens to whatever map or view you were using last, but pressing Ctrl+Home displays your current location, assuming the program knows what that is.

Searching for places and services

To find a location, click the Search tool on the left or press Ctrl+F. You can type an address or the name of a place known to Maps—an institution or a restaurant, for example. As shown in Figure 10-9, Maps displays the location on the map, one or more street-side pictures, and other interesting information—including, in this example, a link to a Wikipedia article. If you search for a restaurant known to Maps, you'll also be rewarded with reviews, hours, and website information. The panel of icons in the What's Nearby section of this information pane offers single-click searches for nearby restaurants, attractions, malls, hotels, banks, hospitals, and parking facilities.

Figure 10-9 In addition to displaying your search item on the map, Maps displays a street-side picture and a considerable amount of related information.

Getting directions

To get directions, click the Directions icon, directly below the Search icon, and then type your starting and ending points. (One of them might already be in place if you just searched for it.) Maps responds with a set of route alternatives:

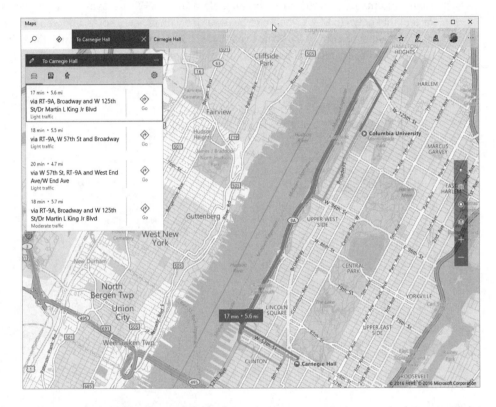

Click or tap the left side of one of these alternatives to see particular steps in the route. Click or tap Go to see and hear turn-by-turn instructions.

Maps defaults to showing driving directions. To see public transportation information instead, click the bus icon near the upper left corner of the directions pane. Maps shows you the best route and includes helpful information about how to watch for your stop on the transit system. For a trip from Columbia University to Carnegie Hall, for example, the resulting instructions include this tip about getting off the train: "Previous stop is 66 St – Lincoln Center. If you reach 50 St., you've gone too far."

If you'd rather walk than ride, click the humanoid icon next to the bus icon. Maps calculates its walking time at a rate of about 2.3 miles per hour. If you usually walk or ride public transit, you can change the default by clicking See More (the ellipsis icon in the upper right corner of the screen), clicking Settings, and opening the Preferred Directions list.

Beginning with the Windows 10 Anniversary Edition, Maps saves all searches and requests for directions in individual tabs. Now you can do such things as save a map of nearby Chinese restaurants on one tab, Korean restaurants on another, and Thai on a third—and switch between them as your mood dictates:

On the right side of a map's display, Maps offers a panel of additional options, allowing you to change the compass heading, switch between plane and elevation views, display your current location, switch between aerial and street views, and zoom in and out.

Picking favorites

Got a favorite place you want to come back to? Search for it once, and then click the Save button in the panel to the left of the map:

Clicking Save adds the place to your favorites list; you can retrieve the items in that list by clicking the star icon near the upper right corner of Maps.

CHAPTER 10

Sharing maps and creating reminders

To send someone a map, display the map, and then click See More > Share. Maps opens a panel of sharing options:

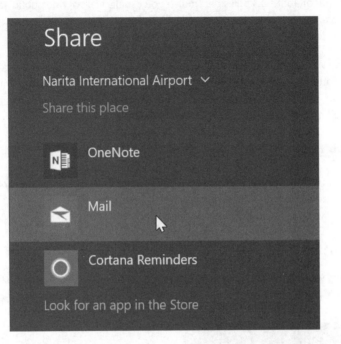

You can email the current map by clicking Mail. Depending on your system, you might find additional sharing options—for example, Facebook. If the person with whom you're sharing doesn't have Maps, you can send a screenshot instead of the map itself. To do this, click the arrow to the right of the name of the place and then click Screenshot, as shown next:

You can create a reminder to yourself associated with a particular place by clicking See More > Share, and then clicking Cortana Reminders. The following appears:

Type what you want to be reminded to do in the box labeled Remember To. Then click Place. On the ensuing screen, you can specify whether you want to be reminded at the time you arrive or the time you depart.

Annotating maps and measuring distances

With a touchscreen and stylus, you can take advantage of Maps' ink support. Click the Windows Ink Toolbar icon, directly to the right of the Favorites icon, in the upper right corner of the display. The toolbar descends:

To draw on the current map, tap the Ballpoint Pen tool, the one at the left end of the toolbar. With the drop-down arrow that appears, you can select a color for your drawing. Then use your stylus to draw. Next to the Ballpoint Pen tool is a Measure Distance tool. Tap that, use the stylus to draw a line between two points, and Maps responds by displaying the distance along that line:

Ink on a map remains until you erase it. That means you can mark up a map, close the program, return later and find your annotations in place. To erase, tap the third tool on the Windows Ink toolbar. To remove everything, tap the Erase All Ink command that appears. To remove a particular annotation, tap it.

Downloading maps for offline use

If you're out and about without a data connection for your portable device, you can still use maps that you previously downloaded. To take advantage of this feature, go to Settings > System > Offline Maps. Figure 10-10 shows the Settings page. To download a map, click the plus sign. On subsequent screens, you can choose the particular map you want.

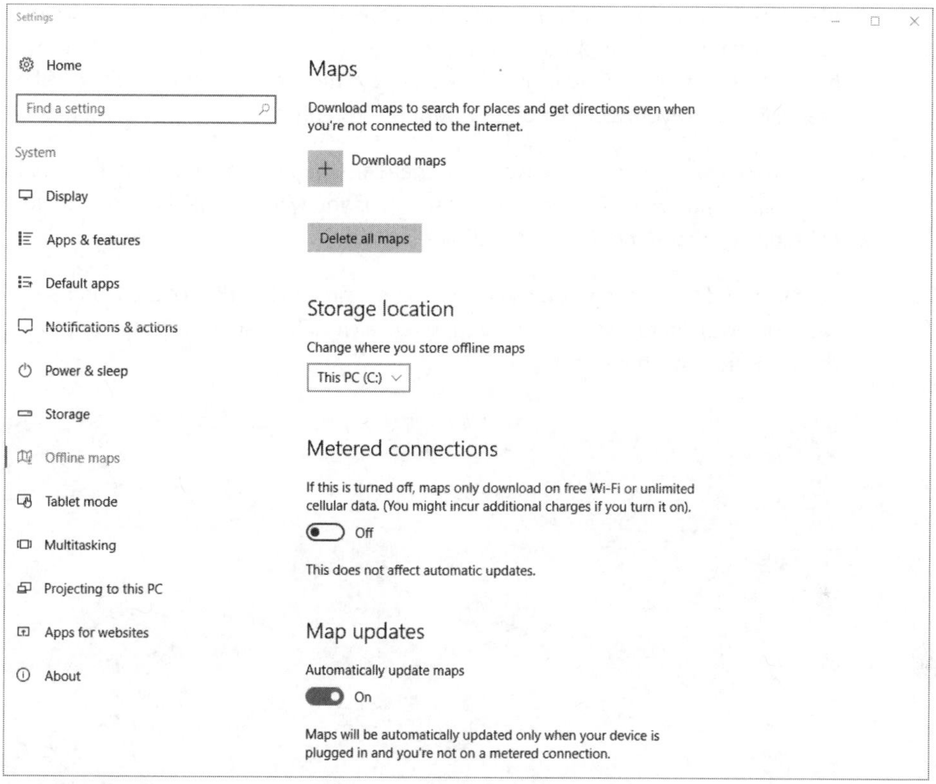

Figure 10-10 The options for downloading offline maps are located at Settings > System > Offline Maps.

Maps are updated frequently. To ensure that you have the most recent data, set the Map Updates switch to on.

Using Alarms & Clock

As the name implies, Alarms & Clock will give you a nudge at a prescribed time. You can configure an alarm to sound once only or to repeat on particular days. For example, if you use an alarm to rouse you from sleep, you can have one alarm for workdays and another for weekends. You can also attach a text message to an alarm—to let you know why you're being roused.

Alarms will also wake your computer from sleep—provided your hardware supports InstantGo. For more information about this feature, previously known as Connected Standby, see *https://bit.ly/InstantGo*. If Alarms & Clock displays the message "Notifications will only show if the PC is awake," your device does not support InstantGo.

To set a new alarm, click the plus sign on the Alarm page. Be sure to click the Save icon on the New Alarm page when you have things set up as you want them. To remove an item from your collection of alarms, right-click it and click Delete.

On the World Clock page, you can check out the time in any part of the world and compare it with your local time. Click the plus sign to add a city. The display uses shading to show where the sun is up and where it's not:

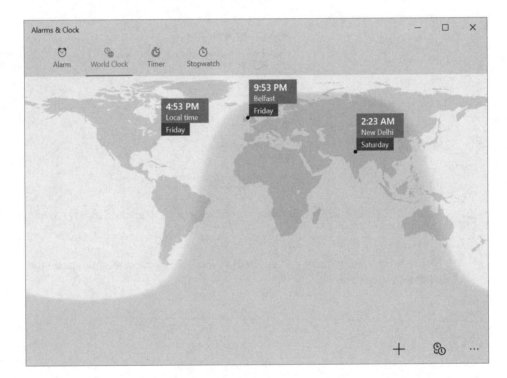

The remaining two pages in Alarms & Clock provide basic timer and stopwatch functionality. Alarms & Clock is a simple app. If you need something more elaborate, visit the Store.

The info apps: News, Weather, Sports, and Money

Windows 10 provides four excellent apps, powered by MSN (*https://www.msn.com*), that can keep you up to date about things going on around you (or lead you down the path to total distraction, depending on your inclinations). You can peruse the current headlines, explore by category, and search for anything you don't immediately find. All the info apps implement live tiles; pin them to your Start menu to get quick headlines and alerts.

News

The News app presents large tiles for recent headline stories, smaller tiles for stories of subordinate interest (be sure to scroll to see the whole list), and a menu across the top you can use to filter by category:

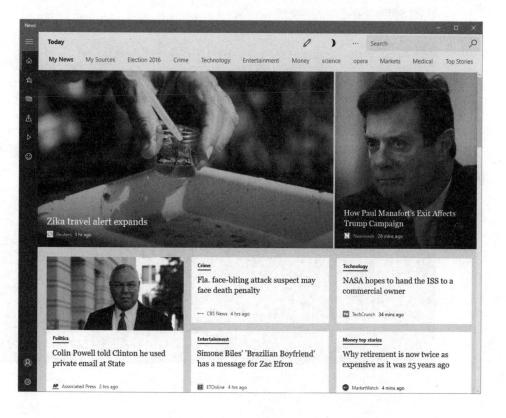

The horizontal menu across the top covers many categories but doesn't include local news. To see stories from news sources closer to home, click the fourth icon on the vertical toolbar at the left side of the window.

If you're looking for a story about a particular topic that doesn't happen to bubble up to the top of one of the category pages, try the Search field. News will present what MSN has about your search topic, along with other items judged to be related.

The horizontal menu of news categories might not include some you'd like to see and others you never want to bother with. To customize, click the second icon on the vertical toolbar. The My Interests page shows all your current categories. To remove a category, click the green check mark. To add others, select one of the items in the menu on the left and then click the plus sign for a category you want to add.

Weather

The Weather app offers a wealth of forecasted and historical information about virtually any city in the world, including your own:

Scroll down the Forecast page to see more details about the day—sunrise, sunset, moonrise, moonset, and more. Below that, you'll find record highs, lows, and rainfall. You might also see such tidbits as the number of times thunderstorms have occurred on this day over the past 30 years. More interesting details await you on the Maps, Historical Weather, and News pages. Click icons in the panel on the left to display these.

If there are cities you regularly track, visit the Favorites page:

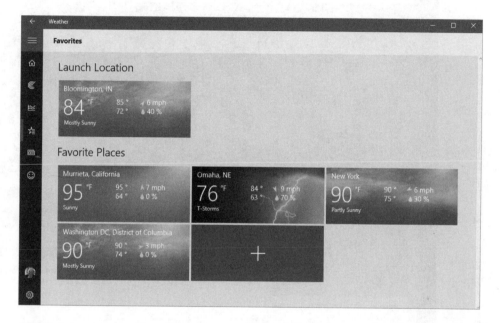

Click the plus sign to add a city. Right-click a city to remove it.

Sports

With the Sports app, you can follow news stories about your favorite teams or sports:

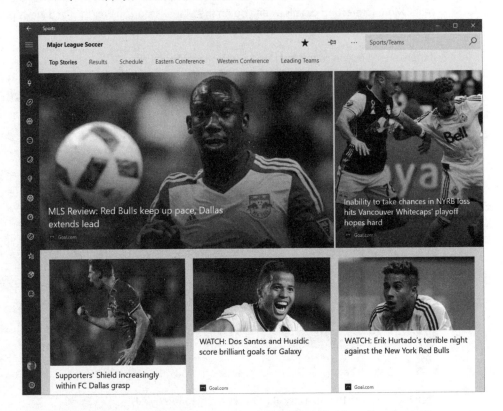

The list of available sports and leagues is truly global. If you like American football, you can follow the NFL, but Europeans who have a different definition of football can choose from no fewer than 42 separate leagues on the continent. You can also track Australian Rules football, cricket, and rugby.

Click Scoreboard, the second item in the horizontal menu at the top of the window, to see tiles for current and imminent games. Click a tile to drill down. For a game in progress, you can see details in something approximating real time.

In your exploration of Sports, don't neglect to visit My Favorites (the third icon from the bottom in the panel at the left). There you can add the teams you're particularly interested in following. Sports will feed updates from these teams to its live tile and to Cortana.

Money

As Sports does for games, Money lets you track market action in an approximation of real time. Below the headline news on the Home page, a dashboard shows the current action in several major markets:

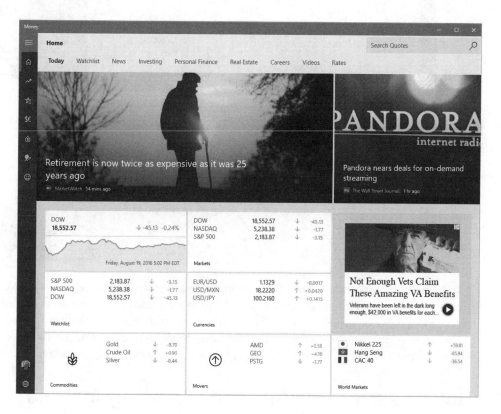

Click a tile to see more detail:

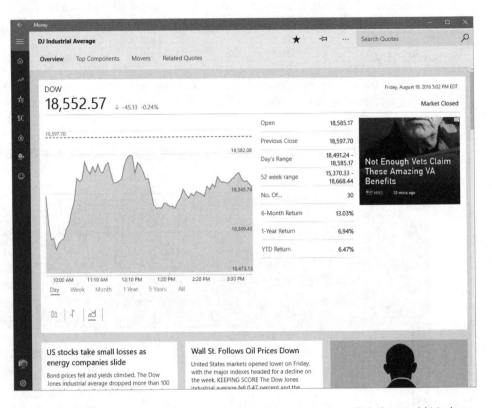

The Money app covers stocks, bonds, commodities, and currencies. Click the World Markets icon (sixth from the top in the panel at the left) to see a map of the world with summaries of many regional markets. Click the Currency Converter icon (fourth in the panel) to check current conversion rates. The Watchlist icon (third from the top) lets you add stock symbols of particular interest. On your Watchlist page, Money supplies news stories as well as price data.

Performing screen captures with Snipping Tool and shortcut keys

Pictures speak louder than words, and sometimes an image capture of the current window or screen can be the ideal way to enhance a PowerPoint presentation, explain a procedure, or remind yourself at some future time of what you were doing and how. All Windows versions, from the very first to the present, have offered two keyboard shortcuts for capturing screens:

- PrtScr captures an image of the entire primary screen.

- Alt+PrtScr captures an image of the current window.

Both of these capture methods post bitmaps to the Clipboard, and you can paste the results into any program that accepts graphics. Recent Windows versions offer a third built-in shortcut:

- Windows key + PrtScr captures an image of all current screens (including secondary screens) and saves that image as a PNG file in the Screenshots subfolder of your Pictures folder.

Of course, there are many situations in which what you want is not a full window or screen capture, but a rectangular or freeform capture of a portion of a window. Many third parties offer richly featured tools for these purposes; we're particularly fond of Techsmith's Snagit and have used it for all recent iterations of our books. Windows, however, includes a lightweight utility called Snipping Tool that serves most basic screen-capture needs.

To run Snipping Tool, type **snip** in the Search box; the program should appear at the top of your search results. Snipping Tool looks like this:

To see your snipping options, click the arrow next to New. The program offers four choices: Free-Form Snip, Rectangular Snip, Window Snip, and Full-Screen Snip. Pick one, click New, and then draw a rectangle or free form or click in the window or screen you want to capture. After capturing the image, Snipping Tool adds editing and file-handling tools to the menu bar:

These tools are straightforward. You can save, copy, or email the current snip. And you can make freehand annotations, apply a highlighter, or erase the edits you already made.

Voice Recorder

The Sound Recorder application that was included with Windows versions dating back to the Middle Ages (well, perhaps not *quite* that long ago) has been replaced by a shiny new modern app called Voice Recorder. The Voice Recorder app, which creates files in the .m4a format, is great for recording speeches, lectures, and interviews. There's no maximum time for a recording, and you can mark the recording at interesting junctures while the speaker is talking. During subsequent playback, a simple click on the marked timeline will bring you back to a place you found noteworthy.

To start recording, click the microphone icon in the left pane. While recording is in progress, Voice Recorder presents a flag icon you can use to mark points of interest. When you have finished recording, Voice Recorder displays the time position you flagged and adds the new recording to the list of those you've already made:

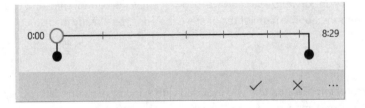

To change a recording's name to something descriptive, click the pencil icon on the toolbar in the right pane.

Voice Recorder includes a Trim command, which you can use to shorten a recording. When you click the second icon on the toolbar, black handles appear at the beginning and end of the timeline:

Drag the handles forward or backward and click the check mark to trim your recording.

CHAPTER 11

Music, photos, movies, and games

Not that long ago, your PC was the indispensable hub of digital media. Music and movies were delivered on shiny discs, and you needed a desktop or laptop PC to rip CDs, watch a movie while traveling, transfer photos from your digital camera, and share your photos on social media.

Today, the explosion of mobile devices and cloud-based entertainment services means the PC is no longer a hub, and shiny discs are now an endangered species. The PC is still uniquely qualified for tasks that involve editing and managing a media collection and syncing it with cloud services, but for playing those files you're more likely to use a smaller mobile device.

The three core media apps included with Microsoft Windows 10—Groove Music, Photos, and Movies & TV—are tightly connected to the cloud. Like other apps built on the Universal Windows Platform, they're touch-friendly but also work well in a window on a conventional PC.

If you're worried that the digital media landscape in Windows 10 will be completely alien, we can reassure you that a few familiar touchstones remain: Windows Media Player is still available for playing music and movies on a desktop or portable PC. Likewise, the venerable Windows Photo Viewer and, yes, Microsoft Paint are still around, virtually unchanged from their Windows 7 incarnations.

In the living room, it's still possible to connect a PC to a home entertainment system directly, although the experience is less enjoyable than it used to be now that Windows Media Center is no longer available with any edition of Windows 10. (In fact, Media Center is removed from your system when you upgrade from a prior edition.) More modern alternatives include streaming content from a Windows tablet or PC to a large display (like your big-screen TV) by using built-in support for the Miracast standard. And if your living room or rec room includes an Xbox One game console, it's easy to connect to a Windows 10 PC.

But before we talk about apps, let's review the basics of how Windows 10 organizes media files.

Managing your digital media libraries

Regardless of whether they're stored on a local drive or in the cloud, digital media files are managed just like other files. As with earlier versions, Windows 10 creates default libraries named Music, Pictures, and Videos, and it uses metadata in files stored within folders in those libraries to organize their contents. In OneDrive, the contents of the Music, Photos, and Videos folders are available for use with the corresponding Windows 10 apps when you sign in to those apps using the same account.

> ➤ For a detailed discussion of how to view and manage metadata in files, see "Managing file properties and metadata" in Chapter 12, "Managing files on PCs and in the cloud."

When you open any of these locations using Details view in File Explorer, files are arranged in columns that reflect their content. The default Music folder, for example, displays song titles, contributing artists, and the name of the album containing those songs. After selecting multiple MP3 files, you can use the properties dialog box to change the album or artist title for the entire group, as shown in Figure 11-1. (This editing capability is supported in all widely used digital media formats, including Windows Media Audio and several lossless formats we discuss later in this chapter.)

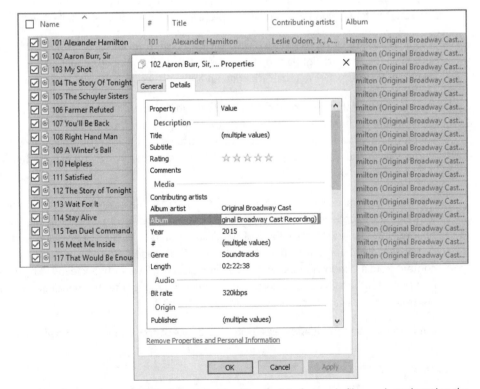

Figure 11-1 Use the properties dialog box to edit metadata for music files, such as changing the album title for a selection of tracks.

Inside OUT

For heavy metadata editing tasks, use third-party tools

File Explorer is fine for basic data touch-up tasks, but it's a poor choice for extensive edit-ing jobs. If you notice a typo in the title of an album or an artist's name, feel free to fix it in File Explorer. But if you're doing maintenance on a large music collection, you'll appreciate a third-party tool for editing tags. You have dozens of choices, including the free Mp3tag package, available at *http://www.mp3tag.de/en*. (Don't let the name fool you—it works with WMA and MP4 file formats as well.) Our favorite commercial package is MediaMonkey (*http://mediamonkey.com*), which also offers robust conversion tools.

When you use File Explorer to open folders that contain music, pictures, or videos, Windows adds a custom tab to the ribbon, with tasks appropriate for that type of data. Figure 11-2, for example, shows the Picture Tools tab, with options to quickly rotate one or more pictures or dis-play them as a slide show; if you have multiple pictures selected, the Set As Background option uses only the most recent selection.

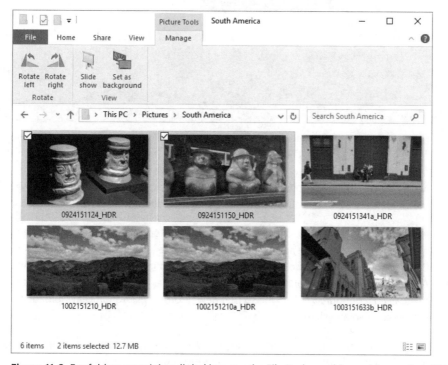

Figure 11-2 For folders containing digital images, the File Explorer ribbon adds a custom Picture Tools tab with an abbreviated set of commands.

Likewise, folders containing digital music and video files contain a custom Music Tools or Video Tools tab, respectively, with an equally limited selection of playback options.

Despite the new look, all the new digital media apps use the tried-and-true library capabilities in Windows 10 to determine which files to display when you open the respective app. You can customize the selection of folders included in each library by clicking the gear icon to open Settings in any of the three apps. Figure 11-3, for example, shows the dialog box that appears when you click or tap Choose Where We Look For Music in the Groove Music app.

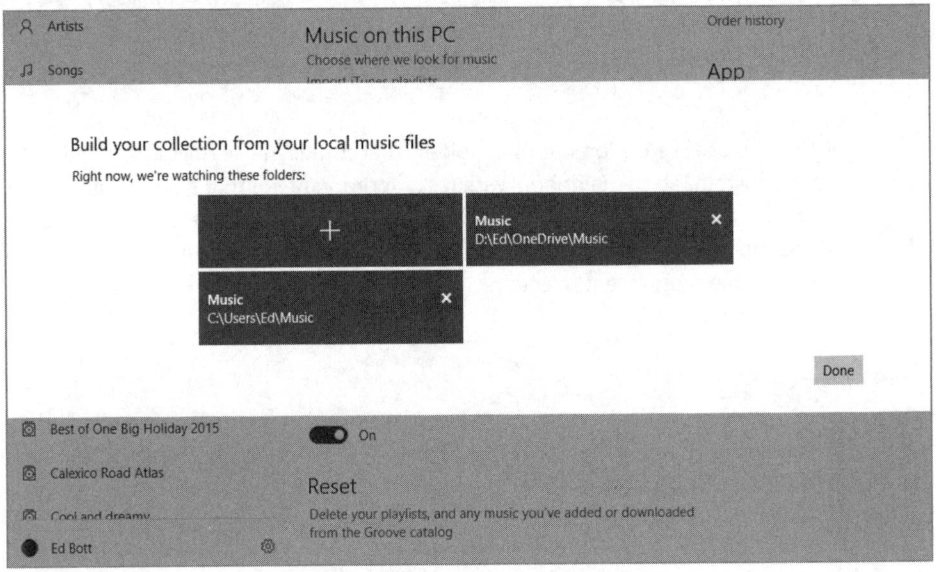

Figure 11-3 Every digital media app in Windows 10 includes a setting to adjust which folders are included in the corresponding library.

Note that any changes you make to the selection of folders in any of the three core digital media apps are automatically reflected in the corresponding Windows 10 library and vice versa.

And, of course, as befits a cloud-centric operating system, all those apps are also integrated with Microsoft OneDrive. The Photos app, for example, includes the contents of your OneDrive Camera Roll folder, which contains photos you upload from mobile devices. (iPhones and Android devices are supported, as are Windows phones.) You can upload pictures to OneDrive manually or configure your phone so that new photos are automatically uploaded to OneDrive for safekeeping and sharing.

Similarly, you can store your music collection in OneDrive and stream or download its contents to any Windows 10 device using the Groove Music app.

Music

No, you're not seeing double. Windows 10 includes two programs whose primary purpose is to play digital music files:

- Groove Music is a Universal Windows app and the default app for playing music files in Windows 10. It's the direct successor to the Xbox Music app from Windows 8.1, and it traces its ancestry (at least indirectly) to the late, lamented Zune Music app. Using Groove Music, you can stream or download your music collection from OneDrive, play music files in various formats, and stream customized playlists from the Groove Music service based on a single track, an album, or an artist. With a Groove Music Pass, you can listen to any album in the service's vast collection and download those album tracks for offline listening on up to four devices.

- Windows Media Player in Windows 10 is virtually identical to the version shipped with Windows 7. (The single, very large exception is support for files saved using formats based on lossless compression.) The most distinctive feature of Windows Media Player compared with Groove Music is its ability to play CDs and rip their contents to digital formats. It can also sync content with some older models of portable music players.

Both programs create indexed libraries from the contents of folders in your Music library. The indexes are stored separately.

Both programs support the same selection of audio formats, most of them compressed. For practical purposes, audio files must be compressed; using the uncompressed WAV format, a typical 60-minute CD will consume more than half a gigabyte of disk space. Compressing the files means you can store more music on your hard disk, and it makes the process of backing up and streaming music files easier and more efficient.

When it comes to compression, Windows 10 supports both lossy and lossless formats. Most popular algorithms used to compress audio (and video) files are lossy, which means that they achieve compression by eliminating data. In the case of audio files in the popular MP3 and AAC formats, the data that's tossed out during the compression process consists mostly of frequencies that are outside the normal range of human hearing. The level of compression is determined by the *bit rate*. Higher bit rates preserve more of the original sound quality of audio tracks but result in larger files on your hard disk or portable player. Lower bit rates pack more music into limited space at a cost in fidelity.

The more compressed a music file is (that is, the lower its bit rate), the more likely you are to notice degradations in audio quality.

Windows 10 supports three different lossless compressed formats: Windows Media Audio Lossless, Apple Lossless Audio Codec (ALAC), and Free Lossless Audio Codec (FLAC). When you have a choice of formats, we recommend FLAC, which is widely supported and stores music files

CHAPTER 11

efficiently without sacrificing any information. In theory, at least, a track saved in any of these lossless formats should be indistinguishable from the original.

NOTE
Although you can play files saved in FLAC format from a local disk, you cannot stream this format from OneDrive.

Using Groove Music

Every installation of Windows 10 sets Groove Music as the default music player, unless you choose a different app when you first set up a user profile. If you used this app in its previous incarnation, the look and feel should be familiar. One major difference (new in the Anniversary Update) is the Your Groove page, which occupies the top slot in the navigation pane. As Figure 11-4 shows, this screen shows tracks you recently played, organized by album, and also recommends custom playlists based on your music collection.

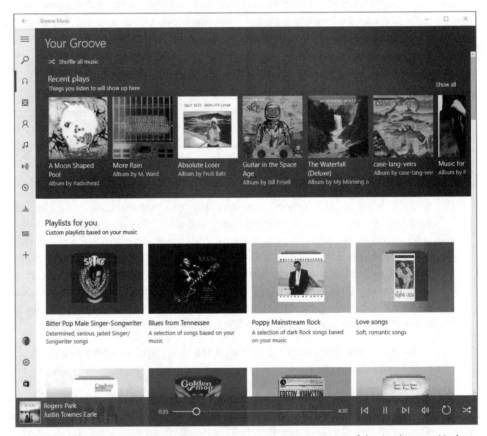

Figure 11-4 This dynamic home page, new in the Groove Music app as of the Anniversary Update, shows recent plays and custom playlists.

The navigation pane—that thin column of icons on the left—follows the same interface conventions as other universal apps. If the app's window is wide enough, the labels for the navigation pane appear automatically; to make those labels visible, or to hide them if you want more room for the current view, click the Maximize/Minimize Navigation (aka "hamburger") button at the top of the pane. Figure 11-5 offers an overview of the Groove interface with the navigation pane expanded to show all its labels.

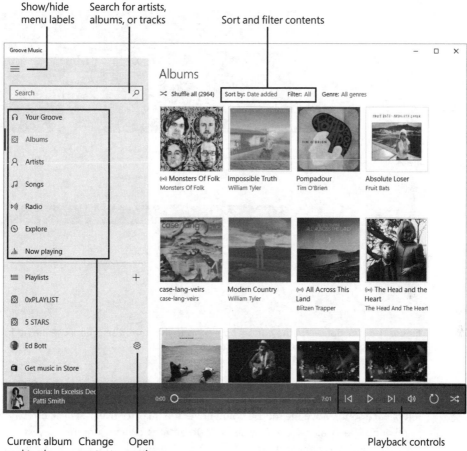

Show/hide menu labels   Search for artists, albums, or tracks   Sort and filter contents

Current album and track   Change contents   Open settings   Playback controls

Figure 11-5 The Groove Music app's contents pane offers multiple views of your collection, available via icons in the navigation pane on the left. Sort or filter the current view using controls at the top.

The design of the Groove Music app isn't difficult to figure out. A menu pane on the left provides a way for you to change the way your collection is displayed (Albums, Artists, or Songs). You can start a customized streaming playlist by clicking Radio, browse new albums available for purchase (or for playback with a Groove Music Pass) by using the Explore button, or display the current album or playlist by clicking Now Playing. Your custom playlists appear at the bottom of the left pane.

Figure 11-6 shows the options that appear when you click to display the contents of an individual album. (The menu of additional options to the right of the album cover is visible because we clicked the ellipsis to the right of the Add To command.)

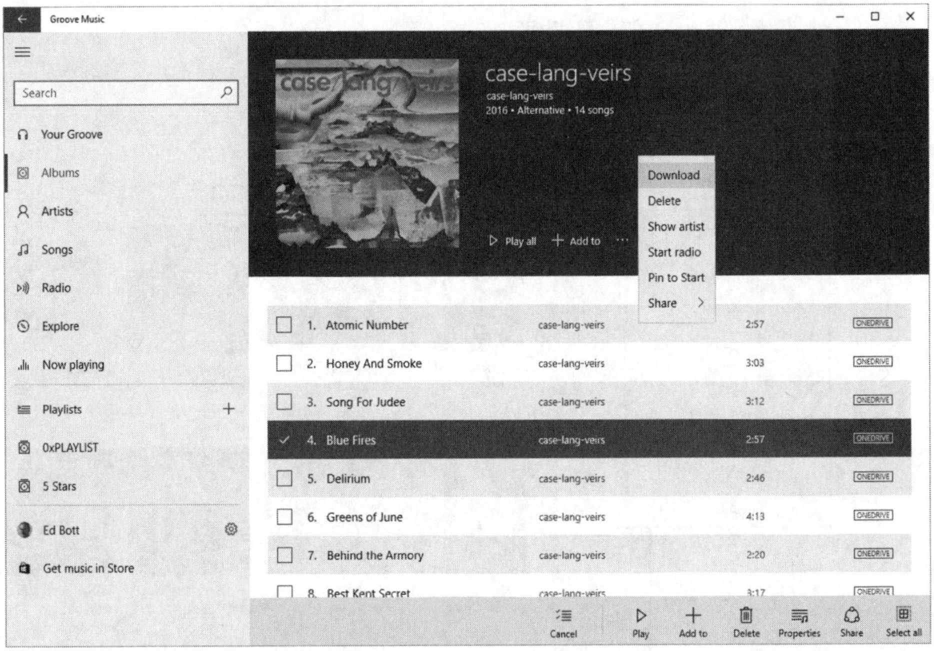

Figure 11-6 The options at the bottom apply only to the current selection. Use the Add To option to send tracks or an entire album to a custom playlist.

The option to select individual songs from an album or playlist (or from the Songs view) isn't immediately obvious. When you select an album, for example, track numbers appear to the left of each song. Move the mouse pointer over the track to reveal a check box where the track number had been, along with Play and Add To buttons. (With songs in a playlist or in the Songs view, the check box appears to the left of the track name.) After you click to select one song, check boxes appear to the left of all other tracks in the current album or playlist.

As we noted earlier, Groove Music integrates neatly with OneDrive. Any compatible files you save to the Music folder in OneDrive are available for playback when you sign in on any Windows 10 device. The resulting collection can be displayed along with locally stored files or maintained separately. Use the Filter menu, as shown in Figure 11-7, to specify your preferences.

Search terms you enter in the box at the top of the navigation pane show artists, albums, and songs from your collection. You can change the scope to Full Catalog to show additional results, which are available for purchase or, with a Groove Music Pass, for streaming and download. Figure 11-8 shows one such search in action.

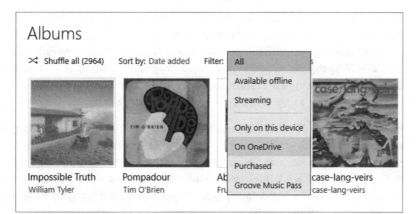

Albums

⤨ Shuffle all (2964)   Sort by: Date added   Filter: All

    Available offline

    Streaming

    Only on this device

    On OneDrive

    Purchased

    Groove Music Pass

Impossible Truth   Pompadour   Ab   case-lang-veirs
William Tyler   Tim O'Brien   Fru   case-lang-veirs

Figure 11-7 Use the Filter menu to show only a subset of your music collection: albums saved in the OneDrive Music folder, for example, or those available offline.

Groove Music   — ☐ ✕

≡

Results for "neko case"

neko case   🔍

In your music | Full catalog (267)

🎧 Your Groove

Artists (2)   Show all

◎ Albums

🔾 Artists

🎵 Songs   Neko Case   Neko Case & Her Boyfriends

▷)) Radio

◔ Explore

Albums (13)   Show all

.ıl Now playing

≣ Playlists   +

◎ 0xPLAYLIST

◎ 5 Stars   Middle Cyclone   Blacklisted   The Worse Things   Fox Confessor Brings   Truckdrive
    Neko Case   Neko Case   Get, The Harder I   The Flood (Reissue)   Mule
    Neko Case   Neko Case   Neko Case

😊 Ed Bott   ⚙

🛍 Get music in Store

    Songs (252)   Show all

Supermoon
case-lang-veirs   0:58 ⎯⎯◯⎯⎯⎯⎯ 3:48 |◁ ▷ ▷| ◁)) ↻ ⤨

Figure 11-8 Searches display results that match artists, albums, and songs from your collection by default. Use the Full Catalog option to see additional results from the Store.

TROUBLESHOOTING

You can't hear any sound from your speakers

Modern PCs often have multiple playback channels, in both digital and analog formats. Audio playback hardware can be found in various locations: on your motherboard; as an optional feature on an add-in video card, with multichannel sound typically delivered over an HDMI cable; on an add-in sound card; or through headphones connected physically or wirelessly using a Bluetooth connection. It's not unusual to find multiple audio playback options in a single PC, especially one that has been upgraded extensively.

If your hardware and drivers appear to be installed correctly but you're unable to hear any sound, right-click the speaker icon in the notification area at the right side of the taskbar and choose Playback Devices. This opens the Sound dialog box from Control Panel, with the Playback tab selected. Look for a green check mark next to the device currently designated as the default playback device. In the following example, the built-in speakers are disabled, and headphones connected via Bluetooth are used for communications programs and for playback. To change the default playback device, click the Speakers/Headphones option that corresponds to the device you want to use (the exact wording varies depending on how the driver developer chose to implement it) and then click Set Default.

➤ For details on how to configure hardware and install drivers to unlock the functionality of those devices, see Chapter 13, "Hardware."

Using Windows Media Player to rip CDs

If you prefer the familiar Windows Media Player interface to the more modern Groove Music app, relief is a search away. We don't recommend Windows Media Player for new Windows 10 users, but if you're already comfortable with its quirks and you don't want or need to access your music collection from the cloud, it's a thoroughly appropriate choice.

We don't include exhaustive instructions for Windows Media Player in this edition. (If you're interested in that, pick up a copy of *Windows 7 Inside Out* from Microsoft Press, 2011). The one task Windows Media Player can perform that Groove Music can't is to convert ("rip") tracks from an audio CD and save them in digital formats on your local hard drive.

Figure 11-9 shows a CD (selected in the left pane in Windows Media Player) with its tracks being ripped to the local hard drive.

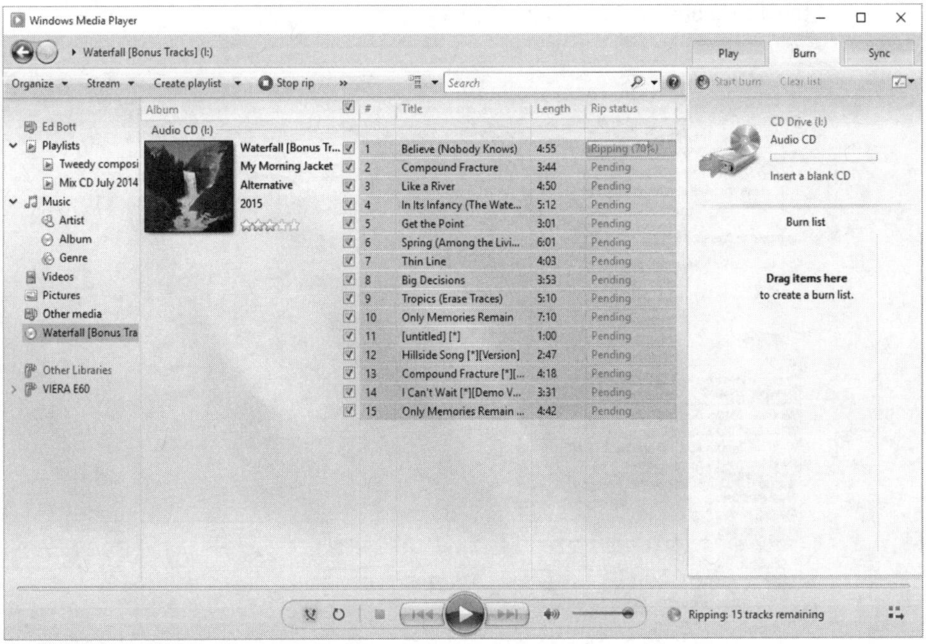

Figure 11-9 The best reason to use Windows Media Player is to rip an audio CD to digital format, a task that Groove Music can't perform.

When you're connected to the internet, Windows Media Player consults its online data sources to determine the name of your disc, as well as the names of the artist or artists and tracks and the genre of music the disc contains. This information is used to automatically tag and name tracks. You can use Windows Media Player or File Explorer to change those tags if necessary.

Windows Media Player copies each CD track to a separate file and stores it, by default, in the Music folder in the user profile of the currently signed-in user (%UserProfile%\Music). Using the album metadata, Windows Media Player creates a folder for each artist and a subfolder for each album by that artist.

The digital files you create by ripping a CD are completely free of technical restrictions on your ability to play them back or make identical copies: you can listen to the saved tracks on your PC or on a mobile device, burn a collection of tracks to a custom CD, or copy those tracks to another PC or to OneDrive. Before you use Windows Media Player to rip a CD, however, it's wise to check the program's settings.

For compatibility with the maximum number of devices, the widely used MP3 format is best.

To set your preferences after inserting a CD, click the Rip Settings button on the Player toolbar. (You can also reach this dialog box by clicking Organize and then Options, and then clicking the Rip Music tab.) Click Format, and then choose one of the eight available formats, as shown in Figure 11-10. If you choose a format that allows lossy compression, use the slider at the bottom of the dialog box to choose a quality level.

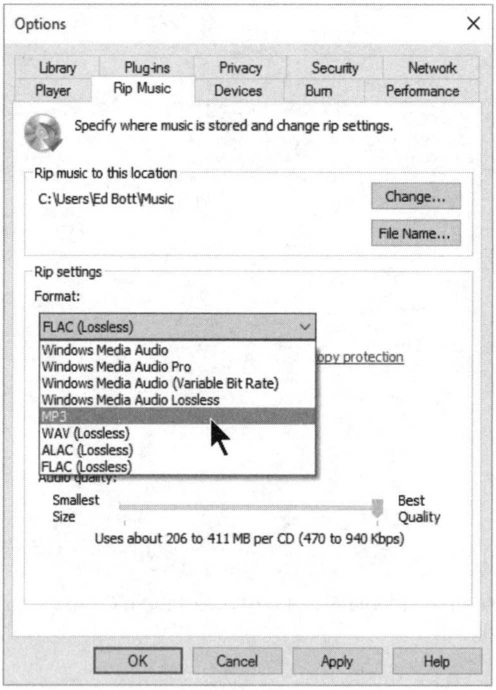

Figure 11-10 Before ripping a CD, be sure to choose a format and quality level here.

As long as you have that dialog box open, use the options at the top to specify the location where you want your ripped files saved and to define the default naming convention for individual tracks.

Managing photos and digital images

Windows 10 includes three built-in apps suitable for viewing, managing, and editing photos in digital image formats. In this section, we concentrate on the Photos app, with a nod to two older desktop programs—Windows Photo Viewer and Paint—that exist primarily for compatibility's sake.

As with its music and movie counterparts, the Photos app displays the contents of all files it finds in your Pictures library. It also includes the option to show photos and videos from OneDrive, even if those files are not synchronized with your PC or tablet.

Figure 11-11 shows the relatively simple user interface of the Photos app, with the entire collection available for browsing and editing.

Figure 11-11 In Collection view, the Photos app displays your collection of digital pictures by date, with newest photos first. Click a month heading to reveal a list you can use to jump to a different month.

The navigation pane on the left includes two alternative views you can use to organize photos into albums or browse the contents of your collection by folder rather than by date. We discuss Albums view in more detail later in this chapter.

CHAPTER 11

Several options in the Photos app's Settings page are worth checking before you invest a lot of time and energy learning its inner workings. Figure 11-12 shows these options, with the two most important ones at the top of the list.

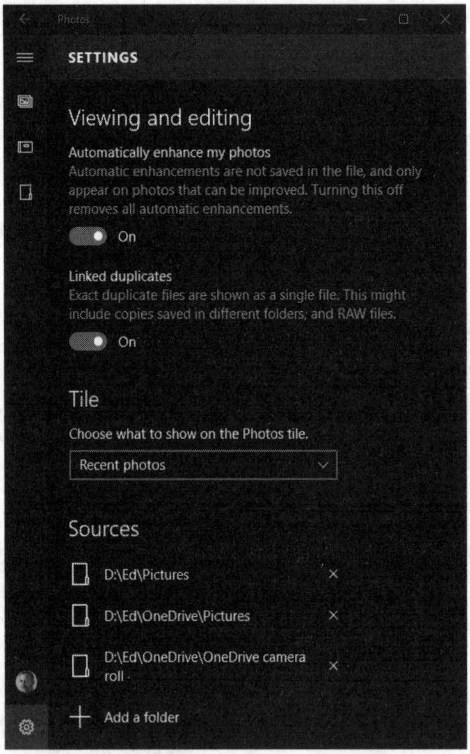

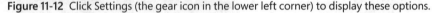

Figure 11-12 Click Settings (the gear icon in the lower left corner) to display these options.

Digital photography purists will probably want to disable both of the options at the top of this list, or at least be aware that they're enabled.

The first option automatically "enhances" photos as they're displayed. The underlying file isn't altered, but the image you (and your audience) see in the app might be changed to make it look better—at least in the eyes of the Photos app's algorithms.

The Linked Duplicates setting is intended to eliminate the frustration of seeing multiple copies of the same image. This can occur if your camera captures images in RAW format but also saves a lower-resolution copy for easier downloading on space-sensitive mobile devices. You can see the full selection of image files by using File Explorer.

Finally, at the bottom of the list is a switch you can use to include photos and videos from One-Drive. Beneath that switch is an option to select which photos and videos are included. If you don't want album art from the Music folder and random images from your Documents folder in the Photos app, select Pictures Folder Only. If you prefer to see only files in selected folders that are synced to your local PC or device, turn this option off and add the local synced OneDrive folders to your Pictures library.

Clicking an individual photo from your collection or from an album opens it for viewing, sharing, and editing, with an array of tools appearing in a bar above the image, as shown in Figure 11-13. Note that we clicked the ellipsis at the end of the menu bar to show a drop-down menu of additional options.

Figure 11-13 By default, the Enhance option is selected in the menu bar. In addition to options for sharing and editing this photo, you can click the ellipsis to the right of the menu bar for more options.

From that menu of additional options, click File Info to see selected details about the image, as shown here. Note that the metadata displayed here is read-only and can't be edited in the Photos app. To work with the file and its metadata directly, click Open Folder under the Folder Path heading; that action opens the folder containing the image in File Explorer.

Using the Photos app to crop and edit pictures

The greatest strength of the Photos app is its collection of lightweight editing tools. After opening an image, click or tap the pen icon to see the full set of editing tools, as shown in Figure 11-14.

For quickly turning a casual shot into something worth keeping and sharing, the tools in the Basic Fixes category are extremely useful. Here's what each one does:

- **Enhance.** Use this option to allow the app's algorithms to analyze the image and make basic changes. You're likely to see the image straightened and the color balance or contrast corrected, for example.

- **Rotate.** You can use this control to shift the angle of the picture 90 degrees at a time, to fix images that are sideways or upside down.

- **Crop.** Cut out extraneous material, using either a freeform selection or a standard aspect ratio. (See more details following this list.)

- **Straighten.** Use this option to move the horizon of the image in either direction, one degree at a time, for those occasions when you were holding the camera at a slight angle when the picture was snapped.

- **Red Eye.** Removes the red-eye effect caused by using a flash when snapping photos of people. (Note that this tool has no effect on pictures of dogs and cats and other nonhuman species.)

- **Retouch.** Click this tool to change the mouse pointer to a tool that blurs anything you click with it. Use it to remove distractions and clutter from an image.

Figure 11-14 Select one of the five options on the left to see a matching collection of editing tools on the right.

The Crop tool is probably the one you'll use most often. Figure 11-15 shows it in action.

Drag any corner to make the crop area larger or smaller. After setting the correct size, click the photo and drag the portion you want to keep into the crop area. Click Apply to see your changes in the contents pane, where you have the option to save the edited image, replacing the original; save a copy; or cancel.

Figure 11-15 For freeform cropping, drag any of these four corners. To choose a predefined aspect ratio, such as square or 4 x 3, click the Aspect Ratio tool on the menu bar before cropping.

The photo editing options available on the right side of the image change based on what you select on the left side. The following options are available in addition to the Basic Fixes tools we listed previously:

- **Filters.** Select from six predefined tones that highlight different shades (blue, gold, and so on); the final choice is black and white.

- **Light.** Change the brightness and contrast or emphasize or de-emphasize highlights and shadows. Figure 11-16, which follows this list, shows an example of this feature in use.

- **Color.** Change the temperature, tint, or saturation of the image—for example, to compensate for a blue tint from indoor lighting. You can use the final option in this group to "color boost" a specific area by dragging a pin icon onto the spot to get the boost.

- **Effects.** The two options here allow you to create a vignette, with the center section you select in focus and the surrounding area slightly out of focus (an effect you can see applied to the image in Figure 11-16), or use the Selective Focus option to highlight a key portion of the image while blurring the rest.

Figure 11-16 shows the editing tools available for the Light category, with the Brightness tool in use.

Figure 11-16 Selecting Light on the left exposes a set of editing tools on the right. Using these tools effectively takes a little practice.

Using these editing controls takes a little practice. When you click or tap Brightness, for example, a circle appears to its left with a large white dot next to it, as shown in Figure 11-17. Drag that circle clockwise or counterclockwise to make the image brighter or dimmer (with the number in the center of the circle increasing or decreasing according to your changes). The other controls work in a similar fashion.

CHAPTER 11

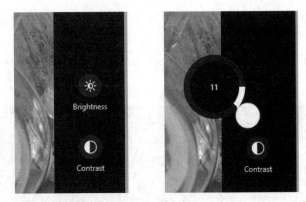

Figure 11-17 Click a photo editing tool, such as Brightness (left), to reveal a circular control (right) with a large handle you can use to adjust the selected attribute.

After making changes to a photo, you can save it (replacing the original) or save a copy. The respective controls are available above the photo itself.

Organizing photos into albums

Previously, we discussed tools for managing an entire collection, which can be organized by date or by folder. Using the second option in the Photos app navigation bar, you can create albums made up of photos and videos you select, which in turn can be uploaded to the cloud for sharing.

The albums feature represents one of the biggest areas of improvement for the Photos app over the past year, specifically the integration between albums in OneDrive and the corresponding feature of the same name in this app. In OneDrive, you create albums manually and can add photos from any folder. The Photos app is capable of sharing those cloud-based albums as well as those stored locally. The Photos app creates some albums automatically, based on dates and events. You can then use those albums as is, customize them, or create new albums manually.

Every album has a cover photo, an album title, and a selection of pictures. You can refine that selection at any time by adding and removing photos, and it's even possible to combine two albums into one, as we explain later. (Note that albums are made up of pointers to files only. Removing an album doesn't remove the photos within it.)

Switching to Albums view in the Photos app produces a scrolling list of all albums, regardless of how they were created, as shown in Figure 11-18.

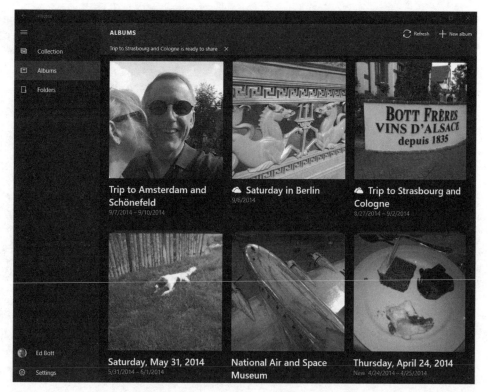

Figure 11-18 The OneDrive icon indicates an album stored in the cloud. Other albums shown here are stored on the device only. Albums with a date for a name were created automatically.

The algorithm that creates albums adds a label to each one, based on the date the photos were taken, and then picks a cover photo and a selection of photos to include in the album. You can customize the name, change the cover photo, and select a different batch of photos. To start, open the album and then click or tap the pen-shaped Edit button. That opens an editing window like the one shown in Figure 11-19.

As with all such changes, be sure to click or tap the check mark (at the top of the page) to save your changes.

Figure 11-19 In this editing view, you can change the title of an album, replace the cover photo, and add or remove photos from the album itself.

Albums you create on OneDrive are available for viewing in Windows 10 if you configured the Photos app to show cloud-only content from OneDrive. To add a local album to OneDrive, open the album, click Share, and then click Upload And Share.

Microsoft Paint (Mspaint.exe) has been a part of Windows since version 1.0. Despite its age, Paint still has a few useful tricks up its sleeve. Its most useful feature is the capability to save an image in an alternative format—if you saved an image in the space-hogging Windows Bitmap format, for example, you can quickly convert it to a much more efficient, compressed format, such as PNG or JPEG, by using the Save As option on the File menu, as shown in Figure 11-20.

You also can use the Paint app to resize an image, a capability that's useful if your original image was captured at a high resolution (with a correspondingly large file size) and you plan to post it on a webpage or share it via email, where the large file size might be unwelcome.

Figure 11-20 Use Paint's File menu to convert an image to a different format.

Inside OUT

Merge two albums

What do you do if Photos automatically created separate albums for each day of your fabulous weekend trip but you want them in a single album? There's no one-button merge feature, but you can accomplish that goal with a few simple steps.

To start, make a note of the album you want to serve as the final destination for the combined collection of photos. Then open the album containing the photos you want to merge into the first album. Click Edit, then click Select from the top menu bar, and then click Select All.

With multiple photos selected, the options on the menu bar change. Click Add To Album (the large plus sign) on the menu bar, and select the name of the album you made a note of earlier. After the photos have been successfully added, you can safely remove the second album.

To shrink an image using Paint, click Resize on the Home tab. That opens the dialog box shown in Figure 11-21, which you use to specify a percentage or an actual height or width, measured in pixels. The decrease in file size can be substantial.

Figure 11-21 Use Paint to change the size of an image file; this option is useful when you plan to post an image online and file size is a concern.

Another legacy tool from bygone days, Windows Photo Viewer, isn't included with a clean Windows 10 installation, but might still be available if you upgraded from Windows 7 or Windows 8.1. We can't really think of a good reason to use this outdated program in favor of the more modern Photos app, and there is no supported way to add it to Windows 10.

Watching movies, recorded TV shows, and video clips

The Movies & TV app is similar in design to Groove Music and Photos. Of the three, it's probably the simplest to use, doing its handful of required tasks very well.

The left-side menu bar in the Movies & TV app allows you to see content you purchased from the Windows Store. (Previous purchases from the Xbox store are also included and can be played back.) Figure 11-22 shows a typical TV library.

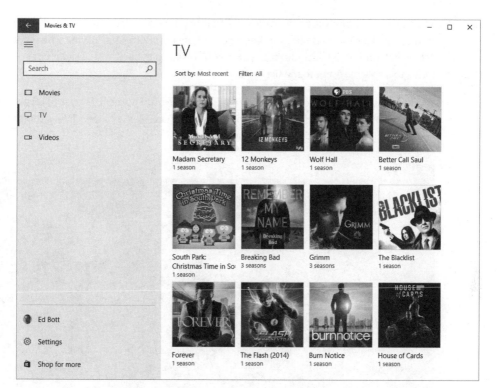

Figure 11-22 Movies and TV programs you purchased through an Xbox or from the Windows Store are available for playback here.

Inside OUT

What about DVDs?

In a significant break from the past, Windows 10 doesn't include the capability to play DVDs (or MPEG-2 files ripped from DVDs). That decision is a reflection of two market realities: Most new PCs don't include optical disc drives at all, and the cost of royalties for DVD play-back software is significant. On the small percentage of PCs that do ship with optical media drives, the manufacturer typically includes playback software.

Microsoft offers a DVD Player app that is available for purchase in the Store. It should be installed automatically (at no charge) when you upgrade a Windows 7, Windows 8, or Windows 8.1 PC that includes Windows Media Center. If your upgrade doesn't qualify for that offer, we recommend the free VLC software, which contains the necessary codecs and is available in a desktop version (from *https://videolan.org*) and also as a universal app in the Windows Store.

You use the Videos page to see your collection of personal video files captured in compatible formats, such as those in MP4 formats recorded on a modern smartphone. The player window, shown in Figure 11-23, includes the typical controls for playback, with a slider bar you can use to move to a specific point in the file.

The More button (indicated by an ellipsis in the lower-right corner of the app) reveals menu options you can use to cast the video to a device such as a large-screen TV—a topic we cover, conveniently enough, in the next section.

Figure 11-23 Click the double-headed diagonal arrow to zoom a video to full screen, hiding elements such as the title bar and playback controls.

Projecting to another screen

You have a high-definition video on your Windows 10 laptop or tablet. That's fine for watching a rented movie or TV show as you fly cross-country, but that laptop screen isn't big enough for the entire family to share. For that, you need the large, high-definition TV connected to a surround-sound system in your living room.

If you have a long enough HDMI cable, you can connect your laptop's video output to a spare HDMI input on the big-screen TV. That option works, but it's an awkward solution at best. So how do you bring that video to the big screen without tripping over a 15-foot cord?

One answer, if you have the right hardware, is to stream your laptop display (with multichannel surround sound) to the larger, louder living-room system. For this task, you can choose from a variety of wireless standards, each one backed by a large hardware or software company. Windows 10 natively supports a standard called Miracast, which is designed for wirelessly mirroring a mobile display and streaming high-quality sound between mobile devices and large displays, with (in theory) perfect fidelity.

In homes, Miracast is mostly an entertainment option, good for projecting YouTube videos and the occasional webcast to a larger screen. This setup is also effective for a conference room or a classroom, where the Miracast adapter can be permanently attached to a large-screen display and available for connection from any Windows 10 device. The Anniversary Update adds the capability for any Windows 10 PC to become a Miracast receiver, allowing you to cast a video from a smaller screen to a larger one.

To project your laptop or tablet display to a TV using Miracast, you need a compatible receiver, such as a TV or Blu-ray player that also supports the standard, or an external adapter that connects to your TV's HDMI port. Although the Miracast standard is relatively new, the technology behind it is well tested, and there are an increasing number of compatible devices on the market. The most versatile option is a thumb drive–sized adapter like the Microsoft Wireless Display adapter shown in Figure 11-24, which plugs into an HDMI input on a TV or monitor and draws power from a USB port on the TV.

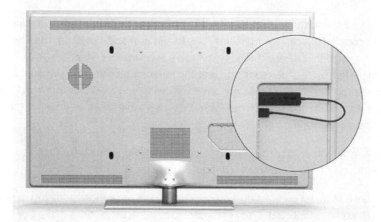

Figure 11-24 The Microsoft Wireless Display adapter plugs into an HDMI port and draws power via a USB connection, turning a TV into a Miracast receiver.

A Miracast receiver uses Wi-Fi Direct to turn itself into a special-purpose wireless hotspot. Connecting a Miracast-compatible device to that invisible hotspot allows the device to mirror or extend its display to the larger screen.

After preparing the Miracast receiver to accept incoming connections (usually a simple matter of turning it on and selecting the matching input on the TV), open Windows 10's Action Center and click or tap the Connect button. That opens up a panel that lists available devices, where you can click or tap the entry for your Miracast receiver, with the goal of making a connection like the one shown in Figure 11-25.

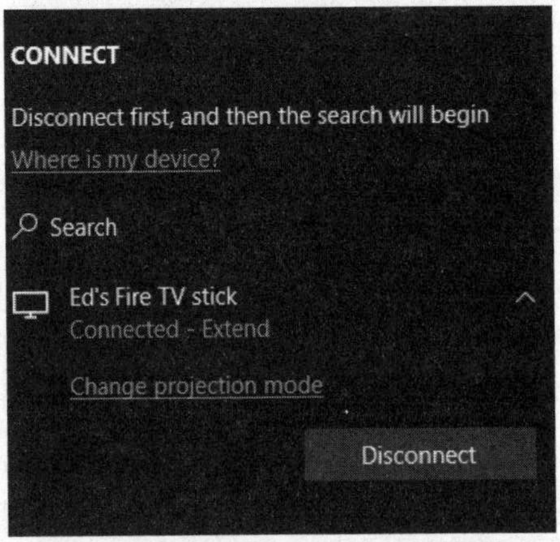

CONNECT

Disconnect first, and then the search will begin

Where is my device?

🔍 Search

🖵   Ed's Fire TV stick   ⌃
     Connected - Extend

     Change projection mode

                              Disconnect

Figure 11-25 Clicking or tapping Connect at the bottom of the Windows 10 Action Center displays this dialog box, from which you can connect to a Miracast device and mirror your laptop or tablet display to a larger device such as a TV.

The first time you encounter a Miracast adapter, you're prompted to add it, installing a device driver in the process. (You can see previously paired and available devices in the Connect pane.) On subsequent visits, that device should be available as a target you can tap or click in the Connect pane. After successfully connecting to the Miracast receiver, you can duplicate the display on your laptop or tablet to the larger screen, allowing you to wirelessly project a Microsoft PowerPoint presentation to a conference room TV, watch a livestream in your living room, or cue up a music playlist for a party.

All three built-in Windows 10 media apps include a Cast option you can use to send the current video and audio output to a previously configured device.

After you make a Miracast connection, you can change the projection mode just as you would with a second display connected directly to your PC. You use the options in the Connect pane to extend the display so that you can watch a webcast or a video conference call on the large screen while you work on your laptop; use the second screen only; or use the PC screen only, severing the Miracast connection.

Xbox and other forms of online entertainment

Microsoft's Xbox One game console doesn't just connect with Windows 10 devices. It actually is one. The November 2015 update for the Xbox One is built on the Windows 10 foundation, and the Anniversary Update adds support for universal apps that target the console.

If you own an Xbox One console, we recommend you check out two apps available for your Windows 10 PC: Xbox One SmartGlass and Xbox app for Windows 10.

Xbox One SmartGlass, shown in Figure 11-26, turns a Windows 10 touchscreen device into a capable remote control for your console. You can tap, slide, and type to control games, navigate the Xbox home screen, and pause or play back media files.

Figure 11-26 The Xbox One SmartGlass app for Windows 10 allows you to use a touchscreen device to control your Xbox One console remotely.

The Xbox app for Windows 10 allows more direct connections to an Xbox One, including the capability to stream games directly from the console to a Windows 10 device for immediate play even if someone else is using the TV that the Xbox One is connected to.

As Figure 11-27 shows, you can see your entire activity feed, connect with friends, and record games by using this versatile app.

CHAPTER 11

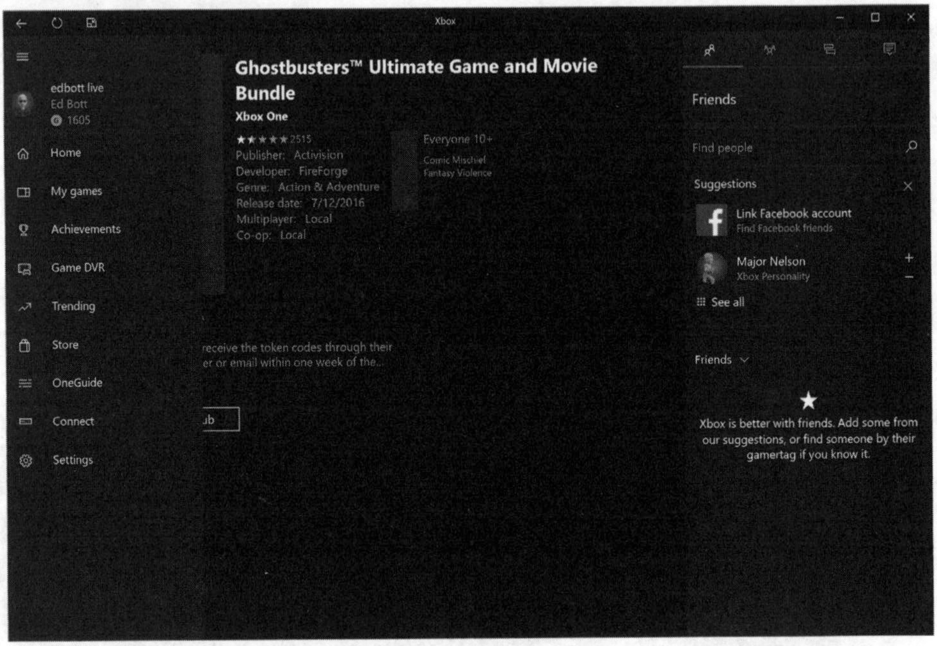

Figure 11-27 The Xbox app includes most capabilities that diehard Xbox gamers want to see.

Managing files on PCs and in the cloud

Unless you use your computer exclusively as a game machine, learning to manage your "stuff"—your documents, programs, and communications—is probably the single most critical computing skill you need to acquire. The addition of cloud services adds extra organizational challenges, especially as you juggle multiple devices with different storage capacities.

The primary tool for managing files in Microsoft Windows 10 is File Explorer (the direct descendant of what was known as Windows Explorer in Windows 7 and earlier versions). File Explorer is an amazingly powerful tool, filled with features that can streamline your work processes and make it easier to find digital music files and photos. Most Windows users barely scratch the surface of File Explorer, which is why we devote a significant section of this chapter to a master class in its rich feature set.

When Windows 10 was released in summer 2015, its support for Microsoft's cloud storage service, OneDrive, was rudimentary, to put it politely. One year later, we're happy to report that the OneDrive sync client is greatly improved. In this chapter, we explain how to configure OneDrive so that your most important files are available when you need them, even if you're not connected to the internet.

Finally, we include an in-depth look at Windows 10's powerful indexing and search tools, which can help you find what you need quickly and with a minimum of effort.

Mastering File Explorer

You can't become a Windows expert without learning how to move quickly and confidently through File Explorer. This general-purpose tool is used throughout Windows for all sorts of file-management tasks, for opening and saving files in Windows programs, and even in parts of the Windows shell. The more you understand about how File Explorer works, the more effective you'll be at speeding through tasks without unnecessary delays. Because it's vital to know your way around, we begin this section with a short tour.

Figure 12-1 shows the default File Explorer layout.

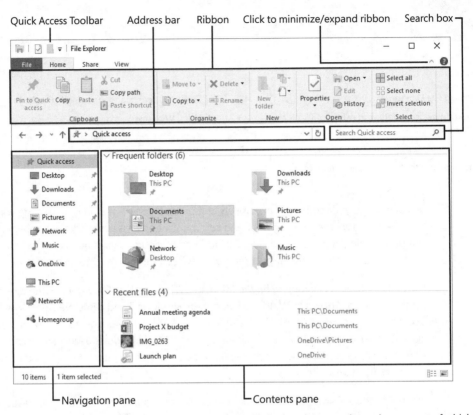

Figure 12-1 File Explorer includes the navigation and display elements shown here, some of which can be customized.

Inside OUT

Use a keyboard shortcut to open File Explorer

You can find File Explorer in various places in Windows 10, but if you're handy with the keyboard, don't bother hunting for it. Press Windows key+E to open a new instance of File Explorer directly. If you want to jump to an open instance of File Explorer, use the taskbar keyboard shortcut, Windows key + *number*, where *number* marks the position of the File Explorer icon on the taskbar. By default, the File Explorer icon is in second position on the taskbar, right after the icon for Microsoft Edge, so unless you've changed the layout, Windows key + 2 should switch between open File Explorer windows.

If you've used any of the recent versions of Microsoft Office, or if you're coming to Windows 10 by way of Windows 8, you won't be startled to see the ribbon atop File Explorer. If, by any chance, this aspect of the user interface is new to you, the only thing you need to know is that it replaces the old system of drop-down and cascading menus with a set of top-level tabs—Home, Share, and View in the example shown in Figure 12-1. Click a tab heading to display available commands for that tab, which are organized into groups—Clipboard, Organize, New, Open, and Select on the Home tab, for example.

More important points to note are the following:

- The command bar from Windows 7 days is gone. The ribbon itself provides the context-specific commands that used to appear on the command bar.

- Unlike its Office counterpart, the commands and groups on the File Explorer ribbon cannot be customized. What you see is what you get.

- The ribbon can be minimized or not, according to your preference. If the ribbon is minimized, it looks very much like a menu, with the commands for a tab appearing only when you click the tab heading. To switch between the full ribbon and this minimized version, use the Expand/Minimize arrow to the right of the tab headings, or just double-click any tab heading.

- When you select folders or files that File Explorer recognizes as pictures, music, or videos, an additional tab appears at the right side of the ribbon, under a color-coded heading. Likewise, selecting a library from the navigation pane or clicking in the search box displays additional tabs with commands relevant to those contexts. These extra tabs can be combined. If you display the contents of the Pictures folder, for example, and then click in the search box, new tabs appear under the Search Tools and Picture Tools headings, as shown here:

- Most of what's on the ribbon is also available on the menus that appear when you right-click files or folders. If you ever become impatient when trying to find a command on the ribbon, right-click in the contents pane and look there. Microsoft adopted the ribbon to reduce the number of cascading submenus that we all used to have to traverse. But sometimes the old ways seem simpler; it's your choice.

CHAPTER 12

To the left of the ribbon tabs, displayed in blue, is the File menu. There you'll find commands for opening a new File Explorer window and for adjusting folder and search options, as well as a list of recently used folders for quick navigation. If you're proficient with managing files at the command line, the most interesting options on this menu are the ones that allow you to open a Command Prompt (Cmd.exe) window or a Windows PowerShell session, using the current folder as the path, with or without administrative privileges.

Inside OUT

Use the keyboard with the ribbon (if you prefer)

Devoted keyboard users will appreciate that any command on the ribbon can be accessed and applied without the mouse. From within File Explorer, tap Alt and notice the letters and numbers that appear under the ribbon tabs and the Quick Access Toolbar. Press one of those letters—V for View, for example—and the appropriate tab itself appears, adorned with its own set of shortcut letters. Follow the shortcuts to your destination.

The design goal of the ribbon is to put the commands you use most often front and center, easy to find. A secondary benefit is that it makes less frequently used commands easier to discover. Here are a few gems that merit your attention:

- The Copy Path command, on the Home tab, puts the path of the current folder or file on the Clipboard. This is handy for sending someone a link to a network share via email. (As an alternative, you can click in the address bar and press Ctrl+C, or you can press Shift as you right-click a file or folder, and then click Copy As Path on the shortcut menu.)

CHAPTER 12

- The Move To and Copy To commands, also on the Home tab, drop down a list of likely targets (recently used folders) for your move and copy operations. If none of those recent folders are appropriate, click Choose Location.

- The Zip command, on the Share tab, instantly creates a Zip (compressed) file from the current selection, thereby providing an alternative to the time-honored approach of right-clicking and choosing Send To, Compressed (Zipped) Folder. (See "Using compressed (zipped) folders" later in this chapter.)

- On the View tab, you'll find handy commands for showing or not showing files and folders with the Hidden attribute. Another command nearby lets you assign the Hidden attribute to the current selection.

Using the navigation pane

In its default arrangement, the navigation pane on the left is arranged into nodes that expand and collapse on demand. Each top-level node offers a starting point for navigating through files on your computer, on your network, and in the cloud.

NOTE

On a Windows 10 device that is joined to a domain, you cannot create a homegroup, but you can join one that has been created by someone else on your home network. In that case, the Homegroup node will be available in File Explorer only if a homegroup is available for you to join. That node remains even if you join and then leave the homegroup.

If you prefer the older, tree-style view with a single hierarchy, click View > Navigation Pane > Show All Folders.

With the Show All Folders option selected, the navigation pane looks like the example shown in Figure 12-2. (Note that the Quick Access menu is collapsed, making the listing even more compact.) The folder hierarchy includes your profile folders (which you can expand by clicking your user name in the navigation pane), any media folders on your network to which you have access (which appear directly under This PC), Control Panel, and the Recycle Bin.

From the Navigation Pane menu on the View tab, you can clear the Navigation Pane entry to make this element completely disappear. Unless you're working on a tiny tablet with extreme space constraints, we can't imagine why you would want to choose this option. This same menu does, however, contain two additional selections you might find useful:

- **Expand To Open Folder.** By default, selecting any item in the navigation pane simply displays its contents in the pane to the right. If you select Expand To Open Folder, File Explorer opens the parent folder of the folder you select in the contents pane, making it easier to see where the selected item fits in the File Explorer hierarchy.

- **Show Libraries.** If you choose to directly manage files stored in libraries (as discussed in "Using libraries" later in this chapter), you might want to include them in your navigation pane. If you select the Show Libraries option, all of your libraries—those that Windows provides and any you create yourself—appear in a node in the navigation pane. If you want to see only particular libraries, click the Libraries node heading, and then right-click each library you want to remove and click Don't Show In Navigation Pane. To restore a library to this node, use the Show In Navigation Pane command. Both commands are also in the Manage group on the Libraries Tools tab.

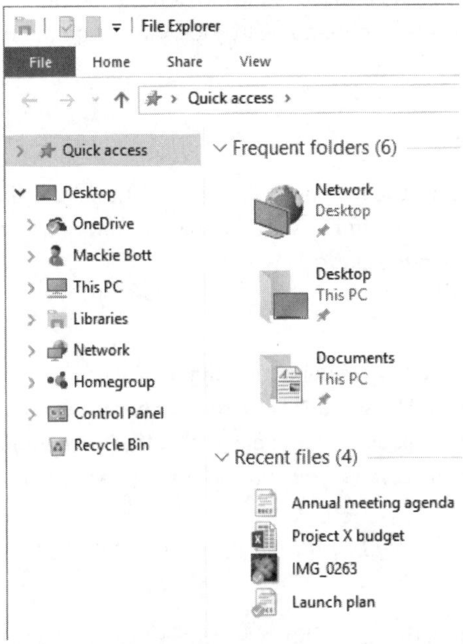

Figure 12-2 Selecting the Show All Folders option changes the navigation pane to one that more closely resembles the file-management tool in older Windows versions.

Navigating faster with Quick Access shortcuts

The Quick Access node, which appears at the top of the navigation pane in all configurations, is new in Windows 10. When it's selected, the contents pane displays two groups of shortcuts: frequently used folders at the top, recently used files beneath it. Windows makes some intelligent choices about what to display under Quick Access, but you can customize this to suit your needs.

In the Frequent Folders section, you'll find some folders marked with pins and others without one. The pinned folders always appear under Quick Access (unless you unpin them). The unpinned folders are ones you recently worked with, and these folders are replaced by others if you begin to use them less frequently. You can unpin a pinned folder by right-clicking it and then clicking Unpin From Quick Access. And you can make any folder anywhere a permanent resident of Quick Access by right-clicking it and then clicking Pin To Quick Access.

The Recent Files section of Quick Access contains files you recently worked with, sorted with the most recently used one at the top. By right-clicking a file name and clicking Open File Location, you can go directly to the folder in which the file resides. If you find that you don't need to see a particular file (and want to make room for another), you can right-click that file and then click Remove From Quick Access.

Quick Access is an extremely handy navigational tool because it gathers together the stuff you're most likely to be concerned with, regardless of where that stuff is actually stored. But if you don't need it, or you're not keen on having passersby see what you've been working on, you can suppress the Frequent Folders section or the Recent Files section, or both. To do this, click View > Options. On the General tab of the Folder Options dialog box, you'll find the check boxes you need in the Privacy section, as shown here:

(If you just want to cover your immediate tracks without changing the overall behavior of File Explorer, it's probably simpler to click Clear in the Privacy section.)

CHAPTER 12

Inside OUT

Customize the Quick Access Toolbar

As its name implies, the Quick Access Toolbar—that set of icons in the upper left corner of File Explorer, above the ribbon—puts commonly used functions close at hand (or close to your mouse pointer). If you'd like those items a few centimeters closer, you can move the Quick Access Toolbar by clicking the arrow at the end and then clicking Show Below The Ribbon.

This menu also includes a short list of six commonly used items you can add to the Quick Access Toolbar, including Undo, Redo, and New Folder. But don't be fooled by that paltry selection. You can add any command or even entire groups of commands to the Quick Access Toolbar. To add a command, right-click it and then click Add To Quick Access Toolbar.

To add an entire group of commands to the Quick Access Toolbar, right-click the name at the bottom of the group and then click Add To Quick Access Toolbar. In this example, we added the Panes group from the View tab, making it easier to add the Preview or Details pane even if the View tab isn't visible:

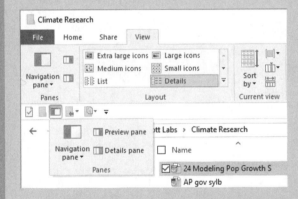

To remove any command or group of commands, right-click the item on the Quick Access Toolbar and then click Remove From Quick Access Toolbar.

Layouts, previews, and other ways to arrange files

You can adjust the display of any individual folder's contents in File Explorer by means of options in the Layout group on the View tab. As Figure 12-3 shows, your choices are numerous: icons in various sizes, Tiles, List, Details, and Content. Display options are folder-specific and persistent.

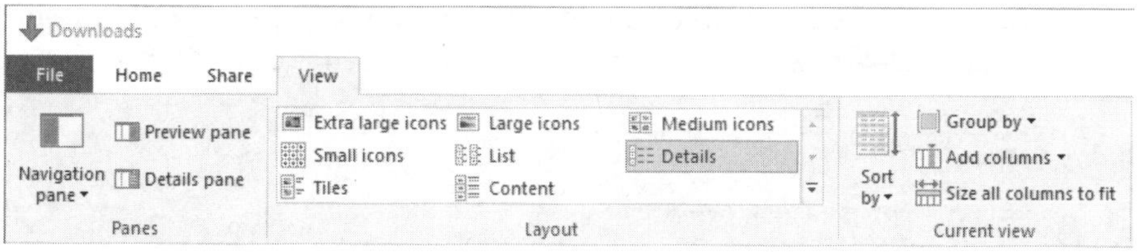

Figure 12-3 The View tab provides a large set of options for displaying content in File Explorer.

You can get a look at each display option by hovering the mouse pointer over it on the View tab. File Explorer gives you a preview of each choice, making it easier for you to decide.

Inside OUT

Switch between File Explorer layouts faster

Each of the eight predefined File Explorer layouts shown on the View tab has its own keyboard shortcut: Ctrl+Shift+*number*, where *number* represents the position of the view in the Layout group, reading from left to right. Thus, Ctrl+Shift+2 is Large Icons view, and Ctrl+Shift+6 is Details view.

In fact, those two views are so important that each has its own one-click shortcut in the lower right corner of every File Explorer window. Clicking the Details icon is by far the fastest way to switch into a view where you can sort and filter using column headings.

The range of options for the various icon views is larger than it looks. Although there are four discrete choices available on the View tab—small, medium, large, and extra large—the actual number of sizes is 76. You can cycle smoothly through all 76 sizes by choosing one of them, holding down the Ctrl key, and turning the wheel on your mouse. With each step, you'll see the icons grow or shrink (although at some of the smaller sizes the change is barely perceptible).

Content view arranges listings in multiline bands that take up the full width of the window, while List view displays file names only, arranged in columns.

Details view is one of the most important alternatives, offering a multicolumn tabulation of your files that unlocks a wide range of sorting, filtering, and search options, as we discuss later in this chapter.

The default arrangement of column headings is determined by the folder type, but you can tailor this arrangement in any folder. To add or remove a column heading while in Details view, right-click anywhere in the row of column headings. (Alternatively, click the View tab and then click Add Columns in the Current View group.) If the list of column headings that appears doesn't include the one you want, click the option at the bottom of the list. As Figure 12-4

CHAPTER 12

shows, the Choose Details dialog box that appears next provides you with a wealth of choices. In fact, Figure 12-4 shows only the first 15 choices in a vast array of possibilities.

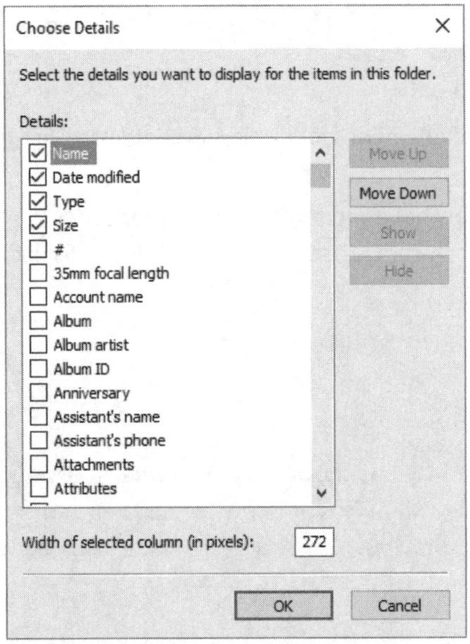

Figure 12-4 Use this dialog box to select which headings are displayed in Details view.

In the Choose Details dialog box, you can use the Move Up and Move Down buttons to change the order in which column headings appear. (You can also change the column order in File Explorer by dragging headings with the mouse.)

As you'll discover later in this chapter (in "Sorting, filtering, and grouping in File Explorer"), headings in Details view are important for sorting and grouping data as well as simply displaying it.

Inside OUT

Change display settings in Open and Save dialog boxes

In many programs, you can change display settings in common file-management dialog boxes (Save As and Open), although the lack of a ribbon means you can't use the View tab to do so. To switch between views in one of these File Explorer–based dialog boxes, use the keyboard shortcuts: Ctrl+Shift+6 for Details view, Ctrl+Shift+2 for Large Icons, and so on. You can also use the unlabeled Change Your View button, with its drop-down list of standard views, which is available in the command bar above the contents pane. As an alternative, right-click an open space in the dialog box (you might have to enlarge the dialog box first) and then click View.

Initially, all folders intended for the storage of user data (including those you create) are assigned one of five folder templates that define the default headings File Explorer considers appropriate for the content type. The logic is straightforward: You'll probably want to sort a folder full of MP3 tracks by track number, and the Date Taken column is extremely useful for filtering digital photos, but neither column would be particularly useful in a folder full of Microsoft Word documents.

Inside OUT

Customize folder templates

Not sure what folder "type" you're in? Right-click a blank space in the folder and then click Customize This Folder, or click View > Customize This Folder. (If this option isn't available, you're viewing a system folder whose template can't be changed.) On the Customize tab of the properties dialog box for the selected folder, look at the selection in the Optimize This Folder For drop-down list, which shows the folder type that's currently in effect.

The View tab also contains commands to show an optional pane on the right side of the contents pane. This pane can either show a preview of the currently selected file—supported file formats include most image files, Microsoft Office documents, and PDF files—or details about the current file (a topic we discuss in the next section). Either command is a toggle. Click once to make the pane visible; click again to hide the pane. If you use either capability regularly, it's worth memorizing the keyboard shortcuts: Alt+P for Preview, Alt+Shift+P for Details.

Using compressed (zipped) folders

Depending on the file type, you can dramatically reduce the amount of disk space used by one or more files by compressing those files into a zipped folder. You can also combine multiple files into a single Zip file while preserving the folder hierarchy of that group of files.

Don't be fooled by the name: A zipped folder (also known as a Zip file or archive) is actually a single file, compressed using the industry-standard Zip format and saved with the .zip file name extension. Any version of Windows can open a file saved in this format, as can other modern operating systems. The format is also accessible with the help of many third-party utilities.

To create a new archive using zipped folders, follow these steps:

1. In File Explorer, display the folder in which you want the new archive to reside.

2. Right-click any empty space in the folder, and then click New > Compressed (Zipped) Folder.

3. Name the folder.

CHAPTER 12

To add files and folders to your archive, drag and drop them onto the zipped folder icon in File Explorer (or double-click to open the zipped folder in its own window and then drag items into it). You can also use the Clipboard to copy and paste items. To remove an item from the zipped folder, double-click the folder to display its contents, right-click the item, and then click Delete.

You can also create a compressed folder from the current selection by clicking Zip on the Share tab in File Explorer. Windows creates an archive file with the same name as the selected object. Use the Rename command (or press F2) to replace the default name with a more descriptive one.

To extract individual files or folders from a zipped folder, open it in File Explorer and then drag the items you want to extract to a new location, or use the Clipboard to copy and paste. To extract all items from a zipped folder to a specific location, right-click the zipped folder icon and then click Extract All, or open the zipped folder in File Explorer and click Extract All on the Extract tab on the ribbon.

Organizing personal data with user profile folders and libraries

The first step on the road to effectively organizing your personal data is to know where it is. Windows uses a logical organizational structure that helps keep data together in known system folders. As we explain in this section, you can change the location of some of these folders to make best use of your available storage. You can also create virtual storage locations called *libraries* to make searching easier.

What's what (and where) in your user profile

Your personal data—settings and files—are stored by default in your *user profile*, which is created by copying the contents of the Default profile to a new folder when you sign in to a user account for the first time on a device. In addition to predefined folders for personal documents and digital media files, this new profile also includes the details that define the desktop environment: the user's own registry settings (HKEY_CURRENT_USER) as well as user data and settings for installed apps and desktop programs.

NOTE
Although you can customize the Default profile, doing so requires the use of enterprise deployment tools and is impractical for home and small business installations.

In addition to individual user profiles, the operating system creates a Public profile containing a group of folders that mirror those in your user profile. You can see the Public Documents, Public Music, Public Pictures, and Public Videos folders in their matching libraries. The advantage of these folders is that other users can save files to these locations from different user accounts on the same computer or from across the network.

Local user profiles are stored in %SystemDrive%\Users. Each user's profile is stored in a sub-folder whose name is based on the user account name (for example, C:\Users\Katy). The entire path for the current user's profile is accessible via another commonly used environment variable, %UserProfile%. If you have File Explorer's navigation pane set to show all folders, you can see the subfolders of your profile by clicking your user name in the navigation pane.

TROUBLESHOOTING

Your user account name and user profile folder name don't match

As we mentioned earlier, Windows creates the user profile folder when you first sign in to a device. If you do so with a local or domain account, the name of the profile folder matches the user name (unless there's already a folder with that name from a previous installation, in which case Windows appends a dot and the name of the PC to the folder name).

This naming convention breaks down if you sign in for the first time using a Microsoft account. In that case, Windows creates a folder name using the first five characters of the user name associated with the Microsoft account. If your user name is six characters or longer, the folder name (which is also shown in File Explorer as the profile name) is truncated. So the profile folder for edbott@example.com becomes C:\Users\edbot.

If that folder name bothers you, we have some bad news: There's no supported way to change the user profile folder name after that first sign-in, unfortunately. But you can make sure it doesn't happen again. The trick is to create a local user account with the same name as what you want to use for your user profile folder. (Follow the instructions in Chapter 2, "Installing, configuring, and deploying Windows 10.) Then, after signing in for the first time using that local account, you can connect your Microsoft account.

To see the folders included in your user profile, open its folder directly from C:\Users or from the drop-down menu at the left of the address bar. As you can see from Figure 12-5, the list includes some familiar destinations. (Because third-party apps can add their own data folders to the user profile, your system might include some additional folders.)

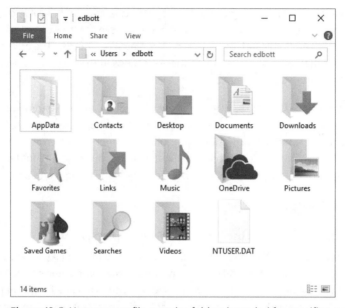

Figure 12-5 Your user profile contains folders intended for specific types of data as well as a hidden AppData folder for data that should be accessed only from within an app.

Inside OUT

What's in the AppData folder?

The hidden AppData folder, introduced in Windows Vista, is used extensively by programs as a way to store user data and settings in a place where they'll be protected from accidental change or deletion. This folder contains application-specific data—customized dictionaries and templates for a word processor, synchronized copies of messages stored on an email server, custom toolbar settings, and so on.

It's organized into three subfolders, named Local, LocalLow, and Roaming. The Roaming folder (which is also accessible via the environment variable %AppData%) is for data that's made available to a roaming profile (a profile stored on a network server; the server makes the profile available to any network computer where the user signs in). The Local folder (which is also accessible via the system variable %LocalAppData%) is for data that should not roam. This location includes the Temp folder (accessible with the environment variable %Temp%), where Windows and apps create files that are strictly for temporary use. The LocalLow folder is used by applications that run at a lower integrity level, such as Internet Explorer in Protected Mode.

The personal data folders (Documents, Downloads, Music, Pictures, and Videos) serve as the default location for applications that use those file types. Here's everything you need to know about the remaining folders:

- **Contacts.** This folder first appeared in Windows Vista and was designed to store contact information used by Windows Mail. It is not used by any programs included in Windows 10 and is maintained for compatibility purposes with third-party personal information management programs.

- **Desktop.** This folder contains items that appear on the user's desktop, including files and shortcuts. (A Public counterpart also contributes items to the desktop.) A link to this location appears in the Quick Access section of the navigation pane.

- **Favorites**. Internet Explorer saves shortcuts to websites here. (Microsoft Edge, as we note in Chapter 9, "Cortana and the web," handles its favorites collection differently.) To manage Internet Explorer favorites in File Explorer, type the shortcut **shell:favorites** in the address bar.

- **Links.** In Windows 7, this folder contains shortcuts that appear in the Favorites list at the top of the navigation pane. Its contents are not used in Windows 10.

- **Saved Games.** This folder is the default storage location for apps that can save a game in progress.

- **Searches.** This folder stores saved search specifications, allowing you to reuse previous searches. (We explain how to use this feature later in this chapter.)

Inside OUT

Expand the Send To menu

The SendTo folder, in %AppData%\Microsoft\Windows, contains shortcuts to some folders and applications that appear on the Send To submenu when you right-click a file or folder in File Explorer (or on the desktop). The SendTo folder is not hidden. You can add your own items to the Send To menu by creating shortcuts here. Type **shell:sendto** in the address bar or in the Run dialog box (Windows key+R) to open this folder and add or delete shortcuts.

Relocating personal data folders

The organizational scheme that Windows uses for personal data folders—keeping documents, music, pictures, and so on in visible subfolders of %UserProfile%—is perfectly appropriate for most configurations. In fact, for portable devices and all-in-one PCs that have only a single storage device, it's the only option.

On desktop PCs that include options for multiple storage devices, some users prefer to separate documents and other profile data from the system drive. This configuration offers the following advantages over a single-volume setup:

- With this configuration, it's easier to organize large collections of data, in particular digital media files, which have a way of overwhelming available space on system volumes. (It's a good idea to keep at least 20 percent of your system drive free for maintenance, such as updates, and for performance, which reduces available data storage even further.)

- Separating data from system files makes restoration easier in the event of system corruption (for example, by malware).

- Separation reduces the size and time devoted to image backups, encouraging their regular use.

- Separation can make it easier, when the time comes, to upgrade the operating system.

This option is especially attractive if you installed Windows on a solid-state drive (SSD) to maximize performance. Adding a conventional hard disk—with a price tag that's typically a fraction of the cost per gigabyte of an SSD—makes it possible to store large amounts of data without compromising system performance.

The easiest, safest way to accomplish this goal is to store personal data in folders on a separate drive, and then include those folders in your libraries and set them as the default save location, a topic we cover in the next section. This approach leaves you with a default set of profile folders, which you can still use when it's convenient to do so, but it keeps the bulk of your data files on a separate drive.

Not everyone loves libraries, however, and there's no requirement to love them. You can still move some or all of your profile subfolders in Windows 10, just as you could in earlier versions. To relocate a user profile folder by editing its properties, follow these steps:

1. Open your user profile folder by starting at This PC, navigating to C:\Users, and then double-clicking your profile name. Alternatively, enter **%UserProfile%** in the address bar.

2. Right-click a folder you want to relocate, and choose Properties. (Or select the folder, and then click Properties on the Home tab.)

3.   On the Location tab of the properties dialog box, enter the address you want to relocate the folder to. For example, to move the Downloads folder from C:\Users\Edbott\ Downloads to X:\Downloads, type or paste the path as shown here:

4.   Click OK. Windows asks permission to create the target folder if it doesn't already exist. Click Yes. A Move Folder dialog box similar to this one appears:

5.   Unless you have some good reason not to move the existing files from the original location to the new one, click Yes.

It's really not a good idea *not* to click Yes in this dialog box. First, it's difficult to imagine why you would want some of your personal documents in a given category on one disk and the rest on another. (If you want to keep your existing files separate from those you save in the future, move the old files to a subfolder in the new location instead of leaving them in the old location.) Second, because %UserProfile% is a system-generated folder, not an ordinary data folder that corresponds to a fixed disk location, leaving some files behind will give you two identically named subfolders in %UserProfile%.

Using libraries

A *library* is a virtual folder that aggregates the contents of multiple folders stored on your computer or on your network. You can sort, filter, group, search, arrange, and share the data in a library as if it were in a single location. Windows 10 gives you several by default: Documents, Music, Pictures, Saved Pictures, and Videos. You can create additional libraries to suit your storage needs, and you can customize any library by changing or adding to the physical folders that make up that library.

The important things to understand about libraries are the following:

- A library can encompass multiple folders on multiple disks.

- All folders in a library must be capable of being indexed, which in turn means you can perform fast searches covering the full contents of a library by entering a search term in its search box. That action quickly pulls up all matching documents, even if they're located on a networked PC or server or on an external drive.

- Library files are automatically backed up by the Windows 10 File History feature.

Libraries are useful for large collections of digital media files, where archived files are stored in a shared network folder or on an external drive, with current work on a local drive. They're also invaluable for keeping team projects organized—create a library that includes your local project folder and the shared folders where your coworkers store graphics and final submissions.

Figure 12-6 illustrates a library search. Here we created a custom library called Research, made up of a synced OneDrive folder, a local folder containing scanned documents, and a shared network folder. Searching for the term *population* returns a single results list containing eight matching items—four Word documents, three Excel worksheets, and a PDF file—stored in three different locations.

To create a new library, right-click the Libraries heading in the navigation pane, and then click New > Library. (If you prefer the ribbon, click Home > New Item > Library.) Give the new library a descriptive name and then press Enter. Your newly created library appears in the navigation pane. Click the Include A Folder button to populate the library.

Using the Include Folder In dialog box, select the folder you want to use as the default location for saving files in this library and then click Include Folder. That opens the library and lists the contents of the folder you just selected.

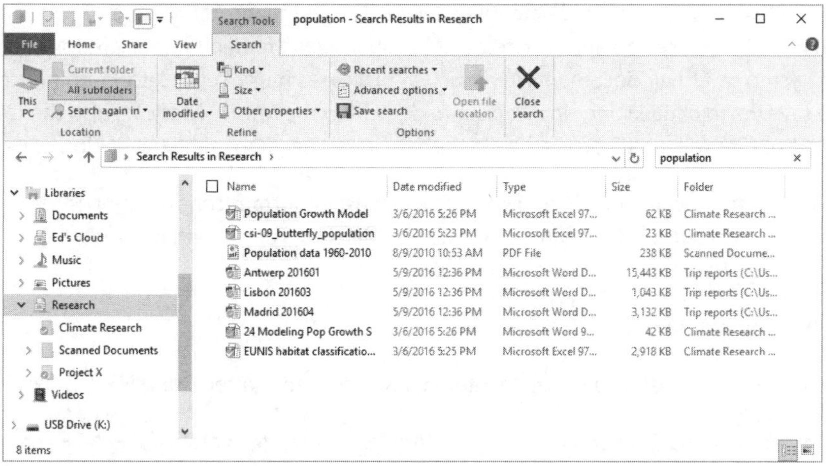

Figure 12-6 The custom library shown here includes folders on two separate local drives and one on a network server. Search results cover all three locations.

To add more folders to the library, click the Manage tab under the Library Tools heading. Then click Manage Library to get to the Library Locations dialog box, shown in Figure 12-7.

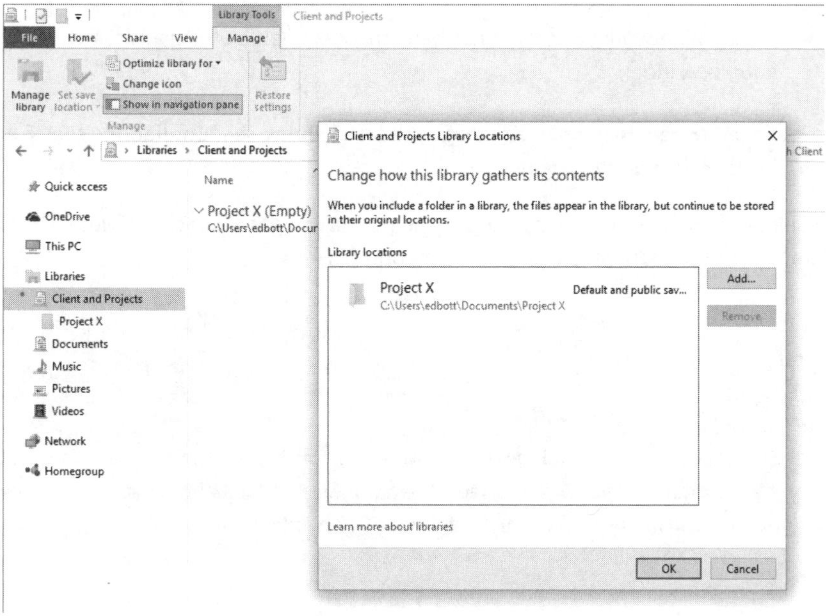

Figure 12-7 The first folder you add to a library becomes the default location for saving files within that library. Use the Manage Library button to add more folders and change settings.

In this dialog box, you can delete folders as well as add them, of course, and you can also change the library's default save folder. The default save folder is important for applications that expect to save their documents in particular places—a music service, for example, that expects to save downloaded songs in a certain folder within the Music library. It's also the folder that File Explorer will use if you drag a file to the library's heading in the navigation pane.

What locations can you add to a library? The most important consideration is that the folder must be indexed so that it can be included in searches. Folders and network shares in any of the following locations are eligible for inclusion:

- The system drive.

- An additional volume on an internal local drive formatted using NTFS or FAT32.

- An external USB or IEEE 1394 (FireWire) hard drive, formatted using NTFS or FAT32.

- A USB flash drive, if the device appears in the navigation pane, under the This PC heading. (Most removable drives do not satisfy this condition.)

- A shared network folder that's indexed using Windows Search; this includes any shared folder from another computer in your homegroup as well as shared folders on Windows-based servers.

- A shared network folder that has been made available offline and is therefore available in your local index.

  ➤ For more details on how to manage the search index, see "Configuring search and indexing options" later in this chapter.

To delete a library, right-click its entry in the navigation pane and click Delete. The library is gone, but its component folders and their contents remain.

Inside OUT

Open a file or folder location from a library

Because libraries are virtual folders, it's sometimes difficult to perform operations directly on their contents. If you want to see a file or folder in its actual location in File Explorer, right-click and choose Open File Location or Open Folder Location.

Managing file properties and metadata

Every file you view in File Explorer has a handful of properties that describe the file itself: the file name and file name extension (which is associated with the program that opens that type of file), the file's size, the date and time it was created and last modified, and any file system attributes. These properties are stored in the file system and are central to displaying the contents of a folder or other location and performing simple searches.

In addition to these basic file properties, many data-file formats can store custom metadata. These additional properties can be added by a device or by software; in some cases, they can be modified by the user. When you take a digital picture, your camera or smartphone might add the device make and model, exposure time, ISO speed, and other details to the file when it's saved. When you buy a digital music track or album, the individual audio files include tags that identify the artist, album, track number, and other details. Microsoft Word automatically adds your name to the Author field in a document you create; you can fill in additional properties such as keywords and comments and save them with the file.

Inside OUT

Rate your favorite digital media files

For digital photos, music, and other media files, you'll notice that the Rating field is available in the details pane. Instead of providing a box to enter free-form text or a number, this field shows five stars, all displayed in gray if this value is empty. You can rate any file on a scale of one to five stars by clicking or tapping the appropriate star in the details pane. Adding ratings is a useful way to filter large media collections so that they show only the entries you previously rated highly. Ratings are also useful for assembling playlists and slide shows.

The details pane, which you can display by clicking Details Pane on the View tab, displays a thumbnail of the selected file (if a thumbnail is available), plus metadata saved as file properties. In the following illustration from a subfolder in the Pictures library, you can see the date the photo was taken, the make of the camera, the dimensions of the picture, the exposure settings, and quite a bit more.

CHAPTER 12

0811161911a_HDR

JPG File

Date taken:	8/11/2016 7:11 PM
Tags:	Add a tag
Rating:	☆ ☆ ☆ ☆ ☆
Dimensions:	5312 x 2988
Size:	5.89 MB
Title:	Add a title
Authors:	Add an author
Comments:	Add comments
Camera maker:	LG Electronics
Camera model:	VS990
Subject:	Specify the subject
F-stop:	f/1.8
Exposure time:	1/30 sec.
ISO speed:	ISO-150
Exposure bias:	0 step
Focal length:	4 mm
Metering mode:	Center Weighted Average
Flash mode:	No flash, compulsory
Date created:	8/11/2016 7:12 PM
Date modified:	8/11/2016 7:11 PM

Saving custom information as metadata can make it easier to find that file (and others like it) using the search tools we describe later in this chapter.

The properties displayed in the details pane are an excellent starting point, but they might not represent every detail available for the selected file. To see the complete list, right-click the item and click Properties (or select the item and press Alt+Enter). Then click the Details tab in the properties dialog box.

Figure 12-8 shows a side-by-side comparison of the properties dialog box and the details pane for a music track. A casual listener might not care that the properties dialog box includes such exotica as Period, Mood, Beats-Per-Minute, and Initial Key, but a professional DJ can certainly find uses for those extra details.

In either place, the details pane or the properties dialog box, you can edit many (but not all) of the item's properties. Some properties, such as file size, are calculated by the file system or are otherwise fixed and cannot be directly modified. But you can edit custom metadata if the format of the underlying file allows you to do so.

To enter or change a property's value, simply click and type. If you add two or more words or phrases to a field that accepts multiple entries (such as Tags or Authors), use semicolons to separate them. Press Enter or click Save to add the new or changed properties to the file.

You can edit properties for multiple files at one time. This is especially useful when you're correcting an error in an album or artist name; just select all the songs in the album's folder. When more than one file is selected, you'll note that some properties in the details pane (such as track numbers and song titles) change to indicate that the specified field contains multiple values. A change you make to any field is written to all the files in your selection.

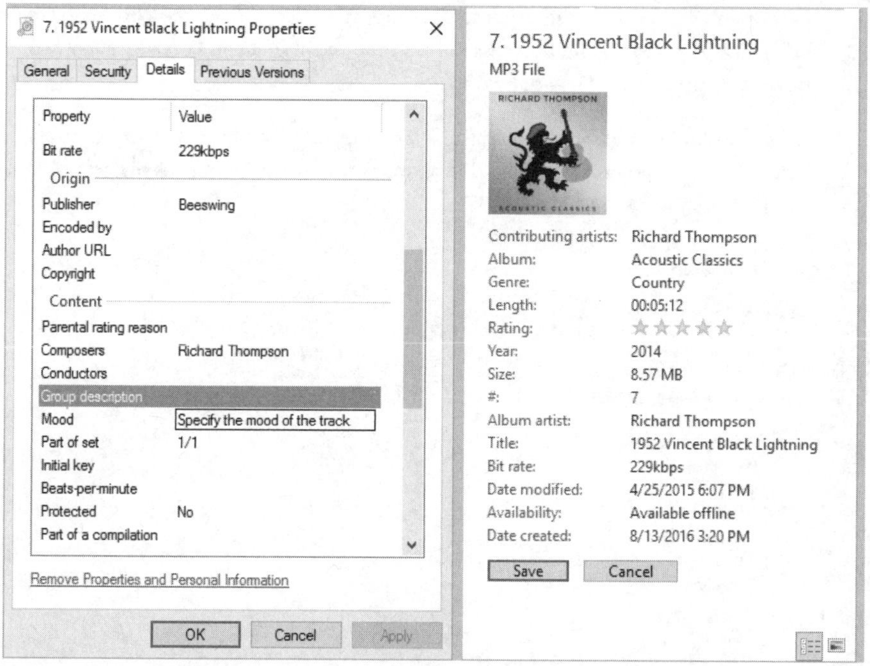

Figure 12-8 The Details tab in a file's properties dialog box (left) offers a more exhaustive set of editable properties than the simpler details pane (right).

Metadata is saved within the file itself, using industry-standard data storage formats. Software developers who need to create a custom file format can make its metadata available to Windows by using an add-in called a property handler, which opens the file format to read and write its properties. Because metadata is saved within the file itself, the properties you edit in File Explorer or a Windows program are fully portable. This opens some useful possibilities:

● You can move files to other computers, even those running other operating systems, without losing the files' tags and other metadata.

● You can edit a file in an application other than the one in which it was created without losing any of the file's properties (assuming the other application properly adheres to the file format's standard for reading and writing metadata).

● A file's properties are visible to anyone who has read access to the file.

CHAPTER 12

Inside OUT

Remove personal metadata for privacy's sake

Metadata within a file can tell a lot about you. Cameras record data about when a picture was taken and what camera or smartphone was used. Microsoft Office automatically adds author and company information to documents and spreadsheets. With user-created tags, you can add personal and business details that might be useful on a local copy but are unwise to disclose to the wider world.

To scrub a file of unwanted metadata, select one or more files in File Explorer, click Home > Properties > Remove Properties. This opens the Remove Properties dialog box, an example of which is shown here:

At this point, you have two choices. The default option creates a copy of your file (using the original file name with the word "Copy" appended to it) and removes all properties that can be changed, based on the file type. With the second option, Remove The Following Properties From This File, you select the check boxes next to individual properties and permanently remove those properties from the file when you click OK. (If no check box is visible, that property is not editable.)

Of course, common sense should prevail when it comes to issues of privacy. This option zeroes out metadata, but it does nothing with the contents of the file itself. You'll need to be vigilant to ensure that a digital photo doesn't contain potentially revealing information in the image itself or that sensitive personal or business details aren't saved within a document's contents.

You can edit custom properties (including tags) only in files saved using a format that accommodates embedded metadata. For digital image files, Windows supports the JPEG, GIF, and TIFF formats, but you cannot save metadata in bitmap images and graphics files saved in PNG format because these formats were not developed with metadata in mind. Among music file formats, MP3, WMA, and FLAC fully support a wide range of properties designed to make it easy to manage a music collection; files saved in the uncompressed WAV (.wav) format do not support any custom tags. Plain text and Rich Text Format (.rtf) files do not support custom metadata; files saved in Word formats expose a rich set of additional properties, as do all other native file formats from Microsoft Office programs.

In some cases, you'll find that you're unable to view or edit metadata in a file even though the underlying format supports metadata. In that case, the culprit is a missing property handler. In some cases, you can lose data in this situation if you're not careful.

Using OneDrive to store, sync, and share files

OneDrive, Microsoft's cloud-based file-storage service, is a crucial part of the Windows 10 experience. When you sign in with a Microsoft account, Windows 10 synchronizes settings and stores recovery keys for encrypted storage using OneDrive. Every free Microsoft account includes 5 GB of OneDrive storage. You can expand that storage capacity with paid upgrades to OneDrive or get a massively increased cloud storage allotment (1024 GB per user) with an Office 365 Home or Personal subscription.

By using OneDrive as the default location for documents, you can have access to your work files from anywhere. If you store your music collection in OneDrive, you can play your favorite tunes using Groove Music. Likewise, you can store, organize, edit, and share one or more digital photos from OneDrive using the Windows 10 Photos app.

The consumer version of OneDrive is separate from OneDrive for Business, which offers enterprise-class management capabilities and 1024 GB of file storage for each Office 365 Business and Enterprise subscription.

OneDrive offers a sync client for every major desktop and mobile operating system. In Windows 10, this sync client is built in and is updated automatically. Before we get to that sync client, though, let's start with an overview of the two OneDrive services.

CHAPTER 12

Inside OUT

Disable OneDrive in Windows 10

Maybe you're philosophically opposed to storing files in the cloud. Maybe you prefer a cloud service from another provider. Or maybe you just don't see the need for OneDrive. Regardless of the reason, if you don't want to use OneDrive, you're free to ignore it. If you're asked to sign in to the sync client, click Cancel, and all your files will remain on your local drive or your network. From OneDrive Settings, you can tell Windows not to load the sync client at startup, making it even easier to steer clear of the cloud.

That option does, however, leave the OneDrive icon in the navigation pane of File Explorer. To make it disappear, you need to make a simple registry edit.

In Windows 10 Pro or Enterprise, you can use Group Policy to make this change. Open Local Group Policy Editor (Gpedit.msc) and go to Computer Configuration > Administrative Templates > Windows Components > OneDrive. Double-click the policy Prevent The Usage Of OneDrive For File Storage and set it to Enabled. After you restart your PC, you'll find that the OneDrive icon is no longer in the navigation pane and the sync client no longer runs.

On devices running Windows 10 Home, where Group Policy isn't available, you must edit the registry manually. Using Registry Editor, navigate to HKLM\Software\Policies\Microsoft\Windows\OneDrive. (If that key doesn't exist, you need to create it.) Add a new DWORD value, DisableFileSyncNGSC, and set it to 1. Restart the PC to make the policy setting effective.

Note that this change applies to every user of the selected device. Any previously synced files stored in the OneDrive folder are still available but are no longer linked to their cloud counterparts.

How OneDrive and OneDrive for Business work

Despite the brand name they share, Microsoft's two cloud-based file-storage services have different origins and different feature sets. Both are designed to allow access to files and folders in a web browser, but there are some big differences in how the two services work.

OneDrive, the consumer service, is designed for personal use, with special views that showcase photo libraries and albums, as well as the ability to store a music collection that can be streamed through Groove Music. OneDrive is the default storage option for Office 365 Home and Personal editions, although nothing prevents you from using it for work. (In fact, the authors, editors, and production professionals who collaborated on this book used OneDrive extensively to exchange and share files.)

Files stored in OneDrive are organized into folders and subfolders just as they would be on a local drive. Figure 12-9 shows the contents of a subfolder in the OneDrive Documents folder, as viewed in a web browser. Note the range of options available in the command bar for the selected file, as well as the additional menu choices available with a click.

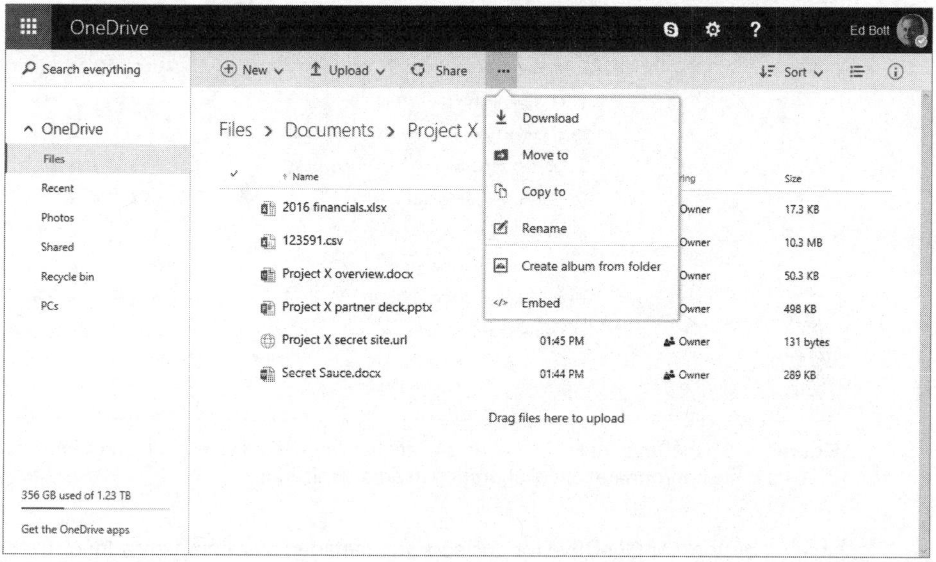

Figure 12-9 When using OneDrive in a web browser, you can perform most file-management tasks, with the ability to create, edit, and collaborate on Office documents.

OneDrive for Business offers a similar web-based view, as shown in Figure 12-10. Note that subscription settings aren't accessible from the navigation pane on the left. That's because a OneDrive for Business subscription is managed by a company administrator, with additional security and collaboration options appropriate for use in an organization.

When you sign in with a Microsoft account, OneDrive is just one of several services available. Clicking the menu button on the left (which looks like a grid of nine squares and is sometimes referred to as the "waffle" button) displays the full range of options, including Mail and Calendar (from Outlook.com) and the Office Online apps—Word, Excel, OneNote, and so on.

When you sign in to an Office 365 Business or Enterprise account, clicking the waffle-shaped menu button in the same location displays a larger group of options, and the OneDrive icon leads to OneDrive for Business.

Both services allow subscribers to share files and folders with other people. The consumer edition of OneDrive allows complete control of sharing, letting you make a file, a photo, or an entire folder public. You can also share access by using a link that doesn't require signing in to a Microsoft account.

CHAPTER 12

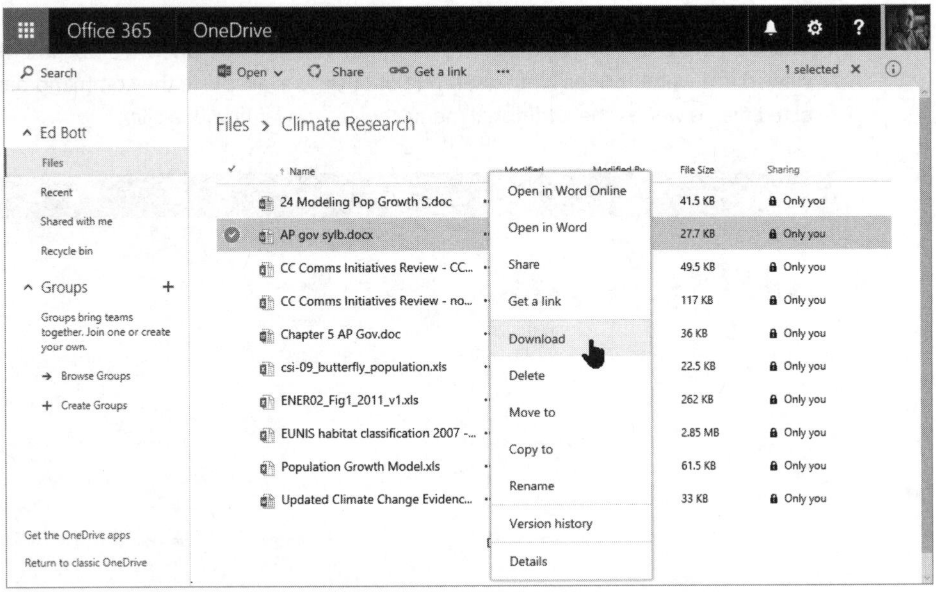

Figure 12-10 OneDrive for Business offers a familiar web-based view of files and folders, with options that are more appropriate for collaboration in an organization.

Sharing options for OneDrive for Business are managed by a company administrator, who might apply restrictions on sharing files with other people, especially in folders that contain confidential company information.

Both OneDrive and OneDrive for Business include built-in versioning, so you can see the history of a document and download an earlier version if you want to recover a portion of an earlier draft. The Recycle Bin for both services makes it possible to retrieve deleted documents.

Synchronizing files with Windows 10 devices

The point of OneDrive's file synchronization is to allow you to store your files in the cloud and then access those files from anywhere. One option, of course, is through a web browser. But Microsoft has also released platform-specific clients you can use to browse, open, and synchronize those files on any device. With files synced locally, you can open and edit those files even if you're offline, with your changes synced back to the cloud the next time you connect.

The Windows 10 Anniversary update includes what Microsoft calls its Next Generation Sync Client (NGSC), which is capable of linking the signed-in account to a single OneDrive account and one or more OneDrive for Business accounts. The NGSC is a significant upgrade over the OneDrive sync client in the initial release of Windows 10, which worked only with OneDrive consumer accounts.

Each OneDrive account you link to Windows 10 shows up as a node in the navigation pane in File Explorer. Each account also gets its own icon in the notification area—white for OneDrive, blue for OneDrive for Business. To begin setup for the first time on a Windows 10 device, click either the OneDrive node in the navigation pane or the gray OneDrive icon in the notification area. Either action opens the Set Up OneDrive dialog box shown here, which is the first step in a straightforward wizard:

After you enter your email address, the setup wizard determines whether that address is associated with a OneDrive personal account or a OneDrive for Business account and prompts you to sign in. After entering your credentials, you see the dialog box shown in Figure 12-11, which recommends a local folder to hold your synced files. Your inclination might be to just click Next and move on quickly; we recommend you stop and consider your options here.

The default location is a folder in your user profile, with the name OneDrive followed by a hyphen and either the word "Personal" or the name of your organization (for OneDrive for Business accounts). (Allow the mouse pointer to hover over the file name if it's truncated.) We can think of two good reasons to click Change Location and select a different drive. First, if your business name is long, consider giving the folder a shorter name to avoid running into problems with lengthy path names. Second, if your system drive is a relatively small SSD and you have a separate data drive with multiple terabytes of storage, you definitely want to choose that data drive for synced files.

Figure 12-11 The default location for storing your synced files is a folder in your user profile. Click Change Location to change the folder name or sync files to a separate data drive.

Inside OUT

Move your local storage folder after setup is complete

Unlike many other data folders in your user profile, the OneDrive sync folders don't include a Location tab as part of the properties dialog box. That's why we recommend you make this configuration decision wisely when you first link your OneDrive account to your PC.

But if you realize after the fact (and after syncing lots of files) that you want to move the OneDrive folder, there's a relatively simple workaround.

Right-click the OneDrive icon in the notification area and then click Settings. On the Account tab of the resulting dialog box, click Unlink This PC—don't worry, your local files and those in the cloud are unaffected. After OneDrive confirms that your account is unlinked, move or rename the (now unsynced) local folder, and then go through OneDrive setup again, specifying the new folder name as your sync location.

When setup is complete, OneDrive confirms that the files in the cloud match those in the new location. The process should go swiftly, with no loss of data.

The final step is choosing which folders you want to sync from the cloud to the local device. If the free space on your data drive is larger than the entire contents of your OneDrive folder, you can accept the default setting, Sync All Files And Folders In My OneDrive, as shown here:

But if your cloud file collection includes hundreds of gigabytes of photos, music and video files, and documents, synchronizing everything is not always a viable option, especially on devices that have limited local storage, such as laptop PCs, phones, and tablets. In that case, you can selectively sync folders in the cloud to the local device, leaving the other files and folders available only from the cloud.

Repeat this process for other accounts you want to set up, bearing in mind you can link only one OneDrive personal account. Note that the Microsoft account you link in OneDrive does not have to be the same one you use to sign in to Windows 10, although that's the most common (and logical) configuration.

At any time, you can change your OneDrive configuration by right-clicking the OneDrive icon in the taskbar and then clicking Settings. From the resulting dialog box, you can add a new account, unlink an existing account, change the selection of folders you're syncing, and limit the amount of bandwidth your system uses.

CHAPTER 12

Sharing OneDrive files with others

On the web, OneDrive offers multiple options for sharing files with others. You can access the same sharing options for files that are synced to your local device. From the OneDrive folder in File Explorer, right-click the file or folder you want to share and then click Share A OneDrive Link. That option creates a link to the shared file or folder, and then copies that link to the Clipboard so that you can paste it into an email message or a chat window.

That type of sharing link is, of course, not secure. Anyone who has the link can access the files, so this option is not appropriate for sharing files that contain confidential information. For cases where you need more security, click the More OneDrive Sharing Options menu item. That opens a web browser with a full range of sharing options, including the capability to manage permissions so that only people you authorize have access to the shared files.

Inside OUT

Share and sync files between accounts

One of OneDrive's best-kept secrets is the capability for friends and coworkers to work together using shared folders. The technique is simple: You mark a folder as shared, giving your colleagues access to it when they sign in with a Microsoft account that has permission to read and write to that folder.

On the other end, your colleague opens OneDrive on the web and clicks Shared in the navigation pane on the left. She then opens the shared folder, clicks the ellipsis button at the end of the command bar, and then clicks Add To My OneDrive. The folder is now available in her list of folders that are eligible to be synced. Both of you now have full access to the contents of the shared folder.

For this technique to be most effective, you should name the shared folder carefully, using a descriptive name like "Shared Files for Budget Committee," so that everyone who sees it knows immediately that it's a shared folder.

Sorting, filtering, and grouping in File Explorer

Regardless of the view settings you've chosen for a folder, you can adjust the way its contents are displayed at any time by changing the sort order, filtering the contents by one or more properties to include only selected items, and grouping and arranging the contents by a particular heading. In any view, the sort and group options are available by right-clicking anywhere in the contents pane and choosing a Sort By or Group By option. In most cases, however, these actions are easier to accomplish by switching to Details view and using the column headings, which is also the preferred way to filter.

Note that all these techniques also work with virtual folders, such as search results and libraries.

Sorting a folder's contents

To sort a folder in Details view, click the heading you want to use as a sort key. For example, to sort by Date Modified, click the Date Modified heading. Click again on the same heading to reverse the sort order. An up arrow or down arrow above the heading indicates whether the folder is sorted in ascending or descending order by the current field.

In all other views, right-click any empty space in the contents pane and select a value from the Sort By menu. A bullet next to Ascending or Descending indicates the current sort order; choose the other option to reverse the sort order.

Filtering folder contents

In Details view only, you can use headings to filter the contents of a folder. If you rest your pointer on a heading, a drop-down arrow appears at the right. Clicking the arrow reveals a set of filter check boxes appropriate for that heading. In most cases, the filter list is built on the fly from the contents of the current file list. If you're looking for a particular type of file—a Word or PDF document, for example, or a text file—you can filter by type to show only those files. Figure 12-12 shows the filter list for the Type field in a folder, with the contents filtered to show only files whose type matches Text Document.

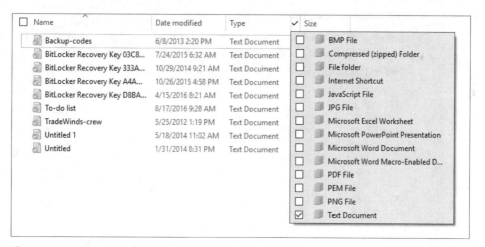

Figure 12-12 When you click the drop-down arrow to the right of a column heading, a set of filtering options appropriate for that heading appears.

Select the check box next to any item to add it to the filter list; clear the check box to remove a previously selected item from the filter. After you filter the list in Details view, you can switch to any other view and the filter will persist. Look in the address bar to see the specific filter applied, and click the folder name to the left of the search term in the address bar (also known as a *breadcrumb*) to remove all filtering without switching back to Details view.

If you filter by Size or Name, you get a much more limited set of choices that includes ranges rather than discrete values.

A single filter can include multiple items from each heading's filter list, which are treated as a logical OR—in other words, File Explorer displays items that match any of the selected check boxes. A filter can also include multiple headings, which together function as a logical AND, with File Explorer displaying only items that satisfy the criteria applied to each heading. So, for example, you can filter a picture folder to show only photos where the value in the Rating column is four or five stars and the value in the Date Taken field is in this year, resulting in a list of your favorite photos of the year, suitable for a year-end newsletter or family photo album.

When a folder is filtered, check marks appear to the right of headings used for filtering. The values on which you have filtered appear in the address bar. You can perform most common file-management tasks on the items in the results list, including renaming individual files or using the Clipboard to copy or move files from their current location to a new folder.

Inside OUT

Use the date navigator to zoom through time

If you click a date heading, the filter options display a date navigator like the one shown next, with common date groupings available at the bottom of the list. You can also click Select A Date Or Date Range and use the calendar to filter the file list that way.

The date navigator is much more powerful than it looks at first glance. Use the calendar to zoom in or out and narrow or expand your view of the contents of a folder or a search. Initially, the calendar shows the current month, with today's date highlighted. Click the month heading to zoom out to a display showing the current year as a heading with the current month highlighted. You can then drag or hold down Ctrl and click to select multiple months, as shown here:

Click the year to zoom out again to show the current decade. Click once more to show the current century. In any calendar view, you can use the arrows to the left and right of the column heading to move through the calendar a month, year, decade, or century at a time. To zoom back in, click any month, year, decade, or century on the calendar control. This technique is especially valuable with folders or search results containing hundreds or thousands of files and folders.

Grouping folder contents

If sorting and filtering don't give you enough ways to organize or locate files, try grouping. When you group items, File Explorer collects all the items that have some common property, displaying each group under a heading that can be expanded or collapsed in most views.

List view offers a particularly interesting perspective, with each group of results appearing under a column heading. The grouped arrangement is saved as part of the custom view settings for that folder; the next time you open the folder, it will still be grouped.

To group items in a File Explorer window, open the View tab, click Group By, and then click the property you want to use. File Explorer displays a dot before the selected property. You can remove the grouping by returning to Group By and choosing None. Figure 12-13 shows a collection of picture files grouped by tags.

Figure 12-13 You can group items in any view. This folder, filled with pictures, is grouped by tag in Details view.

Inside OUT

Use check boxes to simplify file selection

File Explorer offers two modes of file and folder selection—with and without check boxes. You can switch between them by means of the Item Check Boxes command on the View tab.

With check boxes on, you can select multiple items that are not adjacent to one another by clicking or tapping the check box for each one in turn; to remove an item from the selection, clear its check box. In either case, there's no need to hold down the Ctrl key. (This option is especially useful when you're trying to select files using a touchscreen.) In any case, though, Ctrl-selecting and Shift-selecting work as they always have, with or without check boxes.

Inside OUT

Zip through File Explorer with keyboard shortcuts

Pressing Ctrl+N in File Explorer opens a new window on the same folder. Ctrl+W closes the current window. (These keyboard shortcuts function the same way in Internet Explorer.) The following additional keyboard shortcuts work in File Explorer:

- **Alt+Up Arrow.** Go up one level.

- **Alt+Right Arrow.** Go forward.

- **Alt+Left Arrow.** Go back.

- **Alt+D.** Move the focus to the address bar, and select the current path.

- **F4.** Move the insertion point to the address bar, and display the contents of the drop-down list of previous addresses.

- **Alt+Enter.** Show properties of the selected file.

- **Tab.** Cycle through the following elements: navigation pane, file list, column headings, address bar, search box.

- **F11.** Switch in and out of full-screen mode.

- **Ctrl+Shift+N.** Create a new subfolder in the current folder.

- **Ctrl+Shift+E.** Expand the navigation pane to the current folder.

Using Windows Search

Perhaps more than any other feature in Windows, the search tools have the potential to change the way you work. If your filing philosophy involves the digital equivalent of throwing everything into a giant shoebox, you'll be startled at how easy it is to find what you're looking for. Even if you consider yourself an extremely well-organized Windows user, we predict you'll find ways to integrate File Explorer's search tools into your everyday routine.

NOTE

You can search for files and folders with Cortana's help, using the search box on the taskbar. For more details, see "Using Cortana for search and more," in Chapter 9.

Configuring search and indexing options

At its heart, Windows Search relies on a speedy, powerful, and well-behaved indexing service that does a fine job of keeping track of files and folders by name, by properties, and (in supported formats) by contents. All those details are kept in the search index, a database that keeps track of indexed file names, properties, and the contents of files. As a rule, when you do most common types of searches, Windows checks the index first and returns whatever results it finds there.

> ### NOTE
> The search index is stored by default in %ProgramData%\Microsoft\Search\Data. Default permissions for this folder are set to allow access only to the System account and to members of the Administrators group. You can change its location using the Indexing Options dialog box (available by searching from the taskbar or Control Panel). We can't, however, think of a good reason to do so. This folder contains no user-editable files, and we recommend that you leave it in its default location with its contents undisturbed.

Inside OUT

When do searches skip the index?

Although we focus mostly on indexed searches in this section, Windows 10 actually includes two search engines. The second engine is informally known as *grep* search. (The name comes from an old UNIX command derived from the full name *global | regular expression | print.*) Windows Search uses the index whenever you use the search box on the taskbar, in libraries, and in locations that are part of a homegroup. In those circumstances, search looks only in the index and ignores any subfolders that are excluded from the index.

Windows uses the grep search engine if you begin your search from the This PC folder, from the root of any local drive (including the system drive), or from a local file folder. Grep searches include the contents of all subfolders within the search scope regardless of whether they're included in the search index. For a more detailed examination of non-indexed searches, see "Advanced search tools and techniques" later in this chapter.

To build the index that makes its magic possible, Windows Search uses several separate processes. The index is constructed dynamically by the Windows Search service, SearchIndexer.exe. The indexer crawls through all locations that are prescribed to be indexed, converting the content of documents (in supported formats) into plain text and then storing the text and metadata for quick retrieval.

The Windows Search service begins running shortly after you start a new Windows session. From that point on, it runs in the background at all times, creating the initial index and updating it as new files are added and existing ones are changed or deleted. Protocol handlers do the work of cracking open different data stores to add items to the index. Property handlers allow Windows Search to extract the values of properties from items and store them properly in the index. Filters extract the contents of supported file types so that you can do full-text searches for those items.

Which files and folders are in the index?

Indexing every 0 and 1 on your hard disk would be a time-consuming and space-consuming task—and ultimately pointless. When you search for a snippet of text, you're almost always looking for something you wrote, copied, or saved, and you don't want the results to include random program files that happen to have the same snippet embedded in the midst of a blob of code. (Yes, we know some developers might disagree, but they're the exception.) So the default settings for the indexer make some reasonable inclusions and exclusions.

Certain locations are specifically included. These include your user profile (but not the AppData folder), the contents of the Start menu, and your browser history. Locally synced files from One-Drive as well as offline files stored in the client-side cache (CSC) are automatically included in your local index. You can explicitly add other folders to the index, but Windows 10 eliminates the need to do that. Instead, just add the folder to a library; when you do so, Windows automatically adds that folder to the list of indexed locations and begins indexing its contents without requiring any additional steps on your part.

To see which folders are currently being indexed, open the Indexing Options dialog box. You can get there in various ways, including by entering **Indexing Options** in the search box on the taskbar. As Figure 12-14 shows, the Indexing Options dialog box initially shows the top level of folders that are included in the index.

To get more information about what's being indexed, click Modify, which opens the Indexed Locations dialog box.

CAUTION

We strongly recommend that you not try to manage locations manually using the Indexed Locations dialog box. If you add a folder to a library and then remove it from the list of indexed locations, the folder remains in the navigation pane under the associated library, but none of its contents will be visible in the library itself.

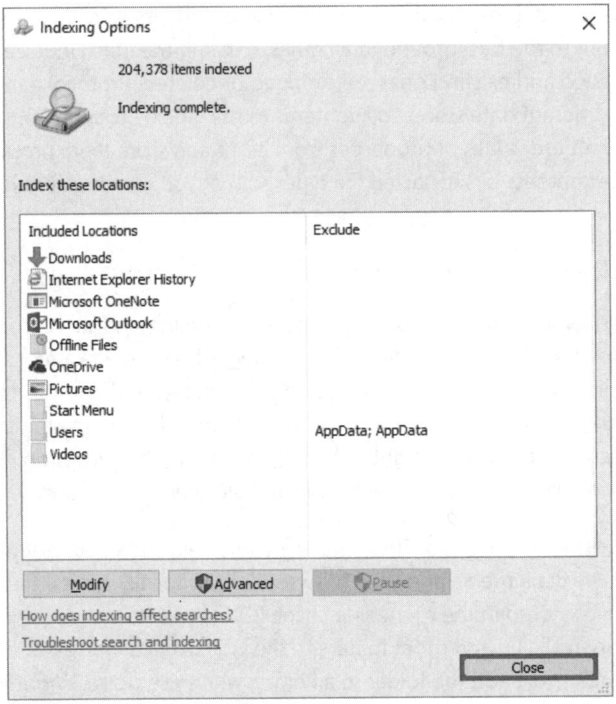

Figure 12-14 The Indexing Options dialog box shows the top level of locations that are included in the index. Subfolders (for example, all the profile subfolders of Users) are not shown here.

In its default view, the list of folders and other data stored on the Indexed Locations dialog box shows only locations that are accessible to your user account. To see (and manage) locations from other user profiles, click Show All Locations. As the User Account Control (UAC) shield icon makes clear, you need to be signed in as an administrator (or provide an administrator's credentials) to continue.

Within that list of indexed locations, the Windows Search service records the file name and properties (size, date modified, and so on) of any file or folder. Files marked as System and Hidden are indexed but are displayed in search results only when you change File Explorer settings to show those file types. Metadata for common music, image, and video file formats is included in the index by default. The indexer also includes the contents of a file and its custom properties if the file format has an associated property handler and filter, as is the case with most popular document formats.

To see if a particular file format supports content indexing, open the Indexing Options dialog box, click Advanced, and then click the File Types tab. Find the extension associated with the file type and then look in the Filter Description column for the name of the filter that handles that extension. If you see File Properties Filter, the file type does not support content indexing. File types that are supported have a named filter, such as Microsoft Office Filter, Open Document Format ODT Filter, HTML Filter, or Reader Search Handler.

The list of formats on the File Types tab on your computer might include more file types if you installed Windows programs that include custom property handlers and filters, such as the Office Open XML Format Word Filter installed with Microsoft Office 365.

Windows Search does not index the content of files that are saved without a file name extension, nor does it index the contents of files that are protected by Information Rights Management (IRM) or digital rights management (DRM).

A handful of locations are specifically excluded from indexing. Even if you manually specify that you want your system drive (normally C) to be included in the index, the following files and folders will be excluded:

- The entire contents of the \Windows folder and all its subfolders. (The Windows.old folder that's created by an upgrade installation of Windows 10 is also excluded.)

- \$Recycle.Bin (the hidden folder that contains deleted files for all user accounts).

- \Users\Default and all of its subfolders. (This is the user profile template used to create a profile for a new user.)

- The entire contents of the \Program Files and \Program Files (x86) folders and all their subfolders.

- The \ProgramData folder (except the subfolder that contains shortcuts for the shared Start menu).

Monitoring the index and tuning indexer performance

The status message at the top of the Indexing Options dialog box offers real-time updates on what the indexer is doing at the moment. "Indexing complete" means there are no pending tasks. The status message lists the number of items (files, folders, and so on) that are currently in the index.

"Indexing paused" means the service has temporarily stopped all indexing tasks; you'll see this message if you check the indexer status shortly after you start the computer because the default setting for the Windows Search service is Automatic (Delayed Start).

If indexing tasks are currently underway, the status message displays an increase or decrease in the number of items indexed as new, changed, and deleted files are processed. The indexer is designed to throttle itself whenever it detects that the system is working on other, presumably more important tasks. As a result, you'll most likely be told that "Indexing speed is reduced due to user activity" when you first check.

CHAPTER 12

That message indicates the indexing service has backed off in response to your activity and is operating at a fraction of its normal speed. If the number of files to be indexed is big enough (if you copied a folder with several thousand documents, for instance), you'll see the indexing speed pick up dramatically after you keep your hands off the keyboard and mouse for a minute or so.

The exact speed of indexing depends on various factors, including the speed of your CPU and storage subsystem as well as the number, size, and complexity of documents and whether their full contents are being indexed. Unfortunately, the status message in the Indexing Options dialog box doesn't include a progress bar and doesn't indicate how many files are yet to be indexed, so there's no easy way to tell whether the current task is barely underway or nearly complete. If you haven't recently added any new folders to the index but have simply been changing a few files in the course of normal work, the index should stay close to complete (assuming you've ever had a complete index).

In the past, some websites for performance-obsessed Windows users complained about the performance hit that Windows Search causes; some even recommended disabling the Windows Search service to improve overall system performance. We recommend you leave it running. In our experience, the Windows Search service uses only a small percentage of available CPU resources even at its busiest. The indexing service is specifically designed to back off when you use your computer for other activities, switching to low-priority input/output (I/O) and allow-ing foreground I/O tasks, such as opening Start, to execute first. When Windows 10 first builds its index, or if you copy a large number of files to the system at once, indexing can take a long time and cause some spikes in CPU and disk activity, but you shouldn't notice any impact on performance.

File Explorer accesses the index directly, so even if the indexer is busy processing new and changed files, it shouldn't affect the speed of a search operation. In normal operation, retrieving search results from even a very large index should take no more than a few seconds. You might notice a delay in opening a folder that contains a large number of compressed folders, includ-ing Zip files and ISO disk images.

TROUBLESHOOTING

You encounter problems finding files that should be in the search index

If you're certain that the files you're looking for are in an indexed location but they don't turn up in search results, the index might have become corrupted. As with so many Windows features, there's a troubleshooter for that.

Open Settings, and type **fix search** in the search box. Then click Find And Fix Problems With Windows Search. The troubleshooter that appears automatically finds and fixes any problems it can detect. If it finds none, it leads you through a series of steps to identify and resolve your problem.

Alternatively, you can manually rebuild the search index. From the Indexing Options dialog box, click Advanced, and then click Rebuild, under the Troubleshooting heading, as shown here:

We recommend you restart your system before trying to rebuild the index, to ensure that no open files are interfering with the indexing process. Rebuilding the index might take a considerable amount of time, especially if you have a large number of files to index. To maximize the efficiency of the reindexing process, start the operation when you know you don't need to use your PC—before lunch or at the end of your workday, for example.

Searching from File Explorer

To use File Explorer's search tools, start by selecting a folder or library to define the *scope* of your search—the set of files from which you want to draw search results. (If you're not sure which folder contains the files you're looking for, choose Libraries or Quick Access from the navigation pane.)

Next, click in the search box in the upper right corner of the File Explorer window. That action displays a new Search tab in the ribbon, under the color-coded Search Tools heading, but you don't need to use any of its tools for now. If you're simply looking for a file whose name, properties, or contents contain a particular word or phrase, just start typing in the search box.

CHAPTER 12

The following rules govern how searches work:

- Whatever text you type as a search term must appear at the beginning of a word, not in the middle. Thus, entering **des** returns items containing the words *desire*, *des*tination, and *des*troy but not un*des*irable or sad*des*t. (You can override this behavior by using wildcard characters, as we explain in "Advanced search tools and techniques" later in this chapter.)

- Search terms are not case sensitive. Thus, entering **Bott** returns items with *Ed Bott* as a tag or property, but the results also include files containing the words *bott*om and *bott*le.

- By default, searches ignore accents, umlauts, and other diacritical marks. If you routinely need to be able to distinguish, say, Händel from Handel, open the Indexing Options dialog box, click Advanced (for which you'll need administrative credentials), and then select Treat Similar Words With Diacritics As Different Words.

- To search for an exact phrase, enclose the phrase within quotation marks. Otherwise, you search for each word individually.

Search results for indexed folders appear so quickly that you might have a substantial number of hits before you type the second or third character in the search string. A complicating factor: If your search term is part of a subfolder name, your results list includes the entire contents of that subfolder.

Inside OUT

See all files in a folder and its subfolders

If you open File Explorer to a particular folder and you want to avoid the tedium of opening subfolders to view their contents, try using the wildcard character that's been around as long as Microsoft has been making operating systems. Entering an asterisk (*) in the search box immediately returns all files and subfolders in the current folder and all its subfolders. Assuming the list is of manageable size, you can then group, filter, sort, or otherwise rearrange the items within the folder to find exactly what you're looking for.

If simply entering a search term doesn't return the needed results, you have two options. The easiest is to build a new search (or refine the current one) using the point-and-click commands on the ribbon's Search Tools tab. The other is to use the powerful but cryptic search syntax to build a search manually.

We start with the Search tab (under the Search Tools heading), which offers a wealth of options to create and refine a search. The choices you make here return results from the current search scope. To change the scope, use the options in the Location group.

In Figure 12-15, for example, OneDrive is selected in the navigation pane, and All Subfolders (the default) is selected in the Location group on the ribbon. Clicking Date Modified and selecting Today from the drop-down list returns all files that were added or changed in all locally synced OneDrive folders today.

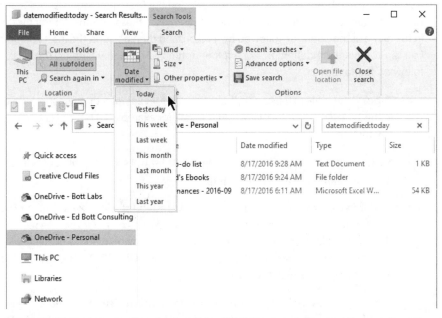

Figure 12-15 To make the Search tab visible, click in the search box, and then use its options to build a search from scratch or refine an existing search.

If you're looking for an invoice you created last month, you can click Last Month from the Date Modified list. If the set of results is still too large to scan, you can use additional options on the Search tab to refine the search or click in the search box and enter a word or phrase that you know was in the file's name or its contents.

Three filters get top billing in the Refine group on the Search tab:

- **Date Modified.** This property represents the most recent date a file or folder was saved. For a downloaded program file, it shows the date you saved the file locally, not the date the developer created it.

- **Kind.** This field shows predefined groups of file types, including those for some items that aren't stored in File Explorer. The most common choice to make here is Document, which includes text files, any file saved in a Microsoft Office format, and PDF files. Try Music, Movie, or Picture if you're looking for digital media files.

- **Size.** This list shows a range of sizes. If you're trying to clear space on your system drive, choosing Huge (16 – 128 MB) or Gigantic (>128 MB) is a good way to locate large files that can safely be deleted or archived on an external drive.

Using any of the previous three filters adds a search operator, followed by a colon and a parameter, in the search box. Clicking Other Properties on the Search tab offers additional, context-specific options to refine the search results. What makes these options different is that they fill in the name of the operator, followed by a colon, and then position the insertion point so that you can complete the definition. For a folder optimized for General Items, this list contains the following four options:

- **Type.** Enter a file extension (pdf, xls, or docx, for example) or any part of the description in the Type field in Details view; enter **Excel**, for example, to return Excel workbooks in any format.

- **Name.** Enter a string of text here. The results list will show any file or folder that contains that exact string anywhere in its name.

- **Folder Path.** Enter a string of text here. The results list will show any file or folder that contains that exact string anywhere in its full path. If you enter *doc*, the results will include all files and folders in your Documents folder and any of its subfolders (because Documents is part of the path for those subfolders), as well as the contents of any other folder whose name contains those three letters.

- **Tags.** Almost every data file contains this field, which is stored as metadata in the file itself. You can add one or more tags to any file using the Details pane or the Details tab in its properties dialog box.

The list of available options changes slightly for other folder types. Documents folders include Authors and Title operators, and Photos folders include Date Taken and Rating, for example.

To run the same search from a different location, click Search Again In and choose an available scope. Or just switch to a different node in the navigation pane and start again.

Advanced search tools and techniques

The search capabilities in Windows 10 are direct descendants of standalone tools and Windows features that date back to the turn of the 21st century. Those original search tools relied on something called Advanced Query Syntax (AQS), which survives, only slightly modified, in a mostly undocumented form today.

You can see some vestiges of AQS when you build a search using the Search tab. Each entry you make from the ribbon adds a corresponding query to the search box. When you learn the query syntax, you can create your own advanced searches and even save them for reuse, as we explain in this section.

NOTE

The advanced search syntax we describe here works in the File Explorer search box but not in searches from the taskbar.

The most basic query typically begins with a keyword (or a portion of a word) typed in the search box. Assuming you begin typing in a location that supports indexed searches (the task-bar search box or your locally synced OneDrive folder, for example), the list of search results will include any item in that location containing any indexed word (in its name or properties or content) that begins with the letters you type. You can then narrow the results list by using additional search parameters.

Advanced queries support the following types of search parameters, which can be combined using search operators:

- **File contents.** Keywords, phrases, numbers, and text strings

- **Kinds of items.** Folders, documents, pictures, music, and so on

- **Data stores.** Specific locations in the Windows file system containing indexed items

- **File properties.** Size, date, tags, and so on

In every case, these parameters consist of a word that the search query recognizes as a property or other index operator, followed by a colon and the value to search for or exclude. (When Windows Search recognizes a word followed by a colon as a valid property, it turns that operator blue.) You can combine search terms using Boolean operators and parentheses.

The value that immediately follows the colon can take several forms. If you want a loose (partial) match, just type a word or the beginning of a word. Thus, **type:Word** turns up files of the type Microsoft Word Document, Microsoft Word 97 – 2003 Document, Microsoft Word 97 – 2003 Template, Microsoft Word Macro-Enabled Document, and so on. To specify a strict (exact) match, use an equal sign and, if necessary, quotation marks, as in this example: **type:="Microsoft Word Document"**.

You can also use Boolean operators (AND, OR, and NOT) and parentheses to combine criteria. If you have fond memories of MS-DOS, you'll welcome using * and ? as wildcards, and you can dramatically change the behavior of a search by means of the innocuous-looking tilde (~) character (which forces Windows to perform a strict character search in indexed locations, as discussed later in this section).

CHAPTER 12

Of course, all these techniques become much more useful when you're able to reuse your carefully crafted search criteria, as we explain in "Saving searches and clearing search history" at the end of this chapter.

Searching by item type or kind

To search for files with a particular file name extension, you can simply enter the extension in the search box, like this:

`*.ext`

(Note that this method of searching does not work for .exe or .msc files.) The results include files that incorporate the extension in their contents as well as in their file names—which might or might not be what you want. You'll get a more focused search by using the ext: operator, including an asterisk wildcard and a period like this:

`ext:*.txt`

> ### NOTE
> As with many properties, you have more than one way to specify an exact file name extension. In addition to ext:, you can use fileext:, extension:, or fileextension:.

File name extensions are useful for some searches, but you'll get even better results using two different search properties: Type and Kind. The Type property limits your search based on the value found in the Type field for a given object. Thus, to look for files saved in any Microsoft Excel format, type this term in the search box:

`type:excel`

To find any music file saved in MP3 format, type this text in the search box:

`type:mp3`

To constrain your search to groups of related file types, use the Kind property, in the syntax kind:=*value*. Enter **kind:=doc**, for example, to return text files, Microsoft Office documents, Adobe Acrobat documents, HTML and XML files, and other document formats. This search term also accepts **folder**, **pic**, **picture**, **music**, **song**, **program**, and **video** as values to search for.

Changing the scope of a search

You can specify a folder or library location by using folder:, under:, in:, or path:. Thus, **folder:documents** restricts the scope of the search to your Documents library, and **in:videos mackie** finds all files in the Videos library that contain *Mackie* in the file name or any property.

Searching for item properties

You can search on the basis of any property recognized by the file system. (The list of available properties for files is identical to the ones we discuss in "Layouts, previews, and other ways to arrange files" earlier in this chapter.) To see the whole list of available properties, switch to Detail view in File Explorer, right-click any column heading, and then click More. The Choose Details dialog box that appears enumerates the available properties.

When you enter text in the search box, Windows searches file names, all properties, and indexed content, returning items where it finds a match with that value. That often generates more search results than you want. To find all documents of which Jean is the author, omitting documents that include the word Jean in their file names or content, you type **author:jean** in the search box. (To eliminate documents authored by Jeanne, Jeannette, or Jeanelle, add an equal sign and enclose jean in quotation marks: **author:="jean"**.)

When searching on the basis of dates, you can use long or short forms, as you please. For example, the search values

modified:9/29/16

and

modified:09/29/2016

are equivalent. (If you don't mind typing the extra four letters, use **datemodified:** instead.)

To search for dates before or after a particular date, use the less-than (<) and greater-than (>) operators. For example,

modified:>09/30/2015

searches for dates later than September 30, 2015. Use the same two operators to specify file sizes below and above some value.

Use two periods to search for items within a range of dates. To find files modified in September or October 2016, type this search term in the Start menu search box:

modified:9/1/2014..10/31/2016

You can also use ranges to search by file size. The search filters suggest some common ranges and even group them into neat little buckets, so you can type **size:** and then click Medium to find files in the range 100 KB to 1 MB.

Again, don't be fooled into thinking that this list represents the full selection of available sizes. You can specify an exact size range—using operators such as >, >=, <, and <=—or you can use the ".." operator. For example, **size:0 MB..1 MB** is the same as **size:<=1 MB**. You can specify values using bytes, KB, MB, or GB.

Inside OUT

Make your searches flexible

You don't need to enter a precise date as part of a search term. Instead, Windows Search recognizes "fuzzy" date qualifiers like *today*, *yesterday*, *this week*, and *last month*. This technique lets you create saved searches you can use to quickly open a window showing only the files you've worked on this week or last week. A search that uses dates picked from the calendar wouldn't be nearly as useful next month for identifying current projects, but one built using these relative dates will continue to be useful indefinitely.

Using multiple criteria for complex searches

You can use the Boolean operators AND, OR, and NOT to combine or negate criteria in the search box. These operators need to be spelled in capital letters (or they will be treated as ordinary text). In place of the AND operator, you can use a plus sign (+), and in place of the NOT operator, you can use a minus sign (–). You can also use parentheses to group criteria; items in parentheses separated by a space use an implicit AND operator. Table 12-1 provides some examples of combined criteria.

Table 12-1 Some examples of complex search values

This search value	Returns
Siechert AND Bott	Items in which at least one indexed element (property, file name, or an entire word within its contents) begins with or equals *Siechert* and another element in the same item begins with or equals *Bott*
title:("report" NOT draft)	Items in which the Title property contains the word *report* and does not contain a word that begins with *draft*
tag:tax AND author:Doug	Items authored by Doug that include *Tax* in the Tags field
tag:tax AND author:(Doug OR Craig) AND modified:<1/1/16	Items authored by Doug or Craig, last modified before January 1, 2016, with *Tax* in the Tags field

NOTE

When you use multiple criteria based on different properties, an AND conjunction is assumed unless you specify otherwise. The search value **tag:Ed Author:Carl** is equivalent to the search value **tag:Ed AND Author:Carl**.

Using wildcards and character-mode searches

File-search wildcards can be traced back to the dawn of Microsoft operating systems, well before the Windows era. In Windows 10, two of these venerable operators are alive and well:

- ***** The asterisk (also known as a star) operator can be placed anywhere in the search string and will match zero, one, or any other number of characters. In indexed searches, which treat your keyword as a prefix, this operator is always implied at the end; thus, a search for **voice** turns up *voice, voices,* and *voice-over.* Add an asterisk at the beginning of the search term (***voice**), and your search also turns up any item containing *invoice* or *invoices.* You can put an asterisk in the middle of a search term as well, which is useful for searching through folders full of data files that use a standard naming convention. If your invoices all start with INV, followed by an invoice number, followed by the date (INV-0038-20160227, for example), you can produce a quick list of all 2016 invoices by searching for **INV*2016***.

- **?** The question mark is a more focused wildcard. In index searches, it matches exactly one character in the exact position where it's placed. Using the naming scheme defined in the previous item, you can use the search term **filename:INV-????-2016*** to locate any file in the current location that has a 2016 date stamp and an invoice number (between hyphens) that is exactly four characters long.

To force Windows Search to use strict character matches in an indexed location, type a tilde (~) as the first character in the search box, followed immediately by your term. If you open your Documents library and type **~??v** in the search box, you'll find any document whose file name contains any word that has a *v* in the third position, such as *saved, level,* and, of course, *invoice.* This technique does not match on file contents.

Searching nonindexed locations

In both the previous examples, we described the behavior of searches in indexed locations, such as a library or a folder within a library. In other locations, the grep search engine kicks in. By default, anything you enter in one of these locations is treated as a character search that can match all or any part of a word. Thus, if you open a data folder that is not in a library and enter the search term **voice**, you get back *voices* and *voice-over* and *invoice.* The behavior of wildcards varies slightly as well. In a grep search, **??voice** matches *invoice* but not *voice.* In an indexed search, the wildcards at the beginning of the term are ignored in favor of loose matches. (Extra question marks at the end of a search term are ignored completely.)

When Windows does a grep search of the folder's contents, a green progress bar traversing your address bar warns you that the search is likely to be slow. While the search is still underway, you can click the Search tab and refine the search.

By default, when searching nonindexed locations, Windows looks at file names and basic properties (date modified and size) only. You can change this behavior so that Windows searches the contents of files that include a property handler and filter. To do this, click the Search tab, click Advanced Options, and then click File Contents, as shown here:

Be aware that choosing this option can add significantly to your search times.

Inside OUT

Search shared remote folders

When you connect to a shared folder on a networked computer, the search engine can detect whether the Windows Search service is running and whether the location you've accessed is already part of the remote index. If it is, great! Your query gets handed off to the remote search engine, which runs it on the other machine and returns its results to your computer. Note that for an indexed search of a shared folder, that folder must be included in the list of indexed locations on the remote computer, and the remote computer must be running version 4.0 or later of Windows Search. All versions of Windows released since 2008 are supported.

Saving searches and clearing search history

After you have completed a search and displayed its results in File Explorer, you can save the search parameters for later reuse. Click Save Search on the Search tab. The saved search is stored, by default, in %UserProfile%\Searches. You can run the search again at any time, using the current contents of the index, by clicking that saved search in the navigation pane or Searches folder.

When you save a search, you're saving its specification (technically, a persistedQuery), not its current results. If you're interested in the XML data that defines the search, right-click the saved search in your Searches folder, choose Open With, and choose Notepad or WordPad.

Recent searches are also included in a history list. To see what you have searched for, click in the search box in File Explorer and then, in the Options group on the Search tab, click Recent Searches. If the list of recent searches gets unwieldy or you want to eliminate older searches that are no longer relevant, click Clear Search History at the bottom of this list.

Recovering lost, damaged, and deleted files and folders

It takes only a fraction of a second to wipe out a week's worth of work. You might accidentally delete a folder full of files or, worse, overwrite an entire group of files with changes that can't be undone. Whatever the cause of your misfortune, Windows includes tools that offer hope for recovery. If a file is simply lost, try searching for it. (See "Using Windows Search" earlier in this chapter.) For accidental deletions, your first stop should be the Recycle Bin, a Windows institution since 1995.

> ➤ **Windows 10 includes a considerably more powerful recovery tool called File History—but it's available only if you set it up in advance. See "Using File History to protect files and folders" in Chapter 16, "Backup, restore, and recovery."**

The Recycle Bin provides protection against accidental erasure of files. In most cases, when you delete one or more files or folders, the deleted items go to the Recycle Bin, not into the ether. If you change your mind, you can go to the bin and recover the thrown-out items. Eventually, when the bin fills up, Windows begins emptying it, permanently deleting the files that have been there the longest.

The following kinds of deletions do not go to the Recycle Bin:

- Files stored on removable disks

- Files stored on network drives, even when that volume is on a computer that has its own Recycle Bin

- Files deleted from a command prompt

- Files deleted from compressed (zipped) folders

You can bypass the Recycle Bin yourself, permanently deleting an item, by holding down the Shift key while you delete the item. You might choose to do this if you're trying to reclaim disk space by permanently getting rid of large files and folder subtrees.

To see and adjust the amount of space currently used by the Recycle Bin for each drive that it protects, right-click the Recycle Bin icon on your desktop and then click Properties. In the Recycle Bin Properties dialog box (shown in Figure 12-16), you can select a drive and enter a different value in the Custom Size box. Windows ordinarily allocates up to 10 percent of a disk's space for recycling. (When the bin is full, the oldest items give way to the newest.) If you think that amount of space is excessive, enter a lower value. If you're certain you don't need to recover files from a particular drive, select the Don't Move Files To The Recycle Bin setting for that drive.

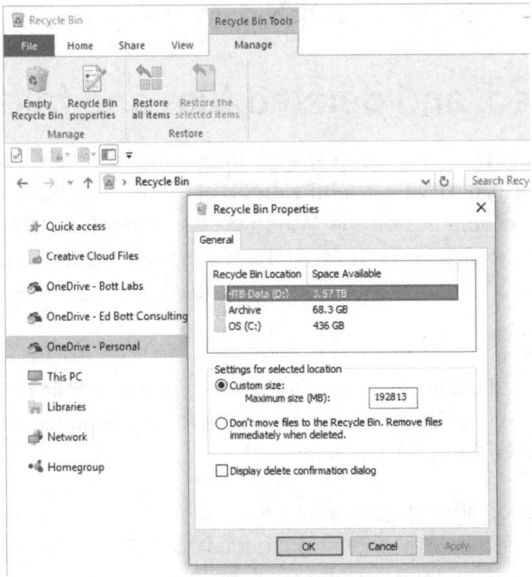

Figure 12-16 You can use the Recycle Bin Properties dialog box to alter the amount of space devoted to the bin—or to turn the feature off for selected drives.

Note that the Recycle Bin for OneDrive folders shows only deleted copies of locally synced files. A separate OneDrive Recycle Bin is available from the browser-based interface and includes all deleted files.

Whether the Recycle Bin is enabled or disabled, Windows normally displays a confirmation prompt when you delete something. If that prompt annoys you, clear the Display Delete Confirmation Dialog check box.

Restoring files and folders

When you open the Recycle Bin, Windows displays the names of recently deleted items in an ordinary File Explorer window. In Details view, you can see when each item was deleted and which folder it was deleted from. You can use the column headings to sort the folder—for example, to display items that have been deleted most recently at the top, with earlier deletions below. Alternatively, you can organize the bin by disk and folder by clicking the Original Location heading. If these methods don't help you find what you're hoping to restore, use the search box.

Note that deleted folders are shown only as folders; you don't see the names of items contained within the folders. If you restore a deleted folder, however, Windows re-creates the folder and its contents.

The Restore commands on the Manage tab (Restore All Items and Restore The Selected Items) put items back in the folders from which they were deleted. If a folder doesn't currently exist, Windows asks your permission to re-create it. Note that if your Recycle Bin contains hundreds or thousands of deleted files dating back weeks or months, Restore All Items can create chaos. That command is most useful if you recently emptied the Recycle Bin and all of its current contents are visible.

If you want, you can restore a file or folder to a different location. Select the item, click the Home tab, click Move To, and then choose a new location. Or, simplest of all, you can drag the item out of the Recycle Bin and drop it in the folder where you want to save it.

Purging the Recycle Bin

A deleted file sitting in your Recycle Bin takes up as much space as it did before it was deleted. If you're deleting files to free up space for new programs and documents, transferring them to the Recycle Bin won't help. You need to remove them permanently. The safest way to do this is to move the items to another storage medium—a different hard disk or a removable disk, for example.

If you're sure you'll never need a particular file again, however, you can delete it in the normal way, and then purge it from the Recycle Bin. Display the Recycle Bin, select the item, and then press Delete.

To empty the Recycle Bin entirely, click Empty Recycle Bin on the Manage tab.

CHAPTER 12

System maintenance and troubleshooting

Hardware

It's probably only a slight exaggeration to say that no two computers are alike. Motherboards, storage devices and controllers, video and network adapters, and peripherals of all shapes and sizes combine to create a nearly infinite number of possible computer configurations.

The good news for anyone using Windows 10 is that most of these devices should just work. For most common hardware upgrades, Windows detects the device automatically and installs a driver so that you can use the device and its full array of features. This chapter covers those installations as well as devices that need to be added manually, those that have optional configuration steps, and of course how to troubleshoot device-related issues.

In this chapter, we cover the traditional nerve center of hardware, Device Manager, as well as the newer hardware configuration options in Settings. We explain how drivers work (and how to work with drivers). We also offer hints on the best ways to set up specific device configurations, including multiple monitors, Bluetooth adapters, and printers.

Adding, configuring, and removing hardware devices

Since its introduction in Windows 95, Plug and Play technology has evolved tremendously. Early incarnations of this technology were notoriously unreliable, leading some users to dismiss the feature as "plug and pray." As this now-mature technology enters its third decade, however, hardware and software standards have converged to make most device configuration tasks completely automatic.

Any computer that was certified as compatible with Windows 7 or later supports the Plug and Play device standard, which handles virtually all the work of configuring computer hardware and attached devices. A Plug and Play device identifies itself to Windows by using unique identifiers in a well-organized hierarchy, listing its required resources (including drivers), and allowing software to configure it.

Plug and Play devices can interact with the operating system, with both sides of the conversation responding to device notification and power management events. A Plug and Play driver can load automatically when Windows detects that a device has been plugged in, and it can suspend its operations when the system sleeps and resume without issue when the system wakes.

> **NOTE**
>
> **Although you still can find older devices that require non–Plug and Play inputs—such as scanners, plotters, and similar peripherals that connect to serial and parallel ports— these legacy devices are becoming increasingly rare. If you own this type of device, we recommend retiring it if possible and replacing it with a supported modern alternative. If you have no choice but to keep it around, look for a community of fellow owners of that device; they're the most likely to be able to help you with configuration issues.**

Installing a new Plug and Play device

When you install a Plug and Play device for the first time, Windows reads the Plug and Play identification tag in the hardware's BIOS or firmware. It then compares that ID tag with a master list of corresponding tags drawn from all the Setup Information files in the %SystemRoot%\Inf folder. If it finds a signed driver with a matching tag, it installs that driver package and makes other necessary system modifications with no intervention required from you. If everything goes as expected, the only subtle indication you might see is a progress dialog box (typically minimized) that displays a green bar over its taskbar icon and then vanishes when its work is complete.

> **NOTE**
>
> **Any user can plug in a new device and begin using it if a driver for that device is included with Windows 10 or is available via Windows Update. Installing a new driver that is downloaded from a third-party site and is digitally signed by a third party rather than by Microsoft requires an administrator's credentials.**

If Windows detects a Plug and Play device (after you've plugged it into a USB port, for instance) but cannot locate a digitally signed driver that matches the device, it doesn't provide any warning notification. Instead, a stub for the device is installed as it awaits the arrival of a proper driver. These partially installed devices appear in Device Manager, under the Other Devices heading, with a yellow exclamation point over the device name, as in Figure 13-1.

Figure 13-1 If Windows 10 can't find drivers for a new Plug and Play device, it adds a yellow exclamation point to the Device Manager listings and files the devices under the Other Devices heading.

> ### TROUBLESHOOTING
>
> **Drivers for built-in devices are missing**
>
> Device Manager might show some devices in the Other Devices category, with a yellow exclamation point indicating that the correct drivers are missing, after a clean installation of Windows 10. This usually occurs on a PC where some low-level devices built into the motherboard aren't recognized during Windows 10 setup. The usual cure for this sort of problem is to check with the device manufacturer to see whether drivers are available for download; pay special attention to chipset drivers, which add the necessary entries to the Windows Plug and Play database to allow the correct built-in drivers to be installed.

When Windows Update can't find a signed driver (and, thankfully, those occasions are becoming rarer as the Windows ecosystem matures), you need to manually install a device driver, a topic we cover in more detail later in this chapter.

The built-in Windows drivers are perfectly adequate for many device classes. Some devices, especially complex ones like scanners and all-in-one printers, might require utility software and additional drivers to enable the full range of features for that device.

How device drivers and hardware work together

Before Windows can work with any piece of hardware, it requires a compatible, properly configured device driver. Drivers are compact control programs that hook directly into Windows and handle the essential tasks of communicating your instructions to a hardware device and then relaying data back to you. After you set up a hardware device, its driver loads automatically and runs as part of the operating system, without requiring any further intervention on your part.

Many individual technologies used in Windows 10 devices use minidriver models, where the device driver is made up of two parts. Typically, Microsoft writes a general class driver that handles tasks that are common to devices in that category. The device manufacturer can then write device-specific code to enable custom features.

Windows 10, even more than its recent predecessors, includes a surprisingly comprehensive library of class drivers that allow most devices to function properly without requiring any additional software. There are class drivers for pieces of hardware that are, these days, typically integrated into a larger system: audio devices, network adapters, webcams, and display adapters, for example. Windows 10 also includes drivers for external add-ons (wired and wireless) including printers, monitors, keyboards, scanners, mice and other pointing devices, smartphones, and removable storage devices.

This core library is copied during Windows setup to a protected system folder, %SystemRoot%\System32\DriverStore. (Driver files and associated elements are stored in the FileRepository subfolder.) Anyone who signs in to the computer has Read & Execute permissions for files that are saved in that location, but only an installation program working with authorization from a member of the Administrators group can create or modify files and folders there.

You can add new drivers to the driver store in a variety of ways, including the following:

- Windows Update offers drivers when it detects that you're running a device that's compatible with that driver but is currently using an older version. (You can also search for the most recent driver via Windows Update when installing a new device.)

- A Windows quality or feature update can refresh the driver store with new and updated drivers.

- As an administrator, you can add signed third-party drivers to the driver store by running an installer program. All drivers added to the driver store in this fashion are saved in their own subfolder within the FileRepository folder, along with some supporting files created by Windows 10 that allow the drivers to be reinstalled if necessary.

Any driver that has been added to the store is considered to be trusted and can be installed without prompts or administrator credentials. All drivers, new or updated, that are downloaded from the Windows Update service are certified to be fully compatible with Windows 10 and are digitally signed by Microsoft.

Inside OUT

Copy the FileRepository folder before a clean reinstall

If you're planning a clean reinstall of Windows 10 using bootable installation media rather than the Reset function, consider copying the FileRepository folder from %SystemRoot%\System32\DriverStore to removable media, such as a USB flash drive. After your clean install is complete, you can quickly reinstall any custom drivers by using the Update Driver option from Device Manager and specifying that saved folder as the location for the new driver files.

A Windows hardware driver package must include a Setup Information file (with the extension .inf). This is a text file that contains detailed information about the device to be installed, including the names of its driver files, the locations where they are to be installed, any required registry settings, and version information. All devices with drivers in the DriverStore folder include Setup Information files in the %SystemRoot%\Inf folder.

Although the Setup Information file is a crucial part of the driver installation process, you don't work with it directly. Instead, this file supplies instructions that the operating system uses during Plug and Play detection, when you use a setup program to install a device or when you manually install a driver update.

CAUTION

The syntax of Setup Information files is complex, and the intricacies of .inf files can trip up even experienced software developers. If you find that a driver setup routine isn't working properly, you might be tempted to try editing the Setup Information file to work around the hang-up. Trust us: That approach is almost certain to fail. In fact, by tinkering with .inf files to install a driver that's not certified to be compatible with your hardware, you run the risk of corrupting registry settings and making your system unstable.

When Windows completes the installation of a driver package, it performs all the tasks specified by the Setup Information file and copies the driver files themselves to %SystemRoot%\System32\Drivers.

Inside OUT

For Windows 10, signed drivers only

Beginning with the release of Windows 10, all new kernel-mode drivers must be submitted to Microsoft and digitally signed by the Windows Hardware Developer Center Dashboard portal. (Kernel-mode drivers run at the same level of privilege as Windows itself, as opposed to user-mode drivers, which run in the context of the currently signed-in user and cannot cause the system to crash.) In an additional change that took effect 90 days after the release of Windows 10, any new drivers submitted to Microsoft must be signed by a valid Extended Validation Code Signing Certificate—a higher-cost option that provides extra assurance about the identity of a software publisher.

The net effect of these changes is to make it extremely difficult for malware to be delivered as part of a driver update. Drivers that were properly signed under the previous rules and were released before those two Windows 10 milestones will continue to work, but Windows 10 will not load new kernel-mode drivers unless they're signed by that Microsoft-controlled portal.

Driver signing establishes an initial threshold of trust, but by itself it's not necessarily an indicator of quality. For that you need to look at the signature a little more closely.

The highest level of quality is found with drivers that have passed compatibility and reliability tests for that category of device, as defined in Microsoft's Hardware Lab Kit. Those devices earn the right to use the Windows logo and can be included on Microsoft's Certified Products List.

Hardware developers who simply want to deliver a signed driver to their customers can submit the driver to Microsoft and "attest" to its quality rather than submitting actual test results. The Attested Signing Service signature is different from the one for a logo-certified device, but Windows 10 treats them the same, allowing either type of signed driver to be installed with no prompts by any user.

In the distant past, users could change default settings to allow installation of unsigned drivers and even completely eliminate warnings about the accompanying security risks. Those options are available by changing advanced startup settings in Windows 10, but they require disabling Secure Boot and fundamentally undermine the device's security. As a result, we strongly recommend against using them.

Getting useful information from Device Manager

The more you know about individual hardware devices and their associated driver versions, the more likely you are to make short work of troubleshooting problems or configuring advanced features for a device. In every case, your starting point is Device Manager, a graphical utility that provides detailed information about all installed hardware, along with controls you can use to configure devices, assign resources, and set advanced options.

> **NOTE**
>
> In Windows 10, Device Manager also includes categories that don't represent actual hardware—print queues, for example, or anything under the Software Devices heading. In this section, we focus only on physical hardware devices and their associated drivers.

The easiest way to open Device Manager (Devmgmt.msc) is to right-click the Start button (or press Windows key+X) and then click the Device Manager shortcut on the Quick Link menu. Alternatively, type **device** in the search box and then click the Device Manager entry from the top of the results list. (Device Manager is also available as a snap-in under the System Tools heading in the fully stocked Computer Management console.)

As Figure 13-2 shows, Device Manager is organized as a hierarchical list that inventories every piece of hardware within or connected to your computer. The default view shows devices by type.

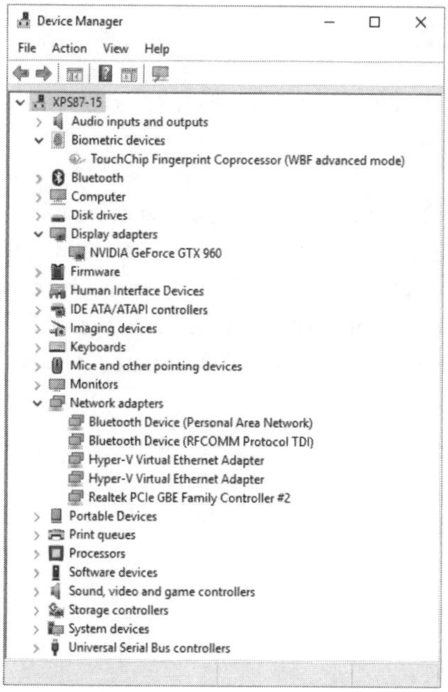

Figure 13-2 Click the arrow to the left of any category in Device Manager to expand or collapse the list of individual devices within that category.

To view information about a specific device, double-click its entry in Device Manager's list of installed devices. Each device has its own multitabbed properties dialog box. Most hardware devices include a selection of tabs, including General and Driver. The General tab lists basic facts about the device, including the device name and type, the name of its manufacturer, and its current status, as in the example in Figure 13-3.

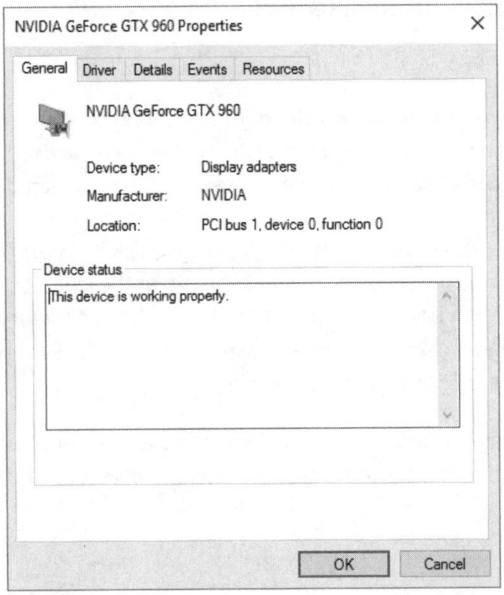

Figure 13-3 The General tab supplies basic information about a device and indicates whether it's currently functioning properly.

The Driver tab, shown in Figure 13-4, lists version information about the currently installed driver for the selected device. Although the information shown here is sparse, it covers the essentials. You can tell at a glance who supplied the driver, and you can see who digitally signed it; you can also determine the date and version number of the driver, which is important when considering whether you should download and install an available update.

Figure 13-4 The Driver tab, which is available for every installed device, offers valuable information and tools for managing installed drivers.

Clicking the Driver Details button on the Driver tab leads to another dialog box that lists the names and locations of all files associated with that device and its drivers. Selecting any file name from this list displays details for that file in the lower portion of the dialog box. (We'll get to the other buttons in the next section.)

Click the Details tab for a potentially overwhelming amount of additional information, arranged in a dialog box in which you can see one property and its associated value at a time. You can see the full list of properties by clicking the arrow to the right of the current entry in the Property box; Figure 13-5 shows the typically dense result.

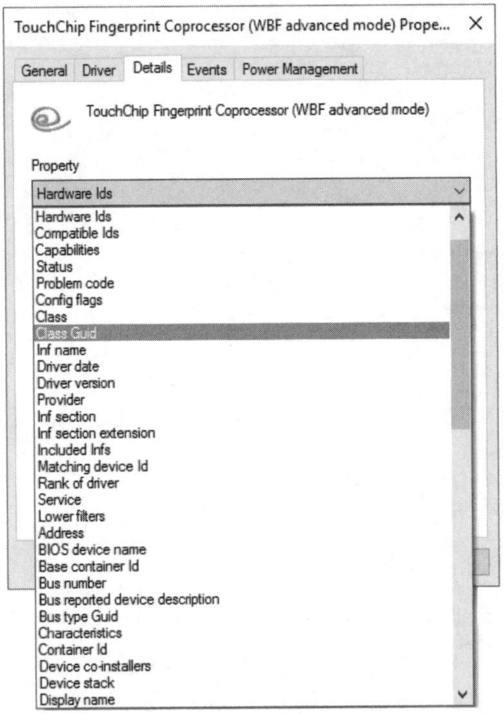

CHAPTER 13

Figure 13-5 Most device properties you can select from this list return obscure details, but a few are useful for troubleshooting purposes.

Choosing a property tucks the list away and displays the value associated with that property, as in the example shown here, which lists the Plug and Play IDs associated with the selected device:

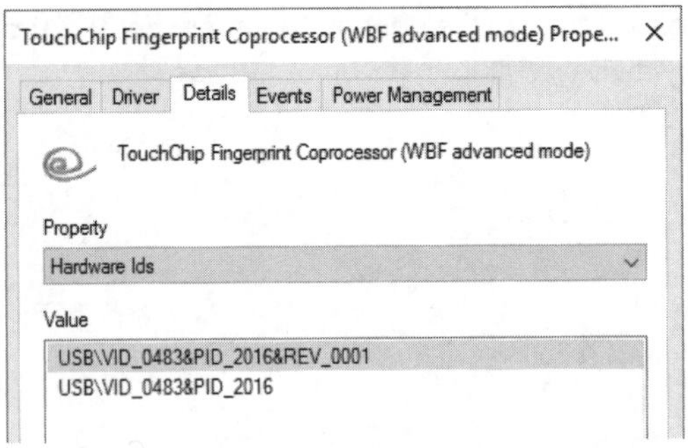

TROUBLESHOOTING

Device Manager shows an unknown device

Most modern hardware built for Windows 7 or later just works with Windows 10. But occasionally you might find mysterious entries under the Other Devices heading in Device Manager, with few or no details, no associated drivers, and no clue about what to do next. This problem is most likely to appear after you perform a clean install of Windows 10 on a device originally designed for another operating system, but the issue can also occur with older external hardware.

You can often get important clues by opening the properties dialog box for the device and looking on the Details tab. The Hardware IDs property, in particular, can be invaluable. The string VID_ followed by a number is a Vendor ID code; PID_ is a Product ID code. Use your favorite search engine to look on the web for a combination of those two values.

In addition to this basic information, the properties dialog box for a given device can include any number of custom tabs. The USB hub built into the motherboard of the PC shown in Figure 13-6, for example, adds a custom tab (Power) that you can use to view how much power is available for devices connected to ports on a particular USB hub (although it might take some further sleuthing and some trial and error to figure out which of the PC's physical ports are associated with that hub).

Figure 13-6 Yes, the properties dialog box for this USB hub includes separate tabs for Power and Power Management.

By design, the information displayed in Device Manager is dynamic. When you add, remove, or reconfigure a device, the information stored here changes as well.

Enabling and disabling devices

Any device listed in Device Manager can be disabled temporarily. You might choose this option if you're certain you won't need an installed device under normal conditions but you want to keep it available just in case. On a desktop PC with a permanent wired Ethernet connection, for example, you can keep a Wi-Fi adapter installed but disabled. That configuration gives you the option to enable the device and use the wireless adapter to connect to a mobile hotspot when the wired network goes out of service.

Right-click any active entry in Device Manager to see a shortcut menu with a Disable command. To identify any device that's currently disabled, look for the black, downward-pointing arrow over its icon in Device Manager, as shown here. To turn a disabled device back on, right-click its entry in Device Manager and then click Enable Device.

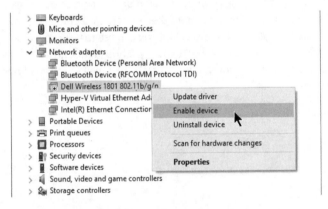

Adjusting advanced device settings

As we mentioned earlier, some devices include specialized tabs in the properties dialog box available from Device Manager. You use the controls on these additional tabs to change advanced settings and properties for devices—for example:

- Network cards, modems, input devices, and USB hubs often include a Power Management tab you can use to control whether the device can force the computer to wake up from Sleep mode. This option is useful if you have fax capabilities (yes, some businesses still use faxes) enabled for a modem or if you use the Remote Desktop feature over the internet on a machine that isn't always running at full power. On both portable and desktop computers, you can also use this option to allow Windows to turn off a device to save power.

- The Volumes tab for a disk drive contains no information when you first display the properties dialog box for that device. Click the Populate button to read the volume information for the selected disk, as shown in Figure 13-7, and click the Properties button to check the disk for errors, run the Defrag utility, or perform other maintenance tasks. Although you can perform these same tasks by right-clicking a drive icon in File Explorer, this option might be useful in situations where you have multiple hard disks installed and you suspect that one of those disks is having mechanical problems. Using this option, you can quickly see which physical disk a given volume is stored on.

ST1000DM003-1ER162 Properties   ✕

| General | Policies | Volumes | Driver | Details | Events |

The volumes contained on this disk are listed below.

Disk:	Disk 0
Type:	Basic
Status:	Online
Partition style:	GUID Partition Table (GPT)
Capacity:	3815448 MB
Unallocated space:	3 MB
Reserved space:	128 MB

Volumes:

Volume	Capacity
4TB-Data (D:)	3745318 MB
Archive	69999 MB

Populate   Properties

OK   Cancel

Figure 13-7 After you click the Populate button, the Volumes tab lists volumes on the selected drive and gives you full access to troubleshooting and maintenance tools.

CAUTION

DVD drives offer an option to change the DVD region, which controls which discs can be played on that drive. The DVD Region setting actually increments a counter on the physical drive itself, and that counter can be changed only a limited number of times. Be extremely careful with this setting, or you might end up losing the capability to play any regionally encoded DVDs in your collection on that device.

- When working with network cards, you can often choose from a plethora of settings on an Advanced tab, as shown in the following example. Randomly tinkering with these settings is almost always counterproductive; however, you might be able to solve specific performance or connectivity problems by adjusting settings as directed by the device manufacturer or a Microsoft Support article.

```
┌─────────────────────────────────────────────────────────────┐
│ Realtek PCIe GBE Family Controller #2 Properties         ✕   │
├─────────────────────────────────────────────────────────────┤
│    Events        Resources        Power Management          │
│  General     Advanced     About     Driver    Details       │
│ ┌─────────────────────────────────────────────────────────┐ │
│ │ The following properties are available for this network │ │
│ │ adapter. Click the property you want to change on the   │ │
│ │ left, and then select its value on the right.           │ │
│ │                                                         │ │
│ │ Property:                     Value:                    │ │
│ │ ┌─────────────────────────┐   ┌──────────────────────┐  │ │
│ │ │ ARP Offload          ▲  │   │ Enabled           ▼  │  │ │
│ │ │ Auto Disable Gigabit    │   └──────────────────────┘  │ │
│ │ │ Energy Efficient Ethernet                             │ │
│ │ │ Flow Control            │                             │ │
│ │ │ Green Ethernet          │                             │ │
│ │ │ Interrupt Moderation    │                             │ │
│ │ │ IPv4 Checksum Offload   │                             │ │
│ │ │ Jumbo Frame             │                             │ │
│ │ │ Large Send Offload v2 (IPv4)                          │ │
│ │ │ Large Send Offload v2 (IPv6)                          │ │
│ │ │ Maximum Number of RSS Queues                          │ │
│ │ │ Network Address         │                             │ │
│ │ │ NS Offload              │                             │ │
│ │ │ Priority & VLAN      ▼  │                             │ │
│ │ └─────────────────────────┘                             │ │
│ └─────────────────────────────────────────────────────────┘ │
│                                    ┌────────┐  ┌────────┐    │
│                                    │   OK   │  │ Cancel │    │
│                                    └────────┘  └────────┘    │
└─────────────────────────────────────────────────────────────┘
```

Updating and uninstalling drivers

If you're having a hardware problem that you suspect is caused by a device driver, your first stop should be Device Manager. Open the properties dialog box for the device, and use the following buttons on the Driver tab to perform maintenance tasks:

- **Update Driver.** This choice opens the Update Driver Software dialog box, which we describe in the next section.

- **Roll Back Driver.** This option uninstalls the most recently updated driver and rolls back your system configuration to the previously installed driver. This option is available from Safe Mode if you need to remove a driver that's causing blue-screen (Stop) errors. Unlike System Restore, this option affects only the selected device. If you have never updated the selected driver, this option is unavailable.

- **Uninstall.** This button completely removes driver files and registry settings for the selected device and, if you select the appropriate option, completely removes the associated driver files as well. Use this capability to remove a driver that you suspect was incorrectly installed and then reinstall the original driver or install an updated driver.

Inside OUT

Create a safety net before tinkering with drivers

When you install a new hardware driver, Windows automatically attempts to create a new System Restore checkpoint. That doesn't mean it will be successful, especially if a problem with your System Restore settings has caused this utility to suspend operations temporarily. To make certain you can roll back your changes if necessary, set a new System Restore checkpoint manually before making any kind of hardware configuration change. (For more details, see "Rolling back to a previous restore point" in Chapter 16, "Backup, restore, and recovery.")

CHAPTER 13

Disabling automatic driver updates

Microsoft uses the Windows Update mechanism to deliver drivers for many devices. Using this feature, you can plug in a new device with relative confidence it will work without extra effort on your part. You also can use it to automatically receive updated drivers, which typically fix reliability, stability, and compatibility problems.

The dark side of driver updates is that they can occasionally cause a previously functional device to act up or even shut down. For that reason, some cautious Windows users prefer to disable automatic driver updates. In previous Windows versions and in the initial release of Windows 10, an advanced setting in Control Panel > System allowed you to specify that you never want to automatically install drivers from Windows Update. In version 1607, this option has been replaced by a Group Policy setting.

If you're willing to accept the burden of manually checking for driver updates in exchange for the assurance of not being inconvenienced by a defective driver update, you can turn on this setting by opening the Local Group Policy Editor (Gpedit.msc) and going to Computer Configuration > Administrative Templates > Windows Components > Windows Update. Double-click the Do Not Include Drivers With Windows Updates policy, and set it to Enabled.

If you want to script this change, or if you're working with Windows 10 Home, where Group Policy is not supported, open the registry editor using an administrator's credentials, and go to the key HKLM\Software\Policies\Microsoft\Windows\WindowsUpdate. Then add a new DWORD value, ExcludeWUDriversInQualityUpdate, and set it to 1.

Updating a device driver manually

Microsoft and third-party device manufacturers frequently issue upgrades to device drivers. In some cases, the updates enable new features; in other cases, the newer version swats a bug that might or might not affect you. New Microsoft-signed drivers are often (but not always) delivered through Windows Update. Other drivers are available only by downloading them from the device manufacturer's website. Kernel-mode drivers must still be digitally signed before they can be installed.

If the new driver includes a setup program, run it first so that the proper files are copied to your system. Then start the update process from Device Manager by selecting the entry for the device you want to upgrade and clicking the Update Driver button on the toolbar or the Update Driver option on the right-click shortcut menu. (You can also click Update Driver on the Driver tab of the properties dialog box for the device.)

That action opens the dialog box shown in Figure 13-8.

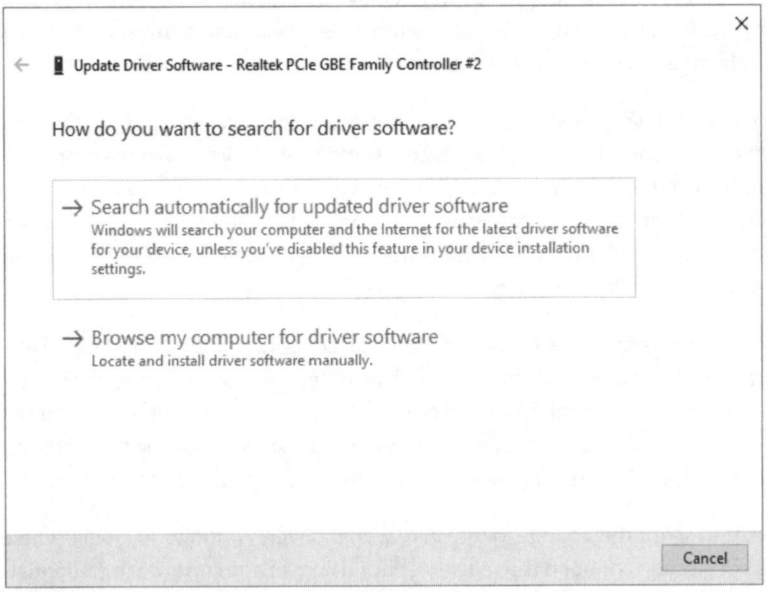

Figure 13-8 When manually updating a driver, try the automatic option first unless you want to select a specific driver you previously downloaded.

Click Search Automatically For Updated Driver Software if you want to look in local removable media and check Windows Update. Click Browse My Computer For Driver Software if you want to enter the location of a downloaded driver package or choose from a list of available drivers in the driver store folder. Clicking the latter option opens a dialog box like the one shown in Figure 13-9, with two options for manually selecting a driver.

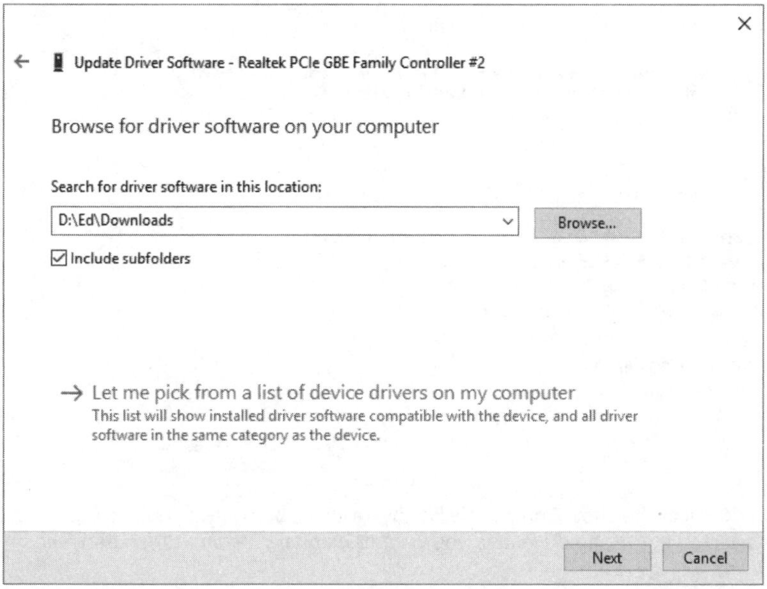

Figure 13-9 If you've downloaded a driver package that doesn't include an installer, select its location here to allow the update to proceed.

If you've downloaded the driver files to a known location or copied them to removable storage, click Browse to select that location, and then click Next to continue. (If you have a copy of the FileRepository folder from a previous Windows installation on the same hardware, you can choose that location.) With the Include Subfolders option selected, as it is by default, the driver update software will do a thorough search of the specified location, looking for a Setup Information file for the selected device; if it finds a match, it installs the specified driver software automatically.

Use the second option, Let Me Pick From A List Of Device Drivers On My Computer, if you know that the driver software you need is already in the local driver store. In general, choosing this option presents a single driver for you to choose. In some cases, as in the example in Figure 13-10, you can see previous versions of a driver, with the option to replace a new driver with an older one for troubleshooting purposes. If you need to install an alternative driver version that isn't listed, clear the Show Compatible Hardware check box and then choose a driver from an expanded list of all matching devices in the device category.

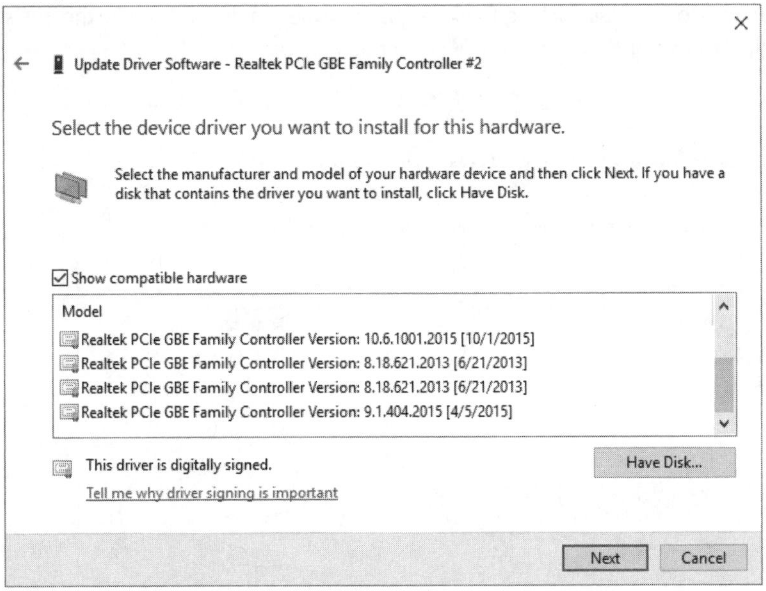

Figure 13-10 Clear the Show Compatible Hardware check box only if you're certain that Plug and Play has selected the wrong driver and you want to manually install a different driver.

Inside OUT

Make sure that update is really an update

How do you know whether a downloaded version is newer than the currently installed driver on your system? A good set of release notes should provide this information and is the preferred option for determining version information. In the absence of documentation, file dates offer some clues, but they're not always reliable. A better indicator is to inspect the properties of the driver files themselves. After unzipping the downloaded driver files to a folder on a local or network drive, right-click any file with a .dll or .sys extension and choose Properties. On the Version tab, you should be able to find details about the specific driver version, which you can compare with the driver details shown in Device Manager.

Rolling back to a previous driver version

Unfortunately, updated drivers can sometimes cause new problems that are worse than the woes they were intended to fix. This is especially true if you're experimenting with prerelease versions of new drivers. If your troubleshooting leads you to suspect that a newly installed driver is the cause of recent crashes or system instability, consider removing that driver and rolling your system configuration back to the previously installed driver.

To do this, open Device Manager and double-click the entry for the device you want to roll back. Then go to the Driver tab and click Roll Back Driver. The procedure that follows is straight-forward and self-explanatory.

Uninstalling a driver

There are at least three circumstances under which you might want to completely remove a device driver from your system:

- You're no longer using the device, and you want to prevent the previously installed drivers from loading or using any resources.

- You've determined that the drivers available for the device are not stable enough to use on your system.

- The currently installed driver is not working correctly, and you want to reinstall it from scratch.

Inside OUT

Manage Plug and Play drivers

Removing and reinstalling the driver for a Plug and Play device requires a little extra effort. Because these drivers are loaded and unloaded dynamically, you can remove the driver only if the device in question is plugged in. Use the Uninstall button to remove the driver before unplugging the device. To reinstall the device driver without unplugging the device, open Device Manager and choose Action, Scan For Hardware Changes.

To remove a driver permanently, open Device Manager, right-click the entry for the device in question, and click Uninstall. (If the entry for the device in question is already open, click the Driver tab and click Uninstall.) Click OK when prompted to confirm that you want to remove the driver, and Windows removes the files and registry settings completely. You can now unplug the device.

If you installed the driver files from a downloaded file, the Confirm Device Uninstall dialog box includes a check box (shown in Figure 13-11) you can select to remove the files from the driver store as well. This prevents a troublesome driver from being inadvertently reinstalled when you reinsert the device or restart the computer.

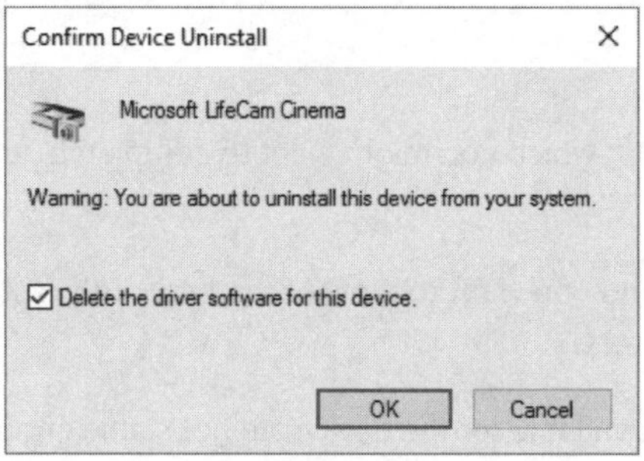

Figure 13-11 Be sure to select this check box so that a troublesome driver doesn't reinstall itself automatically.

Note that you can't delete driver software that's included with Windows 10.

If the troublesome device driver was delivered through Windows Update, removing it is only a temporary fix. The next time Windows checks for new updates, it will download and install that same driver, unless you take steps to exclude that driver. To do that, use the troubleshooting package Microsoft created expressly for this problem. You can download it from *https://bit.ly/wushowhide*.

After downloading the package, run it and follow the prompts, choosing the Hide Updates option. After checking for available updates, the troubleshooter displays a list of driver updates that apply to the current system, as shown next.

← ▓ Show or hide updates	✕

Hide updates

Updates are available. Select the updates that aren't working, Windows will not install hidden updates. Run this troubleshooter again to show hidden updates so they install automatically.

- ☐ Brother - Printers - Brother HL-2240 series
- ☐ AMYUNI Technologies - Printers - Amyuni Document Converter 500
- ☐ Intel - Other hardware - Intel(R) Extreme Tuning Utility Device Driver
- ☐ Intel - Other hardware - Intel(R) Watchdog Timer Driver (Intel(R) WDT)
- ☐ Intel driver update for Intel(R) Management Engine Interface
- ☐ HUAWEI Technologies Co., Ltd. - Other hardware - Huawei System Firmware 1.0
- ☐ Intel - Other hardware - Intel(R) 8 Series/C220 Series PCI Express Root Port #1 - 8C10
- ☐ Intel - Other hardware - Intel(R) 8 Series/C220 Series PCI Express Root Port #8 - 8C1E
- ☐ Intel - Other hardware - Intel(R) Z87 LPC Controller - 8C44
- ☐ Intel - Other hardware - Intel(R) Xeon(R) processor E3 - 1200 v3/4th Gen Core processor

[Next]   [Cancel]

Select the check box to the left of the unwanted driver, and finish the wizard. If you find that a later update has resolved the problem, rerun the troubleshooter and choose the Show Updates option to make the driver available again via Windows Update.

Troubleshooting sporadic hardware errors

When your computer acts unpredictably, chances are good that defective hardware or a buggy device driver is at fault.

In those circumstances, using a powerful troubleshooting tool called Driver Verifier (Verifier.exe) is a terrific way to identify flawed device drivers. Instead of your computer locking up at a most inopportune time with a misleading Blue Screen of Death (BSOD), Driver Verifier stops your computer predictably at startup with a BSOD that accurately explains the true problem. Although this doesn't sound like a huge improvement (your system still won't work, after all), Driver Verifier performs a critical troubleshooting step: identifying the problem. You can then correct the problem by removing or replacing the offending driver. (If you're satisfied that the driver really is okay despite Driver Verifier Manager's warning, you can turn off Driver Verifier for all drivers or for a specific driver. Any driver that Driver Verifier chokes on should be regarded with suspicion, but some legitimate drivers bend the rules without causing problems.)

Driver Verifier works at startup to thoroughly exercise each driver. It performs many of the same tests that are run as part of the Windows certification and signing process, such as checking for the way the driver accesses memory.

Beware: If Driver Verifier finds a nonconforming driver—even one that doesn't seem to be causing any problems—it will prevent your system from starting. Use Driver Verifier only if you're having problems. In other words, if it ain't broke . . .

To begin working with Driver Verifier, open an elevated Command Prompt window and type **verifier.** In the Driver Verifier Manager dialog box, shown below, select Create Standard Settings. (If you want to assess current conditions before proceeding, select the last option, Display Information About The Currently Verified Drivers.)

When you click Next, you get a list of all currently installed drivers that match the conditions you specified. Note that the list might contain a mix of hardware drivers and some file-system filter drivers, such as those used by antivirus programs, CD-burning software, and other low-level system utilities.

At this point, you have two choices:

- Go through the list and make a note of all drivers identified and then click Cancel. No changes are made to your system configuration; all you've done is gather a list of suspicious drivers, which you can then try to remove or disable manually.

- Click Finish to complete the wizard and restart your computer. Don't choose this option unless you're prepared to deal with the consequences, as explained in the remainder of this sidebar.

If your computer stops with a blue screen when you next sign in, you've identified a problem driver. The error message includes the name of the offending driver and an error code.

Driver Verifier has been included with every version of Windows since Windows 2000 and is included with Windows 10. For information about using Driver Verifier, see the Microsoft Support article 244617, "Using Driver Verifier to identify issues with Windows drivers for advanced users," at *https://support.microsoft.com/kb/244617*. To resolve the problem, boot into Safe Mode using Windows 10's Recovery Environment and disable or uninstall the problem driver. You'll then want to check with the device vendor to get a working driver that you can install.

To disable Driver Verifier so that it no longer performs verification checks at startup, run Driver Verifier Manager again and select Delete Existing Settings in the initial dialog box. Alternatively, at a command prompt, type **verifier /reset**. (If you haven't yet solved the driver problem, of course, you'll be stopped at a BSOD, unable to disable Driver Verifier. In that case, boot into Safe Mode and then disable Driver Verifier.)

You can configure Driver Verifier so that it checks only certain drivers. To do that, open Driver Verifier Manager, select Create Standard Settings, click Next, and select the last option, Select Driver Names From A List. With this option, you can exempt a particular driver from Driver Verifier's scrutiny—such as one that Driver Verifier flags but you're certain is not the cause of your problem.

Printers and print queues

To install a modern printer that plugs into a USB port on the PC where you plan to use it, just connect the device. Plug and Play does the rest of the work. (See "Installing a new Plug and Play device" earlier in this chapter.)

NOTE

Although it's nearly certain there are still some non–Plug and Play printers out there, connecting to creaky parallel ports on PCs from the late Cretaceous period, we are happy to bid those devices adieu, and we urge you to do the same. We don't cover manual connection options for legacy devices in this book.

Wireless printers that connect over Wi-Fi or by using Bluetooth also support Plug and Play. Follow the manufacturer's instructions to complete the wireless connection, or skip ahead a few pages to our explanation of the Add A Printer option.

> ➤ **You can share a printer for use by other users on the same local network. The simplest way is using the HomeGroup feature, which we describe in "Sharing files, digital media, and printers in a homegroup" in Chapter 5, "Networking essentials." On business networks, the procedure is more formal; see "Sharing a printer" in Chapter 20, "Advanced networking."**

To configure a printer or work with documents in a print queue, go to Settings > Devices > Printers & Scanners. Click any installed printer to show buttons like those visible in Figure 13-12.

The Open Queue button, naturally, takes you to a list of pages waiting to print. Click Manage to see options that include the familiar printer-queue dialog box as well as links to printer settings and the extremely useful Print A Test Page command. Click Manage > Printer Properties to see status information and other configuration options.

Printers aren't exactly like snowflakes, but there are far too many variations in hardware and software design for us to offer more than the most general advice: Get to know your printer by inspecting these settings, and don't be afraid to read the manual.

To make a wireless or networked printer available locally, go to Settings > Devices > Printers & Scanners and click Add A Printer Or Scanner. If the planets are properly aligned, the autodiscovery software might locate your printer and walk you through setting it up. If you're not so lucky, click The Printer I Want Isn't Listed to open the manual options shown in Figure 13-13.

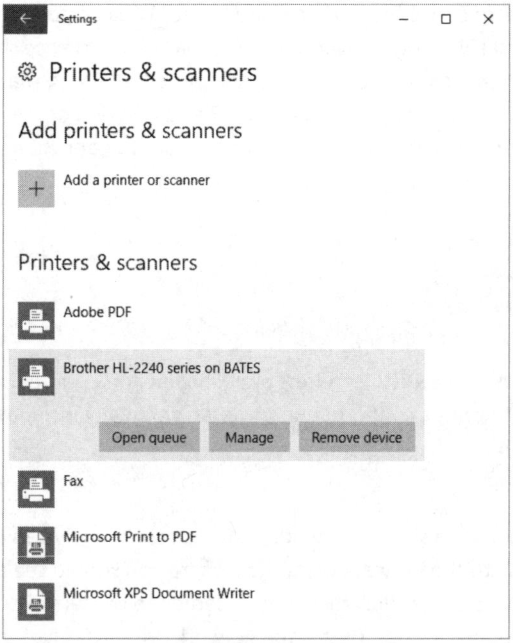

Figure 13-12 This Settings page shows installed printers and scanners. Click any item in the list to reveal management tools.

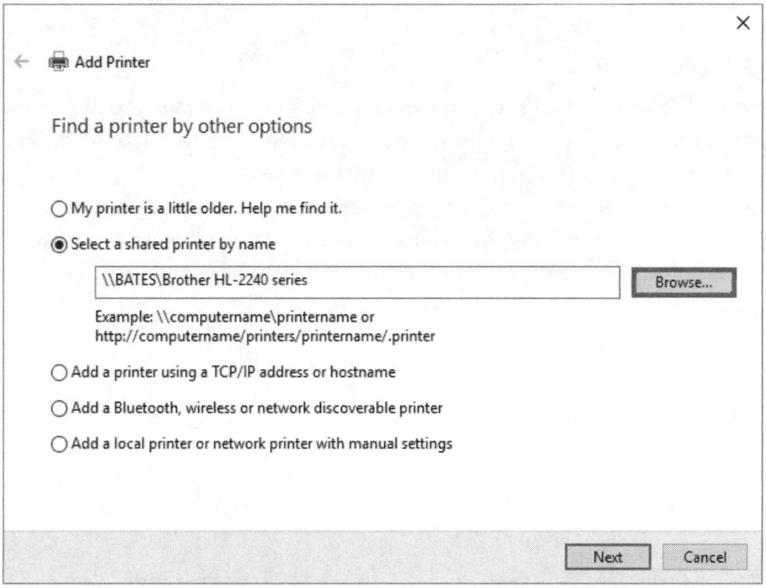

Figure 13-13 The Add Printer Wizard offers numerous paths to connect to a printer, especially those that are available over a network.

Among the "other options" available on this page in the Add Printer Wizard, you can connect to a network printer using its Universal Naming Convention (UNC) name. The device shown in Figure 13-11 earlier, for example, is connected to a printer on a server named Bates, making its UNC address \\BATES\Brother HL-2240 Series. You can also use an IP address for a device that has a permanently assigned address, and you can enlist the help of a wizard to connect a wireless or Bluetooth printer.

Inside OUT

Find a printer's TCP/IP address or host name

Often the easiest way to determine the TCP/IP address or host name for a printer is to use the printer's control panel to print a configuration page, which usually includes this information.

One of the simplest ways to connect to a shared network printer doesn't involve any wizards at all. Just use File Explorer to browse to the network computer, where you should see an entry for any shared printer available to you. Double-click that icon to begin the process of connecting to that printer. Because Windows requires a local copy of the network printer's driver, you'll need an administrator's credentials.

Inside OUT

Use a compatible driver

If you can't find a driver that's specifically designed for your printer, you might be able to get away with using another driver. Check the hardware documentation to find out whether the printer emulates a more popular model, such as a Hewlett-Packard LaserJet. If so, choose that printer driver, and then print some test documents after completing setup. You might lose access to some advanced features available with your model of printer, but this strategy should allow you to perform basic printing tasks.

Configuring displays

On a desktop or portable PC with a single screen (and, in the case of a desktop, the proper cable), you shouldn't need to do anything to configure your display. All modern display adapters deliver up-to-date drivers via Windows Update, and the display is capable of configuring itself as soon as it's connected.

So when do you need to pay attention to these settings? One scenario involves so-called high-DPI displays, which are typically found today on high-end portable PCs. Microsoft's Surface Book, for example, has a screen size of 13.5 inches (measured diagonally) and a native resolution of 3000 by 2000 pixels. That translates to 267 pixels per inch (a measure sometimes referred to in casual usage as dots per inch, or DPI).

That density is far greater (typically more than double) the density of a high-resolution desktop display. If you use a high-DPI system at normal (100 percent) scaling, the icons and text will be so small as to be unreadable. That's why, by default, the Surface Book is configured to run Windows 10 at 200 percent scaling. The result is an impressively sharp display. Everything in the Windows interface and in universal Windows apps is magnified at twice its normal size, using multiple physical pixels to create each effective pixel. The most popular classic desktop apps look great on primary high-DPI displays, as does any desktop app that was built using Windows Presentation Foundation (WPF), although some older desktop apps might look a little blurry.

The problem comes when you try to dynamically scale the display. This can happen in a variety of scenarios: connecting a portable PC with a high-DPI internal display to a larger external monitor, for example, using a video output or a laptop dock; projecting that high-DPI display to a large TV screen; or making a Remote Desktop connection. Any of those scenarios can result in some unfortunate scaling combinations, especially when using desktop apps.

Windows 10 supports scaling factors from 100 percent all the way to 450 percent, with most elements of the user interface looking crystal-clear even at the highest scaling levels. That includes Start, Cortana, File Explorer, and the Windows taskbar.

In general, scaling just works. In some scenarios, however, scaling issues can cause problems, including blurry text, desktop programs that are too large or too small, or interface elements such as menus and toolbars that are clipped or overlap. These problems are common when the scaling factor of a Windows PC changes while you're logged in—if you connect your high-DPI laptop to a dock, for example, and use a larger monitor with a different scaling factor as the primary display.

When that happens, the only cure is to close all running apps, sign out of Windows, and then sign back in. Ironically, the same problem occurs in reverse when you disconnect from the docking station.

Aside from that issue, you can make display changes by going to Settings > System > Display. Here are the three display settings you need to pay attention to:

- **Resolution.** Every display has a native resolution, one where the number of physical pixels matches the number of pixels Windows wants to show. Configuring the display at a non-native resolution generally results in a subpar viewing experience, often with a blurry, stretched display. That's probably why you have to take an extra step and go to the Advanced Display Settings page to see and change resolution. Figure 13-14 shows a Surface Book running at its native resolution of 3000 by 2000 pixels, as indicated by the word "(Recommended)" in the label, with its full list of other supported resolutions open below it.

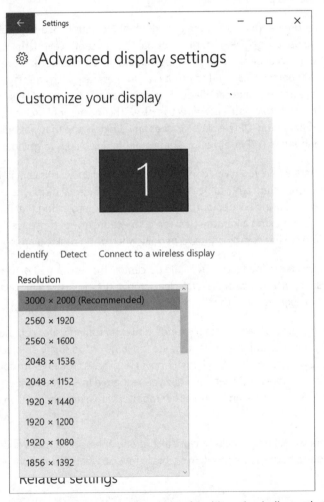

Figure 13-14 The "(Recommended)" after this option indicates that it's the native resolution and usually the correct choice.

Why would you choose a non-native resolution? One common scenario is projecting to a large display—in a conference room, for example, or to a Miracast adapter connected to the HDMI input on a TV. If you choose the option to duplicate displays on both monitors, you need to set the resolution to match what your audience is seeing, even if it looks squashed on your built-in display.

TROUBLESHOOTING

Display options stop at 1920 by 1080 even though your monitor supports higher resolutions

The most likely cause of this problem is an HDMI connection that's incapable of handling the desired resolution. If either the display adapter or the monitor supports the HDMI 1.3 standard, you're limited to Full HD (1920 by 1080) resolution. If both ends of the connection support HDMI 1.4 or later, you need to use a High Speed HDMI cable; a standard HDMI cable is limited to Full HD resolution. In most cases, the best workaround is to use a different connection, if one is available. The DisplayPort 1.2a standard, which uses mini and full-sized connectors and also works with USB-C adapters, supports 4K (3840 by 2160 or 4096 by 2160) resolutions, and the HDMI 1.4 standard will support 5K displays (5120 by 2880).

- **Scaling.** On high-resolution monitors, you can increase the apparent size of apps and text. Here, too, Windows recommends a scaling factor based on the size of the display and the resolution. You might choose a larger or smaller scaling factor for your own personal comfort. On a system with a single display, you can adjust the scaling by using a slider below the thumbnail of the current monitor on the Display page in Settings.

➤ We cover scaling in "Making text easier to read" in Chapter 3, "Using Windows 10."

- **Multiple displays.** When you attach a second (or third or fourth) display to Windows 10, the Display page in Settings changes. Thumbnails in the preview pane (which you can see in Figure 13-15) show each display at its relative size (in terms of resolution), and you can drag the displays to either side of one another (or even stack one on top of the other). You can also adjust the alignment of the two displays to match their actual physical alignment, with the goal of having your mouse pointer move naturally between displays without a jarring shift when crossing the bezels.

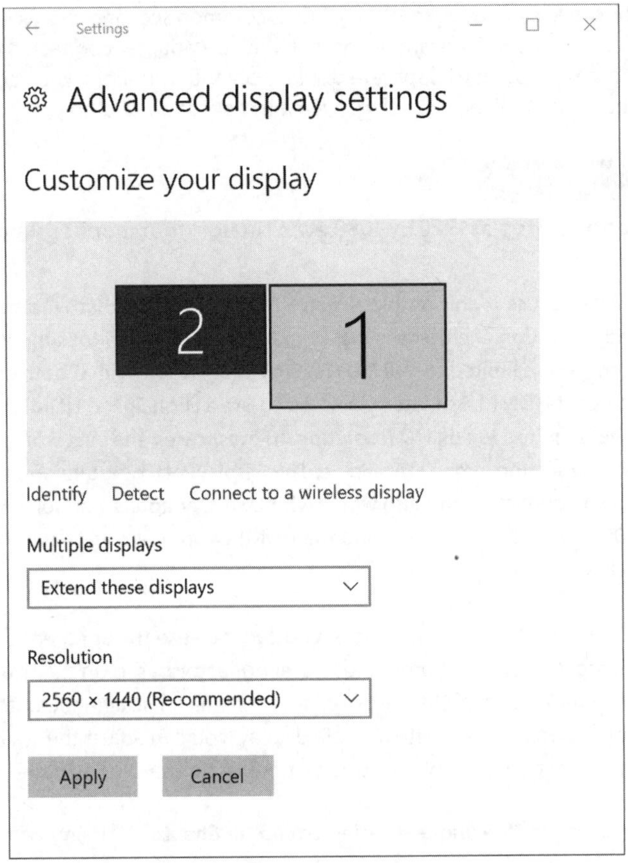

Figure 13-15 With two monitors, you can arrange each so that it matches the physical layout. Drag the monitor thumbnail up, down, or to either side of another display's thumbnail.

Setting up Bluetooth devices

Bluetooth is one of those rare standards that passes the "it just works" test consistently. These days, virtually every portable device supports Bluetooth for wirelessly connecting headsets and pairing fitness devices. Many desktop PCs include Bluetooth support as well, for connecting keyboards and mice.

Before you can use one Bluetooth device with another, you have to pair it, a process that generally involves making the external device discoverable, switching to the Bluetooth tab in Settings > Devices, and then following some instructions. Figure 13-16 shows a Surface pen, made discoverable by holding down a special button combination for several seconds. Tapping Pair completes the connection and makes the device usable with Windows 10, running in this exam-ple on a Surface Book.

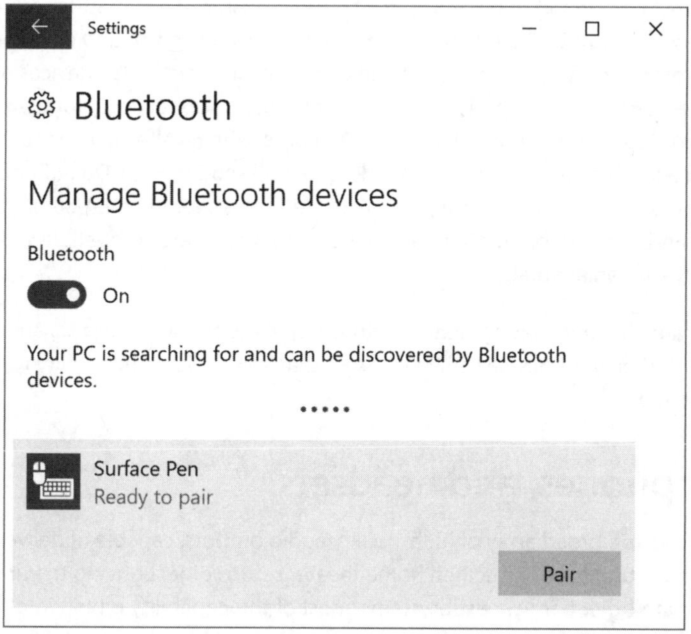

Figure 13-16 Before using a Bluetooth device with a Windows 10 PC, it must be paired.

Bluetooth connections represent a security risk—a low one, to be sure, but a risk nonetheless. That's why pairing a keyboard, for example, requires that you enter a code from the PC's screen. Without that precaution, an attacker might be able to connect a wireless keyboard to your com-puter and then use it to steal data or run unauthorized and potentially dangerous software.

The Bluetooth Settings page contains an on-off switch for the Bluetooth adapter. On mobile PCs, this is a power-saving feature. On a desktop PC, be careful before disabling Bluetooth, because doing so could render your wireless keyboard and mouse—and thus the entire PC—unusable. The only cure in that case is to plug in a wired keyboard or mouse and turn the set-ting back on.

Managing USB devices

Universal serial bus, more commonly known as USB, is one of the oldest and most reliable Plug and Play standards in the world. Through the years, the USB standard has progressed from ver-sion 1.1 to 2.0 to 3.1, with the latest jump making a monumental difference in the speed of data transfer between USB-connected devices. The new USB 3.1 standard is probably the greatest evolution of all, offering the ability to power full-size laptops, transfer data at blistering speeds, and even drive high-resolution displays.

In an unfortunate bit of timing that has inspired some confusion, a new USB Type-C connector arrived at the same time as USB 3.1 began to appear in high-end computing machinery. USB Type-C connectors typically support USB 3.1 and can connect to older USB devices using adapters. However, because the USB Type-C specification mandates support only for the older, slower USB 2.0 standard, you have no guarantee of USB 3.1 compatibility. Alternate modes for USB Type-C support adapters for DisplayPort, Thunderbolt, and Mobile High-Definition Link (MHL) connections. The USB Type-C connector is reversible (no more flipping the USB plug three times until you find the right orientation). These new connectors are compatible with older USB devices, but only with an adapter.

All USB devices are Plug and Play compatible. Knowing the types of connectors and the highest standard supported on your device can help ensure that you avoid compatibility hassles and carry the right cables.

Speakers, microphones, and headsets

Windows 10 supports a broad array of high-quality audio outputs, capable of delivering multi-channel surround sound to sophisticated home theater setups or just driving the tiny speakers on a laptop. As with other hardware subsystems, most of this capability is built into the Windows core drivers and doesn't require custom drivers from hardware manufacturers.

A few useful built-in capabilities are buried deep in the configuration dialog boxes of the Windows 10 audio subsystem.

The first allows you to test your surround-sound (or stereo) audio configuration to confirm that every speaker is working properly. Enter **audio** in the search box in Settings, and open the Playback tab of the Sound dialog box. Choose the default playback device (marked with a green check mark) and then click Configure to open the test app. Pick your speaker layout and then click Test to cycle through all the speakers, with a visual display showing which one should be playing. To end the test, click Stop, as shown in Figure 13-17.

Windows 10 also allows you to designate a playback device, typically a headset, for use as the default communications device, as shown in Figure 13-18. After making that designation, you can change playback behavior so that other sounds automatically reduce their volume when your communication device is in use and the sound of, say, loud music would interfere with your communication.

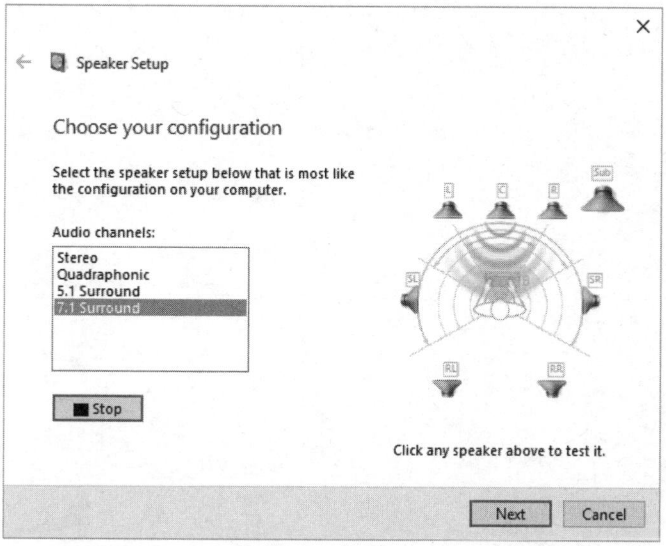

Figure 13-17 You can use this speaker setup test to confirm you haven't accidentally wired the right speakers to left and vice versa.

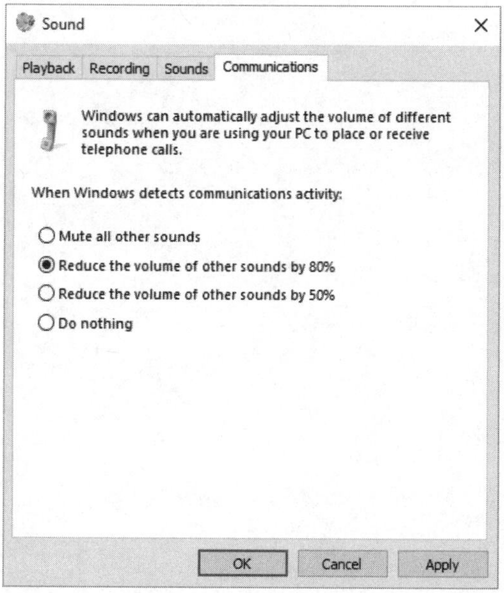

Figure 13-18 Using this well-hidden option, you can reduce other sounds (music and notifications, for example) when Windows detects that you're trying to communicate.

Managing disks and drives

When you get right down to it, storage defines what you can and can't do with Microsoft Windows. A big hard disk (or two or three) makes it possible for you to download and store an enormous amount of digital music, photos, and video; manage large-scale, data-intensive projects; and keep your entire collection of digital resources safely backed up.

Using today's gigantic disks effectively, however, often entails partitioning them intelligently so that separate volumes can be assigned distinct purposes. For various reasons, we recommend, for example, that you keep your operating system and personal data on separate volumes, that (if possible) you make a full image backup of the volume on which the Windows system files are stored, and that you make regular and frequent backups of your valuable data. All of this requires some planning and some familiarity both with disk-management concepts and with management tools that Windows 10 provides.

➤ For more information, see Chapter 12, "Managing files on PCs and in the cloud," and Chapter 16, "Backup, restore, and recovery."

In this chapter, we'll look at the disk-management tools provided by Windows 10 and survey some scenarios under which you might find these tools of use.

The Windows 10 disk-management tools

The principal disk-management tool in Windows 10 is the Disk Management console (Diskmgmt.msc). For those who need to incorporate disk-management tasks in scripts (as well as for those who simply prefer carrying out administrative tasks at the command prompt), Windows also provides a powerful command-line program called DiskPart. Everything you can do with Disk Management you can also do by using DiskPart; you just have to work harder and more carefully. Accessing Windows Management Instrumentation (WMI) through Windows PowerShell provides another method for managing disks. This method offers capabilities that are not available with the Disk Management console or DiskPart, and it has the additional advantage of custom programmability, which can be useful when you need to perform disk-management operations repeatedly on different computers.

Knowing when to use which tool is the secret of disk wizardry in Windows 10. Disk Management, for example, is ideal for shrinking and expanding volumes, while the Clean command in DiskPart makes short work of preparing a disk to be formatted for a new role. That command has no counterpart in Disk Management.

Running Disk Management

To run Disk Management, type **diskmgmt.msc** at a command prompt, or press Windows key+X (or right-click the Start button) and then click Disk Management. You need administrative credentials to run Disk Management. Figure 14-1 illustrates the Disk Management console.

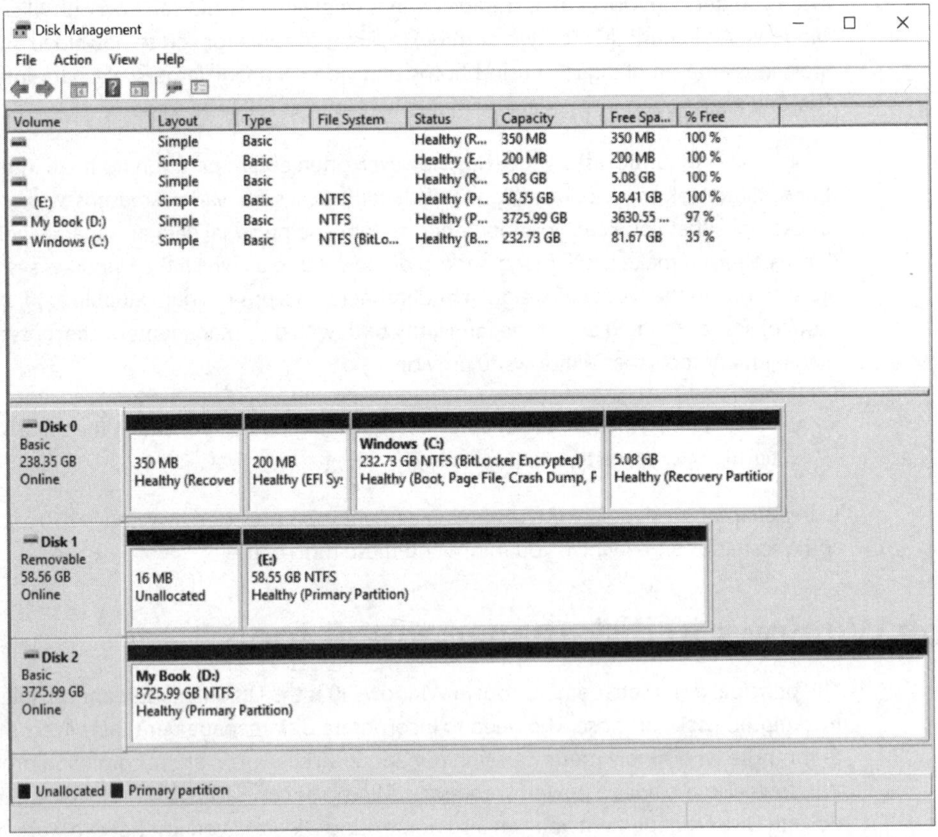

Figure 14-1 Use the Disk Management console to gather information about and manage hard disks and removable disks.

Disk Management provides a wealth of information about physical disks and the volumes, partitions, and logical drives in place on those disks. You can use this utility to perform the following disk-related tasks:

- Check the size, file system, status, and other properties of disks and volumes

- Create, format, and delete partitions, logical drives, and dynamic volumes

- Assign drive letters to hard disk volumes, removable disk drives, and optical drives

- Create mounted drives

- Convert basic disks to dynamic disks and vice versa

- Create spanned and striped volumes

- Extend or shrink partitions

Disk Management displays information in two panes. In its default arrangement, the upper pane lists each volume on your system and provides information about the volume's type, status, capacity, available free space, and so on. You can carry out commands on a volume by right-clicking in the first column of this pane (the column labeled Volume) and choosing a command.

In the lower pane, each row represents one physical device. In the headings at the left of each row, you see the name by which the device is known to the operating system (Disk 0, Disk 1, and so on), along with its type, size, and status. To the right are areas that display information about the volumes of each device. Note that these areas are not by default drawn to scale. To change the scaling used by Disk Management, click View and then Settings. You'll find various options on the Scaling tab of the Settings dialog box.

Right-clicking a heading at the left in the lower pane displays commands pertinent to an entire storage device. Right-clicking an area representing a volume provides a menu of actions applicable to that volume.

Managing disks from the command prompt

To use DiskPart, start by running Cmd.exe with elevated privileges. You can do that by pressing Windows key+X and then clicking Command Prompt (Admin).

➤ **For more information about the command prompt, see Chapter 19, "Automating tasks and activities."**

When you run DiskPart, it switches to a command interpreter, identified by the DISKPART> prompt. If you type **help** and press Enter, you see a screen that lists all available commands, like the one shown next.

CHAPTER 14

```
Administrator: Command Prompt - diskpart                              —    □    ×

DISKPART> help

Microsoft DiskPart version 10.0.14393.0

ACTIVE       - Mark the selected partition as active.
ADD          - Add a mirror to a simple volume.
ASSIGN       - Assign a drive letter or mount point to the selected volume.
ATTRIBUTES   - Manipulate volume or disk attributes.
ATTACH       - Attaches a virtual disk file.
AUTOMOUNT    - Enable and disable automatic mounting of basic volumes.
BREAK        - Break a mirror set.
CLEAN        - Clear the configuration information, or all information, off the
               disk.
COMPACT      - Attempts to reduce the physical size of the file.
CONVERT      - Convert between different disk formats.
CREATE       - Create a volume, partition or virtual disk.
DELETE       - Delete an object.
DETAIL       - Provide details about an object.
DETACH       - Detaches a virtual disk file.
EXIT         - Exit DiskPart.
EXTEND       - Extend a volume.
EXPAND       - Expands the maximum size available on a virtual disk.
FILESYSTEMS  - Display current and supported file systems on the volume.
FORMAT       - Format the volume or partition.
GPT          - Assign attributes to the selected GPT partition.
HELP         - Display a list of commands.
IMPORT       - Import a disk group.
INACTIVE     - Mark the selected partition as inactive.
LIST         - Display a list of objects.
MERGE        - Merges a child disk with its parents.
ONLINE       - Online an object that is currently marked as offline.
OFFLINE      - Offline an object that is currently marked as online.
RECOVER      - Refreshes the state of all disks in the selected pack.
               Attempts recovery on disks in the invalid pack, and
               resynchronizes mirrored volumes and RAID5 volumes
               that have stale plex or parity data.
```

Understanding disk-management terminology

The current version of Disk Management has simplified somewhat the arcane language of disk administration. Nevertheless, it's still important to have a bit of the vocabulary under your belt. The following terms and concepts are the most important:

- **Volume.** A volume is a disk or subdivision of a disk that is formatted and available for storage. If a volume is assigned a drive letter, it appears as a separate entity in File Explorer. A hard disk can have one or more volumes.

- **Mounted drive.** A mounted drive is a volume that is mapped to an empty folder on an NTFS-formatted disk. A mounted drive does not get a drive letter and does not appear separately in File Explorer. Instead, it behaves as though it were a subfolder on another volume.

- **Format.** To format a disk is to prepare it for storage by using a particular file system (such as NTFS).

- **File system.** A file system is a method for organizing folders (directories) and files on a storage medium. Windows 10 supports the following file systems: FAT (File Allocation Table), NTFS, exFAT (Extended File Allocation Table; optimized for use with flash drives), CDFS (Compact Disc File System; also sometimes identified as ISO-9660), and UDF (Universal Disk Format). Windows 10 does not currently support the new Resilient File System (ReFS, for short) but this support is likely to arrive in a future update.

- **Basic disk and dynamic disk.** The two principal types of hard-disk organization in Windows are called basic and dynamic:

  - A basic disk can be subdivided into as many as four partitions. (Disks that have been initialized using a GUID Partition Table can have more than four.) All volumes on a basic disk must be simple volumes. When you use Disk Management to create new simple volumes, the first three partitions it creates are primary partitions. The fourth is created as an extended partition using all remaining unallocated space on the disk. An extended partition can be organized into as many as 2,000 logical disks. In use, a logical disk behaves exactly like a primary partition.

  - A dynamic disk offers organizational options not available on a basic disk. In addition to simple volumes, dynamic disks can contain spanned or striped volumes. These last two volume types combine space from multiple disks.

- **Simple volume.** A simple volume is a volume contained entirely within a single physical device. On a basic disk, a simple volume is also known as a partition.

- **Spanned volume.** A spanned volume is a volume that combines space from physically separate disks, making the combination appear and function as though it were a single storage medium.

- **Striped volume.** A striped volume is a volume in which data is stored in 64-KB strips across physically separate disks to improve performance.

- **MBR and GPT disks.** MBR (master boot record) and GPT (GUID Partition Table) are terms describing alternative methods for maintaining the information regarding a disk's subdivisions. GPT disks support larger volumes (up to 18 exabytes) and more partitions (as many as 128 on a basic disk). You can convert a disk from MBR to GPT (or vice versa) only before a disk has been partitioned for the first time (or after all partitions have been removed). GPT is required on drives that contain the Windows partition on UEFI-based systems.

- **Active partition, boot partition, and system partition.** The active partition is the one from which an x86-based computer starts after you power it up. The first physical hard disk attached to the system (Disk 0) must include an active partition. The boot partition is the partition where the Windows system files are located. The system partition is the partition that contains the bootstrap files that Windows uses to start your system and display the boot menu.

Even if you don't prefer the command line and don't intend to write disk-management scripts, you should know about DiskPart, because if you ever find yourself needing to manage hard disks from the Windows Recovery Environment (Windows RE), you will have access to DiskPart but you won't have access to the Disk Management console. (Windows RE is a special environment you can use for system-recovery purposes if a major hardware or software problem prevents you from starting Windows.)

Windows also includes a second command-line tool for file-system and disk management, called Fsutil. You can use this utility to find files by security identifier (SID), change the short name of a file, and perform other esoteric tasks.

CAUTION

Fsutil and DiskPart are not for the faint of heart or casual experimentation. Both are intended primarily to be incorporated into scripts rather than for interactive use. DiskPart in particular is dense and cryptic, with a complex structure that requires you to list and select objects before you act on them. For more details about DiskPart, see Microsoft Support article 300415, "A Description of the DiskPart Command-Line Utility" (*https://bit.ly/diskpart-commands*). Although this article dates from Windows XP days and some of the comparisons it makes between DiskPart and the Disk Management console are out of date, its tutorial information about the syntax and usage of DiskPart is still accurate.

Setting up a new hard disk

Whether you're installing Windows on a brand new hard disk or simply adding a new disk to an existing system, you should consider how you want to use the new storage space before you begin creating volumes. If your goal is to set up a large space for backup or media storage, for example, you might want to devote the entire disk to a single volume. On the other hand, if your plan is to establish two or more separate volumes—perhaps one for each family member on a shared home computer—decide how many gigabytes you want to assign to each partition. You can change your mind later (see "Managing existing disks and volumes" later in this chapter), but it's easiest to adjust the number of volumes on a disk and their relative sizes before you put a lot of data on the platter.

Installing Windows on a new disk

When you run the Windows 10 setup program on a computer with a single, raw hard disk, you're presented with a screen identifying the disk and its size. If you want to create a single volume encompassing the entire disk, you can click Next to proceed. Otherwise, you can click New, and then in the same screen you can choose the size of the volume you want to create for your Windows installation.

If you decide not to use the entire disk for Windows, you can create additional volumes from within the Setup program. But there's no particular need to do this. After you install Windows, you can use Disk Management to create one or more additional volumes in the unallocated space remaining on the disk.

> ➤ For more information about setting up Windows, see Chapter 2, "Installing, configuring, and deploying Windows 10."

Adding a new disk to an existing Windows installation

In the graphical view pane of Disk Management, a new hard disk, whether internal or external, appears like this:

To make this disk available for storage, you need to create one or more volumes, assign drive letters, label the volumes (if you don't want them to be identified in File Explorer as simply "New Volume"), and format them. You can carry out all these steps from the New Simple Volume Wizard.

Specifying volume capacity

To begin, right-click anywhere in the area marked Unallocated and then click New Simple Volume. The New Simple Volume Wizard appears. Click Next to get past the welcome page. On the Specify Volume Size page, you're shown the maximum and minimum amounts of space you can devote to the new volume:

The wizard doesn't give you the option of designating volume space as a percentage of unallocated space, so if your goal is to create two or more volumes of equal size, you might want to do a bit of arithmetic before going on. In this example, if you want to split the disk into two nearly equal partitions, you enter 476933 in the Simple Volume Size In MB box.

Assigning a drive letter

After you specify the volume size in megabytes and click Next, you are given the opportunity to assign a drive letter to the new volume. Note that the letters A and B, which used to be reserved for floppy disks, are no longer reserved:

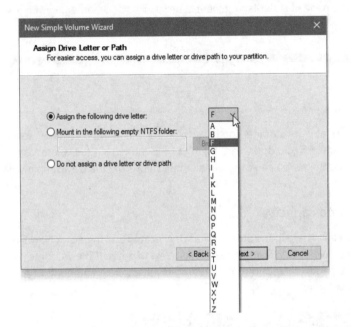

Formatting the new volume

The Format Partition page, which follows the Assign Drive Letter Or Path page, gives you a chance to do just that, but it does not require that you do so. If you prefer to wait, you can always do the formatting later (by right-clicking the area for the volume in the graphical view pane of Disk Management and then clicking Format). Figure 14-2 illustrates the Format Partition page.

Your choices are as follows:

- **File System.** For hard disk volumes larger than 4 GB (4,096 MB), your only options are NTFS (the default) and exFAT. If you're formatting removable media such as USB flash drives or a writable optical disc, other file systems are available. For more information, see "Choosing a file system" later in this chapter.

- **Allocation Unit Size.** The allocation unit size (also known as the cluster size) is the small-est space that can be allocated to a file. The Default option, in which Windows selects the appropriate cluster size based on volume size, is the best choice here.

- **Volume Label.** The volume label identifies the drive in File Explorer. The default label is "New Volume." It's a good idea to give your new volume a name that describes its purpose.

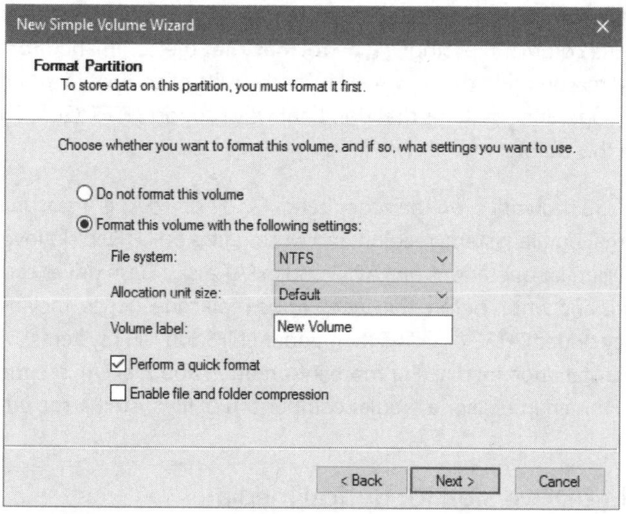

Figure 14-2 You use the Format Partition page to specify your new volume's file system, allocation unit size, and volume label.

Select the Perform A Quick Format check box if you want Disk Management to skip the some-times lengthy process of checking the disk media. Select Enable File And Folder Compression if you want all data on the new volume to use NTFS compression. (This option, which you can also apply later, is available only on NTFS volumes. For more information, see the Inside OUT sidebar "Increase storage space with NTFS compression" later in this chapter.)

The wizard's final page gives you one more chance to review your specifications. You should actually take a moment to read this display before you click Finish.

After Disk Management has done its work and disk formatting is complete, a dark blue bar appears over the new volume in the console's graphical view pane:

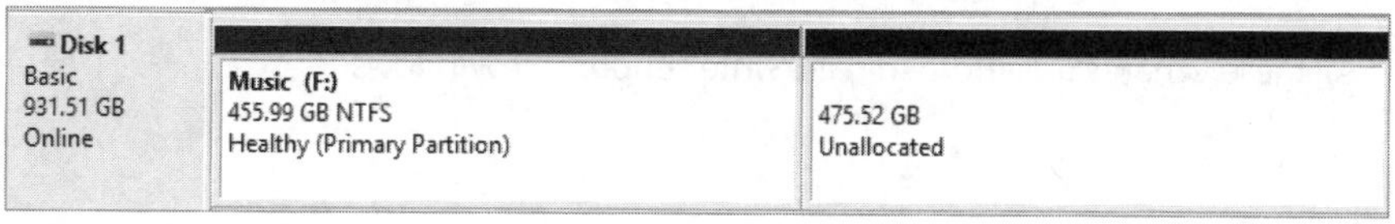

If your disk still has unallocated space (as the disk in this example does), you can add another volume by right-clicking that part of the display and then clicking New Simple Volume again.

Choosing a file system

Whether you're setting up a new disk or reformatting an existing one, the process of formatting entails choosing a file system. The choices available to you depend on the type of media you're formatting. With hard disks, the only options made available by Disk Management are NTFS and exFAT. If you want to format a hard disk in FAT32, you need to use the Format command with the /FS switch at the command prompt. (Type **format /?** at the command prompt for details.) The only good reason to do this, however, is for the sake of compatibility with devices running non-Microsoft operating systems that don't natively support NTFS. (See "The Advantages of NTFS" later in this chapter.)

If you're formatting a USB flash drive, on the other hand, FAT32 or exFAT is a reasonable choice. Because NTFS is a journaling file system, reading and writing files on NTFS disks involves more disk input/output than similar operations on FAT32 and exFAT disks. Flash drives can perform a finite number of reads and writes before they need to be replaced—hence, they might have a longer life expectancy under FAT32 or exFAT than under NTFS. On UEFI systems, FAT32 is required for bootable installation media. (For more information about exFAT, see the "exFAT vs. FAT32" sidebar later in this chapter.) For a tabular comparison of file systems, see *https://bit.ly/ file-systemcomparison*.

Choosing the right UDF version for optical media

If you're formatting a writable CD or DVD disc, your choices are various flavors of the Universal Disk Format (UDF). UDF, a successor to the Compact Disc File System (CDFS), is an evolving specification. Windows 10 can format discs using version 1.50, 2.00, 2.01, or 2.50. (Windows 10 can also use—but not format—discs using the latest version, which is 2.60.) Which to choose? It depends on whether you want the CDs or DVDs that you generate to be readable on systems running earlier versions of Windows or Windows Server. The differences are as follows:

- **Version 1.50.** Can be read on systems running Windows 2000 and later.

- **Version 2.00 or 2.01.** Cannot be read on Windows 2000. Can be read on Windows XP Service Pack 3 or later and Windows Server 2003 or later. Note that version 2.01 is a minor revision of version 2.00. There's no reason to prefer version 2.00.

- **Version 2.50.** Can be read only on computers running Windows Vista or later and Windows Server 2008 or later.

All these variants are afforded read/write support by Windows 10.

Choosing between UDF and mastered optical media

You do not have to format a CD or DVD (using one of the compatible UDF flavors) to store files on it. You can burn files to optical media by copying files to a temporary folder and transferring them en masse to the CD or DVD. Using UDF is somewhat more convenient because it allows you to read and write CD or DVD files as though they were stored on a USB flash drive or floppy disk. But the older method, sometimes called Mastered or ISO, offers greater compatibility with computers running other operating systems, and it's the only method you can use to burn audio files and play them back on consumer audio devices.

The advantages of NTFS

NTFS offers a number of important advantages over the earlier FAT and FAT32 file systems:

- **Security.** On an NTFS volume, you can restrict access to files and folders by using permissions. (For information about using NTFS permissions, see "What are ACLs?" in Chapter 6, "Managing user accounts, passwords, and credentials.") You can add an extra layer of protection by encrypting files if your edition of Windows 10 supports it. On a FAT or FAT32 drive, anyone with physical access to your computer can access any files stored on that drive.

- **Reliability.** Because NTFS is a journaling file system, an NTFS volume can recover from disk errors more readily than a FAT32 volume. NTFS uses log files to keep track of all disk activity. In the event of a system crash, Windows 10 can use this journal to repair file-system errors automatically when the system is restarted. In addition, NTFS can dynamically remap clusters that contain bad sectors and mark those clusters as bad so that the operating system no longer uses them. FAT and FAT32 drives are more vulnerable to disk errors.

- **Expandability.** Using NTFS-formatted volumes, you can expand storage on existing volumes without having to back up, repartition, reformat, and restore.

- **Efficiency.** On partitions greater than 8 GB, NTFS volumes manage space more efficiently than FAT32. The maximum partition size for a FAT32 drive created by Windows 10 is 32 GB; by contrast, you can create a single NTFS volume of up to 16 terabytes (16,384 GB) using default settings, and by tweaking cluster sizes you can ratchet the maximum volume size up to 256 terabytes.

- **Optimized storage of small files.** Files on the order of a hundred bytes or less can be stored entirely within the Master File Table (MFT) record, rather than requiring a minimum allocation unit outside the MFT. This results in greater storage efficiency for small files.

exFAT vs. FAT32

Microsoft introduced the Extended FAT (exFAT) file system first with Windows Embedded CE 6.0, an operating system designed for industrial controllers and consumer electronics devices. Subsequently, exFAT was made available in Windows Vista Service Pack 1 (SP1). Its principal advantage over FAT32 is scalability. The exFAT file system removes the 32-GB volume and 4-GB file-size limitations of FAT32. It also handles more than 1,000 files per directory. Its principal disadvantage is limited backward compatibility. Some non-PC consumer electronics devices might be able to read earlier FAT systems but not exFAT.

If you're formatting a flash drive and you expect to store large video files on it, exFAT might be a good choice for the file system. And if you're planning to take that flash drive to a photo kiosk at your local convenience store, FAT32 is definitely the way to go.

Inside OUT

Formatting does not remove a volume's data

Whatever formatting options you choose, you're warned that the action of formatting a volume makes that volume's data inaccessible. That's true. Whatever data is there when you format will no longer be available to you by normal means after you format. Unless you use the /P switch, the data remains in some form, however. If you're really concerned about covering your tracks, either use the Format /P:x (where x represents the number of passes) or wipe the disk after you format it by using the command-line program Cipher.exe, with the /W switch. (Type **cipher /?** at the command prompt for details.) For information about other ways to clean a disk, see "Permanently wiping all data from a disk" later in this chapter.

Managing existing disks and volumes

No matter how well you plan, your approach to deploying storage resources is likely to change over time. Disk Management can help you adjust to changing requirements. You can expand volumes (assuming space is available), shrink volumes, reformat, relabel, assign new drive letters, and more. We'll consider these options next.

Extending a volume

Disk Management will be happy to make an NTFS volume larger for you, provided unallocated space is available on the same or another hard disk. To accomplish the expansion, right-click the volume you want to expand and then click Extend Volume. Click Next to move past the Extend Volume Wizard's welcome page. The Select Disks page, shown in Figure 14-3, appears.

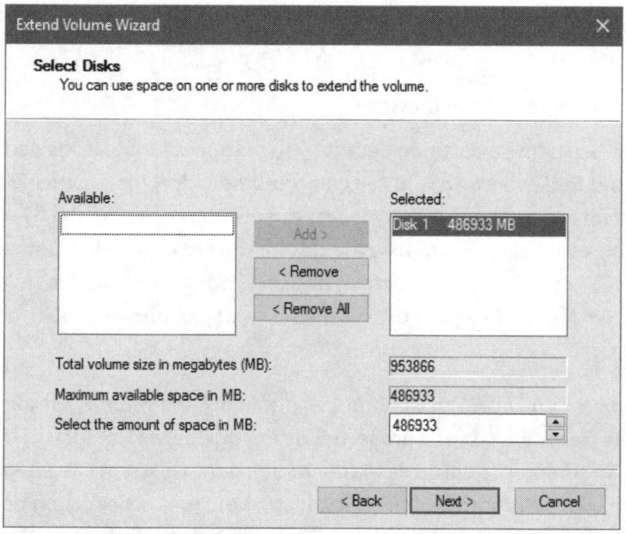

Figure 14-3 Use the Extend Volume Wizard to extend a volume into unallocated space on the same disk or another hard disk with free space.

The Selected list, on the right side of this dialog box, initially shows the disk whose volume you intend to extend. The Maximum Available Space In MB box shows you how much larger you can make the volume, assuming you want to confine your expansion to the current disk. The Select The Amount Of Space In MB box, initially set to equal the maximum available space, is where you declare the number of megabytes you want to add to the volume, and the Total Volume Size In Megabytes (MB) box shows you how big your volume is about to become.

When you're ready to continue, click Next, review your orders on the ensuing page, and then click Finish. If your volume resided on a basic disk to begin with, it remains basic after the expansion—provided that the space into which you expanded was contiguous with the original volume. Note that no separate formatting step is required; the new territory acquires the same formatting as the original.

Volume extension is subject to the following limitations:

- Only NTFS-formatted volumes can be extended.

- A logical drive can be extended only within the extended partition that contains it.

- The system and boot partitions can be extended only into contiguous unallocated space.

- You cannot extend a striped volume.

Inside OUT

Increase storage space with NTFS compression

If you're thinking of expanding a partition because you're short of space, consider compressing your files and folders instead. You can compress individual files, particular folders, or entire volumes. Items compressed in this manner are decompressed on the fly when you open them and compressed again when they are closed. You won't achieve huge savings in storage space this way—less than you would get by using compressed (zipped) folders—but the convenience of NTFS is high and the cost, in terms of performance, is virtually unnoticeable.

To compress a volume, open This PC in File Explorer, right-click the volume, click Properties, and then, on the General tab of the properties dialog box, select Compress This Drive To Save Disk Space. To compress a particular folder or file, right-click it in File Explorer, click Properties, and then click Advanced on the General tab of the properties dialog box. In the Advanced Attributes dialog box, select Compress Contents To Save Disk Space. Note that this form of compression is available only on NTFS volumes and that NTFS compression is incompatible with encryption that uses the Encrypting File System. You can have one or the other, but not both.

Shrinking a volume

Provided space is available, you can shrink an NTFS-formatted volume to make more space available for other volumes. To do this, right-click the volume in either the volume list or graphical view pane and then click Shrink Volume. Disk Management responds by analyzing the disk, and then it reports the amount of shrinkage possible, as shown next:

Shrink F:	×
Total size before shrink in MB:	466933
Size of available shrink space in MB:	463811
Enter the amount of space to shrink in MB:	463811
Total size after shrink in MB:	3122

ⓘ You cannot shrink a volume beyond the point where any unmovable files are located. See the "defrag" event in the Application log for detailed information about the operation when it has completed.

See "Shrink a basic volume" in Disk Management help for more information

[Shrink]   [Cancel]

Enter the number of megabytes by which you want to reduce your volume, and then click Shrink. Disk Management defragments the disk, moving all its data to a contiguous block, and then performs the shrink.

Be aware that page files and volume shadow copy files cannot be moved during the defragmentation process. This means you might not have as much room to shrink as you would like. Microsoft also advises that the amount by which you can shrink a volume is "transient" and depends on what is happening on the volume at the time. In other words, if you're trying to eliminate, say, 10 GB from the volume and Disk Management can manage only 7, take the 7 and then try for more later.

Deleting a volume

Deleting a volume is easy—and irreversible. All data is lost in the process, so be sure you have backed up or no longer need whatever the volume currently contains. Then right-click the volume and click Delete Volume. The volume reverts to unallocated space, and if it happens to have been the last volume on a dynamic disk, the disk itself is converted to basic.

Converting a FAT32 disk to NTFS

To convert a FAT or FAT32 disk to NTFS, use the command-line Convert utility. The essential syntax is

```
convert d: /fs:ntfs
```

where *d* is the drive letter you want to convert. For information about optional parameters, type **convert /?** at the command prompt.

The Convert utility can do its work within Windows if the drive to be converted is not in use. However, if you want to convert the system volume or a volume that holds a page file, you might see an error message when you run Convert. In that case, you must schedule the conversion to occur the next time you start Windows. After you restart the computer, you see a prompt that warns you that the conversion is about to begin. You have 10 seconds to cancel the conversion. If you allow it to proceed, Windows runs the Chkdsk utility and performs the conversion automatically. During this process, your computer will restart twice.

Assigning or changing a volume label

In Windows 10, as in previous versions of Windows, you can assign a descriptive text label to any volume. Assigning a label is purely optional, but it's a good practice, especially if you have a multi-boot system or if you set up separate volumes to keep your data organized. You can use Data as the label for your data drive, Music for the drive that holds your collection of digital tunes, and so on.

You can enter a volume label when you format a new volume, or you can do it at any time afterward by right-clicking a volume (in Disk Management or in File Explorer), clicking Properties, and entering text in the edit field near the top of the General tab.

Assigning and changing drive letters

You can assign one and only one letter to a volume. For all but the following volumes, you can change or remove the drive letter at any time:

- The boot volume

- The system volume

- Any volume on which the page (swap) file is stored

To change a drive-letter assignment, right-click the volume in Disk Management and then click Change Drive Letter And Paths. (You can do this in either the upper or lower pane.) To replace an existing drive letter, select it and click Change. To assign a drive letter to a volume that currently has none, click Add. Select an available drive letter from the Assign The Following Drive Letter list, and then click OK twice.

> ### TROUBLESHOOTING
> **The drive letter for my card reader has disappeared**
>
> Windows 10 does not display empty drives by default. If your computer has a set of drives for memory cards, you might be accustomed to seeing those drives listed in File Explorer whether the drives are empty or not. If you want to make the empty drives visible, open File Explorer, click the View tab, and then select Hidden Items.

Mapping a volume to an NTFS folder

In addition to (or in place of) a drive letter, you can assign one or more paths to NTFS folders to a volume. Assigning a drive path creates a mounted volume (also known as a mounted drive, mounted folder, or volume mount point). A mounted volume appears as a folder within an NTFS-formatted volume that has a drive letter assigned to it. Besides allowing you to sidestep the limitation of 26 drive letters, mounted volumes offer these advantages:

- You can extend storage space on an existing volume that's running low on free space. For instance, if your digital music collection has outgrown your drive C, you can create a subfolder of your Music folder and call it, say, More Music. Then you can assign a drive path from a new volume to the More Music folder—in effect increasing the size of your original Music folder. The More Music folder in this example appears to be part of the original Music folder but actually resides on the new volume.

- You can make commonly used files available in multiple locations. Say you have an enormous collection of clip art that you store on drive X, and each user has a subfolder in his or her Documents folder where desktop publishing files are stored. In each of those personal folders, you can create a subfolder called Clip Art and assign that folder's path to volume X. That way, the entire clip art collection is always available from any user's desktop publishing folder, and no one has to worry about creating shortcuts to X or changing drive letters while they work.

To create a mounted volume, follow these steps:

1. In Disk Management, right-click the volume you want to change (in either the graphical view pane or the volume list pane), and then click Change Drive Letter And Paths.

2. Click Add to open the Add Drive Letter Or Path dialog box.

3. Select Mount In The Following Empty NTFS Folder. (This is the only option available if the volume already has a drive letter assigned.)

4. Click Browse. The Browse For Drive Path dialog box that appears shows only NTFS volumes, and the OK button is enabled only if you select an empty folder or click New Folder to create one.

5. Click OK to add the selected location in the Add Drive Letter Or Path dialog box, and then click OK to create the drive path.

You can manage files and subfolders in a mounted volume just as though it were a regular folder. In File Explorer, the folder icon will be marked by a shortcut arrow. And as Figure 14-4 shows, when you right-click the folder icon and then click Properties, the General tab reveals that the folder is actually a mounted volume and provides more details about the drive to which the folder is mapped.

Click the Properties button within that properties dialog box to see more details about the drive to which the folder is mapped.

If you use the Dir command in a Command Prompt window to display a folder directory, a mounted volume is identified as <JUNCTION> (for junction point, yet another name for a mounted volume), whereas ordinary folders are identified as <DIR> (for directory, the MS-DOS term for a folder).

CAUTION

When creating mounted volumes, avoid establishing loops in the structure of a drive—for example, by creating a drive path from drive X that points to a folder on drive D and then creating a drive path on drive D that points to a folder on drive X. Windows allows you to do this, but it's invariably a bad idea, because an application that opens subfolders (such as a search) can go into an endless loop.

CHAPTER 14

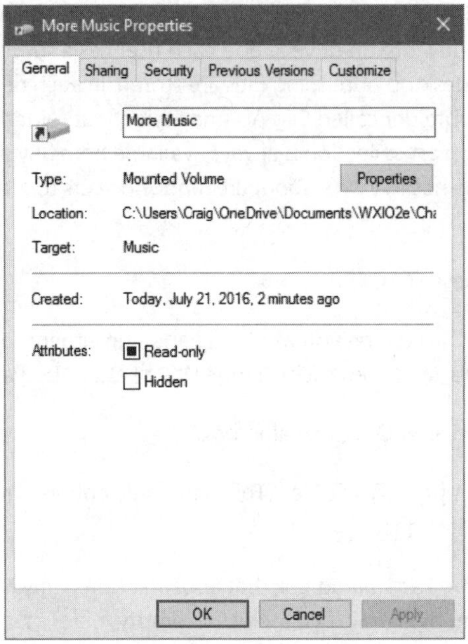

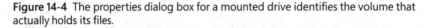

Figure 14-4 The properties dialog box for a mounted drive identifies the volume that actually holds its files.

To see a list of all the mounted drives on your system, click View, Drive Paths in Disk Management. A dialog box like the one shown in Figure 14-5 appears. Note that you can remove a drive path from this dialog box; if you do so, the folder remains in the same spot it was previously located, but it reverts to being a regular, empty folder.

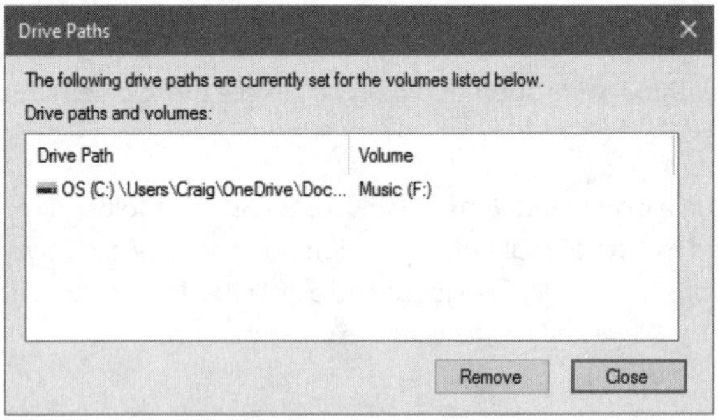

Figure 14-5 This dialog box lists all the mounted drives on a system and shows the volume label, if any, of each mounted drive.

➤ For instructions on how to make a USB flash drive bootable so that you can use it to install Windows 10, see "Build (or buy) installation media" in Chapter 2. For details on how to mount an ISO file so you can run the setup program without requiring external media, see the Inside OUT sidebar "Upgrade directly from an ISO file," also in Chapter 2.

Checking the properties and status of disks and volumes

You can check the properties of any drive—including the volume label, file system, and amount of free space available—by right-clicking the drive in File Explorer's This PC folder and then clicking Properties. You can see the same details and more in Disk Management. Most of the crucial information is visible in the volume list, the tabular pane that appears by default at the top of the Disk Management window. Slightly less information is available in the graphical view at the bottom of the window. Of particular interest is information about the status of a disk or volume. Figure 14-6 shows where to look for this information.

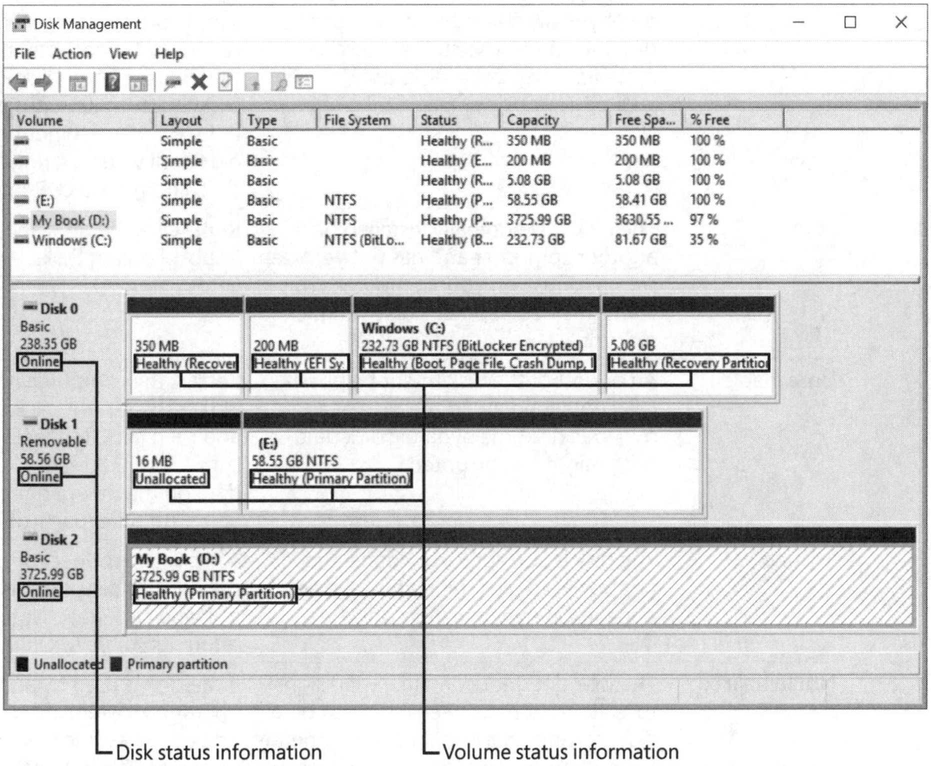

Figure 14-6 Disk Management displays information about the status of each disk and volume.

Under normal circumstances, the status information displayed here should report that each disk is online and each volume is healthy. Table 14-1 lists all possible disk status messages you might see on a system running Windows 10, along with suggested actions for resolving possible errors.

Table 14-1 Disk status messages

Status	Description	Action required
Online	The disk is configured correctly and has no known problems.	None.
Online (Errors)	The operating system encountered errors when reading or writing data from a region of the disk. (This status message appears on dynamic disks only.)	Right-click the disk, and then click Reactivate Disk to return its status to Online. If errors continue to occur, check for damage to the disk.
Offline	The disk was once available but is not currently accessible. The disk might be physically damaged, or it might be disconnected. (This status message appears on dynamic disks only.)	Check the physical connections between the disk and the power supply or disk controller. After repairing connections, right-click the disk and then click Reactivate Disk to return its status to Online. If the damage cannot be repaired, delete all volumes, right-click the disk, and then click Remove Disk.
Foreign	The disk was originally installed on another computer and has not yet been set up for use on your computer. (This status message appears on dynamic disks only.)	Right-click the disk, and then click Import Foreign Disks.
Unreadable	All or part of the disk might be physically damaged, or (in the case of a dynamic disk) the dynamic disk database might be corrupted.	Restart the computer. If the problem persists, right-click the disk and then click Rescan Disks. If the status is still Unreadable, some data on the disk might be recoverable with third-party utilities.
Missing	The disk is corrupted, disconnected, or not powered on. (This status message appears on dynamic disks only.)	After you reconnect or power on the missing disk, right-click the disk and click Reactivate Disk to return its status to Online.
Not Initialized	The disk does not contain a valid signature. It might have been prepared on a system running a non-Microsoft operating system, such as Unix or Linux, or the drive might be brand new.	If the disk is used by another operating system, do nothing. To prepare a new disk for use with Windows 10, right-click the disk and click Initialize Disk.
No Media	A disc is not inserted in the drive. (This status message appears only on removable media drives, such as CD and DVD drives.)	Insert a disc in the drive, and then click Action, Rescan Disks.

Table 14-2 describes volume status messages you're likely to see.

Table 14-2 Volume status messages

Status	Description	Action required
Healthy	The volume is properly formatted and has no known problems.	None.
Healthy (At Risk)	Windows encountered errors when reading from or writing to the underlying disk. Such errors are often caused by bad blocks on the disk. After encountering an error anywhere on the disk, Disk Management marks all volumes on that disk as Healthy (At Risk). (This status message appears on dynamic disks only.)	Right-click the disk, and then click Reactivate Disk. Persistent errors often indicate a failing disk. Back up all data, and run a thorough diagnostic check using the hardware manufacturer's software; if necessary, replace the disk.
Healthy (Unknown Partition)	Windows does not recognize the partition; this occurs with some partitions created by another operating system or by a computer manufacturer that uses a partition to store system files. You cannot format or access data on an unknown partition.	If you're certain the partition is unnecessary, use Disk Management to delete it and create a new partition in the free space created.
Initializing	Disk Management cannot determine the disk status because the disk is initializing. (This status message appears on dynamic disks only.)	Wait. The drive status should appear in a few seconds.
Failed	The dynamic disk is damaged or the file system is corrupted.	To repair a failed dynamic volume, check to see whether the disk is online. (If it's not, right-click the disk, and then click Reactivate Disk.) Right-click the volume, and then click Reactivate Volume. If the failed volume is on a basic disk, be sure that the disk is properly connected.
Unknown	The boot sector for the volume is corrupted, and you can no longer access data. This condition might be caused by a virus.	Use an up-to-date virus-scanning program to check for the presence of a boot-sector virus.

Permanently wiping all data from a disk

Formatting a volume results in a root folder that appears to be empty. However, as we mentioned earlier in this chapter, someone with data-recovery tools might be able to restore deleted files even after you format the volume. If you're discarding or recycling an old computer or hard disk, you don't want to risk the possibility of it landing in the hands of someone who might search it for recoverable data that can be used for identity theft or other nefarious purposes.

If your old disk is headed for the dumpster, you can ensure that the data can't be recovered by removing the disk drive from the computer and physically destroying the disk. Using tools as varied as a power saw, drill, torch, or sledge hammer, you can render the disk inoperable. Although this method is effective, it has several disadvantages: it takes time and considerable physical effort, and it has all the usual risks associated with tools. (Be sure you're wearing safety goggles.) Perhaps most important, you're left with a disk that can't be sold or donated to someone who can use it.

As we mentioned earlier, the Format command (with the /P switch) and the Cipher command (with the /W switch) can be used to overwrite everything on a disk, but these tools are impractical for cleaning the system partition.

A better solution is to use a third-party disk-wiping tool. A free one that we like is Darik's Boot And Nuke (DBAN), which you can download from *http://www.dban.org*. DBAN is a bootable disk that securely wipes a computer's hard disks. If you're worried that DBAN or another purported disk-wiping utility might surreptitiously steal your data before destroying it, remove your concerns by disconnecting your computer from your network before using the program.

If your disk contains highly sensitive material and you want to be absolutely sure its data can't be recovered, search for a utility that conforms to the United States Department of Defense DoD 5220.22-M standard for clearing and sanitizing media. This standard requires each sector to be overwritten with different characters several times, thus defeating even the most sensitive data-recovery tools. Programs that meet the standard include Active@ KillDisk (*http://www.kill-disk.com*) and BCWipe (*https://www.jetico.com*).

Working with virtual hard disks

Disk Management can create virtual hard disks in the VHD format used by the Windows 10 Hyper-V Manager program. A .vhd file encapsulates all the characteristics of a simple disk volume in a single file. Once created, initialized, and formatted, it appears as a disk drive in File Explorer and Disk Management, but you can copy it, back it up, and do anything else with it that you might do with an ordinary file.

➤ **For more information about Hyper-V Manager, see Chapter 22, "Running virtual machines with Hyper-V."**

To create a virtual hard disk, open Disk Management and click Action, Create VHD. Disk Management responds with the Create And Attach Virtual Hard Disk dialog box:

Specify a file name with a fully qualified path. It's easiest to do this with the help of the Browse button, but note that the file cannot be stored in your %SystemRoot% (usually C:\Windows) folder. If you want the disk to expand in size as you add files to it, select Dynamically Expanding. Otherwise, select Fixed Size (Recommended). Either way, you must also specify a size (that's a maximum size if you select Dynamically Expanding). The minimum size is 3 MB; the maximum is the amount of free space available on your (real) disk.

New in Windows 10 is the option to create a virtual hard disk in either of two formats. The VHD format supports disks up to 2 TB, which can be used on systems running Windows 7, Windows 8 or 8.1, or Windows 10. The VHDX format supports much larger disks, up to 64 TB, but it's not supported by earlier versions of Windows. The VHDX format was introduced with Windows Server 2012, and the option to create gigantic virtual disks is perhaps primarily of interest to server administrators. VHD is still the default format in Windows 10. However, because metadata in VHDX disks continuously tracks changes (a service not provided in VHD), they are, as the dialog box indicates, more resilient to power failures. For that reason, you might prefer the newer format even if your size requirements are well under 2 TB. Provided that you don't require

CHAPTER 14

interoperability with Windows 7 or Windows 8 or 8.1, we don't know of a good reason not to prefer VHDX.

After you finish with the Create And Attach Virtual Hard Disk dialog box, Disk Management adds the new virtual disk to its graphical view pane as an unknown, uninitialized disk with unallocated space:

Right-click the area at the left side of this display (with the disk number), and then click Initialize Disk. The Initialize Disk dialog box that appears gives you the option of setting up a disk with a master boot record or a GUID Partition Table:

Select MBR (Master Boot Record) unless you're working with a very large disk. After completing these steps, you can follow the procedures described earlier in this chapter to create one or more volumes on the new disk. After you have created a volume, formatted it, and assigned it a drive letter, the disk appears like any other in Disk Management and File Explorer.

To remove a virtual hard disk, right-click the disk-number box at the left side of Disk Management's graphical view pane, and then click Detach VHD. Disk Management informs you that deleting the disk will make it unavailable until you reattach it. The dialog box also reminds you of the location of the file that encapsulated your virtual hard disk.

To reattach a deleted virtual disk, click Action, Attach VHD in Disk Management. Then type or browse to the location of the VHD or VHDX file. (It will be identified in File Explorer as Hard Disk Image File.)

Checking disks for errors

Errors in disk media and in the file system can cause a wide range of problems, from an inability to open or save files to blue-screen errors and widespread data corruption. Windows is capable of recovering automatically from many disk errors, especially on drives formatted with NTFS.

To perform a thorough inspection for errors, you can run the Windows Check Disk utility (Chkdsk.exe). Two versions of this utility are available—a graphical version that performs basic disk-checking functions, and a command-line version that provides a much more extensive set of customization options.

To check for errors on a local disk, follow these steps:

1. In File Explorer, open This PC, right-click the icon belonging to the drive you want to check, and then click Properties.

2. On the Tools tab, click Check. (If you're using a standard account, you need to supply credentials for an account in the Administrators group to execute this utility.) Unless Windows is already aware of problems with the selected disk, you're likely to see a message similar to the following:

Error Checking (OS (C:))

You don't need to scan this drive

We haven't found any errors on this drive. You can still scan the drive for errors if you want.

→ Scan drive
You can keep using the drive during the scan. If errors are found, you can decide if you want to fix them.

Cancel

3. If you want to go ahead and check the disk, click Scan Drive. Windows will perform an exhaustive check of the entire disk. If there are bad sectors, Windows will locate them and recover readable information where it can.

The command-line version of Check Disk gives you considerably more options. You can also use it to set up regular disk-checking operations using Task Scheduler (as described in "Using Task Scheduler" in Chapter 19). To run this command in its simplest form, open a Command Prompt window using the Run As Administrator option, and then type **chkdsk** at the prompt. This command runs Chkdsk in read-only mode, displaying the status of the current drive but not making any changes. If you add a drive letter after the command (*chkdsk d:*, for instance), the report applies to that drive.

To see descriptions of the command-line switches available with the Chkdsk command, type **chkdsk /?**. Here is a partial list of the available switches:

- **/F** Instructs Chkdsk to fix any errors it detects. This is the most commonly used switch. The disk must be locked. If Chkdsk cannot lock the drive, it offers to check the drive the next time you restart the computer or to dismount the volume you want to check before proceeding. Dismounting is a drastic step; it invalidates all current file handles on the affected volume and can result in loss of data. You should decline the offer. When you do, Chkdsk makes you a second offer—to check the disk the next time you restart your system. You should accept this option. (If you're trying to check the system drive, the only option you're given is to schedule a check at the next startup.)

- **/V** On FAT32 volumes, /V displays verbose output, listing the name of every file in every directory as the disk check proceeds. On NTFS volumes, this switch displays cleanup messages (if any).

- **/R** Identifies bad sectors and recovers information from those sectors if possible. The disk must be locked. Be aware that this is a time-consuming and uninterruptible process.

The following switches are valid only on NTFS volumes:

- **/I** Performs a simpler check of index entries (stage 2 in the Chkdsk process), reducing the amount of time required.

- **/C** Skips the checking of cycles within the folder structure, reducing the amount of time required.

- **/X** Forces the volume to dismount, if necessary, and invalidates all open file handles. This option is intended for server administrators. Because of the potential for data loss, it should be avoided.

- **/L[:size]** Changes the size of the file that logs NTFS transactions. If you omit the size parameter, this switch displays the current size. This option is intended for server administrators. Because of the potential for data loss, it also should be avoided in normal use.

- **/B** Reevaluates bad clusters and recovers readable information.

Optimizing disks for better performance

On a relatively new system with a speedy processor, plenty of physical memory, and a conventional hard disk drive with spinning platters, disk performance is the single biggest bottleneck in everyday operation. Even with a zippy hard drive, it takes time to load large data files into memory so that you can work with them. The problem is especially noticeable with movies, video clips, DVD-burning projects, databases, ISO image files, and virtual hard disks, which can easily take up multiple gigabytes, sometimes in a single file.

On a freshly formatted disk, files load fairly quickly, but performance can degrade over time because of disk fragmentation. To understand how fragmentation works, it helps to understand the basic structure of a hard disk. The process of formatting a disk divides it into sectors, each of which contains space for 512 bytes of data. The file system combines groups of sectors into clusters, which are the smallest units of space available for holding a single file or part of a file.

On any NTFS volume greater than 2 GB in size, the cluster size is 4 KB. Thus, when you save a 200-MB video clip, Windows divides the file into roughly 50,000 pieces. When you save this file for the first time on a freshly formatted, completely empty hard disk, Windows writes it in contiguous clusters. Because all the clusters that hold individual pieces of the file are physically adjacent to one another, the mechanical components of the hard disk can work very efficiently, scooping up data in one smooth operation. As a bonus, the hard disk's onboard cache and the Windows disk cache are able to anticipate the need for data and fetch nearby clusters that are likely to contain other parts of the file, which can then be retrieved from fast cached memory rather than from the relatively slow disk.

Unfortunately, hard disks don't stay neatly organized for long. When you add data to an existing file, the file system has to allocate more clusters for storage, typically in a different physical location on the disk. As you delete files, you create gaps in the once-tidy arrangement of contiguously stored files. As you save new files, especially large ones, the file system uses all these bits of free space, scattering the new files over the hard disk in many noncontiguous pieces. The resulting inefficiency in storage is called fragmentation; each time you open or save a file on a badly fragmented disk, disk performance suffers, sometimes dramatically, because the disk heads have to spend extra time moving from cluster to cluster before they can begin reading or writing data.

The Optimize Drives service in Windows 10 runs as a low-priority background task that defragments your disks at regularly scheduled intervals. By default, the program kicks off once a week in the middle of the night, without requiring any attention from you. If you would like a different schedule, or if you want to optimize certain disks and not others, type **dfrgui** at a command prompt. The Optimize Drives dialog box appears:

Here you can analyze the fragmentation level of particular disks, optimize a disk ad hoc, or reconfigure the system's background defragmentation schedule. To reconfigure, click Change Settings. The frequency options are Daily, Weekly, and Monthly:

By clicking the Choose button, you can turn optimization on or off for particular drives:

Optimize Drives   ✕

Select the drives you want to optimize on a regular schedule:

- ▣ Select all
- ☑ OS (C:)
- ☑ 4TB-Data (D:)
- ☑ Archive (D:\Ed\Archive)
- ☑ PBR Image
- ☐ WINRETOOLS
- ☐ \\?\Volume{50397e5d-b2ca-44ff-b0e8-85a67819442d}\

Only drives that can be scheduled for automatic optimization are shown.

☑ Automatically optimize new drives

OK   Cancel

Working with solid state drives

Many newer computers are equipped with a solid state drive (SSD), which is a chunk of flash memory instead of a spinning magnetic disk coupled with an onboard disk controller and the requisite power and data connectors. Such drives can provide improved performance, increased battery life, better durability, reduced likelihood of damage caused by drops and shocks, faster startup times, and reductions in noise, heat, and vibration. These benefits come at a price: SSDs typically cost more and have less storage capacity than current hard disk drive (HDD) models, although the gap is closing.

Conventional hard disk drives are typically the biggest performance bottleneck in any computing environment. If you can speed up disk activity, especially reads, the effects on system startup and application launch times can be breathtaking. On our test platform, which has a conventional hard disk and an older solid state drive configured for dual booting, the total boot time when using the SSD is roughly one-fourth the time required to boot from the HDD. On very recent hardware, with the latest generation of SSDs, we routinely see boot times of less than 15 seconds. Close examination of log files created by the Windows System Assessment Tool (WinSAT), which are stored in %SystemRoot%\Performance\WinSAT\DataStore, shows radically higher throughput and faster times in the DiskMetrics section of the SSD-based system.

Although the underlying technology in SSDs and HDDs is completely different, for the most part the devices are treated identically by Windows, and you don't need to concern yourself

CHAPTER 14

with the differences. Behind the scenes, Windows does several things differently on SSDs, including the following:

- SuperFetch, ReadyBoost, ReadyBoot, and ReadyDrive, features designed to overcome hard disk bottlenecks, are unnecessary and are disabled by default on most SSDs. (Windows analyzes disk performance and disables these features only on SSDs that are fast enough to make these features superfluous.)

- When creating a partition on an SSD, Windows properly aligns the partition for best performance.

- Windows 10 supports the TRIM command. SSDs have to erase blocks of data before those blocks can be reused; they can't write directly over deleted data as rotating disks can. The TRIM command makes this process more efficient by reclaiming deleted space in the background. You can find more details in this Wikipedia article: *https://en.wikipedia.org/wiki/Trim_(computing)*.

Optimizing solid state drives

If your system includes one or more SSDs and you have read that defragmentation is inappropriate with such drives, you might be surprised to see that SSDs are listed in the Optimize Drives dialog box.

Rest assured that the optimization that Windows performs automatically at (by default) weekly intervals is primarily retrimming, not defragmenting. (See the comments about the TRIM command in the preceding section.) For an interesting discussion of the application of TRIM to SSDs and the issues in general surrounding optimization with such drives, see Scott Hanselman's blog post at *https://bit.ly/defrag-ssd*.

That blog post includes a quotation from an unnamed Microsoft spokesperson indicating that Windows *does* defragment SSDs once a month, provided System Restore is enabled. This is done to improve performance of the System Restore process on drives that have become fragmented. In our view, there's no good reason to interfere with this optimization.

Monitoring disk usage

The Windows 10 Storage page lets you see at a glance how your various storage assets are being consumed. Go to Settings, System, click on Storage in the list of subsections at the left, and you're presented with a display comparable to the following:

This initial display shows a bar graph for each volume, letting you see at a glance how much storage is in use and how much remains. The controls below the bar graphs provide an easy way to change the default storage locations for various categories of files—documents, music, pictures, and so on.

> ➤ For a detailed discussion of how this feature works, see "Managing disk space" in Chapter 15, "System maintenance and performance."

Changing default save locations

In the Save Locations section of the initial Storage display, you'll find a set of drop-down lists for various categories of files—apps and games, documents, music, pictures, and videos. Using these controls, you can change the locations where new items are saved by default. All these categories, except for apps and games, represent libraries, and changing the default storage location simply adds a new location to the library. Opening the Save New Music To list and switching from This PC to Music (F:), for example, expands the Music Library to include drive F, as Figure 14-7 shows.

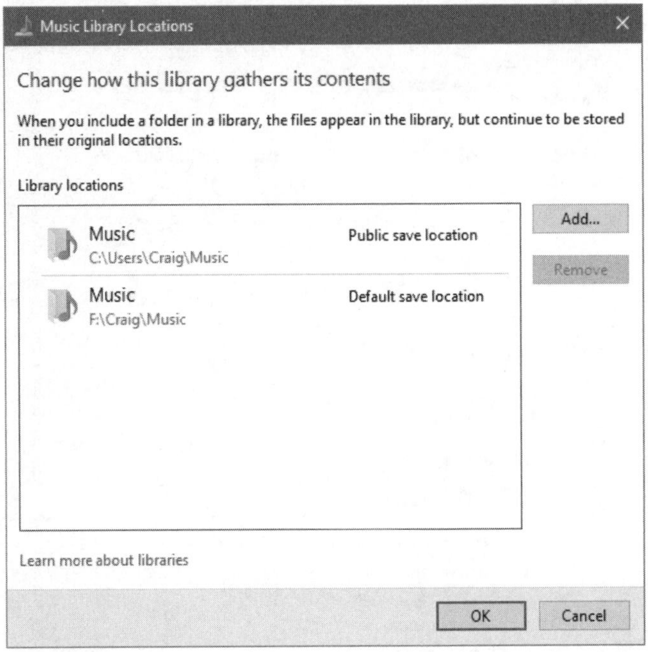

Figure 14-7 Changing the default save location for a file type expands the library, if any, associated with that file type.

Note that if the volume to which you redirect new saves does not already include an appropriate folder for the selected document type, Windows creates the folder. In Figure 14-7, for example, the folder F:\Craig\Music did not exist before we changed the default save location for music. Also note that the previous save folder (in this case, C:\Users\Craig\Music) becomes a public save location. If you subsequently change the default save location again, the previous save location remains in the library (and, of course, the folder and its contents also remain). You can change the library locations by selecting a library in the Navigation pane and then selecting Library Tools > Manage Library.

➤ **For information about libraries, see "Using libraries" in Chapter 12.**

Using Storage Spaces

Storage Spaces is a technology introduced with the server editions of Windows in 2012 and with Windows 8 and Windows 8.1. With this technology you can aggregate collections of disks into "storage pools" and then create virtualized disks ("storage spaces") within those pools. For example, you could take two 3-TB disks (Serial-Attached SCSI, Serial ATA, or USB) and use Storage Spaces to create from them a single 6-TB virtualized disk.

You can also use Storage Spaces to establish resiliency for critical data. For example, using your two 3-TB disks, you could create a mirrored storage space in which each file saved on one of the physical disks is mirrored on the other; if one of the physical disks fails, your data is preserved.

Three types of resiliency are available:

- **Two-way mirror.** The system writes two copies of your data. You can lose one physical disk without data loss. A minimum of two physical disks is required. The amount of storage available is half of the total storage pool.

- **Three-way mirror.** The system writes three copies of your data. You can lose two physical disks without data loss. A minimum of three physical disks is required, and the amount of storage available is one-third of the storage pool.

- **Parity.** The system stripes data across physical disks while also maintaining parity information that allows it to protect and recover your data more efficiently in the event of drive failure. A minimum of three drives is required.

Simple (nonresilient) storage spaces are recommended if you prefer a large virtual disk to separate physical disks. You might make this choice, for example, if you have a large media collection and several older (hence smaller) disks that are not currently in service. Simple storage spaces are also a good choice for space-intensive operations (video editing, for example) that do not require resiliency. Files in a simple storage space are striped across physical disks, resulting in better performance.

Use parity for maximum resiliency, but note that write performance is degraded by the requirement for the system to calculate and store parity information. This choice might be ideal for archival storage.

Note the following:

- You can create a storage space only on freshly formatted blank disks. Storage Spaces will erase all data on the physical components of a pool (with due warning to you, of course) before setting up the storage space, and such erased data cannot be recovered via the Recycle Bin or other data-recovery tools.

- Storage spaces should not be used as a substitute for backups. They do not protect you against theft, fire, or other comparable adversities.

To set up a storage space, type **storage spaces** in the search box. (Or you can go to Control Panel and search for it there.) Click Create A New Pool And Storage Space, and respond to the UAC prompt. A display comparable to the one shown next appears.

CHAPTER 14

After noting the warning about the erasure of existing data on the available drives, select the drives you want to use, and then click Create Pool. The Create A Storage Space window appears, as shown next:

Choose a drive letter, file system, and resiliency type, and then click Create Storage Space.

➤ For much more information about Storage Spaces, see *https://bit.ly/storage-spaces* and *https://bit.ly/storage-spaces-faq*.

System maintenance and performance

Expectations for how a Microsoft Windows 10 device should perform are defined by a host of factors. Among them is your threshold of patience, but for big jobs, such as converting and editing video files, time is literally money. For those tasks, it's worth spending a little effort tweaking and tuning to shave a few minutes off the time needed to complete them.

For the most part, Windows 10 works acceptably out of the box. Yes, it's possible to improve performance for some tasks, but we don't believe there's a secret formula, magic bullet, or special MakeRocketShipGoFast registry value that will suddenly send your system into warp speed. Our formula for getting great performance out of a Windows PC is much more prosaic: Start with quality parts, make sure everything has the right drivers and is up to date, and then look at ways to speed yourself through your workday and make games go faster after hours.

We also know that performance problems can crop up unexpectedly. This chapter covers a number of tools you can use to establish a performance baseline and identify the cause of performance issues. Our goal in this chapter is to help you measure performance accurately and to understand the routine maintenance tasks that can keep a system running smoothly and prevent performance problems from occurring in the first place.

We begin with the single most important maintenance tool of all: Windows Update.

Keeping Windows up to date

In Windows 10, the Windows Update service delivers security fixes, performance and reliability improvements, and updated device drivers, just as its predecessors have done for two decades. But this release also assigns a crucial new role to this core Windows feature. In the "Windows as a Service" model, Windows Update delivers regular upgrades to Windows 10, with new and improved features alongside the bug fixes.

Windows Update and its associated services, such as the Background Intelligent Transfer Service (BITS), should run automatically, with little or no attention required from you. We strongly suggest checking in at regular intervals to confirm that updates are being delivered as expected

CHAPTER 15

and that the various Windows Update services are working properly. To do this, go to Settings > Update & Security > Windows Update. The text below the Update Status heading tells you whether your system was up to date as of the most recent check. If an update has recently been delivered but your device needs to be restarted to complete the update process, you'll see words to that effect. Windows Update will restart your system at a time outside of your active hours, but you can go ahead and restart manually if you want.

Inside OUT

Don't fear automatic updates

Over the past decade, Microsoft and other software companies, large and small, occasionally delivered updates that caused new problems. Among conservative IT pros and Windows experts, it became practically dogma to stand out of the line of fire when updates were first released. Historically, problematic updates are usually identified within the first week or two and either pulled or fixed, making it safe to deploy them after a suitable delay.

So why are things different this time around? Are monthly updates in Windows 10 more trustworthy than their predecessors? The crucial difference is the introduction of the Windows Insider program, which allows a large group of early adopters to test updates in the Fast and Slow Insider tracks before updates are released to the general population.

Yes, it's still possible for a seemingly innocuous update to cause problems for some users, but the risk is much lower now because those updates will have been tested more fully than ever before. A policy-based option in Windows 10 Pro and Enterprise can help you avoid the occasional flawed update that sneaks into circulation. See "Using Windows Update for Business" in Chapter 21, "Managing Windows 10 in business," for details. For truly mission-critical systems, where any downtime could be disastrous and a conservative approach is imperative, consider upgrading to Windows Enterprise edition, where the Long Term Servicing Branch is available.

How updates are delivered

If you're accustomed to using Windows Update in earlier versions of Windows, you might be startled by one major change in Windows 10. Whereas Windows 7 and Windows 8.1 users were offered a menu of updates periodically and could pick and choose which updates they wanted to install, Windows 10 bundles all its available updates into cumulative updates. A cumulative update includes all fixes that Microsoft has previously released. When you install the update, the system downloads and applies only those updates you have not previously installed. This major change in the servicing model for Windows is likely to dismay traditionalists who want the option to sort through updates at their leisure, accepting some, delaying others, and rejecting still others.

In recent years, most newly discovered vulnerabilities in Windows have been patched quickly—usually before they became widespread problems. In fact, many of the worst outbreaks were based on vulnerabilities that had been patched months or years earlier. Windows users who installed the updates promptly avoided infection, whereas those who failed to keep their systems updated fell victim. With Windows 10, Microsoft has taken additional steps to ensure that more systems are updated quickly—namely, by installing updates automatically in many cases.

Inside OUT

Other software needs updates, too

On a typical Windows PC, it's not unusual to find many apps, services, plug-ins, and utilities that also update themselves automatically. Microsoft Edge and Internet Explorer include Adobe Flash Player, for example, which is updated automatically through Windows Update. Third-party browsers that support Flash-based content require separate updates for the Flash Player plug-in. Likewise, it's crucial to ensure that Oracle's Java, which is regularly targeted by malware writers, has the most recent security updates.

Other programs and features you're likely to use on a PC running Windows 10 also require updates. This list includes Microsoft Office and Office 365 and offline content for the Maps app. Apps acquired from the Windows Store automatically update themselves as well. Many third-party programs and services, including web browsers and cloud-based file-storage services, include their own updaters, which typically run in the background or as scheduled tasks.

In general, it's a good idea to allow these updaters to run. Studies have shown repeatedly that most malware arrives through exploits that target vulnerabilities for which security patches have long been available. Keeping all installed software up to date is an excellent way to avoid being a victim.

Managing the update process

The level of control you have over how and when updates are installed depends on which edition of Windows you have and on settings controlled by your network administrator:

- With Windows 10 Home, new features, bug fixes, and security updates are pushed to your computer automatically. You don't need to take any additional action aside from observing the occasional reminders to restart your computer. (When Windows does require a restart, you can control when it occurs.) As a result, Windows 10 Home systems are always up to date; users who want to skip or postpone certain updates do not have that option. In Microsoft parlance, this servicing "ring" is called the Current Branch.

- Users of Windows 10 Pro can use the default settings and receive Current Branch servicing. An additional option, not available in Windows 10 Home, allows you to select Defer Feature Updates from the Windows Update Advanced Options page. This option shifts update delivery to the Current Branch for Business; security updates arrive through Windows Update when they are released, but feature upgrades are delayed several months, until they have been thoroughly tested by users in the Windows Insider Program and by the general public in the Current Branch. (For more information about the Current Branch for Business, see "Using Windows Update for Business" in Chapter 21.) Note that the Defer Feature Updates option does not affect security updates. Fixes for security issues, which are typically included in cumulative updates delivered around the second Tuesday of each month, are always automatically installed.

- Organizations that deploy Windows 10 Enterprise get the same servicing options as Windows 10 Pro, plus one significant extra: In addition to the Current Branch and Current Branch for Business, they can choose the Long Term Servicing Branch, which we describe in "Servicing options for Windows" in Chapter 21.

- Windows 10 Education, which most closely resembles Windows 10 Enterprise in terms of features, has the same update servicing options as Windows 10 Pro.

> ➤ For a full discussion of how Microsoft delivers security updates, see "Staying on top of security updates" in Chapter 7, "Securing Windows 10 devices."

The tools for managing updates are no longer in the old-style Control Panel. Search for **Windows Update** and the following results, all included as part of the modern Settings app, should appear at the top of the results list:

Click or tap Check For Updates to open the Windows Update page in Settings. A list of available updates appears at the top of the page. If the updates have been installed and require a restart, you might see a screen similar to the one shown in Figure 15-1.

Windows proposes to restart your machine outside of your designated active hours. If you need to change your active hours settings, click Change Active Hours. However you set those active hours, Windows checks to see if your machine is actually idle before performing the reset.

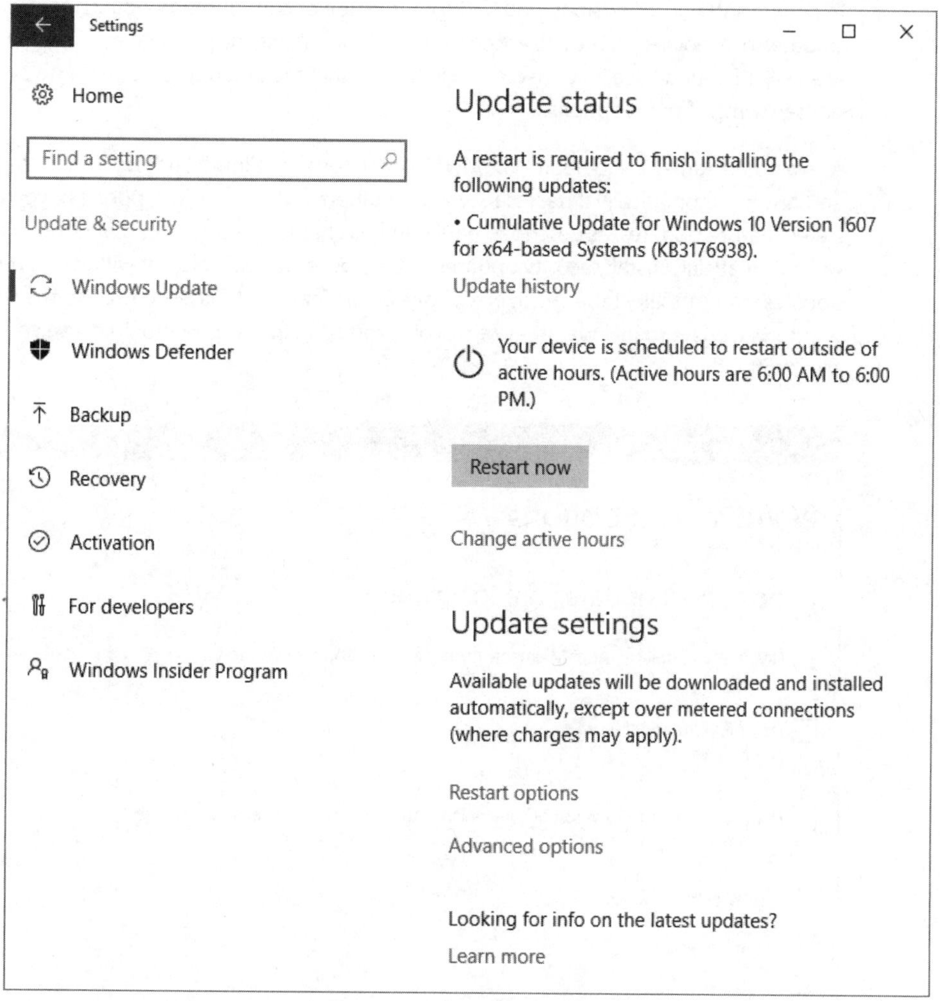

Figure 15-1 In Windows 10, updates are installed automatically. If one or more updates require a restart, Windows proposes a restart time when you're not likely to be using the machine.

You also have the option of restarting manually. This option is ideal if you know you're going to be away from the PC for a meeting or lunch break that will last longer than the few minutes it takes to install a batch of updates. (But watch out for feature updates, which are equivalent to full upgrades and typically take an hour or more.) Save your existing work and close any open files, and then click Restart Now. Be sure to wait for all open apps to close before you head out the door. It's highly annoying (and a big drag on productivity) to come back from a meeting and discover that the restart hasn't taken place because a dialog box was open, waiting for your okay.

In previous Windows versions, you had a wide range of configuration options for Windows Update. In Windows 10, the Advanced Options list contains the three items shown in Figure 15-2. (If your device is connected to a domain and managed by System Center, you might not see some of these options.)

As we noted earlier, the default Windows Update settings allow Windows 10 to install updates and restart automatically if necessary. If your edition of Windows 10 supports it, you can select Defer Feature Updates, as described earlier in this chapter. If you select that check box, Windows will automatically install security updates as they become available but will postpone feature updates. You can select the check box above Defer Feature Updates to expand the scope of Windows Update to include other Microsoft products, such as perpetual-license versions of Microsoft Office.

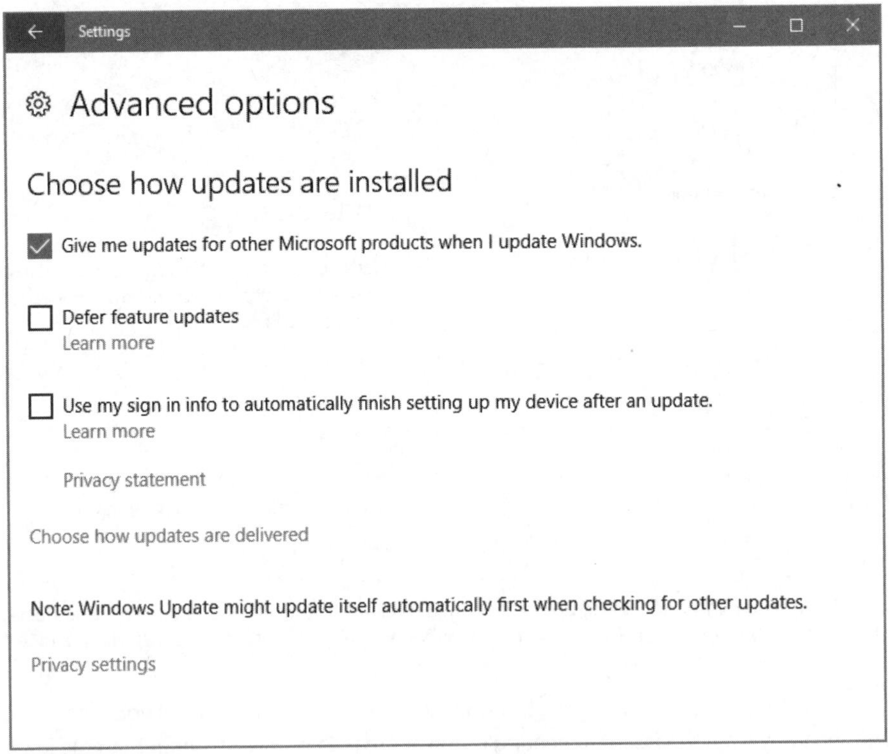

Figure 15-2 Windows 10 is designed for automatic delivery of updates, with only a few configuration options available.

When installing an update entails a restart of your system, Windows normally requires you to sign in before the installation finishes. If you're away from your machine while an upgrade is in progress, you might find the system waiting at the sign-in screen when you return. You can streamline the process by selecting the third check box, Use My Sign In Info To Finish Setting Up My Device After An Update.

You can exert slightly more control over the upgrade process by clicking Choose How Updates Are Delivered. This opens the page shown in Figure 15-3. With this peer-to-peer feature, which is new in Windows 10, you can share updates with devices on your local network rather than requiring a connection to Microsoft's update servers. In a small office or lab, this option can significantly reduce the amount of data you download through your internet connection. You can use the last option to share updates over the internet at large, using Microsoft's peer-to-peer service.

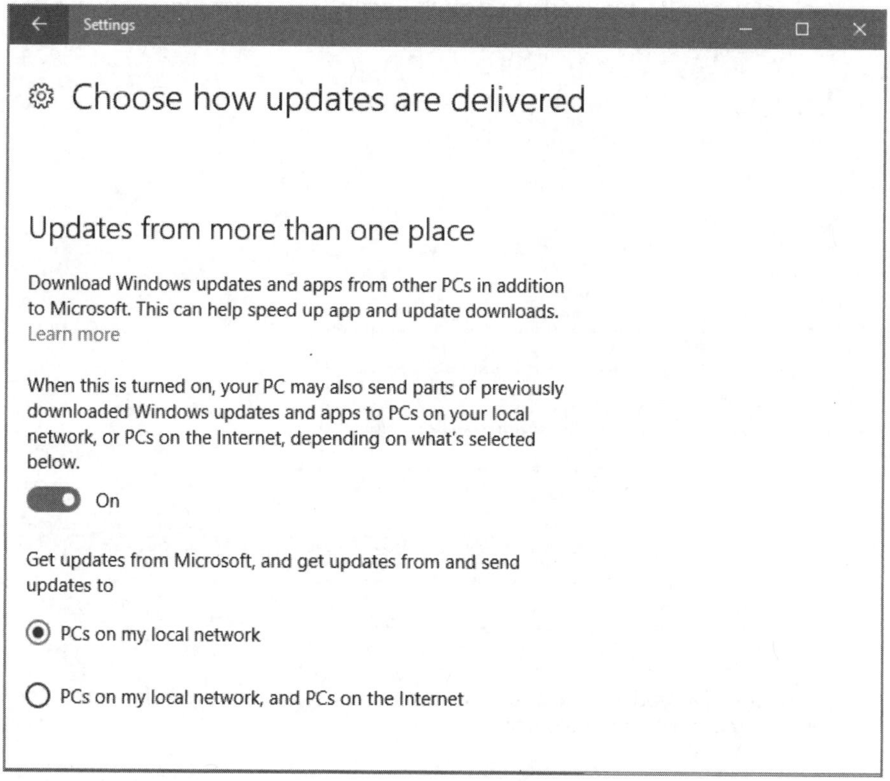

Figure 15-3 Enabling this peer-to-peer option can speed up installation of large updates on a small network, reducing the demands on your internet connection.

Clicking the Update History link shown in Figure 15-1 reveals a list that includes the name of each installed Windows update, the date on which it was installed, and a link that includes the update's Knowledge Base (KB) number.

Most options for Windows Update have been moved to the modern Windows 10 Settings app. Clicking the Uninstall Updates option on the Update History page reveals a noteworthy exception, as shown in Figure 15-4. This list, which uses the old-style Control Panel interface, displays an inventory of everything that Windows Update has installed for Windows itself, for other Microsoft products, and for compatible third-party updates.

From this page, you can confirm a particular update has been installed by referring to its KB number in the list of installed items. If you click the support link at the bottom of the page, you can see details about the selected update. The Uninstall option appears above the list and allows you to remove an update. This option should be a last resort for troubleshooting and used only when you suspect that a recently installed update is causing serious performance or reliability issues.

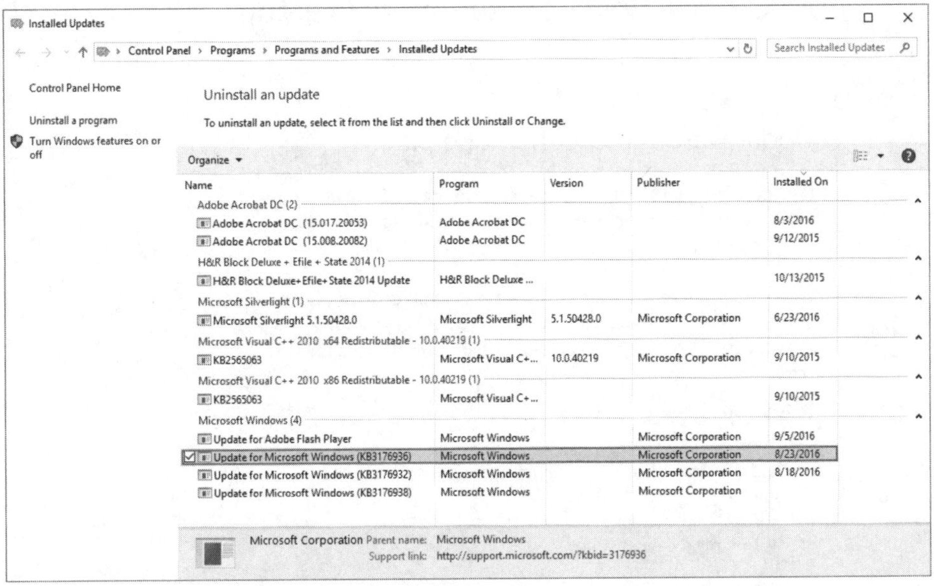

Figure 15-4 If an update is causing problems, you can select it from this list and use the Uninstall option to remove it for troubleshooting purposes.

If a device driver is causing problems, you can uninstall it as follows: Right-click the Start button, click Device Manager, and double-click the device with the problem driver. On the driver tab of the Properties dialog box, click Uninstall.

Inside OUT

Hide troublesome updates so that Windows Update doesn't try repeatedly to install them.

Suppose the latest update includes an unwanted driver or some other component that wreaks havoc on your system. You can uninstall it, as just described. But because of the way cumulative updates work, Windows Update will reinstall the unwanted item the next time it delivers a cumulative update. You can interrupt this Sisyphusian loop by "hiding" the item.

To do this, you need to run the Show Or Hide Updates troubleshooter package, which you can download from *https://support.microsoft.com/kb/3073930*. The troubleshooter presents a list of updates that can be hidden. Select the item that you don't want to reinstall. The ruse is temporary, but it should give you respite until an updated driver or component becomes available. For more details about how to use this troubleshooter with problematic hardware drivers, see "Uninstalling a driver," in Chapter 13, "Hardware."

CHAPTER 15

TROUBLESHOOTING

Windows Update is stuck in a reboot loop

In some cases, Windows Update can get stuck in a loop, failing to complete the installation of one or more updates and continually repeating the unsuccessful update process each time you restart.

The solution? Reset Windows Update completely, removing content from the update cache and starting with fresh downloads. In most cases, that's enough to get things unstuck.

Microsoft created a help resource for diagnosing and fixing Windows Update problems, which is available at *https://support.microsoft.com/kb/971058*. The process involves stopping several services, removing the folder containing updates in progress, and reregistering a list of system files. You can download a troubleshooter that performs these steps automatically from *https://aka.ms/diag?wu*.

Mastering Task Manager

The easiest way to open Task Manager is with its keyboard shortcut, Ctrl+Shift+Esc. (You can also press Ctrl+Alt+Delete and then click or tap Task Manager.) Task Manager's instant accessibility is its most endearing trait, especially when something appears to have gone awry. Its executable file, Taskmgr.exe, runs at a Base Priority of High, allowing it to kick into action even when another program running at Normal priority is refusing to surrender control. When you need to stop an application (or process) that doesn't respond to the usual measures, or if your system suddenly slows down and you want to know who's eating your processor cycles, Task Manager is your best friend.

If you're upgrading from Windows 7, you're in for a treat. The new Task Manager debuted in Windows 8, and in our humble opinion it is awesome. We'll repeat that keyboard shortcut, Ctrl+Shift+Esc, because we think every Windows user should memorize it. Pressing that combination opens Task Manager using the simple view shown in Figure 15-5.

The short list shows only processes that were started by and can be directly controlled by the current user account. If a program has stopped responding, you'll see "Not responding" after its entry in the list, and you can use the End Task button to kill the app and start fresh.

Click More Details to see Task Manager in all its multitabbed, information-rich glory. Figure 15-6 shows this dramatically expanded display, with the Processes tab selected.

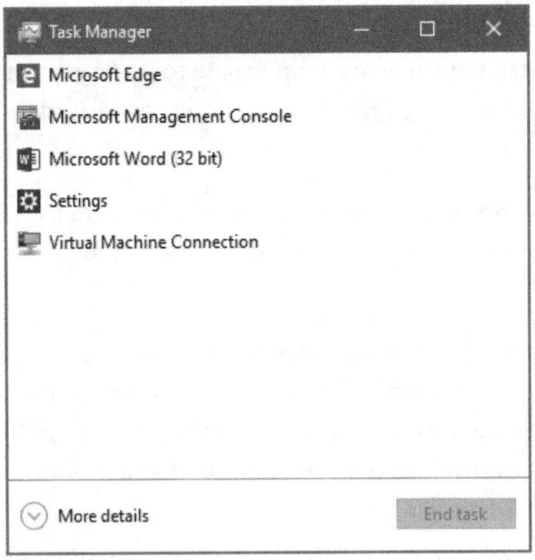

Figure 15-5 In its Fewer Details view, Task Manager shows only apps that were started by the current user, with the option to end a task that is nonresponsive.

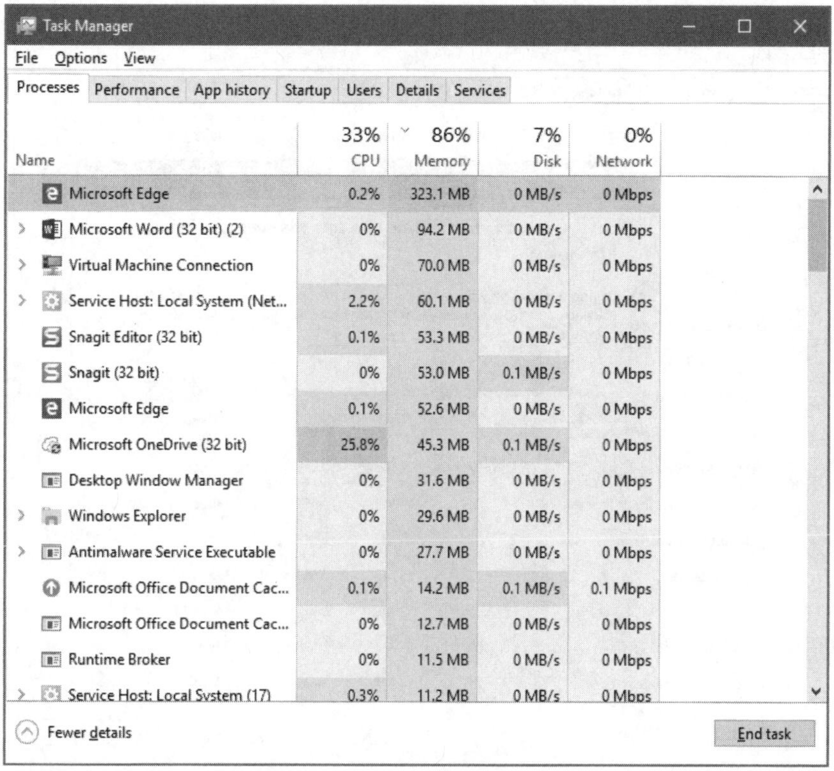

Name	33% CPU	86% Memory	7% Disk	0% Network
Microsoft Edge	0.2%	323.1 MB	0 MB/s	0 Mbps
> Microsoft Word (32 bit) (2)	0%	94.2 MB	0 MB/s	0 Mbps
> Virtual Machine Connection	0%	70.0 MB	0 MB/s	0 Mbps
> Service Host: Local System (Net...	2.2%	60.1 MB	0 MB/s	0 Mbps
Snagit Editor (32 bit)	0.1%	53.3 MB	0 MB/s	0 Mbps
Snagit (32 bit)	0%	53.0 MB	0.1 MB/s	0 Mbps
Microsoft Edge	0.1%	52.6 MB	0 MB/s	0 Mbps
Microsoft OneDrive (32 bit)	25.8%	45.3 MB	0.1 MB/s	0 Mbps
Desktop Window Manager	0%	31.6 MB	0 MB/s	0 Mbps
> Windows Explorer	0%	29.6 MB	0 MB/s	0 Mbps
> Antimalware Service Executable	0%	27.7 MB	0 MB/s	0 Mbps
Microsoft Office Document Cac...	0.1%	14.2 MB	0.1 MB/s	0.1 Mbps
Microsoft Office Document Cac...	0%	12.7 MB	0 MB/s	0 Mbps
Runtime Broker	0%	11.5 MB	0 MB/s	0 Mbps
> Service Host: Local System (17)	0.3%	11.2 MB	0 MB/s	0 Mbps

Figure 15-6 In the More Details view, Task Manager includes a much longer list of running processes, with real-time performance information for each one.

Although the list of running apps in Figure 15-6 looks similar to the one in the simpler view, scrolling down reveals a much longer list, grouped into three categories: Apps, Background Processes, and Windows Processes. Processes that have multiple child windows have an arrow at their left, which you can click to expand the entry and see the titles of Microsoft Office document windows, Skype sessions, and the like.

You can end a task in the Apps group with minimal consequences. (You'll lose any unsaved work.) However, attempting to end a task in the Windows Processes group is equivalent to pulling the plug on Windows, as the stern warning message, shown next, makes clear.

In the More Details view, the totals at the top of each of the four performance-related headings show total resource use for that category. You can click any column heading to sort by that value, making it possible to see at a glance which program is hogging the CPU or using more memory than its fair share. (For more information about performance monitoring, using Task Manager and other tools, see "Monitoring and improving system performance," later in this chapter.)

Inside OUT

Why is the System process using so much memory?

Any experienced Windows user who has tracked per-process memory usage in previous versions of Windows might be startled to see the System process using far more RAM than it seemingly should. Relax. That's not a bug; it's a feature, specifically a new memory-management subsystem that improves performance by compressing memory pages for processes you haven't used recently. If the system needs the memory, it will reclaim it quickly by flushing those compressed pages to disk.

When you right-click any item in the Processes list, you see several choices on a shortcut menu. Click Go To Details to jump to Task Manager's Details tab.

Windows veterans will feel right at home on the Details tab, which is a dense, data-rich list that was the default view in Task Manager in Windows 7 and earlier editions. It shows the executable file for the original process, along with technical details like those shown in Figure 15-7.

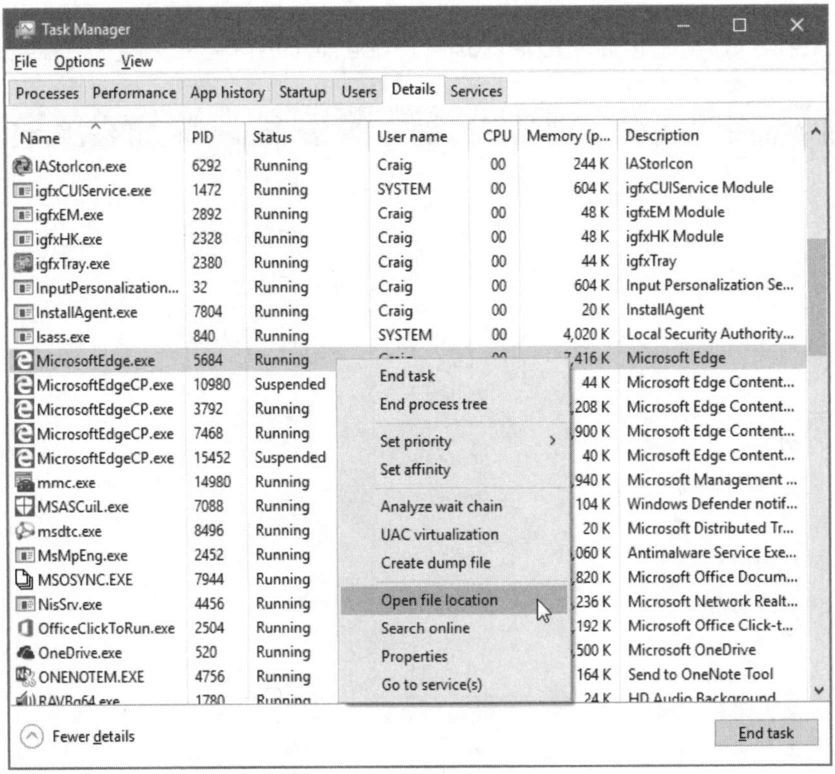

Figure 15-7 To show an executable file in its parent folder, select the item on the Details tab and then use the Open File Location option on the shortcut menu.

Inside OUT

Restart Explorer.exe to fix shell-related problems

In the expanded view of Task Manager, you'll find an entry for Windows Explorer under the Name heading on the Processes tab. If you have multiple File Explorer windows open, each of them will be listed as a child task under that heading. Occasionally, for any of a variety of reasons, the main Windows shell process (Explorer.exe) can become unresponsive. When that happens, clicking the taskbar or Start button does nothing, and the search box is unusable as well.

The cure? Open Task Manager, select Windows Explorer on the Processes tab (it might be in any of the three groups), and look in the lower right corner, where the button normally labeled End Task now reads Restart. Click this button to close all existing instances of Explorer.exe, and restart the Windows shell. If the shell doesn't restart automatically, go to File > Run New Task, type **explorer.exe**, and click OK or press Enter.

As with the Processes tab, right-clicking any entry on this list displays a shortcut menu with some technical options. The four options at the bottom of the menu are most useful for troubleshooting:

- Click Open File Location to locate the file responsible for the running process. Often, just knowing which folder this file appears in is enough to help ease your mind about a process with a name and description that don't provide useful details.

- Click Search Online to open a browser window and pass the name and description of the selected executable file to the default search engine. This is a useful way to get additional information about a mysterious file, but beware of information from unknown and untrusted sources—watch out for search results that lead to scam sites bent on convincing you to buy bogus security software.

- The Properties menu choice leads directly to the properties dialog box for the associated executable file, where the Details tab includes copyright information and other relevant data drawn from the file itself. That information can help you decide whether a file is legitimate or needs further investigation.

- Finally, for processes that are running as Windows services, you can click the Go To Service(s) option, which takes you to the Services tab and highlights all the individual services associated with that process. For an instance of Svchost.exe, the list might number a dozen individual services.

Inside OUT

Get to know the Process ID column

The default arrangement of columns on the Processes tab does not include the Process Identifier (PID) column, although you can add it by right-clicking any visible column heading and clicking PID in the list of available columns. The PID column is shown by default on the Details and Services tabs, where it's extremely useful in enabling you to see which processes are running as part of the same Svchost.exe instance. To find out what's inside a particularly busy Svchost process, make a note of its PID and then switch to the Services tab and sort by the PID column. The associated services will appear in a block using that PID.

As was true with its predecessors, the Task Manager Details tab includes the option to display many more columns than the handful that are shown by default. To add or remove columns, right-click any visible column heading and then click Select Columns. That action opens the dialog box shown in Figure 15-8.

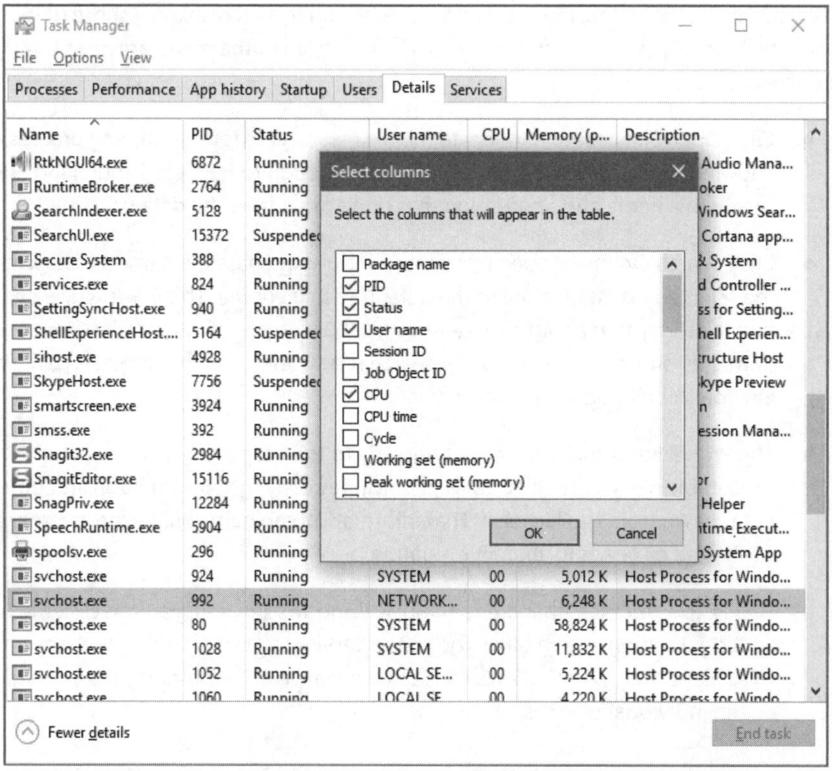

Figure 15-8 If you're comfortable interpreting technical information about resources associated with a running process, you can add columns to the Details tab in Task Manager.

The list of available columns is overwhelming and highly technical. Some provide interesting information you can't find elsewhere, though. For example, on a device running 64-bit Windows 10, the Platform column lets you sort 32-bit and 64-bit processes quickly, while the Elevated column identifies processes that are running with full administrative privileges (usually in the context of the SYSTEM account). If you're experiencing issues with display corruption, show the GDI Objects column and then sort its values in descending order to locate processes that might be to blame.

Managing startup programs and services

One of the most common performance problems occurs when Windows automatically loads an excessive number of programs at startup. The result, especially on systems with limited resources, can be unpleasant: startup takes an unnecessarily long time, applications you never use steal memory from programs you use frequently, and the page file, which swaps programs and data from memory to disk when RAM fills up, gets more of a workout than it should. Some programs, such as antivirus utilities, need to start up automatically. But in many cases, you're better served by running programs when you need them and closing them when they're not needed.

An overstuffed auto-start list is often a "feature" on computer systems sold in retail outlets, where Windows is preinstalled along with a heaping helping of applications. In some cases, the bundled programs are welcome, but a free software program is no bargain if it takes up memory and you never use it.

On the Task Manager Startup tab, shown in Figure 15-9, you can see at a glance which programs are starting automatically. Using the Disable button or the equivalent option on the shortcut menu, you can disable any option that you determine is slowing down your system.

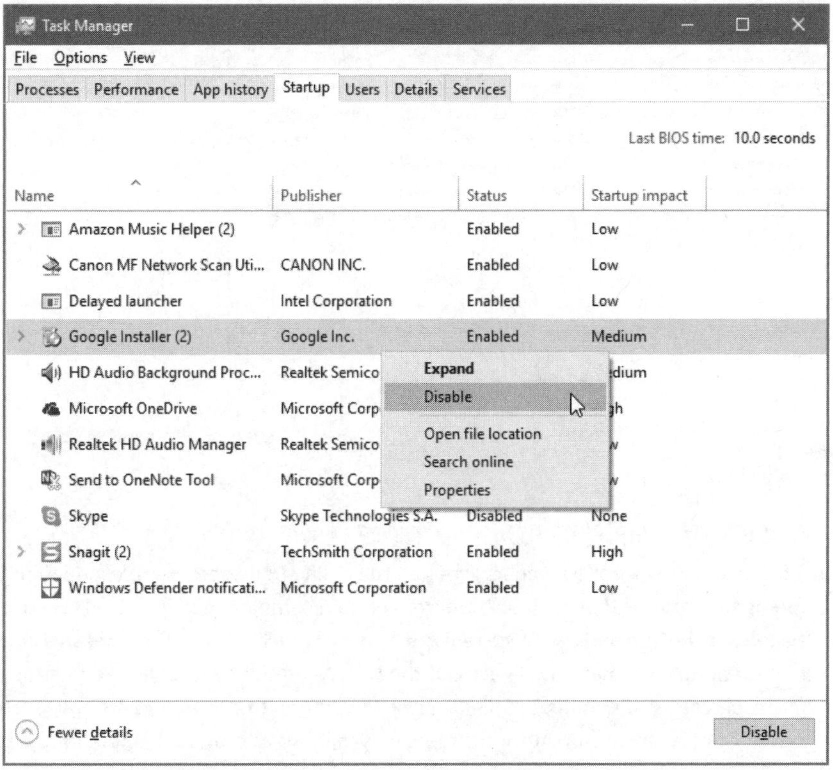

Figure 15-9 The Startup tab in Task Manager shows all programs that start automatically with Windows, with an easy option to disable those you prefer to start manually.

By default, the Startup tab shows only a gross measurement of the effect of a program on startup time. This value is displayed under the Startup Impact heading as High, Medium, or Low. To discover more details about the precise impact of an app that runs at startup, right-click the column headings on the Startup tab and add the two columns shown next—Disk I/O At Startup and CPU At Startup—which quantify just how much disk activity and CPU usage occur when the program starts.

CHAPTER 15

Inside OUT

For complete control of startup items, download Autoruns

The Startup tab in Task Manager gives you the ability to inspect, disable, and reinstate programs and services that are launched from certain common locations, such as your startup folder and the Run and RunOnce registry keys. For much more comprehensive control over items that run automatically, check out the Autoruns utility, available free at *https://technet.microsoft.com/sysinternals/bb963902.aspx*. In addition to controlling programs launched at system startup or sign-in, Autoruns reports such items as browser helper objects, toolbars, and Windows Explorer shell extensions. As in Task Manager, you can disable items you don't think you need, but once you're sure you don't need something, you can also use Autoruns to remove it from the list of programs that start automatically, without having to edit the registry yourself.

Managing disk space

At the dawn of the Windows 10 era, several long-term trends converged to make data storage more of a performance issue than it has been in years.

For many years, the trend with conventional hard disks was simple: more storage space at a lower cost per gigabyte. Each new Windows version required more space than its predecessor, but the accompanying new generation of hardware meant there was plenty of room for system files and data.

The advent of solid state drives (SSDs) and flash memory changed all that. SSDs are dramatically faster than conventional hard disks. They're also more reliable than hard disks because they have no moving parts. But SSDs are far more expensive per gigabyte than conventional hard disks, causing PC makers to choose smaller default disks for new PCs. Couple that trend with the arrival of small, cheap tablets that run Windows 10 with 32 GB of total storage or less and you have a recipe for chronic space shortage.

On a desktop PC, you have the option to expand storage by replacing the primary drive with one that's faster, larger, or both; on most full-size desktop PCs, you can also install additional drives to make room for extra data files. Many portable devices, on the other hand, provide built-in primary storage that is soldered to the system board and can't be replaced. For some portable devices, the option to expand storage using inexpensive removable media is available. Microsoft's Surface Pro PCs, for example, include a slot that accepts up to 128 GB of removable storage in the form of a MicroSD card, which can be treated as dedicated storage and used for File History.

> ➤ For a full discussion of the ins and outs of managing hard drives and SSDs in Windows 10, see Chapter 14, "Managing disks and drives." For a discussion of how to use removable storage for backup, see "Using File History to protect files and folders" in Chapter 16, "Backup, restore, and recovery."

Managing storage on a Windows 10 device involves two separate challenges:

- Setting default file locations to make best use of available storage

- Performing occasional maintenance to ensure useful space (especially on the system drive) isn't being wasted with unnecessary files

For an overview of how much total storage is available and what's in use on a Windows 10 device, open Settings > System > Storage to see a page like the one shown in Figure 15-10. This example shows a desktop PC with a 1-TB system drive (C) and a second 1-TB external drive, on which a 32-GB partition has been created for archival purposes (F), with the remainder devoted to File History and image backups (G).

CHAPTER 15

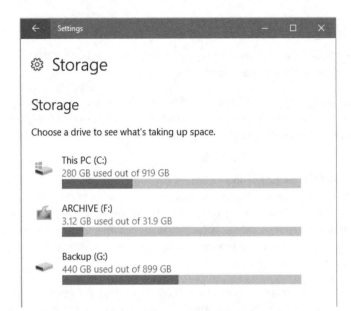

Figure 15-10 The Storage page in Settings shows all available volumes, with an indication of how much space is currently in use on each.

Inside OUT

Why is actual storage capacity lower than advertised disk sizes?

When you use Microsoft's built-in disk utilities to view the storage capacity of a disk, the capacity is reported by using the binary system (base 2) of measurement: 1 KB is 1,024 bytes, 1 MB is 1,024 KB, 1 GB is 1,024 MB, and so on. Thus, measured in binary terms, 1 GB is calculated as 1,073,741,824 bytes. But the makers of storage devices and the PC makers who build SSDs and hard disks into their products typically advertise storage using the convenient metric that 1 GB is equal to 1 billion bytes. That difference is why a system advertised with 32 GB of storage displays only about 28 GB when detailed in Disk Management and other Windows tools. Fortunately, those same tools also report the number of bytes of storage, which allows more accurate comparisons with the advertised space.

Regardless of how many drives are available, you can see which types of files are using that space, color coded by file type. Open Storage in Settings and click any drive to show a breakdown of storage space in use, as in Figure 15-11.

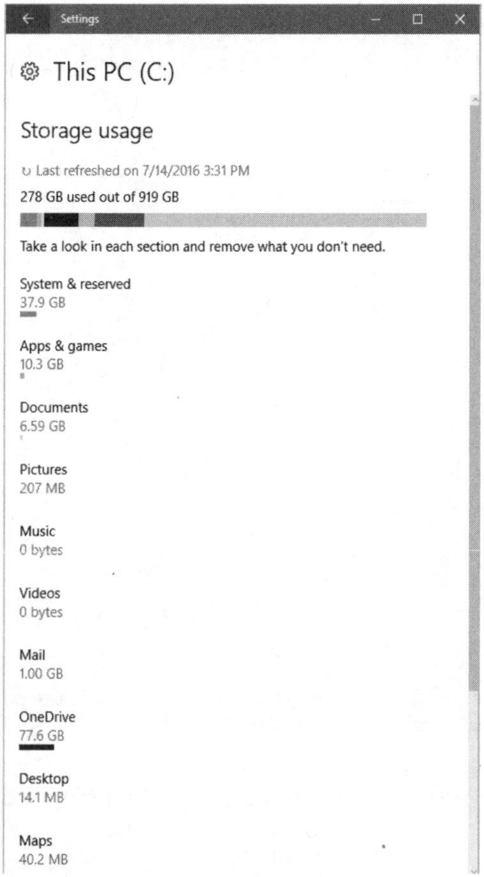

Figure 15-11 This screenshot shows just the start of a long list that displays a detailed breakdown of how much space is in use, grouped by type of file.

Click or tap any category to see more details about what's in it. Here are some examples of what you'll find in each category:

- **System And Reserved.** This category is typically large and includes files that are essential to the operation of the system. The actual amounts of storage in use depend on the type of device and how much memory it contains. Figure 15-12, for example, shows the breakdown for this category on a Windows 10 desktop PC with 8 GB of RAM.

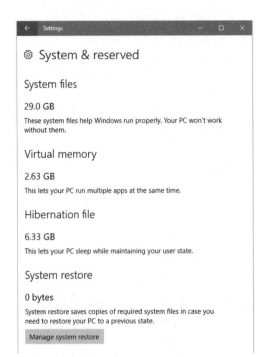

Figure 15-12 The System & Reserved category shows how much space is in use by Windows, space reserved for virtual memory, and hibernation files.

- **Apps And Games.** This category includes default apps as well as those you downloaded from the Windows Store.

- **Documents, Pictures, Music, Videos.** These separate categories show how much space is in use in the default save locations for the respective file types. Note that this value is not the total found in the libraries of the same names.

- **Mail.** This value measures the space used by local copies of messages saved using the default mail app. Clicking or tapping the Manage Mail button takes you to the default email app: Mail or Microsoft Outlook, for example.

- **OneDrive.** The total amount of space used by local copies of files synced from OneDrive.

- **Desktop.** This total should be small unless you use the desktop as a dumping ground for downloads and other potentially large files.

- **Maps.** If you have a large collection of offline maps, this category can get fairly large.

- **Other Users.** This category displays the total amount of space in use for data files from other user accounts, not broken down by file types.

- **Temporary Files.** This category includes files that are managed by Windows but are not typically necessary for the operation of a Windows 10 device. On the system shown in Figure 15-13, with just a few clicks, you can recover almost 20 GB of storage space from the Recycle Bin.

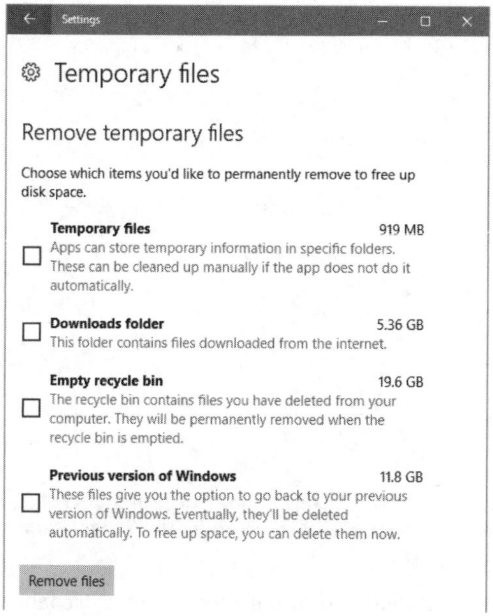

Figure 15-13 With several options in this category, you can free up large amounts of disk space.

- **Other.** If you have large collections of files that don't slot into the standard categories, you might see a very large Other category. Figure 15-14 shows an example of the types of large files that might show up in this category, including Hyper-V virtual machines and associated VHD files, ISO files, and recorded TV programs.

As you click to navigate deeper into the categories in the Storage section of Settings, you'll find buttons and links for managing files contained in that category by using File Explorer.

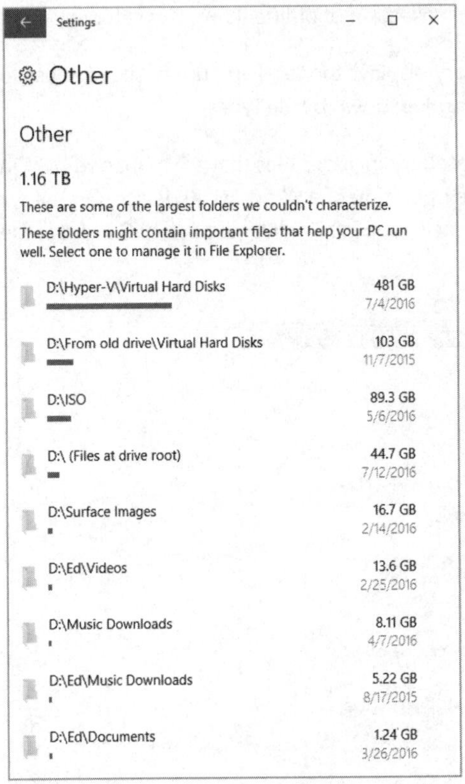

Figure 15-14 Developers and IT pros are likely to have large amounts of space in use for files that don't fit into standard categories and wind up under the Other heading.

On systems with multiple drives (including removable media), you can change the default location for specific file types. If you have a large music collection, for example, you might prefer to store MP3 files on an SD card rather than on your main system drive. To make that possible, open the Storage page in Settings and adjust the options under the Save Locations heading, as shown in Figure 15-15.

NOTE

Changing the default location for a file type affects the storage of new items. It does not move current items.

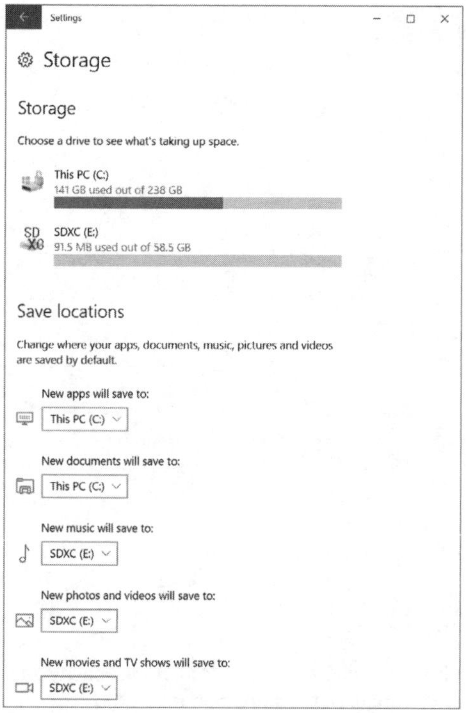

Figure 15-15 You can change the default location for new files you save in default categories. Existing files remain in their current locations.

When you set the default save location for these categories to a secondary drive, Windows 10 creates folders on the secondary drive, with subfolders that correspond to the category name for each file type within a folder named after your user account name.

You can also examine how much storage is currently available and in use by opening File Explorer, right-clicking a disk icon in This PC, and then clicking Properties. Figure 15-16 shows an example of what you might see.

Click Disk Cleanup to run the utility of the same name (Cleanmgr.exe). Note that this utility initially opens in standard user mode, allowing you to manage files available to your user account but blocking access to system files. To enable the full range of Disk Cleanup options, click Clean Up System Files and enter the credentials for an administrator account if necessary. That restarts the utility and unlocks access to the full range of cleanup options, as shown in Figure 15-17.

CHAPTER 15

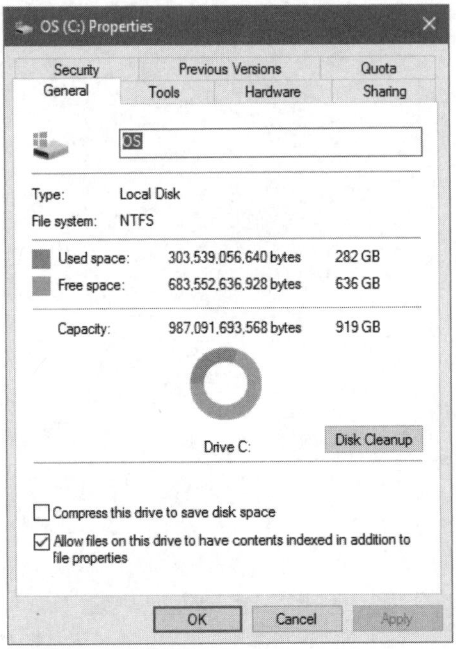

Figure 15-16 Open the properties dialog box for a disk to see the total disk capacity and how much space is in use. Click Disk Cleanup to open the utility of the same name.

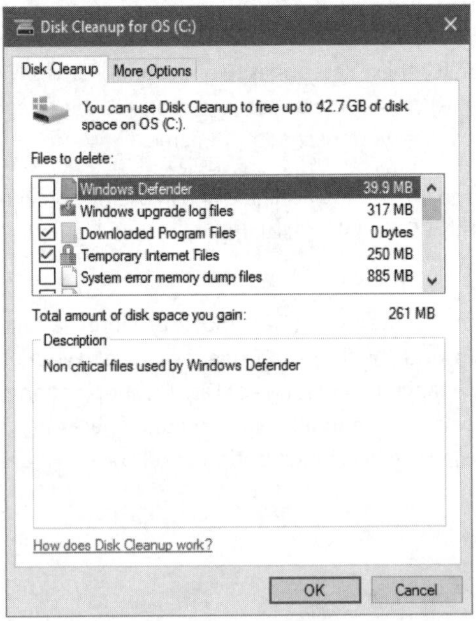

Figure 15-17 When you start Disk Cleanup using administrative credentials, you have the option to remove Windows installation files and previous Windows versions.

CAUTION

You might be tempted to obsess over disk space usage and use every trick to create as much free space as possible. That strategy might come back to haunt you, however. If you remove previous Windows installations, for example, you lose the ability to roll back to a previous version to recover from compatibility problems. As a general rule, you should keep at least 20 percent of total disk capacity free. That allows enough room to process temporary files properly without affecting performance dramatically. Beyond that baseline, think long and hard before deleting what might be important files.

Power management and battery life

Power-management features in Windows 10 can be broadly divided into two groups. Features in the first group apply universally to all Windows devices, even those that are permanently tethered to AC power. Allowing a PC or tablet to sleep or hibernate cuts the amount of power it consumes, which translates into monetary savings for you and a benefit for society at large.

For portable devices—including Ultrabooks, hybrid devices, and tablets—paying attention to power management has additional productivity benefits. Anything you do to extend the battery life of a portable device helps you avoid having to quit working because your battery gave up the ghost.

On a portable device, a flyout control, visible with a tap of the battery icon in the notification area, shows how much charge your battery is currently holding. If the device is disconnected from AC power, this display offers an estimate of how many hours and minutes you can continue working. If you're plugged in, the display shows how much longer until the battery is fully charged, as in the example in Figure 15-18.

That battery indicator isn't just a status box, however. It's actually an entry point to multiple settings where you can fine-tune how a portable device uses power.

The screen brightness button, for example, cycles through brightness settings (25 percent, 50 percent, 75 percent, and 100 percent). Lowering the display brightness saves energy but makes the display dimmer and hence possibly more difficult to see well. For watching movies on a long-haul flight in a darkened jumbo jet, the power-saving setting has many advantages.

To adjust additional settings, click or tap Power & Sleep Settings. Figure 15-19 shows the corresponding options on a battery-equipped device—in this case, a Microsoft Surface Pro 3. Other portable PCs might show a slightly different set of options, depending on which power-saving features are supported in hardware.)

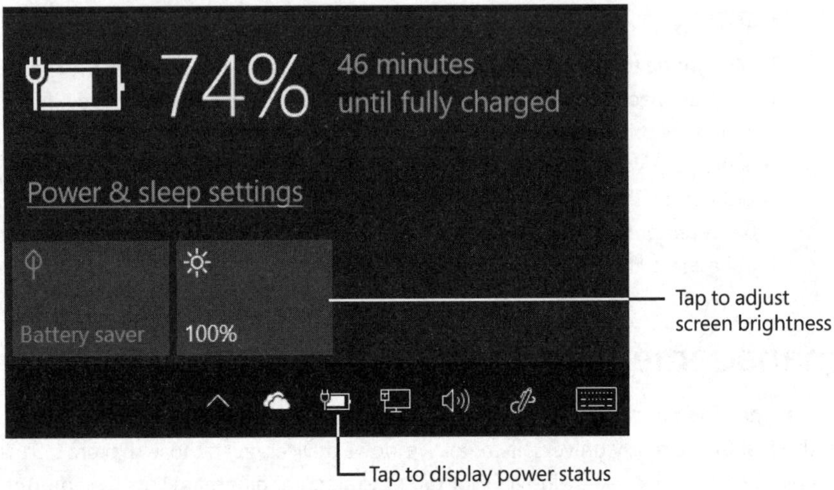

Tap to adjust screen brightness

Tap to display power status

Figure 15-18 Tap the battery icon on a portable device running Windows 10 to display this flyout control, which gives an up-to-date picture of your current battery status.

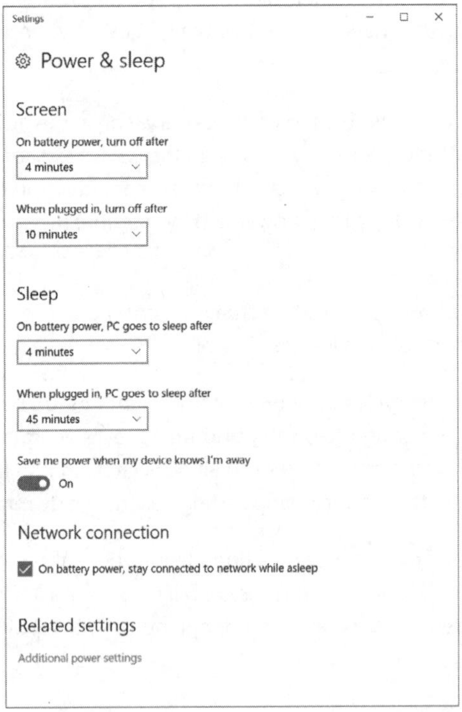

Figure 15-19 On a battery-powered device, you can fine-tune these settings for better performance when the device is plugged in to AC power and longer battery life when it's unplugged.

As with several other Windows features, the transition of power-management settings from the traditional Control Panel to the modern Settings app is not yet complete. Clicking the Additional Power Settings link at the bottom of the Power & Sleep page in Settings opens the Power Options page in Control Panel, where you'll find an extensive selection of power settings, some extremely esoteric.

The old-school Power Options in Control Panel, shown in Figure 15-20, is based on power plans, which represent a collection of saved settings. With older versions of Windows, it was common to find at least three power plans, with a hardware maker sometimes defining its own plan as well. In the Windows 10 era, you're likely to find a single Balanced plan that should work for most use cases.

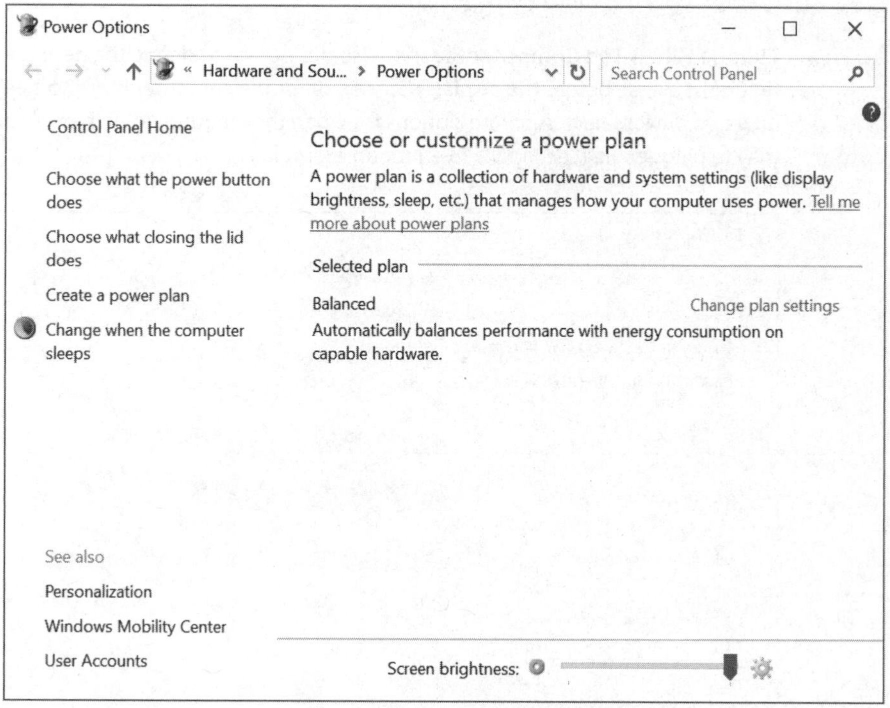

Figure 15-20 Default power options in Windows 10 include a single Balanced power plan. You can create additional plans for special purposes.

Your options here include the following (but note that the list you see on a PC or mobile device will vary from this one depending on the capabilities of your hardware):

- **Require A Password On Wakeup.** This is an essential security option for a portable device or one that is in a place where it can be accessed by strangers or coworkers. For a home PC, you might choose the convenience of not requiring a password.

- **Choose What The Power Button Does.** Use these settings to define whether pressing the power button shuts down the device, puts it to sleep, hibernates the device, turns off the display, or does nothing. If your device has any combination of power, sleep, and standby buttons, you might see additional options here.

- **Choose What Closing The Lid Does.** This option, available on laptop devices, has the same choices as the previous option.

- **Create A Power Plan.** Click to copy the current settings to a new power plan, which then appears in the list of available plans and can be customized separately.

- **Choose When To Turn Off The Display.** With this option, typically found on desktop systems, you can blank the screen to save energy.

- **Change When The Computer Sleeps.** Use this option to define the period of inactivity that must elapse before the display is turned off or the computer is put to sleep. Battery-powered devices have separate options for when they're running on battery and when they're plugged in. (See Figure 15-21 for an example.)

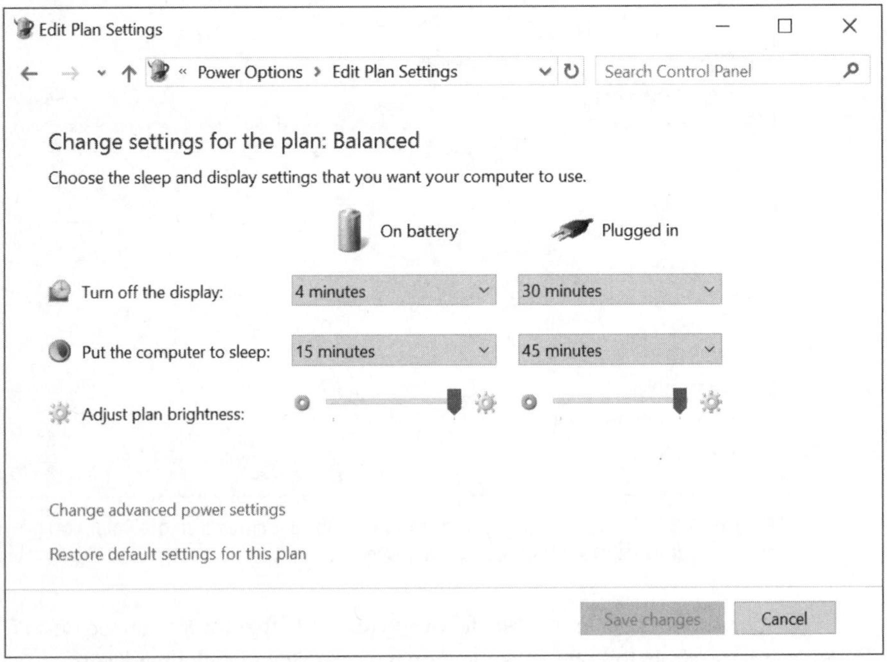

Figure 15-21 To maximize battery life on a portable PC, set the sleep option to the minimum acceptable amount. When the PC is plugged in, you might prefer to set the sleep option to a higher value for the convenience of instant access.

For each option, the choices in the drop-down list range from 1 minute (probably more annoying than most people will accept) to 5 hours (useful if you want the computer to sleep only when you're away for a long time). To disable either option, choose Never from the drop-down list.

If those options aren't sufficient, click the Change Advanced Power Settings option to open the advanced options dialog box shown in Figure 15-22.

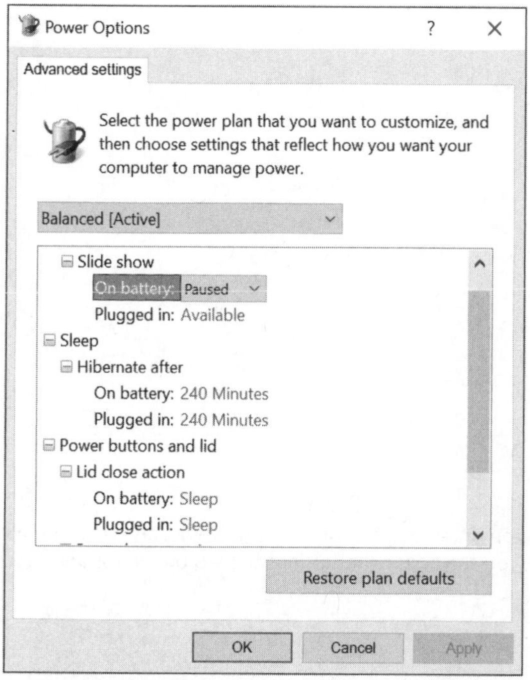

Figure 15-22 These advanced options give you incredibly granular control over power-management settings in Windows 10.

A new feature in Windows 10, Battery Saver mode, allows you to apply a group of power-saving settings with a single click or tap. Battery Saver mode, which stops many background processes and limits notifications, kicks in automatically when the battery level drops below a predefined threshold; you can also turn on Battery Saver mode manually, even on a device with a fully charged battery, as a preventive measure.

To change settings for this feature (available only on a battery-powered device), search for **Battery Saver** and open the Settings page shown in Figure 15-23. For aggressive management of battery life, set the threshold higher than the default 20 percent. You can also define exceptions for background operation for critical apps.

Figure 15-23 By default, your laptop or tablet goes into an aggressive battery-saving mode when your battery drops to 20 percent. You can adjust the settings to be more or less aggressive.

Inside OUT

Adjust Hibernate options for maximum battery life

To maximize battery life on a portable device, use the Hibernate option, which shifts from Sleep mode at an interval you define. Hibernation saves the current state of the system as well as the contents of memory to a hidden file (Hiberfil.sys), and then shuts down the computer. That effectively cuts power use to zero. Resuming from hibernation is much faster than a cold start, and when you resume you're back where you left off, with apps and files open exactly as they were. To adjust this option, open the Advanced Settings dialog box and change the values in the Hibernate After setting under On Battery. Switching from the default 240 minutes to, say, 30 minutes can significantly extend the battery life of a device you use intermittently.

Configuring power options from the command line

If your work entails managing power settings for multiple systems and users, you'll find the powercfg command-line utility invaluable. With powercfg, you can query and set power schemes and parameters, export power settings to a file, import the file on remote systems, and more. Even if your concerns are only with your own systems, you might find **powercfg /batteryreport**, **powercfg /energy**, and **powercfg /sleepstudy** useful. These commands generate reports that are not available via the interactive power-management features described earlier in this section.

Table 15-1 lists the commands available with powercfg. (To generate this list for yourself, open a Command Prompt window and type **powercfg /?**.) For syntax details and usage examples of any powercfg command, type **powercfg /?** *command*.

Table 15-1 Powercfg commands

Command	Description
/List, /L	Lists all power schemes
/Query, /Q	Displays the contents of a power scheme
/Change, /X	Modifies a setting value in the current power scheme
/Changename	Modifies the name and description of a power scheme
/Duplicatescheme	Duplicates a power scheme
/Delete, /D	Deletes a power scheme
/Deletesetting	Deletes a power setting
/Setactive, /S	Makes a power scheme active on the system
/Getactivescheme	Retrieves the currently active power scheme
/Setacvalueindex	Sets the value associated with a power setting while the system is powered by AC power
/Setdcvalueindex	Sets the value associated with a power setting while the system is powered by DC power
/Import	Imports all power settings from a file
/Export	Exports a power scheme to a file
/Aliases	Displays all aliases and their corresponding GUIDs
/Getsecuritydescriptor	Gets a security descriptor associated with a specified power setting, power scheme, or action
/Setsecuritydescriptor	Sets a security descriptor associated with a power setting, power scheme, or action
/Hibernate, /H	Enables and disables the hibernate feature
/Availablesleepstates, /A	Reports the sleep states available on the system
/Devicequery	Returns a list of devices that meet specified criteria

Command	Description
/Deviceenablewake	Enables a device to wake the system from a sleep state
/Devicedisablewake	Disables a device from waking the system from a sleep state
/Lastwake	Reports information about what woke the system from the last sleep transition
/Waketimers	Enumerates active wake timers
/Requests	Enumerates application and driver power requests
/Requestsoverride	Sets a power request override for a particular process, service, or drive
/Energy	Analyzes the system for common energy-efficiency and battery-life problems
/Batteryreport	Generates a report of battery usage
/Sleepstudy	Generates a diagnostic connected standby report
/Srumutil	Dumps energy estimation data from System Resource Usage Monitor (SRUM)
/Systemsleepdiagnostics	Generates a diagnostic report of system sleep transitions

Monitoring and improving system performance

As we noted at the beginning of this chapter, the out-of-the-box performance of a Windows 10 PC should be acceptable, assuming that the device you're using is capable of the work you're asking it to perform. A small tablet with a low-power mobile processor will almost certainly struggle at a processor-intensive task like video processing, for example.

But even a workstation-class PC can perform poorly if you have a problem with a major subsystem or if Windows is configured incorrectly. In our experience, the most common causes of poor performance (in no particular order) are these:

- **Defective hardware.** Memory and disk errors are most obvious when they cause system crashes, but hardware-related problems can also cause performance to drag. Check with your hardware manufacturer to see what diagnostic tools are available.

- **Outdated or flawed device drivers.** PC and device makers are responsible for supplying drivers for the individual hardware components that go into their hardware. If you do a clean install, Windows might install a generic driver instead of one written specifically for that device. We have seen performance problems vanish immediately after a simple driver upgrade. Always be certain you're using the best possible drivers for all system devices. (Don't assume that a newer driver is automatically better than an older one, however; any driver update has the potential to cause new problems.)

- **Inadequate hardware resources.** Windows 10 should perform basic tasks well on even low-end hardware that was designed and built five or more years ago. But more demanding tasks, such as digital media encoding, can push some systems to the breaking point. The performance-monitoring tools we identify later in this chapter should help you identify areas where hardware resources are being pushed to the limit.

- **Out-of-control processes or services.** Sometimes, a program or background task that normally runs just fine will spin out of control, consuming up to 100 percent of CPU time or grabbing increasing amounts of memory or other system resources. In the process, of course, performance of all other tasks slows down or grinds to a halt. Knowing how to identify and kill this sort of process or service and prevent it from recurring is a valuable troubleshooting skill.

  ➤ **For instructions on how to identify programs that run automatically at startup or when you sign in, see "Managing startup programs and services" earlier in this chapter.**

- **Malware.** Viruses, Trojan-horse programs, spyware, and other forms of unwanted software can wreak havoc on system performance. Be sure to check for the possibility that malware is present on a system that exhibits otherwise unexplained performance problems.

Windows 10 offers two valuable tools for monitoring the performance of your system in real time, Task Manager and Resource Monitor. Task Manager has been a mainstay of Windows through many versions. We described its use for terminating recalcitrant processes and disabling unwanted startup programs. (See "Mastering Task Manager," earlier in this chapter.) It also includes valuable performance-monitoring tools, which we describe here. For zeroing in on performance issues with even more detail, you can use an advanced tool called Resource Monitor. In combination, these tools help you to keep an eye on CPU, memory, disk, and network usage and give you the ability to isolate troublesome processes.

Monitoring performance with Task Manager

The Performance tab of Task Manager gives you a quick overview of your system's performance as measured in multiple dimensions, including CPU, memory, disk, and network usage. The small thumbnail graphs at the left report current data in real time; clicking any of these thumbnails displays a much larger version, with additional information below the chart. Figure 15-24 shows the performance data for a desktop PC, roughly 30 seconds after opening Task Manager.

The graphs to the right show 60 seconds' worth of data, with updates at one-second intervals. In Figure 15-24, for example, the CPU graph shows a large spike to 100 percent usage (which occurs, ironically, when you open Task Manager), followed by several additional spikes as other activities make demands on the CPU.

CHAPTER 15

By keeping this pane open as you work, you can see what the impact of a given activity is. For example, you might monitor CPU usage when encoding a video file to see whether the operation pins CPU usage at 100 percent; if so, that might be evidence that you need to upgrade your desktop PC to one with a more powerful CPU that's capable of doing the same work faster, generating less heat, and allowing you to do other things while the task completes in the background.

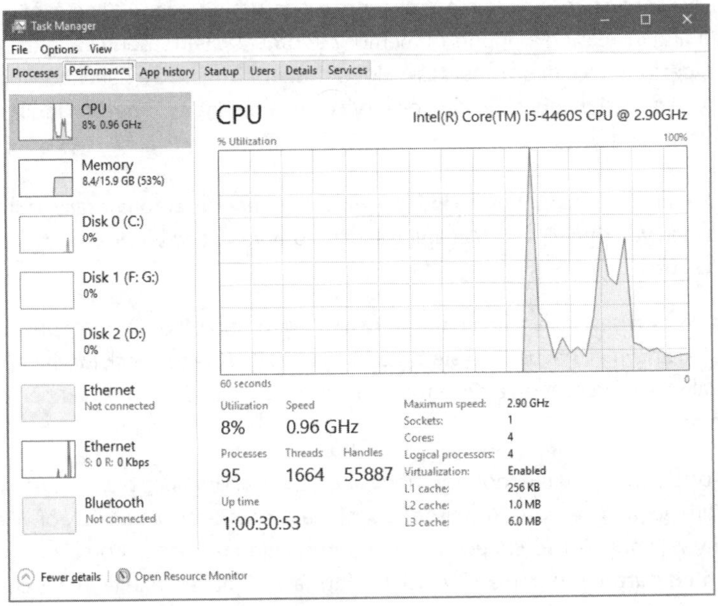

Figure 15-24 The Performance tab of Task Manager gives you a big-picture view of resource usage.

Inside OUT

How long has your PC been running?

Many of the details below the performance graph on the CPU tab in Task Manager are obscure and only of use to developers. You probably don't need to know how many handles are in use by your current workload, for example. But one detail here is interesting as a benchmark of stability. The Up Time measure shows the amount of time that has elapsed—in days, hours, minutes, and seconds—since the machine was last restarted. Thanks to monthly updates that usually include mandatory restarts, it's unlikely you'll ever see this number go beyond 30 days.

The Memory option offers a snapshot of memory usage, as shown in Figure 15-25. Note that the total amount of memory is visible above the graph, with details about the physical memory itself (number of sticks and slots, for example) below, alongside the amount of RAM in use and the amount available.

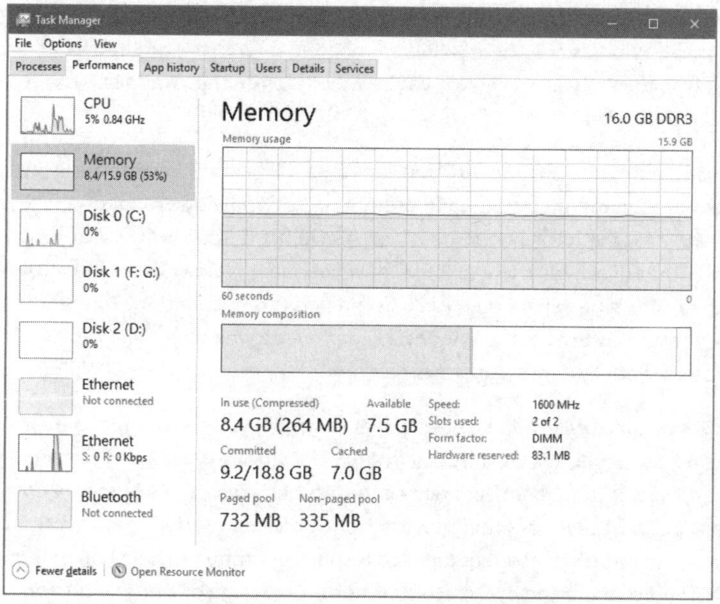

Figure 15-25 Use the Memory option on the Performance tab to see how much of your system's RAM is in use. If the value is at 100 percent, it's time to close some apps to improve performance.

On this page, a detailed Memory Composition bar chart appears below the main graph. At first glance, it appears to be just an alternate view of the main Memory Usage chart, but hover the mouse pointer over any segment to see its real purpose. The ScreenTips that appear over each segment explain what each one represents.

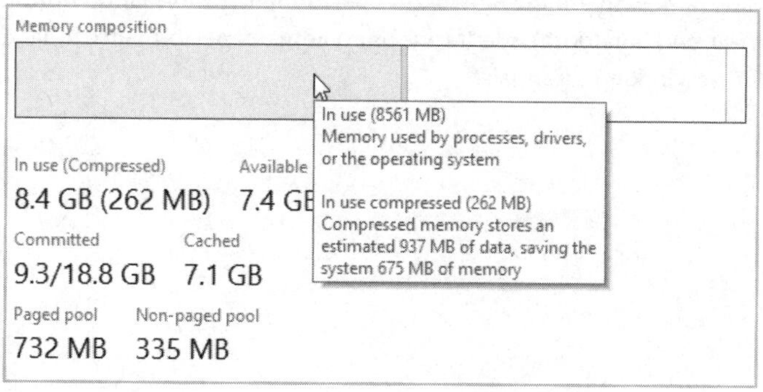

Inside OUT

What happened to the Windows Experience Index?

Beginning with Windows Vista, Microsoft published a set of numbers purporting to quantify your system's performance in five distinct areas. These numbers were merged into an overall score. In Windows 10, these values are no longer reported on the System Properties page. However, they're still available if you're willing to run the Windows System Assessment Tool (Winsat.exe).

Using WinSAT, as it's known for short, you can run a full performance analysis (by typing **winsat formal** at an elevated command prompt) or test individual Windows subsystems (type **winsat –?** for the full syntax). You can also save the output as an XML file or redirect the verbal output of the tests to a text file for subsequent review. To see the most recent set of detailed results, type **winsat query** in a Command Prompt window. This report shows the raw test results instead of the Windows Experience Index scores and provides a more detailed look at your system's performance.

Windows keeps a history of WinSAT performance results you can use for comparisons. You'll find them in %SystemRoot%\Performance\WinSAT\DataStore, each one stamped with the date and time it was run. Minor variations in results between WinSAT runs are normal, and they usually occur because of other processes and services interfering with resource usage. Keeping even an informal record of detailed results over time can help you determine whether a significant change in test scores is normal or a sign of a problem to be found and fixed.

The Disk options, likewise, graph the performance of all nonremovable disks on the current system. Each disk gets its own entry on the left side, with details about the selected disk's performance on the right, as shown in Figure 15-26. The top graph depicts the percentage of time the disk is busy processing read or write requests; the bottom graph shows the disk transfer rate.

➤ For a discussion of how to use the networking performance information from Task Manager (Ethernet, Wi-Fi, and Bluetooth), see "Monitoring network performance in Task Manager" in Chapter 5, "Networking essentials."

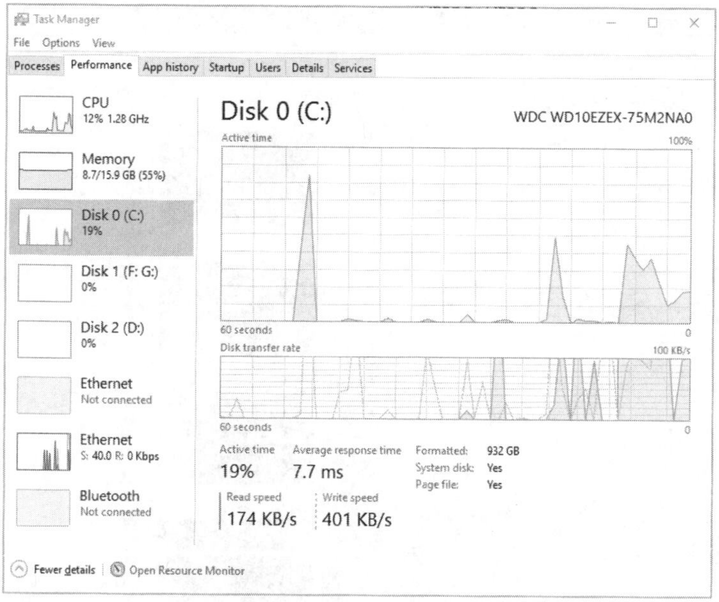

Figure 15-26 The Disk options in Task Manager let you see the throughput of a fixed disk and determine whether a particular activity is causing a bottleneck.

Using Resource Monitor to pinpoint performance problems

Like the Performance tab in Task Manager, Resource Monitor gives you both instantaneous and recent-history readouts of key performance metrics. Also like Task Manager, Resource Monitor can show you, in excruciating detail, what each process is doing.

To open Resource Monitor, you can search for it from the Start menu or use its command line, **perfmon /res**, from an elevated Command Prompt window. But the fastest way is to click the link at the bottom of the Task Manager Performance tab. This is, in our opinion, the preferred way to use this utility. Start with a quick overview from Task Manager, and if you need more information, call on Resource Monitor.

When you first open Resource Monitor, you see the Overview tab shown in Figure 15-27, which provides both detailed tables and charts that summarize performance in four areas.

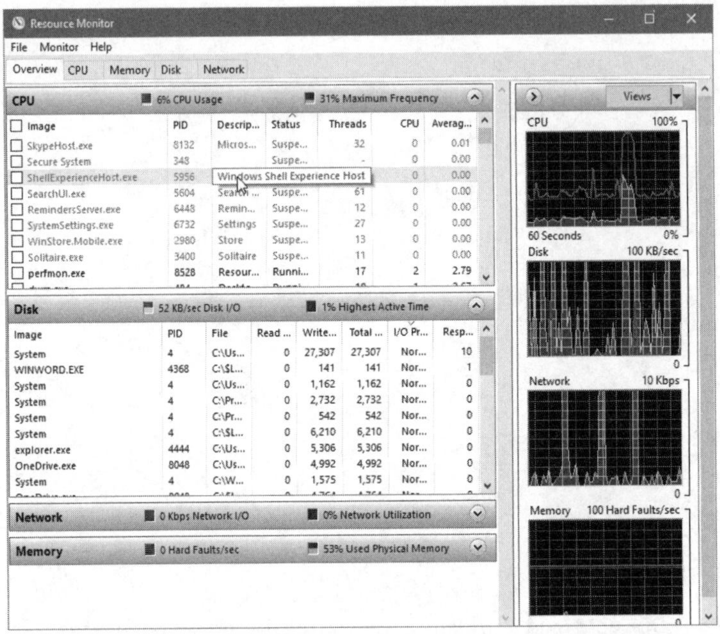

Figure 15-27 Use the check boxes in the top section of Resource Monitor to limit the results to a specific process. ScreenTips show details for files that are truncated in the list below.

Using the tabs along the top of the Resource Monitor window, you can switch to a different context and focus on a specific type of resource usage. The basic layout of each tab is similar and consists of a handful of common elements.

One or more tables contain details about the resource featured on that tab. The first table on each tab is called the key table; it contains a list of all processes currently using the selected resource, with a check box to the left of each process you use to filter the data displayed in additional tables on the tab. The key table at the top of the Overview tab lists all running processes in a display that is similar to the Processes tab of Task Manager.

Resource Monitor is overkill for most performance troubleshooting tasks. But it shines when you want to see exactly which process or file is responsible for an unexplained burst of activity.

CHAPTER 16

Backup, restore, and recovery

In the Unabridged Edition of Murphy's Law, you'll find an entire chapter of corollaries that apply to computers in general and your important data files in particular. Murphy says, "Anything that can go wrong will go wrong." That's certainly true of storage devices, where it's not a matter of whether they'll fail but when. When a hard drive fails catastrophically or a solid-state drive (SSD) suddenly becomes unreadable, any data files on that device are gone, as are your Microsoft Windows installation and all your apps and settings.

Even if your hardware never lets you down, human error can wreak havoc with data. You can press the wrong key and inadvertently delete a group of files you meant to move. If you're not paying attention, you might absent-mindedly click the wrong button in a dialog box, saving a new file using the same name as an old one, wiping out a week's worth of work in the process.

Some of the most important new features in Windows 10 let you recover quickly from either type of disaster.

In this chapter, we explain how to use the backup tools included with Windows 10, which allow you to prepare for the inevitable day when you need to restore a lost file (or an entire drive's worth of files). We also explain your options for resetting Windows when the operating system becomes damaged, for whatever reason. And finally, we offer a guide to the venerable but still useful System Restore feature.

An overview of Windows 10 backup and recovery options

Through the years, the backup and recovery tools in Windows have evolved, but their fundamental purpose has not changed. How well you execute your backup strategy will determine how easily you're able to get back to where you were after something goes wrong—or to start over with an absolutely clean slate. When you reach into the recovery toolkit, you're hoping to perform one of the following three operations:

- **Full reset.** If you're selling or giving away a PC or other device running Windows 10, you can reset it to a clean configuration, wiping personal files in preparation for the new owner. Some Windows users prefer this sort of clean install when they just want to get a fresh start, minus any cruft from previous installations.

- **Recovery.** The "stuff happens" category includes catastrophic hardware failure, malware infection, and system corruption, as well as performance or reliability problems that can't easily be identified with normal troubleshooting. The recovery process involves reinstalling Windows from a backup image or a recovery drive.

- **File restore.** When (not if) you accidentally delete or overwrite an important data file or (ouch) an entire folder, library, or drive, you can call on a built-in Windows 10 tool to bring back the missing data. You can also use this same feature to find and restore earlier versions of a saved file—an original, uncompressed digital photo, for example, or a Microsoft Word document that contains a section you deleted and now want to revisit.

In Windows 10, the primary built-in tool for backing up files is called File History. Its job is to save copies of your local files—every hour is the default frequency—so that you can find and restore your personal documents, pictures, and other data files when you need them.

Inside OUT

Integrating the cloud into your backup strategy

It's tempting to think of Microsoft OneDrive and other cloud-based storage services as a primary backup. But that strategy is potentially dangerous as well. Cloud services are generally reliable, but it's not out of the question that one might fail or be temporarily unavailable. Moreover, online accounts can be compromised. There are risks associated with using the cloud as your only backup medium. And even when you think you have a backup, it might not be what you expect. Your cloud backups of photos, for example, might be converted to a lower resolution than the original images, meaning that your only copy of a priceless photo is an inferior compressed version.

Having a complete archive of files backed up to the cloud does offer the reassurance that you can recover any or all those saved files in the event of an accident or natural disaster, such as a fire or flood, that wipes out your primary device and its separate local backup. Given the ubiquity and relatively low cost of online storage services, in fact, it's probably prudent to keep copies of important files in two separate cloud-based services. Just remember that those distant archives are not a replacement for comprehensive local backups on an external storage device or a networked PC.

File History has evolved since its introduction in Windows 8. Still, it's designed to be simple and not full featured, which is why Windows 10 also includes the old-style Windows 7 Backup

And Restore tool. You'll find both backup solutions by opening Settings > Update & Security > Backup, as shown in Figure 16-1.

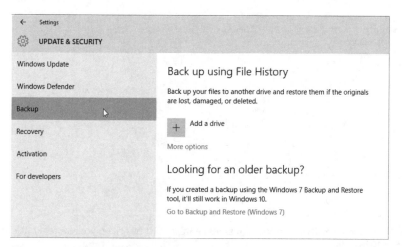

Figure 16-1 After you designate an external drive for File History, its controls are deceptively simple. For fine-tuning, click the More Options link.

Despite its advanced age, the Windows 7 backup tool can still do one impressive digital magic trick that its newer rivals can't: it can create an image of the system drive that can be restored to an exact copy of the original saved volume, complete with Windows, drivers and utilities, desktop programs, settings, and data files. System image backups were once the gold standard of backup and are still a perfect way to capture a known good state for quick recovery.

The disadvantage of a full image backup is that it's fixed at a moment in time and doesn't capture files created, changed, or deleted since the image was created. If your primary data files are located in the cloud or on a separate volume from the system drive, that might not be a problem.

Over the decades, the clean install has taken on almost magical properties among some Windows users. This classic recovery option involves reinstalling Windows from installation media, installing custom drivers, rebuilding connections to network resources, restoring data files, reinstalling apps, and redoing individual preferences. You can still follow that old-school routine if you're willing to spend the time and energy. But there are faster, easier ways in Windows 10.

In Windows 8, Microsoft formally introduced a "push-button reset" feature with two options. Windows 10 simplifies this feature under a single reset heading, which you can use to reinstall Windows with the option to keep or discard personal data files. With this option, you can reset a misbehaving system on the fly, rolling back with relative ease to a clean, fully updated Windows 10 installation minus any third-party programs or drivers that might be causing problems. You'll

CHAPTER 16

find the Reset This PC option on the Recovery page in Settings, which sits next to Backup in the Update & Security group. (See Figure 16-2.)

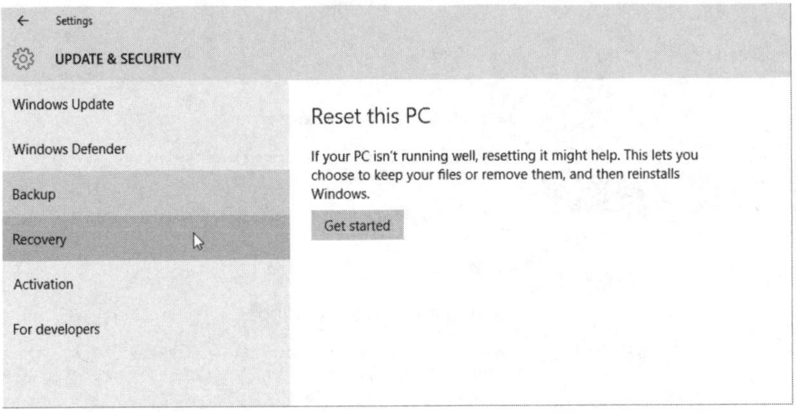

← Settings

⚙ UPDATE & SECURITY

Windows Update

Windows Defender

Backup

Recovery

Activation

For developers

Reset this PC

If your PC isn't running well, resetting it might help. This lets you choose to keep your files or remove them, and then reinstalls Windows.

[Get started]

Figure 16-2 The Reset This PC option gives you a fresh start by rolling your system back to a clean Windows 10 installation.

Inside OUT

Do you need the OEM recovery image?

The Windows 10 Reset feature, in a major change from Windows 8.1, is capable of reinstalling Windows without requiring a recovery partition or any external media. Instead, it uses the existing Windows system files to create a new, clean, side-by-side copy. The result, at least in theory, allows you to recover the sometimes significant disk space used by original equipment manufacturer (OEM) recovery images.

The OEM image restores the device to its original, factory-installed configuration, complete with custom drivers and utilities as well as bundled (and potentially unwanted) software. Depending on when the machine left the factory, this option is likely to be significantly out of date. Unless you're running short of space for storing data, this partition is worth keeping on any device that's still under warranty.

You can safely remove the OEM recovery image if you're confident you have a reliable way to restore your system to a clean image (to pass it along to a new owner, for example). Creating your own recovery drive or system image, as we explain in this chapter, fills either bill. Removing the OEM partition might require a trip to the Command Prompt window and some judicious use of the DiskPart utility, as we explain in "Managing disks from the command prompt" in Chapter 14, "Managing disks and drives."

Windows 10 also includes a built-in option to turn a USB flash drive into a bootable recovery drive. Using this recovery drive, you can restore Windows, even after a complete system drive failure.

In the remainder of this chapter, we discuss these backup and recovery options in more detail.

Using File History to protect files and folders

As we noted earlier, the File History feature was introduced in Windows 8 as a replacement for the Backup And Restore tool in Windows 7. Although you can delve into advanced settings if you dig deeply enough, File History is designed as a "set it and forget it" feature. After you enable this backup application, it first copies all files in the backup location and then scans the file system at regular intervals (hourly, by default), looking for newly created files and changes to existing files. Copies of each new or changed file are stored on a secondary drive, usually an external device.

You can browse the backed-up files by date and time—or search the entire history—and then restore any or all of those files to their original location or to a different folder.

But first, you have to go through a simple setup process.

Setting up File History

Although the File History feature is installed by default, it's not enabled until you designate a drive to serve as the backup destination. This drive can be a second internal hard disk or an external storage device, such as an external hard drive, or a network location.

CAUTION

Be sure you specify a File History volume that is on a separate physical drive from the one that contains the files you're backing up. Windows will warn you, sternly, if you try to designate a separate volume on the same physical drive as your system drive. The problem? One sadly common cause of data loss is failure of the drive itself. If the backups and original files are stored on the same drive, a failure wipes everything out. Having backups on a separate physical drive allows them to remain independent.

To turn on File History for the first time, open Settings > Update & Security > Backup. Click Add A Drive to scan for available File History drives. The File History wizard responds by showing you all available drives. To add a list of network shares for which you have read/write permission, click Show All Network Locations. (This link appears after the list of available non-networked drives has been populated.) Figure 16-3 shows a system that has no attached drives but includes three network shares. Selecting one of the available locations turns on the File History service and begins the backup process, with the backup frequency set to one hour.

CHAPTER 16

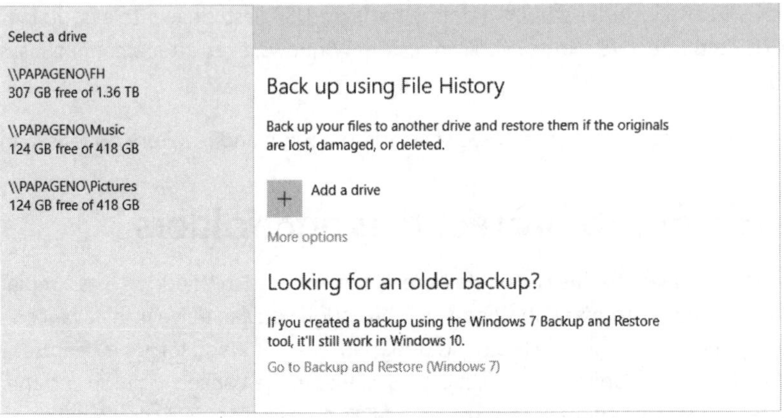

Figure 16-3 Before you can enable File History, you must specify a location (preferably an external drive or a network share) to hold the backed-up files.

When you first enable File History, it creates a full copy of all files in the locations you designated for backup. That list contains either the default locations or your customized list. (We describe how to create a custom backup list in the next section.)

The drive you designate as a File History drive must be either an internal or external hard drive (a category that includes SSDs). Removable drives, such as USB flash drives, are not eligible. The File History setup wizard will show you only eligible drives when you set up File History for the first time.

There's nothing complicated or proprietary about File History volumes:

- When you use an external drive, Windows creates a FileHistory folder, with a separate subfolder for each user. Thus, on a device that includes multiple user accounts, each user's files can be backed up separately.

- Within each user's private folder are separate subfolders, one for each device backed up. This folder arrangement allows you to use a single external drive to record File History backups on different devices.

- Each individual backup set includes two folders. The Configuration folder contains XML files and, if necessary, index files to allow speedier searches. The Data folder contains backed-up files, which are stored in a hierarchy that matches their original location.

- Backed-up files are not compressed. File names are the same as the original, with a date and time stamp appended (in parentheses) to distinguish different versions. As a result, you can browse a File History drive in File Explorer and use search tools to locate a file or folder without using the File History app.

CAUTION

Files stored on a File History drive are not encrypted by default. Anyone who has physical possession of the drive can freely read any files stored there. If you're concerned about confidential information contained in an external File History drive, we recommend you encrypt the drive. (See "Encrypting with BitLocker and BitLocker To Go" in Chapter 7, "Securing Windows 10 devices," for detailed instructions.) As an alternative, consider saving File History to a shared network folder for which you have appropriate permissions.

File History is yet another example of a feature caught in the transition from the classic Windows Control Panel to the new Settings app. The overlap between old interface and new is more pronounced here than elsewhere. From the old Control Panel (in File History, click Advanced Settings) or the new Settings app (on the Backup page, click More Options), you can change the backup interval and time period for saving backups. The options, identical in effect but different in appearance, are shown here and on the next page.

Backup options

Overview

Size of backup: 90.4 GB

Total space on Backup disk: 1.36 TB

Last backup: 9/6/2016 1:40 PM

Back up now

Back up my files

Every hour (default)

Keep my backups

Forever (default)

By default, File History checks your designated drives and folders once an hour, saving copies of any new or changed files as part of the operation. You can adjust this setting in either direction, choosing from nine intervals that range from every 10 minutes (if you really hate the idea of ever losing a saved file) to once daily.

File History backups are saved by default forever. (You receive a warning when your File History drive is full.) However, you can alter the Keep Saved Versions setting to 1, 3, 6, or 9 months or 1 or 2 years. The "set it and forget it" Until Space Is Needed setting allows File History to automatically jettison old backups to make way for new ones when the drive is full.

The options in Settings and Control Panel overlap but aren't identical. For example, the options to share a File History drive with others in a homegroup and to quickly view File History event logs are available only in the Advanced Settings section of the classic Control Panel.

TROUBLESHOOTING

Some files are missing from File History backups

Because of the unique way File History organizes and names backed-up files, you might find that some files aren't backed up properly. This can happen, for example, if you append a version date and time to the name of a file, particularly if the file is deeply nested within multiple subfolders. Those extra characters added to an already long path can cause the file name in the File History folder to exceed the maximum path limit of 260 characters. You can spot these errors easily in the File History event logs and resolve them by moving the original files or subfolders to a location with a path name that's sufficiently shorter.

Choosing locations to back up

By default, File History backs up all folders in the current user profile (including those created by third-party apps) as well as the contents of local folders that have been added to custom libraries.

> ➤ For an overview of what's in a default user profile and instructions on how to work with libraries, see Chapter 12, "Managing files on PCs and in the cloud."

To manage the list of folders backed up by File History, open Settings > Update & Security > Backup > More Options. Scroll down to view the folder list on the Backup Options page, as shown in Figure 16-4.

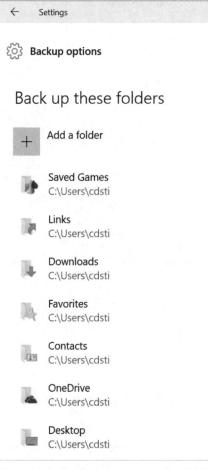

Figure 16-4 File History presents a list of folders that it is set to back up, allowing you to add to the list or delete particular folders.

To remove any folder from this list, select its name and then click or tap Remove. To add a folder from any local drive, click or tap Add A Folder and then select the location using the Select Folder dialog box.

NOTE
Although the OneDrive folder is included by default in the list of folders to be backed up by File History, only files that are synced to the local drive are actually backed up.

At the end of the list is an Exclude These Folders option, shown in Figure 16-5. It's useful when you want to avoid filling your File History drive with large files that don't require backing up. If you routinely put interesting but ephemeral video files into a subfolder in your Downloads folder, for example, you might choose to exclude that Videos subfolder completely from File History, while leaving the rest of the Downloads folder to be backed up.

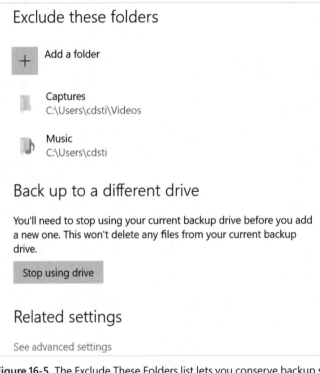

Figure 16-5 The Exclude These Folders list lets you conserve backup space by leaving out folders you don't need to back up.

A quicker way to exclude a folder from the backup list is simply to click it in the include list and then click the Remove button that appears:

Unfortunately, although this approach does remove folders from the list to be backed up, it does not add them to the list that appears under Exclude These Folders. In most cases, the end result is the same. But if the folder you remove happens to be a subfolder of an included folder, it will continue to be backed up unless you explicitly add it to the exclusion list.

When a File History drive fills up, you can either change the settings to remove old backed-up files and make room for new ones or swap in a new drive. If you choose the latter option, click or tap the Stop Using Drive button on the Backup Options page, remove the old drive, and set up the new one.

Restoring files and folders

There are several ways to find and restore a backed-up file, folder, or drive. From File Explorer, you can right-click an item, choose Properties, and then click the Previous Versions tab. This sequence of steps generates a list of available backed-up versions sorted by date, as shown in Figure 16-6.

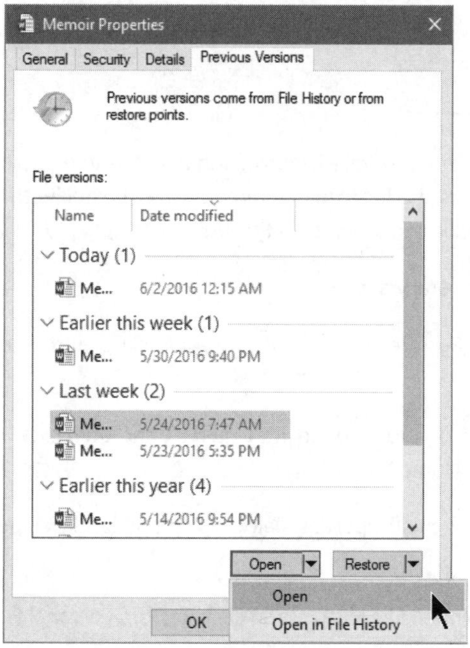

Figure 16-6 When you know exactly what you want to restore, it's often quickest to get it from the Previous Versions tab in File Explorer.

The Open button at the bottom of the Previous Versions list gives you a choice of opening the selected item in its original application and opening it in the File History application; we'll say more about the File History application in a moment. If you open the document in its original application, what you get is a read-only copy of the document. That way, you won't accidentally overwrite the current version of the document with the older one you just opened.

The Restore button, to the right of Open, also provides a pair of choices. You can restore the document to its original location, or you can restore it to a new location of your choice. If you restore to the original location and the original file still exists, you'll see the Replace Or Skip Files dialog box, which gives you an opportunity to change your mind or save the new file as a copy in the same location. (If you want to restore a copy without deleting the original, click Compare Info For Both Files and then select the check box for both the original file and the restored previous version. The restored copy will have a number appended to the name to distinguish it from the original.)

The File History app offers a distinctly different take on browsing backed-up files. Although it resembles File Explorer in some respects, it adds a unique dimension—the ability to choose a set of saved files from a specific date and time to scan, scroll through, or search.

You can start the File History app in several ways:

- From the Settings app, look for Restore Files From A Current Backup, at the bottom of the Backup Options page.

- From File Explorer, select the file or folder you're interested in, and then click History, in the Open group of the ribbon's Home tab.

- From the Previous Versions tab in the Properties dialog box for a file, click Open In File History.

- Using the classic Control Panel, open File History and click Restore Personal Files in the links at the left of the settings.

Figure 16-7 shows the File History app, which has an address bar, navigation controls, and a search box along the top, very much like File Explorer. What's different are the time stamp (above the file browsing window) and three controls below the window that allow time control without the need for flux capacitors or other imaginary time-machine components.

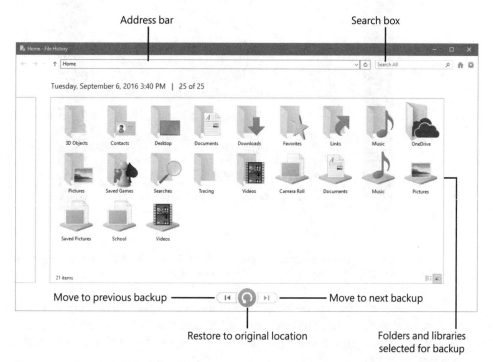

Figure 16-7 In its Home view, the File History app shows all files and folders set for regular backup. Scroll left for older files, right for more recent backups.

The legend at the top of the window tells you the date and time of the currently displayed backup. You can use controls at the bottom of the window to move between backups. So, for example, to restore a file or folder you regret having deleted, you can move backward through the backups until you find one that includes the longed-for item and then restore it from there.

Within the backup window, you can open folders to see their contents. An address bar at the top, along with the invaluable up arrow beside it, lets you navigate as you might in File Explorer. As with File Explorer, you can use the search box in the upper right to narrow the results by file type, keyword, or file contents. Because file names rarely provide enough detail to determine whether a specific file is the one you're looking for, File History has a preview function. Double-click a file to show its contents in the File History window. Figure 16-8 shows one such preview of a PowerPoint presentation, with the full path and file name in the address bar and a scroll bar along the right for moving through the document in the preview window.

CHAPTER 16

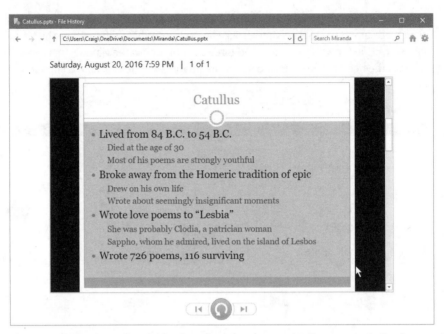

Figure 16-8 File History is capable of previewing most popular file types, including images, PDF files, and Microsoft Office documents like this PowerPoint presentation.

The option to restore entire folders is especially useful when you're switching to a new PC. After you complete one last backup on your old PC, plug the File History drive into your new PC, and then use the big green Restore button to copy your backed-up files to corresponding locations on the new PC.

As with File Explorer, you can change the view of files in the File History browsing window. By using the two shortcuts in the lower right corner, you can quickly switch to Details or Large Icons view, although you have a total of eight predefined views, available from the well-hidden shortcut menu shown in Figure 16-9.

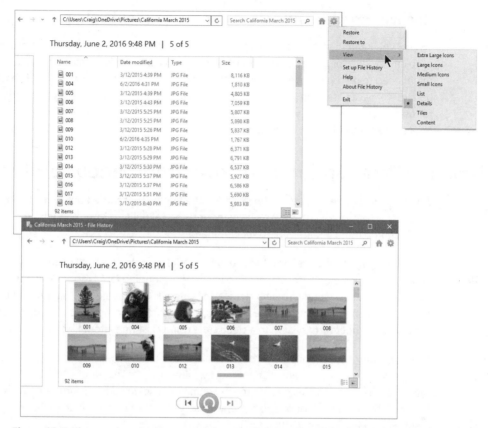

Figure 16-9 The gear icon in the upper right corner of the File History app leads to a menu with eight view settings. Details view (top) and Large Icons (bottom) work the same as in File Explorer.

Inside OUT

Transfer your File Explorer smarts to File History

There's no need to open a menu or click a tiny icon to change the view in File History. Any of the eight predefined views, from Content through Extra Large Icons, can be invoked with its keyboard shortcut, Ctrl+Shift+*number*. Any number between 1 and 8 works, with Ctrl+Shift+2 switching to Large Icons view and Ctrl+Shift+6 to Details view. These same shortcuts work in File Explorer as well.

Recovering files and folders from an older backup

What if you need to recover documents from a File History drive that's no longer in use? No problem. In File Explorer, open the old File History drive and navigate to the files you need. You might need to go through several layers of subfolders to get there. Your previously backed-up files will have dates and times appended to their original names to help you decide which to resurrect. Copy the files you want to restore, using a destination folder of your choosing; rename the files, if desired, to remove the date and time stamp.

Using the Reset option to recover from serious problems

One of the signature features of Windows 8 was a feature that turned out to be quietly revolutionary: a way for any user, even one without technical skills, to reset Windows to its original configuration using a Refresh or Reset command.

Windows 10 significantly refines that capability under a single Reset command. The most important change eliminates the need to have a disk-hogging OEM recovery image in a dedicated partition at the end of the hard drive. In Windows 10, that recovery image and its associated partition are no longer required. Instead, Windows 10 accomplishes recovery operations by rebuilding the operating system to a clean state using existing system files.

This push-button reset option has the same effect as a clean install, without the hassles of finding drivers and without wiping out potentially valuable data. The Reset This PC option is at the top of the list on the Recovery page in Settings, as shown earlier in Figure 16-2. It's also the featured choice on the Troubleshoot menu when you restart in the Windows Recovery Environment, as shown in Figure 16-10.

When you reset a PC, Windows 10 and its drivers are restored to the most recent rollup state. The reset PC includes all updates except those installed in the last 28 days, a design that allows recovery to succeed when a freshly installed update is part of the problem.

For PCs sold with Windows 10 already installed, any customized settings and desktop programs installed by the manufacturer are restored with the Windows 10 reset. These customizations are saved in a separate container, which is created as part of the OEM setup process.

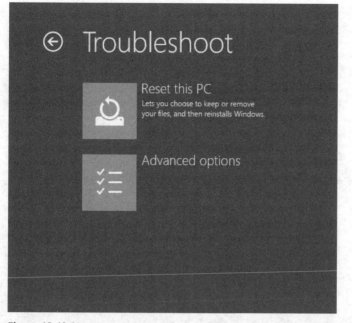

Figure 16-10 You can reset your Windows 10 PC by starting the Windows Recovery Environment and choosing the top option shown here.

All Windows apps included with Windows 10 by default (Photos, Weather, Groove Music, Mail, and Calendar, for example) are restored, along with any Windows apps that were added to the system by the OEM or as part of an enterprise deployment. App updates are downloaded and reinstalled via the Store automatically after recovery.

Windows desktop programs are not restored and must be manually reinstalled. Likewise, any previously purchased Windows apps are discarded and must be reinstalled from the Store.

Resetting a PC isn't something you do accidentally. The process involves multiple confirmations, with many opportunities to bail out if you get cold feet or realize that you need to do just *one* more backup before you irrevocably wipe the disk. The first step offers you the option to keep your personal files or remove everything, as shown in Figure 16-11.

CHAPTER 16

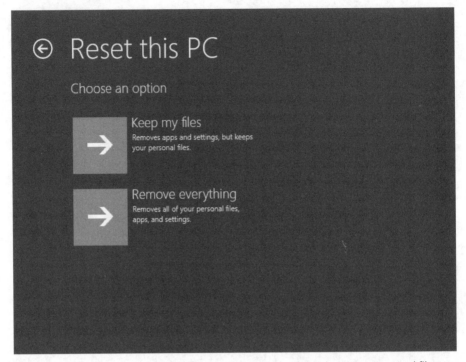

Figure 16-11 The Reset This PC options let you choose whether to keep your personal files or remove everything and start with a completely clean slate.

If you're performing the reset operation in preparation for selling or donating your computer, you'll probably want to use the second option. Otherwise, choose the first option to retain your personal files.

If you're removing everything, the reset process also includes an option to scrub data from the drive so that it cannot easily be recovered using disk utilities. As the explanatory text in Figure 16-12 makes clear, the Remove Files And Clean The Drive option can add hours to the process. Note that this option, while thorough, is not certified to meet any government or industry standards for data removal.

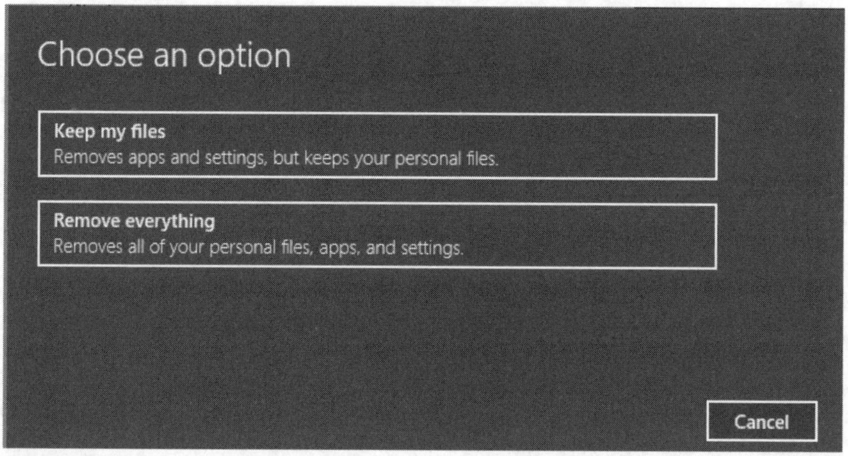

Choose an option

Keep my files
Removes apps and settings, but keeps your personal files.

Remove everything
Removes all of your personal files, apps, and settings.

Cancel

Figure 16-12 Choose the first option if you're resetting a PC for a trusted friend or family member to use. The second option might be worth the time if your PC was used for work or contained sensitive information.

If you made it this far through the process, you have only one more confirmation to get through. That dialog box, shown in Figure 16-13, shows the choices you made, with one last Cancel option. To plunge irreversibly ahead, click Reset.

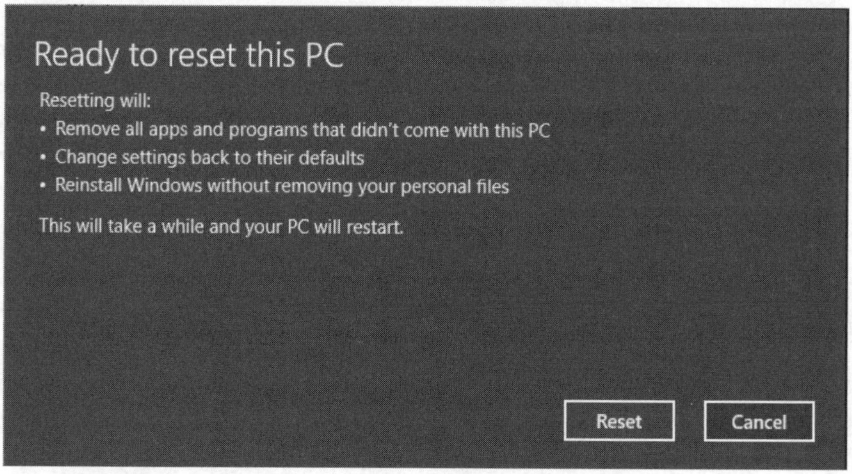

Ready to reset this PC

Resetting will:
• Remove all apps and programs that didn't come with this PC
• Change settings back to their defaults
• Reinstall Windows without removing your personal files

This will take a while and your PC will restart.

Reset   Cancel

Figure 16-13 This is your last chance to back out when resetting a PC.

CHAPTER 16

The reset option is a tremendous time-saver, but it's not all-powerful. Your attempts to reset Windows can be thwarted by a handful of scenarios:

- If operating system files have been heavily corrupted or infected by malware, the reset process will probably not work.

- If the problem is caused by a cumulative update that is more than 28 days old, the reset might not be able to avoid that problem.

- If a user chooses the wrong language during the out-of-box-experience (OOBE) phase on a single-language Windows version (typically sold in developing countries and regions), a complete reinstallation might be required.

If the reset option doesn't work, it might be time for a more drastic solution: reinstalling with the assistance of a recovery drive.

Creating and using a recovery drive

If you took advantage of the free upgrade offer in the first year after Windows 10 was released, the one thing you didn't get out of the deal was a shiny disk. Relax—you don't need it. Windows 10 includes the capability to turn a USB flash drive into a recovery drive you can use to perform repairs or completely reinstall Windows.

The Recovery Media Creator creates a bootable drive that contains the Windows Recovery Environment. To get there, open Control Panel, search for Recovery, and select Create A Recovery Drive. If you select the Back Up System Files To The Recovery Drive check box, as shown in Figure 16-14, the utility creates a bootable drive that can be used to fully restore Windows, skipping most of the setup process.

CHAPTER 16

Inside OUT

Turn a recovery drive into installation media

The Recovery Media Creator creates a FAT32-formatted drive that's fully capable of booting and installing Windows 10. In fact, you can use that drive as a shortcut to turn an ISO file, such as those available to MSDN subscribers, into a full-fledged Windows installer. Skip the option to back up system files to the recovery drive. Open the newly created recovery drive in one File Explorer window. Double-click the ISO file to mount it as a virtual drive in a separate File Explorer window, and then copy the entire contents of the mounted ISO drive by dragging them to the recovery drive, overwriting any existing files. The resulting drive can be used for clean installs on any PC.

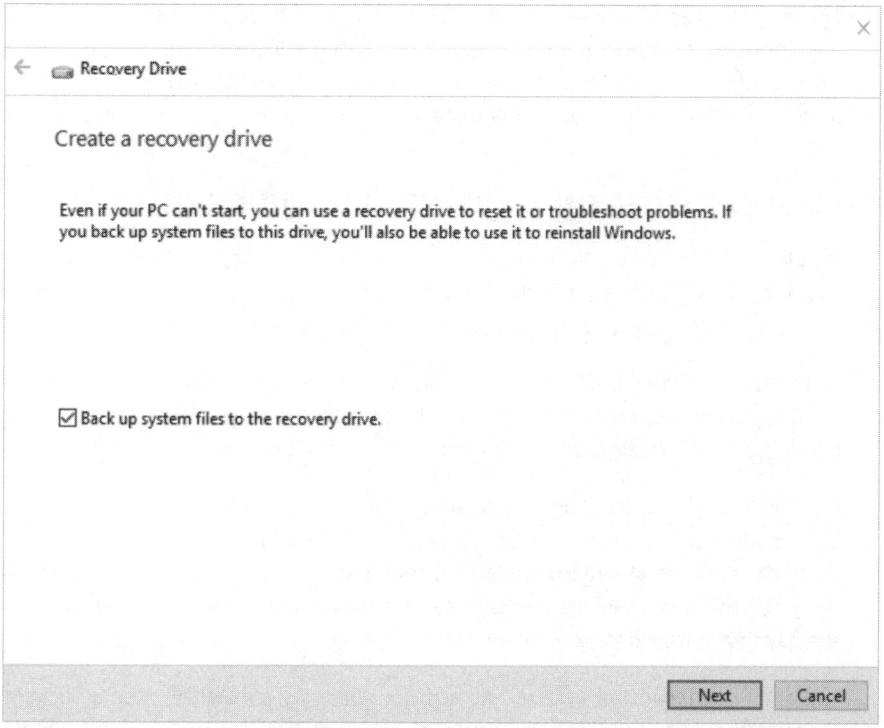

Figure 16-14 You'll typically need a USB flash drive with a capacity of at least 8 GB to create a recovery drive that includes backed-up system files.

To use the recovery drive, configure your PC so that you can boot from the USB flash drive. (That process, which is unique for many machines, might involve tapping a key or pressing a combination of buttons such as Power+Volume Up when restarting.)

If you see the Recover From A Drive option when you restart, congratulations—the system has recognized your recovery drive and you are (fingers crossed) a few minutes away from being back in business.

Inside OUT

Download a recovery image

If your system won't start but you can get to the internet on another machine, you might be able to download a recovery image from your hardware vendor and then copy that to a flash disk. Microsoft, for example, offers this service for its Surface models. (Go to *https://surface.com*, and search for Download Recovery Image.) For other vendors, check support offerings to see if an image is available.

CHAPTER 16

The menu that appears when you start from a recovery drive allows you to repair a PC that has startup issues. Choose Troubleshoot to get to the Advanced Options menu, where you can choose to perform a startup repair, use System Restore to undo a problematic change, or open a Command Prompt window to use system tools such as DiskPart from the command line.

Creating and restoring a system image backup

Windows 10 includes the Windows Backup program (Sdclt.exe) originally released as part of Windows 7. Its feature set is basically the same as its predecessor, and it's included primarily for compatibility with backups created using that older operating system.

If you have a working backup routine based on the Windows 7 Backup program, we don't want to stand in your way. The version included with Windows 10 does all the familiar tasks you depend on, and we suggest you carry on. After all, the best backup program is the one you use.

For Windows 10, there are better backup utilities, but we continue to recommend the Windows Backup program for the one task it does exceptionally well: Use it to make a system image backup that can re-create a complete PC configuration, using a single drive or multiple drives. Restoring that system image creates a perfect copy of the system configuration as it existed on the day that system image was captured.

You don't need to install, update, and activate Windows; reinstall all your applications; and then configure your applications to work the way you like. Instead, you boot into the Windows Recovery Environment, choose an image file to restore, and then complete the process by restoring from your latest file backup, which is likely to be more recent than the image. The image files that Windows Backup creates are largely hardware independent, which means that—with some limitations—you can restore your backup image to a new computer of a different brand and type. (Just be prepared to jump through some activation hoops on the new PC.)

Inside OUT

Use a system image to save your custom configuration

The single greatest use for a system image backup is to clean up an OEM configuration, leaving Windows intact, removing unwanted software, and installing your favorite apps. Being able to return to a baseline configuration quickly is a trick that IT pros learned long ago as a way of deploying Windows in large organizations. By mastering the system image backup feature, you can accomplish the same result even in an environment with a few PCs instead of a thousand.

Creating a system image backup

Type **backup** in the search box to find the Windows 7 Backup And Restore (Windows 7) tool, shown in Figure 16-15.

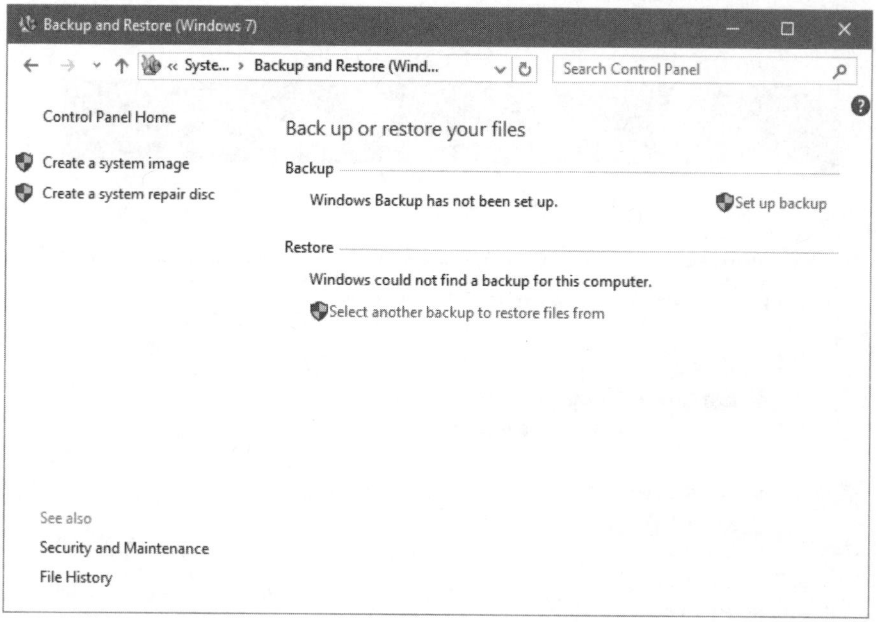

Figure 16-15 The vintage Windows 7 backup tool isn't necessary for file backup tasks, but it's ideal for capturing a complete image of a Windows installation for disaster recovery.

NOTE

When you first open Windows Backup, a message alerts you that the program has not been set up. You can ignore the Set Up Backup link forever if you simply want to create a system image backup (an excellent idea if you just finished performing a clean installation with all your drivers and programs installed and ready to use). Click the Create A System Image link in the left pane.

Ignore the options in the center of that window, and instead click the Create A System Image link at the left side of the window. That opens the efficient Create A System Image wizard. The first step asks you to define a destination for your system image, as shown in Figure 16-16.

The ideal destination for a system image backup is a local hard disk, internal or external. If the Windows Backup program detects a drive that qualifies, it suggests that destination in the list of hard disks at the top of the dialog box.

CHAPTER 16

The second option lets you choose a DVD writer as the target for the backup operation. You'll need to supply two, three, and maybe more blank discs to store the image backup. Although this option might have made sense in a bygone era, it's downright quaint today. Most new PCs don't even include a DVD drive, making backups stored on that media inconvenient at best and potentially useless. Even when a DVD drive is available, a single corrupted disc in the series can ruin the whole backup.

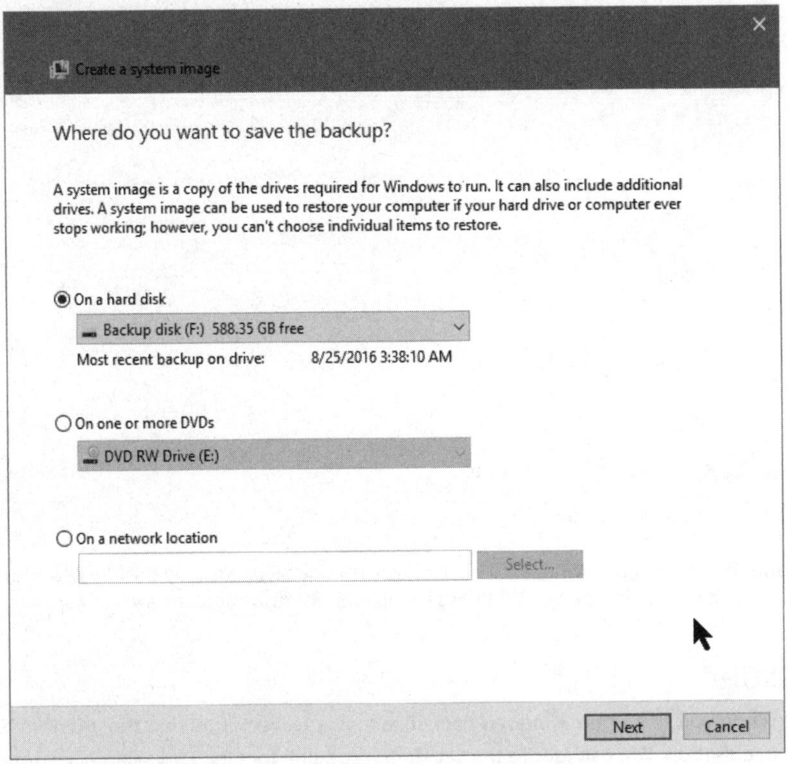

Figure 16-16 The best location for a system image backup is an external hard disk. Avoid the DVD option.

CHAPTER 16

TROUBLESHOOTING

Windows Backup says your drive is not a valid backup location

If you try to choose a removable drive that is not a hard drive, such as a USB flash drive or SD card, Windows Backup will return this error message: "The drive is not a valid backup location." In its conventional backup role, Windows Backup can save data files on just about any storage medium. System image backups, however, must be saved on a hard disk, a DVD, or a network location.

When you create a system image backup, the resulting image file stores the complete contents of all selected drives during its first backup. If the backup target is a local (internal or external) hard drive, subsequent backup operations store only new and changed data. Therefore, the subsequent, incremental backup operation typically runs much faster, depending on how much data has been changed or added since the previous image backup operation.

If you choose a shared network folder as the backup destination, you can save only one image backup. Any subsequent image backup wipes out the previous image backup.

If you have multiple hard drives, Windows displays a dialog box like the one shown in Figure 16-17, in which you choose the volumes you want to include in the backup. By default, any volume that contains Windows system files is selected. If other drives are available, you can optionally choose to include them in the image backup as well.

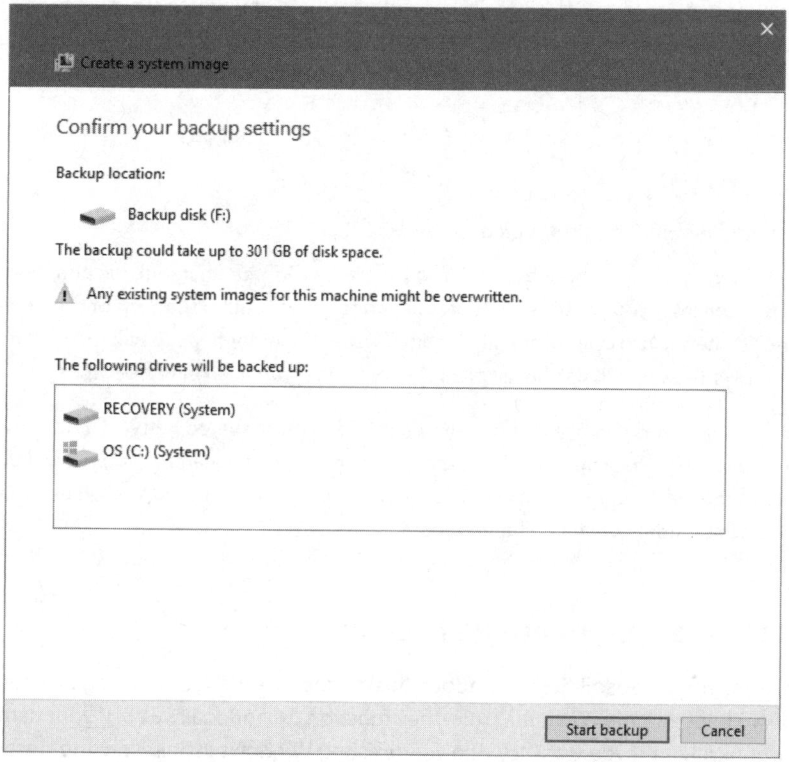

Figure 16-17 The Windows boot volume (indicated by the logo on the drive icon) and other system volumes must be included in a system image. Other volumes, such as a dedicated data drive, are optional.

The disk space requirements for an image-based backup can be substantial, especially on a well-used system that includes lots of user data files. Windows Backup estimates the amount of disk space the image will use (as shown in Figure 16-17) and will warn you if the destination you choose doesn't have sufficient free disk space.

After you confirm your settings, click Start Backup to begin the process of building and saving your image.

System images are stored in virtual hard disk (.vhd) format. Although the data is not compressed, it is compact because the image file does not include the hard drive's unused space and some other unnecessary files, such as hibernation files, page files, and restore points. Incremental system image backups on a local drive are not written to a separate folder. Instead, new and updated files (actually, the changed blocks in those files) are written to the same .vhd file. The older blocks are stored as shadow copies in the .vhd file, allowing you to restore any previous version.

The final step of the image backup process offers to help you create a system repair disc on a writable CD or DVD. This option might be useful for an older PC, but it's redundant if you already created a recovery drive as described in the previous section.

Inside OUT

Save multiple image backups on a network

If you specify a shared network folder as the destination for an image backup, beware of the consequences if you try to reuse that location for a subsequent backup of the same computer. If the backup operation fails for any reason, the older backup will be overwritten, but the newer backup will not be usable. In other words, you'll have no backup.

You can avoid this risk by creating a new subfolder in the shared network folder to hold each new image backup. The disadvantage, of course, is that each image file will occupy as much space as the original disk, unlike an incremental image backup on an external hard drive, which stores only the changed data.

Restoring a system image backup

The system image capabilities in Windows Backup are intended for creating an emergency recovery kit for a single PC. In that role, they function exceptionally well. If your hard drive fails catastrophically, or if you want to wipe your existing Windows installation and start with a clean custom image you created a few weeks or months ago, you've come to the right place.

Your options (and potential gotchas) become more complex if you want to use these basic image backup and restore tools to work with a complex set of physical disks and partitions, especially if the disk layout has changed from the time you created the original image.

In this chapter, we assume you created an image backup of your system disk and want to restore it to a system that is essentially the same (in terms of hardware and disk layout) as the one you started with. In that case, you can restart your computer using a recovery drive or a Windows 10 installation drive and then choose the Repair Your Computer option.

Choose Advanced Options and then select System Image Recovery, as shown in Figure 16-18.

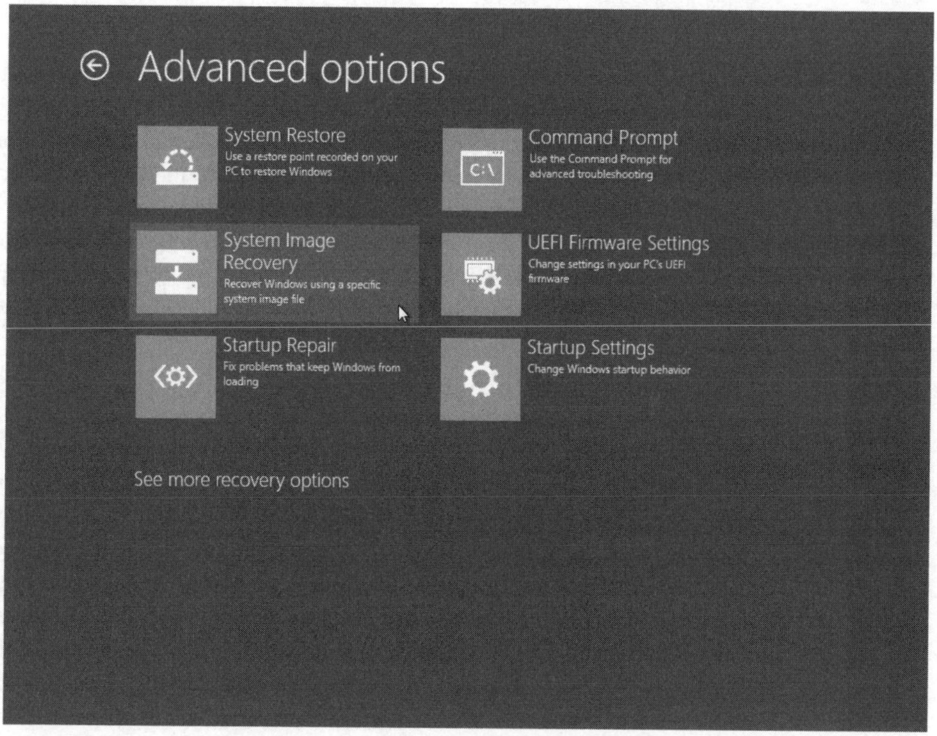

Figure 16-18 By booting into the Windows Recovery Environment, you can wipe the current device clean and replace its contents with a saved system image backup.

If the backup deities are smiling, you should see a dialog box proposing the most recent available system image backup. If you're restoring the most recent image backup to the same system on which it was originally created and the backup is stored on an external hard drive attached to the computer, your job is easy. Verify that the date and time and other details of the image match the one you want to restore, and then click Next to continue.

If the image file you're planning to restore from is on a network share or if you want to use a different image, choose Select A System Image and then click Next. You'll see a dialog box that lists additional image files available on local drives. Select the correct file, and click Next to select an image created on a specific date if more than one is available. If the image file you're looking for is in a shared network folder, click the Advanced button and then click Search For A System Image On The Network. Enter the network location that contains your saved image, along with a user name and password that have authorized access to that location.

Restoring an image backup completely replaces the current contents of each volume in the image file. The restore program offers to format the disk or disks to which it is restoring files before it begins the restore process; if you have multiple drives or volumes and you're nervous about wiping out valuable data files, it offers an option to exclude certain disks from formatting.

The important point to recognize about restoring a system image is that it replaces the current contents of system volumes with the exact contents that existed at the time of the image backup you select. That means your Windows system files and registry will be returned to healthy (provided the system was in good shape when you performed your most recent backup and that no hardware-related issues have cropped up since then). Whatever programs were installed when you backed up your system will be restored entirely. All other files on the restored disk, including your documents, will also be returned to their prior states, and any changes made after your most recent backup will be lost.

CAUTION

If you keep your documents on the same volume as your system files, restoring a system image is likely to entail the loss of recent work—unless, of course, you have an up-to-date file backup or you have the good fortune to have made an image backup almost immediately before your current troubles began. The same is true if you save documents on a volume separate from your system files but have included that data volume in your image backup. If you have documents that have not been backed up, you can avoid losing recent work by copying them to a disk that will not be affected by the restore process—a USB flash drive, for example, or some other form of removable media. You can use the Command Prompt option in the Windows Recovery Environment to copy these documents. (For details about using the Command Prompt option, see "Working at the Command Prompt" in Chapter 19, "Automating tasks and activities.") If you do have a recent file backup, you can restore files after you restore the image backup and your system is running again.

NOTE

The main hardware limitation for restoring a system image backup is that the target computer must have at least as many hard drives as the source system, and each drive must be at least as big as its corresponding drive in the source system. This means, for example, that you can't restore a system image from a system that has a 500-GB hard drive to a system with a 256-GB SSD, even if the original system used far less than 256 GB of drive space. Keep in mind also that on a system with multiple hard drives, the BIOS determines which one is the bootable drive, and this is the one on which Windows will

CHAPTER 16

restore the image of your system volume. (You have no choice in the matter, aside from reconnecting the drives or, if your BIOS permits it, selecting a different bootable drive.)

If your new computer meets the space requirements, restoring a system image should work. This is true even when the source and target computers use different disk controllers. Similarly, other differences—such as different graphics cards, audio cards, processors, and so on—shouldn't prevent you from restoring a system image to a different computer, because hardware drivers are isolated from the rest of the image information and are rebuilt as part of the restore process. (You might need to reactivate Windows because of hardware changes.)

TROUBLESHOOTING

Your backup folders are "empty"

If you use File Explorer to browse to the folder containing your system image backup, when you rest the mouse pointer over a folder name, the pop-up tip might identify it as an "Empty folder." Alarmed, you right-click the folder and choose Properties, only to find that the folder apparently contains 0 bytes, 0 files, and 0 folders. Don't worry. This is the normal condition when your backups are stored on an NTFS volume because, by default, only the System user account has permission to view the files. (That's a reasonable security and reliability precaution, which prevents you or another user from inadvertently deleting a key backup file.) If you're confident in your ability to work safely with backup files in their native format, the solution is simple: Double-click the folder name. Follow the prompts, including a User Account Control (UAC) consent dialog box, to permanently add your user account to the folder's permissions list, giving you Full Control access to the folder.

Configuring system protection options

The System Restore feature has been part of Windows since the turn of the twenty-first century. It's a relatively minor part of the recovery toolkit now, but it can be useful for quickly undoing recent changes that introduced instability. When System Restore is enabled, the Volume Shadow Copy service takes occasional snapshots of designated local storage volumes. These snapshots occur before Windows Update installs new updates and when supported software installers run. You can also create snapshots manually—a sensible precaution before you make system-level changes.

System Restore snapshots take note of differences in the details of your system configuration—registry settings, driver files, third-party applications, and so on—allowing you to undo changes and roll back a system configuration to a time when it was known to work correctly.

CHAPTER 16

NOTE

In Windows 7, the volume snapshots created by System Restore also included a record of changes to data files on designated drives, allowing you to restore previous versions of those data files. In Windows 10, this capability has been moved into the File History feature, which we described in detail earlier in this chapter.

Note that System Restore monitors all files it considers system-related, which includes executable files and installers. If you download the latest version of a favorite utility and store it in your Downloads folder, it will be removed if you roll back to a System Restore checkpoint from before it was downloaded.

Inside OUT

What's in a restore point?

Restore points in Windows 10 include a full copy of the registry at the time of the snapshot as well as information about changes made to specific files on that volume since the previous snapshot was created. Historically, files are monitored if they include any of 250+ file-name extensions specifically designated for monitoring. This list (which cannot be modified) contains many file types that are clearly programs and system files, with extensions such as .exe, .dll, and .vbs. But it also includes other files you might not think of as system files, including .inf and .ini, and some that are truly head-scratchers, such as .d01 through .d05 and .d32. (Apparently .d06 through .d31 are unmonitored.) You can see the entire list at *https://bit.ly/monitored-extensions*. The information there is most useful for programmers and system administrators, but you might want to browse the extension list if you're curious why System Restore deleted a file.

To check the status of System Protection, start typing **System Protection** in the search box and follow the Create A Restore Point link to the System Protection tab of the System Properties dialog box in Control Panel. There you'll find a list of internal and external NTFS-formatted drives. (See Figure 16-19.) The value under Protection Settings indicates whether restore points are being created automatically for each drive.

Using the System Properties dialog box, you can enable or disable automatic monitoring for any local drive. By design, system protection is fully enabled for the system drive and is disabled for all other local drives.

You can also manually create a restore point at any time for all drives that have system protection enabled. Click the Create button at the bottom of the System Protection tab to open the Create A Restore Point dialog box shown in Figure 16-20. Enter a meaningful description.

(You can't leave the box blank, although you can tap the spacebar to leave that box effectively blank.) Then click Create to enter the descriptive text.

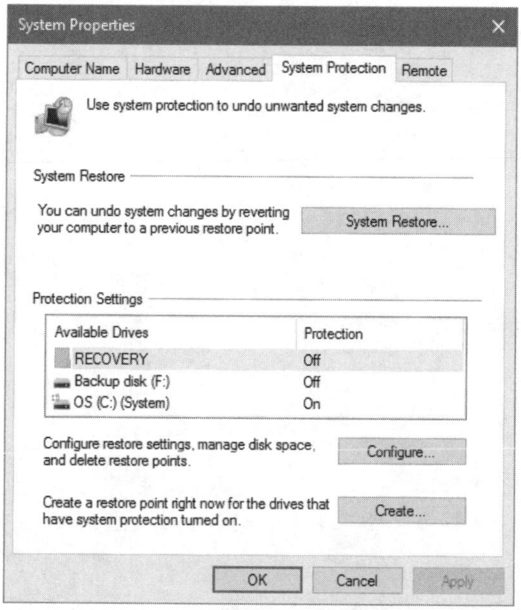

Figure 16-19 By default, System Restore monitors changes to the system drive. Select another drive and click Configure to enable System Protection for that drive.

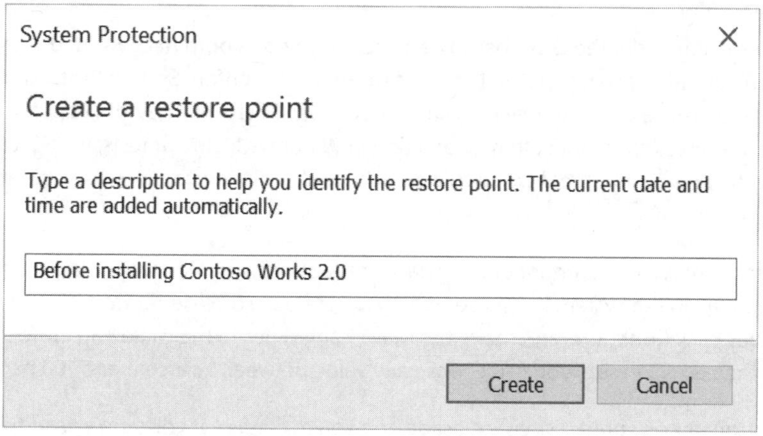

Figure 16-20 When you create a restore point manually, you're required to enter a description that will help you identify it later.

To turn system protection on or to adjust the amount of space it uses, select a drive from the Available Drives list and then click Configure. That opens the dialog box shown in Figure 16-21.

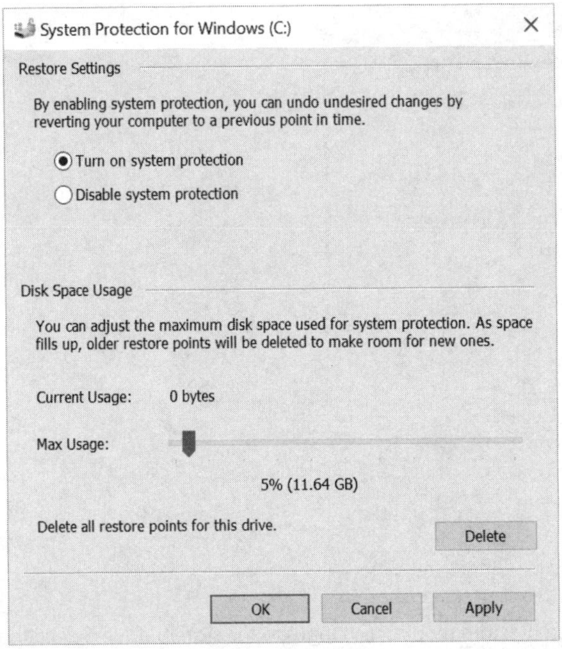

Figure 16-21   Use the Max Usage slider to adjust the amount of disk space used by System Restore snapshots.

The information under the Disk Space Usage heading shows both the current usage and the maximum amount of space that will be used for snapshots before System Protection begins deleting old restore points to make room for new ones. Microsoft has not yet published its rules for how it reserves space for system protection in Windows 10. In our tests, we typically see this value set to 5 percent of the disk, up to a maximum of 10 GB, on volumes that are larger than 64 GB.

To adjust the maximum amount of disk space available for volume snapshots, click the System Protection tab in the System Properties dialog box, select a drive letter from the list of available drives, click Configure, and move the Max Usage slider to the value you prefer. For drives greater than 64 GB in size, you can choose any value between 1 percent and 100 percent.

If you're concerned about disk space usage and you're confident you won't need to use any of your currently saved restore points, you can click the Delete button in the lower right corner under the Disk Space Usage heading to remove all existing restore points without changing other System Protection settings.

NOTE

The default location for System Restore data is *d*:\System Volume Information, where *d* is the letter of each drive. Each restore point is stored in its own subfolder, under a name that includes a unique 32-character alphanumeric identifier called a GUID. This location cannot be changed. On an NTFS drive, these files are not accessible to users, even those in the Administrators group; the default NTFS permissions grant access only to the System account, and there is no easy way to view these files or to take ownership of them (nor should you even consider doing so, because these data structures are not intended for use by anything other than a program working through tightly controlled application programming interfaces).

Rolling back to a previous restore point

After you configure System Protection, it runs silently and automatically, making as-needed snapshots of your system configuration. In this section, we explain how to make use of those snapshots.

The System Restore utility provides controlled access to snapshots created by the System Protection feature. It can't perform miracles—it won't bring a dead hard drive back to life, unfortunately—but it can be a lifesaver in any of the following situations:

- You install a program that conflicts with other software or drivers on your system. If uninstalling the program doesn't cure the problem, you can restore your system configuration to a point before you installed the program. That should remove any problematic files or registry settings that were left behind by the uninstaller.

- You install one or more updated drivers that cause performance or stability problems. Rather than using the Roll Back Driver command in Device Manager, use System Restore to replace the new, troublesome driver (or drivers) with those that were in place the last time you saved a restore point.

- Your system develops performance or stability problems for no apparent reason. This scenario is especially likely if you share a computer with other family members or coworkers who have administrator accounts and are in the habit of casually installing untested, incompatible software and drivers. If you know the system was working properly on a certain date, you can use a restore point from that date, undoing potentially harmful changes made since then and, if all goes well, returning your system to proper operation.

CAUTION

Don't count on System Restore to protect you from viruses, worms, Trojan horses, and other malware. Use Windows Defender or a reliable and up-to-date third-party antivirus program.

CHAPTER 16

The quickest way to get to System Restore is to type **rstrui** at a command prompt. You can also click System Restore on the System Protection tab of the System Properties dialog box to find this well-hidden feature.

If you're running under a standard user account, you'll need to enter an administrator's credentials in a UAC dialog box to continue.

When the System Restore wizard appears, it might recommend the most recent restore point. To see a complete list of available restore points, select Show More Restore Points and click Next. That displays a list of recent restore points, as shown in Figure 16-22.

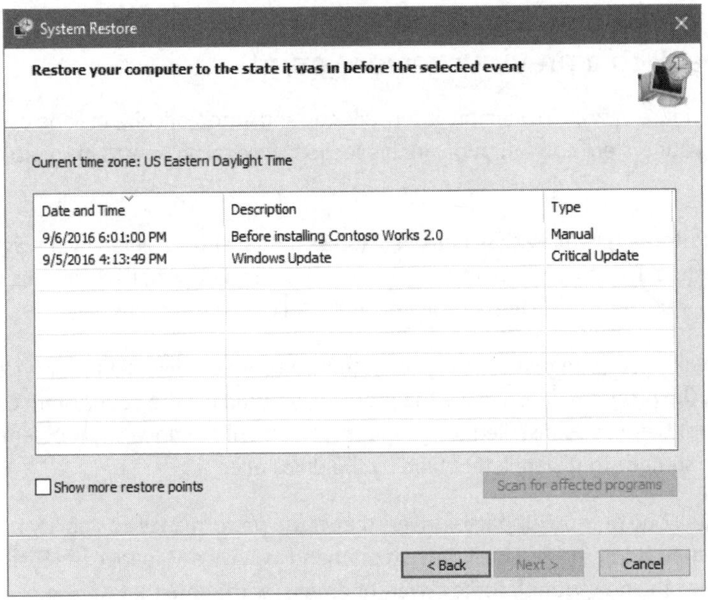

Figure 16-22 You must select the check box at the bottom of this dialog box to see more than the five most recent restore points.

If the restore point you're looking for is older than the oldest entry in the list, select Show More Restore Points to see the full list.

What impact will your choice of restore points have? To see a full list of programs and drivers that will be deleted or restored, select the restore point you're planning to use, and then click Scan For Affected Programs. That displays a dialog box like the one shown in Figure 16-23, highlighting every change you made since that restore point was created. (Note that this list does not warn you about any executable files that might be deleted from your Desktop, Downloads, or other folders.)

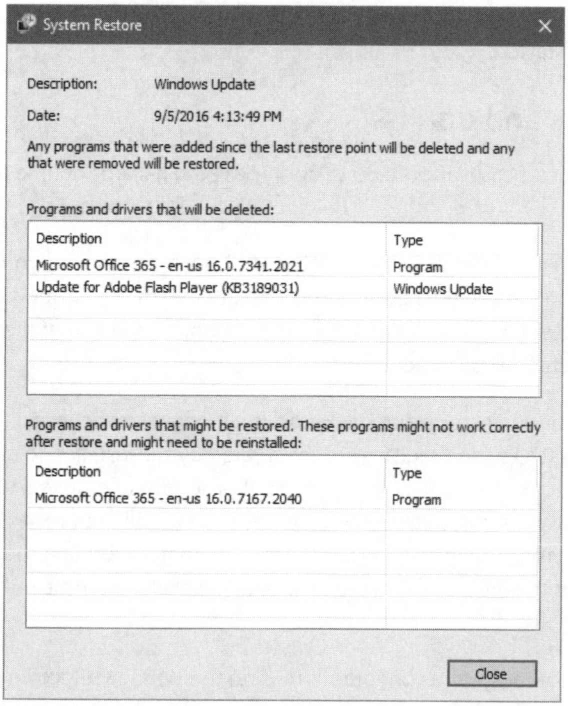

Figure 16-23 Look at this report before using System Restore to roll back to an earlier configuration so that you know what changes the operation will make.

After selecting a restore point, click Next to display a series of confirmation dialog boxes. After you successfully convince the system that, yes, you really want to do this, it creates a new restore point and then begins replacing system files and registry settings with those in the restore point you selected. As part of the process, your computer will restart and various messages will appear, all counseling patience and asking you not to interfere with the goings-on.

When System Restore reinstates a previously saved configuration using a restore point, your data files—documents, pictures, music files, and the like—are not tampered with in any way. (The only exception is if you or a program created or saved a file using file-name extensions from the list of monitored extensions, as described in the previous section.) Before System Restore begins the process of returning your system to a previous restore point, it creates a new restore point—making it possible for you to return to the present if this time machine doesn't meet your expectations.

When the process is complete, do some testing to see whether the restoration fixed the problem you were encountering. If it has not and you want to return the system to the state it was in before you restored it, retrace your steps to System Restore. At or near the top of the list of available restore points, you will find one labeled Undo: Restore Operation. Choose that one and you're back where you started.

System Restore do's and don'ts

You don't have to be a science-fiction aficionado to appreciate the hazards of time travel. Here are some to be aware of:

- If you create a new user account and then use System Restore to roll back your system configuration to a point before the new account was created, the new user will no longer be able to sign in, and you will receive no warning. (The good news is that the new user's unencrypted documents will be intact.)

- System Restore does not uninstall programs, although it does remove executable files, dynamic-link libraries (DLLs), and registry entries created by the installer. To avoid having orphaned program shortcuts and files, view the list of programs and drivers that will be affected when you return to the restore point you're about to roll back to. If you don't want the program anymore, uninstall it in the normal way before running the restore operation. If you want to continue using the program, reinstall it after the restore is complete.

- Any changes made to your system configuration using the Windows Recovery Environment are not monitored by System Protection. This can produce unintended consequences if you make major changes to system files and then roll back your system configuration with System Restore.

- Although you can restore your system to a previously saved restore point from the Windows Recovery Environment, you cannot create a new restore point from that location. As a result, you cannot undo a restore operation that you perform by starting from the Windows Recovery Environment. You should use System Restore in this mode only if you are unable to start Windows normally to perform a restore operation.

Troubleshooting

As they say, stuff happens. That might not be exactly the way you remember that quote, but it's certainly true whenever hardware and software are involved.

Although Microsoft Windows generally has become more stable and reliable over time, it will never be perfect. Apps hang (stop responding) or crash (shut down unexpectedly). Once in a while, a feature of Windows walks off the set without warning. And on rare occasions, the grim BSOD ("Blue Screen of Death," more formally known as a *Stop error* or *bugcheck*) arrives, bringing your whole system to a halt.

In a fully debugged, perfect world, such occurrences would never darken your computer screen. But you don't live there, and neither do we. So the prudent course is to prepare for the unexpected. That starts with enabling File History so that your documents are backed up at regular intervals and, if possible, creating periodic image backups. But it also entails learning to use the many tools Windows provides for diagnosing errors and recovering from problems. These tools are the subject of this chapter.

> ➤ For information about backing up with File History and creating image backups, see
> Chapter 16, "Backup, restore, and recovery."

Getting to know your troubleshooting toolkit

As any detective will tell you, solving a mystery requires evidence. If your mystery involves inexplicably slow performance or crashes, you have several places to look for clues.

Built-in troubleshooters

The most obvious first step on the road to resolving performance issues is the aptly named Troubleshooting section in the classic Control Panel. By default, it displays a list of the most commonly used troubleshooters included with Windows 10, as shown in Figure 17-1.

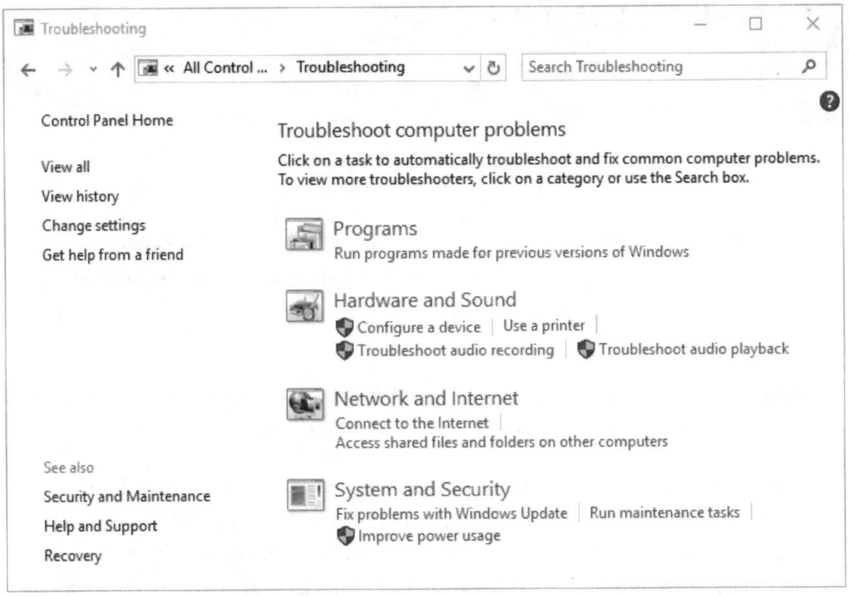

Figure 17-1 Each troubleshooter included with Windows 10 launches an interactive problem-solving tool that steps you through diagnoses of and resolutions to common problems.

Click the View All link on the left side of the Troubleshooting page to see an expanded list that includes modules for fixing more esoteric problems, such as issues with search and indexing or with the Background Intelligent Transfer Service.

There's nothing magical about any of these troubleshooters. Their purpose is to ensure that you check the most common causes of problems, including some that might seem obvious. (Is the network cable plugged in? Is the printer turned on?) Running a troubleshooter can result in easy fixes for some issues; more importantly, it establishes a baseline for further troubleshooting.

A troubleshooter might lead you through several steps and ask you to check settings or connections. At the end, it displays its results, which include a View Detailed Information link that leads to troubleshooting report similar to the one shown in Figure 17-2.

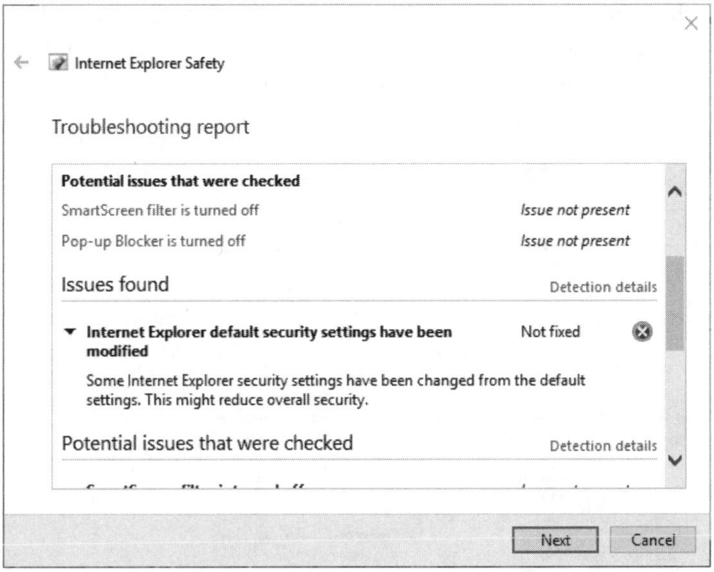

Figure 17-2 The troubleshooting report lists issues and indicates whether they were fixed. Click the Detection Details link to see more granular information about that item.

Windows Error Reporting

Often an early indication that something is amiss is an error message informing you that an application is "not responding"—as if you hadn't figured that out already. If the application doesn't come back to life, you kill the process with Task Manager and move on—ideally, without losing any data.

While all that's happening, the Windows Error Reporting (WER) service runs continuously in the background, keeping track of software and driver installations (successful and otherwise) as well as crashes, hangs, and other system events that indicate a possible problem with Windows. (In fact, although the service and programs that enable the feature are called Windows Error Reporting, the term you're more likely to see in Windows is *problem reporting*.) Microsoft provides this diagnostic information to the developers of the program that caused the error (including Microsoft developers when the issue occurs with a feature in Windows, Office, or another Microsoft program). The goal, of course, is to improve quality by identifying problems and delivering fixes through Windows Update.

In previous versions, Windows was downright chatty about reporting crashes, successful updates, and minor speed bumps. In Windows 10, most of these problem reports (including diagnostic reports sent after successful upgrades) are completely silent, but each report is logged. You can use the history of problem reports on a system to review events and to see whether any patterns demand additional troubleshooting.

To open the Problem Reports log, type **problem reports** in the search box and then click View All Problem Reports. Figure 17-3 shows a portion of the error history for a computer that was upgraded to the Windows 10 Anniversary Update, version 1607, in August 2016.

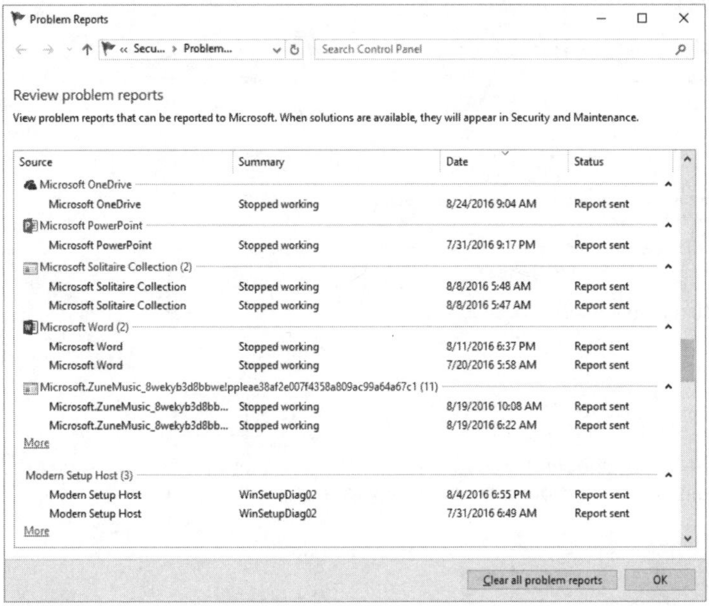

Figure 17-3 The list of saved problem reports displays the two most recent reports in each group.

If more than two reports for a given heading are available, a More link appears below the group. The number in parentheses to the right of the group heading tells you how many there are. In Figure 17-3, for example, you can see the system has recorded 11 problems with the Groove Music app, which goes by an unwieldy name that starts with Microsoft.ZuneMusic.

If the words *Solution Available* appear in the Status column for an item, right-click that item and then click View Solution. Note also that the shortcut menu includes commands to group the entries in the list of problem reports by source (which is the default view, shown in Figure 17-3), summary, date, or status—or you can choose Ungroup to see the entire, uncategorized list. With the list grouped or not, you can sort by any field by clicking the field's column heading.

You can see a more detailed report about any event in this log by double-clicking the event. (See Figure 17-4.) The Description field usually is written clearly enough to provide potentially useful information. The rest of the details might or might not be meaningful to you, but they could be helpful to a support technician. Some reports include additional details sent in a text file you can inspect for yourself.

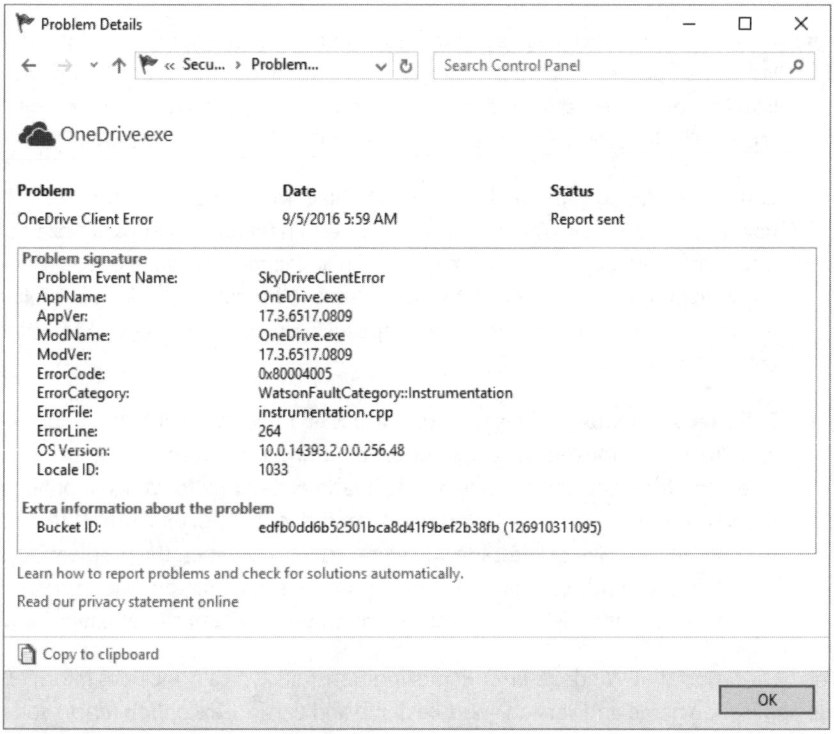

Figure 17-4 Double-clicking an entry in the problem reports list displays details about the problem that might be useful to a support technician.

By default, Windows 10 configures your system so that it sends a generous amount of diagnostic and feedback information, including error reports that could inadvertently contain personal information. If you're concerned about data use or privacy, you can dial back the amount of diagnostic information by using the Feedback & Diagnostics page under the Privacy heading in Settings. We describe these and other privacy settings in more detail in "Configuring privacy options," in Chapter 6, "Managing user accounts, passwords, and credentials."

The Feedback Frequency setting at the top of this page controls how often Microsoft asks you about your use of features. If you prefer to be left alone, set this to Never.

By selecting preferences under the second heading, Diagnostic And Usage Data, you specify how much diagnostic information your Windows 10 device sends to Microsoft servers as part

CHAPTER 17

of its normal operation. Much of that information is from problem reports, which rarely mean much by themselves but can be tremendously important as part of a larger data set to pinpoint the cause of problems. There are three available settings:

- **Basic.** This level includes data that is fundamental to the operation of Windows and Windows Update. It includes information about the capabilities of your device, what is installed, and whether Windows is operating correctly (which includes sending basic error reports to Microsoft). No personally identifiable information is included.

- **Enhanced.** Along with the data sent with the Basic setting, this setting adds data about how you use Windows (how often you use certain features or apps, for example) and collects enhanced diagnostic information, such as the memory state of your device when a system or app crash occurs. Information sent to Microsoft also includes reliability data for devices, the operating system, and apps. This is the default setting for Windows 10 Enterprise edition.

- **Full (Recommended).** This setting, which is enabled by default on Windows 10 Home and Pro installations, includes the full set of information from the Basic and Enhanced levels and turns on advanced diagnostic features that provide much more detailed error reports. These reports might include system files or memory snapshots that could include the contents of a file or message you were working on when the problem occurred. If a report inadvertently contains personal or sensitive information, Microsoft's privacy policy says the information will not be used to identify, contact, or target advertising to you.

The basic report that Windows Error Reporting transmits typically includes information such as the application name and version, module name and version, exception (error) code, and offset. Hardware reports include Plug and Play IDs, driver versions, and other system details. The likelihood that any of these items will convey personally identifiable information is essentially nil. The process does transmit your IP address to a Microsoft server, but Microsoft's privacy statement asserts that the IP address is used only to generate aggregate statistics and will not be used to identify you.

In work environments, your network administrators will almost certainly disable the sending of advanced error reports that might inadvertently disclose confidential information.

In addition to this automated feedback, Windows 10 also includes a Feedback app that anyone can use to send problem reports and suggestions to Microsoft. This app was previously available only to registered members of the Windows Insider program. From the app, you can search for existing feedback, as we've done in Figure 17-5. You can filter and sort the list of search results to see if your specific issue has already been reported.

CHAPTER 17

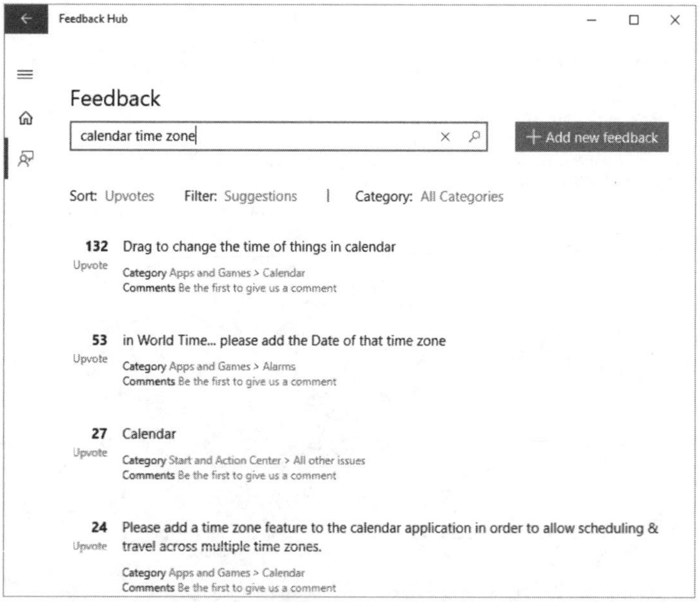

Figure 17-5 Use the Feedback Hub app to find problem reports and suggestions from others or add your own comments in Microsoft's virtual suggestion box.

If you find an existing feedback entry that describes your issue, you can add a comment and an upvote. If you discover a new issue, feel free to create your own feedback item by clicking Add New Feedback. In the spirit of setting expectations, we are compelled to add that items you submit here are not the same as support tickets. You won't get personal support from a Microsoft engineer or support tech, although your feedback will be considered, especially if the number of upvotes hits double or triple digits.

Reliability Monitor

Windows 10 keeps track of a wide range of system events. For a day-by-day inventory of these events, type **reliability** in the search box and then click the top result, View Reliability History. That opens Reliability Monitor, shown in Figure 17-6.

Each column in the graphical display represents events of a particular day (or week, if you click that option in the upper left corner). Each red X along the first three lines below the graph (the various "Failures" lines) indicates a day on which problems occurred. The "Warnings" line describes minor problems unrelated to system reliability, such as a program whose installation process didn't complete properly. The last line below the graph—the line marked Information— identifies days on which an app or an update was installed or removed. You can see the details about the events of any day by clicking on the graph for that day. Reliability Monitor retains its system stability records for one year, giving you plenty of history to review.

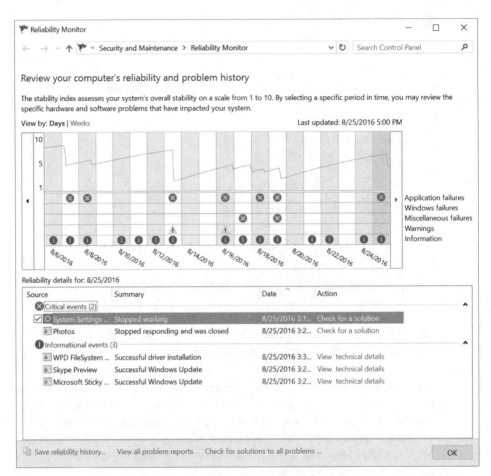

Figure 17-6 Reliability Monitor rates your system's stability on a scale of 1 (wear a crash helmet) through 10 (smooth sailing). This PC has had a rough couple of weeks.

This history is most useful when you begin experiencing a new problem and are trying to track down its cause. Examine the critical events for the period when the problem began, and see whether they correspond with an informational item, such as a program installation. The alignment of these events could be mere coincidence, but it could also represent the first appearance of a long-term problem. Conjunctions of this sort are worth examining. If you think a new software application has destabilized your system, you can try uninstalling it.

Double-clicking any item exposes its contents, which are filled with technical details that are potentially useful, confusing, or both:

Although the various signatures and details for each such incident by themselves are probably just baffling, they're much more useful in the aggregate. Armed with a collection of similar reports, an engineer can pin down the cause of a problem and deliver a bug fix. If a previously common error suddenly stops appearing in the logs, chances are it was resolved with an update.

Note also that you can click the link in the Action column to take additional steps, such as searching for a solution or viewing the technical details of a particular event.

Event Viewer

Technically, we probably should have included Event Viewer (Eventvwr.msc) in the previous section. It is, after all, just another troubleshooting tool. But we think that this, the most powerful of all the diagnostic tools in Windows 10, deserves its own section in this chapter.

In Windows, an *event* is any occurrence that is potentially noteworthy—to you, to other users, to the operating system, or to an application. Events are recorded by the Windows Event Log service, and their history is preserved in one of several log files, including Application, Security, Setup, System, and Forwarded Events. You can use Event Viewer, a Microsoft Management Console (MMC) snap-in supplied with Windows, to review and archive these event logs, as well as other logs created by the installation of certain applications and services.

CHAPTER 17

You can examine the history of errors on your system by creating a filtered view of the Application log in Event Viewer. Why would you want to do this? The most likely reasons are to troubleshoot problems that have occurred, to keep an eye on your system to forestall problems, and to watch out for security breaches. If a device has failed, a disk has filled close to capacity, a program has crashed repeatedly, or some other critical difficulty has arisen, the information recorded in the event logs can help you—or a technical support specialist—figure out what's wrong and what corrective steps are required.

To start Event Viewer, find it by searching for **event** and then click Event Viewer or View Event Logs in the search results. (Alternatively, enter **eventvwr.msc** or **eventvwr.exe** in the Run box or at a command prompt.)

> ### NOTE
>
> **Event Viewer requires administrator privileges for full functionality. If you start Event Viewer while signed in as a standard user, it starts without requesting elevation. However, the Security log is unavailable, along with some other features. To get access to all logs, right-click and choose Run As Administrator.**

Figure 17-7 offers an overview of Event Viewer.

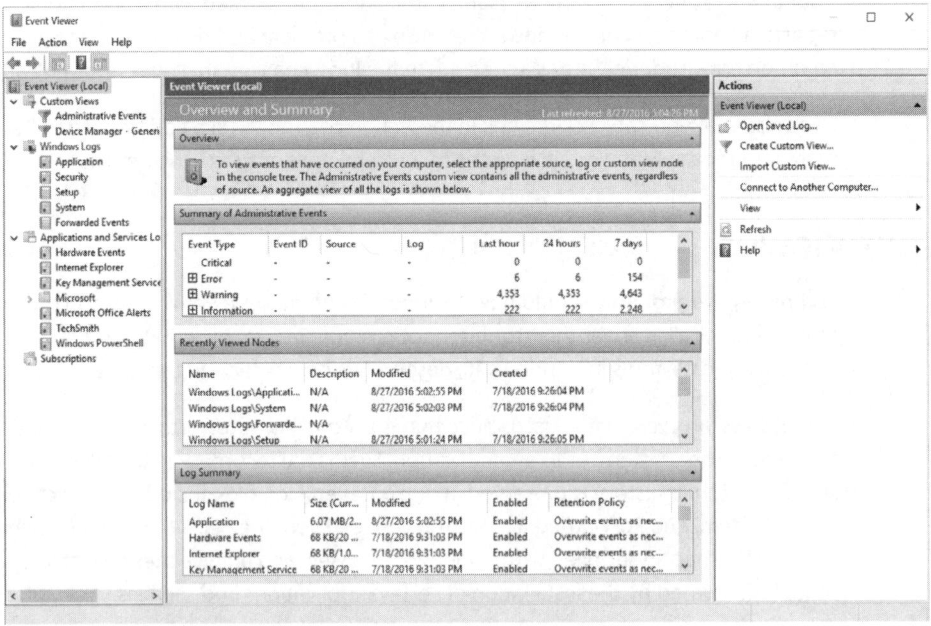

Figure 17-7 Event Viewer's console tree (left) lists available logs and views; the details pane (center) displays information from the selected log or view; and the Actions pane (right) provides a menu of tasks relevant to the current selection.

When you select the top-level folder in Event Viewer's console tree, the details pane displays summary information, as shown in Figure 17-7. With this view, you can see at a glance whether any significant events that might require your attention have occurred in the past hour, day, or week. You can expand each category to see the sources of events of that event type. Seeing a count of events of various types in various time periods is interesting—but not particularly useful in and of itself. But if, for example, you see an unusually large number of recent errors from a particular source, you might want to see the full list to determine whether a particular error needs closer examination. To do that, you can right-click an event type or an event source under Summary Of Administrative Events, and then click View All Instances Of This Event, as shown here:

The resulting filtered list of events is drawn from multiple log files, sparing you from having to search in multiple places. Armed with this information, you can quickly scroll through and examine the details of each one, perhaps identifying a pattern or a common factor that will help you find the cause and, eventually, the cure for whatever is causing the event.

Types of events

As a glance at the console tree confirms, events are recorded in one of several logs. Logs are organized in the console tree in folders, and you can expand or collapse the folder tree using the customary outline controls. The following default logs are visible under the Windows Logs heading:

- **Application.** Application events are generated by applications, including programs you install, programs that are preinstalled with Windows, apps from the Windows Store, and operating system services. Program developers decide which events to record in the Application log and which to record in a program-specific log under Applications And Services Logs.

- **Security.** Security events include sign-in attempts (successful and failed) and attempts to use secured resources, such as an attempt to create, modify, or delete a file.

- **Setup.** Setup events are generated by application installations.

- **System.** System events are generated by Windows itself and by installed features, such as device drivers. If a driver fails to load when you start a Windows session, for example, that event is recorded in the System log.

- **Forwarded Events.** The Forwarded Events log contains events gathered from other computers.

Under the Applications And Services Logs heading, you'll find logs for individual applications and services. The difference between this heading and the Windows Logs heading is that logs under Applications And Services record events related only to a particular program or feature, whereas the logs that appear under Windows Logs generally record events that are systemwide.

If you expand the Microsoft entry under Applications And Services Logs, you'll find a Windows subfolder, which in turn contains a folder for each of hundreds of features that are part of Windows 10. Each of these folders contains one or more logs.

Viewing logs and events

When you select a log or a custom view from the console tree, the details pane shows a list of associated events, sorted (by default) in reverse chronological order, with each event occupying a single line. A preview pane below the list displays the contents of the saved event record. Figure 17-8 shows one such listing from the System log.

NOTE
The Windows Event Log service records the date and time each event occurred in coordinated universal time (UTC), and Event Viewer translates those time values into dates and times appropriate for your own time zone.

Events in most log files are classified by severity, with one of three entries in the Level field: Error, Warning, or Information. *Error* events represent possible loss of data or functionality. Examples of errors include events related to a malfunctioning network adapter and loss of functionality caused by a device or service that doesn't load at startup. *Warning* events represent less significant or less immediate problems than error events. Examples of warning events include a nearly full disk, a timeout by the network redirector, and data errors on local storage. Other events that Windows logs are identified as *Information* events.

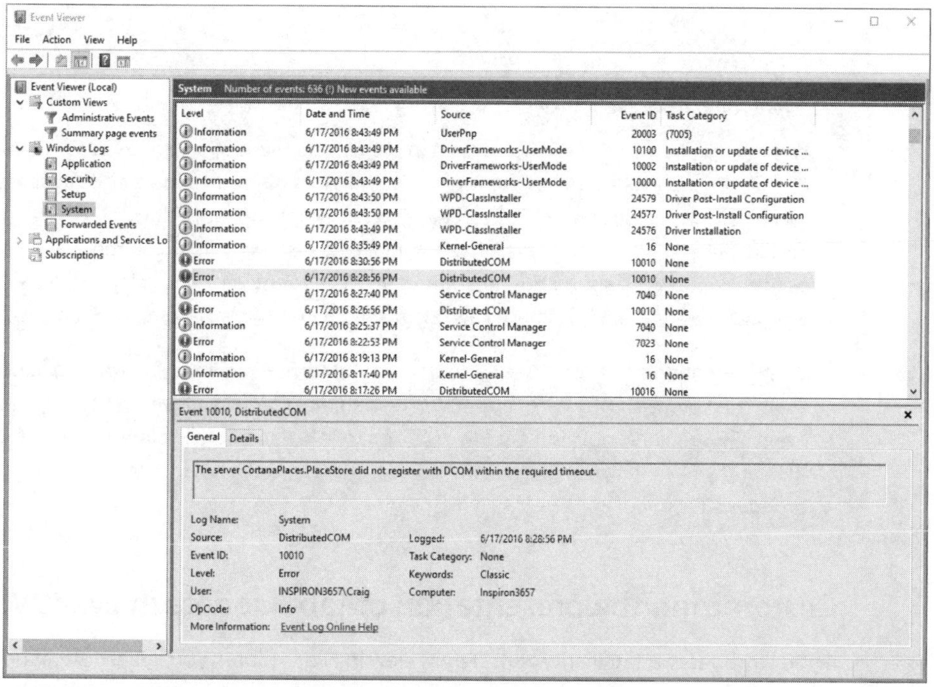

Figure 17-8 All the details you need for an individual event are visible in this preview pane. Double-click an event to see those same details in a separate window.

The Security log file uses two different icons to classify events: A key icon identifies Audit Success events, and a lock icon identifies Audit Failure events. Both types of events are classified as Information-level events; "Audit Success" and "Audit Failure" are stored in the Keywords field of the Security log file.

The preview pane shows information about the currently selected event. (Drag the split bar between the list and preview pane up to make the preview pane larger so that you can see more details, or double-click the event to open it in a separate dialog box that includes Next and Previous buttons and an option to copy the event to the Clipboard.)

The information you find in Event Viewer is evidence of things that happened in the past. Like any good detective, you have the task of using those clues to help identify possible issues. One hidden helper, located near the bottom of the Event Properties dialog box, is a link to more information online. Clicking this link opens a webpage that might provide more specific and detailed information about this particular combination of event source and event ID, including further action you might want to take in response to the event.

Inside OUT

Export data from Event Viewer

You can save selected events, all events in the current view, or all events in a particular log to a file for archival purposes, for further analysis in a different program, or to share with a technical support specialist. (To select events for exporting, hold down the Ctrl key and click each event you want to include.) The command to export events is on the Action menu, but the command name varies depending on the current view and selection: Save Selected Events, Save Filtered Log File As, Save Events In Custom View As, or Save Events As.

Saving event data in Event Viewer's native (.evtx) format creates a file you can view only in Event Viewer (or a third-party application capable of reading native event logs). However, Event Viewer can export log data to XML and to tab-delimited or comma-delimited text files, and you can import these easily into database, spreadsheet, or even word-processing programs.

Customizing the presentation of tabular data in Event Viewer

If you have passing familiarity with Details view in File Explorer, you'll feel right at home with the many tabular reports in Event Viewer. You can change a column's width by dragging its heading left or right. You can sort on any column by clicking its heading; click a second time to reverse the sort order. Right-click a column heading and choose Add/Remove Columns to make more or fewer columns appear. As you'll see, the choices are many:

As with files and folders in File Explorer, you also have the option to group events in Event Viewer. To do that, right-click the column heading by which you want to group and then click Group Events By This Column. Here, for example, we grouped by Source.

Filtering the log display

As you can see from a cursory look at your System log, events can pile up quickly, obscuring those generated by a particular source or those that occurred at a particular date and time. Sorting and grouping can help you to find that needle in a haystack, but to get the hay out of the way altogether, use filtering. With filtering, you can select events based on multiple criteria; all other events are hidden from view, making it much easier to focus on the items you currently care about.

To filter the currently displayed log or custom view, click Filter Current Log or Filter Current Custom View in the Action pane on the right. A dialog box like the one shown in Figure 17-9 appears. To fully appreciate the flexibility of filtering, click the arrow by each filter. You can, for example, filter events from the past hour, 12 hours, day, week, month, or any custom time period you specify. In the Event Sources, Task Category, and Keywords boxes, you can type text to filter on (separating multiple items with commas), but you'll probably find it easier to click the arrow and then click each item you want to include in your filtered view. In the Includes/Excludes Event IDs box, you can enter multiple ID numbers and number ranges, separated by commas; to exclude particular event IDs, precede their number with a minus sign.

Click OK to see the filtered list. If you think you'll use the same filter criteria again, click Save Filter To Custom View in the Action pane on the right. To restore the unfiltered list, in the Event Viewer window, click Clear Filter.

CHAPTER 17

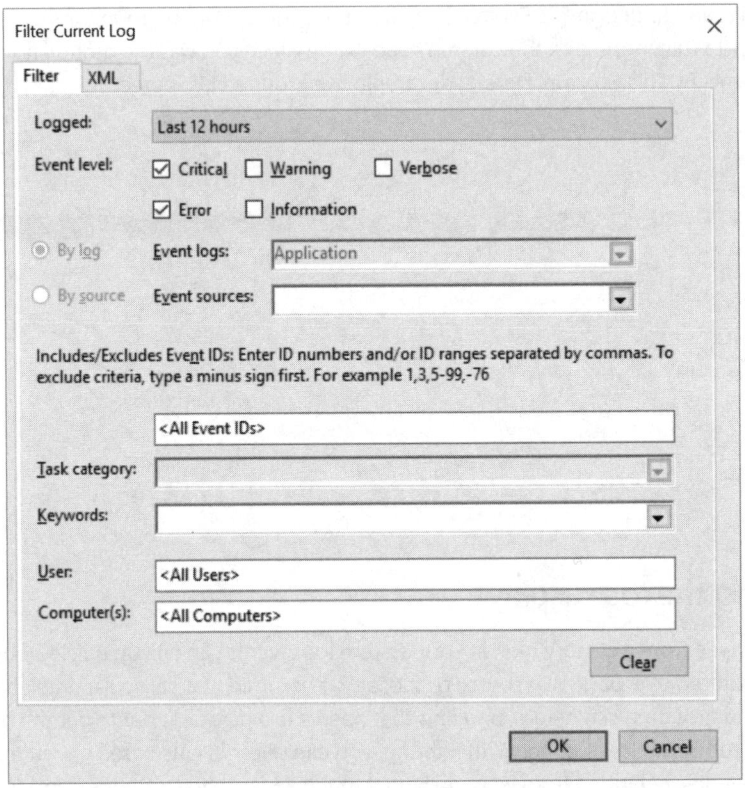

Figure 17-9 If you don't select any Event Level check boxes, Event Viewer includes all levels in the filtered results. Similarly, any other field you leave blank includes all events without regard to the value of that property.

NOTE

Event Viewer also includes an anemic search capability, which you access by clicking Action, Find. You can perform more precise searches by filtering.

Working with event logs on a remote computer

Event Viewer, like many other Microsoft Management Console applications, gives the option of viewing logs on a remote computer as well as your local computer. You might find this useful if you run a help desk and need to troubleshoot a remote user's system. To point Event Viewer to another computer, select the top heading in the outline tree, click Action, and then click Connect To Another Computer. In the Select Computer box, type the IP address or name of the computer you want to connect to.

To manage logs on a remote computer, you need to enable the Remote Event Log Management exception in the Windows Firewall settings on the remote computer. For other details about using Event Viewer remotely, see *https://technet.microsoft.com/library/cc766438.aspx*.

Dealing with Stop errors

If Windows has ever suddenly shut down, you've probably experienced that sinking feeling in the pit of your stomach. When Windows 10 encounters a serious problem that makes it impossible for the operating system to continue running, it does the only thing it can do, just as every one of its predecessors has done in the same circumstances. It shuts down immediately and displays an ominous text message whose technical details begin with the word *STOP*. Because a Stop error typically appears in white letters on a blue background, this type of message is often referred to as a *blue-screen error* or the *Blue Screen of Death (BSOD)*. When a Stop error appears, it means there is a serious problem that demands your immediate attention.

Windows 10 collects and saves a variety of information in logs and dump files, which a support engineer or developer armed with debugging tools can use to identify the cause of Stop errors. You don't have to be a developer to use these tools, which are available to anyone via download from *https://bit.ly/windows-debugging-tools*. (Don't worry; you can't break anything by simply inspecting a .dmp file.) If you know where to look, however, you can learn a lot from these error messages alone, and in many cases you can recover completely by using standard troubleshooting techniques.

Customizing how Windows handles Stop errors

When Windows encounters a serious error that forces it to stop running, it displays a Stop message and then writes debugging information to the page file. When the computer restarts, this information is saved as a crash dump file, which can be used to debug the specific cause of the error.

You can customize two crucial aspects of this process by defining the size of the crash dump files and specifying whether you want Windows to restart automatically after a Stop message appears. By default, Windows automatically restarts after a Stop message and creates a crash dump file optimized for automatic analysis. That's the preferred strategy in response to random, isolated Stop errors. But if you're experiencing chronic Stop errors, you might have more troubleshooting success by changing these settings to collect a more detailed dump file and to stop after a crash.

To make this change, type **advanced** in the search box and then click View Advanced System Settings in the results list. (Or, in the Run or search box, type the undocumented command **systempropertiesadvanced** and press Enter.)

On the Advanced tab of the System Properties dialog box, under Startup And Recovery, click Settings. Adjust the settings under the System Failure heading, as shown in Figure 17-10.

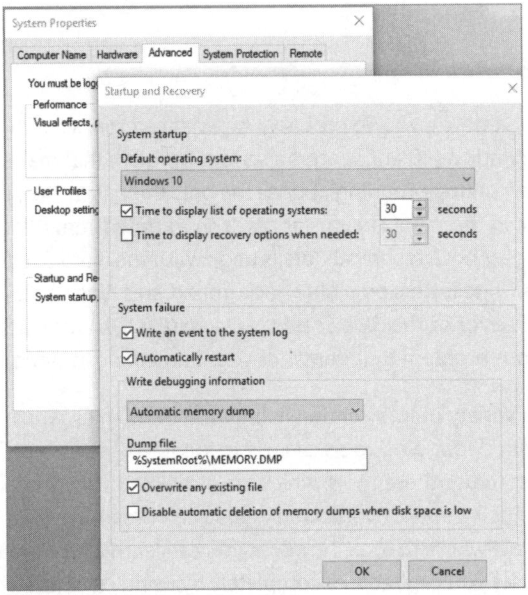

Figure 17-10 By default, Windows keeps a kernel memory dump and restarts automatically after a Stop error. You can pick a larger or smaller dump file here.

If you want Windows to pause at the Stop error message page, clear the Automatically Restart check box and click OK.

From the same dialog box, you can also define the settings for crash dump files. By default, Windows sets this value to Automatic Memory Dump, which saves a kernel memory dump after a crash. This option includes memory allocated to kernel-mode drivers and programs, which are most likely to cause Stop errors. Because this file does not include unallocated memory or memory allocated to user-mode programs, it usually will be smaller in size than the amount of RAM on your system. The exact size varies, but in general you can expect the file to be no larger than one-third the size of installed physical RAM, and much less than that on a system with 16 GB of RAM or more. The crash files are stored in %SystemRoot% using the file name Memory.dmp. (If your system crashes multiple times, each new dump file replaces the previous file.)

If disk space is limited or you're planning to send the crash dump file to a support technician, you might want to consider setting the system to store a small memory dump (commonly called a *mini dump*). A small memory dump contains just a fraction of the information in a kernel memory dump, but it's often enough to determine the cause of a problem.

What's in a Stop error

The exact text of a Stop error varies according to what caused the error. But the format is predictable. Don't bother copying down the error code from the blue screen itself. Instead, look through Event Viewer for an event with the source BugCheck, as shown in the example in Figure 17-11.

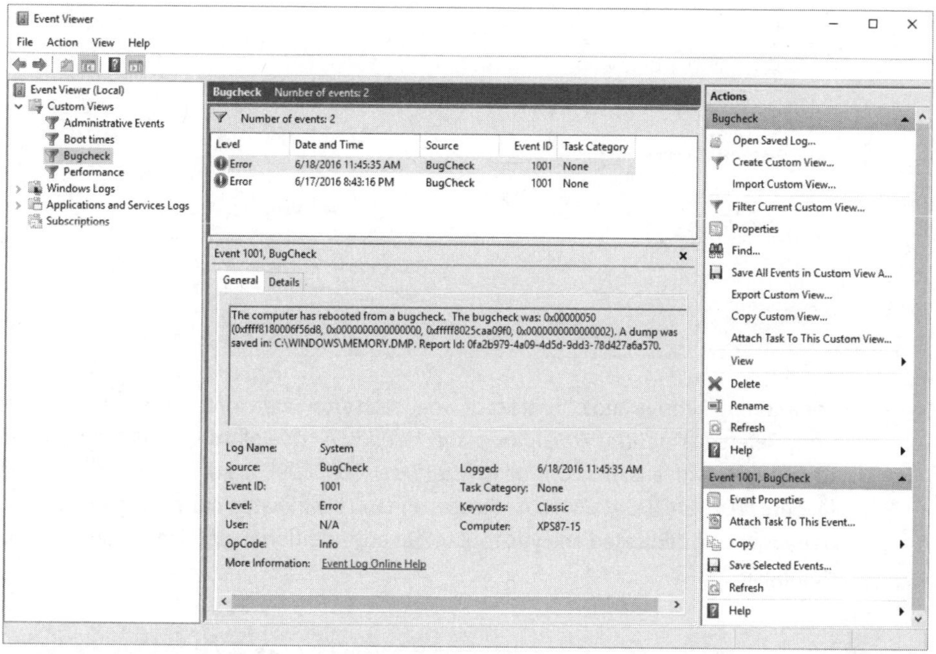

Figure 17-11 Decoding the information in a Stop error can help you find the underlying problem and fix it. Start with the error code—0x00000050, in this example.

You can gather important details from the bugcheck information, which consists of the error number (in hexadecimal notation, as indicated by the *0x* at the beginning of the code) and up to four parameters that are specific to the error type.

Windows 10 also displays the information in Reliability Monitor, under the heading Critical Events. Select the day on which the error occurred, and double-click the "Shut down unexpectedly" entry for an event with Windows as the source. That displays the bugcheck information in a slightly more readable format than in Event Viewer, as shown next, even using the term

BlueScreen as the Problem Event Name. (For more information, see "Reliability Monitor," earlier in this chapter.)

For a comprehensive and official list of what each error code means, see the MSDN "Bug Check Code Reference" at *https://bit.ly/bug-check-codes*. A code of 0x00000144, for example, points to problems with a USB 3 controller, whereas 0x0000009F is a driver power state failure. (Our favorite is 0xDEADDEAD, which indicates a manually initiated crash.) In general, you need a debugger or a dedicated analytic tool to get any additional useful information from a memory dump file.

Inside OUT

Create your own Stop error

If for any reason—curiosity, a desire to test debugging procedures, or whatever—you want to generate a Stop error on demand, Windows 10 will accommodate you. As outlined at *https://bit.ly/force-Stop*, the steps involve making a small registry edit and then pressing a multikeystroke sequence on your USB or PS/2 keyboard.

Inside OUT

Troubleshoot Stop errors with DaRT

Microsoft Windows Volume Licensing customers who have purchased a Software Assurance subscription have access to a powerful Crash Analyzer tool, which is included with the Microsoft Diagnostics and Recovery Toolset, otherwise known as DaRT. Crash Analyzer can examine the memory dump file created by a Stop error and, usually, pinpoint the cause of the problem. For details about DaRT, see *https://technet.microsoft.com/itpro/mdop/dart-v10*.

Isolating the cause of a Stop error

If you experience a Stop error, don't panic. Instead, run through the following troubleshooting checklist to isolate the problem and find a solution:

- **Don't forget to rule out hardware problems.** In many cases, software is the victim and not the cause of blue-screen errors. Common hardware failures such as a damaged hard disk or a corrupted solid state disk (SSD), defective physical RAM, an overheated CPU chip, or even a bad cable can result in Stop errors. If the errors seem to happen at random and the message details vary each time, there's a good chance you're experiencing hardware problems.

- **Check your memory.** Windows 10 includes a memory diagnostic tool you can use if you suspect a faulty or failing memory chip. To run this diagnostic procedure, type **memory** in the search box and click Windows Memory Diagnostic in the search results. This tool, shown here, requires a restart to run its full suite of tests, which you can perform immediately or defer until your next restart.

- **Look for a driver name in the error details.** If the error message identifies a specific file name and you can trace that file to a driver for a specific hardware device, you might be able to solve the problem by disabling, removing, or rolling back that driver to an earlier version. The most likely offenders are network interface cards, video adapters, and disk controllers. For more details about managing driver files, see "Updating and uninstalling drivers" in Chapter 13, "Hardware."

- **Ask yourself, "What's new?"** Be suspicious of newly installed hardware and software. If you added a device recently, remove it temporarily and see whether the problem goes away. Take an especially close look at software in the categories that install services or file-system filter drivers; these hook into the core operating system files that manage the file system to perform tasks such as scanning for viruses. This category includes backup programs, multimedia applications, antivirus software, and DVD-burning utilities. You might need to permanently uninstall or update the program to resolve the problem.

- **Search Microsoft Support.** Make a note of the error code and all parameters. Search Microsoft Support using both the full and short formats. For instance, if you're experiencing a KMODE_EXCEPTION_NOT_HANDLED error, use 0x1E and 0x0000001E as your search keywords.

- **Check your system BIOS or firmware.** Is an update available from the manufacturer of the system or motherboard? Check the BIOS or firmware documentation carefully; resetting all BIOS options to their defaults can sometimes resolve an issue caused by overtweaking.

- **Are you low on system resources?** Stop errors are sometimes the result of a critical shortage of RAM or disk space. If you can start in Safe Mode, check the amount of physical RAM installed and look at the system and boot drives to see how much free disk space is available.

- **Is a crucial system file damaged?** To reinstall a driver, restart your computer in Safe Mode. (See the following section.) If your system starts in Safe Mode but not normally, you very likely have a problem driver. Try running Device Manager in Safe Mode and uninstalling the most likely suspect. Or run System Restore in Safe Mode. If restoring to a particular day cures the problem, use Reliability Monitor to determine what changes occurred on or shortly after that day.

CHAPTER 17

Troubleshooting in Safe Mode

In earlier times, holding down the F8 key while restarting gave you the opportunity to start your system in Safe Mode, with only core drivers and services activated. On modern hardware, with UEFI firmware, that's no longer possible. Safe Mode is still available, but you have to work a little harder to get there.

If you can start Windows and get to the sign-in screen, you can then click the Power button in the lower right corner of that screen. Clicking Restart while holding down Shift takes you to the Windows Recovery Environment, where you can take various actions, including restoring Windows from an image backup (if one is available), running System Restore to revert to a saved Restore Point, and resetting your PC.

➤ **For information about creating and using an image backup, using System Restore, and resetting your PC, see Chapter 16.**

When you first arrive in the Windows Recovery Environment, the following menu appears:

To get to Safe Mode, click Troubleshoot in this menu, and then click Advanced Options. On the Advanced Options menu that appears, click Startup Settings, and then click Restart. You will then see the Startup Settings menu, shown in Figure 17-12.

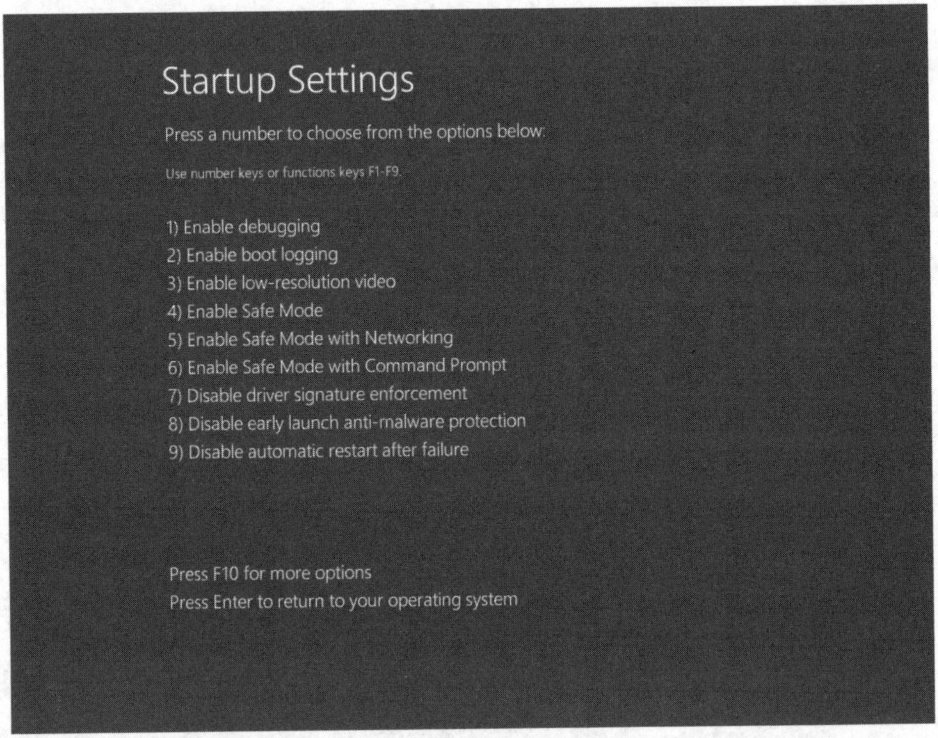

Startup Settings

Press a number to choose from the options below:

Use number keys or functions keys F1-F9.

1) Enable debugging
2) Enable boot logging
3) Enable low-resolution video
4) Enable Safe Mode
5) Enable Safe Mode with Networking
6) Enable Safe Mode with Command Prompt
7) Disable driver signature enforcement
8) Disable early launch anti-malware protection
9) Disable automatic restart after failure

Press F10 for more options
Press Enter to return to your operating system

Figure 17-12 Use the Startup Settings menu to boot into Safe Mode to remove a troublesome program or driver that is preventing you from signing in normally.

In Safe Mode, you can access certain essential configuration tools, including Device Manager, System Restore, and Registry Editor. If Windows appears to work properly in Safe Mode, you can safely assume there's no problem with the basic services. Use Device Manager, Driver Verifier, and Event Viewer to try to figure out where the trouble lies. If you suspect that a newly installed device or program is the cause of the problem, you can remove the offending software while you're running in Safe Mode. Use Device Manager to uninstall or roll back a hardware driver; use Control Panel to remove a desktop program or utility. Then try restarting the system normally to see whether your changes have resolved the problem.

If you need access to network connections, choose the Safe Mode With Networking option, which loads the base set of Safe Mode files and adds drivers and services required to start Windows networking.

The third Safe Mode option, Safe Mode With Command Prompt, loads the same stripped-down set of services as Safe Mode, but it uses the Windows command interpreter (Cmd.exe) as a shell instead of the graphical Windows Explorer (Explorer.exe, which also serves as the host for File Explorer). This option is unnecessary unless you're having a problem with the Windows graphical interface. The default Safe Mode also provides access to the command line. (Press Windows key+R, and then type **cmd.exe** in the Run dialog box.)

The six additional choices on the Startup Settings menu are of use in specialized circumstances:

- **Enable Boot Logging.** With this option enabled, Windows creates a log file that lists the names and status of all drivers loaded into memory. To view the contents of this file, look for Ntbtlog.txt in the %SystemRoot% folder. If your system is hanging because of a faulty driver, the last entry in this log file might identify the culprit.

- **Enable Low-Resolution Video.** This option starts the computer in 640-by-480 resolution using the current video driver. Use this option to recover from video problems that are caused not by a faulty driver but by incorrect settings, such as an improper resolution or refresh rate.

- **Disable Driver Signature Enforcement.** Use this option if Windows is refusing to start because you installed an unsigned user-mode driver. Windows will start normally, not in Safe Mode. (Note that you cannot disable the requirement for signed kernel-mode drivers.)

- **Disable Early Launch Antimalware Protection.** This is one of the core security measures of Windows 10 on a UEFI-equipped machine. Unless you're a security researcher or a driver developer, we can't think of any reason to disable this important security check.

- **Disable Automatic Restart After Failure.** Use this option if you're getting Stop errors (blue-screen crashes) and you want the opportunity to see the crash details on the Stop error screen instead of simply pausing there before restarting.

CHAPTER 17

Connecting to another computer with Quick Assist

With Quick Assist, an inconspicuous new tool introduced with the Anniversary Update to Windows 10, you can connect to another computer to give or receive assistance. If you are the helper, you can see the other computer's screen on your system, run diagnostic tools such as Task Manager, edit the remote system's registry, and even use a stylus to annotate the remote display. With roles reversed, you can let another user troubleshoot problems on your own system and help you find your way out of difficulty.

The technology behind Quick Assist is not new. In the guise of Windows Remote Assistance, it was present in versions of Windows dating back to Windows XP and Windows Server 2003. But earlier incarnations were complex and difficult to use. With Quick Assist, Windows 10 provides a simpler if less ambitious tool, one that a novice in need of help can use with ease.

Two ground rules apply: The computer giving assistance must be able to sign in with a Microsoft account (Quick Assist will prompt for one if the user is signed in using a local account), and both systems have to be running Windows 10, version 1607 or later.

The simplest way to run Quick Assist is to start typing **quick** in the Search box. The program should quickly appear at the top of the search results. Both parties run the program in this manner, and both see the following:

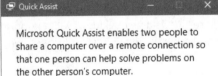

The user needing help clicks Get Assistance; the helper clicks Give Assistance. The helper is then given a six-digit security code:

The user to be assisted sees the following:

CHAPTER 17

If you're the helper, you have 10 minutes to communicate the security code to your friend or colleague. You can use the Send Email link to do this, but it's probably simpler to use the phone. The two of you are likely to want to be in touch via phone in any case.

When the code has been delivered and entered, the user to be helped must give permission to make his system visible:

With permission granted, the helper sees the other system on his or her own display. A toolbar appears as well, at the top of the helper's screen:

From left to right, the buttons are as follows:

- Annotate opens a second toolbar with pen tools. The helper can use stylus or mouse to make freehand annotations on the other screen. These are erased at the end of the session.

- To accommodate systems of differing resolutions, the remote system is sized to fit the helper system. The Actual Size button switches from fitted to actual.

- The Restart button restarts the remote system. The connection between the two systems is reinstated after the remote system logs back on; no additional exchange of security code is required.

- The Task Manager button lets you display that invaluable utility on the remote system. (Pressing Ctrl+Shift+Esc launches the helper's own Task Manager, not that of the remote computer.)

- The Reconnect button is there to help you reestablish connection in the event the connection is broken.

- The Pause button, which changes to Resume when used, gives you a means of taking time out. Either party can pause. During the pause, the systems remain connected, but the remote system is not visible to the helper.

- The End button terminates the connection. Either party can also terminate by clicking the usual close button in the upper right corner of the screen.

CHAPTER 17

Windows 10 for experts and IT pros

Using advanced system management tools

In this chapter, we look at a handful of programs and management consoles that can help you attain greater mastery over Microsoft Windows. We start with tools for unearthing details about your system—its hardware, software environment, running programs and services, and other elements. In the remainder of the chapter, we discuss the Services console, Registry Editor, and various specialized tools that use Microsoft Management Console (MMC).

NOTE

These aren't the only programs included with Windows that could be considered as system management tools, of course. Some others include File Explorer, which is discussed in Chapter 12, "Managing files on PCs and in the cloud"; Disk Management, discussed in "Running Disk Management" in Chapter 14, "Managing disks and drives"; Event Viewer, which we cover in "Event Viewer" in Chapter 17, "Troubleshooting"; and Windows PowerShell, covered in "An introduction to Windows PowerShell" in Chapter 19, "Automating tasks and activities."

Viewing details about your system

For answers to basic questions about your operating system and computer, there's no better place to start than System, which displays the current Windows edition and whether it is a 32-bit or 64-bit version; basic system details, including processor type and installed memory; details about the computer name and network membership (domain or workgroup); and the current activation status.

Windows 10 offers two versions of this information. On a tablet or touchscreen-enabled system, you'll probably use the new Settings app. Open Settings > System > About to display details like those shown in Figure 18-1.

Figure 18-1 This About page, found in the new Settings app, includes basic details about the local PC along with options to change its name and join a corporate network.

An alternative display that includes most of the same information is in the old-style Control Panel, shown in Figure 18-2. The simplest way to get to the System settings page in Control Panel is to right-click the Start button (or press Windows key+X) and then click System. If File Explorer is open, right-click This PC and click Properties to reach the same destination.

For the most exhaustive inventory of system configuration details in a no-frills text format, Windows offers three tools that provide varying levels of technical information: Systeminfo, Windows Management Instrumentation, and System Information. We describe these tools in the following sections.

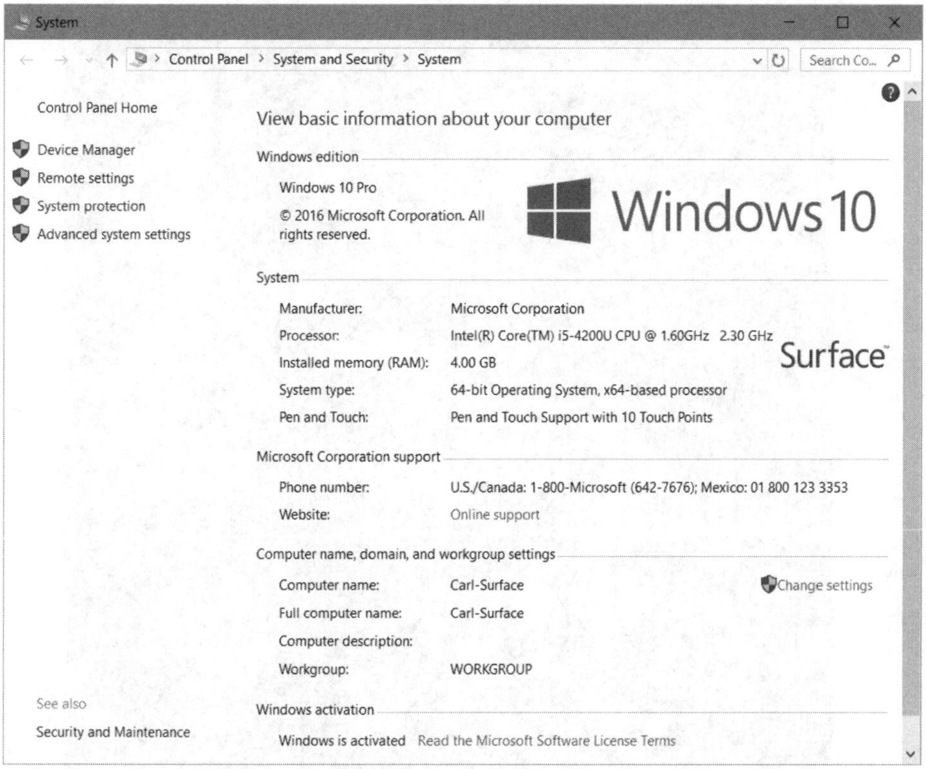

Figure 18-2 The System page in Control Panel provides basic details about your computer's configuration.

Systeminfo

Systeminfo.exe is a command-line utility, installed in the Windows\System32 folder, that displays information about your Windows version, BIOS, processor, memory, network configuration, and a few more esoteric items. Figure 18-3 shows sample output.

To run Systeminfo, open a Command Prompt window, type **systeminfo**, and then press Enter. In addition to the list format shown in Figure 18-3, Systeminfo offers two formats that are useful if you want to work with the information in another program: Table (fixed-width columns) and CSV (comma-separated values). To use one of these formats, append the /FO switch to the command, along with the Table or Csv parameter. You also need to redirect the output to a file. For example, to store comma-delimited information in a file named Info.csv, enter the following command:

```
systeminfo /fo csv > info.csv
```

CHAPTER 18

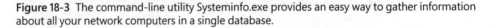

```
Command Prompt                                                         —    □    ×

C:\Users\Carl>systeminfo

Host Name:                  CARL-SURFACE
OS Name:                    Microsoft Windows 10 Pro
OS Version:                 10.0.14383 N/A Build 14383
OS Manufacturer:            Microsoft Corporation
OS Configuration:           Standalone Workstation
OS Build Type:              Multiprocessor Free
Registered Owner:           carl@example.com
Registered Organization:
Product ID:                 00330-80000-00000-AA610
Original Install Date:      7/7/2016, 6:52:35 PM
System Boot Time:           7/8/2016, 2:17:36 PM
System Manufacturer:        Microsoft Corporation
System Model:               Surface Pro 2
System Type:                x64-based PC
Processor(s):               1 Processor(s) Installed.
                            [01]: Intel64 Family 6 Model 69 Stepping 1 GenuineIntel ~1600 Mhz
BIOS Version:               American Megatrends Inc. 2.05.0250, 4/10/2015
Windows Directory:          C:\WINDOWS
System Directory:           C:\WINDOWS\system32
Boot Device:                \Device\HarddiskVolume2
System Locale:              en-us;English (United States)
Input Locale:               en-us;English (United States)
Time Zone:                  (UTC-08:00) Pacific Time (US & Canada)
Total Physical Memory:      4,016 MB
Available Physical Memory:  1,027 MB
Virtual Memory: Max Size:   5,424 MB
Virtual Memory: Available:  1,716 MB
Virtual Memory: In Use:     3,708 MB
Page File Location(s):      C:\pagefile.sys
Domain:                     WORKGROUP
Logon Server:               \\CARL-SURFACE
Hotfix(s):                  N/A
Network Card(s):            5 NIC(s) Installed.
                            [01]: Surface Ethernet Adapter
                                  Connection Name: Ethernet 4
                                  Status:          Media disconnected
                            [02]: Marvell AVASTAR 350N Wireless Network Controller
                                  Connection Name: Wi-Fi
                                  DHCP Enabled:    Yes
```

Figure 18-3 The command-line utility Systeminfo.exe provides an easy way to gather information about all your network computers in a single database.

Using the /S switch, you can get system information about another computer on your network. (If your user name and password don't match that of an account on the target computer, you also need to use the /U and /P switches to provide the user name and password of an authorized account.) When you've gathered information about all the computers on your network, you can import the file you created into a spreadsheet or database program for tracking and analysis. The following command appends information about a computer named Bates to the original file you created:

```
systeminfo /s Bates /fo csv >> info.csv
```

Windows Management Instrumentation command-line utility

This tool with the extra-long name is better known by the name of its executable, Wmic.exe, which is located in the Windows\System32\Wbem folder. Wmic provides an overwhelming amount of information about hardware, system configuration details, and user accounts. It can be used in either of two ways.

Enter **wmic** from a command prompt, and the utility runs in console mode, wherein you can enter commands and view output interactively. Alternatively, you can add global switches or aliases, which constrain the type of output you're looking for, and see the output in a Command Prompt window or redirect it to a file. For example, use the following command to produce a neatly formatted HTML file:

```
wmic qfe list brief /format:htable > %temp%\hotfix.html
```

You can then open that file in a web browser to see a list of all installed updates on the current system. To see the full syntax for Wmic, open a Command Prompt window and type **wmic /?**.

System Information

System Information—often called by the name of its executable, Msinfo32.exe—is a techie's paradise. It displays a wealth of configuration information in a simple tree-and-details arrangement, as shown in Figure 18-4. You can search for specific information, save information, view information about other computers, and even view a list of changes to your system.

To start System Information, begin typing **system information** in the search box or type **msinfo32** at a command prompt.

You navigate through System Information much as you would through File Explorer: Click a category in the left pane to view its contents in the right pane. To search for specific information, use the Find What box at the bottom of the System Information window. (If the Find bar is not visible, press Ctrl+F, or click Edit and then clear the check box next to Hide Find.)

The Find feature is basic but effective. Here are a couple of things you should know:

- Whenever you type in the Find What box to start a new search, Find begins its search at the top of the search range (which is the entire namespace unless you select Search Selected Category Only)—not at the current highlight.

- Selecting Search Category Names Only causes the Find feature to look only in the left pane. When this check box is cleared, the text in both panes is searched.

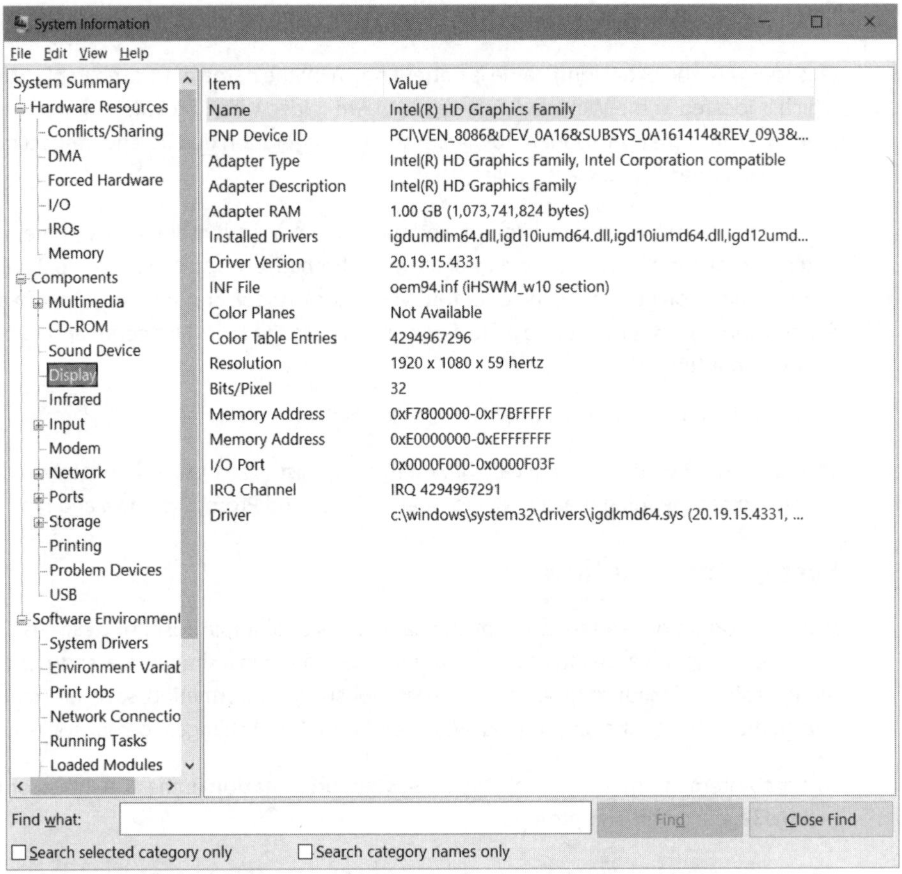

Figure 18-4 System Information is for viewing configuration information only; you can't use it to actually configure settings.

Using the System Information tool, you can preserve your configuration information—which is always helpful when reconstructing a system—in several ways:

- **Save the information as an .nfo file.** You can subsequently open the file (on the same computer or on a different computer with System Information) to view your saved information. To save information in this format, click File, Save. Saving this way always saves the entire collection of information.

- **Save all or part of the information as a plain-text file.** To save information as a text file, select the category of interest and click File, Export. To save all the information as a text file, select System Summary before you export it.

- **You can print all or part of the information.** Select the category of interest; click File, Print; and be sure that Selection is selected under Page Range. To print everything, select All under Page Range—and be sure to have lots of paper on hand. Depending on your system configuration and the number of installed applications, your report could top 100 pages. (Even better, consider "printing" to PDF and saving the results.)

Regardless of how you save your information, System Information refreshes (updates) the information immediately before processing the command.

Inside OUT

Save your system information periodically

Saving system configuration information when your computer is working properly can turn out to be useful when you have problems. Comparing your computer's current configuration with a known good baseline configuration can help you spot possible problem areas. You can open multiple instances of System Information to display the current configuration in one window and a baseline configuration in another. Save the configuration in OneDrive, and you'll be able to retrieve the information even after a hard-disk replacement.

Managing services

A *service* is a specialized program that performs a function to support other programs. Many services operate at a low level (by interacting directly with hardware, for example) and need to run even when no user is signed in. For this reason, they're often run by the System account (which has elevated privileges) rather than by ordinary user accounts. In this section, you'll learn how to view installed services; start, stop, and configure them; and install or remove them. We'll also take a closer look at some services used in Windows 10 and show you how to configure them to your advantage.

For the most complete view of services running on your computer, use the Services console. You can also view running services and perform limited management functions by using Task Manager. In this section, we discuss both tools.

Using the Services console

You manage services with the Services snap-in (Services.msc) for Microsoft Management Console, shown in Figure 18-5. To view this snap-in, type **services** in the search box and then click the Services desktop app at the top of the results list. (You must have administrator privileges to gain full functionality in the Services console. Running it as a standard user, you can view service settings, but you can't start or stop most services, change the startup type, or make any other configuration changes.)

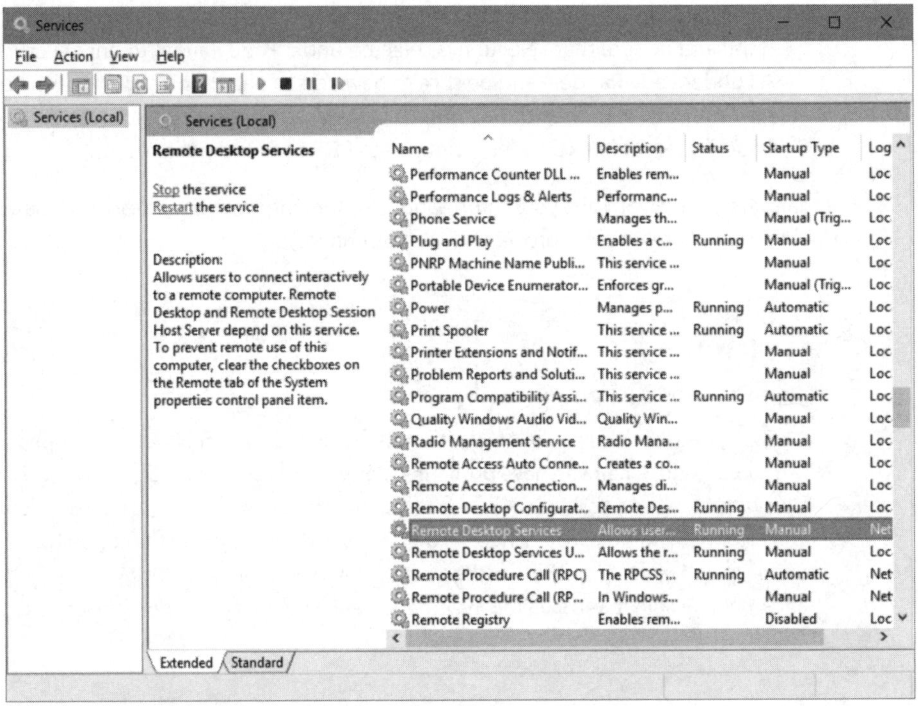

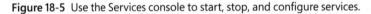

Figure 18-5 Use the Services console to start, stop, and configure services.

The Extended and Standard views in the Services console (selectable by clicking a tab near the bottom of the window) have a single difference: The Extended view provides descriptive information of the selected service in the space at the left edge of the details pane. This space also sometimes includes links for starting, stopping, or pausing the selected service. Unless you need to constrain the console display to a small area of your screen, you'll probably find the Extended view preferable to the Standard view.

The Services console offers plenty of information in its clean display. You can sort the contents of any column by clicking the column title, as you can with similar lists. To sort in reverse order, click the column title again. In addition, you can do the following:

- Start, stop, pause, resume, or restart the selected service, as described in the following section.

- Display the properties dialog box for the selected service, in which you can configure the service and learn more about it.

Most essential services are set to start automatically when your computer starts, and the operating system stops them as part of its shutdown process. A handful of services that aren't typically used at startup are set with the Automatic (Delayed Start) option, which starts the associated service two minutes after the rest of startup completes, making the startup process smoother. The Trigger Start option allows Windows to run or stop a service as needed in response to specific events; the File History service, for example, doesn't run unless you enable the File History feature.

But sometimes you might need to manually start or stop a service. For example, you might want to start a seldom-used service on the rare occasion when you need it. (Because running services requires system resources such as memory, running them only when necessary can improve performance.) On the other hand, you might want to stop a service because you're no longer using it. A more common reason for stopping a service is because it isn't working properly. For example, if print jobs get stuck in the print queue, sometimes the best remedy is to stop and then restart the Print Spooler service.

Inside OUT

Pause instead of stopping

If a service allows pausing, try pausing and then continuing the service as your first step instead of stopping the service. Pausing can solve certain problems without canceling jobs in process or resetting connections.

Starting and stopping services

Not all services allow you to change their status. Some prevent stopping and starting altogether, whereas others permit stopping and starting but not pausing and resuming. Some services allow these permissions to only certain users or groups. For example, most services allow only members of the Administrators group to start or stop them. Which status changes are allowed and who has permission to make them are controlled by each service's discretionary access control list (DACL), which is established when the service is created on a computer.

NOTE

In Windows 10, software installers can stop and restart running applications and services by using a feature called Restart Manager (introduced in Windows Vista). A handful of system services are considered critical, however, and cannot be restarted manually or programmatically except as part of a system restart. These critical services include Smss.exe, Csrss.exe, Wininit.exe, Logonui.exe, Lsass.exe, Services.exe, Winlogon.exe, System, Svchost.exe with RPCSS, and Svchost.exe with DCOM/PnP.

To change a service's status, select it in the Services console. Then click the appropriate link in the area to the left of the service list (if you're using the Extended view and the link you need

CHAPTER 18

appears there). Alternatively, you can use the Play/Pause/Stop controls on the toolbar or right-click and use the corresponding command.

You can also change a service's status by opening its properties dialog box and then clicking one of the buttons on the General tab. Taking the extra step of opening the properties dialog box to set the status has only one advantage: You can specify start parameters when you start a service by using this method. This is a rare requirement.

Configuring services

To review or modify the way a service starts up or what happens when it doesn't start properly, view its properties dialog box. To do that, double-click the service in the Services console. Figure 18-6 shows an example.

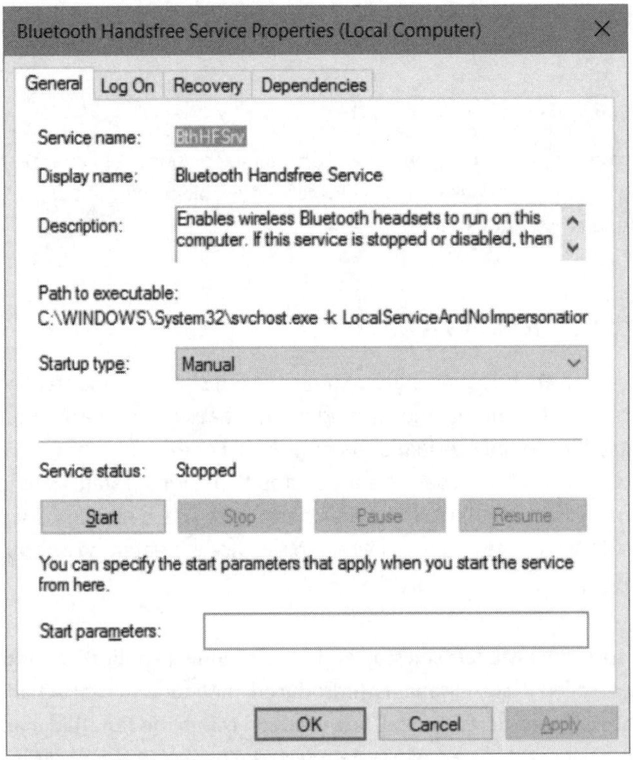

Figure 18-6 Specify a service's startup type on the General tab, where you can also find the actual name of the service (in this case, BthHFSrv) above its display name.

Setting startup options

On the General tab of the properties dialog box (shown in Figure 18-6), you specify the startup type:

- **Automatic (Delayed Start).** The service starts shortly after the computer starts in order to improve startup performance and user experience.

- **Automatic.** The service starts when the computer starts.

- **Manual.** The service doesn't start automatically at startup, but it can be started by a user, program, or dependent service.

- **Disabled.** The service can't be started.

The Trigger Start option cannot be configured manually from the Services console. Instead, you have to use SC (Sc.exe), a command-line program that communicates with the Service Control Manager. If you'd rather not tinker with the arcane syntax of this command, try the free Service Trigger Editor, available from Core Technologies Consulting, at *https://bit.ly/servicetriggereditor*.

You'll find other startup options on the Log On tab of the properties dialog box, as shown in Figure 18-7.

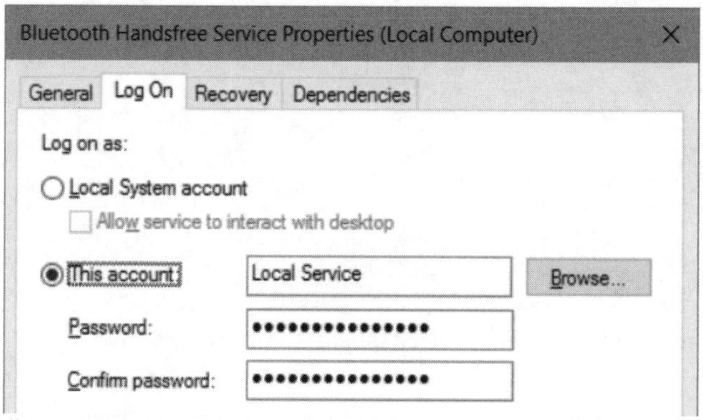

Figure 18-7 On the Log On tab, you specify which user account runs the service.

NOTE

If you specify a sign-in account other than the Local System account, be sure that account has the requisite rights. Go to the Local Security Policy console (at a command prompt, type **secpol.msc**), and then go to Security Settings\Local Policies\User Rights Assignment and assign the Log On As A Service right to the account.

CHAPTER 18

Specifying recovery actions

For various reasons—hardware not operating properly or a network connection being down, for example—a service that's running smoothly might suddenly stop. By using settings on the Recovery tab of the properties dialog box, you can specify what happens if a service fails. Figure 18-8, for example, shows the default settings for the Bluetooth Handsfree service.

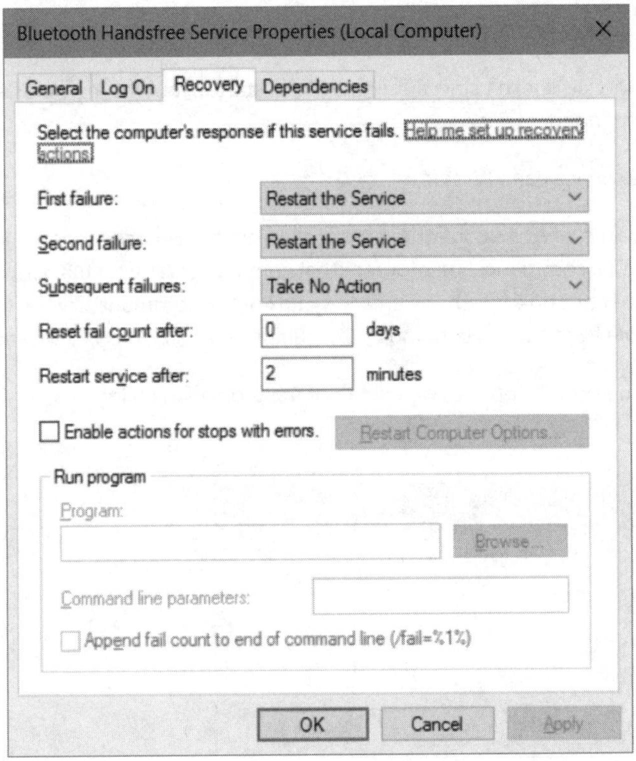

Figure 18-8 Use the Recovery tab to specify what happens if a service fails.

You might want to perform a different action the first time a service fails than on the second or subsequent failures. The Recovery tab enables you to assign a particular response to the first failure, the second failure, and all subsequent failures, from among these options:

- **Take No Action.** The service gives up trying. In most cases, the service places a message in the event log. (Use of the event log depends on how the service was programmed by its developers.)

- **Restart The Service.** The computer waits for the time specified in the Restart Service After box to elapse and then tries to start the service.

- **Run A Program.** The computer runs the program you specify in the Run Program box. For example, you could specify a program that attempts to resolve the problem or one that alerts you to the situation.

- **Restart The Computer.** Drastic but effective, this option restarts the computer after the time specified in the Restart Computer Options dialog box elapses. In that dialog box, you can also specify a message to be broadcast to other users on your network, warning them of the impending shutdown.

Viewing dependencies

Many services rely on the functions of another service. If you attempt to start a service that depends on other services, Windows first starts the others. If you stop a service upon which others are dependent, Windows also stops those services. Before you either start or stop a service, therefore, it's helpful to know what other services your action might affect. To obtain that information, go to the Dependencies tab of a service's properties dialog box, as in the example shown in Figure 18-9.

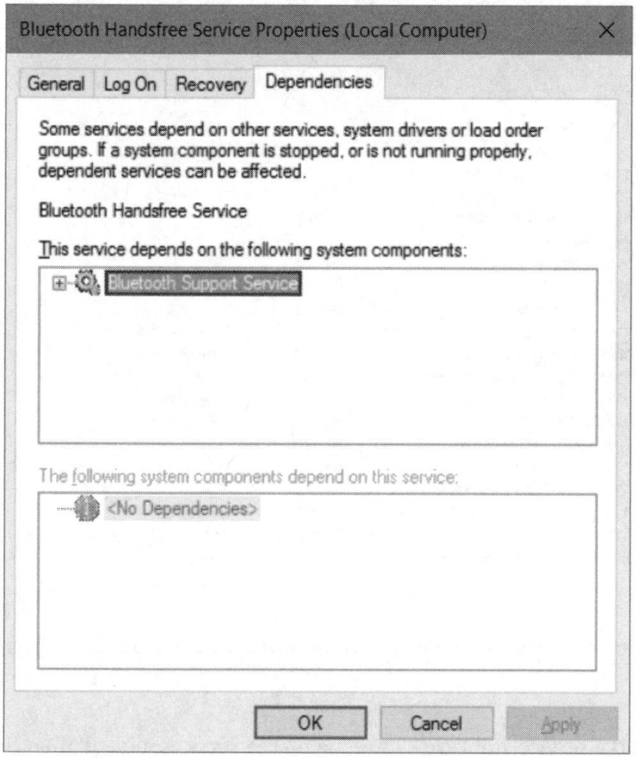

Figure 18-9 The Dependencies tab shows which services depend on other services or drivers.

Managing services from Task Manager

Using the Services tab in Windows Task Manager, you can start and stop services and view several important aspects of the services, both running and available, on your computer. You can also use this tab as a shortcut to the Services console.

To open Task Manager, use any of the following techniques:

- Right-click Start (or press Windows key+X), and then click Task Manager on the Quick Link menu.

- Right-click the taskbar, and then click Task Manager.

- Press Ctrl+Alt+Delete, and then click Task Manager.

- Press Ctrl+Shift+Esc.

The Services tab is shown in Figure 18-10.

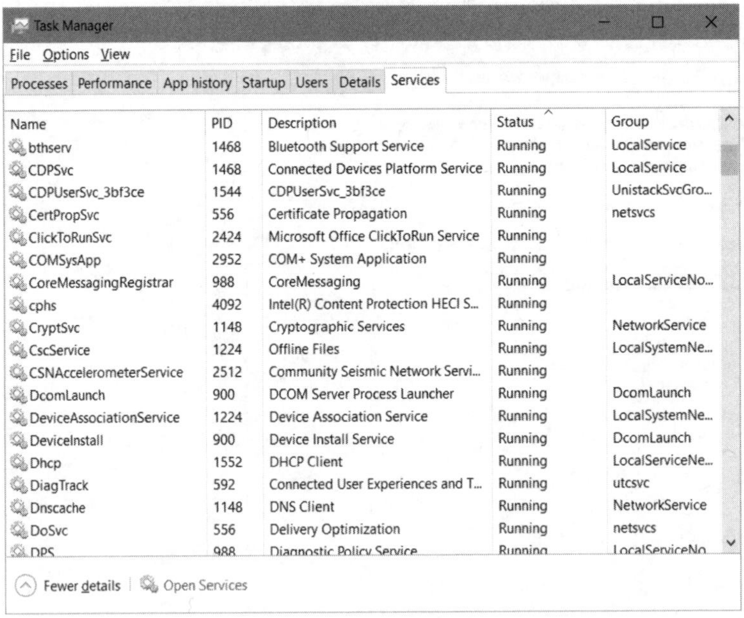

Figure 18-10 By sorting on the Status column, you can see which services are running and which are stopped.

To start, stop, or restart a service, right-click its name on the Services tab and then click Start, Stop, or Restart.

Using the Services tab, you can also associate a running service with its process identifier (PID) and then further associate that PID with other programs and services being run under that PID. For example, Figure 18-10 shows a couple of services running with PID 1468. Right-clicking one of the services with PID 1468 gives you two options: one to stop the service and one called Go To Details. Clicking the latter option opens the Details tab in Task Manager with the particular process (typically, Svchost.exe) highlighted.

Determining the name of a service

As you view the properties dialog box for different services, you might notice that the service name (shown at the top of the General tab) is often different from the name that appears in the Services console (the display name) and that neither name matches the name of the service's executable file. (Many services run as part of a service group, under Services.exe or Svchost.exe.) The General tab (shown earlier in Figure 18-6) shows all three names.

So how does this affect you? When you work in the Services console, you don't need to know anything other than a service's display name to find it and work with it. But if you use the Net command to start and stop services from a Command Prompt window, you might find using the actual service name more convenient; it's often much shorter than the display name. You'll also need the service name if you're ever forced to work with a service's registry entries, which can be found in the HKLM\System\CurrentControlSet\Services*service* subkey (where *service* is the service name).

And what about the executable name? You might need it if you have problems running a service; in such a case, you need to find the executable and check its permissions. Knowing the executable name can also be useful, for example, if you're using Windows Task Manager to determine why your computer seems to be running slowly. Although the Processes tab and the Services tab show the display name (under the Description heading), because of the window size it's sometimes easier to find the more succinct executable name.

Editing the Windows registry

The Windows registry is the central storage location that contains configuration details for hardware, system settings, services, user customizations, applications, and every detail—large and small—that makes Windows work.

> ### NOTE
> The registry is the work of many hands, over many years, and capitalization and word spacing are not consistent. With readability as our goal, we made our own capitalization decisions for this book, and our treatment of names frequently differs from what you see in Registry Editor. No matter. Capitalization is irrelevant. Spelling and spacing must be correct, however.

Although it's convenient to think of the registry as a monolithic database, its contents are actually stored in multiple locations as separate *hive* files, alongside logs and other support files. Some of those hive files are read into memory when the operating system starts; hive files that contain user-specific settings are stored in the user profile and are loaded when a new user signs in.

The Boot Configuration Data (BCD) store has its own file on the boot drive. The core hives for Windows—the Security Account Manager (SAM), Security, Software, and System—are securely stored in %SystemRoot%\System32\Config. Two hives that contain settings for local and network services are located in %SystemRoot%\ServiceProfiles\LocalService and %SystemRoot%\ServiceProfiles\NetworkService, respectively. User-specific hives are stored as part of the user profile folder.

The Hardware hive is unique in that it has no associated disk file. This hive, which contains details about your hardware configuration, is completely volatile; that is, Windows 10 creates it anew each time you turn your system on.

NOTE

You can see where the hives of your system physically live by examining the values associated with HKLM\System\CurrentControlSet\Control\HiveList. Windows assigns drive letters after assembling the registry, so these paths do not specify drive letters.

You can't work with hive files directly. Windows 10 is designed in such a way that direct registry edits by end users are generally unnecessary. When you change your configuration by using the Settings app or Control Panel, for example, Windows writes the necessary updates to the registry for you. Likewise, when you install a new piece of hardware or a new program, the setup program makes the required registry changes; you don't need to know the details.

On the other hand, because the designers of Windows couldn't provide a user interface for every conceivable customization you might want to make, sometimes working directly with the registry is the only way to make a change. Even when it's not the only way, it might be the fastest way. Removing or modifying registry entries is occasionally a crucial part of troubleshooting and repair as well. Windows includes a registry editor you should know how to use—safely. This section tells you how.

CAUTION

Most Microsoft support articles contain a dire warning about the risks associated with editing the registry. We echo those warnings here. An incorrect registry modification can render your system unbootable and in some cases might require a complete reinstall of the operating system. Use Registry Editor at your own risk.

Understanding the Registry Editor hierarchy

Registry Editor (Regedit.exe) offers a unified view of the registry's contents as well as tools for modifying its contents. You won't find this important utility on the All Apps list, however, and it doesn't show up when you type its name in the search box. To start Registry Editor, you must use the name of its executable file, Regedit.exe, or type **regedit** at a command prompt.

Figure 18-11 shows a collapsed view of the Windows 10 registry, as seen through Registry Editor.

The Computer node appears at the top of the Registry Editor tree listing. Beneath it, as shown here, are five root keys: HKEY_CLASSES_ROOT, HKEY_CURRENT_USER, HKEY_LOCAL_MACHINE, HKEY_USERS, and HKEY_CURRENT_CONFIG. For simplicity's sake and typographical convenience, this book, like many others, abbreviates the root key names as HKCR, HKCU, HKLM, HKU, and HKCC, respectively.

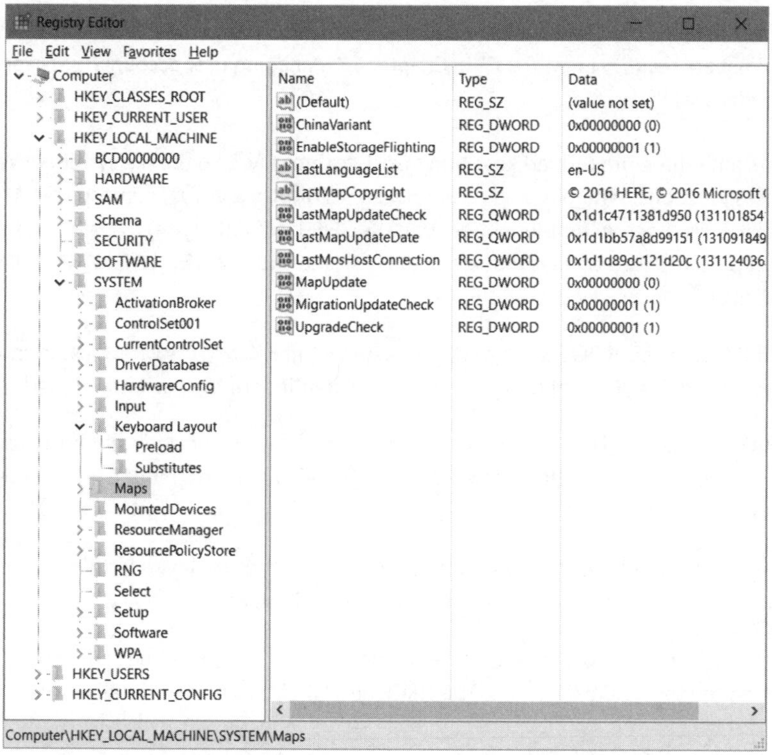

Figure 18-11 The registry consists of five root keys, each of which contains many subkeys.

Root keys, sometimes called *predefined keys*, contain subkeys. Registry Editor displays this structure in a hierarchical tree in the left pane. In Figure 18-11, for example, HKLM is open, showing its top-level subkeys.

Subkeys, which we call *keys* for short, can contain subkeys of their own, which can be expanded as necessary to display additional subkeys. The status bar at the bottom of the Registry Editor window shows the full path of the currently selected key: HKLM\System\Maps, in the previous figure.

The contents of HKEY_LOCAL_MACHINE define the workings of Windows itself, and its subkeys map neatly to several hives we mentioned at the start of this section. HKEY_USERS contains an entry for every existing user account (including system accounts), each of which uses the security identifier, or SID, for that account.

> ### NOTE
>
> **For a detailed discussion of the relationship between user accounts and SIDs, see "What are security identifiers?" in Chapter 6, "Managing user accounts, passwords, and credentials."**

The remaining three predefined keys don't exist, technically. Like the file system in Windows—which uses junctions, symlinks, and other trickery to display a virtual namespace—the registry uses a bit of misdirection (implemented with the REG_LINK data type) to create these convenient representations of keys that are actually stored within HKEY_LOCAL_MACHINE and HKEY_USERS:

- HKEY_CLASSES_ROOT is merged from keys within HKLM\Software\Classes and HKEY_USERS*sid*_Classes (where *sid* is the security identifier of the currently signed-in user).

- HKEY_CURRENT_USER is a view into the settings for the currently signed-in user account, as stored in HKEY_USERS*sid* (where *sid* is the security identifier of the currently signed-in user).

- HKEY_CURRENT_CONFIG displays the contents of the Hardware Profiles\Current subkey in HKLM\SYSTEM\CurrentControlSet\Hardware Profiles.

Any changes you make to keys and values in these virtual keys have the same effect as though you had edited the actual locations. The HKCR and HKCU keys are generally more convenient to use.

Registry values and data types

Every key contains at least one value. In Registry Editor, that obligatory value is known as the default value. Many keys have additional values. The names, data types, and data associated with values appear in the right pane.

The default value for many keys is not defined. You can think of an empty default value as a placeholder—a slot that could hold data but currently does not.

All values other than the default always include the following three components: name, data type, and data. Figure 18-12, for example, shows customized settings for the current user's lock screen. (Note the full path to this key in the bottom of the Registry Editor window.)

The SlideshowEnabled value (near the bottom of the list) is of data type REG_DWORD. The data associated with this value (on the system used for this figure) is 0x00000000. The prefix 0x denotes a hexadecimal value. Registry Editor displays the decimal equivalent of hexadecimal values in parentheses after the value.

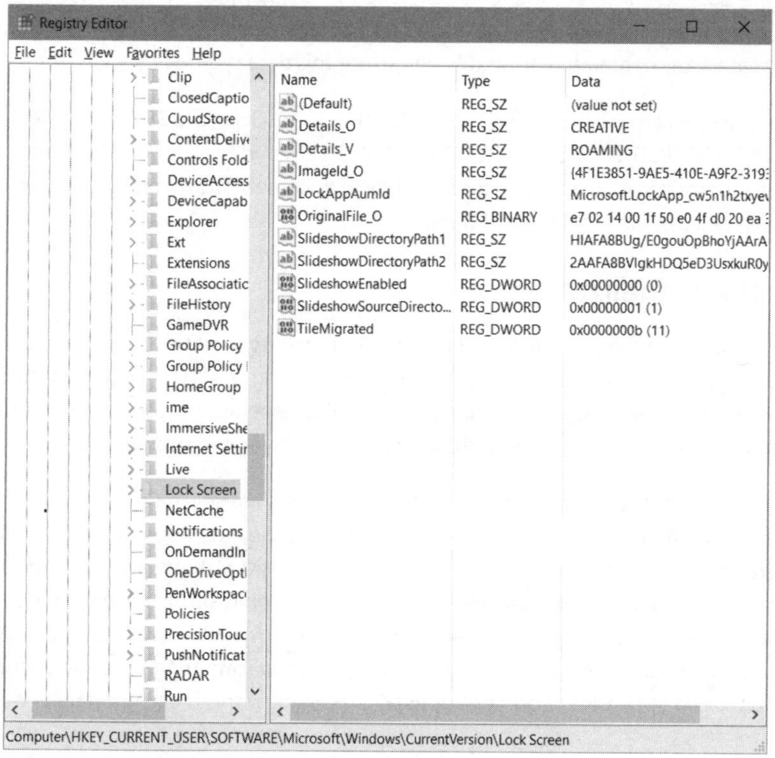

Figure 18-12 Selecting a key on the left displays all of its values on the right.

CHAPTER 18

The registry uses the following data types:

- **REG_SZ**   The SZ indicates a zero-terminated string. This variable-length string can contain Unicode as well as ANSI characters. When you enter or edit a REG_SZ value, Registry Editor terminates the value with a 00 byte for you.

- **REG_BINARY**   The REG_BINARY type contains binary data—0s and 1s.

- **REG_DWORD**   This data type is a "double word"—that is, a 32-bit numeric value. Although it can hold any integer from 0 to 2^{32}, the registry often uses it for simple Boolean values (0 or 1) because the registry lacks a Boolean data type.

- **REG_QWORD**   This data type is a "quadruple word"—a 64-bit numeric value.

- **REG_MULTI_SZ**   This data type contains a group of zero-terminated strings assigned to a single value.

- **REG_EXPAND_SZ**   This data type is a zero-terminated string containing an unexpanded reference to an environment variable, such as %SystemRoot%. (For information about environment variables, see "Interacting with PowerShell" in Chapter 19.) If you need to create a key containing a variable name, use this data type, not REG_SZ.

Internally, the registry also uses REG_LINK, REG_FULL_RESOURCE_DESCRIPTOR, REG_RESOURCE_LIST, REG_RESOURCE_REQUIREMENTS_LIST, and REG_NONE data types. Although you might occasionally see references in technical documentation to these data types, they're not visible or accessible in Registry Editor.

Registry virtualization

One of the longstanding fundamental principles of security in Windows is that it prevents applications running under a standard user's token from writing to system folders in the file system and to machine-wide keys in the registry, while at the same time enabling users with a standard account to run applications without running into "access denied" roadblocks.

Many applications that require administrator-level access are still in use in Windows 10, but standard users can run them without hassle. That's because User Account Control uses registry virtualization to redirect attempts to write to subkeys of HKLM\Software. (Settings in HKLM apply to all users of the computer, and therefore only administrators have write permission.) When an application attempts to write to this hive, Windows writes instead to a per-user location, HKCR\VirtualStore\Machine\Software. Like file virtualization, this is done transparently; the application (and all but the most curious users) never know this is going on behind the scenes.

NOTE

When an application requests information from HKLM\Software, Windows looks first in the virtualized key if it exists. Therefore, if a value exists in both the VirtualStore hive and in HKLM, the application sees only the one in VirtualStore.

Note that because the virtualized data is stored in a per-user section of the registry, settings made by one user do not affect other users. Running the same application in Windows XP, which doesn't use virtualization and therefore looks only at the actual HKLM hive, presents all users with the same settings. This difference in behavior can lead to confusion by users who are accustomed to sharing an application in Windows XP and find that it works differently in Windows 10.

Inside OUT

Copy virtualized registry entries to other user accounts

The hive that stores virtualized registry data, HKCR\VirtualStore\Machine\Software, can also be found in HKU*sid*_Classes\VirtualStore\Machine\Software, where *sid* is the security identifier of the user who is currently signed in. If you want to make sure that a certain application works identically for a different user, you can copy that application's subkey to the corresponding HKU subkey for the other user.

➤ For more information about UAC and virtualization, see "Preventing unsafe actions with User Account Control" in Chapter 7, "Securing Windows 10 devices."

NOTE

Registry virtualization is an interim solution to application compatibility problems. It was introduced with Windows Vista; at that time, nearly 10 years ago, Microsoft announced its intention to remove the feature from a future version of the operating system. It is still a feature in Windows 10. For more information about registry virtualization, see *https://bit.ly/registry-virtualization*.

Backing up and restoring parts of the registry

The two most important things to know about Registry Editor are that it copies your changes immediately into the registry and that it has no Undo command. Registry Editor doesn't wait for you to issue a File, Save command (because it has no such command) before making changes in the registry files. And after you alter some bit of registry data, the original data is gone forever—unless you remember it and restore it yourself or unless you have some form of backup you can restore. Registry Editor, therefore, is a tool to be used sparingly and cautiously; it should not be left open when not in use.

Before you make any changes to the registry, consider using System Restore to set a restore point, which includes a snapshot of the registry as it currently exists. Taking this precaution allows you to roll back any ill-advised changes.

> ➤ **For information about using System Restore, see "Rolling back to a previous restore point" in Chapter 16, "Backup, restore, and recovery."**

In addition, you can use the Export command in Registry Editor to back up the branch of the registry where you plan to work.

Registry Editor can save all or portions of your registry in any of the four different formats described here:

- **Registration Files.** The Registration Files option creates a .reg file, which is a text file that can be read and edited in Notepad or a similar program. A .reg file can be merged into the registry of a system running any version of Windows. When you merge a .reg file, its keys and values replace the corresponding keys and values in the registry. By using .reg files, you can edit your registry "offline" and add your changes to the registry without even opening Registry Editor. You can also use .reg files as an easy way to share registry settings and copy them to other computers.

- **Registry Hive Files.** The Registry Hive File format saves a binary image of a selected portion of the registry. You won't be able to read the resulting file (although you can choose one of the text-file options if that's what you need to do), but if you need to restore the keys you worked on, you can be confident that this format will do the job correctly.

  Registry Hive File is the format of choice if you want to create a backup before working in Registry Editor. That's because when you import a registry hive file, it restores the entire hive to exactly the way it was when you saved it. (The .reg file types, when merged, restore all the saved keys and values to their original locations, which repairs all deletions and edits. But the process does not remove any keys or values you added.) Note, however, that a registry hive file has the potential to do the greatest damage if you import it to the wrong key; see the caution in the following section.

- **Win9x/NT4 Registration Files.** The Win9x/NT4 Registration Files option also generates a .reg file, but one in an older format used by earlier versions of Windows. The principal difference between the two formats is that the current format uses Unicode and the older format does not. We can't think of a real-world scenario in which you would actually want to use this legacy format.

- **Text Files.** The Text Files option, like the Registration Files option, creates a file that can be read in Notepad or another text editor. The principal advantage of this format is that it cannot accidentally (or intentionally) be merged into the registry. Thus, using this option is a good way to create a record of your registry's state at a particular time. Its disadvantage, relative to the .reg file format, is the size of the files it creates. Text files are considerably larger than corresponding .reg files, and they take longer to create.

To export all or part of a registry hive, select a key in the left pane, and then on the File menu, click Export. (Easier yet: Right-click a key and click Export.) In the Save As Type list in the Export Registry File dialog box, select one of the four file types. Under Export Range, select Selected Branch. The resulting file includes the selected key and all its subkeys and values.

If you need to restore the exported hive from a registry hive file, select the same key in the left pane of the Registry Editor window, click Import on the File menu, and specify the file. You'll see a confirmation prompt letting you know that your action will overwrite (replace) the current key and all its subkeys. This is your last chance to make sure you're importing the hive into the right location, so take a moment to make sure you selected the correct key before you click Yes.

CAUTION

> Importing a registry hive file replaces the entire contents of the selected key with the contents of the file—regardless of its original source. That is, it wipes out everything in the selected key and then adds the keys and values from the file. When you import, be absolutely certain you selected the correct key.

If you saved your backup as a .reg file, you use the same process to import it. (As an alternative, you can double-click the .reg file in File Explorer without opening Registry Editor.) Unlike with a registry hive file, however, the complete path to each key and value is stored as part of the file and it always restores to the same location. This approach for recovering from registry editing mishaps is fine if you did not add new values or subkeys to the section of the registry you're working with; it returns existing data to its former state but doesn't alter the data you added.

TROUBLESHOOTING

You used a registry cleaner and your system is no longer working properly

The registry is often inscrutable and can appear messy. Misguided attempts at cleanup can cause unexpected problems that are nearly impossible to troubleshoot, which explains why Microsoft is so insistent with its warnings that improper changes to the registry can prevent your computer from operating properly or even booting. We've never found a so-called registry cleaner that justifies the risk it inevitably entails. If you find yourself with a misbehaving system after using a registry cleaner, use the Reset option to recover your system and start over. And this time, don't bother to install that unnecessary utility.

CHAPTER 18

Browsing and editing with Registry Editor

Because of the registry's size, looking for a particular key, value, or data item can be daunting. In Registry Editor, the Find command (on the Edit menu and also available by pressing Ctrl+F) works in the forward direction only and does not wrap around when it gets to the end of the registry. If you're not sure where the item you need is located, select the highest level in the left pane before issuing the command. If you have an approximate idea where the item you want is located, you can save time by starting at a node closer to (but still above) the target.

After you locate an item of interest, you can put it on the Favorites list to simplify a return visit. Open the Favorites menu, click Add To Favorites, and supply a friendly name (or accept the default). If you're about to close Registry Editor and know you'll be returning to the same key the next time you open the editor, you can skip the Favorites step because Registry Editor always remembers your last position and returns to that position in the next session.

Registry Editor includes a number of time-saving keyboard shortcuts for navigating the registry:

- To move to the next subkey that starts with a particular letter, simply type that letter when the focus is in the left pane; in the right pane, use the same trick to jump to the next value that begins with that letter.

- To open a key (revealing its subkeys), press the Right Arrow key.

- To move up one level in the subkey hierarchy, press the Left Arrow key; a second press collapses the subkeys of the current key.

- To move to the top of the hierarchy, press Home.

- To quickly move between the left and right panes, use the Tab key.

- In the right pane, press F2 to rename a value, and press Enter to open that value and edit its data.

Once you are comfortable using these keyboard shortcuts, you'll find it's usually easier to zip through the subkey hierarchy with a combination of arrow keys and letter keys than it is to open outline controls with the mouse.

Changing data

You can change the data associated with a value by selecting a value in the right pane and pressing Enter or by double-clicking the value. Registry Editor pops up an edit window appropriate for the value's data type:

Adding or deleting keys

To add a key, select the new key's parent in the left pane, open the Edit menu, point to New, and click Key. The new key arrives as a generically named outline entry, exactly the way a new folder does in File Explorer. Type a new name.

To delete a key, select it and then press Delete.

Adding or deleting values

To add a value, select the parent key, open the Edit menu, and point to New. On the submenu that appears, click the type of value you want to add. A value of the type you select appears in the right pane with a generic name. Type over the generic name, press Enter twice, enter your data, and press Enter once more.

To delete a value, select it and press Delete.

Using the Reg command

One expert-level option is to use the Reg command in a Command Prompt window or in a batch file or script. Type **reg /?** to see the full list of eligible arguments for the reg command (query, add, export, import, and so on). Each of those variants has its own syntax help. Try **reg add /?** to see the correct syntax for adding a value.

CHAPTER 18

Using .reg files to automate registry changes

The .reg files created by the Export command in Registry Editor are plain text, suitable for reading and editing in Notepad or any similar editor. Therefore, they provide an alternative method for editing your registry. You can export a section of the registry, change it offline, and then merge it back into the registry. Or you can add new keys, values, and data to the registry by creating a .reg file from scratch and merging it. A .reg file is particularly useful if you need to make the same changes to the registry of several computers. You can make and test your changes on one machine, save the relevant part of the registry as a .reg file, and then transport the file to the other machines that require it.

Figure 18-13 shows a .reg file. In this case, the file was exported from the HKCU\Software\Microsoft\Windows\CurrentVersion\Explorer\Advanced key, shown in Figure 18-14.

```
Explorer-Advanced.reg - Notepad                               —    □    ×
File  Edit  Format  View  Help
Windows Registry Editor Version 5.00

[HKEY_CURRENT_USER\SOFTWARE\Microsoft\Windows\CurrentVersion\Explorer\Advanced]
"Start_SearchFiles"=dword:00000002
"ServerAdminUI"=dword:00000000
"Hidden"=dword:00000001
"ShowCompColor"=dword:00000001
"HideFileExt"=dword:00000000
"DontPrettyPath"=dword:00000000
"ShowInfoTip"=dword:00000001
"HideIcons"=dword:00000000
"MapNetDrvBtn"=dword:00000000
"WebView"=dword:00000001
"Filter"=dword:00000000
"ShowSuperHidden"=dword:00000000
"SeparateProcess"=dword:00000000
"AutoCheckSelect"=dword:00000000
"IconsOnly"=dword:00000000
"ShowTypeOverlay"=dword:00000001
"ShowStatusBar"=dword:00000001
"ListviewAlphaSelect"=dword:00000001
"ListviewShadow"=dword:00000001
"TaskbarAnimations"=dword:00000001
"StartMenuInit"=dword:0000000d
"ReindexedProfile"=dword:00000001
"TaskbarSizeMove"=dword:00000001
"DisablePreviewDesktop"=dword:00000001
"TaskbarGlomLevel"=dword:00000000
"MMTaskbarEnabled"=dword:00000001
```

Figure 18-13 A .reg file is a plain-text file suitable for offline editing. This .reg file was exported from the key shown in Figure 18-14.

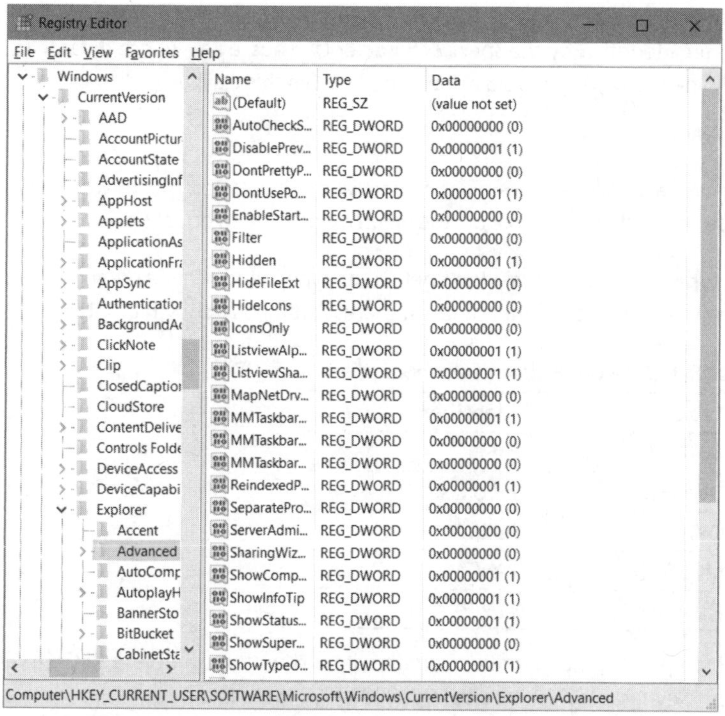

Figure 18-14 This key's name, values, and data are recorded in the .reg file shown in Figure 18-13.

Identifying the elements of a .reg file

As you review the examples shown in the two figures, note the following characteristics of .reg files:

- **Header line.** The file begins with the line "Windows Registry Editor Version 5.00." When you merge a .reg file into the registry, Registry Editor uses this line to verify that the file contains registry data. Version 5 (the version used with Windows 7 and later versions, including Windows 10) generates Unicode text files, which can be used with all supported versions of Windows as well as the now-unsupported Windows XP and Windows 2000.

- **Key names.** Key names are delimited by brackets and must include the full path from the root key to the current subkey. The root key name must not be abbreviated. (Don't use HKCU, for example.) Figure 18-13 shows only one key name, but you can have as many as you want.

- **The default value.** Undefined default values do not appear in .reg files. Defined default values are identified by the special character @. Thus, a key whose default REG_SZ value was defined as MyApp would appear in a .reg file this way:

```
"@"="MyApp"
```

- **Value names.** Value names must be enclosed in quotation marks, whether or not they include space characters. Follow the value name with an equal sign.

- **Data types.** REG_SZ values don't get a data type identifier or a colon. The data directly follows the equal sign. Other data types are identified as shown in Table 18-1.

Table 18-1 Data types identified in .reg files

Data type	Identifier
REG_BINARY	hex
REG_DWORD	dword
REG_QWORD	hex(b)
REG_MULTI_SZ	hex(7)
REG_EXPAND_SZ	hex(2)

A colon separates the identifier from the data. Thus, for example, a REG_DWORD value named "Keyname" with value data of 00000000 looks like this:

```
"Keyname"=dword:00000000
```

- **REG_SZ values.** Ordinary string values must be enclosed in quotation marks. A backslash character within a string must be written as two backslashes. Thus, for example, the path C:\Program Files\Microsoft Office\ is written like this:

```
"C:\\Program Files\\Microsoft Office\\"
```

- **REG_DWORD values.** DWORD values are written as eight hexadecimal digits, without spaces or commas. Do not use the 0x prefix.

- **All other data types.** Other data types—including REG_EXPAND_SZ, REG_MULTI_SZ, and REG_QWORD—appear as comma-delimited lists of hexadecimal bytes (two hex digits, a comma, two more hex digits, and so on). The following is an example of a REG_MULTI_SZ value:

```
"Addins"=hex(7):64,00,3a,00,5c,00,6c,00,6f,00,74,00,00,75,00,73,00,5c,00,\
31,00,32,00,33,00,5c,00,61,00,64,00,64,00,64,00,69,00,6e,00,73,00,5c,00,\
64,00,71,00,61,00,75,00,69,00,2e,00,31,00,32,00,61,00,00,00,00,00,00,00
```

- **Line-continuation characters.** You can use the backslash as a line-continuation character. The REG_MULTI_SZ value just shown, for example, is all one stream of bytes. We added backslashes and broke the lines for readability, and you can do the same in your .reg files.

- **Line spacing.** You can add blank lines for readability. Registry Editor ignores them.

- **Comments.** To add a comment line to a .reg file, begin the line with a semicolon.

Using a .reg file to delete registry data

.Reg files are most commonly used to modify existing registry data or add new data. But you can also use them to delete existing values and keys.

To delete an existing value, specify a hyphen character (minus sign) as the value's data. For example, to use a .reg file to remove the value ShellState from the key HKCU\Software\Microsoft\Windows\CurrentVersion\Explorer, add the following lines to the .reg file:

```
[HKEY_CURRENT_USER\Software\Microsoft\Windows\CurrentVersion\Explorer]
"ShellState"=-
```

To delete an existing key with all its values and data, insert a hyphen in front of the key name (inside the left bracket). For example, to use a .reg file to remove the key HKCR\.xyz\shell and all its values, add the following to the .reg file:

```
[-HKEY_CLASSES_ROOT\.xyz\shell]
```

Merging a .reg file into the registry

To merge a .reg file into the registry from within Registry Editor, open the File menu and click Import. Registry Editor adds the imported data under the appropriate key names, overwriting existing values where necessary.

The default action for a .reg file is Merge—meaning merge with the registry. Therefore, you can merge a file into the registry by simply double-clicking it in File Explorer and answering the confirmation prompt.

Using Microsoft Management Console

Microsoft Management Console (MMC) is an application that hosts tools for administering computers, networks, and other system components. By itself, MMC performs no administrative services. Rather, it acts as the host for one or more modules, called *snap-ins*, which do the useful work. MMC provides user-interface consistency so that you or the users you support see more or less the same style of application each time you need to carry out some kind of computer

CHAPTER 18

management task. A combination of one or more snap-ins can be saved in a file called a Microsoft Common Console Document or, more commonly, an MMC console.

Creating snap-ins requires expertise in programming. You don't have to be a programmer, however, to make your own custom MMC consoles. All you need to do is run MMC, start with a blank console, and add one or more of the snap-ins available on your system. Alternatively, you can customize some of the MMC consoles supplied by Microsoft or other vendors simply by adding or removing snap-ins. You might, for example, want to combine the Services console with the Event Viewer console, the latter filtered to show only events generated by services. You might also want to include a link to a website that offers details about services and service-related errors. Or perhaps you would like to simplify some of the existing consoles by removing snap-ins you seldom use.

MMC consoles use, by default, the file-name extension .msc, and .msc files are associated by default with MMC. Thus, you can run any MMC console by double-clicking its file name in a File Explorer window or by entering the file name at a command prompt. Windows 10 includes several predefined consoles; the most commonly used ones, described in Table 18-2, can be easily found by typing their name in the search box.

Inside OUT

Avoiding User Account Control problems with MMC consoles

Consoles can be used to manage all sorts of computer hardware and Windows features: With a console, you can modify hard-drive partitions, start and stop services, and install device drivers, for example. In other words, MMC consoles perform the types of tasks that User Account Control (UAC) is designed to restrict. In the hands of someone malicious (or simply careless), consoles have the power to wreak havoc on your computer.

Therefore, when using an MMC console, you're likely to encounter a User Account Control request for permission to continue. If UAC is enabled on your computer, the type of request you get and the restrictions that are imposed depend on your account type and the console you're using. Some consoles, such as Device Manager (Devmgmt.msc), display a message box informing you that the console will run with limitations. (In effect, it works in a read-only mode that allows you to view device information but not make changes.) Others block all use by nonadministrative users. To ensure you don't run into an "access denied" roadblock when performing administrative tasks while signed in with a standard account, always right-click and then click Run As Administrator.

Table 18-2 Useful predefined consoles

Console name (file name)	Description
Computer Management (Compmgmt.msc)	Includes the functionality of the Task Scheduler, Event Viewer, Shared Folders, Local Users And Groups, Performance Monitor, Device Manager, Disk Management, Services, and WMI Control snap-ins, providing control over a wide range of computer tasks.
Certificate Manager (Certmgr.msc)	Uses the Certificates snap-in to view and manage security certificates for the current user. A similar console, Certlm.msc, manages certificates on the local machine.
Device Manager (Devmgmt.msc)	Uses the Device Manager snap-in to enable administration of all attached hardware devices and their drivers. See Chapter 13, "Hardware," for more information on configuring hardware.
Disk Management (Diskmgmt.msc)	Uses the Disk Management snap-in for configuring disk volumes and partitions. For details, see Chapter 14.
Event Viewer (Eventvwr.msc)	Uses the Event Viewer snap-in to display all types of logged information. See "Event Viewer" in Chapter 17 for details.
Hyper-V Manager (Virtmgmt.msc)	Uses the Hyper-V Manager snap-in to provide an environment for creating, modifying, and running virtual machines. See Chapter 22, "Running virtual machines with Hyper-V," for details.
Local Users and Groups (Lusrmgr.msc)	Uses the Local Users and Groups snap-in to manage local user accounts and security groups. For more information, see "User accounts and security groups" in Chapter 6.
Performance Monitor (Perfmon.msc)	Uses the Performance Monitor snap-in to provide a set of monitoring tools. See Chapter 15, "System maintenance and performance," for details.
Print Management (Printmanagement.msc)	Uses the Print Management snap-in for managing printers and print jobs.
Services (Services.msc)	Uses the Services snap-in to manage services in Windows. For details, see "Managing startup programs and services" in Chapter 15 and "Managing services," earlier in this chapter.
Task Scheduler (Taskschd.msc)	Uses the Task Scheduler snap-in for managing tasks that run automatically. For details, see "Using Task Scheduler" in Chapter 19.
Trusted Platform Module (TPM) Management (Tpm.msc)	Displays information about and enables configuration of a computer's TPM chip.
Windows Firewall With Advanced Security (Wf.msc)	Uses the Windows Firewall With Advanced Security snap-in to configure rules and make other firewall settings. For details, see "Advanced tools for managing Windows Firewall" in Chapter 7.

CHAPTER 18

Automating tasks and activities

If you use your computer very often—and if you're reading this book you probably do—you likely find yourself performing certain ordinary tasks repeatedly. Such tasks might include routine maintenance activities, such as backing up your data or cleaning deadwood from your hard disk, or they might be jobs that require many steps. If you're a system administrator or help desk technician, you undoubtedly have management or troubleshooting tasks you need to perform on a recurrent basis.

Microsoft Windows 10 provides several ways to automate tasks. We'll dive into a couple of them in this chapter. Task Scheduler is an interactive graphical application you can use to set up automated routines, triggered by events or by a schedule. Task Scheduler requires no programming expertise. Windows PowerShell is a .NET-based command-line shell and scripting language tailored to work with every facet of Windows, including Task Scheduler. (You can use PowerShell to create, inspect, manage, and delete Task Scheduler tasks—among many other things.) This chapter provides an introduction to the PowerShell language, with pointers to additional online and printed learning resources.

If you're an old hand with a library of MS-DOS or Cmd.exe batch programs, you'll have no need to forsake that investment in Windows 10; such programs run just as they always have. Batch programming is a decades-old technology, and we'll give it a fond salute in passing without stopping for a detailed look. We do, however, provide an overview of techniques and tips for working in Command Prompt windows.

Using Task Scheduler

Task Scheduler is a Microsoft Management Console (MMC) snap-in that supports an extensive set of triggering and scheduling options. You can run programs or scripts at specified times, launch actions when a computer has been idle for a specified period of time, run tasks when particular users sign in or out, and so on. Task Scheduler is also tightly integrated with the Event Viewer snap-in, making it easy for you to use events (an application crash or a disk-full error, for example) as triggers for tasks.

➤ **For more information about Event Viewer, see Chapter 17, "Troubleshooting."**

To launch Task Scheduler, in the search box, type **sched**. In the results list, click Task Scheduler. Alternatively, press Windows key+R and type **taskschd.msc** in the Run box.

Figure 19-1 shows a sample of Task Scheduler in its default layout. As you can see, the window is divided into three regions—a console tree on the left, the Actions pane on the right, and, in between, various informative windows in the details pane. The console tree shows you which computer you're working with (the local machine or a network computer) and provides a folder tree of currently defined tasks. You can create your own folders here to organize the tasks you create yourself, or you can add new tasks to existing folders.

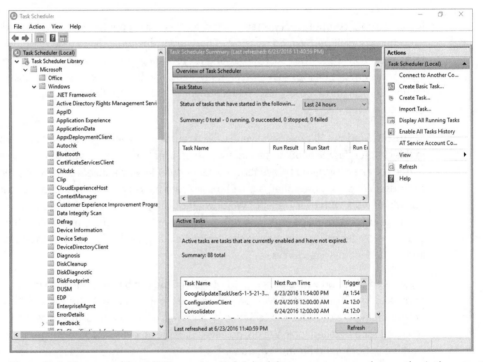

Figure 19-1 Like many other MMC snap-ins, Task Scheduler presents a console tree, the Actions pane, and various informative windows.

The Actions pane provides a menu of things you can do. Some, but not all, of the items here are also available on the menus at the top of the window. If your screen is too crowded with the Actions pane displayed, you can hide—and redisplay—it using the button at the right end of the toolbar, directly below the menu bar.

In the center part of the window, initially you see an overview message (which is a bit of static text you can hide by clicking the collapse arrow at the right), a status report of all tasks that have run (or were scheduled to run) during some period of time (by default, the most recent 24 hours), and a summary of all the currently enabled tasks. Entries in the Task Status list have outline controls; click an item's plus sign to see more details.

The Task Status and Active Tasks areas are not updated automatically. To get the latest information, click Refresh at the bottom of the screen, in the Actions pane, or on the Action menu.

If this is your first visit to Task Scheduler, you might be surprised by the number of active tasks that Windows and your applications have already established. Windows and third-party apps make extensive use of Task Scheduler to set up maintenance activities that run on various schedules. You can see which tasks managed by Task Scheduler are currently running by clicking Display All Running Tasks in the Actions pane.

To satisfy your curiosity about what an active task does and how it has been set up, you need to locate it in the console tree. Expand the outline entries as needed, and browse to an item of interest. The entries in the console tree are virtual folders, each of which can contain subfolders or one or more tasks. When you select a folder, the upper part of the details pane lists all tasks stored in the folder. The lower area of the pane, meanwhile, shows a tabbed display of the properties of the selected task.

Figure 19-2 shows the Customer Experience Improvement Program folder selected in the console tree, the task named KernelCeipTask selected in the upper area of the details pane, and the General tab of the KernelCeipTask properties displayed in the lower area. (The Actions pane has been hidden in this figure.)

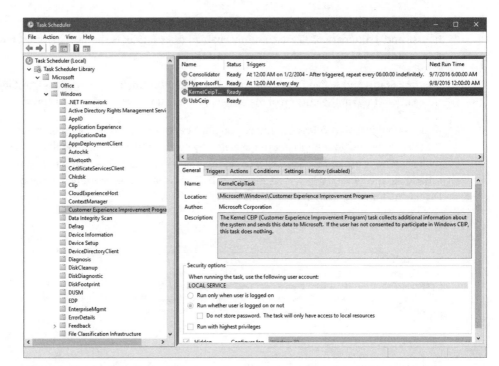

Figure 19-2 Selecting a folder in the console tree produces a list of that folder's tasks in the upper part of the details pane and a properties display in the lower part.

The properties display that appears is read-only. To edit the properties associated with a task, right-click the task name and then click Properties (or double-click the task's entry). That will open a read/write dialog box in a separate window.

With the exception of the History tab, the properties dialog box is identical to the Create Task dialog box, one of the tools you can use to create a new task; we'll explore that dialog box in some detail in the following section, "Creating a task." On the History tab, you can see exactly how, whether, and when a task has run. Figure 19-3 shows the History tab for the Notifications task in the Microsoft\Windows\Location folder.

> ### NOTE
> If the History tab is disabled, click Enable All Tasks History in the Actions pane.

When you display the History tab, the relevant portion of the Event Viewer snap-in snaps in, showing you all the recent events related to the selected task. This is exactly what you see if you run Eventvwr.msc, navigate in the console tree to Applications And Services Logs\Microsoft\Windows\TaskScheduler\Operational, and filter the resulting log to show events related to the selected task. (Obviously, if you want this information, it's quicker to find it in the Task Scheduler console than in the Event Viewer console.) If a task you set up is not being triggered when you expect it to or not running successfully when it should, you can double-click the appropriate event entry and read whatever details the event log has to offer.

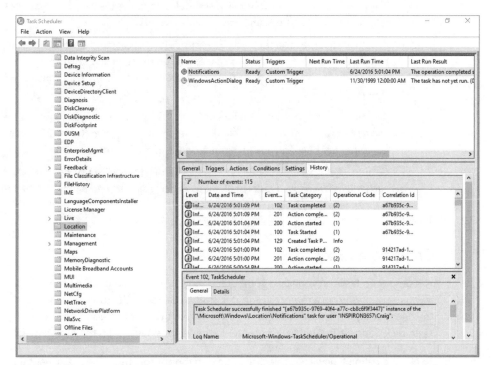

Figure 19-3 The History tab is where you confirm that a scheduled task is running as expected.

Inside OUT

Use the History tab to troubleshoot tasks

The Windows 10 Task Scheduler maintains an ample history of the events generated by each task. If a task is failing regularly or intermittently, you can review all the causes by scrolling through the History tab on the task's properties display.

Task Scheduler terminology

As you go through the steps to create or edit a task, you'll encounter the following terms:

- **Trigger.** The time at which a task is scheduled to run or the event in response to which a task runs. A task can have multiple triggers.

- **Action.** What the task does. Possible actions include starting a program, sending an email message, and displaying a message on the screen. A task can have multiple actions, in which case the actions occur sequentially in the order in which you assign them.

- **Condition.** An additional requirement that, along with the trigger, must be met for the task to run. For example, a condition might stipulate that the task run only if the computer has been idle for 10 minutes or only if it's running on AC power.

- **Setting.** A property that affects the behavior of a task. With settings, you can do such things as enable a task to run on demand or set retry parameters to be followed if a task fails to run when it's triggered.

Creating a task

You can set up tasks on your own computer or any other computer to which you have access. If you're administering a remote computer, start by selecting the top item in the console tree—the one that says Task Scheduler (Local) if you haven't yet connected to a remote computer. Then click Connect To Another Computer in the Actions pane or on the Action menu.

To begin creating a new task, select the folder in the console tree where you want the task to reside. (If you want to create a new folder for this purpose, right-click the folder's parent in the console tree and click New Folder.)

You can create a new task in the Task Scheduler snap-in by using a wizard or by filling out the Create Task dialog box. The wizard, which you launch by clicking Create Basic Task (in the Actions pane or on the Action menu), is ideal for time-triggered tasks involving a single action. It's also fine for setting up a task to run when you sign in or when Windows starts. For a more complex task definition, you need to work through the Create Task dialog box. Select the folder where you want the task to appear (in the console tree), and then click Create Task in the Actions pane or on the Action menu. Figure 19-4 shows the General tab of the Create Task dialog box.

The one required entry on the General tab is a name for the task; everything else is optional. The task's author is you (you can't change that), and unless you specify otherwise, the task will run in your own security context. If you want it to run in the security context of a different user or group, click Change User Or Group and fill out the ensuing dialog box.

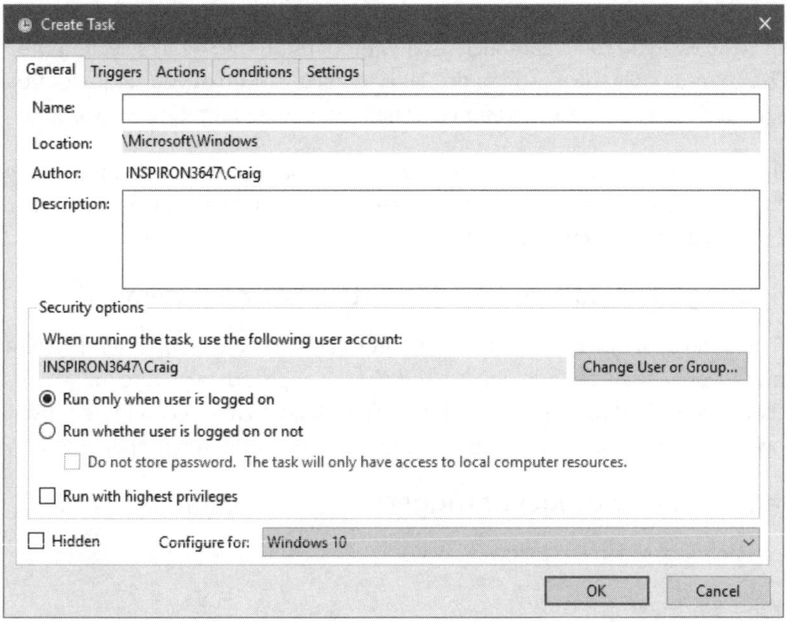

Figure 19-4 On the General tab, type a name for your new task and indicate the security context it should run in.

The circumstance under which you're most likely to need to change the security context is when you're setting up tasks to run on another computer. If you intend to run programs with which another user can interact, you should run those in the other user's security context. If you run them in your own, the tasks will run noninteractively (that is, the user will not see them).

Regardless of which user's security context the task is to run in, you have the option of allowing the task to run whether that user is signed in or not. If you select Run Whether User Is Logged On Or Not, you will be prompted for the user's password when you finish creating the task. If you don't happen to have that password, you can select Do Not Store Password. As the text beside this check box indicates, the task will have access to local resources only.

Creating a task to run with elevated privileges

If the task you're setting up is one that would generate a User Account Control (UAC) prompt if it is run interactively, you'll want to select Run With Highest Privileges. If you're setting up a task to run with elevated privileges in the context of a user who does not have administrative credentials, you're asked to supply credentials when you complete the task-setup process.

Creating a hidden task

Windows XP Service Pack 2 introduced the ability to create hidden tasks—tasks that did not ordinarily appear in the Windows XP Scheduled Tasks folder. Such tasks could be created only by means of an application programming interface (API). In Windows 10 and other recent versions of Windows, you can create such tasks without using the API by selecting the Hidden check box. Presumably the reason to do this is to make tasks that you set up for other users less visible (hence, less subject to alteration or deletion) on their target machines.

Note, however, that anyone with administrative credentials can make hidden tasks visible by clicking View, Show Hidden Tasks. And anyone running Task Scheduler can alter or delete tasks at will, regardless of who created them.

Configuring a task to run in a different operating system

If you're setting up a task on a remote computer that's running an operating system other than Windows 10, open the Configure For list and choose appropriately. Note that some applications that create scheduled tasks as part of their installation might configure those tasks for Windows 7, Windows Vista, or Windows XP. These tasks should run properly on Windows 10.

Setting up a task's trigger or triggers

Tasks can be triggered in the following ways:

- On a schedule

- At logon

- At startup

- On idle

- On an event

- At task creation or modification

- On connection to a user session

- On disconnection from a user session

- On workstation lock

- On workstation unlock

You can establish zero, one, or several triggers for a task. If you don't set any triggers, you can still run the task on demand (unless you clear the Allow Task To Be Run On Demand check box on the Settings tab of the Create Task dialog box). Running the task on demand gives you a way to test a new task before committing it to a schedule, for example. If you set multiple triggers, the task runs when any one of the triggers occurs.

To set up a trigger, click the Triggers tab in the Create Task dialog box, and then click New. In the New Trigger dialog box (shown in Figure 19-5), choose the type of trigger you want from the Begin The Task list.

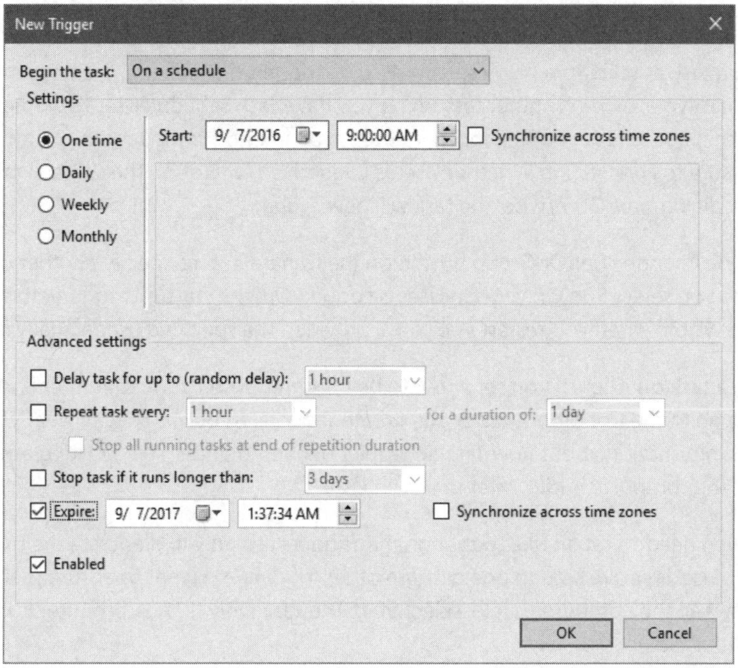

Figure 19-5 A task can have zero, one, or several triggers. You can use the Advanced Settings options to set delay, repeat, and expiration parameters.

Note the Advanced Settings options at the bottom of the dialog box shown in Figure 19-5. These choices—which you use to establish delay, repeat, and expiration parameters (among other things)—are not so easy to find when you're reviewing a task that you or someone else has already created. They don't appear in the read-only version of a task's properties, and in the read/write version of the properties dialog box, you need to select a trigger (on the Triggers tab) and click Edit to see or change the advanced settings.

Triggering a task on schedule   Time-triggered tasks can be set to run once or recur at regular intervals. The choices are probably self-explanatory, with the possible exception of the Synchronize Across Time Zones check box. Time triggers are governed by the clock of the machine on which the task is to run, unless you select this check box—in which case, they're based on coordinated universal time (UTC). You might want to go with UTC if you're trying to coordinate time-triggered tasks on multiple machines in multiple time zones.

Triggering a task at log on   Logon tasks can be set for any user or a specific user or user group. If the user whose logon triggers the task is not the one in whose security context the task is running, the task will be noninteractive—in other words, essentially invisible. (The user can note the presence of the task—and terminate it—by running Windows Task Manager, going to the Users tab, and expanding the current user to see a list of running processes.)

Triggering a task at startup   If you set a task to be triggered at startup, the trigger takes effect when you start your own computer (assuming you have Task Scheduler set to configure the local machine) but before you sign in. Therefore, if you intend for the task to run on your own system, be sure to choose Run Whether User Is Logged On Or Not on the General tab of the Create Task dialog box. Otherwise, the task will never run.

If you use the Change User Or Group button on the General tab to specify another user on your domain and you select Run Only When User Is Logged On, the startup-triggered task runs on the remote system when you restart your own, provided the specified user actually is signed in.

Triggering a task on idle   If you set a task to be triggered when your computer is idle, you should also go to the Conditions tab of the Create Task dialog box to specify what you mean by idle. For information about how Task Scheduler defines idleness, see "Starting and running a task only if the computer is idle" later in this chapter.

Note that you need to set an idle trigger on the Triggers tab only if idleness is the only trigger you want to use. If you're setting one or more other triggers but want to ensure that the task starts only when the computer is idle, select Start The Task Only If The Computer Is Idle For on the Conditions tab.

Using an event to trigger a task   Anything that generates an item in an event log can serve as a task trigger. The simplest way to use this feature is to launch Event Viewer (Eventvwr.msc), find the event you want to use as a trigger, right-click it in Event Viewer, and click Attach Task To This Event. This action launches the Create Basic Task Wizard, with the trigger portion of the wizard already filled out. The new task appears in a folder called Event Viewer Tasks (newly created for you if it doesn't already exist), and you can modify the task if needed by selecting it there and opening its properties dialog box.

➤ For information about events and event logs, see "Event Viewer" in Chapter 17.

It's possible, of course, to create an event-driven task directly in Task Scheduler—by selecting On An Event in the New Trigger dialog box. If you set up the task in this fashion, you need to supply the Log, Source, and Event ID information yourself. It's more trouble to do it this way, and there's no need.

Triggering at task creation or modification   The option to trigger a task at task creation or modification gives you an easy way to run a task the moment you finish setting it up or edit it subsequently. You can use this setting for testing purposes or, by combining it with other triggers, to make a task run immediately as well as subsequently.

Triggering a task at user connection or disconnection   The options On Connection To A User Session and On Disconnect From A User Session give you some flexible ways to run tasks in response to user activities. By using the option buttons associated with these choices, you can specify whether the settings apply to any user or to a particular user or group. Additional options make the trigger apply to remote connections and disconnections or to local connections and disconnections. Setting a trigger to a particular user on the local computer, for example, enables you to run a task in response to that user's connection via Remote Desktop Connection or the Switch User command.

Triggering a task at workstation lock or unlock   Like several other triggering choices, the On Workstation Lock and On Workstation Unlock options can be configured to apply to a particular user or group or to anyone who locks or unlocks the computer.

Setting up a task's action or actions

In addition to the task name (which you supply on the General tab of the Create Task dialog box), the only other task parameter you must provide is the action or actions the task is supposed to perform. This you do by clicking New on the Actions tab and filling out the rest of the dialog box.

Opening the Start A Program drop-down menu, you will find three choices: Start A Program, Send An E-Mail, and Display A Message. The second and third of these, however, have been deprecated since Windows 8. So leave Action set at Start A Program, and then supply the program (or script) name, optional arguments, and an optional start location.

You can specify one or several actions. Multiple actions are carried out sequentially, with each new action beginning when the previous one is complete.

The Start A Program option can be applied to anything Windows can execute—a Windows program, a batch program or script, a document associated with a program, or a shortcut. You can use the Browse button to simplify entry of long path specifications, add command-line parameters for your executable on the Add Arguments line, and specify a start-in folder for the executable. If your program needs elevated privileges to run successfully, be sure you select Run With Highest Privileges on the General tab of the Create Task dialog box.

Starting and running a task only if the computer is idle

On the Conditions tab of the Create Task dialog box (shown in Figure 19-6), you can require that the computer be idle for a specified period of time before a triggered task can begin. To do this, select Start The Task Only If The Computer Is Idle For and specify the time period in the field to the right. Other check boxes in the Idle section of the Conditions tab let you specify what should happen if the task starts to run during a required idle period but the computer subsequently becomes active again.

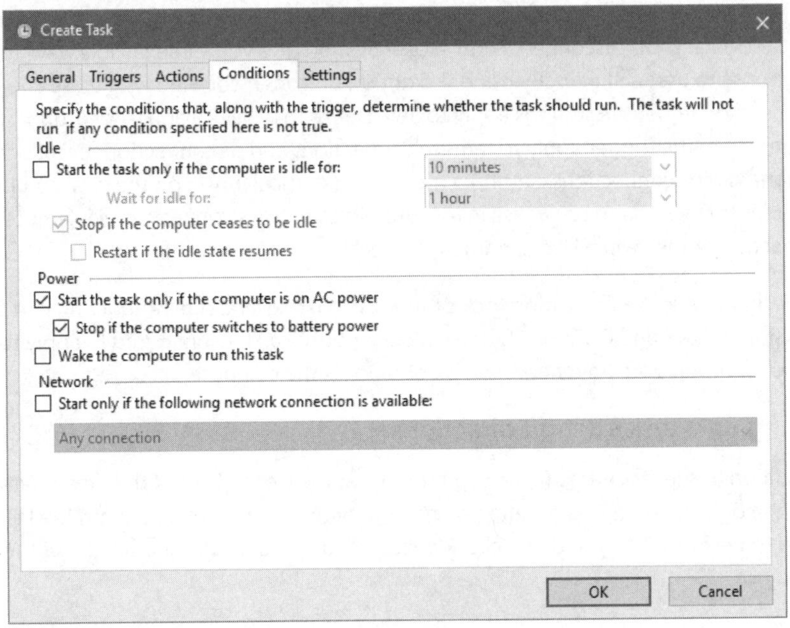

Figure 19-6 You can configure a task to run only when the computer is idle, only when it's running on AC power, or only when it's connected to a network.

Task Scheduler defines idleness as follows:

- If a screen saver is running, the computer is presumed to be idle.

- If a screen saver is not running, the system checks for idleness every 15 minutes, considering the machine to be idle if no keyboard or mouse input has occurred during that interval and if the disk input/output (I/O) and CPU usage figures were 0 percent for 90 percent of that time.

In addition to specifying a required period of idleness, you can tell Windows to wait some period of time after a task has been triggered before beginning to determine whether the computer is idle. Clearly, adjusting the idle parameters is a bit of an art; if you have precise requirements for some reason, you might need to experiment and test to get things just the way you want them.

Requiring AC power

If you're setting up a task to run on a portable computer, consider whether you want the task to begin running while the computer is running on battery power. If you do not, select Start The Task Only If The Computer Is On AC Power in the Power section of the Conditions tab. You can use a second check box below this one to specify whether the task, once it begins, should cease if the computer switches to battery power.

Waking the computer to run a task

If it's essential that your task run at some particular time, whether or not the computer is asleep, be sure to select Wake The Computer To Run This Task on the Conditions tab. Once roused, the computer will then perform whatever duties you've assigned, returning to sleep on completion in accordance with whatever power plan is in effect.

If you do not want to disturb your computer's rest, you might want to stipulate that the task run as soon as possible after the machine wakes. You can do that by selecting Run Task As Soon As Possible After A Scheduled Start Is Missed on the Settings tab of the Create Task dialog box.

Requiring a network connection

If your task requires access to network resources, be sure to select Start Only If The Following Network Connection Is Available on the Conditions tab. Then use the drop-down list directly below this check box to specify which network connection is required. You might want to use this option in conjunction with Run Task As Soon As Possible After A Scheduled Start Is Missed, a check box on the Settings tab.

Running a task on demand

You can run a scheduled task on demand as well as in response to various time or event triggers. You can turn this feature off for a task by clearing the Allow Task To Be Run On Demand check box on the Settings tab. But unless you're concerned that another user with access to your system might run a task against your wishes, it's hard to imagine why you would want to disallow on-demand execution.

To run a task on demand, assuming you have not disallowed it, locate the task's folder in the console tree, right-click the task in Task Scheduler's upper pane, and then click Run.

Scheduling tasks with the Schtasks command

Task Scheduler provides a friendly and versatile method of creating and managing scheduled tasks. In some instances, however, you might find it easier to manage scheduled tasks from a command prompt. For these occasions, Windows provides the Schtasks command, a replacement for the venerable At command that was included with earlier versions of the Windows NT platform. With Schtasks, you can create, modify, delete, end, view, and run scheduled tasks—and, of course, you can incorporate the command in batch programs and scripts. (As we discuss later in this chapter, you can also do all these things from a Windows PowerShell script.)

Tasks created via Schtasks appear in the top-level folder (Task Scheduler Library) in the Task Scheduler console tree, and you can edit, run, or delete them from there as well as from the command prompt.

Schtasks is a complex command with lots of command-line switches and other parameters, but it has only six main variants:

- **Schtasks /Create.** This variant, which you use to create a new scheduled task, is the most complex because of all the available triggering options, conditions, and settings. For details, type **schtasks /create /?** at the command prompt.

- **Schtasks /Change.** This variant is the one you use to modify an existing task. Among other things, you can change the program that the task runs, the user account under which the task runs, or the password associated with that user account. For details, type **schtasks /change /?** at the command prompt.

- **Schtasks /Delete.** This variant deletes an existing task or, optionally, all tasks on a computer.

- **Schtasks /End.** This variant stops a program that was started by a scheduled task.

- **Schtasks /Query.** This variant displays, with optional verbosity, all scheduled tasks on the local computer or a remote computer. You can use arguments to restrict the display to particular tasks or tasks running in particular security contexts. For details, type **schtasks /query /?** at the command prompt.

- **Schtasks /Run.** This variant runs a specified task on demand.

Automating command sequences with batch programs

A batch program (also commonly called a *batch file*) is a text file that contains a sequence of commands to be executed. You execute the commands by entering the file name at a command prompt. Any action you can take by typing a command at a command prompt can be encapsulated in a batch program.

When you type the name of your batch program at the command prompt (or when you specify it as a task to be executed by Task Scheduler and the appropriate trigger occurs), the command interpreter opens the file and starts reading the statements. It reads the first line, executes the command, and then goes on to the next line. On the surface, this seems to operate just as though you were typing each line yourself at the command prompt. In fact, however, the batch program can be more complicated because the language includes replaceable parameters, conditional and branching statements, the ability to call subroutines, and so on. Batch programs can also respond to values returned by programs and to the values of environment variables.

Automating tasks with Windows Script Host

Microsoft Windows Script Host (WSH) provides a way to perform more sophisticated tasks than the simple jobs that batch programs are able to handle. You can control virtually any component of Windows and of many Windows-based programs with WSH scripts.

To run a script, you can type a script name at a command prompt or double-click the script's icon in File Explorer. WSH has two nearly equivalent programs—Wscript.exe and Cscript.exe—that, with the help of a language interpreter dynamic-link library such as Vbscript.dll, execute scripts written in VBScript or another scripting language. (Cscript.exe is a command-line program; Wscript.exe is its graphical counterpart.)

With WSH, the files can be written in several languages, including VBScript (a scripting language similar to Microsoft Visual Basic) and JScript (a form of JavaScript). All the objects are available to any language, and in most situations you can choose the language with which you are most comfortable. WSH doesn't care what language you use, provided the appropriate interpreter dynamic-link library is available. VBScript and JScript interpreters come with Windows 10; interpreters for Perl, KiXtart (Kix), Python, Rexx, and other languages are available elsewhere.

Working at the command prompt

To get to the command prompt, run Cmd.exe. You can do this by double-clicking any shortcut for Cmd.exe, but because you like to type, you might find it easiest to press Windows key+R, and then type **cmd**. To open a second or subsequent Command Prompt window when one is already open, you can type **start** in the window that's already running.

Running with elevated privileges

Your activities in a Command Prompt session are subject to the same User Account Control (UAC) restrictions as anything else you do in Windows. If you use Command Prompt to launch a program (for example, Registry Editor) that requires an administrative token, you'll be asked to confirm a UAC prompt before moving on. If you plan to run several such tasks from Command Prompt, you might prefer to run Cmd.exe itself with elevated privileges. To do this, right-click any shortcut for Command Prompt and then click Run As Administrator. Or right-click the Start button and click Command Prompt (Admin). Windows displays the word *Administrator* in the title bar of any Command Prompt window running with elevated privileges.

Starting Command Prompt at a particular folder

If you run Cmd.exe from a shortcut or from %SystemRoot%\System32, the session begins with that folder as the current directory. (*Directory* is the MS-DOS-era term for *folder*, and you'll encounter it frequently in command names, help files, and so on.) If you run Cmd from the Start menu, it begins in your %UserProfile% folder. To run a Command Prompt session at a different folder, hold down the Shift key while you right-click the folder in File Explorer. On the shortcut menu, click Open Command Window Here.

Starting Command Prompt and running a command

By using the /C and /K command-line arguments, you can start a Command Prompt session and immediately run a command or program. The difference between the two is that **Cmd /C commandstring** terminates the Command Prompt session as soon as *commandstring* has finished, whereas **Cmd /K commandstring** keeps the Command Prompt session open after *commandstring* has finished. Note the following:

- You must include either /C or /K if you want to specify a command string as an argument to Cmd. If you type **cmd commandstring**, the command processor simply ignores *commandstring*.

- While *commandstring* is executing, you can't interact with the command processor. To run a command or program and keep the Command Prompt window interface, use the Start command. For example, to run Mybatch.bat and continue issuing commands while the batch program is running, type

  ```
  cmd /k start mybatch.bat
  ```

- If you include other command-line arguments along with /C or /K, /C or /K must be the last argument before *commandstring*.

Using AutoRun to execute commands when Command Prompt starts

By default, Command Prompt executes on startup whatever it finds in the following two registry values:

- The AutoRun value in HKLM\Software\Microsoft\Command Processor

- The AutoRun value in HKCU\Software\Microsoft\Command Processor

The AutoRun value in HKLM affects all user accounts on the current machine. The AutoRun value in HKCU affects only the current user account. If both values are present, both are executed—HKLM before HKCU. Both AutoRun values are of data type REG_SZ, which means they can contain a single string. To execute a sequence of separate Command Prompt statements, therefore, you must use command symbols or store the sequence as a batch program and then use AutoRun to call the batch program.

You can also use Group Policy objects to specify startup tasks for Command Prompt.

Editing the command line

When working at a command prompt, you often enter the same command multiple times or enter several similar commands. To assist you with repetitive or corrective tasks, Windows includes a feature that recalls previous commands and allows you to edit them on the current command line. Table 19-1 lists these editing keys and what they do.

Table 19-1 Command-line editing keys

Key	Function
Up Arrow or F3	Recalls the previous command in the command history
Down Arrow	Recalls the next command in the command history
Page Up	Recalls the earliest command used in the session
Page Down	Recalls the most recently used command
Left Arrow	Moves left one character
Right Arrow	Moves right one character
Ctrl+Left Arrow	Moves left one word
Ctrl+Right Arrow	Moves right one word
Home	Moves to the beginning of the line
End	Moves to the end of the line
Esc	Clears the current command
F7	Displays the command history in a scrollable pop-up box
F8	Displays commands that start with the characters currently on the command line
Alt+F7	Clears the command history

Using command symbols

Old-fashioned programs that take all their input from a command line and then run unaided can be useful in a multitasking environment. You can turn them loose to perform complicated processing in the background while you continue to work with other programs in the foreground.

To work better with other programs, many command-line programs follow a set of conventions that control their interaction:

- By default, programs take all of their input as lines of text typed at the keyboard. But input in the same format also can be redirected from a file or any device capable of sending lines of text.

- By default, programs send all of their output to the screen as lines of text. But output in the same format also can be redirected to a file or another line-oriented device, such as a printer.

- Programs set a number (called a *return value*) when they terminate to indicate the results of the program.

When programs are written according to these rules, you can use the symbols listed in Table 19-2 to control a program's input and output or chain programs together.

Table 19-2 Command symbols

Symbol	Function
<	Redirects input
>	Redirects output
>>	Appends redirected output to existing data
|	Pipes output
&	Separates multiple commands in a command line
&&	Runs the command after && only if the command before && is successful
||	Runs the command after || only if the command before || fails
^	Treats the next symbol as a character
(and)	Groups commands

The redirection symbols

Command Prompt sessions in Windows allow you to override the default source for input (the keyboard) or the default destination for output (the screen).

Redirecting output   To redirect output to a file, type the command followed by a greater-than sign (>) and the name of the file.

Using two greater-than signs (>>) redirects output and appends it to an existing file.

Redirecting input   To redirect input from a file, type the command followed by a less-than sign (<) and the name of the file.

Redirecting input and output   You can redirect both input and output in a command line. For example, to use Batch.lst as input to the Sort command and send its output to a file named Sorted.lst, type the following:

```
Sort < batch.lst > sorted.lst
```

Standard output and standard error   Programs can be written to send their output either to the standard output device or to the standard error device. Sometimes programs are written to send different types of output to each device. You can't always tell which is which because, by default, both devices are the screen.

The Type command illustrates the difference. When used with wildcards, the Type command sends the name of each matching file to the standard error device and sends the contents of the file to the standard output device. Because they both go to the screen, you see a nice display with each file name followed by its contents.

However, if you try to redirect output to a file by typing something like this:

```
type *.bat > std.out
```

the file names still appear on your screen because standard error is still directed to the screen. Only the file contents are redirected to Std.out.

With Windows, you can qualify the redirection symbol by preceding it with a number. Use 1> (or simply >) for standard output and 2> for standard error. For example:

```
type *.bat 2> err.out
```

This time the file contents go to the screen and the names are redirected to Err.out.

The pipe symbol

The pipe symbol (|) is used to send, or pipe, the output of one program to a second program as the second program's input. Piping is commonly used with the More command, which displays multiple screenfuls of output one screenful at a time. For example:

```
help dir | more
```

This command line uses the output of Help as the input for More. The More command filters out the first screenful of Help output, sends it to the screen as its own output, and then waits for a keystroke before sending more filtered output.

> ## Inside OUT
> ### Pipe command-line output to the Clipboard
>
> Using the Clip utility, introduced with Windows Vista, you can pipe the output of a command to the Windows Clipboard, from whence you can paste it into any program that accepts Clipboard text. Typing **dir | clip**, for example, puts a listing of the current directory's files on the Clipboard. You can also redirect the contents of a file to the Clipboard using the < symbol. Typing **clip < myfile.txt**, for example, transfers the contents of myfile.txt to the Clipboard.

Customizing Command Prompt windows

You can customize the appearance of a Command Prompt window in several ways. You can change its size, select a font, and even use eye-pleasing colors. And you can save these settings independently for each shortcut that launches a Command Prompt session so that you can make appropriate settings for different tasks.

To customize a Command Prompt window, you make settings in a properties dialog box that you can reach in any of three ways:

- Right-click a shortcut that opens a Command Prompt window, and then click Properties on the shortcut menu. Changes you make here affect all future Command Prompt sessions launched from this shortcut.

- Click the Control menu icon at the left side of the title bar in a Command Prompt window, and then click Properties on the Control menu. (If Command Prompt is running in full-screen mode, press Alt+Enter to switch to window display.) Changes you make here affect the current session. When you leave the properties dialog box, you'll be given the option of propagating your changes to the shortcut from which this session was launched.

- Click the Control menu icon in a Command Prompt window, and then click Defaults on the Control menu. Changes here do not affect the current session. Instead, they affect all future sessions, except those launched from a shortcut whose properties you have modified.

Setting the window size and position

To change the screen position where a newly launched Command Prompt window appears, open the window's properties dialog box and click the Layout tab.

The dialog box maintains two different sizes: the screen buffer size and the window size. The width for both sizes is specified in columns (characters); the height is specified in rows (text lines).

The screen buffer settings control the size of the "virtual screen," which is the maximum extent of the screen. Standard screen sizes are 80 by 25, 80 by 43, or 80 by 50, but you can set your Command Prompt session to any size you want.

The window size settings control the size of the Command Prompt window on your screen. In most cases, you'll want it to be the same size as the screen buffer. But if your screen is crowded, you can reduce the window size. If you do, scroll bars are added. The window size settings cannot be larger than the screen buffer size settings.

Because you size a window by specifying how many rows and columns of characters it should have, the size of those characters also affects the amount of space the window occupies on your display. For information about changing the character size, see the upcoming "Selecting a font" section.

Setting the window size and position visually

Rather than guess at the settings for window size and position, you can drag the borders of a Command Prompt window to adjust its size and drag its title bar to adjust its position. To retain the settings for future sessions, click the Control menu icon, click Properties, and click the Layout tab. You'll see the settings that reflect the window's current condition. Click OK to apply these settings.

Selecting a font

Applications in a Command Prompt window can display only one font at a time. Your choice is limited, as you'll see if you click the Font tab in the Command Prompt window's properties dialog box.

Make a selection in the Font list first because your choice here determines the contents of the Size list. If you select the Consolas or Lucida Console font, you'll find point sizes to choose from in the Size list. If you select Raster Fonts, you'll find character widths and height in pixels.

Inside OUT

Run the Bash shell natively in Windows

In March 2016, Microsoft announced it would be offering developers the ability to work with the Ubuntu user space and Bash shell, running natively (not in a virtualized environment) in Windows 10. The technology, which relies on a new Windows Subsystem for Linux (WSL), enables developers to use command-line utilities such as grep, awk, and sed, and run Bash scripts that rely on these utilities.

For more information, see the Windows Developer blog post at *https://blogs.windows.com/buildingapps/2016/03/30/run-bash-on-ubuntu-on-windows*. Note that at the time this book was in production, the implementation of Ubuntu and Bash was still in beta.

Setting colors

You can set the color of the text and the background of the Command Prompt window. You can also set the color of the text and the background of pop-up windows that originate from the command prompt, such as the command history window.

To set colors, click the Colors tab in the Command Prompt window's properties dialog box. Here you can set separate foreground and background colors for the Command Prompt window and pop-up windows, such as the command history window.

An introduction to Windows PowerShell

Microsoft describes Windows PowerShell as a "task-based command-line shell and scripting language designed especially for system administrators." That means you can use PowerShell for the same kinds of tasks you're accustomed to performing with Cmd.exe, and you can use its scripting power to automate routine work. If you're a Windows user who occasionally likes to take advantage of the power of text-based command-line tools such as Ipconfig or Netsh, you'll find that PowerShell lets you interact with the operating system in all the old familiar ways—and a good many new ones as well. If you're accustomed to using batch programs, VBScript, or JScript to automate administrative tasks, you can retain your current scripting investment but take advantage of the additional capabilities afforded by PowerShell's object orientation and .NET Framework foundation as your scripting needs grow.

Among the advantages PowerShell offers over previous shells and scripting platforms are the following:

- **Integration with the Microsoft .NET Framework.** Like more traditional development languages, such as C#, PowerShell commands and scripts have access to the vast resources of the .NET Framework.

- **Object orientation and an object-based pipeline.** All PowerShell commands that generate output return .NET Framework objects rather than plain text, eliminating the need for text parsing when the output of one command provides input to a second.

- **A consistent, discoverable command model.** All of PowerShell's commands (or "cmdlets," as they are called) use a verb-noun syntax, with a hyphen separating the two components. All cmdlets that read information from the system begin with Get; all those that write information begin with Set. These and other similar consistencies make the language easy to learn and understand. Each cmdlet has a help topic that can be retrieved by typing **get-help** *cmdletname* (where *cmdletname* is the name of a cmdlet). You can use a –Whatif parameter to test the effect of a cmdlet before you execute it.

- **Universal scripting capability.** A PowerShell script is a text file, with the extension .ps1, containing PowerShell commands. Any commands that can be used interactively can be incorporated into a script, and scripting structures, such as looping, branching, and variables, can also be used interactively—that is, outside the context of a script.

- **A focus on administrators.** PowerShell includes features of particular interest to system administrators, such as the ability to work with remote computers; access to system resources such as files, folders, registry keys, events, and logs; and the ability to start and stop services.

- **Extensibility.** Developers can extend the PowerShell language by importing modules—packages of PowerShell commands and other items.

The following pages introduce PowerShell. Our discussion focuses primarily on the use of PowerShell as an interactive command shell, because PowerShell scripting is itself a book-length subject. For sources of additional information, see "Finding additional PowerShell resources" later in this chapter.

Starting PowerShell

To launch Windows PowerShell, type **powershell** into the search box; the Windows PowerShell application should appear at or near the top of the results list. Nearby you'll also find the 64-bit and 32-bit versions of the Windows PowerShell Integrated Scripting Environment (ISE). The ISE is a multitabbed graphical environment of particular use for developing and debugging scripts.

As Figure 19-7 shows, PowerShell's default appearance differs minimally from that of Cmd.exe. The caption *Windows PowerShell* and the letters *PS* at the beginning of the command prompt might be the only details you notice.

Figure 19-7 An uncustomized (default) PowerShell window looks a lot like Cmd.exe.

Interacting with PowerShell

If you're an old hand at the command prompt but new to PowerShell, the first thing you might want to try is using some of Cmd.exe's familiar internal commands. You'll discover that such items—for example, *dir*, *cd*, *md*, *rd*, *pushd*, and *popd*—still work in PowerShell. Redirection symbols, such as > to send output to a file and > > to append output to a file, work as well, and you can pipe lengthy output to More, just as you're accustomed to doing in Cmd.exe. PowerShell uses aliases to map Cmd.exe commands to its own cmdlets. Thus, for example, *dir* is an alias for the PowerShell cmdlet *Get-Childitem*; *cd* is an alias for PowerShell's *Set-Location*. You can create your own aliases to simplify the typing of PowerShell commands that you use often; for details, see "Using and creating aliases" later in this chapter.

Like any other command prompt, PowerShell can be used to launch executables. Typing **regedit**, for example, launches Registry Editor; typing **taskschd** launches Task Scheduler. (Note that with PowerShell you also can work directly with the registry without the use of Registry Editor; for details, see "Working with the registry" later in this chapter.)

Using cmdlets

The core of PowerShell's native vocabulary is a set of cmdlets, each consisting of a verb, followed by a hyphen, followed by a noun—for example, *Start-Service*. A cmdlet can be followed by one or more parameters; each parameter is preceded by a space and consists of a hyphen connected to the parameter's name followed by a space and the parameter's value. So, for example,

```
Get-Process -Name iexplore
```

returns information about any currently running processes named iexplore.

With parameters that accept multiple values, you can use a comma to separate the values. For example,

```
Get-Process -Name iexplore, winword, excel
```

generates information about Microsoft Word and Excel as well as Internet Explorer.

Many cmdlets use positional parameters. For example, the –Name parameter for *Get-Process* is positional. PowerShell expects it to come first, so you can omit –Name and simply specify the names of the processes in which you're interested.

If you omit both the first positional parameter and its value, PowerShell typically assumes a value of *. So, for example,

```
Get-Process
```

returns information about all running processes, as shown in Figure 19-8.

In some cases, if you omit values for an initial positional parameter, PowerShell prompts you to supply the parameter. For example, in response to

```
Get-Eventlog
```

PowerShell will do you the courtesy of prompting for the name of an event log. (Event logs are large; it wouldn't be reasonable to ask for all of them at once.)

For information about any particular cmdlet, type **get-help** followed by the cmdlet name.

```
Windows PowerShell                                                    -  □  ×
PS C:\Users\Craig> get-process

Handles  NPM(K)    PM(K)     WS(K)     CPU(s)     Id  SI ProcessName
-------  ------    -----     -----     ------     --  -- -----------
    357      16     5268     12960       0.56   8596   1 Amazon Music Helper
    710      32    26400     35188      26.17    220   1 ApplicationFrameHost
    143       8     1800      7024       0.02   7228   1 AppVShNotify
    129       8     1268      5628              2568   0 armsvc
    839      18    26032     21824     499.09   6736   0 audiodg
    271      14     3396      7036       1.00   6224   1 CastSrv
    138       9     1484      7260       0.05   8028   1 CNMFSUT6
    169      11     3648     12920       1.09   7416   1 conhost
    848      34    26772     38468       2.88   7800   1 CSISYNCCLIENT
    448      14     1372      3512              636   0 csrss
    558      19     2044      4384              716   1 csrss
    424      19     4984     13136             1664   0 dasHost
    227      13     4424     10668             2660   0 dllhost
    127       9     3808      7400             3408   0 dllhost
    182      20     4708     11264       0.22   5256   1 dllhost
    245      12     3132     16576       0.20   9680   1 dllhost
    134       8     1836      9640            10808   0 dllhost
    672      37    52004     41032              628   1 dwm
   2954     149    70968    123944     204.30   2364   1 explorer
    185      14     2120      1104       0.39   8640   1 GoogleUpdate
    418      37    30680     34244             3896   0 IAStorDataMgrSvc
    316      28    19996     28712       2.27   1740   1 IAStorIcon
      0       0        0         4                0   0 Idle
    164       9     1788      7564             1808   0 igfxCUIService
    179      13     3808     11148       0.66   2488   1 igfxEM
    114       9     2436      7808       0.31   3884   1 igfxHK
    154      11     3236      9988       0.66   3820   1 igfxTray
    364      18     3964     12640       1.09    892   1 InputPersonalization
    140       9     1628      5988             2724   0 IntelCpHeciSvc
   1293      22     6688     14536              876   1 lsass
      0       0      544    133292             2636   0 Memory Compression
    224      14     3040     10880       0.34   6468   1 MSASCuiL
    197      13     2872      8084             3796   0 msdtc
    567      67   182292     63300             1972   0 MsMpEng
    680     100    27460     38464      34.63   6648   1 Music.UI
    278      26    15244      7300             2868   0 NisSrv
    736      28    39780     33748             6316   0 OfficeClickToRun
    728      40    69784     64992     311.48   9596   1 OneDrive
    150      10     3404      2284       0.13   8304   1 ONENOTEM
```

Figure 19-8 Typing **Get-Process** without parameters produces information about all running processes.

Using the pipeline

You can use the pipe operator (|) to supply the output of one cmdlet as input to another. You can connect as many cmdlets as you please in this manner, as long as each cmdlet to the right of a pipe operator understands the output of the cmdlet to its left. Because PowerShell cmdlets return full-fidelity .NET objects rather than text, a cmdlet to the right of a pipe operator can operate directly on properties or methods of the preceding cmdlet's output.

The following paragraphs provide examples of the use of piping to format, filter, and sort the output from various Get- cmdlets.

Formatting output as a list   The default output from many Get- cmdlets is a table that presents only some of the resultant object's properties (about as many as the width of your display is likely to accommodate). For example, the cmdlet

```
Get-Service
```

generates a three-column display that includes only the Status, Name, and DisplayName properties.

If you pipe the same output to *Format-List*,

```
Get-Service | Format-List
```

PowerShell, no longer constrained by display width, can display more of the object's properties (as shown in Figure 19-9), including in this case such useful items as the dependencies of each service and whether the service can be paused or stopped.

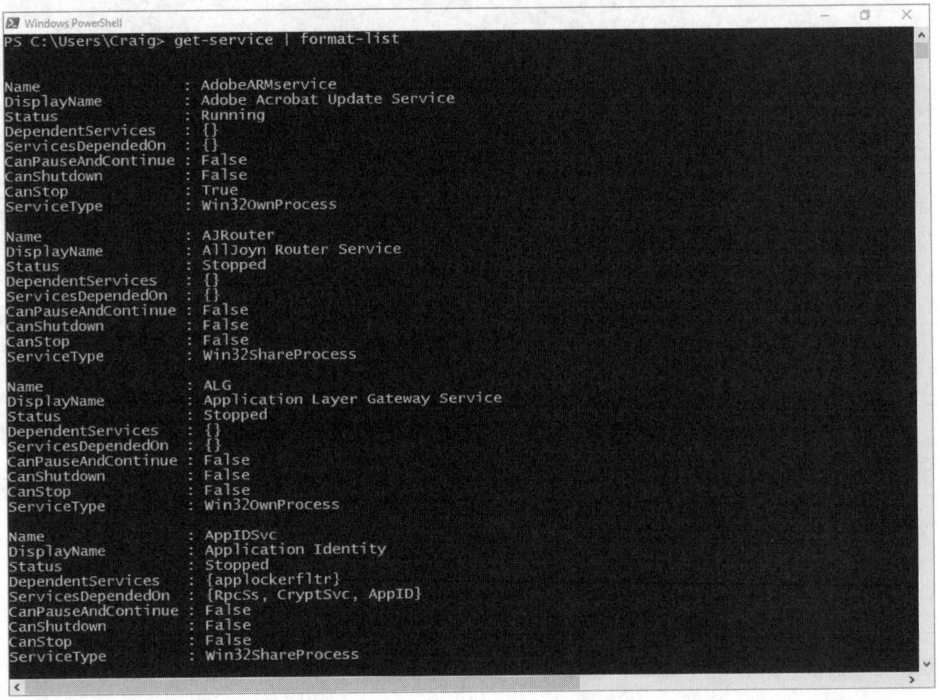

Figure 19-9 By piping a cmdlet to *Format-List*, you can see more of a resultant object's properties.

In some cases, you'll find the *Format-List* cmdlet, with no parameters, is equivalent to *Format-List –Property *. But this is by no means always the case. For example,

```
Get-Process | Format-List
```

returns four properties for each process: ID, Handles, CPU, and Name. Asking for all properties produces a wealth of additional information.

To generate a list of particular properties, add the –Property parameter to *Format-List* and supply a comma-separated list of the properties you want to see. To see what properties are available for the object returned by a cmdlet, pipe that cmdlet to *Get-Member*:

```
Get-Process | Get-Member -Itemtype property
```

(Omitting the –Itemtype parameter returns methods as well as properties.)

Formatting output as a table   Perhaps you want tabular output but with different properties from those that your cmdlet gives you by default. *Format-Table* does the trick. For example,

```
Get-Service | Format-Table -Property name, dependentservices, servicesdependedon
```

generates a table consisting of these three enumerated properties. Note that PowerShell's console output is constrained by your console width, no matter how many properties you ask to see. For results that are too wide to display, redirect output to a file (using the > operator) or try the *Out-Gridview* cmdlet, described next.

Generating an interactive graphical table with *Out-Gridview*   Piping the output to *Out-Gridview* generates a graphical tabular display you can filter, sort, and copy easily into other programs, such as Excel, that accommodate tabular data. For example,

```
Get-Process | Select-Object * | Out-Gridview
```

produces output comparable to that shown in Figure 19-10. Note that in this example, *Get-Process* is piped first to *Select-Object* * because *Out-Gridview*, unlike *Format-Table*, does not include a –Property parameter. *Select-Object* * passes all properties of the object returned by *Get-Process* along the pipeline to *Out-Gridview*.

Name	Id	PriorityClass	FileVersion	HandleCount	WorkingSet	PagedMemorySize	PrivateMemorySize	VirtualMemorySize	Tota
Amazon Music Helper	8,596	Normal		357	12,939,264	5,394,432	5,394,432	104,398,848	00:0
ApplicationFrameHost	220	Normal	10.0.14379.0 (rs1_release.160627-1607)	705	36,589,568	26,910,720	26,910,720	195,153,920	00:0
AppVShNotify	7,228	Normal	5.0.10334.0	143	6,770,688	1,843,200	1,843,200	82,599,936	00:0
armsvc	2,568			129	5,341,184	1,298,432	1,298,432	59,629,568	
audiodg	6,736			827	19,881,984	27,377,664	27,377,664	144,687,104	00:0
CastSrv	6,224	Normal	10.0.14379.0 (rs1_release.160627-1607)	271	7,045,120	3,477,504	3,477,504	102,891,520	00:0
CNMFSUT6	8,028	Normal	1.02	138	7,032,832	1,519,616	1,519,616	90,255,360	00:0
conhost	3,232	Normal	10.0.14379.0 (rs1_release.160627-1607)	182	12,271,616	3,780,608	3,780,608	116,133,888	00:0
CSISYNCCLIENT	7,800	Normal	16.0.7070.2022	848	39,874,560	27,410,432	27,410,432	415,674,368	00:0
csrss	636			434	3,457,024	1,409,024	1,409,024	52,039,680	
csrss	716			547	4,202,496	2,093,056	2,093,056	88,326,144	
dasHost	1,664			424	13,557,760	5,103,616	5,103,616	60,596,224	
dllhost	2,660			227	10,878,976	4,526,080	4,526,080	61,526,016	
dllhost	3,408			127	7,241,728	3,899,392	3,899,392	45,436,928	
dllhost	5,256	Normal	10.0.14379.0 (rs1_release.160627-1607)	141	8,491,008	2,256,896	2,256,896	72,044,544	00:0
dllhost	10,...			133	9,879,552	1,921,024	1,921,024	74,907,648	
dwm	628			664	56,754,176	65,941,504	65,941,504	295,583,744	
explorer	2,364	Normal	10.0.14379.0 (rs1_release.160627-1607)	2,870	124,993,5...	70,815,744	70,815,744	690,028,544	00:0
GoogleUpdate	8,640	Idle	1.3.29.1	185	983,040	2,170,880	2,170,880	99,983,360	00:0
IAStorDataMgrSvc	3,896			418	41,271,296	31,416,320	31,416,320	215,175,168	
IAStorIcon	1,740	Normal	14.5.0.1081	316	28,938,240	20,475,904	20,475,904	260,132,864	00:0
Idle	0			0	4,096	0	0	65,536	
igfxCUIService	1,808			164	7,684,096	1,830,912	1,830,912	50,573,312	
igfxEM	2,488	Normal	6.15.10.3682	179	11,386,880	3,899,392	3,899,392	112,951,296	00:0
igfxHK	3,884	Normal	6.15.10.3682	114	7,610,368	2,494,464	2,494,464	65,400,832	00:0
igfxTray	3,820	Normal		154	10,063,872	3,305,472	3,305,472	106,958,848	00:0
InputPersonalization	892	BelowNor...	10.0.14379.0 (rs1_release.160627-1607)	364	13,099,008	4,091,904	4,091,904	126,238,720	00:0
IntelCpHeciSvc	2,724			140	5,783,552	1,667,072	1,667,072	44,544,000	
lsass	876			1,274	14,680,064	6,815,744	6,815,744	51,216,384	

Figure 19-10 The *Out-Gridview* cmdlet produces a graphical tabular display you can sort, filter, and copy into a spreadsheet.

You can manipulate the *Out-Gridview* display with techniques comparable to those used by many other programs:

- To sort the display, click a column heading; click a second time to reverse the sort.

- To change the position of a column, drag its heading. You can also rearrange columns by right-clicking any column head, choosing Select Columns, and then using the Move Down and Move Up buttons in the Select Columns dialog box.

- To remove columns from the display, right-click any column heading, click Select Columns, and then use the < < button in the Selected Columns dialog box.

- To perform a quick filter, enter text in the line labeled Filter. For example, to limit the display in Figure 19-10 to processes with properties containing the word Microsoft, type **Microsoft** on the Filter line.

- To filter on one or more specific columns, click the Add Criteria button. In the drop-down list that appears, select check boxes for the columns on which you want to filter and then click Add.

Filtering output with *Where-Object*   To filter output from a cmdlet, pipe it to the *Where-Object* cmdlet. With *Where-Object*, you encapsulate filtering criteria in a script block, between curly braces. The following example filters output from *Get-Service* so that only services whose status is Stopped are displayed:

```
Get-Service | Where-Object {$_.Status -eq "Stopped"}
```

Sorting output with *Sort-Object*   You can use the *Sort-Object* cmdlet to sort the output from a cmdlet on one or more of the resultant object's properties in a variety of useful ways. If you omit the –Property parameter, *Sort-Object* sorts on the default property. For example,

```
Get-Childitem | Sort-Object
```

sorts the contents of the current directory by Name, the default property in this case. To sort on multiple properties, follow –Property with a comma-separated list. *Sort-Object* sorts on the first named property first, sorting items with identical values for the first property by the second property, and so on. Sorts are ascending by default; to sort in descending order, add the parameter –Descending.

By piping *Sort-Object* to *Select-Object*, you can do such things as return the largest or smallest *n* items in a resultant object. For example,

```
Get-Process | Sort-Object -Property WS | Select-Object -Last 10
```

returns the processes with the 10 largest values of the working set (WS) property. Using –First 10 instead of –Last 10 gives you the items with the smallest values.

Piping output to the printer To redirect output to the default printer, pipe it to *Out-Printer*. To use a nondefault printer, specify its name, in quotation marks, after *Out-Printer*. For example,

```
Get-Content C:\Users\Craig\Documents\Music\Sonata.sib | Out-Printer
"Microsoft Print To PDF"
```

sends the content of C:\Users\Craig\Documents\Music\Sonata.sib to the device named Microsoft Print To PDF.

Using PowerShell features to simplify keyboard entry

PowerShell is a wordy language and doesn't take kindly to misspellings. Fortunately, it includes many features to streamline and simplify the task of formulating acceptable commands.

Using and creating aliases An alias is an alternative formulation for a cmdlet. As mentioned earlier, PowerShell uses aliases to *translate* Cmd.exe commands to its own native tongue—for example, *cd* to *Set-Location*. But it includes a great many more simply for your typing convenience; *gsv*, for example, is an alias for *Get-Service*. And you can create aliases of your own.

To see what aliases are currently available (including any you created yourself during the current session), type **get-alias**. To see whether an alias is available for a particular cmdlet, pipe *Get-Alias* to *Where-Object*, like this:

```
Get-Alias | Where-Object { $_.definition -eq "Set-Variable" }
```

This particular command string inquires whether an alias is available for the *Set-Variable* cmdlet. If you type this, you'll discover that PowerShell offers two: *sv* and *set*.

To create a new alias, type **set-alias *name value***, where *name* is the alias and *value* is a cmdlet, function, executable program, or script. If *name* already exists as an alias, *Set-Alias* redefines it. If *value* is not valid, PowerShell won't bother you with an error message—until you try to use the alias.

Aliases you create are valid for the current session only. To make them available permanently, include them in your profile. See "Using your profile to customize PowerShell" later in this chapter.

Abbreviating parameter names Aliases are dandy for cmdlets, but they're no help for parameter names. Fortunately, with PowerShell you can abbreviate such names. The commands *Get-Process –name iexplore* and *Get-Process –n iexplore* are equivalent. As soon as you've typed enough of a parameter name to let PowerShell recognize it unambiguously, you can give your fingers a rest. And, of course, you can combine aliases with parameter abbreviations to further lighten your load.

Using Tab expansion   As a further convenience, with PowerShell you can complete the names of files, cmdlets, or parameters by pressing Tab. Type part of a name, press Tab, and PowerShell presents the first potential completion. Continue pressing Tab to cycle through all the possibilities. Note, however, that Tab expansion works only with the noun portion of a cmdlet; type the verb and the hyphen, and then you can use Tab expansion for the noun.

Using wildcards and regular expressions   Like all its Windows-shell predecessors, PowerShell supports the * and ? wildcards—the former standing in for any combination of zero or more characters, the latter for any single character. PowerShell also provides a vast panoply of "regular expressions" for matching character strings. For details about regular expressions in PowerShell, type **get-help about_regular_expressions**.

Recalling commands from the command history   PowerShell maintains a history of your recent commands, which makes it easy to reuse (or edit and reuse) a command you already entered. To see the history, type **get-history**. Each item in the history is identified by an ID number. Type **invoke-history *ID*** to bring an item to the command line. On the command line, you can edit an item before executing it. With the exception of Alt+F7, the editing keys available in Cmd.exe (which are listed in Table 19-1) work the same way in PowerShell.

The number of history items retained in a PowerShell session is defined by the automatic variable $MaximumHistoryCount. By default, that variable is set to 64. If you find you need more, you can assign a larger number to the variable. For example, to double the default for the current session, type **$MaximumHistoryCount = 128**. To change the history size for all sessions, add a variable assignment to your profile. For more information, see "Using your profile to customize PowerShell" later in this chapter.

Using PowerShell providers for access to file-system and registry data

PowerShell includes a set of built-in providers that gives you access to various kinds of data stores. Providers are .NET Framework–based programs, and their data is exposed in the form of drives, comparable to familiar file-system drives. Thus, for example, you can access a key in the HKLM registry hive with a path structure similar to that of a file-system folder; for example, the path HKLM:\Hardware\ACPI specifies the ACPI key of the Hardware key of the HKLM hive. Or, to use a quite different example, you can use the command *Get-Childitem env:* to get a list of current environment variables and their values.

Table 19-3 lists PowerShell's built-in providers. For more information about providers, type **get-help about_providers**.

Table 19-3 Built-in providers

Provider	Drive	Data store
Alias	Alias:	Currently defined aliases
Certificate	Cert:	X509 certificates for digital signatures
Environment	Env:	Windows environment variables
FileSystem	(varies)	File-system drives, directories, and files
Function	Function:	PowerShell functions
Registry	HKLM:, HKCU:	HKLM and HKCU registry hives
Variable	Variable:	PowerShell variables
WSMan	WSMan:	WS-Management configuration information

The following paragraphs provide some basic information about working with the file system and registry.

Working with the file system   For very simple file-system operations, you might find that familiar Cmd.exe commands are adequate and easier to use than PowerShell cmdlets. The built-in aliases listed in Table 19-4 let you stick with time-honored methods. PowerShell supports the familiar single period (.) and double period (..) symbols for the current and parent directories, and it includes a built-in variable, $Home, that represents your home directory (equivalent to the HomePath environment variable).

Table 19-4 File-system aliases

Alias	PowerShell cmdlet
cd, chdir	*Set-Location*
copy	*Copy-Item*
del	*Remove-Item*
dir	*Get-Childitem*
move	*Move-Item*
md, mkdir	*New-Item*
rd, rmdir	*Remove-Item*
type	*Get-Content*

The PowerShell cmdlets, however, include valuable optional parameters:

- **–Confirm and –Whatif.** The –Confirm parameter, used with *Copy-Item*, *Move-Item*, *Remove-Item*, or *Clear-Content*, causes PowerShell to display a confirmation prompt before executing the command. (*Clear-Content* can be used to erase the contents of a file.) If you use the –Whatif parameter, PowerShell shows you the result of a command without executing it.

- **–Credential.** Use the –Credential parameter to supply security credentials for a command that requires them. Follow –Credential with the name of a user, within double quotation marks. PowerShell will prompt for a password.

- **–Exclude.** You can use the –Exclude parameter to make exceptions. For example, *Copy-Item directory1*.* directory2 –Exclude *.log* copies everything, excluding all .log files, from Directory1 to Directory2.

- **–Recurse.** The –Recurse parameter causes a command to operate on subfolders of a specified path. For example, *Remove-Item x:\garbagefolder*.* –Recurse* deletes everything from X:\Garbagefolder, including files contained within that folder's subfolders.

- **–Include.** By using the –Include parameter in conjunction with –Recurse, you can restrict the scope of a command. For example, *Get-Childitem c:\users\craig\documents* –Recurse –Include *.xlsx* restricts a recursive listing of C:\Users\Craig\Documents to files with the extension .xlsx.

- **–Force.** The –Force parameter causes a command to operate on items that are not ordinarily accessible, such as hidden and system files.

For detailed information about using these parameters with *Set-Location*, *Get-Childitem*, *Move-Item*, *Copy-Item*, *Get-Content*, *New-Item*, *Remove-Item*, or *Get-Acl*, type **get-help cmdletname**.

Working with the registry   The built-in registry provider provides drives for two registry hives, HKLM and HKCU. To change the working location to either of these, type **set-location hklm:** or **set-location hkcu:**, respectively. Use standard path notation to navigate to particular subkeys, but enclose paths that include spaces in quotation marks—for example, *set-location "hkcu:\control panel\accessibility"*.

To display information about all subkeys of a key, use *Get-Childitem*. For example,

```
Get-Childitem -Path hkcu:\software\microsoft
```

returns information about all the subkeys of HKCU:\Software\Microsoft.

To add a key to the registry, use *New-Item*. For example,

```
New-Item -Path hkcu:\software\mynewkey
```

adds the key mynewkey to HKCU:\Software. To remove this key, type **remove-item –path hkcu:\software\mynewkey**.

To copy a key, use *Copy-Item* and specify the source and destination paths; like this, for example,

```
Copy-Item -Path hkcu:\software\mykey hkcu:\software\copyofmykey
```

To move a key, use *Move-Item*. The command

```
Move-Item -Path hkcu:\software\mykey -Destination hkcu:\software\myrelocatedkey
```

copies all properties and subkeys associated with HKCU:\Software\Mykey to HKCU:\Software\ Myrelocatedkey and deletes HKCU:\Software\Mykey.

To display the security descriptor associated with a key, use *Get-Acl*. To see all the properties of the security descriptor, pipe this to *Format-List –Property *. For example,

```
Get-Acl -Path hkcu:\software\microsoft | Format-List -Property *
```

generates a display comparable to this:

For more information about working with the registry, type **get-help registry**.

Using PowerShell to manage scheduled tasks

PowerShell includes a set of cmdlets you can use to create, register, enable, disable, and get information about scheduled tasks. Table 19-5 lists these cmdlets.

Table 19-5 Cmdlets for managing scheduled tasks

Cmdlet	Description
Disable-ScheduledTask	Disables a scheduled task
Enable-ScheduledTask	Enables a scheduled task
Export-ScheduledTask	Exports a scheduled task as an XML string
Get-ClusteredScheduledTask	Gets clustered scheduled tasks for a failover cluster
Get-ScheduledTask	Gets the task definition object of a scheduled task that is registered on the local computer
Get-ScheduledTaskInfo	Gets run-time information for a scheduled task
New-ScheduledTask	Creates a scheduled task instance
New-ScheduledTaskAction	Creates a scheduled task action
New-ScheduledTaskPrincipal	Creates an object that contains a scheduled task principal
New-ScheduledTaskSettingsSet	Creates a new scheduled task settings object
New-ScheduledTaskTrigger	Creates a scheduled task trigger object
Register-ClusteredScheduledTask	Registers a scheduled task on a failover cluster
Register-ScheduledTask	Registers a scheduled task definition on a local computer
Set-ClusteredScheduledTask	Changes settings for a clustered scheduled task
Set-ScheduledTask	Modifies a scheduled task
Start-ScheduledTask	Starts one or more instances of a scheduled task
Stop-ScheduledTask	Stops all running instances of a scheduled task
Unregister-ClusteredScheduled-Task	Removes a scheduled task from a failover cluster
Unregister-ScheduledTask	Unregisters a scheduled task

Here are a few examples:

```
disable-scheduledtask -taskname "MyTask"
```

disables the task MyTask, which is stored in Task Scheduler's root folder.

```
get-scheduledtaskinfo -taskname "Microsoft\XblGameSave\XblGameSaveTask"
```

returns information, including the last run time and result for the task XblGameSaveTask, which is stored in the Microsoft folder.

```
get-scheduledtask -taskpath "\Microsoft\Office" | export-scheduledtask
```

returns task definition information about all tasks stored in the folder \Microsoft\Office and pipes that information to *export-scheduledtask*, which renders that information as an XML string.

For detailed information and examples concerning the use of the scheduled tasks cmdlets, see *https://bit.ly/schtask-cmdlets* or use the *Get-Help* cmdlet, as described in the following section.

Discovering PowerShell

PowerShell provides plenty of resources to help you learn as you go. You can display help information about any cmdlet by typing **get-help** *cmdletname*. For example, to read help about *Get-Help*, type **get-help get-help**. If you omit the first *get*, PowerShell helpfully pipes the help text to More. So, for example, if you type **help get-help**, PowerShell pauses the output after each screenful.

Among the useful parameters for *Get-Help* are the following:

- **–Examples.** To display only the name, synopsis, and examples associated with a particular help text, add the –Examples parameter.

- **–Parameter.** To get help for a particular parameter associated with a cmdlet, include –Parameter. Specify the parameter name in quotation marks.

- **–Detailed.** To get the description, syntax, and parameter details for a cmdlet, as well as a set of examples, use the –Detailed parameter. (Without this parameter, the examples are omitted; with –Examples, the syntax information is omitted.)

- **–Full.** For the works, including information about input and output object types and additional notes, specify –Full.

- **–Online.** For the latest information that Microsoft has, including additions or corrections to the native output of *Get-Help*, specify –Online. The relevant information, from the Microsoft TechNet Script Center, will appear in your browser.

PowerShell includes a compiled HTML (.chm) help file, which you can run from the Jump List that appears on the recent items or pinned items section of your Start menu (or on the taskbar if you pin PowerShell there). But the information made available via the –Online parameter is more current and more accurate than that provided in the .chm file. For the most recent updates, visit the "Scripting with Windows PowerShell" page at Microsoft TechNet, *https://bit.ly/scripting-with-powershell*.

Finding the right cmdlet to use

The *Get-Command* cmdlet can help you figure out which cmdlet is the right one to use for a given task. Type **get-command** with no arguments to get the names and definitions of all available cmdlets, functions, and aliases. *Get-Command* can also give you information about non-PowerShell executables. If you type **get-command ***, for example, you'll get a huge list including all files in all folders included in your current Path environment variable.

Either global list (with or without the non-PowerShell executables) is likely to be less than useful when you just want to know which cmdlets are available for use with a particular object. To get such a focused list, add the –Noun parameter. For example, type **get-command –noun eventlog** to get a list of the cmdlets that use that noun; you'll be rewarded with the names and definitions of *Clear-Eventlog*, *Get-Eventlog*, *Limit-Eventlog*, *New-Eventlog*, *Remove-Eventlog*, *Show-Eventlog*, and *Write-Eventlog*. You can get a list focused similarly on a particular verb by using the –Verb parameter.

Scripting with PowerShell

A PowerShell script is a text file with the extension .ps1. You can create a script in any plain text editor (Notepad will do fine), or you can use the Integrated Scripting Environment (ISE).

Anything you do interactively with PowerShell you can also do in a script. The reverse is true as well; you can take lines from a script, including those that involve looping or branching structures, and execute them individually outside the context of a script. For example, if you type

```
For ($i=1; $i -le 5; $i++) { "Hello, World" }
```

at the PowerShell command prompt, PowerShell performs the familiar greeting five times.

Using PowerShell's history feature, you can easily transfer commands you have used interactively into a script. That way you can test to see what works and how it works before committing text to a .ps1 file.

For example, the command

```
Get-History | Foreach-Object { $_.commandline } >> c:\scripts\mynewscript.ps1
```

appends the Commandline property from each item in your current history to the file C:\Scripts\Mynewscript.ps1. (If the path doesn't exist, the command returns an error.) Once you have transferred your history to Mynewscript.ps1 in this manner, you can edit it in Notepad by typing **notepad c:\scripts\mynewscript.ps1**.

Running PowerShell scripts

Although files with the extension .ps1 are executable PowerShell scripts, running one is not quite as straightforward as double-clicking a .bat file. In the first place, if you double-click a .ps1 file in File Explorer, you'll get an Open File—Security Warning dialog box, from which the only forward step leads to Notepad. In effect, the default action for a PowerShell script in File Explorer is Edit.

Second, the first time you try to run a script by typing its name at the PowerShell command prompt, you might see a distressing message displayed in red letters and with possibly unwelcome detail. This means that PowerShell has declined to run your script "because the execution of scripts is disabled on this system." You need to change PowerShell's execution policy, as described next.

Third, even after you've cleared the execution-policy hurdle, you might still be rebuffed if you try to run a script stored in the current directory. That's because PowerShell requires a full path specification, even when the item you're running is stored in the current directory. For example, to run Displayprocessor.ps1, which resides in the current directory, you must type **.\displayprocessor**.

Getting and setting the execution policy

PowerShell's power can be used for evil ends. The majority of Windows users will never run PowerShell, but many will have .ps1 files lying about on their system or will download them inadvertently. To protect you from malice, PowerShell disables script execution until you explicitly enable it. Enabling execution requires a change to the execution policy.

Note that your profile script (if you have one) is subject to the same execution policy as any other script. (See "Using your profile to customize PowerShell" later in this chapter.) Therefore, it's pointless to set an execution policy by means of a profile script; that script itself will not run until you've enabled script execution elsewhere.

The following execution policies, listed here from least permissive to most, are available:

- **Restricted.** The default policy. No scripts are allowed to run.

- **AllSigned.** Any script signed by a trusted publisher is allowed to run. PowerShell presents a confirmation prompt before running a script signed by a publisher that you have not designated as "trusted."

- **RemoteSigned.** Scripts from local sources can run. Scripts downloaded from the internet (including scripts that originated as email or instant-messaging attachments) can run if signed by a trusted publisher.

- **Unrestricted.** All scripts can run, but PowerShell presents a confirmation prompt before running a script from a remote source.

- **Bypass.** All scripts are allowed to run.

Execution policies can be set separately for the following scopes:

- **Process.** Affects the current PowerShell session only. The execution policy is stored in memory and expires at the end of the session.

- **CurrentUser.** The execution policy is stored in a subkey of HKCU and applies to the current user only. The setting is retained between PowerShell sessions.

- **LocalMachine.** The execution policy is stored in a subkey of HKLM and applies to all users at this computer. The setting is retained between PowerShell sessions.

If policies are set at two or more of these scopes, the Process policy takes precedence over the CurrentUser policy, which takes precedence over the LocalMachine policy. Execution policy can also be set via Group Policy, however, and settings made in that manner trump any of the foregoing scopes. (Group Policy settings can be made in either the Computer Configuration or User Configuration node; a Computer Configuration setting trumps any other.)

To see the execution policies in effect at all scopes, type **get-executionpolicy –list**.

To set an execution policy, use *Set-ExecutionPolicy*. To set a policy at the LocalMachine scope, you need to be running PowerShell with administrative privileges.

The default scope for *Set-ExecutionPolicy* is LocalMachine, so if you're planning to apply a policy to all users at your computer, you can omit the –Scope parameter. For example, if you're comfortable disabling all of PowerShell's script-execution security measures, including warning prompts, you can type **set-executionpolicy bypass.** For a slightly more protective environment, type **set-executionpolicy unrestricted**.

To set a policy at the CurrentUser or Process scope, add –Scope followed by CurrentUser or Process. Note that you can also set an execution policy at the Process scope by adding an –Executionpolicy argument to a command that launches PowerShell. For example, from a command prompt in Cmd.exe, in PowerShell, or on the Start menu, you can type **powershell –executionpolicy unrestricted** to launch PowerShell with the Unrestricted execution policy at the Process scope.

To remove an execution policy from a particular scope, set that scope's policy to Undefined. For example, if you set a Process policy to, say, Bypass, and you would like PowerShell to revert to the policy at the next level of precedence (CurrentUser, if a policy is set there, or LocalMachine, if not), type **set-executionpolicy undefined –scope process**.

Using your profile to customize PowerShell

Your profile is a script that PowerShell executes at the beginning of each session. You can use it to tailor your PowerShell environment to your preferences. Your profile must have the following path and file name:

$Home\Documents\WindowsPowerShell\Profile.ps1

where $Home is a system-generated *PowerShell* variable corresponding to the environment variable UserProfile. You can see where this is on your system by typing **$profile**, and you can edit an existing profile by typing **notepad $profile**. If you have not yet created a profile, you can type the following:

```
if (!(test-path $profile)){New-Item -Type file -Path $profile -Force}
```

PowerShell will create the file for you in the appropriate folder. Then you can type **notepad $profile** to edit the blank file.

You can use your profile to customize PowerShell in a variety of ways. Possibilities to consider include changing the default prompt and creating new aliases.

PowerShell's prompt is derived from a built-in function called Prompt. You can overwrite that function with your own. For example, the function

```
Function prompt {"PS [$env:computername] $(Get-Date) > "}
```

replaces the built-in PowerShell prompt with the letters PS, followed by your computer name, followed by the current date and time. For more information about PowerShell prompts, type **get-help about_prompts**.

To add new aliases to the ones PowerShell already offers, include *Set-Alias* statements in your profile. (See "Using and creating aliases" earlier in this chapter.)

Using the PowerShell ISE

A feature introduced with PowerShell 2.0 allows you to issue commands and work with scripts in a graphical environment. This ISE includes a command pane, a script pane, and an output pane. The output pane displays the results of any commands you issue in the command pane or any scripts you run in the script pane.

The ISE supports multiple tabs, so you can open several scripts at once. Click File, New to open a new blank tab (for example, to write a new script) or File, Open to open an existing script in a new tab. To run the current script, click Run/Continue on the Debug menu, press F5, or click the green arrow in the middle of the toolbar. You can use other commands on the Debug menu to set and remove breakpoints and step through execution.

The ISE offers all the usual amenities of a graphical environment. You can resize and rearrange the panes, for example. You can use the View menu's Zoom commands (or adjust the slider in the lower right corner of the window) to make the text display larger or smaller. And you can easily select and copy text from one pane to another or from the ISE to another application.

The ISE uses its own profile, separate from the one you use to customize PowerShell itself. The path and file name are as follows:

$Home\Documents\WindowsPowerShell\ProfileISE.ps1

and you create the file by typing:

```
if(!(Test-Path $profile)){New-Item -Type file -Path $profile -Force}
```

Finding additional PowerShell resources

This chapter's discussion of PowerShell has barely nicked the surface. For further exploration, we recommend the following:

- *Windows PowerShell 3.0 First Steps*, by Ed Wilson (Microsoft Press, 2013)

- *Windows PowerShell Cookbook*, third edition, by Lee Holmes (O'Reilly Media, 2013)

- "Windows PowerShell Scripting" (part of the Microsoft TechNet Script Center) at *https://bit.ly/ps-script-center*

- The "Hey, Scripting Guy!" blog at *https://bit.ly/scripting-guy*

- "Getting Started with Windows PowerShell" (part of the MSDN Script Center) at *https://msdn.microsoft.com/powershell/scripting/getting-started/getting-started-with-windows-powershell*

Advanced networking

For most users of Microsoft Windows at home or in a small office, HomeGroup and the other networking methods and procedures described in Chapter 5, "Networking essentials," provide all the needed connectivity. In these environments, accessing shared files, media, and printers throughout a local area network is easily achieved.

But there's much more to networking, enough to fill another book the size of this one. In this chapter, we touch upon a few of these more complex features.

We begin with a look at other ways to share resources over a network. Although HomeGroup has the advantage of being easy to set up and use, it doesn't allow you to apply resource permissions on a granular level. If you need to provide different types of access to individual users, you can use the procedures in this section. Another limitation of HomeGroup is that it works only with Windows 7 and later versions; if your network includes computers running other operating systems or—gasp!—older versions of Windows, this section is for you.

In this chapter, we also look at situations in which accessing shared files and printers is not enough; you want access to an *entire computer*. With Remote Desktop, you can do exactly that, and a section of this chapter is devoted to showing you how.

Networked devices don't always communicate the way they should, so we conclude with a survey of network troubleshooting tools included with Windows and explain sound procedures for using them.

Viewing network status

If you're familiar with earlier Windows versions, you probably know Network And Sharing Center as the place to go for a quick overview of your network connections and the condition of your network. And, if you're experiencing problems with your network, it serves as a launch pad to various diagnostic tools.

> ➤ **For more information, see "Network And Sharing Center" in Chapter 5.**

As you've seen with other Control Panel applications, much of the functionality of Network And Sharing Center from previous Windows versions has made the transition to Settings in Windows 10, and the Anniversary Update, version 1607, further advances the cause. Take a look by opening Settings > Network & Internet, which is shown in Figure 20-1.

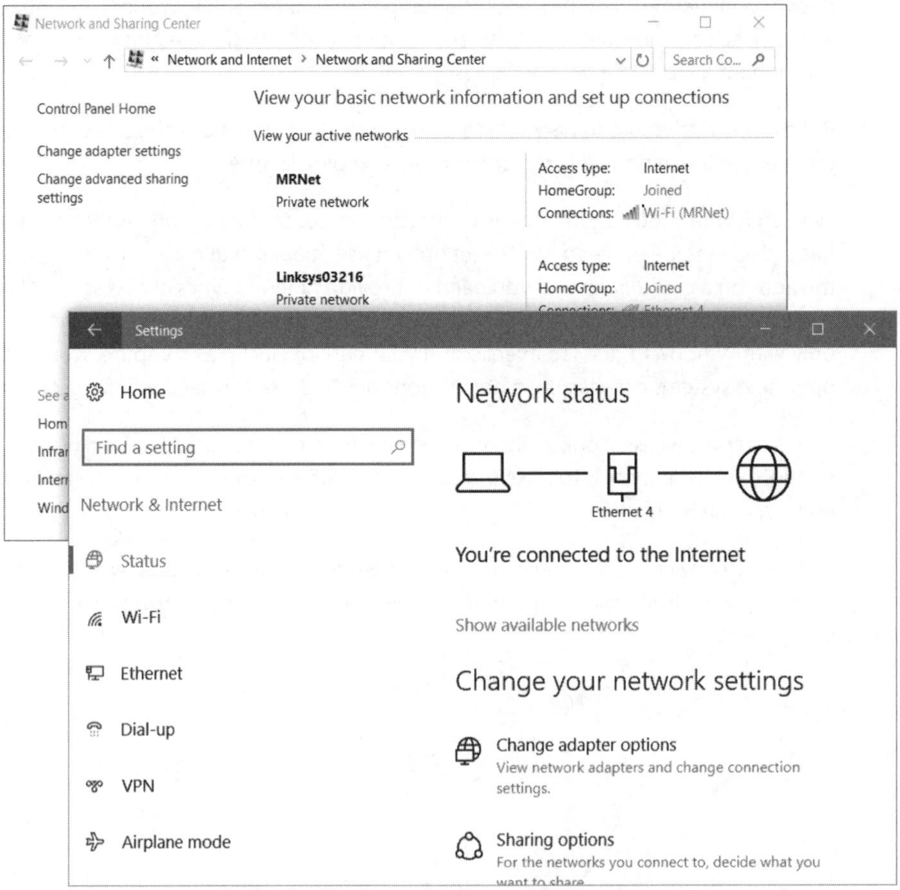

Figure 20-1 Network & Internet in Settings will someday supplant Network And Sharing Center. In the meantime, a link in Settings leads to the Control Panel page.

Inside OUT

Easily open Network & Internet or Network And Sharing Center

The quickest way to get to either network settings app is to click or tap the network icon in the notification area of the taskbar. To open Network & Internet in Settings, click the icon, click Network Settings, and then click Status. To open Network And Sharing Center in Control Panel, right-click or long tap the network icon in the taskbar and then choose Open Network And Sharing Center.

Inside OUT

Rename a network connection

In Network And Sharing Center, each network connection is assigned a name, which appears next to the Connections label. The name is typically Wi-Fi or Ethernet, but after you've messed around with your networking configuration a bit, you might see a name like Ethernet 4, as shown in Figure 20-1. If you want to get rid of the number or use a name that makes more sense to you, in Network And Sharing Center, click Change Adapter Settings. Right-click the connection and choose Rename.

Sharing resources with other users

The simplest way to share files, digital media, printers, and other resources in a small network is with HomeGroup, a feature we cover in Chapter 5. Convenient as it is, however, HomeGroup isn't appropriate for all networks. First, it's designed for use in a home, where you fully trust everybody. Hence, it has limited abilities for applying different access requirements to various objects and for various users. Second, HomeGroup works only on computers running Windows 7 and later. Computers running earlier versions of Windows or other operating systems must use different methods for sharing and accessing network resources.

These other methods are fully supported in Windows 10, and you can use them alongside HomeGroup if you want to. The underlying system of share permissions and NTFS permissions for controlling access to objects remains in Windows 10, working much like it has in previous versions of Windows going all the way back to Windows NT in the early '90s.

➤ For more information about the HomeGroup feature and its idiosyncratic spelling, see "Sharing files, digital media, and printers in a homegroup" in Chapter 5.

Understanding sharing and security models in Windows

Much like Windows 7, Windows 10 offers two ways (aside from HomeGroup) to share file resources, whether you're doing so locally or over the network:

- **Public folder sharing.** When you place files and folders in your Public folder or its sub-folders, those files are available to anyone who has a user account on your computer. Each person who signs in has access to his or her own profile folders (Documents, Music, and so on), and *everyone* who signs in has access to the Public folder. (You need to dig a bit to find the Public folder, which doesn't appear by default in the left pane of File Explorer. Navigate to C:\Users\Public. If you use the Public folder often, pin it to the Quick Access list in File Explorer.)

  By default, all users with an account on your computer can sign in and create, view, mod-ify, and delete files in the Public folders. The person who creates a file in a Public folder (or copies an item to a Public folder) is the file's owner and has Full Control access. All others who sign in locally have Modify access.

  Settings in Advanced Sharing Settings (accessible from Settings > Network & Internet, discussed in the next section) determine whether the contents of your Public folder are made available on your network and whether entering a user name and password is required for access. If you turn on password-protected sharing, only network users who have a user account on your computer (or those who know the user name and password for an account on your computer) can access files in the Public folder. Without password-protected sharing, everyone on your network has access to your Public folder files if you enable network sharing of the Public folder.

  You can't select which network users get access, nor can you specify different access levels for different users. Sharing via the Public folder is quick and easy—but it's inflexible.

- **Advanced sharing.** By choosing to share folders or files outside the Public folder, you can specify precisely which user accounts are able to access your shared data, and you can specify the types of privileges those accounts enjoy. You can grant different access privileges to different users. For example, you might enable some users to modify shared files and create new ones, enable other users to read files without changing them, and lock out still other users altogether.

You don't need to decide between sharing the Public folder and sharing specific folders because you can use both methods simultaneously. You might find that a mix of sharing styles works best for you; each has its benefits:

- Sharing specific folders is best for files you want to share with some users but not with others—or if you want to grant different levels of access to different users.

- Public folder sharing provides a convenient, logical way to segregate your personal documents, pictures, music, and so on from those you want to share with everyone who uses your computer or your network.

Configuring your network for sharing

If you plan to share folders and files with other users on your network through options other than those available in the HomeGroup feature, you need to take a few preparatory steps. (If you plan to share only through HomeGroup and with others who use your computer by signing in locally, you can skip these steps. And if your computer is part of a domain, some of these steps—or their equivalent in the domain world—must be done by an administrator on the domain controller. We don't cover those details in this book.)

1. **Be sure that all computers use the same workgroup name.** With versions of Windows newer than Windows XP, this step isn't absolutely necessary, although it does improve network discovery performance. For details, see the sidebar, "Renaming your workgroup."

2. **Be sure that your network's location is set to Private.** This setting provides appropriate security for a network in a home or an office. For details, see "Setting network locations" in Chapter 5.

3. **Be sure that Network Discovery is turned on.** This should happen automatically when you set the network location to Private, but you can confirm the setting—and change it if necessary—in Advanced Sharing Settings, which is shown in Figure 20-2. To open Advanced Sharing Settings, go to Settings > Network & Internet > Sharing Options. Alternatively, open Network And Sharing Center and click Change Advanced Sharing Options.

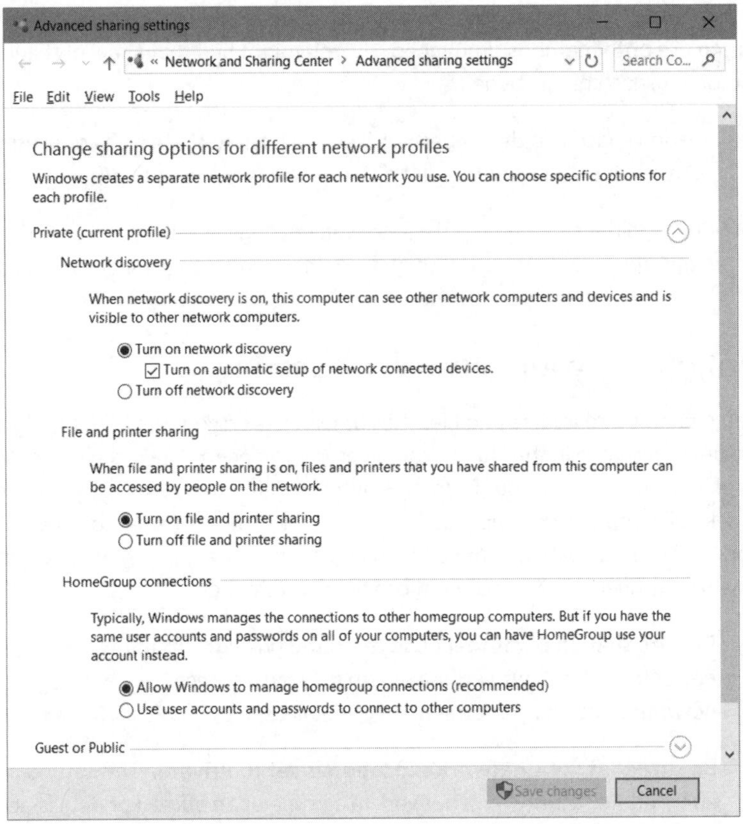

Figure 20-2 After you review settings for the Private profile, click the arrow by All Networks (below Guest Or Public) to see additional options.

4. **Select your sharing options.** In Advanced Sharing Settings, make a selection for each of the following network options. You'll find the first two options under the Private profile; to view the remaining settings, expand All Networks.

    ▪ **File And Printer Sharing.** Turn on this option if you want to share specific files or folders, the Public folder, or printers; it must be turned on if you plan to share any files (other than media streaming) over your network.

       The mere act of turning on file and printer sharing does not expose any of your computer's files or printers to other network users; that occurs only after you make additional sharing settings.

    ▪ **HomeGroup Connections.** If you use a homegroup for sharing, it's generally best to use the default setting, Allow Windows To Manage Homegroup Connections (Recommended). With this setting, when a user at a computer that's also part of a homegroup attempts to use a shared resource on your computer, Windows connects using the HomeGroupUser$ account.

When a user connects from a computer that's not a member of the homegroup, Windows first tries to authenticate using that person's sign-in credentials; if that fails, Windows uses the built-in Guest account (if password-protected sharing is off) or prompts for credentials (if password-protected sharing is on). If you select Use User Accounts And Passwords To Connect To Other Computers, homegroup computers work like non-homegroup computers instead of using the Home-GroupUser$ account.

- **Public Folder Sharing.** If you want to share items in your Public folder with all network users (or, if you enable password-protected sharing, all users who have a user account and password on your computer), turn on Public folder sharing. If you do so, network users will have read/write access to Public folders. With Public folder sharing turned off, anyone who signs in to your computer locally has access to Public folders, but network users do not.

- **Media Streaming.** Turning on media streaming provides access to pictures, music, and video through streaming protocols that can send media to computers or to other media playback devices.

- **File Sharing Connections.** Unless you have very old computers on your network, leave this option set to 128-bit encryption, which has been the standard for most of this century.

- **Password Protected Sharing.** When password-protected sharing is turned on, network users cannot access your shared folders (including Public folders, if shared) or printers unless they can provide the user name and password of a user account on your computer. With this setting enabled, when another user attempts to access a shared resource, Windows sends the user name and password that the person used to sign in to her own computer. If that matches the credentials for a local user account on your computer, the user gets immediate access to the shared resource (assuming permissions to use the particular resource have been granted to that user account). If either the user name or the password does not match, Windows asks the user to provide credentials.

  With password-protected sharing turned off, Windows does not require a user name and password from network visitors. Instead, network access is provided by using the Guest account. As we explain in Chapter 6, "Managing user accounts, passwords, and credentials," this account isn't available for interactive use but can handle these tasks in the background.

5. **Configure user accounts.** If you use password-protected sharing, each person who accesses a shared resource on your computer must have a user account on your computer. Use the same user name as that person uses on his or her own computer and the same password as well. If you do that, network users will be able to access shared resources without having to enter their credentials after they've signed in to their own computer.

CHAPTER 20

Renaming your workgroup

A workgroup is identified by a name; all computers in a workgroup must be in the same local area network and subnet, and all must share the same workgroup name. In Windows 10, the workgroup name is largely invisible and irrelevant; when you open the Network folder or look at a network map, Windows displays all computers in the network, regardless of which workgroup they're in. (However, network discovery is faster when all computers are in the same workgroup.) The default name for a workgroup in recent Windows versions is WORKGROUP.

To set the workgroup name, follow these steps:

1. In the search box or in Control Panel, type **workgroup**, and then click Change Workgroup Name.

2. On the Computer Name tab of the System Properties dialog box, click Change, which displays the following dialog box:

3. In the Computer Name/Domain Changes dialog box, select Workgroup and type the name of the workgroup (which has a 15-character maximum and can't include any of these characters: ; : < > * + = \ | / ? ,). Then click OK in each dialog box.

4. Restart your computer.

Sharing files and folders from any folder

Whether you plan to share files and folders with other people who share your computer or those who connect to your computer over the network (or both), the process for setting up shared resources is the same as long as the Sharing Wizard is enabled. We recommend you use the Sharing Wizard even if you normally disdain wizards. It's quick, easy, and certain to make all the correct settings for network shares and NTFS permissions—a sometimes daunting task if undertaken manually. After you configure shares with the wizard, you can always dive in and make changes manually if you need to.

To be sure the Sharing Wizard is enabled, open File Explorer Options. (Type **folder** in the search box, and choose File Explorer Options. Or, in File Explorer, click View > Options.) In the dialog box that appears, shown next, click the View tab. Near the bottom of the Advanced Settings list, see that Use Sharing Wizard (Recommended) is selected.

With the Sharing Wizard at the ready, follow these steps to share a folder or files:

1. In File Explorer, select the folders or files you want to share. (You can select multiple objects.)

2. Right-click and choose Share With > Specific People. (Alternatively, click or tap the Share tab and then click Specific People in the Share With box. You might need to click the arrow in the Share With box to display Specific People.) The File Sharing dialog box appears, as shown in Figure 20-3.

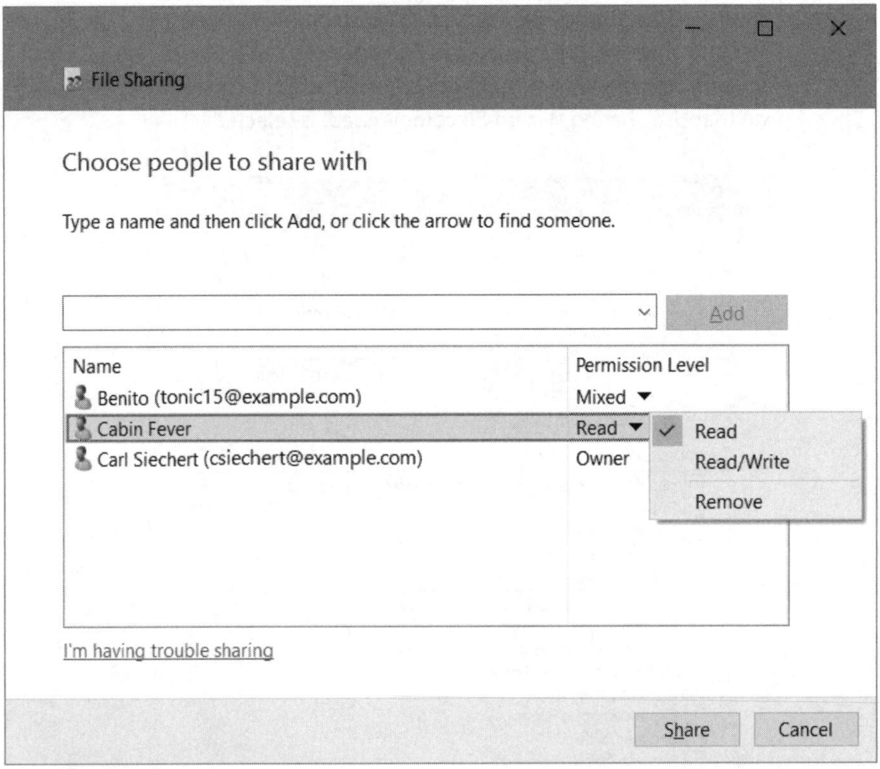

Figure 20-3 For each name in the list, you can click the arrow to set the access level—or remove that account from the list.

3. In the entry box, enter the name or Microsoft account for each user with whom you want to share. You can type a name in the box or click the arrow to display a list of available names; then click Add. Repeat this step for each person you want to add.

The list includes all users who have an account on your computer, plus Everyone. If you've joined a homegroup, the list also includes any Microsoft accounts that have been linked to user accounts on any PC that's part of the homegroup. Guest is included if password-protected sharing is turned off. If you want to grant access to someone who doesn't appear in the list, click Create A New User, which takes you to User Accounts in Control Panel. (This option appears only if your computer is not joined to a homegroup.)

NOTE

If you select Everyone and you have password-protected sharing enabled, the user must still have a valid account on your computer. However, if you turned off password-protected sharing, network users can gain access *only* if you grant permission to Everyone or to Guest.

4. For each user, select a permission level. Your choices are

   - **Read.** Users with this permission level can view shared files and run shared programs, but they cannot change or delete files. Selecting Read in the Sharing Wizard is equivalent to setting NTFS permissions to Read & Execute.

   - **Read/Write.** Users assigned the Read/Write permission have the same privileges you do as owner: they can view, change, add, and delete files in a shared folder. Selecting Read/Write sets NTFS permissions to Full Control for this user.

NOTE

You might see other permission levels if you return to the Sharing Wizard after you set up sharing. Contribute indicates Modify permission. Custom indicates NTFS permissions other than Read & Execute, Modify, or Full Control. Mixed appears if you select multiple items and they have different sharing settings. Owner, of course, identifies the owner of the item.

5. Click Share. After a few moments, the wizard displays a page like the one shown in Figure 20-4.

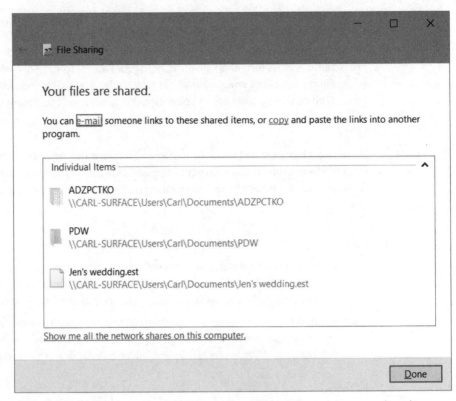

Figure 20-4 The Sharing Wizard displays the network path for each item you shared.

6. In the final step of the wizard, you can do any of the following:

   ■ Send an email message to the people with whom you're sharing. The message includes a link to the shared items.

   ■ Copy the network path to the Clipboard. This is handy if you want to send a link via another application, such as a messaging app. (To copy the link for a single item in a list, right-click the share name and choose Copy Link.)

   ■ Double-click a share name to open the shared item.

   ■ Open File Explorer with your computer selected in the Network folder, showing each network share on your computer.

   When you're finished with these tasks, click Done.

Creating a share requires privilege elevation, but after a folder has been shared, the share is available to network users no matter who is signed in to your computer—or even when nobody is signed in.

Inside OUT

Use advanced sharing to create shorter network paths

Confusingly, when you share one of your profile folders (or any other subfolder of %SystemDrive%\Users), Windows creates a network share for the Users folder—not for the folder you shared. This behavior isn't a security problem; NTFS permissions prevent network users from seeing any folders or files except the ones you explicitly share. But it does lead to some long Universal Naming Convention (UNC) paths to network shares. For example, sharing the PDW subfolder of Documents (as shown in Figure 20-4) creates the network path \\CARL-SURFACE\Users\Carl\Documents\PDW. If this same folder had been anywhere on your computer outside the Users folder, no matter how deeply nested, the network path would instead be \\CARL-SURFACE\PDW. Other people to whom you granted access wouldn't need to click through a series of folders to find the files in the intended target folder.

Network users, of course, can map a network drive or save a shortcut to your target folder to avoid this problem. But you can work around it from the sharing side too: Use advanced sharing to share the folder directly. (Do this after you've used the Sharing Wizard to set up permissions.) For more information, see "Setting advanced sharing properties" following the next section. (And while you're doing that, be sure the share name you create doesn't have spaces. Eliminating them makes it easier to type a share path that works as a link.)

Stopping or changing sharing of a file or folder

If you want to stop sharing a particular shared file or folder, select it in File Explorer and on the Share tab, click Stop Sharing. (Or right-click and choose Share With > Stop Sharing.) Doing so removes access control entries that are not inherited. In addition, the network share is removed; the folder will no longer be visible in another user's Network folder.

To change share permissions, right-click and choose Share With > Specific People. In the File Sharing dialog box (shown earlier in Figure 20-3), you can add users, change permissions, or remove users. (To stop sharing with a particular user, click the permission level by the user's name and choose Remove.)

Setting advanced sharing properties

With Advanced Sharing, you configure network shares independently of NTFS permissions. (For more information about this distinction, see the sidebar "How shared resource permissions and NTFS permissions work together" later in this chapter.) To open Advanced Sharing, right-click a folder, choose Properties, and click the Sharing tab. Or, if the Sharing Wizard is disabled, select a folder in File Explorer and on the ribbon's Share tab (or the right-click Share With menu) choose Advanced Sharing. Both methods display the Sharing tab, which is shown in Figure 20-5.

Figure 20-5 The Share button under Network File And Folder Sharing summons the Sharing Wizard, but it's available only when the wizard is enabled.

NOTE

The Sharing tab is part of the properties dialog box for a folder, but not for files. Also, when the Sharing Wizard is disabled, the Advanced Sharing button appears on the ribbon only when you select a single folder. Only the Sharing Wizard is capable of making share settings for files and for multiple objects simultaneously.

To create or modify a network share using advanced settings, follow these steps:

1.   On the Sharing tab, click Advanced Sharing to display the Advanced Sharing dialog box.

2.   Select Share This Folder, as shown next:

3. Accept or change the proposed share name.

NOTE

If the folder is already shared and you want to add another share name (perhaps with different permissions), click Add and then type the name for the new share.

The share name is the name that other users will see in their own Network folders. Windows initially proposes to use the folder's name as the share name. That's usually a good choice, but you're not obligated to accept it. If you already have a shared folder with that name, you need to pick a different name.

4. Type a description of the folder's contents in the Comments box.

    Other users will see this description when they inspect the folder's properties dialog box in their Network folder (or use Details view).

5. To limit the number of users who can connect to the shared folder concurrently, specify a number in the box. Windows 10 permits up to 20 concurrent network connections. (If you need to share a resource with more users, you must use Windows Server.)

6. Click Permissions.

The default shared resource permission associated with a new share is Read access to Everyone.

CAUTION

When you share a folder, you also make that folder's subfolders available on the network. If the access permissions you set for the folder aren't appropriate for any of its subfolders, either reconsider your choice of access permissions or restructure your folders to avoid the problem.

7. In the Group Or User Names list, select the name of the user or group you want to manage.

   The shared resource permissions for the selected user or group appear below in the permissions list.

8. Select Allow, Deny, or neither for each access control entry:

   - **Full Control.** Allows users to create, read, write, rename, and delete files in the folder and its subfolders. In addition, users can change permissions and take ownership of files on NTFS volumes.

- **Change.** Allows users to read, write, rename, and delete files in the folder and its subfolders but not create new files.

- **Read.** Allows users to read files but not write to them or delete them.

If you select neither Allow nor Deny, it's still possible that the user or group can inherit the permission through membership in another group that has the permission. If the user or group doesn't belong to another such group, the user or group is implicitly denied permission.

NOTE

To remove a name from the Group Or User Names list, select it and click Remove. To add a name to the list, click Add to open the Select Users Or Groups dialog box, where you can enter the names of the users and groups you want to add.

How shared resource permissions and NTFS permissions work together

The implementation of shared resource permissions and NTFS permissions is confusingly similar, but you need to recognize that these are two separate levels of access control. Only connections that successfully pass through both gates are granted access.

Shared resource permissions control *network* access to a particular resource. Shared resource permissions do not affect users who sign in locally. You set shared resource permissions in the Advanced Sharing dialog box, which you access from the Sharing tab of a folder's properties dialog box.

NTFS permissions (also known as discretionary access control lists, DACLs) apply to folders and files on an NTFS-formatted drive. For each user to whom you want to grant access, you can specify exactly what that user is allowed to do: run programs, view folder contents, create new files, change existing files, and so on. You set NTFS permissions on the Security tab of the properties dialog box for a folder or file.

Keep in mind that the two types of permissions are combined in the most restrictive way. If, for example, a user is granted Read permission on the network share, even if the account has Full Control NTFS permissions on the same folder, the user gets only read access when connecting over the network. In effect, the two sets of permissions act in tandem as "gatekeepers" that winnow out incoming network connections. An account that attempts to connect over the network is examined first by the shared resource permissions gatekeeper. The account is either rejected or allowed to enter with certain permissions. It's then confronted by the NTFS permissions gatekeeper, which might strip away (but not add to) some or all the permissions granted at the first doorway. In many advanced sharing scenarios, it's common practice to simply configure the shared folder with Full Control permissions for Everyone and then configure NTFS permissions to control access as desired.

In determining the effective permission for a particular account, you must also consider the effect of group membership. Permissions are cumulative; an account that's a member of one or more groups is granted all the permissions that are granted explicitly to the account as well as all permissions granted to each group of which it's a member. The only exception to this rule is Deny permissions, which take precedence over any conflicting Allow permissions.

Inside OUT

Review and change your sharing and NTFS permissions settings

A tool in File Explorer opens a dialog box, shown next, that displays NTFS permissions and share permissions in a format that's sometimes easier to decipher than the properties dialog box. Select a single folder or file in File Explorer and then, on the ribbon's Share tab, click Advanced Security. Here, in addition to viewing each type of permission, you can determine the *effective access*, which shows for a specific user or group the cumulative effect of various permissions and group memberships. (On a small network, the easiest way to specify a user on the Effective Access tab is to click Select A User > Advanced > Find Now.)

Advanced Security Settings for PDW					□ X
Name:	C:\Users\Carl\Documents\PDW				
Owner:	Carl Siechert (csiechert@example.com) 🛡 Change				

Permissions	Share	Auditing	Effective Access

For additional information, double-click a permission entry. To modify a permission entry, select the entry and click Edit (if available).

Permission entries:

	Type	Principal	Access	Inherited from	Applies to
👤	Allow	Benito (tonic15@example.com)	Read & execute	None	This folder, subfolders and files
👥	Allow	SYSTEM	Full control	None	This folder, subfolders and files
👥	Allow	Administrators (Carl-Surface\Ad...	Full control	None	This folder, subfolders and files
👤	Allow	Carl Siechert (csiechert@examp...	Full control	None	This folder, subfolders and files
👤	Allow	Cabin Fever (Carl-Surface\Cabin ...	Read & execute	None	This folder, subfolders and files

Add   Remove   View

Enable inheritance

☐ Replace all child object permission entries with inheritable permission entries from this object

OK   Cancel   Apply

Sharing a printer

Although Windows doesn't have a wizard for sharing a printer over the network, the process is pretty simple. You configure all options for a printer—whether you plan to share it or not—by using the printer's properties dialog box, which you access from Devices And Printers in Control Panel.

To make a printer available to other network users, right-click a printer and click Printer Properties. (If you prefer Settings over Control Panel, you can reach this same dialog box by following a lengthier route: Settings > Devices > *printer name* > Manage > Printer Properties.) On the Sharing tab, select Share This Printer and provide a share name, as shown in Figure 20-6.

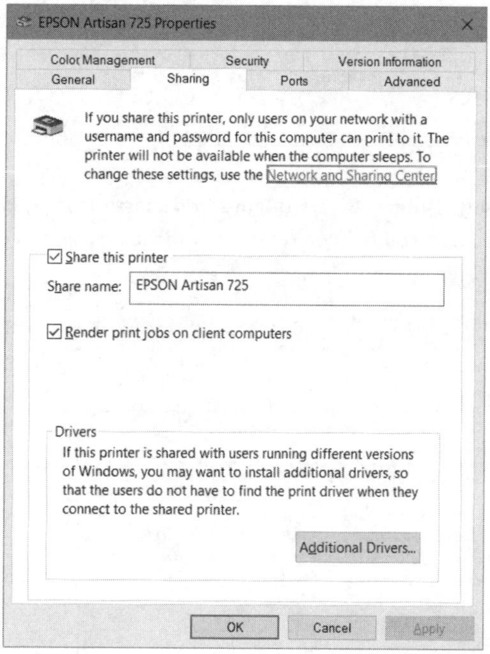

Figure 20-6 The share name for a printer can include spaces.

Unlike for shared folders, which maintain separate share permissions and NTFS permissions, a single set of permissions controls access to printers, whether by local users or by network users. (Of course, only printers that have been shared are accessible to network users.)

When you set up a printer, initially all users in the Everyone group have Print permission for documents they create, which provides users access to the printer and the ability to manage their own documents in the print queue. By default, members of the Administrators group also have Manage Printers permission—which allows them to share a printer, change its properties, remove a printer, and change its permissions—and Manage Documents permission, which lets them pause, restart, move, and remove all queued documents. As an administrator, you can view or modify permissions on the Security tab of the printer properties dialog box.

Setting server properties

In addition to setting properties for individual printers by using their properties dialog boxes, you can set other properties by visiting the Print Server Properties dialog box. To get there, select a printer in the Devices And Printers folder, and then click Print Server Properties.

Inside OUT

Use the Print Management console

Users of Windows 10 Pro and Enterprise editions have a tool that places all print management tasks in one convenient console. Print Management (Printmanagement.msc), shown here, provides a place for managing printers, drivers, queues, and shares. If your edition includes Print Management, you can start it by typing **print** in the search box and then clicking Print Management.

The first three tabs control the list of items you see in the properties dialog box for a printer:

- The Forms tab controls the list of forms you can assign to trays using the Device Settings tab in a printer's properties dialog box. You can create new form definitions and delete any you create, but you can't delete any of the predefined forms.

- On the Ports tab, you can configure the ports that appear on the Ports tab in a printer's properties dialog box.

- The Drivers tab offers a list of all the installed printer drivers and provides a centralized location where you can add, remove, or update drivers.

On the Advanced tab, you can specify the location of spool files. (You might want to change to a folder on a different drive if, for example, you frequently run out of space on the current drive when you attempt to print large documents.) You can also set notification options on this tab.

Finding and using shared resources on a Windows network

The Network folder is your gateway to all available network resources, just as This PC is the gateway to resources stored on your own system. The Network folder (shown in Figure 20-7) contains an icon for each computer that Windows discovers on your network; double-click a computer icon to see that computer's shared resources, if any.

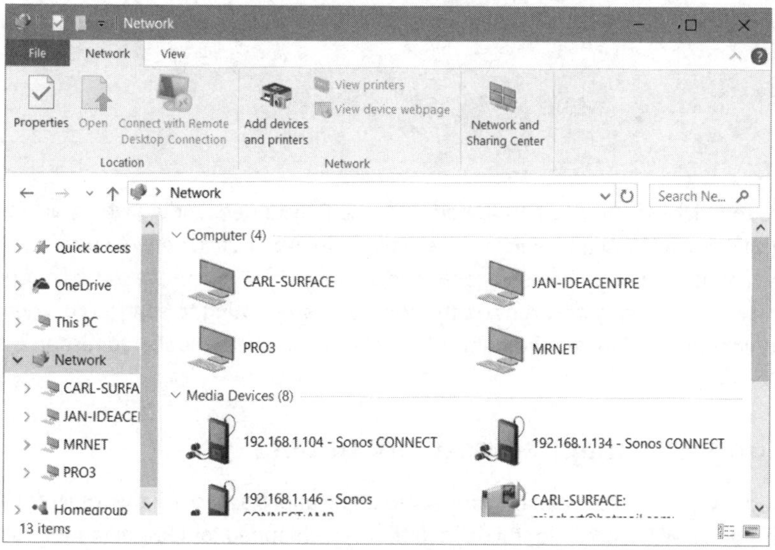

Figure 20-7 The Network folder shows all computers on your network, not just those in your workgroup.

To open a shared folder on another computer, double-click its icon in the Network folder. If you have the proper permissions, this action displays the folder's contents in File Explorer. It's not always that easy, however. If the user account with which you signed in doesn't have permission to view a network computer or resource you select, a dialog box (shown next) asks you to provide the name of an account (and its password, of course) that has permission. Don't be fooled by the Domain reference below the User Name and Password boxes; in a workgroup, that value refers to the local computer.

Windows Security	✕

Enter network credentials

Enter your credentials to connect to: JAN-IDEACENTRE

> ⍝   User name

> Password

Domain:

☐ Remember my credentials

The user name or password is incorrect.

OK	Cancel

Perhaps the trickiest part of using shared folders is fully understanding what permissions have been applied to a folder and which credentials are in use by each network user. It's important to recognize that *all network access is controlled by the computer with the shared resources*; regardless of what operating system runs on the computer attempting to connect to a network share, it must meet the security requirements of the computer where the shared resource is actually located.

Working with mapped network folders

Mapping a network folder makes it appear to applications as though the folder is part of your own computer. Windows assigns a drive letter to the mapped folder, making the folder appear like an additional hard drive. You can still access a mapped folder in the conventional manner by navigating to it through the Network folder. But mapping gives the folder an alias—the assigned drive letter—that provides an alternative means of access.

To map a network folder to a drive letter, follow these steps:

1. Open This PC in File Explorer, and on the ribbon's Computer tab, click Map Network Drive. (Alternatively, after you open a computer in the Network folder, right-click a network share and choose Map Network Drive.)

2. Select a drive letter from the Drive list. You can choose any letter that's not already in use.

3. In the Folder box, type the path to the folder you want or, more easily, click Browse and navigate to the folder.

4. Select Reconnect At Sign-In if you want Windows to connect to this shared folder automatically at the start of each session.

5. If your regular sign-in account doesn't have permission to connect to the resource, select Connect Using Different Credentials. (After you click Finish, Windows asks for the user name and password you want to use for this connection.)

6. Click Finish.

In File Explorer, the "drive" appears under This PC.

If you change your mind about mapping a network folder, right-click the folder's icon in your This PC folder. Choose Disconnect on the resulting shortcut menu, and the connection will be severed.

Connecting to a network printer

To use a printer that has been shared, open the Network folder in File Explorer and double-click the name of the server to which the printer is attached. If the shared printers on that server are not visible, return to the Network folder, click to select the server, and then, on the ribbon's Network tab, click View Printers. Right-click the printer and choose Connect. Alternatively, from the Devices And Printers folder, click Add A Printer and use the Add Printer Wizard to add a network printer.

Connecting to another computer with Remote Desktop

Sharing computer resources over a network, when properly configured, gives you access to all the files you might need, wherever they're stored. But sometimes even that's not enough. You might need to run a program that's installed only on another computer, or you might need to configure and manage another computer's files and settings in ways that can be done only by sitting down in front of that computer. As it turns out, there's an alternative to direct physical access: Remote Desktop. By using a Remote Desktop session, you can operate a computer by remote control over a local network or over the internet.

> ### NOTE
> Windows includes a desktop program for remote access called Remote Desktop Connection. Although this program's appearance remains largely unchanged since its inclusion in Windows XP, it's still perfectly suitable for remote connections. A newer alternative, called Remote Desktop, is available through the Store. This Universal Windows Platform app works on a wide variety of Windows 10 device types, and it includes some capabilities not available in Remote Desktop Connection. In this section, we describe how to use both programs.

With Remote Desktop, applications run on the remote computer; your computer is effectively used as a dumb terminal. You can use a low-powered computer—an inexpensive laptop or an old desktop clunker—and enjoy the speed and power of the remote computer. With the Remote Desktop app, you can even use your phone or other mobile device to connect to a remote computer. Remote Desktop connections are encrypted, so your information is secure, even if you're making a connection over the internet.

The basic requirements for using Remote Desktop are pretty simple: you need two computers that are connected via a local area network, the internet, or a dial-up connection.

NOTE

The computer that you want to control—the one at the remote location—is called the *remote computer*. The computer you want to use to control the remote computer is called the *client computer*.

These are the requirements for the two computers:

- **Remote computer.** You need a computer running Windows 10 Pro, Enterprise, or Education. (Windows 10 Home does not include the software required for hosting Remote Desktop sessions.) The remote computer can also use Windows 8 or 8.1 (Pro or Enterprise editions), Windows 7 (Professional, Enterprise, or Ultimate editions), Windows Vista (Business, Enterprise, or Ultimate editions), Windows XP Professional (or Windows XP Media Center or Tablet PC editions), Windows Home Server, or Windows Server. This computer must have a connection to a local area network or to the internet. If you're going to connect to this computer over the internet, its internet connection must have a known, public IP address. (For ways around this last requirement, see the next section, "Configuring your network for Remote Desktop connections.")

- **Client computer.** You can access Remote Desktop from a computer running any version of Windows or Windows Phone. Remote Desktop client software from Microsoft is also available for iOS, OS X, and Android; third-party apps are available for Linux and other operating systems. To find one, search for "RDP apps." (RDP is short for *Remote Desktop Protocol*, the networking protocol that enables Remote Desktop.)

Configuring your network for Remote Desktop connections

When you enable Remote Desktop on Windows 10 Pro, Enterprise, or Education, the remote computer listens for incoming connections on port 3389. Enabling Remote Desktop also creates an exception in Windows Firewall that allows authenticated traffic on this port.

That makes Remote Desktop easy to use over a local network where no third-party security software is installed. But it doesn't solve the many problems you face when trying to connect to Remote Desktop over the internet. To connect through the internet, you must be able to reach the remote computer by using a known public IP address, and you have to get through a router and past any security software in between the two computers. If you're sitting in a hotel room or an airport, connecting to Remote Desktop poses several challenges imposed by firewalls, routers, and IP addresses. The solutions to these issues depend on your specific hardware configuration, but we can offer some general advice.

If the remote computer is connected to the internet through a router, you need to accomplish two tasks. First, you have to ascertain the router's public IP address. (Depending on your internet service provider [ISP], this public address can change over time. See the following tip for a workaround.) Then you have to configure the router to forward Remote Desktop Protocol traffic it receives on port 3389 to the remote computer.

To find the router's IP address, open its browser-based administration interface and find the status screen. The public IP address is typically labeled as the WAN (wide area network) address; don't use the local area network (LAN) address, which is the private IP address used to forward traffic to computers on your local network.

To make sure RDP traffic reaches your remote PC, look for a "port forwarding" page in the same router administration interface. (It's often buried within an advanced configuration section.) You need to specify the local (private) IP address of the remote computer and tell the router you want all traffic on port 3389 to be forwarded to that PC instead of being discarded. Figure 20-8 shows this configuration on a Linksys router, allowing incoming Remote Desktop requests to be forwarded to a computer with a local (private) IP address of 192.168.10.25. (You might also want to configure the remote computer with a static IP address.)

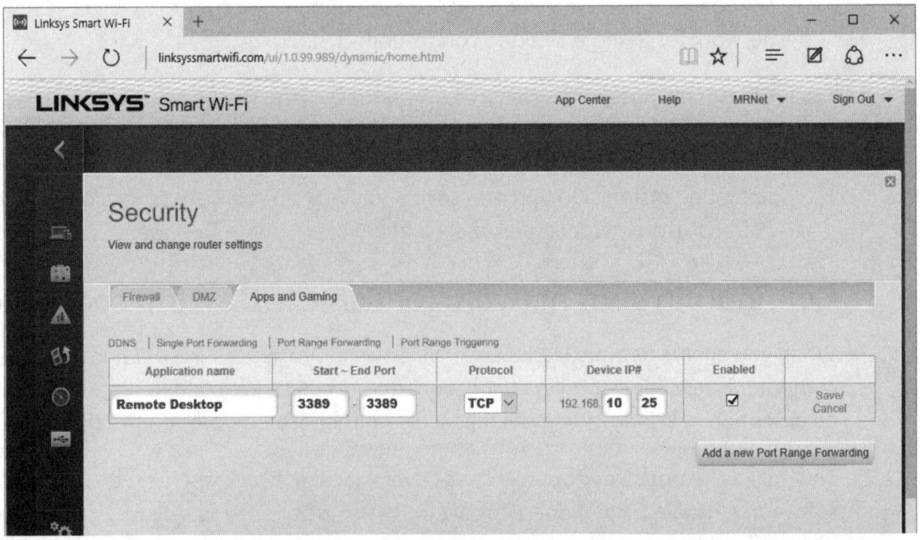

Figure 20-8 Every router has a different configuration interface, but the basic concepts of port forwarding are similar to the one shown here, which will forward traffic on port 3389 to a local PC with the specified private IP address.

Inside OUT

Use dynamic DNS to avoid IP address confusion

Using a bare IP address for Remote Desktop connections is easy but potentially risky. If you forget the public IP address assigned to your computer, you'll be unable to make a connection. Worse, if your ISP decides to change your IP address, you'll be stymied until you discover the new address, which is a challenge if you're away from home. The solution is to use a dynamic DNS service, such as those offered by Dyn (*http://dyndns.com*), No-IP (*http://noip.com*), and Duck DNS (*https://duckdns.org*). (A web search for "dynamic DNS service" will turn up many more options.)

Such services map the public IP address on your router to a domain name that doesn't change. Dynamic DNS services typically rely on software installed on your remote computer, which notifies the service provider's domain name servers if your IP address changes. Because the domain name server correlates your domain name with its current IP address, you (or anyone you designate) can always find your computer by using your registered domain name instead of a numeric IP address.

Enabling inbound remote desktop connections

If you intend to connect to a remote computer—whether it's at home while you're away, at work when you're out of the office, or just down the hall—you must first enable Remote Desktop on that computer. To set up a computer running Windows 10 Pro, Enterprise, or Education to accept Remote Desktop connections, follow these steps:

1. Open Control Panel > System And Security > System, or use this shortcut to get to the same place: Right-click the Start button and choose System. In the left pane, click Remote Settings. (Or use the undocumented command **systempropertiesremote**.)

2. Under Remote Desktop, select Allow Remote Assistance Connections To This Computer, as shown next.

CHAPTER 20

CHAPTER 20

System Properties   ✕

Computer Name   Hardware   Advanced   System Protection   **Remote**

Remote Assistance

☑ Allow Remote Assistance connections to this computer

What happens when I enable Remote Assistance?

Ad_v_anced...

Remote Desktop

Choose an option, and then specify who can connect.

○ _D_on't allow remote connections to this computer

◉ A_l_low remote connections to this computer

☑ Allow connections only from computers running Remote Desktop
with _N_etwork Level Authentication (recommended)

Help me choose   Select Users...

OK   Cancel   Apply

Unless you anticipate you'll need to access your computer from a computer running
an ancient version of Remote Desktop Connection, leave Allow Connections Only From
Computers Running Remote Desktop With Network Level Authentication (Recom-
mended) selected. This requires Remote Desktop version 6 or later, but all versions of
Windows and Windows Server released since 2007 (that is, Windows Vista or later, or
Windows Server 2008 or later) meet this requirement. In addition, versions of Remote
Desktop that support Network Level Authentication are available for earlier Windows ver-
sions and for other operating systems.

At this point, the current user account and any user account that's a member of the local
Administrators group can be used to connect remotely to the computer, provided that
the account has a sign-in password. (As a security precaution, accounts that use a blank
password cannot be enabled for remote connections.)

3.   If you want to change which users can connect remotely, click Select Users. The Remote
Desktop Users dialog box appears:

Remote Desktop Users   ?   ✕

The users listed below can connect to this computer, and any members of the Administrators group can connect even if they are not listed.

Cabin Fever

csiechert@example.com already has access.

Add...   Remove

To create new user accounts or add users to other groups, go to Control Panel and open User Accounts.

OK   Cancel

- To add a user to the Remote Desktop Users group, click Add. Then type the user's name in the Select Users dialog box that appears (or click Advanced, Find Now to select names from a list). You can type the name of any local user account or, if your computer is in a domain, any domain user account. You can add multiple users by separating each user name with a semicolon.

- To delete a user from the Remote Desktop Users group, select the user's name in the Remote Desktop Users dialog box and click Remove.

That's all you need to do to set up the remote computer. Windows configures rules for Remote Desktop in Windows Firewall when Remote Desktop is enabled, allowing connection requests on port 3389 to be received from any IP address.

If your connection has to pass through a router to get to your computer, be sure you take the additional steps outlined earlier in "Configuring your network for Remote Desktop connections." If you replaced Windows Firewall with a third-party software firewall, you need to configure it to allow incoming access to TCP port 3389.

Using the Remote Desktop app

Remote Desktop is a modern app that's not included with Windows; it is, however, available as a free download via the Store. Remote Desktop offers several features not found in Remote Desktop Connection. Its visual approach shows all your remote connections on the home screen, allowing you to open one with a single click or tap. In addition, Remote Desktop includes several performance enhancements that optimize your connection quality. And, of course, as a modern app, it's touch friendly.

Install the Remote Desktop app, and after you've enabled incoming remote connections on your PC at home or in the office and verified that your network and firewall have the welcome mat out (for visitors with suitable credentials only, of course), you're ready to begin using Remote Desktop.

To begin using Remote Desktop, click the Add (+) button and then click Desktop. Add A Desktop appears in the right pane, as shown in Figure 20-9.

> ### NOTE
> You'll notice when you click Add that Remote Desktop also supports connections to apps on Azure RemoteApp, a cloud-based app-hosting service. For more information, visit *http://remoteapp.windowsazure.com*. In August 2016, Microsoft and Citrix jointly announced that the RemoteApp service would be replaced by XenApp Express in 2017.
>
> Similarly, you can connect to "remote resources," which are server-based apps used by some large organizations. Visit *https://bit.ly/remoteresources* for more information.

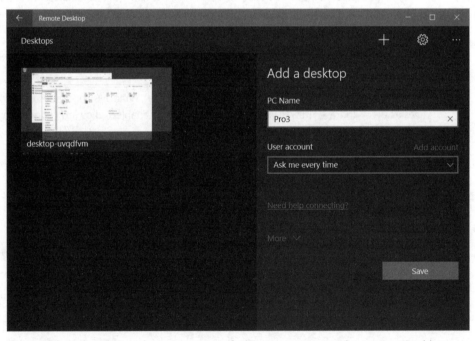

Figure 20-9 In the PC Name box, you can specify the remote computer by name or IP address.

To set up a connection to a remote desktop, enter this information in the Add A Desktop pane:

- **PC Name**   Enter the name or IP address of the remote computer.

- **User Account**   Select Ask Me Every Time to be prompted for your user name and password each time you connect to the desktop. Alternatively, you can click the arrow at the right side and select a user account, and Remote Desktop uses that account without asking for credentials. If the account you want to use doesn't appear in the list, click Add Account.

At this point you've entered all the information necessary to make the connection and you can click Save. However, you can set additional parameters, including some that come into view when you click More:

- **Display Name**   You can provide a friendly name that appears under the icon for a remote computer in the main Remote Desktop window.

- **Audio**   Here you choose where sounds should emanate from when an app on the remote computer plays audio. You can have it play on the remote computer, on your client computer, or nowhere.

- **Switch Mouse Buttons**   This option, sure to induce confusion, swaps the functionality of the left and right mouse buttons while you work in the remote desktop. They maintain their normal functionality while you work in your own local desktop.

Working in a Remote Desktop session

After you save a connection in the Add A Desktop pane, an icon for that connection appears in Remote Desktop. Click the icon to open a connection to the remote computer. Along the way, you might encounter a couple of obstacles:

- If you specified Ask Me Every Time in the User Account box, Remote Desktop asks for the user name and password of an account authorized on the remote computer to make a connection. Select Remember Me, and you won't need to enter this information in future sessions.

- If the remote computer doesn't have a digital certificate that's trusted by your computer to positively identify it, you'll be asked whether you want to accept the untrusted certificate, as shown next. If you're certain that you're connecting to the right computer, select the check box (so you won't be bothered in future sessions) and click Connect, as shown next.

CHAPTER 20

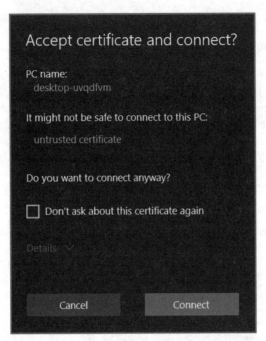

Accept certificate and connect?

PC name:
desktop-uvqdfvm

It might not be safe to connect to this PC:

untrusted certificate

Do you want to connect anyway?

☐ Don't ask about this certificate again

Details ∨

| Cancel | Connect |

After bounding past those hurdles, Remote Desktop attempts to open a connection. If the account you use for the remote connection is already signed in to the remote computer—or if no one is signed in to the remote computer—the remote computer's desktop then appears on your computer.

If a different user account is signed in to the remote computer, Windows lets you know that you'll be forcing that person to sign out and gives you a chance to cancel the connection. On the other end, the signed-in user sees a similar notification that offers a short time to reject the remote connection before it takes over. Note that only one user at a time can control the desktop of a computer running Windows. Whoever is currently signed in has the final say on whether someone else can sign in.

While you're connected to the remote computer, the local display on that computer (if it's turned on) does not show what you see on the client computer but instead shows the lock screen. A person who has physical access to the remote computer can't see what you're doing (other than the fact that you're signed in remotely).

When you connect to a remote computer using the universal Remote Desktop app, the remote computer takes over your entire screen. It uses the resolution of the client computer, regardless of the resolution set on the remote computer. At the top of the screen, in the center, a button with three dots appears, as shown in Figure 20-10.

Figure 20-10 This screenshot is cropped to show the upper right corner of the screen. When you click the button with three dots, the buttons on the right appear.

The buttons that appear on the right side offer these functions:

- **Disconnect**. Clicking this button ends your remote session and returns you to the main Remote Desktop window. The remote computer remains locked, ready for someone to sign in locally.

- **Full-Screen**. This button toggles between full-screen and windowed views of the remote desktop. Figure 20-11 shows a Remote Desktop window.

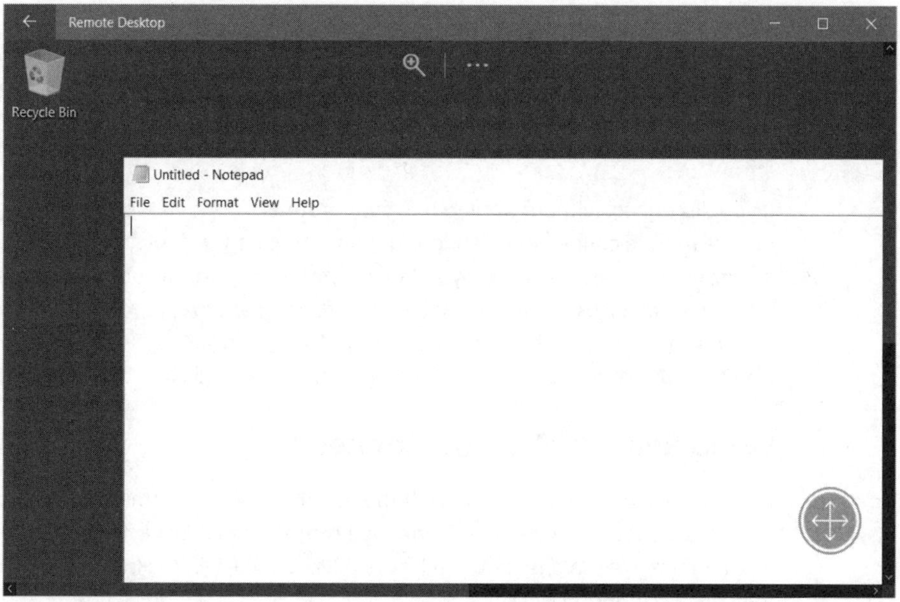

Figure 20-11 When you use a windowed display and enable touch, arrows appear in the lower right corner, as shown here. Tap the arrow and drag to move the screen within the window.

- **Touch**. If your client computer has a touchscreen, clicking this button enables touch control of the remote computer. When you switch to this mode, a magnifier icon appears along the top edge of the screen; use this to enlarge the display so that it's easier to hit touch targets.

While in full-screen mode, two more controls are less obvious. Move the mouse pointer to the top edge of the screen, and a small button appears; click it to display the Remote Desktop title bar, which includes the usual window controls (minimize, resize, and close) as well as a button at the left end that disconnects your session and returns to the main window. Move the mouse pointer to the bottom edge of the screen and a similar button appears; click it to display the taskbar for your local computer. If your computer has a touchscreen, you can see these buttons by dragging in from the top or bottom edge of the screen.

Ending a remote session

When you're through with a Remote Desktop Connection session, you can lock, sign out, or disconnect. If the remote computer is running Windows 10, you'll find these options in the usual places where comparable options appear on your local computer: Lock and Sign Out appear when you click the user name at the top of Start on the remote computer, and Disconnect appears when you click Power on Start. For remote machines running earlier Windows versions, these options appear in the lower right corner of the remote session's Start menu. (You must click the arrow to see all the options.)

Locking the computer keeps the remote session connected and all programs running, but it hides everything behind a sign-in screen that requests a password; this is comparable to pressing Windows key+L to lock your computer.

Signing out closes all your programs, exits your user session, and disconnects.

If you disconnect without signing out, your programs continue to run on the remote computer, but the remote connection is ended. The sign-in screen is visible on the remote computer, and it's available for another user. If you sign in later—either locally or through a remote connection—you can pick up right where you left off. As an alternative to the Start commands, you can disconnect by clicking the Disconnect button (shown in Figure 20-10), displaying the Remote Desktop title bar and clicking the Back button, or simply closing the Remote Desktop window.

Using Remote Desktop Connection

Remote Desktop Connection is a desktop app that might be familiar to longtime remote desktop users. To start it, in the search box, type **remote** and then click Remote Desktop Connection. A dialog box like the one shown in Figure 20-12 appears. In the Computer box, type the name of the remote computer or its IP address.

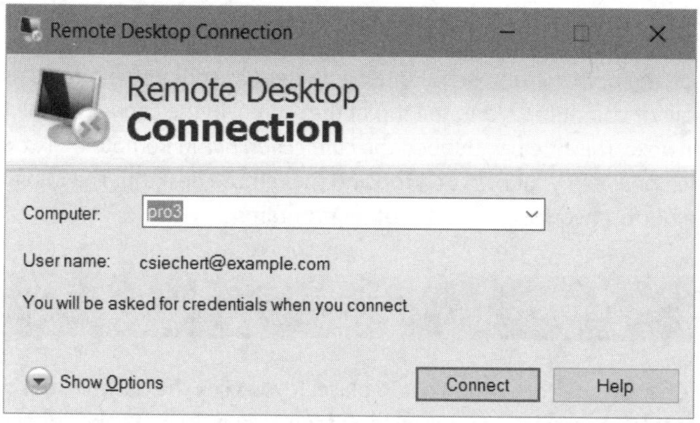

Figure 20-12 You can specify the remote computer by name or IP address.

NOTE

After a successful connection to a remote desktop, the name of the remote computer is added to the drop-down list in the Computer box. Thereafter, you can simply select it from the list (if it isn't already selected) instead of typing the name each time.

In addition, if Remote Desktop Connection is pinned to your taskbar or Start menu (or if it's in the Start menu's recently used list), the name of each computer to which you've successfully connected appears on the Jump List. By using the Jump List and saved sign-in credentials, you can bypass this dialog box completely.

If you're willing to accept the default settings, you can click Connect at this point.

If you're signed in to the client computer using an account other than one that's authorized on the remote computer, Windows first displays a request for credentials. After you enter your credentials and they're approved, Windows initiates the Remote Desktop Connection session.

The remote computer's sign-in screen then appears on your computer, either in a window or a full-screen display. Enter your password; other sign-in options (that is, PIN, picture password, or biometric sign-in) are not available for a remote connection.

As with Remote Desktop (described in the preceding sections), Windows warns if your connection will knock off another user who's signed in to the remote computer.

Changing screen resolutions and display settings

When you connect, the display from the remote computer fills your entire screen, using the resolution of the client computer. Along the top of the screen, in the center, a small title bar appears, as shown next. This title bar, dubbed the *connection bar* in Remote Desktop Connection, lets you switch between your own desktop and the remote desktop. The Minimize, Maximize, and Restore buttons work as they do in other programs.

The pushpin button locks the connection bar in place. If you click the pushpin, the connection bar disappears completely, retracting into the top of the screen. To make the connection bar reappear, "bump" the mouse pointer to the top edge of the screen. To keep the connection bar visible at all times, click the pushpin again. The Close button disconnects the remote computer (but does not sign you out of the remote computer) and closes Remote Desktop Connection. You can pick up where you left off by reopening Remote Desktop Connection and reconnecting or by signing in locally at the remote computer.

Inside OUT

Move the connection bar

If the connection bar covers a part of the screen you need to see, you can move it instead of hiding it altogether with the pushpin button. Simply slide it left or right.

You might prefer to use less than your full screen resolution for the remote desktop. (This option is especially useful if you have a large monitor and the work you want to do with Remote Desktop is just another task among several.) You must set the resolution—along with a number of other options—before you connect to the remote computer. After you start Remote Desktop Connection, click the Show Options button (shown in Figure 20-12) to expand the dialog box. Then click the Display tab, which is shown in Figure 20-13. You can set the screen resolution to any size that's supported on the client hardware, from 640 by 480 up to the current resolution of the client computer (not the remote computer). Set it to full screen by moving the slider all the way to the right.

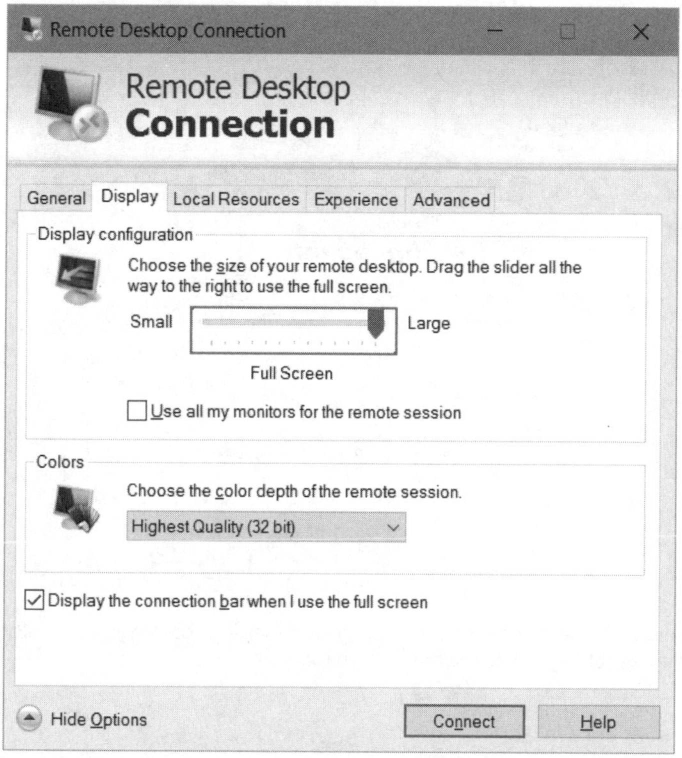

Figure 20-13 Screen resolution is determined by the client computer.

Remote Desktop Connection allows the use of multiple monitors, as long as the remote computer is running Windows 7 or later. To configure the connection for use with more than one monitor, select Use All My Monitors For The Remote Session.

Accessing local resources

While you use Remote Desktop Connection, it's immediately apparent you have control of the remote computer. That's terrific if the remote computer has everything you need. But you'll often want to use local resources and information from the client computer as well as from the remote computer. In addition, you might want to move information between the two computers. With Remote Desktop Connection, you can do so easily by clicking Show Options to expand the Remote Desktop Connection dialog box and then adjusting any of the options on the Local Resources tab, shown in Figure 20-14.

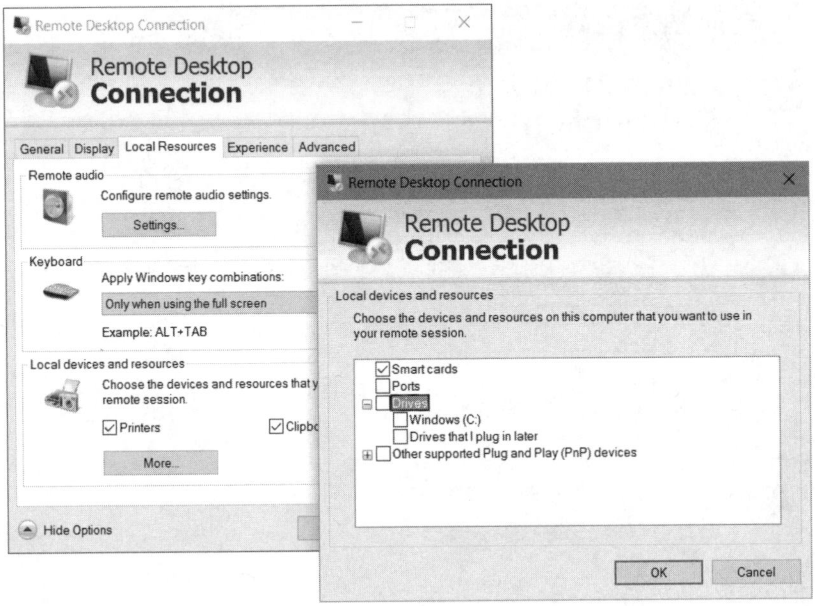

Figure 20-14 Configure these Remote Desktop Connection settings before you make the connection—you can't change settings while the connection is active.

The following options are available:

- **Remote Audio.** If your music collection is on the remote PC and you want some tunes at your current location, click Settings and select Play On This Computer. If you want both computers to be silent, choose Do Not Play. After clicking Settings, you can also tell Remote Desktop Connection whether to pay attention to the microphone (or other audio input) on the client computer.

- **Keyboard.** When you press a Windows keyboard shortcut such as Alt+Tab, do you want the shortcut to take effect on the remote machine or on your client computer?

- **Printers.** When this option is selected, your local printers appear in the remote computer's Printers folder. Their entries have "(from *clientcomputername*)" appended to each printer name. To print to a local printer, select its name in the Print dialog box from any application.

- **Clipboard.** When you copy or cut text or graphics on either the remote computer or the local computer, it's saved on the Clipboard in both locations. The Clipboard contents are then available for pasting in documents on either computer. Similarly, you can cut or copy files or folders from a File Explorer window on either computer and paste them into a folder on the other computer. Clear this option if you want to keep the contents of the two Clipboards separate.

The More button leads to additional devices in the Local Devices And Resources category. Smart cards are automatically enabled, and serial ports are disabled by default. Local drives and Plug and Play devices are also disabled by default. They can be enabled individually, as shown in Figure 20-14. These options are most useful if you're expecting to do most or all of your work with the Remote Desktop session in full-screen view and you don't want to continually flip back to your local desktop for file-management tasks.

Inside OUT

Use your pen in Remote Desktop Connection

In addition to keyboard, mouse, and touch input, if your client computer supports the use of a pen or stylus, you can use it in a Remote Desktop session. You won't see pens mentioned on the Local Resources tab because no configuration is required. You need to have Windows 10 or Windows Server 2016 on the remote computer and the client computer. You can use this feature to add handwriting and other drawings even if the remote computer has no built-in pen capability. You can use the full pen capabilities of the local computer; for example, pens that vary in line width based on the pressure you apply to the screen can use this feature on remote documents.

Using the keyboard with Remote Desktop Connection

When the Remote Desktop Connection window is active, almost every key you press is passed to the remote computer. Certain key combinations, however, can be processed by the client computer, depending on the setting you make in the Keyboard section of the Local Resources tab of the Remote Desktop Connection dialog box (shown in Figure 20-14). You can specify that the key combinations shown in the first column of Table 20-1 are sent to the remote computer all the time, only when the remote desktop is displayed in full-screen mode, or never.

If you select On This Computer, key combinations from the first column of Table 20-1 are always applied to the client computer. To get the equivalent function on the remote computer, press the key combination shown in the second column. The same is true if you select Only When Using The Full Screen and the remote session is displayed in a window.

If you select On The Remote Computer, key combinations from the first column are applied to the remote computer. Key combinations in the second column are ignored (unless they have some function in the active application on the remote desktop). The same is true if you select Only When Using The Full Screen and the remote session is displayed in full-screen mode. One exception is the Ctrl+Alt+Delete combination, which is always applied to the client computer. Regardless of your Local Resources tab setting, you must press Ctrl+Alt+End to obtain the same result on the remote computer.

Table 20-1 Special keys in Remote Desktop Connection

Key combination for a local session	Equivalent key combination for a Remote Desktop session	Description
Alt+Tab	Alt+Page Up	Switches between programs
Alt+Shift+Tab	Alt+Page Down	Switches between programs in reverse order
Alt+Esc	Alt+Insert	Cycles through programs in the order they were started
N/A	Ctrl+Alt+Break	Switches the remote desktop between a window and full screen
Ctrl+Alt+Delete	Ctrl+Alt+End	Displays the Windows Security screen
Ctrl+Esc	Alt+Home	Displays the Start menu
Alt+Spacebar	Alt+Del	Displays the Control menu of the active window (does not work when using Remote Desktop in full-screen mode)
Shift+Print Screen	Ctrl+Alt+Plus Sign (on numeric keypad)	Captures a bitmap image of the remote desktop and places it on the remote computer's Clipboard
Alt+Print Screen	Ctrl+Alt+Minus Sign (on numeric keypad)	Captures a bitmap image of the active window and places it on the remote computer's Clipboard

Configuring performance options

When you first use Remote Desktop Connection, you might notice that the remote desktop doesn't display a background. Disabling the background is one of several settings you can make that affect the perceived performance of your remote session. How you set these options depends in large measure on the speed of the connection between the two computers. If you're using a slow, bandwidth-challenged, or metered connection, you should disable as many features as possible to reduce the amount of information that must be transmitted across the wire and keep the mouse and windows movements responsive. On the other hand, if you're connecting to another desktop over a fast local area network, you might as well enable all features to enjoy the full experience of working at the remote computer.

The performance-related options are on the Experience tab of the Remote Desktop Connection dialog box. To quickly select an appropriate set of prepackaged options, select the speed of your connection from the list box. Use those settings or select your own options.

Saving a Remote Desktop configuration

Changes you make in the expanded Remote Desktop Connection dialog box are automatically saved in a hidden file named Default.rdp (stored in your default save location for documents), and they're used the next time you open Remote Desktop Connection. But you might want to have several different Remote Desktop Connection configurations for connections to different computers. If you have a portable computer, you might want different settings for use with different connections to the same computer (for example, a slow Wi-Fi connection from a hotel versus a fast LAN at your branch office).

You can also save your credentials (user name and password) along with the other settings. To do so, enter your user name under Logon Settings on the General tab and select Allow Me To Save Credentials. You'll be prompted to save the password (in encrypted form, of course) when you sign in. Note that not all remote operating systems allow the use of saved credentials.

To save a configuration, after you make all your settings, click the General tab, and click Save As.

To reuse a stored configuration at a later time, start Remote Desktop Connection, click Show Options, click Open, and then double-click the stored file. More simply, select it from the Jump List for Remote Desktop Connection (on the taskbar or Start menu), or double-click the stored file in File Explorer.

Troubleshooting network problems

Network connectivity problems can be a source of great frustration. Fortunately, Windows 10 includes several tools and wizards that can help you identify and solve problems. Even better, Windows has built-in network diagnostic capabilities, so in many cases, if there is a problem with your network connection, Windows knows about it before you do, displays a message, and often solves the problem.

When a network-dependent activity (for example, browsing to a website) fails, Windows works to address the most common network-related issues, such as problems with file sharing, website

CHAPTER 20

access, newly installed network hardware, connecting to a wireless network, and using a third-party firewall.

If you encounter network problems that don't trigger an automatic response from Windows, you should first try to detect and resolve the problem with one of the built-in troubleshooters. Open Settings > Network & Internet > Network Troubleshooter to fix an issue. If the options shown in that troubleshooter don't address your problem, go to Settings > Network & Internet > Network And Sharing Center > Troubleshoot Problems to display the choices shown in Figure 20-15.

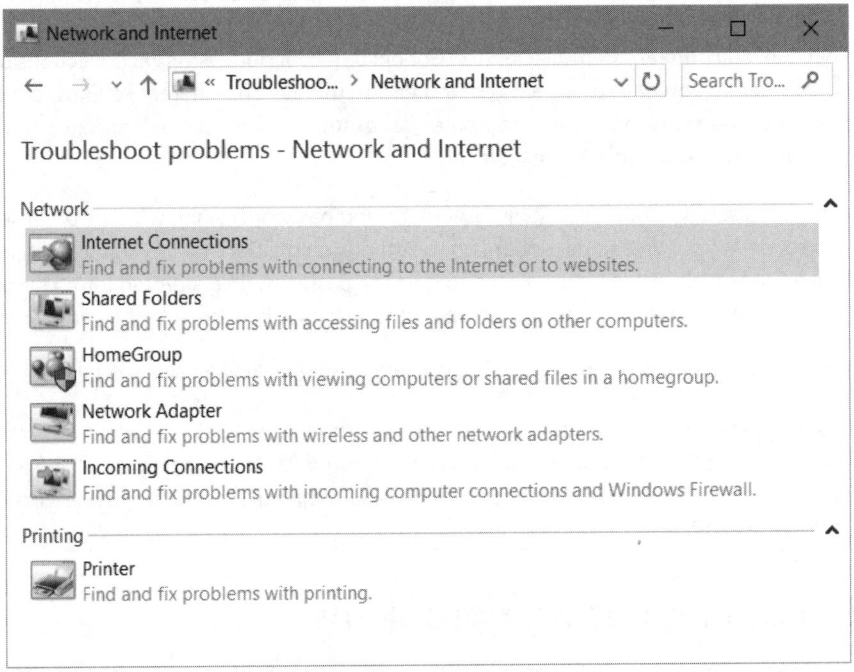

Figure 20-15 Click any of these options to launch a troubleshooter that performs numerous diagnostic and corrective steps.

Inside OUT

Skip the troubleshooting menu

You can bypass Network And Sharing Center and the troubleshooting menu shown in Figure 20-15. Simply right-click the network icon in the notification area and choose Troubleshoot Problems; doing so launches right into a network troubleshooter.

Each of the troubleshooting wizards performs several diagnostic tests, corrects some conditions, suggests actions you can take, and ultimately displays a report that explains the wizard's findings. Sometimes, the problem is as simple as a loose connection:

Windows Network Diagnostics   ✕

Plug an Ethernet cable into this computer

An Ethernet cable looks like a telephone cable but with larger connectors on the ends. Plug this cable into the opening on the back or side of the computer.
Make sure the other end of the cable is plugged into the router. If that does not help, try using a different cable.

→ **Check to see if the problem is fixed**
Click here after you follow the instructions above.

→ **Skip this step**
Continue trying to fix the problem.

Cancel

CHAPTER 20

Other situations might point to problems outside your network:

> ✕
>
> 📡 Internet Connections
>
> Your broadband modem is experiencing connectivity issues
>
> ⚠️ Restart your broadband modem:
> 1. Unplug or turn off the modem.
> 2. After all the lights on the modem are off, wait at least 10 seconds.
> 3. Turn the modem on or plug it back into the power outlet.
>
> Why can't I connect to the Internet?
>
> Next   Cancel

If the diagnostic capabilities leave you at a dead end, you'll find that restarting the affected network hardware often resolves the problem, because the hardware is forced to rediscover the network. Here's a good general troubleshooting procedure:

1. Isolate the problem. Does it affect all computers on your network, a subset of your network, or only one computer?

2. If it affects all computers, try restarting the internet device (that is, the cable or DSL modem). If the device doesn't have a power switch, unplug it for a few moments and plug it back in.

3. If the problem affects a group of computers, try restarting the router to which those computers are connected.

4. If the problem affects only a single computer, try repairing the network connection for that computer. In Network And Sharing Center, click Change Adapter Settings. (Alternatively, open Settings > Network & Internet > Change Adapter Options.) Then, in Network Connections, select the connection and click Diagnose This Connection. If the troubleshooter doesn't resolve the problem, select the connection and click Disable

This Network Device; then click Enable This Network Device, which causes Windows to reinitialize it.

If all else fails, open Settings > Network & Internet > Network Reset. Network Reset removes all your network adapters, reinstalls them, sets other networking components to their default settings, and restarts your computer.

Troubleshooting HomeGroup problems

The HomeGroup troubleshooting wizard provides a good example of how these troubleshooters work. If you're having problems seeing shared resources in a homegroup and you didn't have the benefit of the troubleshooter's assistance, you'd need to check the following settings, among others:

- The network location profile must be set to Private.

- In Windows Firewall With Advanced Security, you need to ensure the following groups of rules are enabled on private networks:
    - Core Networking
    - Network Discovery
    - HomeGroup
    - File/Printer Sharing
    - Windows Media Player
    - Windows Media Player Network Sharing

- The following services must be configured so that they can run:
    - HomeGroup Listener
    - HomeGroup Provider
    - Function Discovery Provider Host
    - Function Discovery Resource Publication
    - Peer Name Resolution Protocol
    - Peer Networking Grouping
    - Peer Networking Identity Manager

Running the HomeGroup troubleshooter—which you can launch from HomeGroup or by right-clicking HomeGroup in File Explorer as well as from the list of troubleshooters shown in Figure 20-15—checks each of these items and more. When you get to the wizard's last window, you can click View Detailed Information to see a troubleshooting report that lists the potential problems that the wizard attempted to identify and fix.

CHAPTER 20

Network troubleshooting tools

When the troubleshooters don't solve the problem, it might be time to dig deeper into the Windows toolbox. Windows contains an assortment of utilities you can use to diagnose, monitor, and repair network connections. Table 20-2 lists the more useful networking-related command-line utilities and summarizes how you can use them. To learn more about each utility, including its proper syntax, open a Command Prompt window and type the executable name followed by **/?**.

Table 20-2 Windows network command-line utilities

Utility name	What it's used for
Get MAC Address (Getmac.exe)	Discovers the Media Access Control (MAC) address and lists associated network protocols for all network cards in a computer, either locally or across a network.
Hostname (Hostname.exe)	Displays the host name of the current computer.
IP Configuration Utility (Ipconfig.exe)	Displays all current Transmission Control Protocol/Internet Protocol (TCP/IP) network configuration values and refreshes Dynamic Host Configuration Protocol (DHCP) and DNS settings.
Name Server Lookup (Nslookup.exe)	Displays information about Domain Name System records for specific IP addresses, host names, or both so that you can troubleshoot DNS problems.
Net services commands (Net.exe)	Performs a broad range of network tasks. Type **net** with no parameters to see a full list of available command-line options.
Netstat (Netstat.exe)	Displays active TCP connections, ports on which the computer is listening, Ethernet statistics, the IP routing table, and IPv4/IPv6 statistics.
Network Command Shell (Netsh.exe)	Displays or modifies the network configuration of a local or remote computer that's currently running. This command-line scripting utility has a huge number of options, which are fully detailed in Help.
PathPing (Pathping.exe)	Combines the functions of Traceroute and Ping to identify problems at a router or network link.
TCP/IP NetBIOS Information (Nbtstat.exe)	Displays statistics for the NetBIOS over TCP/IP (NetBT) protocol, NetBIOS name tables for both the local computer and remote computers, and the NetBIOS name cache.
TCP/IP Ping (Ping.exe)	Verifies IP-level connectivity to another internet address by sending Internet Control Message Protocol (ICMP) packets and measuring the response time in milliseconds.
TCP/IP Route (Route.exe)	Displays and modifies entries in the local IP routing table.
TCP/IP Traceroute (Tracert.exe)	Determines the path to an internet address and lists the time required to reach each hop. It's useful for troubleshooting connectivity problems on specific network segments.

As is the case with other command-line utilities, the Windows PowerShell environment includes cmdlets that offer much of the same functionality along with the scripting capability of PowerShell. (Indeed, one of the commands shown in Table 20-2—Netsh—displays a notice that it might be removed from future versions of Windows. The trend in Windows command-line utilities, certainly, is moving away from Command Prompt toward PowerShell. However, because of the one-off nature of troubleshooting tasks—the topic of this section—our emphasis here is on command-line utilities that run in a Command Prompt window.)

You can get a list that includes many of the more commonly used network-related cmdlets by entering the following at a PowerShell prompt:

```
get-command -module nettcpip, netadapter
```

➤ For more information about PowerShell, see "An introduction to Windows PowerShell" in Chapter 19, "Automating tasks and activities." For details about the Net TCP/IP cmdlets, go to *https://bit.ly/netcmdlets*. On that page, you'll also find (using the navigation pane on the left) details about other network-related cmdlets, including those for Network Adapter, Network Connection, and Network Connectivity Status.

Troubleshooting TCP/IP problems

Transmission Control Protocol/Internet Protocol (TCP/IP) is the default communications protocol of the internet; in Windows 10, it's installed and configured automatically and cannot be removed. Most of the time, your TCP/IP connection should just work, without requiring any manual configuration. When you encounter problems with TCP/IP-based networks, such as an inability to connect with other computers on the same network or difficulty connecting to external websites, the problems might be TCP/IP related. You'll need at least a basic understanding of how this protocol works before you can figure out which tool to use to uncover the root of the problem.

Setting IP addresses

Networks that use the TCP/IP protocol rely on *IP addresses* to route packets of data from point to point. On a TCP/IP network, every computer has a unique IP address for each protocol (that is, TCP/IPv4 and TCP/IPv6) in use on each network adapter. An IPv4 address consists of four 8-bit numbers (each one represented in decimal format by a number from 0 through 255) separated by periods. An IPv6 address consists of eight 16-bit numbers (each one represented in hexadecimal format) separated by colons. In addition to the IP address, each computer's TCP/IP configuration has the following additional settings:

- A *subnet mask*, which tells the network how to distinguish between IP addresses that are part of the same network and those that belong to other networks

- A *default gateway*, which is a computer that routes packets intended for addresses outside the local network

CHAPTER 20

- One or more *Domain Name System (DNS) servers*, which are computers that translate domain names (such as *www.microsoft.com*) into IP addresses

Windows provides several methods for assigning IP addresses to networked computers:

- **Dynamic Host Configuration Protocol (DHCP).** This is the default configuration for Windows 10. A DHCP server maintains a pool of IP addresses for use by network devices. When you connect to a network, the DHCP server assigns an IP address from this pool and sets subnet masks and other configuration details. Many corporate networks use DHCP to avoid the hassle of managing fixed addresses for constantly changing resources; all versions of Windows Server include this capability. Most routers and residential gateways also incorporate DHCP servers that automatically configure computers connected to those devices.

- **Automatic Private IP Addressing (APIPA).** When no DHCP server is available, Windows automatically assigns an IP address in a specific private IP range. (For an explanation of how private IP addresses work, see the sidebar "Public and private IP addresses" later in the chapter.) If all computers on a subnet are using APIPA addresses, they can communicate with one another without requiring any additional configuration. APIPA was introduced with Windows 98 and works the same in all versions of Windows released since that time.

- **Static IP Addressing.** By entering an IP address, subnet mask, and other TCP/IP details in a dialog box, you can manually configure a Windows workstation so that its address is always the same. This method takes more time and can cause some configuration headaches, but it allows a high degree of control over network addresses.

  Static IP addresses are useful if you plan to set up a web server, a mail server, a virtual private network (VPN) gateway, or any other computer that needs to be accessible from across the internet. Even inside a local network, behind a router or firewall, static IP addresses can be useful. For instance, you might want to configure the router so that packets entering your network on a specific port get forwarded to a specific computer. If you use DHCP to assign addresses within the local network, you can't predict what the address of that computer will be on any given day. But by assigning that computer a static IP address that's within the range of addresses assigned by the DHCP server, you can ensure the computer always has the same address and is thus always reachable.

- **Alternate IP Configuration.** Use this feature to specify multiple IPv4 addresses for a single network connection (although only one address can be used at a time). This feature is most useful with portable computers that regularly connect to different networks. You can configure the connection to automatically acquire an IP address from an available DHCP server, and you can then assign a static backup address for use if the first configuration isn't successful.

To set a static IP address, follow these steps:

1. In the Network Connections folder, select the connection whose settings you want to change. On the command bar, click Change Settings Of This Connection. (Alternatively, right-click the icon and choose Properties.)

2. In the list of installed network items, select Internet Protocol Version 4 (TCP/IPv4) or Internet Protocol Version 6 (TCP/IPv6), and then click Properties.

3. In the Internet Protocol (TCP/IP) Properties dialog box, select Use The Following IP Address and fill in the blanks. You must supply an IP address, a subnet mask (for IPv6, the length of the subnet prefix, which is usually 64 bits), and a default gateway.

4. Select Use The Following DNS Server Addresses, and then fill in the numeric IP addresses for one or more DNS servers as well. Figure 20-16 shows the dialog box with all fields filled in.

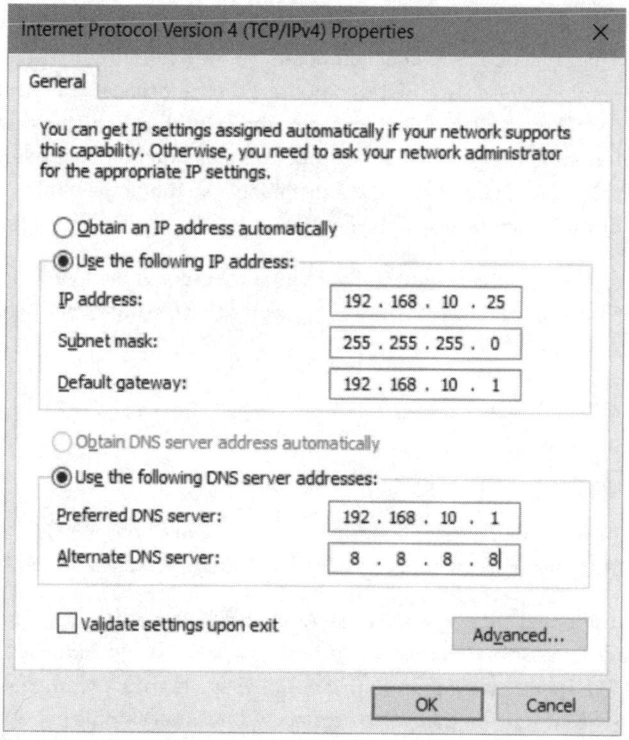

Figure 20-16 When assigning static IP addresses, you must fill in all fields correctly. To avoid making a mistake that could cause you to lose your network connectivity, select Validate Settings Upon Exit.

5. Click OK to save your changes.

CHAPTER 20

Public and private IP addresses

Any computer that's directly connected to the internet needs a public IP address—one that can be reached by other computers on the internet—so that information you request (webpages and email, for instance) can be routed back to your computer properly. When you connect to an internet service provider, you're assigned a public IP address from a block of addresses registered to that ISP. If you use a dial-up connection, your ISP probably assigns a different IP address to your computer (drawn from its pool of available addresses) each time you connect. If you have a persistent connection to your ISP via a DSL or cable modem, your IP address might be permanent—or semipermanent if you turn off your computer when you leave your home or office to travel and your assigned IP address is changed when you reconnect on your return.

On a home or small office network, you don't need to have a public IP address for each computer on the network. In fact, configuring a network with multiple public addresses can increase security risks and often requires an extra fee from your ISP. A safer, less costly solution is to assign a single public IP address to a router or residential gateway (or a computer that performs that function). All other computers on the network connect to the internet through that single address. Each of the computers on the local network has a private IP address that's not directly reachable from the outside world. To communicate with the internet, the router on the edge of the network uses a technology called Network Address Translation (NAT) to pass packets back and forth between the single public IP address and the multiple private IP addresses on the network.

The Internet Assigned Numbers Authority (IANA) has reserved the following three blocks of the IPv4 address space for use on private networks that are not directly connected to the internet:

- 10.0.0.0–10.255.255.255
- 172.16.0.0–172.31.255.255
- 192.168.0.0–192.168.255.255

In addition, the Automatic Private IP Addressing feature in all post-1998 Windows versions uses private IP addresses in the range 169.254.0.0 through 169.254.255.255.

Routers and residential gateways that use NAT almost always assign addresses from these private ranges. Linksys routers, for instance, typically assign addresses starting with 192.168.1.x. If you're setting up a small business or a home network that will not be connected to the internet, or that will be connected through a single proxy server, you can freely use these addresses without concern for conflicts. Just make sure that all the addresses on the network are in the same subnet.

Checking for connection problems

Any time your network refuses to send and receive data properly, your first troubleshooting step should be to check for problems with the physical connection between the local computer and the rest of the network. Assuming your network connection uses the TCP/IP protocol, the first tool to reach for is the Ping utility. When you use the Ping command with no parameters, Windows sends four echo datagrams—small Internet Control Message Protocol (ICMP) packets—to the address you specify. If the machine at the other end of the connection replies, you know that the network connection between the two points is alive.

To use the Ping command, open a Command Prompt window (Cmd.exe) and type the command **ping *target_name*** (where *target_name* is an IP address or the name of another host machine). The return output looks something like this:

```
C:\>ping www.example.com

Pinging www.example.com [93.184.216.34] with 32 bytes of data:
Reply from 93.184.216.34: bytes=32 time=54ms TTL=51
Reply from 93.184.216.34: bytes=32 time=40ms TTL=51
Reply from 93.184.216.34: bytes=32 time=41ms TTL=51
Reply from 93.184.216.34: bytes=32 time=54ms TTL=51

Ping statistics for 93.184.216.34:
    Packets: Sent = 4, Received = 4, Lost = 0 (0% loss),
Approximate round trip times in milli-seconds:
    Minimum = 40ms, Maximum = 54ms, Average = 47ms
```

If all the packets you send come back and the time values are roughly equal, your TCP/IP connection is fine and you can focus your troubleshooting efforts elsewhere. If some packets time out, a "Request timed out" message appears, indicating your network connection is working but one or more hops between your computer and the target machine are experiencing problems. In that case, repeat the Ping test using the –n switch to send a larger number of packets; **ping –n 30 192.168.1.1**, for example, sends 30 packets to the computer or router at 192.168.1.1.

NOTE

The –n switch is case-sensitive; don't capitalize it.

A high rate of timeouts, also known as *packet loss*, usually means the problems are elsewhere on the network and not on the local machine. (To see the full assortment of switches available for the Ping command, type **ping** with no target specified.)

If every one of your packets returns with the message "Request timed out," the problem might be the TCP/IP connection on your computer or a glitch with another computer on that network. To narrow down the problem, follow these steps, in order, stopping at any point where you encounter an error:

1. Ping your own machine by using any of the following commands:

    ```
    ping ::1
    ping 127.0.0.1
    ping localhost
    ```

    These are standard addresses. The first line is the IPv6 address for your own computer; the second line is the IPv4 address; the third line shows the standard host name. If your local network components are configured correctly, each of these three commands should allow the PC on which the command is run to talk to itself. If you receive an error, TCP/IP is not configured properly on your system. For fix-it details, see "Repairing your TCP/IP configuration" later in this chapter.

2. Ping your computer's IP address.

3. Ping the IP address of another computer on your network.

4. Ping the IP address of your router or the default gateway on your network.

5. Ping the address of each DNS server on your network. (If you don't know these addresses, see the next section for details on how to discover them.)

6. Ping a known host outside your network. Well-known, high-traffic websites are ideal for this step, assuming that they respond to ICMP packets.

7. Use the PathPing command to contact the same host you specified in step 6. This command combines the functionality of the Ping command with the Traceroute utility to identify intermediate destinations on the internet between your computer and the specified host or server.

Inside OUT

Choose your test site carefully

In some cases, pinging an external website results in a string of "Request timed out" messages, even when you have no trouble reaching those sites. Don't be misled. Some popular sites block all ICMP traffic, including Ping packets, as a routine security measure. Some routers and residential gateways are also configured to block certain types of ICMP traffic. Try pinging several sites before concluding that your internet connection is broken.

If either of the two final steps in this process fails, your problem might be caused by DNS prob-lems, as described later in this chapter. (For details, see "Resolving DNS issues.") To eliminate this possibility, ping the numeric IP address of a computer outside your network instead. (Of course, if you're having DNS problems, you might have a hard time finding an IP address to ping!) If you can reach a website by using its IP address but not by using its name, DNS problems are indicated.

If you suspect that there's a problem on the internet between your computer and a distant host or server, use the Traceroute utility (Tracert.exe) to pinpoint the problem. Like the Ping command, this utility works from a command line. You specify the target (a host name or IP address) by using the syntax **tracert *target_name***, and the utility sends out a series of packets, measuring the time it takes to reach each hop along the route. Timeouts or unusually slow per-formance indicate a connectivity problem. If the response time from your network to the first hop is much higher than the other hops, you might have a problem with the connection to your internet service provider; in that case, a call to your ISP's support line is in order. Problems far-ther along in the traceroute might indicate congestion or hardware problems in distant parts of the internet that are out of your ISP's hands. These symptoms might disappear when you check another URL that follows a different path through the internet.

If your testing produces inconsistent results, rule out the possibility that a firewall program or NAT device (such as a router or residential gateway) is to blame. If you're using Windows Firewall or a third-party firewall program, disable it temporarily. Try bypassing your router and connecting directly to a broadband connection such as a DSL or cable modem. (Use this con-figuration only for testing and only very briefly because it exposes your computer to various attacks.)

If the Ping test works with the firewall or NAT device out of the picture, you can rule out net-work problems and conclude that the firewall software or router is misconfigured. After you complete your testing, be sure to enable the firewall and router again!

Diagnosing IP address problems

On most networks, IP addresses are assigned automatically by Dynamic Host Configuration Pro-tocol (DHCP) servers; in some cases, you might need (or prefer) to use static IP addresses, which are fixed numeric addresses. Problems with DHCP servers or clients can cause network connec-tions to stop working, as can incorrectly assigned static IP addresses.

To see details of your current IP configuration, follow these steps:

1. Open Settings > Network & Internet > Change Adapter Options.

2. Double-click the icon for the connection about which you want more information. (Alternatively, you can select the icon and click View Status Of This Connection on the command bar.)

3. Click Details to see the currently assigned IP address, subnet mask, and default gateway for this connection. (If you have IPv4 and IPv6 connectivity, the Network Connection Details dialog box shows information for both.) In the following example, you can tell that the IP address was automatically assigned by the DHCP server in a router; details indicate that DHCP is enabled and the DHCP server address matches that of the router:

Network Connection Details   ✕

Network Connection Details:

Property	Value
Connection-specific DNS S...	charter.com
Description	Marvell AVASTAR 350N Wireless Network C
Physical Address	28-18-78-59-56-B5
DHCP Enabled	Yes
IPv4 Address	192.168.1.149
IPv4 Subnet Mask	255.255.255.0
Lease Obtained	Sunday, July 31, 2016 11:24:22 PM
Lease Expires	Monday, August 01, 2016 11:24:21 PM
IPv4 Default Gateway	192.168.1.1
IPv4 DHCP Server	192.168.1.1
IPv4 DNS Server	192.168.1.1
IPv4 WINS Server	
NetBIOS over Tcpip Enabl...	Yes
Link-local IPv6 Address	fe80::cde9:dbe8:1217:4a8d%14
IPv6 Default Gateway	
IPv6 DNS Server	

Close

CHAPTER 20

You can also get useful details of your IP configuration by using the IP Configuration utility, Ipconfig.exe, in a Command Prompt window. Used without any parameters, typing **ipconfig** at a command prompt displays the DNS suffix; IPv6 address, IPv4 address, or both; subnet mask; and default gateway for each network connection. To see exhaustive details about every available network connection, type **ipconfig /all**.

The actual IP address you see might help you solve connection problems:

- If the address is in the format 169.254.*x.y*, your computer is using Automatic Private IP Addressing (APIPA). This means your computer's DHCP client was unable to reach a DHCP server to be assigned an IP address. Check the connection to your network.

- If the address is in one of the blocks of IP addresses reserved for use on private networks (for details, see the sidebar "Public and private IP addresses" earlier in this chapter), make sure that a router or residential gateway is routing your internet requests to a properly configured public IP address.

- If the address of your computer appears as 0.0.0.0, the network is either disconnected or the static IP address for the connection duplicates an address that already exists on the network.

- Make sure you're using the correct subnet mask for computers on your local network. Compare IP settings on the machine that's having problems with those on other computers on the network. The default gateway and subnet mask should be identical for all network computers. The first one, two, or three sets of numbers in the IP address for each machine should also be identical, depending on the subnet mask. A subnet mask of 255.255.255.0 means the first three IP address numbers of computers on your network must be identical—192.168.0.83 and 192.168.0.223, for instance, can communicate on a network using this subnet mask, but 192.168.1.101 will not be recognized as belonging to the network. The gateway machine must also be a member of the same subnet. (If you use a router, switch, or residential gateway for internet access, the local address on that device must be part of the same subnet as the machines on your network.)

NOTE

Are you baffled by subnets and other related technical terms? For an excellent overview of these sometimes confusing topics, read Knowledge Base article 164015, "Understanding TCP/IP Addressing and Subnetting Basics" (*https://support.microsoft.com/kb/164015*), which offers information about IPv4. For comparable details about IPv6, see the "Introduction to IPv6" white paper at TechNet (*https://bit.ly/ipv6-intro*).

Repairing your TCP/IP configuration

If you suspect a problem with your TCP/IP configuration, try either of the following repair options:

- **Use the automated repair option.** Right-click the connection icon in Network Connections and click Diagnose.

- **Release and renew your IP address.** Use the **ipconfig /release** command to let go of the DHCP-assigned IPv4 address. Then use **ipconfig /renew** to obtain a new IP address from the DHCP server. To renew an IPv6 address, use **ipconfig /release6** and **ipconfig /renew6**.

NOTE

If these methods don't work, you can use the Netsh utility to restore the TCP/IP stack to its original configuration when Windows was first installed. The utility restores all registry settings relating to the TCP/IP stack to their original settings, which is effectively the same as removing and reinstalling the protocol. The utility records a log of the changes it makes. For details about this drastic, but effective, solution, see Microsoft Knowledge Base article 299357 (*https://support.microsoft.com/kb/299357*). Another option is to reset the network adapter; go to Settings > Network & Internet > Network Reset.

Inside OUT

Translate names to IP addresses and vice versa

The Nslookup command is a buried treasure in Windows. Use this command-line utility to quickly convert a fully qualified domain name to its IP address. You can tack on a host name to the end of the command line to identify a single address; for instance, you can type **nslookup ftp.microsoft.com** to look up the IP address of Microsoft's File Transfer Protocol (FTP) server. Or type **nslookup** to switch into interactive mode. From this prompt, you can enter any domain name to find its IP address.

If you need more sophisticated lookup tools, you can find them with the help of any search engine. A good starting point is DNSstuff (*http://dnsstuff.com/tools*), which offers an impressive collection of online tools for looking up domains, IP addresses, and host names. The site also offers form-based utilities that can translate obfuscated URLs and dotted IP addresses, both of which are widely used by spammers to cover their online tracks.

Resolving DNS issues

The Domain Name System (DNS) is a crucial part of the internet. DNS servers translate host names (*www.microsoft.com*, for instance) into numeric IP addresses so that packets can be routed properly over the internet. If you can use the Ping command to reach a numeric address outside your network but are unable to browse websites by name, the problem is almost certainly related to your DNS configuration.

Here are some questions to ask when you suspect DNS problems:

- **Do your TCP/IP settings point to the right DNS servers?** Inspect the details of your IP configuration, and compare the DNS servers listed there with those recommended by your internet service provider. (You might need to call your ISP to get these details.)

- **Is your ISP experiencing DNS problems?** A misconfigured DNS server (or one that's offline) can wreak havoc with your attempts to use the internet. Try pinging each DNS server to see whether it's available. If your ISP has multiple DNS servers and you encounter problems accessing one server, remove that server from your TCP/IP configuration temporarily and use another one instead.

- **Have you installed any "internet accelerator" utilities?** Many such programs work by editing the Hosts file on your computer to match IP addresses and host (server) names. When Windows finds a host name in the Hosts file, it uses the IP address listed there and doesn't send the request to a DNS server. If the owner of the server changes its DNS records to point to a new IP address, your Hosts file will lead you to the wrong location.

Temporary DNS problems can also be caused by the DNS cache, which Windows maintains for performance reasons. If you suddenly have trouble reaching a specific site on the internet and you're convinced there's nothing wrong with the site, type this command to clear the DNS cache: **ipconfig /flushdns**.

A more thorough solution is offered by **ipconfig /registerdns**, which renews all DHCP leases (as described in the previous section) *and* reregisters all DNS names.

CHAPTER 21

Managing Windows 10 in business

Throughout this book, our emphasis has been on how individuals can get the most out of Microsoft Windows: learn how to use its many features, save time with shortcuts and work-arounds, and customize it to suit specific needs. Most of this information applies equally to a wide variety of devices—including tablets, laptops, and desktop PCs—in a wide variety of environments. Whether you use Windows as a standalone system, in a home network, in a small business network, or as a tiny cog in a ginormous enterprise-scale operation, you can make use of this knowledge.

In this chapter, however, we depart from that focus on the individual to provide an overview of topics, products, and techniques that are useful primarily on business networks. Most require a business edition of Windows: Windows 10 Pro or Windows 10 Enterprise. (Windows 10 Education editions can also use these features.) And many rely on Active Directory services, which are available only on centrally managed networks running Windows Server or via Azure Active Directory.

Of course, we don't have the space in this book—or any other single book—to fully document the wealth of business tools Microsoft makes available for Windows 10. Instead, our goal here is to provide a survey of some widely used tools along with pointers to more in-depth information.

Using a domain-based network

Elsewhere in this book, we describe setup, configuration, and usage of peer-to-peer (or *workgroup*) networks. This is the type of network most commonly found in homes and small businesses, and it does not require a server; each computer on the network is an equally empowered peer.

Windows 10 Pro, Enterprise, and Education editions can also be configured in an Active Directory domain. The traditional Active Directory domain-based network requires at least one computer running a version of Windows Server. This is sometimes called *on-premises Active Directory* to differentiate it from a newer, cloud-based alternative called Azure Active Directory (Azure AD).

Both variants of Active Directory provide identity and access services, allowing users to sign on to any cloud or on-premises web application using a wide variety of devices, and to sign on to domain-joined devices. All computers and user accounts on the network can be centrally managed through the server or through a web-based Azure AD dashboard. An on-premises domain controller offers full, policy-based management capabilities. Azure AD, in its current incarnation, provides a more limited set of management tools. When you have more than a handful of computers in a network, they become much easier to manage when configured as a domain.

If you use a business-focused Microsoft cloud service such as Office 365 or Microsoft Dynamics CRM (among others), your subscription already includes Azure AD.

A detailed description of domains and Active Directory is (well) beyond the scope of this book. Here are some resources to get you started:

- Microsoft Azure: *https://azure.microsoft.com*

- Azure Active Directory: *https://azure.microsoft.com/services/active-directory*

- Identity and access services in Azure AD: *https://bit.ly/AzureAD-identity*

- Windows Server: *http://www.microsoft.com/windowsserver*

Managing computers with Group Policy

Group Policy lets administrators configure computers throughout sites, domains, or organizational units. In addition to setting standard desktop configurations and restricting what settings users are allowed to change, administrators can use Group Policy to centrally manage software installation, configuration, updates, and removal; specify scripts to run at startup, shutdown, sign in, and sign out; and redirect users' profile folders (such as Documents) to network server drives. Administrators can customize all these settings for different computers, users, or groups.

In a domain environment, Group Policy enables an administrator to apply policy settings and restrictions to users and computers (and groups of each) in one fell swoop. With a workgroup, you must make similar Group Policy settings on each computer where you want such restrictions imposed. Nonetheless, Group Policy can be a useful tool for managing computers on a small network or even for managing a single computer.

Using Local Group Policy Editor

In this book's examples, we use Local Group Policy Editor (Gpedit.msc) to make policy settings. That way, you can follow along even if you don't have access to a domain controller or don't need the power of Active Directory. Setting Group Policy in an Active Directory domain uses similar methods and policies.

To begin exploring Group Policy, in the Start search box type **group policy** and then tap or click Edit Group Policy. As shown in Figure 21-1, Local Group Policy Editor appears in the familiar Microsoft Management Console format.

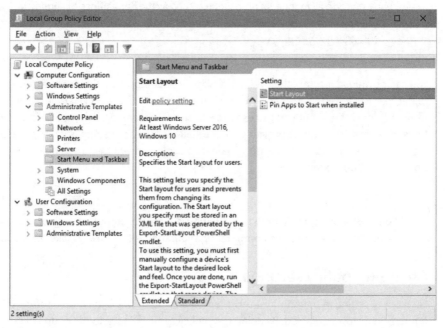

Figure 21-1 Selecting a folder in the left pane shows its policy settings in the right pane. When you select a setting, a description of the setting appears.

The Computer Configuration branch of Group Policy includes various computer-related settings, and the User Configuration branch includes various user-related settings. The line between computer settings and user settings is often blurred, however. Your best bet for discovering the policies you need is to scan them all. You'll find a treasure trove of useful settings, including many that can't be made any other way short of manually editing the registry. In the Administrative Templates folders, you'll find several hundred computer settings and even more user settings, which makes this sound like a daunting task—but you'll find that you can quickly skim the folder names in Local Group Policy Editor, ignoring most of them, and then scan the policies in each folder of interest.

To learn more about each policy, simply select it in Local Group Policy Editor, as shown in Figure 21-1. If you select the Extended tab at the bottom of the window, a description of the selected policy appears in the center pane.

Inside OUT

Customize Start and taskbar behavior and appearance

The policy setting shown in Figure 21-1 controls one aspect of Start. Many more policies—most of them located in User Configuration > Administrative Templates > Start Menu And Taskbar—manage all manner of Start details, such as the appearance of suggestions and most-used apps in the app list on Start. For more information about these policy settings, go to *https://bit.ly/start-policy*

You can download a comprehensive list of all policy settings from the Administrative Templates folder, in Microsoft Excel format, by visiting *https://bit.ly/group-policy-settings*. The list is huge—thousands of entries—but you can use Excel to sort, filter, or search the list to find policy settings of interest. The list also provides other details about each setting, such as the scope of the setting (machine or user), the registry value it controls, and whether a setting change requires a sign-off or reboot to take effect.

NOTE

Some settings appear in both User Configuration and Computer Configuration. In a case of conflicting settings, the Computer Configuration setting always takes precedence.

Changing policy settings

Each policy setting in the Administrative Templates folders has one of three settings: Not Configured, Enabled, or Disabled. By default, all policy settings in the local Group Policy objects are initially set to Not Configured.

To change a policy setting, in Local Group Policy Editor, simply double-click the name of the policy setting you want to change or click the Policy Setting link that appears in the center pane of the Extended tab. A dialog box then appears, as shown in Figure 21-2.

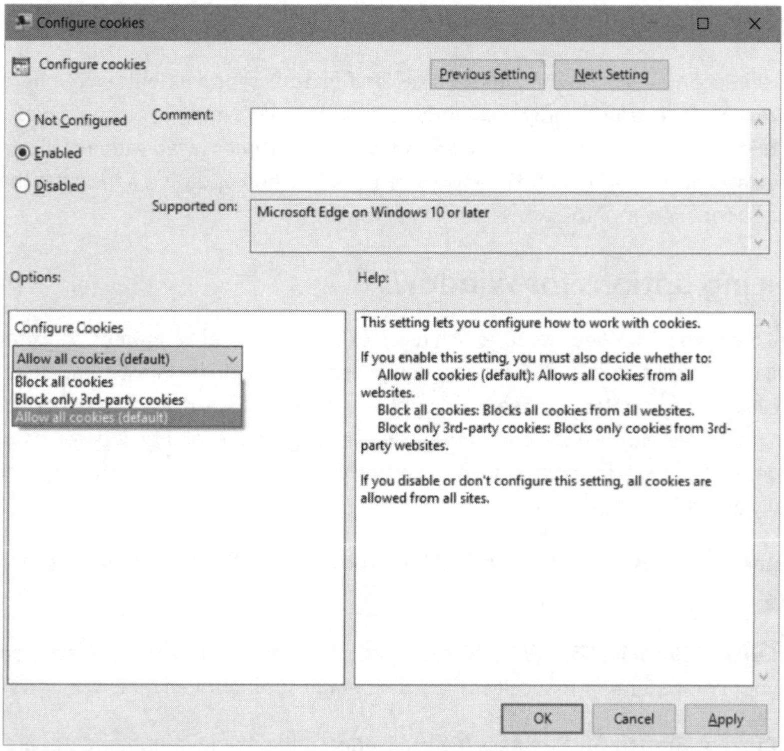

Figure 21-2 When a policy setting has configurable options, like those shown here under Options, they're available only when the policy is set to Enabled.

Beside the settings option buttons is a large area where you can write a comment. The Help pane below this Comment area includes detailed information about the policy setting (the same information that appears in the center pane of the Extended tab). The pane to the left of the Help pane offers options relevant to the current policy. Previous Setting and Next Setting buttons make it convenient to go through an entire folder without opening and closing individual dialog boxes.

Managing updates

In earlier versions of Windows, updates, fixes, and feature improvements were offered as an ever-growing collection of individual updates. This approach meant you could pick and choose which updates to install. But it also meant you were sometimes faced with installing scores of updates (and performing multiple reboots), especially when updating a machine that hadn't been used for a few months.

Servicing options for Windows

That all changes with Windows 10, which receives so-called quality updates, to fix security and reliability issues, in cumulative packages. When you install the latest cumulative update, it retrieves all the updates you need and applies them en masse. If you use Windows 10 Home edition, that's pretty much the end of the story: Security and reliability updates, as well as major upgrades (called *feature updates*) such as version 1607 (Anniversary Update), are installed automatically at the first opportunity.

With other Windows editions, you might have the ability to choose among these servicing options:

- **Current Branch (CB).** With CB, security updates and feature upgrades are pushed to your computer automatically. This is the default setting for all retail Windows editions.

- **Current Branch for Business (CBB).** Under CBB, only definition updates are installed immediately. Security, reliability, and driver updates can be postponed for up to 30 days to allow time for testing before deployment throughout your organization. Feature updates are not even offered to CBB clients until they've been road tested by CB clients for a period of time—at least four months. Even then, installation of feature updates can be deferred for up to eight months. Because CBB allows for controlled rollout of both quality and feature updates over a longer period of time, it's often the best option for the majority of users in an organization. CBB is available only on Pro, Enterprise, and Education editions of Windows 10. Deferring updates for CBB is most easily done with Windows Update for Business, which we describe in the next section.

- **Long Term Servicing Branch (LTSB).** Each LTSB release includes the usual monthly security and reliability updates, but no new features are added for up to 10 years. LTSB is not intended for general-purpose workstations; rather, it's targeted at specialized devices (such as manufacturing control systems or point-of-sale systems) that run mission-critical applications and where high reliability is the primary goal. For this reason, LTSB editions lack several Windows components that are included in other editions, including Windows Store, Microsoft Edge, Cortana, and the built-in universal apps such as Mail, Weather, Photos, Alarms & Clock, and Groove Music.

LTSB is a licensing option for Windows 10 Enterprise and is available only for customers with a Volume License agreement. Because you don't get feature updates with LTSB, the only way to get a new Windows version is to pay for a new license (unless you have Software Assurance) and upgrade to a newer LTSB release when it's available.

NOTE

A fourth servicing option is available for those who want to be ahead of the curve. The Windows Insider Program delivers updates *before* they're distributed to the masses. Insider Preview builds allow you to get an early look at new features, test them, and provide feedback to Microsoft—but it also means you install software that hasn't been as widely tested and might cause severe problems. If you want to be a guinea pig, go to Settings > Update & Security > Windows Insider Program.

➤ To learn the version number and build number of the current release in each servicing option, go to *https://bit.ly/windows-release*.

➤ For more information about Windows Update, see "Keeping Windows up to date" in Chapter 15, "System maintenance and performance." For additional details about Windows servicing options, visit *https://bit.ly/servicing-options*. We describe the Windows Insider Program in more detail in Chapter 23, "What's next for Windows 10?"

Using Windows Update for Business

Windows Update for Business is a set of configuration options for the free Windows Update service that allows users of Windows 10 Pro, Enterprise, and Education editions to defer most updates and upgrades. You configure Windows Update for Business through Group Policy. In Windows 10 version 1607, you'll find two policy settings in Computer Configuration > Administrative Templates > Windows Components > Windows Update > Defer Windows Updates:

- **Select when Feature Updates are received.** Configure this policy, shown in Figure 21-3, to defer feature updates. If you enable this policy, you can then select the "branch readiness level": Current Branch (which is the default setting and refers to the feature update currently in wide public release) or Current Branch For Business (in which feature updates are typically released about four months later, after Microsoft declares an update ready for this branch).

  With either branch, you can then specify an amount of time to defer the update after release. You enter the number of days, up to 180.

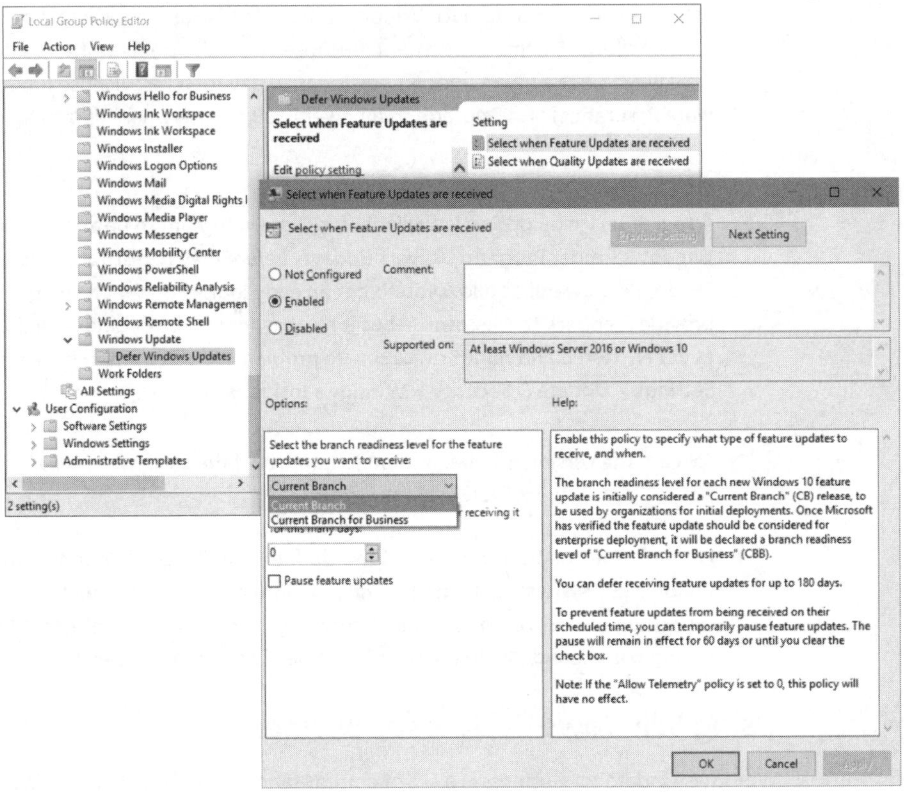

Figure 21-3 Windows Update for Business originally appeared in version 1511 with a single policy setting. In version 1607 (Anniversary Update), two policy settings control this feature.

- **Select when Quality Updates are received.** With this policy, you can defer the regular cumulative updates (which include security, reliability, and driver updates) for up to 30 days. Although this gives you an opportunity to test the latest update on a smaller ring in your organization, it can also put your other machines at risk because potentially important security fixes are delayed.

Managing apps

You might want to control the apps that are installed on employees' computers. Of course, you want to be sure that the apps they install and run are safe; the last thing you need is malware spreading throughout your organization. Perhaps you want to limit availability of productivity-killing apps. Or maybe you need a way to manage licenses throughout your company.

Managing distribution with Windows Store for Business

Windows Store for Business provides a way for organizations to make volume purchases of Windows apps. App licenses can be allocated to certain users in your organization, and licenses can be reclaimed and reused. Organizations can create a private store for their employees that includes a curated collection of apps from Windows Store. In addition, you can add and distribute your own private line-of-business apps.

As with Windows Store, Windows Store for Business manages updates for apps, ensuring that all your users automatically receive the most recent updates.

The requirements for using Windows Store for Business are not too rigorous: To set up Windows Store for Business, you must have an Azure AD account for your organization. To install apps from the Store, employees must be running Windows 10 version 1511 or later on a PC or mobile device and must have an Azure AD account.

For complete details about Windows Store for Business, including how to set up your store and "stock" it with apps, visit *https://bit.ly/windows-store-for-business*.

Securing apps with AppLocker

AppLocker is a feature of Windows Enterprise and Education editions that lets an administrator control which apps and files users can run. AppLocker rules apply to all types of executable files, including scripts, app installers, and dynamic-link libraries (DLLs) as well as program files; it's a comprehensive tool for dictating what is allowed to run. AppLocker rules can be applied to security groups or individual users.

➤ For complete information about AppLocker, start at *https://bit.ly/applocker-overview*.

CHAPTER 21

Managing the browsing experience

In Windows 10, Microsoft Edge has replaced Internet Explorer as the default browser. Microsoft Edge offers improvements in security and speed over Internet Explorer. Nevertheless, some line-of-business web applications were designed specifically for Internet Explorer; upgrading these applications can be expensive and impractical. Likewise, you might find some public websites that rely on Internet Explorer. For these sites, Enterprise Mode in Microsoft Edge automatically opens sites in Internet Explorer.

> ➤ **For complete details about Microsoft Edge, see Chapter 9, "Cortana and the web." For information about the differences between Microsoft Edge and Internet Explorer, see "Why the new browser?" in Chapter 9.**

To use Enterprise Mode, you must first create a list of sites you want to open in Internet Explorer. The easiest way to create the list (an XML file) is with Enterprise Mode Site List Manager, a free tool from Microsoft that you can download from *https://bit.ly/emslm-v2*.

With the list in place, you must then turn on a Group Policy setting that causes Microsoft Edge to use the Enterprise Mode site list. In the Group Policy editor, go to Administrative Templates > Windows Components > Microsoft Edge and open the Configure The Enterprise Mode Site List setting, as shown in Figure 21-4.

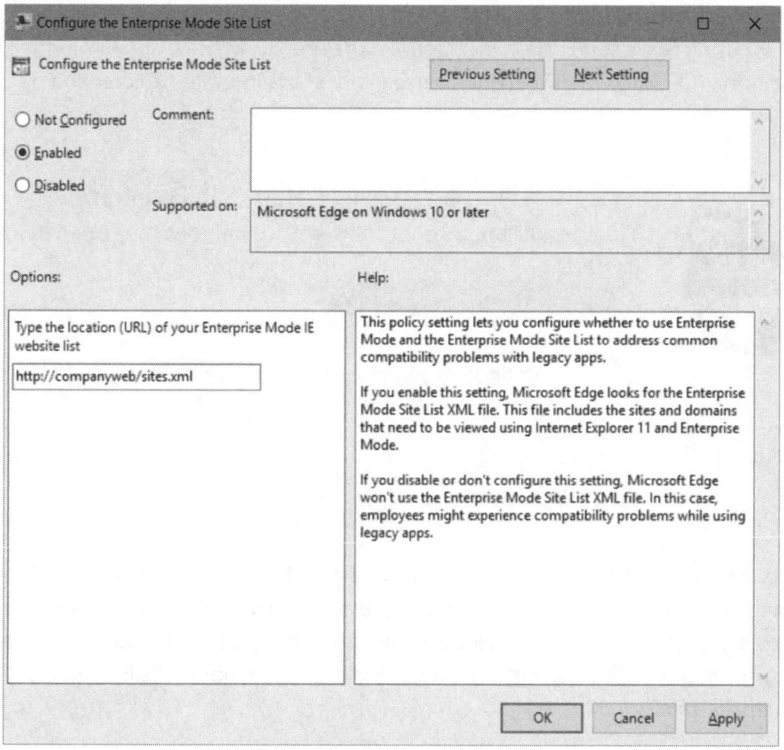

Figure 21-4 To configure this policy, select Enabled and then enter the URL of the site list you created with Enterprise Mode Site List Manager.

Inside OUT

Manage other browsing features

While you have your Group Policy editor open to Administrative Templates > Windows Components > Microsoft Edge, this is an excellent time to look at other policy settings that control the way Microsoft Edge works. You can, for example, disable the use of extensions, specify home pages, prevent the use of InPrivate browsing, and so on.

With an Enterprise Mode site list in place and enabled by Group Policy, when a user visits a site on the list using Microsoft Edge, a message like the one shown next appears in the Microsoft Edge window. Clicking Open With Internet Explorer starts Internet Explorer and opens the page in a new window.

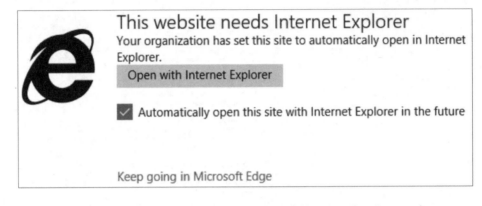

Enterprise Mode has other capabilities that make it useful in some situations, such as an option to open intranet sites in Internet Explorer, the ability to automatically open a site in Microsoft Edge from Internet Explorer, compatibility with sites that depend on rendering engines as ancient as Internet Explorer 5, and more. For more details, visit *https://bit.ly/ie11enterprise-mode-1607*.

Managing special-purpose computers

Nowadays, it's a rare business whose fleet of computers consists solely of a desktop PC on the desk of each worker. In the following sections, we look at a couple of other common computer use cases: shared PCs and kiosk devices.

Using shared PC mode

In your business, you might find it useful to have a shared PC—one that can be used by employees as they work at different locations within your business, or one that you want to make available for temporary use by customers and visitors. A new feature in version 1607 (Anniversary Update) called *shared PC mode* makes this easier than ever on domain-joined computers.

In shared PC mode, you can configure how temporary users sign on, what apps and other resources are available to them, and what to do with the user's data when he or she signs off.

➤ For complete information about setting up and using shared PC mode, go to *https://bit.ly/shared-pc-mode*.

Setting up a kiosk device

Another common scenario in business is to set up a kiosk device—a computer that is set up to do only one thing. You might use this computer as a device in the lobby or on the retail floor that customers can use to view your product catalog or check prices. Or it might be a single-purpose device used by an employee in your organization, such as a data-entry device for warehouse workers or a map app for drivers.

You configure a kiosk device to run a single app. If that app is a Universal Windows Platform (UWP) app, you can use any Windows 10 edition. A desktop app can be used only on a kiosk device running the Enterprise or Education edition.

To set up a kiosk device to run a UWP app, you use a feature called *assigned access*. There are several methods for enabling assigned access, including Windows PowerShell, mobile device management, and tools in the Windows Assessment and Deployment Kit (ADK). But you can also configure a single device by going to Settings > Accounts > Family & Other People > Set Up Assigned Access. See Figure 21-5.

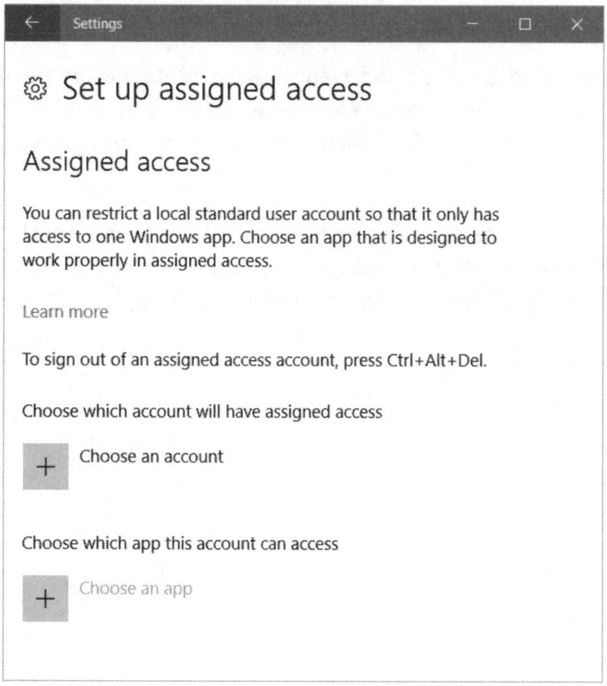

Figure 21-5 After you select an account to use for assigned access, you select an app that runs automatically.

NOTE

For assigned access configured using Settings or PowerShell, you must use a local standard account. With the other methods, you can use any account type, including domain accounts and local administrator accounts. For information about creating an account, see "Working with user accounts" in Chapter 6, "Managing user accounts, passwords, and credentials."

Click Choose An Account and select the account you'd like to use. Then click Choose An App and select a UWP app.

You might also want to configure the account to sign in automatically each time you start the computer. To do that, in Registry Editor open HKLM\Software\Microsoft\Windows NT\CurrentVersion\Winlogon and set values for these three keys:

- AutoAdminLogon: Set value to 1

- DefaultUserName: Set to the name of the account to sign in

- DefaultPassword: Set to the password for the account

With your device thus configured, turn it on and it launches directly to the app you selected, running in a full screen and lacking all the usual Windows accoutrements, including the Start button and taskbar. To escape, press Ctrl+Alt+Delete, whereupon you can sign in using another account.

To undo this setup, return to Settings > Accounts > Family & Other People > Set Up Assigned Access. Click the name of the assigned access user, and then click Don't Use Assigned Access. If you configured automatic sign in, return to Registry Editor and change the value of AutoAdminLogon to 0.

← Settings   — □ ✕

⚙ S

Assig

Choose an account

If the selected account is currently signed in,
you must sign out and sign in again to apply
the changes.

Don't use assigned access

You ca   y has
access   d to
work p

Learn n   [icon] Cabin Fever

To sign   Del.

Choose

[icon] Cabin Fever

Choose which app this account can access

[icon] Maps

➤ For more details about setting up a kiosk device, including a list of settings to lock down for secure kiosk use, visit *https://bit.ly/kiosk-setup*.

CHAPTER 21

Running virtual machines
with Hyper-V

You can use Hyper-V to create and run *virtual machines*—effectively, computers within a computer. A console on your computer acts as a monitor for a virtual machine (sometimes called a *VM*), which generally has most of the features and capabilities of a standalone computer. The only difference is that a virtual machine runs as a program on a host computer, under the control of a system-level software layer called a *hypervisor*.

Hyper-V has long been a power feature in server editions of Microsoft Windows, allowing IT managers to use a single server machine to host various server roles, each in its own virtual machine. Beginning with Windows 8, Client Hyper-V is included in Pro and Enterprise editions of Windows, to the great delight of IT professionals, developers, security researchers, and tech enthusiasts.

Client Hyper-V has most, but not all, of the features of Hyper-V Server. In Windows 10, Client Hyper-V gains some additional features, such as production checkpoints, better support of older operating systems, and the ability for users to change memory and other settings without first shutting down a virtual machine. The November 2015 update to Windows 10 (version 1511) provided support for Secure Boot and Trusted Platform Modules in VMs. The Anniversary Update (version 1607) introduces nested virtualization, allowing virtual environments to host additional virtual machines. One noteworthy use of this new capability is a feature called *Hyper-V Containers*, which we discuss at the end of this chapter.

Virtual machines running under Hyper-V are useful in the following situations, among many others:

- People who have programs that do not work properly in Windows 10 can run them in a virtual machine using an older version of Windows.

- Developers who need to test their programs in different Windows versions or under different resource configurations can set up a virtual machine for each target platform.

- Security researchers and curious users who want to test software of unknown provenance or explore potentially dangerous websites can do so safely within the confines of a virtual machine (assuming it's properly isolated from the host and the host network). If a virus or other malware is found, the host machine remains unscathed, and the virtual machine can be rolled back to a safe state.

- Tech enthusiasts who want to test a new beta (prerelease) version of Windows or other software can install it in a virtual machine. This way, they can try the software without having to dedicate a physical machine (or worse, upgrading their main system to run an operating system that still has issues).

- Authors of books like this one can use virtual machines not only to test various setups, but also to capture images of screens that would be impossible to grab using ordinary screen-capture tools (for example, images showing sign-in screens or even Windows setup before Windows itself is fully functional).

To use Hyper-V, your system must meet certain minimum requirements and you might need to enable the Hyper-V feature, as described in the next section. After that is done, you use Hyper-V Manager to create virtual machines. With enough system resources, you can then run one or more virtual machines, each in its own window. Because they function as independent computers, each virtual machine can run a different version of Windows—32-bit or 64-bit, old or new, server or desktop—or even other operating systems that work on PC-compatible hardware.

Inside OUT

Determine whether your computer supports Hyper-V

On a PC that's already running Windows 10, checking for Hyper-V support is as easy as opening the System Information app (Msinfo32.exe). Scroll to the bottom of the System Summary tab to see four entries that begin with "Hyper-V," as shown here:

Item	Value
Installed Physical Memory (RAM)	16.0 GB
Total Physical Memory	15.9 GB
Available Physical Memory	13.3 GB
Total Virtual Memory	18.3 GB
Available Virtual Memory	15.8 GB
Page File Space	2.38 GB
Page File	C:\pagefile.sys
Hyper-V - VM Monitor Mode Extensions	Yes
Hyper-V - Second Level Address Translation Extensions	Yes
Hyper-V - Virtualization Enabled in Firmware	Yes
Hyper-V - Data Execution Protection	Yes

System Summary
Hardware Resources
Components
Software Environment

System Information
File Edit View Help

If you see the value *Yes* for every item on that list, you can turn on Hyper-V.

To check Hyper-V compatibility before upgrading a PC running an older version of Windows, use the CoreInfo utility from Windows Sysinternals, which is available from *https://bit.ly/sysinternals-coreinfo*. At an elevated command prompt, enter **coreinfo –v** to see results similar to this:

```
Administrator: Command Prompt                                    —    □    ×

Microsoft Windows [Version 10.0.10586]
(c) 2015 Microsoft Corporation. All rights reserved.

C:\windows\system32>coreinfo -v

Coreinfo v3.31 - Dump information on system CPU and memory topology
Copyright (C) 2008-2014 Mark Russinovich
Sysinternals - www.sysinternals.com

Intel(R) Core(TM) i7-6600U CPU @ 2.60GHz
Intel64 Family 6 Model 78 Stepping 3, GenuineIntel
Microcode signature: 00000082
HYPERVISOR     -        Hypervisor is present
VMX            *        Supports Intel hardware-assisted virtualization
EPT            *        Supports Intel extended page tables (SLAT)
```

For an Intel processor (as shown here), an asterisk in the EPT line indicates support for Second Level Address Translation (SLAT), a requirement for running Hyper-V; a hyphen in that space indicates that the processor does *not* support SLAT. For an AMD processor, the line to look for is NP. Note that you'll get valid results only if Hyper-V is *not* already running. (But if it's already running, you didn't need to run this diagnostic test anyway, did you?)

Setting up Hyper-V

Before you get started with Hyper-V, be sure your computer meets the system requirements. Because each virtual machine uses system resources on a par with a standalone computer, the requirements are somewhat steep:

- **64-bit version of Windows 10 Pro, Enterprise, or Education.** Hyper-V is unavailable on 32-bit versions and is also not part of Windows 10 Home.

- **At least 4 GB of RAM.** With 4 GB of total RAM, you can probably run one or two low-resource virtual machines simultaneously. In our experience, you need at least 8 GB of total RAM for satisfactory performance with one or more virtual machines running Windows 10.

- **Copious disk space.** Each virtual machine is stored in files on your hard drive. The size can vary considerably depending on how you configure your virtual machines (for example, the operating system and the size of the VM's virtual hard disks), how many checkpoints you save, and so on—but expect to use at least 20 GB of disk storage for each virtual machine.

- **A CPU with Hyper-V features enabled.** Your computer must have a 64-bit processor that supports virtualization in the firmware and has Data Execution Prevention enabled. Most 64-bit processors sold by Intel and AMD in the past few years have this capability. In addition, Second Level Address Translation (SLAT) is essential for acceptable performance.

With those prerequisites in place, you're ready to turn on the Hyper-V features, which are installed but are off by default. To do so, open Windows Features, shown in Figure 22-1. (In the search box, type **features** and then click Turn Windows Features On Or Off.)

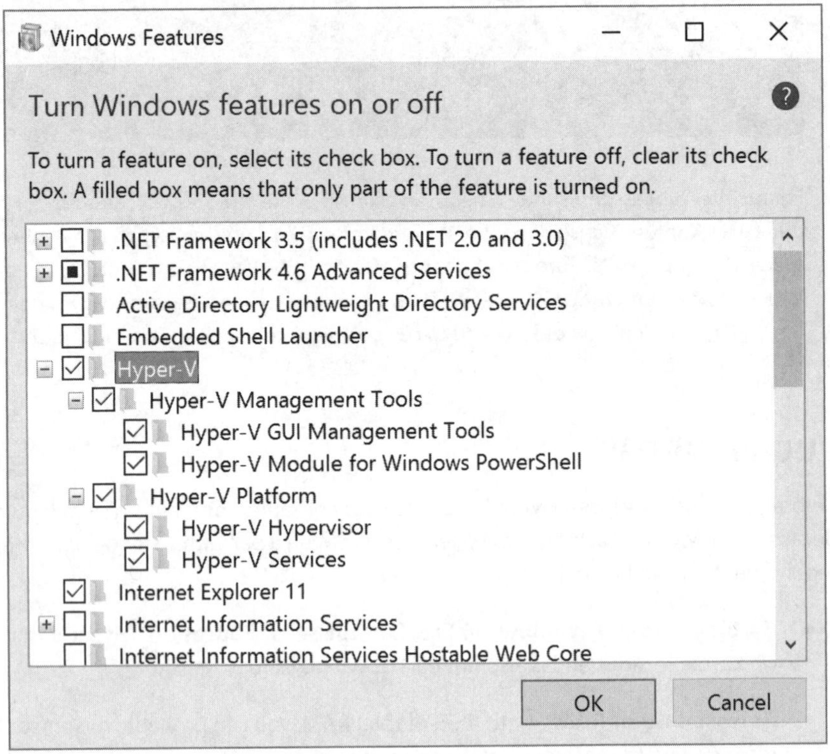

Figure 22-1 To select all the Hyper-V-related entries, select the top-level Hyper-V check box.

Click the plus sign by the top-level Hyper-V entry to show all the subentries. If your computer does not fully support Hyper-V, the Hyper-V Hypervisor entry is not available.

> ## Inside OUT
>
> ### Using Hyper-V on a computer that lacks hardware support
>
> Hyper-V Management Tools, the first subentry under Hyper-V, can be installed on any computer running any edition of Windows 10. Therefore, even if the Hyper-V Hypervisor entry is dimmed (which means your computer isn't capable of hosting virtual machines), you can use Hyper-V Management Tools to manage virtual machines that are hosted on a different physical computer (in most cases, a computer running Window Server). To run virtual machines on your own computer, you must enable the Hyper-V Hypervisor.

Select Hyper-V (which also selects all the available subentries) to enable it, and then click OK. After a few moments, Windows asks you to restart your computer.

Alternatively, you can enable Hyper-V by using Windows PowerShell. Use this cmdlet:

```
Enable-WindowsOptionalFeature –Online –FeatureName Microsoft-Hyper-V –All
```

Using Hyper-V Manager

Hyper-V Manager is the program you use to create, run, and manage your virtual machines. When you start Hyper-V Manager, the initial view, shown here, might leave you scratching your head. You're faced with a barren console window, one that has only one available action:

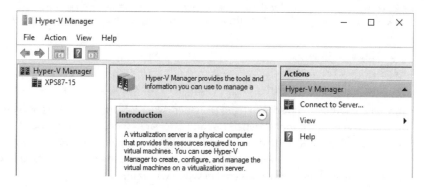

The trick is to select a "server" (in this case, your local computer) in the left pane, the console tree. (On computers that do not have Hyper-V Platform enabled, the only option is to choose the Connect To Server action, which lets you connect to a different computer running Hyper-V Platform.) Lots more information and options then appear, as shown in Figure 22-2.

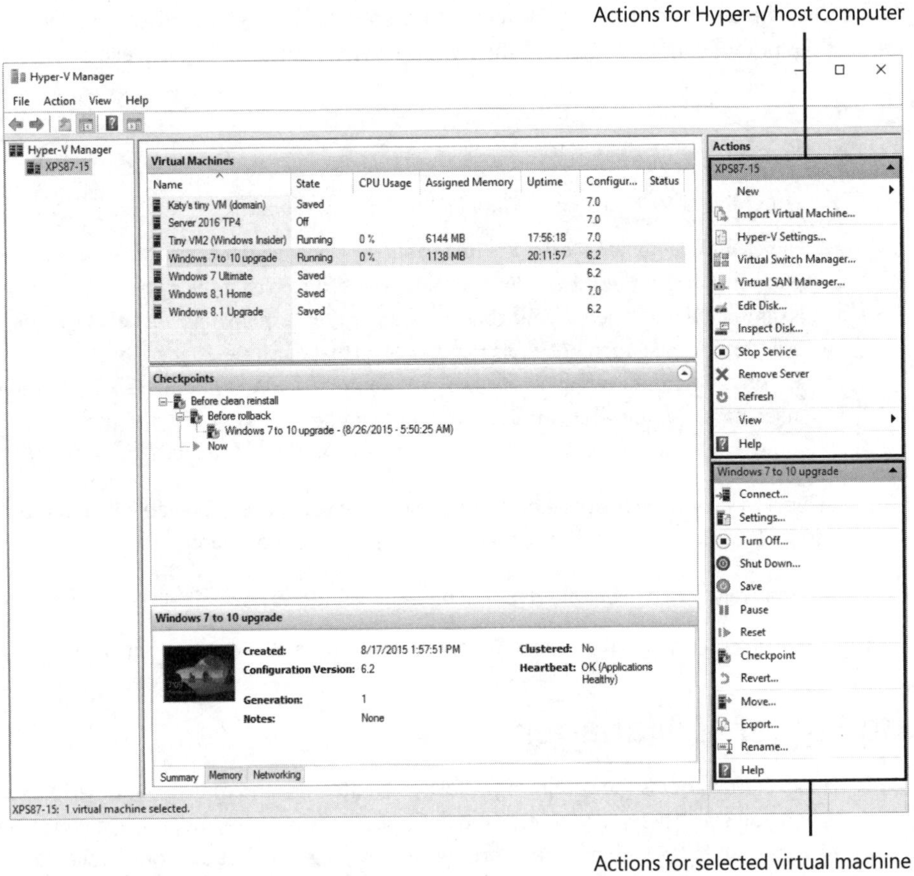

Actions for Hyper-V host computer

Actions for selected virtual machine

Figure 22-2 When you select a local machine or remote server in the console tree (XPS87-15 in this example), Hyper-V Manager shows the virtual machines stored on that physical computer.

TROUBLESHOOTING

The name of your computer doesn't appear in the console tree

If your computer's name doesn't appear under Hyper-V Manager in the console tree, it's not running the Hyper-V Hypervisor and associated services. Be sure you're running a 64-bit version of Windows 10, and be sure your computer supports Hyper-V, as described in the previous section. If your computer meets the requirements, check to be sure that Hyper-V Platform is selected in Windows Features.

When you select a Hyper-V host in the console tree (in this case, your PC running Windows 10 Pro or Enterprise), the center pane lists the virtual machines available on that host and shows a bit of information about the current state of each one. Below that, you'll see a list of checkpoints for the selected virtual machine. (A *checkpoint* captures the configuration and data of a virtual machine at a point in time. For more information, see "Working with checkpoints" later in this chapter.) At the bottom of the center pane, the Summary, Memory, and Networking tabs show additional details about the selected virtual machine. Here you can see at a glance what IP address has been assigned to the virtual machine, how much memory is in use, and so on. The thumbnail image on the Summary tab also provides a convenient launching method for the virtual machine; double-click it to connect to that virtual machine.

As in other console applications, the right pane shows available actions for the items selected in the left and center panes. Figure 22-2, for example, shows the actions that apply to the Hyper-V host running on the local computer named XPS87-15 and to the virtual machine named Windows 7 to 10 Upgrade.

Creating a network switch

By default, a new virtual machine is set up as a standalone computer with no network connection. It can't connect to the internet or to other computers on your network. That disconnected configuration might be useful for some testing scenarios, but for most situations you'll probably want to give your virtual machines access to a network connection.

To do that, you must first have a bit of networking infrastructure in place—namely, a *virtual switch*. A virtual switch connects the virtual network adapter in your virtual machine to the physical network adapter in your physical computer, thereby allowing the virtual machine to connect to the outside world.

> ## NOTE
>
> You can create and manage a virtual switch *after* you set up a virtual machine and then modify your virtual machine to use the virtual switch. Setting up the virtual switch before you set up your virtual machines simply saves a few steps. In addition, you can create multiple virtual switches using different network adapters or configurations and choose the type of virtual switch you need for each VM, at startup time or while the VM is running.

To create a virtual switch or make changes to an existing one, in the Actions pane (or on the Action menu) click or tap Virtual Switch Manager. Then select the type of switch you want to create:

- **External.** This is the most common type for a VM that you want to use as if it were another PC on your local network. This configuration binds the virtual switch to your computer's physical network adapter so that you can access your physical network. Assuming your physical network adapter is connected to the internet, your virtual machines using this type of switch also have internet access.

- **Internal.** An internal virtual switch can be used only to make a connection among the virtual machines running on your physical computer, and between the virtual machines and your physical computer.

- **Private.** Use a private virtual switch to set up a network that comprises only the virtual machines running on your physical computer and using the same virtual switch. This network is isolated from all physical computers, including the Hyper-V host on which it's installed.

When you click or tap Create Virtual Switch, you're asked for more details, as shown in Figure 22-3. Click OK to complete the switch creation.

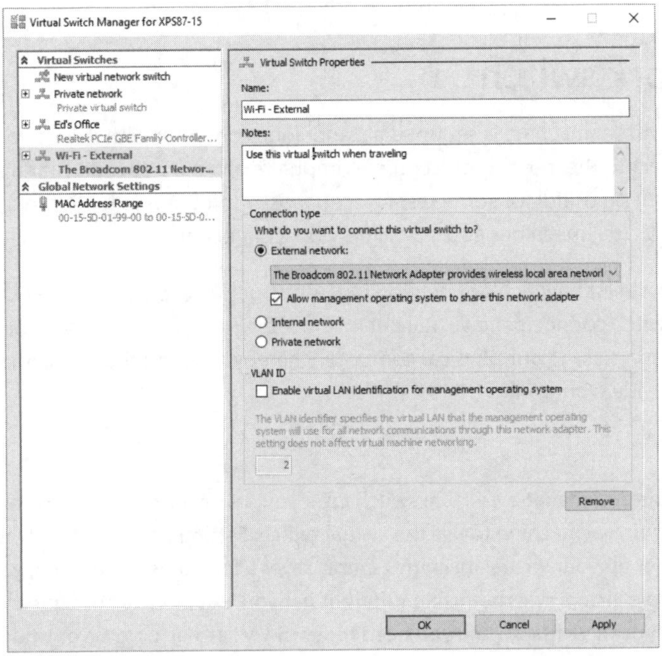

Figure 22-3 If your computer has more than one physical network adapter, specify the one you want to use under External Network.

Creating a virtual machine

To create a new virtual machine, open Hyper-V Manager and, in the Actions pane, click or tap New > Virtual Machine, which launches the New Virtual Machine Wizard. Navigating through the wizard leads you through the process of setting up a virtual machine, by using the Next and Previous buttons or the links along the left side. At any point in the wizard, you can click Finish to create a virtual machine that uses default values for any wizard pages you skip.

NOTE

The absolute fastest way to create a new virtual machine is to open the New Virtual Machine Wizard and immediately click Finish. As it turns out, however, that up-front efficiency is just an illusion, as you'll need to spend time and effort later manually changing the generic default name for the VM and the virtual hard disk, adjusting the size of available memory, and attaching installation media. In addition, the default settings create a generation 1 VM, which can't be changed to a generation 2 configuration. For those reasons, we recommend going through the wizard fully when creating any new VM.

Specify name and location

After you step through the Before You Begin page, the wizard asks you to provide a name for your virtual machine. Enter a name or description that'll help you differentiate this virtual machine from others you might create. (The wizard will use this entry again later, as the suggested name for the virtual hard disk you create.) If you don't like the proposed storage location for the virtual machine files, select the check box and specify another, as shown in Figure 22-4.

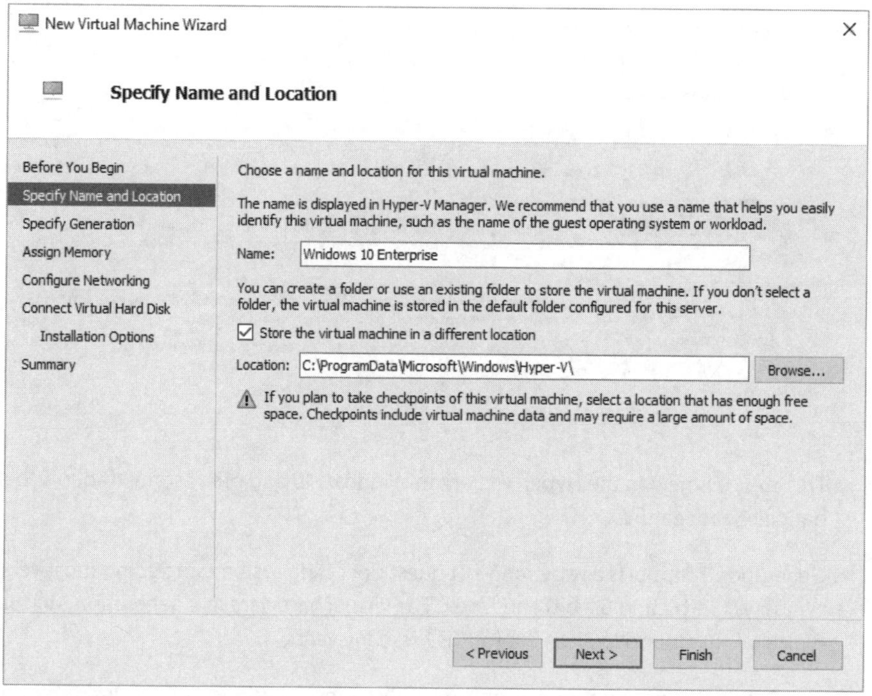

Figure 22-4 For our purposes, the operating-system name provides a good name for a virtual machine, but you might have different needs.

The default location is %ProgramData%\Microsoft\Windows\Hyper-V\. (%ProgramData% is an environment variable that is set to C:\ProgramData on a standard Windows installation.) If your computer has a small system drive—a common configuration in some desktop systems that use a solid state drive for system files and a large hard disk for data files—you might want to store the files elsewhere. Keep in mind that a virtual machine can occupy 10–40 GB or more, and each checkpoint can consume equivalent amounts of space.

It's possible to move the virtual machine files after you create the machine, but it's not easy. Although some parts of a virtual machine (the virtual hard disk and the paging file, for example) can be moved by changing the settings of the virtual machine, this option isn't available for some of the core files. To completely move a machine at a later time, you can import a virtual machine, copy it, and store it in a different location. You're much better off choosing a suitable location *before* you create the virtual machine.

Specify generation

On the Specify Generation page, shown here, select either Generation 1 or Generation 2 for the style of virtual machine you need:

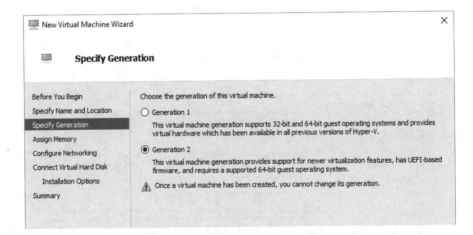

This choice is new to the Hyper-V client in Windows 10 and offers some tradeoffs between compatibility and features.

Generation 1 supports a wide range of guest operating systems, including most versions of Windows (32-bit and 64-bit) and Linux. The virtual hardware in a generation 1 virtual machine is typical of that found in BIOS-based PCs for many years.

Generation 2 currently supports only 64-bit Windows versions: among desktop operating systems, Windows 8, Windows 8.1, and Windows 10 are supported; support for Windows Server as a guest operating system is restricted to Windows Server 2012 and later versions. In addition, generation 2 removes support for attaching physical DVD drives and other older hardware to a virtual machine. But a generation 2 virtual machine has modern UEFI-based firmware, which enables Secure Boot and booting from a network adapter, SCSI hard drive, or virtual DVD. In addition, generation 2 virtual machines enable new Hyper-V features, such as the ability to adjust memory or add a network adapter while the virtual machine is running.

If you're going to install one of the newer supported operating systems in your virtual machine, select Generation 2 to enable additional features. For an older operating system, you must stick with the default option, Generation 1.

NOTE

If you select Generation 2, you must install the operating system from an ISO file; you can't use the physical DVD drive on the Hyper-V host.

Assign memory

On the Assign Memory page, shown in Figure 22-5, you specify the amount of RAM your virtual machine will have.

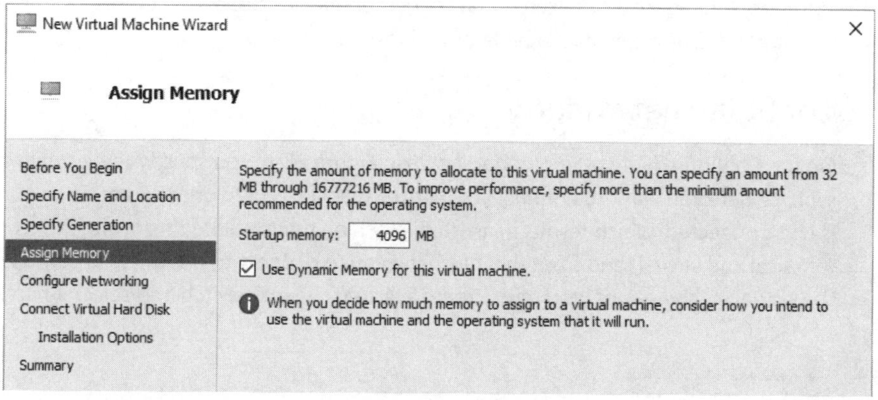

Figure 22-5 By selecting the Use Dynamic Memory For This Virtual Machine check box, you can use memory more efficiently, which improves performance when running multiple virtual machines.

If you enable Dynamic Memory, Hyper-V uses memory as a shared resource that can be reallocated as needed among running virtual machines. This way, each machine gets as much memory as it needs, but it doesn't reserve a fixed amount of memory (which would preclude other virtual machines or the host operating system from using that memory).

Therefore, if you plan to run more than one virtual machine at once, we recommend you select Use Dynamic Memory For This Virtual Machine to get the best performance. Then set Startup

Memory to at least the minimum amount required for the operating system you plan to install in this virtual machine.

> ### TROUBLESHOOTING
>
> **Installing a guest operating system fails with Dynamic Memory turned on**
>
> In some configurations, turning on Dynamic Memory might cause the installation of the guest operating system to fail. The problem occurs when the system assigns a minimal amount of dynamic memory to the VM at startup, and that amount causes the installer to believe the system doesn't meet minimum requirements. The solution is to turn off Dynamic Memory temporarily while installing the operating system. After installation is complete, return to the settings for that VM and turn Dynamic Memory on again.

If you plan to run only one virtual machine, or if you know how much memory your virtual machine will need to perform its given tasks, you can turn off Dynamic Memory and specify a fixed amount of memory. This setup works more like a physical computer, in that whatever memory you specify is the total amount of installed RAM in the virtual machine.

Note that the options for configuring memory in the New Virtual Machine Wizard are extremely limited. You can exercise far more granular control over memory by adjusting the settings for a VM, as we explain a bit later in this section.

Configure networking

On the Configure Networking page, shown in Figure 22-6, you specify the virtual network switch where you want to connect your virtual machine's network adapter. The default option is Not Connected, which results in a virtual machine that's isolated from all other computers (physical and virtual) and from the internet. Even to connect to the physical computer on which the virtual machine runs, you must create a virtual network switch and select it here.

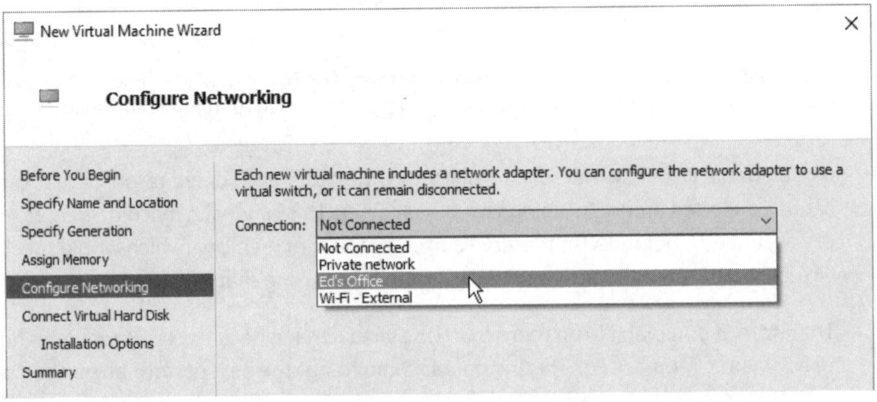

Figure 22-6 Select a virtual network switch to connect to the outside world.

The only available option is Not Connected

Before you can connect to a network, you must create a virtual network switch, as described earlier in "Creating a network switch." Each virtual network switch you create appears in the Connection list. You can't create a new virtual switch while the New Virtual Machine Wizard is running. In that case, you can continue creating the VM and then, after the configuration is complete, create a new virtual switch and attach it using the Settings page for the newly created VM.

To determine which type of network switch you're using (External, Internal, or Private), you need to return to the Virtual Switch Manager.

Connect virtual hard disk

On the Connect Virtual Hard Disk page, shown in Figure 22-7, you set up the virtual machine's first virtual hard disk. A virtual hard disk is actually a file in the VHD or VHDX format. By default, the New Virtual Machine Wizard creates a dynamically expanding virtual hard disk (VHDX). If you want a fixed-size virtual hard disk (VHD), you need to create it separately.

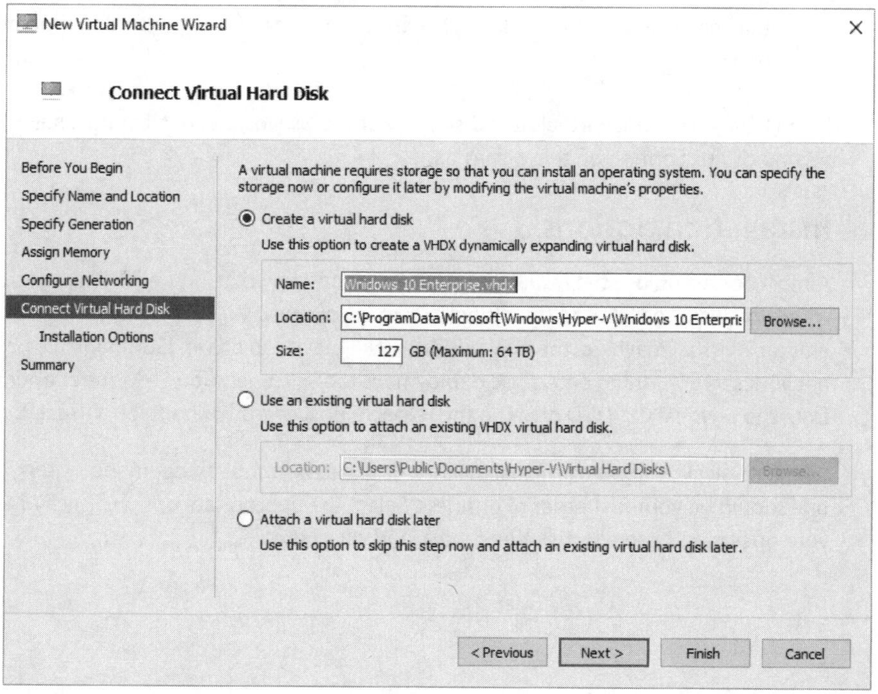

Figure 22-7 With the first option, you create a virtual hard disk. Choose one of the other options to use an existing virtual hard disk.

Just like a physical computer, a virtual machine can have multiple hard drives; the wizard allows you to create or attach the system drive only. By default, this drive is created in a subfolder of the virtual machine location you specified earlier. But you can override that default and store the virtual hard disk on any physical disk that's accessible to the host computer running Hyper-V.

In addition to specifying the name and location of your virtual hard disk file, you must specify the disk's capacity, in gigabytes. Be sure you create a virtual hard disk that's big enough to store the operating system, programs, and data you plan to use on the virtual machine. Although you don't want to go overboard, don't worry too much about specifying a size that's too big. Because of the way data is stored in a dynamically expanding virtual hard disk, the size of the VHDX file roughly corresponds with the amount of disk space in use rather than the size you specify, which is the maximum. However, its dynamically expanding nature also means that the VHDX file can grow to that maximum size; be sure that the physical hard drive where you store it has enough room to accommodate growth.

NOTE

You can change the location later, but it's a multistep process. And it's possible to resize a virtual hard disk after it has been created, but doing so brings some risk of data loss. (For more information, select the virtual hard disk in the Settings window for the virtual machine, and then click Edit.) Therefore, it's best to get this setting right from the beginning.

If you have an existing virtual hard disk you want to use instead of creating a new one, select the second or third option on this wizard page.

Installation options

Almost done! You use the Installation Options page, shown in Figure 22-8, to specify how and when you want to install an operating system in your new virtual machine. Because this is a generation 2 virtual machine, the only options available are to use an ISO image file or install from a network server running enterprise deployment tools. (Generation 1 VMs offer options to install from the physical CD/DVD drive on the Hyper-V host or from a bootable virtual floppy disk.)

Like a physical computer, a virtual machine is useless without an operating system, so installing one should be your first order of business. Select the appropriate option, specify the location of your operating system installation media, and click Next.

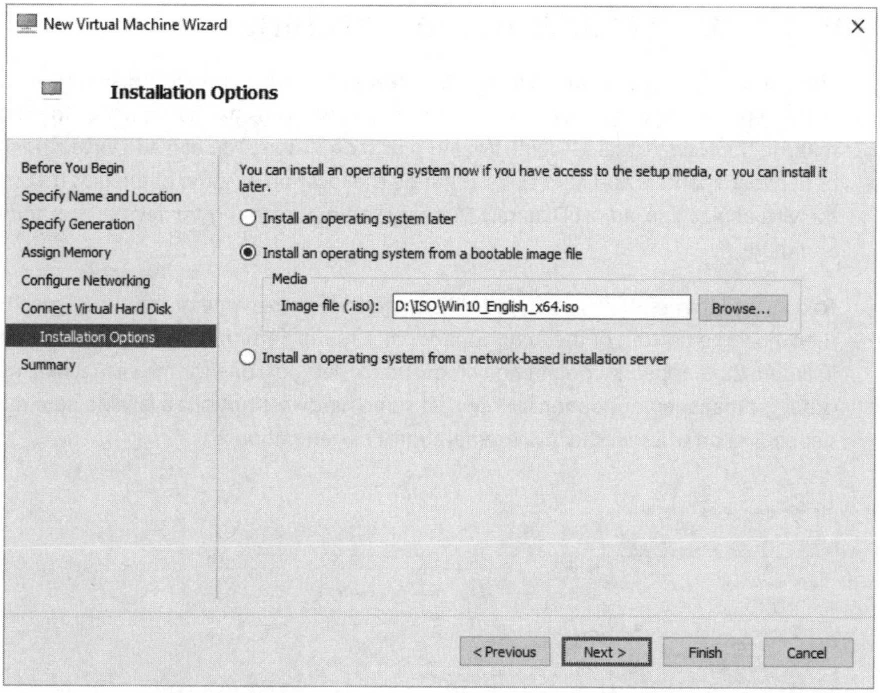

Figure 22-8 These options appear if you chose Generation 2 on the previous Specify Generation page. Options for installing from a physical CD/DVD drive or floppy disk are available only for generation 1 VMs.

This brings you to a Summary page, where you can review your settings before clicking Finish to complete the wizard.

At this point, even though you specified installation options, you still don't have a working virtual machine. Now back in Hyper-V Manager, you have two choices: You can select the newly created VM and then fine-tune its settings (as described in the next section). Or you can double-click the new virtual machine to open it in a Virtual Machine Connection window. Then click or tap the Start button on the toolbar or choose Start on the Action menu. This "powers on" your virtual machine and launches the operating-system setup from the location you specified in the wizard.

Changing settings for a virtual machine

The options you specify when you use the New Virtual Machine Wizard are but a small subset of the settings you can apply to a virtual machine. You can change almost all the settings you make in the New Virtual Machine Wizard plus scores more. You can add virtual devices such as network adapters and hard drives, change the location of some of the files that make up the virtual machine, adjust Dynamic Memory settings, reconfigure devices at a granular level, and more.

To dive into these settings, in Hyper-V Manager select the name of the virtual machine and then, near the bottom of the Actions pane, click or tap Settings. A dialog box like the one shown in Figure 22-9 appears, containing two groups of settings, one for the virtual hardware and the other for management options. Note that some hardware options available here differ slightly, depending on whether the VM is generation 1 or generation 2.

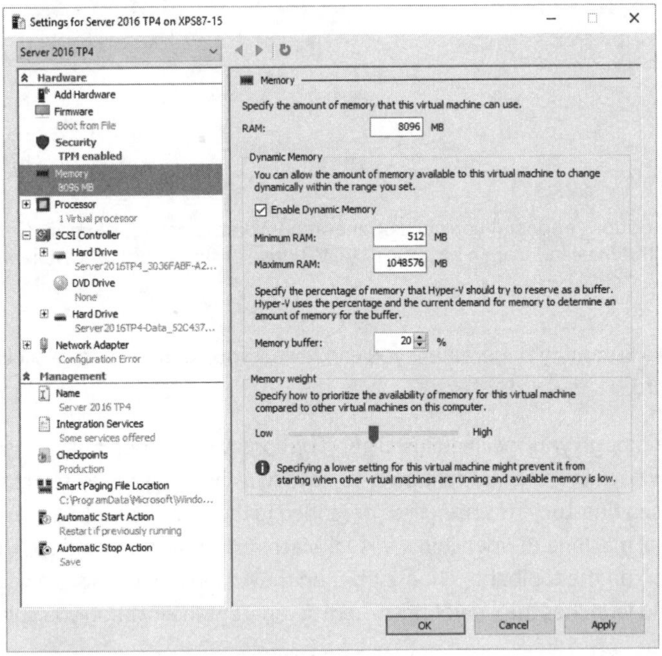

Figure 22-9 Use this Settings dialog to adjust a wide array of options, such as these detailed on the Memory page, that are not available when using the New Virtual Machine Wizard.

Some settings can be changed even while a machine is running (which is important for virtual machines running critical tasks), especially on generation 2 virtual machines. Other configuration changes, however, require that the VM be turned off (not just saved).

Inside OUT

Mount or unmount a virtual DVD quickly

Any disk image in ISO format can appear as a virtual DVD drive, and there's no need to go through the Settings dialog box to mount or unmount a virtual drive. Instead, to attach an ISO file as a drive, click Media from the VMConnect console, and then click DVD Drive > Insert Disk. Choose an ISO file, and click OK. To unmount a virtual drive, use the Eject <*ISO filename*> option from the DVD Drive menu.

The following sections highlight some of the many options you can set using this dialog box.

Changing boot order

If you want a VM to start from something other than the default system drive, such as a virtual DVD or a secondary virtual hard disk, use the BIOS tab (for a generation 1 VM) or the Firmware tab (in generation 2 VMs).

Advanced security options

On generation 2 VMs only, the Security tab offers the same security features you get with Windows 10 running on a UEFI-based physical PC. Figure 22-10 shows these options for a virtual machine running a preview release of Windows Server. Note that Secure Boot is enabled using the Microsoft Windows template. For a virtual machine running a distribution of Linux that supports Secure Boot, choose the Microsoft UEFI Certificate Authority template instead.

This tab also contains an option to enable a virtual Trusted Platform Module (TPM), which allows the disks in a virtual machine to be encrypted with BitLocker Disk Encryption. Enabling this feature requires some special preparation, as described in the TechNet article "Virtual machine security settings in Hyper-V Manager," at *https://technet.microsoft.com/library/ mt403347.aspx*. That same article also describes setup steps for high-security "shielded" virtual machines.

CHAPTER 22

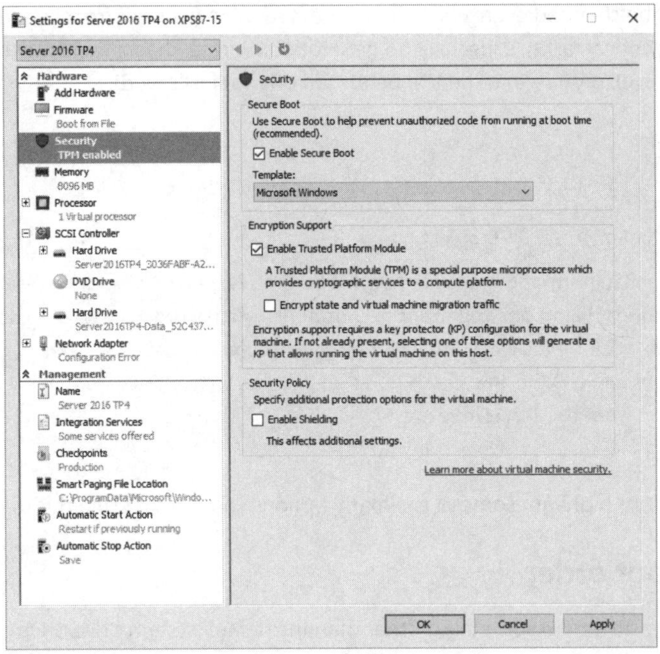

Figure 22-10 On a generation 2 virtual machine, you can turn on Secure Boot and, optionally, create a virtual Trusted Platform Module to use BitLocker Disk Encryption on virtual disks.

Fine-tuning virtual memory usage

Options on the Memory tab are identical for both generations of virtual machines. When Dynamic Memory is enabled, you can specify minimum and maximum amounts of memory to be available to that VM. If you're obsessed with memory tuning, you can also change buffer sizes for Dynamic Memory and adjust the priority for memory usage when multiple virtual machines compete for a limited supply of physical RAM.

Adding, removing, and adjusting virtual hard disks

To work with existing virtual hard disks and create new ones, click SCSI Controller in the console tree on a generation 2 machine, or select an IDE Controller on a generation 1 machine. Choose an unused location on the controller and click New to open the New Virtual Hard Disk Wizard. The default option, Dynamically Expanding, is the same type of VHDX file you create with the New Virtual Machine Wizard. Fixed Size disks, as the name implies, reserve the full allotted disk space, marginally improving performance and avoiding the risk of running out of actual disk space on the Hyper-V host.

The Differencing option is an advanced type of disk configuration intended for scenarios where you want to use a base disk that remains intact, with changes to the operating system or data saved to a separate file, making it easy to reverse those changes.

To expand a virtual disk or convert it to a different format, you need to first remove any checkpoints from the virtual machine. After doing so, shut down the VM, select the hard disk from the Settings dialog box, and click Edit. That opens yet another wizard, with Compact, Convert, and Expand options that are relatively easy to follow.

It's also possible to connect a volume on a physical disk to a virtual machine. The drive must be offline on the Hyper-V host to be available here.

CHAPTER 22

Automatic start and stop actions

You use the final two options under the Management heading to specify what happens to a virtual machine when you shut down or start the Windows 10 Hyper-V host. For most purposes, the correct setting for Automatic Stop Action is Save; for Automatic Start Action, you can configure a VM to start automatically (with or without a delay) or start the VM only if it was running when the system shut down previously.

Running a virtual machine

As the final step in creating a virtual machine, as described earlier in this chapter, you double-click the name of a virtual machine in Hyper-V Manager to open the machine in a Virtual Machine Connection window. You then click the Start button on the toolbar to power on the machine. You can run the virtual machine session in a Virtual Machine Connection (VMConnect) window using one of two session types:

- Basic sessions run in the VMConnect console window, which can be expanded to any resolution supported by the virtual display adapter. This type of session accepts keyboard and mouse input and displays the contents of the VM display; there's also no access to audio hardware or external USB devices.

- Enhanced sessions, which debuted with Hyper-V in Windows 8.1, provide a significantly richer experience, with the ability to share the Clipboard with the host machine, redirect audio from the VM to the host PC's speakers or headphones, share local drives and some USB devices in the VM, connect to a printer through the host PC, and sign in with a smart card. Enhanced sessions can also use multitouch displays and multiple-monitor configurations.

Enhanced session mode uses Remote Desktop Protocol over the virtual machine bus (VMBus); as a result, it requires a supported guest operating system: Windows 8.1 or Windows 10 (Pro, Enterprise, or Education); or Windows Server 2012 R2 or later. Remote Desktop connections do not have to be enabled in the guest operating system. For operating systems that don't support enhanced sessions, such as Windows 7 Pro, the only option is to configure a network connection in the VM and use the Remote Desktop client to connect to it.

Using basic session mode

As shown in Figure 22-11, a virtual machine running in a Virtual Machine Connection window looks (and, for the most part, acts) just like a separate physical computer, except that it's contained in a window on your desktop.

Virtual Machine Connection menu and toolbar   Windows 7 running in a basic session window

Virtual Machine Connection status bar

Figure 22-11 To run a legacy program that doesn't run properly on newer operating systems, you can run Windows 7 in a Virtual Machine Connection window.

CHAPTER 22

Use the toolbar at the top of the window (or the corresponding commands on the Action menu) to operate the virtual machine.

Tiny VM2 (Windows Insider) on XPS87-15 - Virtual Machine Connection

File   Action   Media   Clipboard   View   Help

From left to right, the buttons have the following functions:

- **Ctrl+Alt+Del.** Because the Ctrl+Alt+Del key combination is reserved by Windows 10 on your physical computer, when you press it while you're using a virtual machine, the key combination goes to your host computer. To mimic the effect of Ctrl+Alt+Del within a virtual machine, press Ctrl+Alt+End, or click or tap this toolbar button.

- **Start.** This button turns on a virtual machine that is off.

- **Turn Off.** This button turns the virtual machine off, but it does so by effectively unplugging the machine. This, of course, is a quick but not graceful way to shut down a computer, and you'll lose any unsaved data.

- **Shut Down.** Clicking this button is equivalent to using the Shut Down command on the Start menu, and the machine goes through the usual shutdown process. Note that some (usually older) operating systems do not support Shut Down, even with Integration Services enabled. For a virtual machine without this support, use commands within the virtual machine to shut down properly.

- **Save.** This button saves the virtual machine state and then turns it off, much like hibernation on a physical computer. When you next start the virtual machine, you return immediately to where you left off.

- **Pause/Resume.** Pausing a virtual machine stops it temporarily but does not fully release its resources, as the Turn Off, Shut Down, and Save options do.

- **Reset.** Resetting a virtual machine discards any changes and reboots using the last saved version.

- **Checkpoint.** This button creates a checkpoint, which is a snapshot of the virtual machine's state and its data. For more information, see "Working with checkpoints" later in this chapter.

- **Revert.** This button restores the virtual machine to its condition at the previous checkpoint and restarts the virtual machine.

- **Enhanced Session.** On guest operating systems that support it, this button toggles the virtual machine between basic session mode and enhanced session mode. For more information, see the next section, "Using enhanced session mode."

Within the Virtual Machine Connection window, you use the virtual machine just as you would a physical computer, with only a few exceptions:

- When you run a guest operating system that does not include integration services, using a mouse is not as fluid as it is when your guest operating system is Windows 7 or later. That's because once you click inside the virtual machine window, the mouse becomes trapped in that window. To release it, press Ctrl+Alt+Left Arrow.

- Not all of your physical computer's hardware is available in all virtual machines.

  For example, access to the physical DVD drive on the Hyper-V host is not available in generation 2 virtual machines. (You can, however, mount an ISO image as a DVD drive.) For generation 1 machines, only one virtual machine can use a physical DVD drive at any given time. (To release the DVD drive from one virtual machine so that you can use it in another, use commands on the Media menu.)

  USB devices, audio devices, and some other local resources work only in enhanced session mode. (For more information, see "Using enhanced session mode.")

When you close the Virtual Machine Connection window, note that your virtual machine continues to run. By closing the window, all you're doing, in effect, is turning off the monitor. To shut down or turn off the virtual machine, you should use the appropriate buttons on the Virtual Machine Connection window. If that window is closed, reopen it by using Hyper-V Manager.

Using enhanced session mode

As we noted earlier, Hyper-V support in earlier versions of Windows included severe limitations on access to physical hardware from a VM. You could overcome some of these limitations (specifically, audio playback and file copying) by using Remote Desktop Connection to connect to a virtual machine, but that option requires a working network connection to the virtual machine.

The solution in Windows 10 is *enhanced session mode*, which solves many of these shortcomings. With enhanced session mode, you can redirect the following resources from your physical computer to a virtual machine in a Virtual Machine Connection window:

- Audio devices

- Printers

- Plug and Play devices

- Clipboard (which you use to copy and paste files and other information between the virtual machine and your physical computer)

CHAPTER 22

Inside OUT

Determine at a glance whether you're in enhanced session mode

Need a quick way to tell whether your machine is running in enhanced session mode? Look at the speaker icon in the notification area of your virtual machine's taskbar. If it has a red X, that's because no audio device is available, which means you're in basic session mode.

Inside OUT

Get ready-to-run virtual machines

As part of its support for developers, Microsoft offers fully configured virtual machines you can download and run. Each one has a different guest operating system with certain software installed. These virtual machines are for testing and evaluation and expire after a limited time, but instructions provided with the virtual machine files explain how to use the files after expiration. You can find these virtual machine files at *https://bit.ly/virtualmachines*.

Alas, enhanced session mode comes with its own limitations. As noted earlier, it works only with Windows 8.1 (or Windows Server 2012 R2) and later versions. And in enhanced session mode you can't readily change the resolution of the virtual machine's monitor. (For a workaround, see the tip on the next page.)

If your virtual machine is running an operating system that supports enhanced session mode, you can switch between basic and enhanced session mode by clicking or tapping the rightmost button on the Virtual Machine Connection toolbar.

You can enable and disable enhanced session mode on a per-server or per-user basis. To view or change either setting, in Hyper-V Manager select the host name from the tree on the left and then, under the host name in the Actions pane, click or tap Hyper-V Settings. In the Hyper-V Settings dialog box that appears, you'll find enhanced-session-mode settings under Server and User.

Inside OUT

Change screen resolution for an enhanced mode session

Within an enhanced session mode window, using the normal Windows settings for chang-ing screen resolution leads to this message: "The display settings can't be changed from a remote session." (Enhanced session mode, in effect, uses Remote Desktop Connection to connect to the virtual machine; hence, the message about a "remote session.")

If you need to change the screen resolution, switch to basic session mode and then close the Virtual Machine Connection window. In Hyper-V Manager, click Connect to open a new Virtual Machine Connection window, and you'll be greeted by a dialog box in which you can specify the screen resolution:

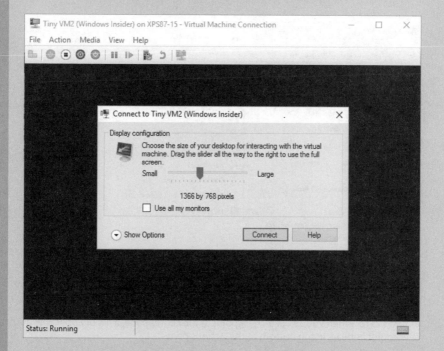

In this same dialog box, clicking Show Options adds a Local Resources tab to the dialog box. On that tab, you specify which local resources—that is, printers, drives, and other devices from the host computer—you want to use within the virtual machine. For more information about these settings, see "Using Remote Desktop Connection" in Chapter 20, "Advanced networking."

CHAPTER 22

Working with checkpoints

A *checkpoint* captures the data and configuration of a running virtual machine—a snapshot in time. Indeed, in earlier versions of Hyper-V, checkpoints were called *snapshots*. A checkpoint can be restored so that you can quickly and easily return your virtual machine to an earlier time—this capability is particularly valuable for providing a consistent test environment for evaluating software. After the testing is complete, revert to the previous checkpoint to start another round of testing under conditions that are exactly the same as they were before the previous test.

To capture a checkpoint, click or tap the Checkpoint button on the Virtual Machine Connection toolbar, or use the keyboard shortcut Ctrl+N. You can provide a descriptive name for the checkpoint, but no other interaction is required. The checkpoints you collect for a given virtual machine appear in the center of the Hyper-V window, as shown in Figure 22-12. To revert to an earlier checkpoint, select the checkpoint and, in the Actions pane, click or tap Apply.

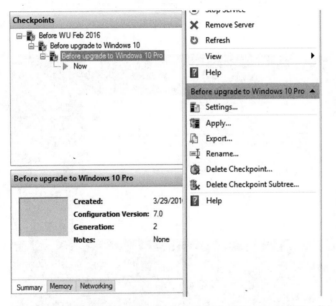

Figure 22-12 When you select a checkpoint in the center pane, a list of applicable actions for that checkpoint appears in the bottom of the Actions pane.

Microsoft engineers discovered that droves of Hyper-V users use checkpoints as a form of backup. (Although it doesn't provide the full capabilities of a more traditional backup program—such as the ability to restore individual folders and files—it's convenient and easy.) However, the checkpoint feature as implemented in earlier Hyper-V versions is far from ideal for backup. Because those checkpoints (now called *standard checkpoints*) include information on the virtual machine state, running applications, and network connections, restoring one often takes you to an unstable condition (for example, the same network connections might not be available).

In response, Client Hyper-V in Windows 10 adds a new type of checkpoint called a *production checkpoint*. A production checkpoint uses the Volume Snapshot Service (VSS) backup technology to save the data and configuration of a running virtual machine but not its state. This provides a much better backup solution, and it's now the default checkpoint in Hyper-V. You can still use standard checkpoints if you prefer; to make the switch, open Settings for a virtual machine and, under Management, click Checkpoints:

Alternatives to Hyper-V

Client Hyper-V is the easiest way to work with virtual machines in Windows 10, but it's not the only way. Two relatively new options provide alternatives that might make sense if you're a candidate for virtualization.

Effective with version 1607, Windows 10 supports the use of Hyper-V Containers, which are self-contained virtual environments that can manage workloads without requiring the overhead (and licensing cost) of a full operating system.

Container support is new and still developing. For an overview, see the information at *https://bit.ly/Windows10-containers*.

Microsoft Azure is a cloud-based service that is capable of running virtual machines that don't require any local resources. Azure VMs are charged on a pay-as-you-go basis, making them ideal for test environments and important servers where downtime is not an acceptable option. If you have an MSDN subscription, your account includes a monthly allowance for Azure usage, with ready-made Windows 10 virtual machines available. For more details, see *https://azure.microsoft.com/en-us/services/virtual-machines/*.

What's next for Windows 10?

Don't get too comfortable with your current Microsoft Windows 10 installation. Microsoft says it plans to release two "feature updates" to Windows 10 in 2017. These are full upgrades, delivered at no charge through Windows Update to properly licensed devices running Windows 10.

This accelerated release schedule is a key part of the "Windows as a Service" model for Windows 10, where upgrades arrive far more frequently than before.

Each new release has its own code name, which you can use to track an upcoming Windows 10 version as it works its way through the development process. The initial release of Windows 10, in July 2015, was code-named Threshold, and the second release, version 1511, was identified as Threshold 2. The Anniversary Update, version 1607, was code-named Redstone. The next release is, not surprisingly, code-named Redstone 2.

Those code names are mostly useful to those who have enrolled in the Windows Insider Program and are actively testing upcoming versions. The first public preview release from the Redstone 2 branch arrived within weeks after version 1607 began rolling out on August 2, 2016. If you see "rs2" in the file name for a download of a preview build, that's what it means.

This open development process makes it significantly easier than in previous years to track the development process and see what's coming next. You can learn by reading or by doing—specifically, by joining the Windows Insider Program.

The Windows roadmap

If your organization uses Windows, you should make a special effort to check the official Windows 10 Roadmap for Business every so often. You'll find it at *https://bit.ly/windows-roadmap*.

This page offers a regularly updated snapshot of new Windows features—those recently made available in a Windows feature update as well as those that are in a public preview or are in development. The information under the In Development heading can be skimpy—for example, when we checked a few weeks after the release of the Anniversary Update, version 1607, we found only three items there. One was simply listed as "Enhancements to Azure AD

Join" accompanied by the promise that the changes will "improve its functionality in enterprise environments," with no further details. But that's at least a starting point for further information-gathering.

Figure 23-1 shows items from the roadmap that were listed as In Development shortly after the Anniversary Update's release.

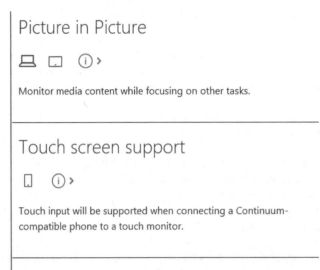

Figure 23-1 Yes, Windows 10 is a multiplatform operating system. The icons for each entry on the Windows Roadmap for Business indicate which platforms the feature applies to.

The icons associated with each item tell you which Windows 10 device types it's associated with: laptop/PC, tablet, mobile/handheld, Surface Hub, Hololens, IoT Core, or industry devices (a catchall category that includes the old Windows Embedded line).

As we noted in Chapter 9, "Cortana and the web," Microsoft Edge has its own roadmap as well, at *https://bit.ly/ms-edge-platform-status*.

In addition to reading those engineering documents, you can check in regularly at Microsoft's network of official blogs covering the Windows ecosystem. The following represent valuable information sources we recommend adding to your reading list:

- Microsoft runs its own mini-network of Windows blogs that includes the Windows Experience blog, Windows For Your Business, the Microsoft Edge Dev Blog, and the Microsoft Devices Blog. Separate blogs are available in German, Chinese, Spanish (Latin America), Italian, Russian, Polish, and Japanese. A comprehensive directory is located at *https://blogs.windows.com/windows-blog-directory/*.

- You'll find announcements for OneDrive at the OneDrive Blog, *https://blogs.office.com/onedrive/*.

- Skype has its own network of blogs as well, with product announcements, updates, tips and tricks, and more. Start at *https://blogs.skype.com/*.

- Developers can go to *https://blogs.msdn.microsoft.com/* for content on Azure, Visual Studio, PowerShell, the Universal Windows Platform, and of course Windows 10. The MSDN network includes official blogs from product teams as well as personal, sometimes highly technical blogs by individual Microsoft employees.

And, of course, there are dozens of unofficial online news sources of varying credibility that will happily keep you up to date on Windows 10 rumors and news. (Sometimes what appears to be news is really just a rumor.)

Do you need a bit of help keeping track of news topics? Feel free to enlist Cortana's assistance. Open Cortana's Notebook, click News, scroll to the bottom of the list, and add Windows 10 as a topic to track.

How the Windows Insider Program works

Reading about what's coming in the next Windows feature update is one thing. Seeing it first-hand is even better. That's where the Windows Insider Program comes in.

You don't need to pay a fee or pass a test to join the Windows Insider Program. All you have to do is go to *https://insider.windows.com*, read the terms and conditions, and sign up using a Microsoft account. After completing that prerequisite, you can configure any device running Windows 10 to install Insider Preview builds of the next major release before the final version reaches the public in the Current Branch.

Inside OUT

Stop unauthorized users from switching to Insider builds

If you manage PCs in an office or home, you probably don't want them installing Insider Preview builds without your permission. On any PC running Windows 10 Pro, Enterprise, or Education, you can apply a Group Policy setting to block changes to Insider settings on that PC. Go to Computer Configuration > Administrative Templates > Windows Components > Data Collection And Preview Builds, and then set the policy Toggle User Control Over Insider Builds to Disabled. On devices running Windows 10 Home, your best option is to configure standard user accounts, which don't have access to the Windows Insider Program settings.

Unless you're an experienced software tester, you should approach these preview builds with caution. By definition, they are unfinished, with known and unknown issues that can potentially expose you to system crashes and data loss. The best test platforms are secondary PCs or virtual machines that are properly backed up.

Another significant issue associated with setting up access to Insider Preview builds is the need to install feature updates frequently. A device that was configured for Insider Preview builds throughout the development process for the Anniversary Update, for example, would have received 28 separate builds, each equivalent to a full upgrade.

Finally, if you decide you want to stop receiving Insider Preview builds and go back to the Current Branch before the Release Preview stage, you'll almost certainly have to back up apps and data and then reinstall Windows. Once an Insider build is declared a Release Preview, you can safely switch to the Current Branch.

If you're cognizant of the risks and willing to accept the trade-offs, follow the instructions in this section to set up a Windows 10 PC to receive Insider builds.

Beginning with Windows 10 version 1607, the Windows Insider settings get their own highly visible access point. Go to Settings > Update & Security > Windows Insider Program. By default, the Microsoft account you use to sign in to Windows 10 is listed here. To switch to another account, click the account name to reveal the buttons shown in Figure 23-2. After confirming that you're using the Microsoft account you registered with the Windows Insider Program, click Get Started.

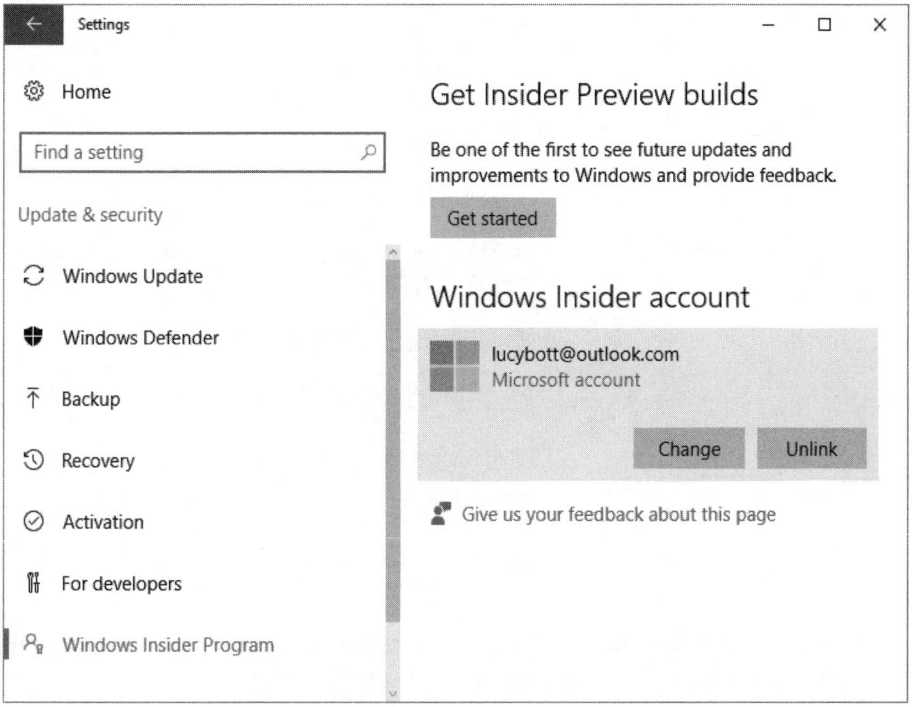

Figure 23-2 If you're willing to accept the risks of installing preview builds in exchange for the opportunity to influence the direction of Windows, click Get Started.

Before you can complete the configuration process, you must click through two bold and very stern warnings, which list the risks we discussed earlier. After a restart, you're ready to begin receiving new builds. Go back to Settings, where you should see some new options in the Windows Insider Program section. Select one of the three Insider Level choices, as shown next.

What's the difference between the three levels? Each represents a release ring that is in between Microsoft's internal testing groups and the Current Branch:

- **Fast.** Preview builds go to this group of Insiders first. The benefit of being first to see a new feature is balanced by the risk of being the first to experience a new bug. You can report those bugs using the Feedback Hub.

- **Slow.** Devices configured for this level receive preview builds after they've had a chance to be thoroughly tested by the Fast ring. These builds are likely to be more stable, because they incorporate fixes based on feedback from testers in the Fast ring.

- **Release Preview.** This is the most conservative ring of all, typically releasing new builds only near the end of the development cycle. Insiders who choose this level can also receive updated Microsoft apps and driver updates.

Insider Preview builds arrive via Windows Update, as normal. After installing an Insider Preview build, you can see a few changes. For starters, a watermark with the words "Evaluation copy" and the Insider Preview build number appears in the lower right corner of the screen, above the clock in the notification area. In addition, some privacy settings can't be adjusted. The Diagnostic And Usage Data settings, for example, are set to the default levels, where they provide the maximum feedback to Microsoft. As you can see in Figure 23-3, the corresponding Settings pages disclose that the Windows Insider Program has taken control of those options.

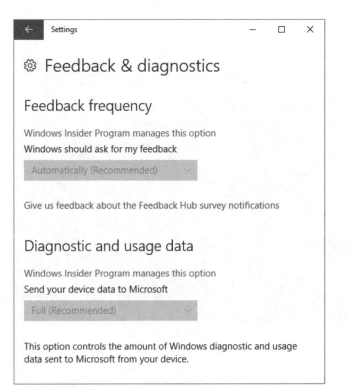

Figure 23-3 When a device is configured to receive Insider Preview builds, you cannot change the settings shown here.

Those options return to normal when you change the configuration of a device so that it no longer receives Insider Preview builds and is back on the Current Branch.

When running an Insider Preview build, you can temporarily suspend delivery of new builds for up to seven days. You might choose to make that change if you're in the midst of a big project and don't want your work to be interrupted by a large download that could take an hour or more to install. You might also choose to stop updates temporarily if you're traveling.

CHAPTER 23

To see your options, go back to Settings >Update & Security > Windows Insider Program and click the Stop Insider Preview Builds button at the top of the page. That opens a dialog box like the one shown next, where you can choose to take a break for 1, 3, 5, or 7 days:

The option at the bottom of that dialog box doesn't actually stop you from receiving preview builds. Instead, it takes you to a pinned post from Microsoft that explains how to opt out of Insider builds and why you might have to reinstall Windows from a saved system image or recovery media.

Windows 10 editions at a glance

Microsoft's lineup of Windows 10 editions is refreshingly simple.

Consumers and businesses that acquire Windows on a new device or as a retail upgrade have their choice of two and only two editions: Windows 10 Home and Windows 10 Pro.

On corporate networks, you have the option to enable additional features by upgrading to the Enterprise edition as part of a volume license agreement. At universities and other institutions of learning, administrators can enable advanced features by upgrading to specialized Education editions, which are, except for a few small details, essentially equivalent to the Pro and Enterprise editions.

That makes a grand total of five editions, of which you're still likely to encounter only two.

NOTE

In some markets, you might find Single Language, KN, and N variations of the two retail and original equipment manufacturer (OEM) editions. Using a Single Language version means you can't install an additional language pack or change the base language unless you update to the full, language-neutral version. KN and N versions are available in South Korea and the European Union, respectively, as a requirement of legal proceedings. Those versions have had several media playback features removed. For most Windows installations in developed countries and regions, the standard Home and Pro editions are the correct choices.

Yes, the Windows 10 family also includes Windows 10 Mobile, which runs on a select group of smartphones and, at least in theory, on other small devices that have not yet appeared in the market. Windows 10 Mobile Enterprise is the same package, with the inclusion of enterprise-management capabilities. Sometime in the future, you might encounter the Windows 10 IoT (Internet of Things) edition, which is for use in specialized hardware (such as automated teller machines) and wearables. But our focus in this appendix is on the editions of Windows 10 designed for use on traditional PCs and PC-like devices such as tablets.

That simple lineup is a stark and welcome improvement over the sometimes confusing assortment of previous Windows editions, and it makes our job in this appendix simple. We start with a recitation of the features you can find in all Windows 10 desktop editions and then, in separate sections, list the additional features available in individual editions.

You can use this information to decide whether to upgrade from Home to Pro when you're shopping for a new PC, for example. You can also use the data in these tables to help decide which PCs on a corporate network should be upgraded to the Enterprise edition using your organization's Volume License agreement.

We start with a brief discussion of hardware configurations. Table A-1 lists technical limits related to CPU and memory support that might affect your purchase or upgrade decision.

Table A-1 Supported hardware configurations in Windows 10

Hardware component	Supported configurations
Number of CPUs/cores	Windows 10 Home: One physical processor. Windows 10 Pro, Enterprise, or Education: One or two physical processors. Both editions support multicore processors, up to a maximum of 32 (x86) or 64 (x64) cores per physical processor.
Addressable memory (RAM)	32-bit (x86) editions: 4 GB maximum (because of 32-bit memory architecture, usable memory is typically 3.5 GB or less). 64-bit (x64) editions: 128 GB for Windows 10 Home, 2 TB for Windows 10 Pro, Enterprise, or Education.

Features available in all Windows 10 editions

With some minor exceptions, which are noted here, the features listed in Table A-2 are available in all retail editions of Windows 10 sold worldwide, including Windows 10 Home edition.

Table A-2 Features available in all Windows 10 editions

Feature	Description
Core Windows features	
Customizable Start menu and taskbar	Similar in concept to the Windows 7 Start menu, with the additional ability to pin apps as Windows 8–style live tiles.
Windows Update	Provides regular security updates, device drivers, and new features. Business editions have limited options to delay reliability updates and defer feature updates.
Fast User Switching	Allows a user to sign in to another user account without requiring the current user to sign out.
Hiberboot and InstantGo	These features, which are supported on most modern devices, allow faster startup as well as low-power, always-on updates even when a device is sleeping.
Settings app	Offers access to many system settings previously available only in Control Panel; uses an interface that scales to devices of different sizes and is especially usable on touch devices.

Feature	Description
Virtual desktops	Allows collections of running apps to be arranged on separate virtual desktops, with keyboard shortcuts or gestures for switching between desktops.
Window snap	An upgrade to the classic Aero Snap behavior, with Snap Assist improving the usability of displaying two windows side by side. Allows snapping of up to four windows to any corner or side of a display; also supports multiple displays.
Task View	Enables users to quickly switch between running programs and virtual desktops with a taskbar button, keyboard shortcuts, or touch gestures.
Power management	In addition to providing support for classic Windows power schemes, includes new Battery Saver options for more aggressive control over battery life.
Ease Of Access features	Includes high-contrast themes, Ease Of Access Center, Magnifier, Narrator, and On-Screen Keyboard.
Windows Mobility Center	The central location for managing power, display, network, and other settings on a notebook PC.
Windows PowerShell and Integrated Scripting Environment	The command-line shell and graphical host application for scripting administrative tasks.
Virtual hard drive (VHD) support	Creates a new VHD; attaches (mounts) an existing VHD.
Windows Subsystem for Linux	Adds a software subsystem, based on Ubuntu Linux 14.04, that runs Linux command-line tools, including the Bash console, without the need to use a virtual machine or third-party tools.
Display	
Touchscreen/pen support	With appropriate hardware and drivers, adds support for touch, multitouch, and pen input.
Tablet Mode	Changes the layout of the Start menu, taskbar, and running programs for easier use on touch devices that do not have a physical keyboard attached. Hybrid devices can be configured to switch modes automatically when the keyboard is attached or removed.
Continuum	Connects a Windows 10 Mobile device to a monitor, mouse, and keyboard so that it works like a laptop.
Miracast and Project To This PC	Allows streaming of audio and video from a Windows 10 device to a Miracast receiver, such as the Microsoft Wireless Display Adapter, or to a Windows 10 device that has had the feature turned on and configured.
Multimonitor support	With properly configured hardware, extends the main display to include a second (or third, fourth, and so on) monitor.

APPENDIX A

Feature	Description
Windows Ink Platform	Supports pen input with compatible apps and hardware; adds Windows Ink Workspace to the notification area for quick access to ink-compatible apps.
Cortana and Search	
Windows Search	Provides the capability to perform an indexed search of local files, programs, and settings, with the ability to expand search to include cloud-based items and the web.
Cortana	Adds a "personality" and a natural language interface to Windows Search, and allows access to an ever-expanding collection of web services.
Speech-based interaction	Allows hands-free activation with the "Hey Cortana" trigger phrase, as well as intelligent and trainable speech recognition.
Interest-based suggestions	A proactive display of news, sports scores, weather forecasts, traffic reports, and more, based on defined interests and linked calendars or other activities. Requires that Cortana be on.
Intelligent actions	Creates reminders, appointments, tasks, and spoken notes from speech, typed input, or messages. Requires that Cortana be on.
Security and reliability	
Trusted Platform Module (TPM) support	Supports the latest TPM specification for the secure storage of system secrets, such as encryption keys and configuration information.
Secure Boot and Early Launch Antimalware	On UEFI devices, ensures the integrity of boot files and prevents malicious software from acting before Windows has fully loaded.
Device encryption	Allows full disk encryption of the system volume on any Windows 10 edition, when signing in with a Microsoft account on devices that support InstantGo. BitLocker Drive Encryption and related administration tools are available only with Pro, Enterprise, and Education editions.
BitLocker To Go	All editions support unlocking of BitLocker-encrypted removable drives, including USB flash drives. Managing encryption on removable drives requires the Pro, Enterprise, or Education edition.
Windows Hello	Biometric sign-in and authentication options enabled through support for compatible fingerprint readers, facial-recognition devices, and iris scanners. A related feature, Windows Hello for Business (formerly known as Microsoft Passport) supports authentication to online resources using biometric credentials without transmitting passwords.
User Account Control	Allows the use of standard accounts for day-to-day activity; includes Enhanced Protected Mode in Internet Explorer 11.
Security and maintenance notifications	Delivers messages and updates about security and maintenance issues.

Feature	Description
Windows Defender	Provides real-time antivirus and antispyware protection, with free updates.
Windows Firewall	Blocks unsolicited inbound network connections; includes an advanced security interface to manage inbound and outbound connections.
System recovery drive/ Windows Recovery Environment	Provides the ability to access a troubleshooting and repair environment at startup without requiring the original installation media.
Reset	Allows the user to recover from system corruption or compromise by reinstalling Windows, with options to keep or remove personal files and account information.
File History	Provides the ability to recover changed or deleted files from automatic or manual backups.
System image backup	A legacy feature, compatible with Windows 7, which includes the capability to create a system image and restore Windows from a previously saved image.
Family safety	For accounts you designate as family members, provides the ability to set time limits on computer usage and block access to specific games, programs, and websites. Requires a Microsoft account for all users.
Windows Remote Assistance and Quick Assist	Allows direct network connections between two Windows PCs for troubleshooting and repair. Remote Assistance is a legacy feature; Quick Assist works only with and between Windows 10 devices running version 1607 or later.
Sideloading of line-of-business apps	In managed environments, supports the deployment of custom Windows apps directly, without requiring access to the Windows Store.
Mobile device management	Allows administrators to manage Windows 10 devices (including PCs and mobile devices running any Windows 10 edition) from a management console.
Installed apps	
Microsoft Edge	The default web browser for retail editions of Windows 10, updated through Windows Store; supports a reading view, PDF viewing, ink comments, and Cortana integration.
Internet Explorer 11	A secondary web browser for Windows 10; provides compatibility with older websites and allows use of ActiveX controls and browser plug-ins.
Mail & Calendar	Allows sending, receiving, and managing email messages, appointments, and meeting invitations; supports industry-standard protocols as well as cloud services from Microsoft, Google, Apple, and Yahoo.

APPENDIX A

Feature	Description
Maps	Provides online and offline support for maps covering the entire world; supports navigation functions on devices equipped with a GPS.
Photos	Allows viewing and basic editing of photos stored locally or in the cloud.
Alarms & Clock	Shows the current time, with the option to display multiple time zones; also includes stopwatch, alarm, and countdown features.
Calculator	A full-featured calculator that performs basic arithmetic as well as advanced statistical functions; also includes programmer and scientific modes and has the ability to convert units of measurement.
News, Weather, Sports, Money	A suite of information apps powered by MSN and connected via the current Microsoft account.
Phone Companion	Manages synchronization with mobile devices, including those running non-Windows operating systems.
Xbox and other games	Allows access to casual games, including a preinstalled modern version of Solitaire; also can stream games from an Xbox One console.
Groove Music	Plays supported audio file formats, including MP3, WMA, AAC, and FLAC; also connects to the Groove Music Pass subscription service.
Camera	Controls built-in camera (front and back) for taking photos or communicating via programs such as Skype.
Scan	A feature used to scan documents and send and receive faxes. Requires a properly configured scanner, fax modem, or both.
XPS Document Writer and XPS Viewer	Provides the capability to create and view documents using the XML Paper Specification.
Voice Recorder	Creates simple voice memos.
Networking	
Remote Desktop client	Enables you to connect via a network to a Remote Desktop host.
SMB network connections	Provides for a maximum of 20 simultaneous connections. Because each PC or device requires two Server Message Block (SMB) connections, 10 PCs or devices can be connected at once.
Ability to join a homegroup	Enables you to share local resources and access shared resources on other devices running Windows 7 or newer versions that are part of the same homegroup.
Microsoft Wi-Fi	Automatically connects to Microsoft-managed Wi-Fi hotspots; requires a subscription.

Windows 10 Pro

Windows 10 Pro includes the same core features as Windows 10 Home, with the addition of features that are primarily of interest to business users and corporate network administrators. All the features listed in Table A-3 are also available in the Enterprise and Education editions.

Table A-3 Features available only in Windows 10 Pro, Enterprise, and Education editions

Feature	Description
Core Windows features	
Client Hyper-V	With proper hardware support, this hypervisor-based virtualization software allows users to create a virtual machine (VM), install Windows or another operating system on the VM, and use it as if it was a separate physical device. The Windows 10 Anniversary Update adds support for Hyper-V Containers.
Boot from virtual hard drive (VHD)	Enables you to configure a VHD as a boot device.
Language packs	Changes the Windows 10 interface to add language packs and switch between languages for displaying menus, dialog boxes, and other elements.
Subsystem for Unix-based Applications	A compatibility subsystem for compiling and running custom Unix-based applications.
Encrypting File System	Enables strong encryption of files and folders on an NTFS-formatted volume.
Management, security, and networking features	
BitLocker	Allows an entire drive to be encrypted, protecting its contents from unauthorized access if the computer is lost or stolen.
BitLocker To Go	Encrypts data on removable media such as USB flash drives and external drives.
Domain join/Group Policy management	Allows the device to join a Windows domain and be managed by using Active Directory and Group Policy.
Windows Information Protection	Provides advanced control over data files, including encryption and remote wipe.
Enterprise Mode Internet Explorer (EMIE)	Using network configuration files, administrators can define compatibility settings for sites accessed using Internet Explorer, including those on corporate intranets, enabling the continued use of older web apps that aren't compatible with Microsoft Edge.
Assigned Access	A special configuration mode, primarily for use on tablets and task-specific workstations, that restricts the ability of a user to run any apps except those on an approved list.

Feature	Description
Remote Desktop (server)	Allows remote access to the full Windows experience on the current PC; the connection is made over the network using Remote Desktop Protocol from a client program running on any Windows PC, Mac, or supported mobile device.
Offline Files	Used to synchronize, cache, and index network files locally so that they're available when the computer is disconnected from the network.
Deployment features	
Azure Active Directory support	Allows a Windows 10 device to join Azure Active Directory, with a single sign-in to cloud-hosted apps.
Business Store for Windows 10	Using this feature, an organization can provision apps and packaged Windows desktop programs in a restricted area of the Windows Store for installation by employees.
Windows Update for Business	Allows central management of security updates and new features delivered through Windows Update, allowing limited delays for feature updates and quality updates. Moving a device to the Current Branch for Business enhances stability by delaying the delivery of new features until they have been thoroughly tested in the Current Branch.

Windows 10 Enterprise and Education

The Windows 10 Enterprise edition is available as an upgrade to Volume License customers; it requires an underlying license for Windows 10 Pro. The Windows 10 Education edition provides equivalent features for large networks in academic environments and allows upgrades from Windows 10 Home or Pro editions. Table A-4 lists features available only in these editions.

Table A-4 Features available only in Windows 10 Enterprise and Education editions

Feature	Description
Management and security features	
Granular control of user experience	Provides standard Start menu layouts defined by administrators and prevents users from altering the standard user experience.
AppLocker	Enables administrators of enterprise networks to create an authorized list of programs that users can install and run.
Credential Guard	Supports multifactor authentication using smart cards and biometric information.

Feature	Description
Device Guard	Allows organizations to lock down a Windows 10 device so that only approved apps and desktop programs can be installed or run, preventing the installation of most forms of malware and any unauthorized software.
Windows To Go Creator	Allows the installation of Windows 10 Enterprise or Education on certified, high-performance USB drives that can boot and run in secure, self-contained mode, isolated from access by the host PC.
Long Term Servicing Branch	Allows administrators to limit deployment of new features in Windows 10, installing reliability and security updates only; this feature is designed for use in mission-critical environments and is available only in the Enterprise edition.
Windows 10 Defender Advanced Threat Protection	Available only with Windows 10 Enterprise E5 subscriptions, provides detection of online threats and attacks.
Networking	
BranchCache	Increases network responsiveness of applications in environments running on Windows Server 2008 R2 and later.
DirectAccess	Provides secure connections (without a virtual private network, or VPN) between a client PC running Windows 10 and a remote server running Windows Server 2008 R2 or newer.
Location-aware printing	Helps domain-joined computers find the correct printer when a user moves between office and home networks.

Help and support resources

We hope this book is helpful. We also know that even if we had unlimited pages and multiple volumes to fill, there's no way we could answer every question or cover every nook and cranny of a product as rich and diverse as Microsoft Windows 10. And, of course, in the "Windows as a Service" model, Windows 10 continues to evolve with new and reworked features and apps that we weren't able to describe in this edition because they didn't exist when we wrote it.

So we've put together this appendix to serve as a compendium of places where you can go to find help, troubleshooting tips, how-to guides, drivers, utilities, and advice.

Our list starts with official resources, collated and curated by Microsoft, but we also include community-based resources where you're likely to find reliable answers.

Online help

Over the years, what longtime Windows users call "the Help file" has evolved, with the internet serving as the greatest agent of change. As recently as Windows 7, a Help And Support link on the Start menu led to Compiled HTML Help (.chm) files, readable with a built-in Windows utility (Hh.exe) that acts like a special-purpose browser.

That utility is still included with Windows 10, and you can still find a few .chm files (mostly for third-party products) if you search hard enough, but for Windows 10 itself most help is available online, where it's easily updated without the hassle of having to deliver those updated files to a billion or so PCs.

So for most questions, your first stop should be the web—specifically, Microsoft's search engine, Bing, which delivers results directly from Microsoft Help when you ask a question about Windows. Figure B-1 shows one such question, with the answer in a box above all other search results and the source clearly labeled as "Help from Microsoft."

If a specific search doesn't return the official answer you're looking for, you can try browsing through Windows Help online (*http://windows.com/help*), which contains tutorials and instructions for common tasks, organized by category, with a search box to help deliver more refined results, as shown in Figure B-2.

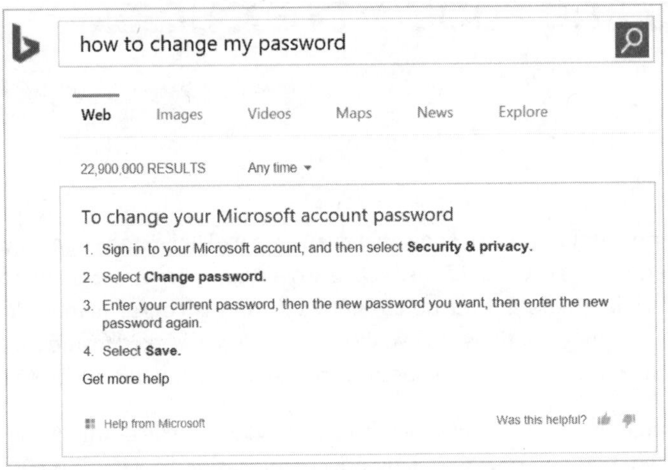

Figure B-1 Microsoft's Bing search engine delivers results directly from its collection of online Help from Microsoft if you ask the right questions.

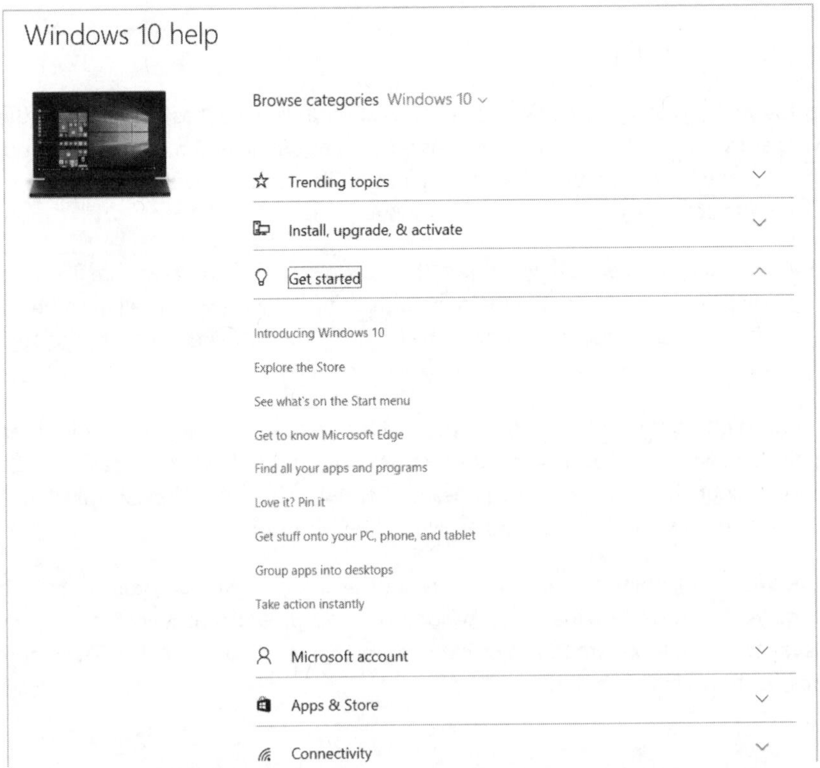

Figure B-2 Windows Help online is organized by category. Use the arrow to the right of each heading, as in the "Get Started" example shown here, to see a list of topics containing explanations and instructions.

Inside OUT

Ask Cortana for help

Cortana doesn't have the entire Windows 10 help library memorized, but you can get help with some tasks. Ask the right question, and you might get a search result that has a large question mark icon to its left. That's your indication you've found a Help topic, which looks like this when you click the search result:

Most of the time, those quick instructions should be sufficient. If you need more information, click the See More Results On Bing.com link.

Sometimes, of course, you're not looking for a detailed explanation or step-by-step instructions but simply trying to find a Windows setting without having to dig through menus or dialog boxes. For that type of chore, you have your choice of no fewer than three separate places to start a search:

- **The search box on the taskbar.** Entering a search term (in this case, the word **display**) in the search box on the taskbar returns a short but usually well-focused set of results. The results are the same regardless of whether you have enabled Cortana, as shown next.

- **The Settings search box.** Click Start > Settings (or use the keyboard shortcut Windows key+I), and enter a word or phrase in the search box in the upper right corner. Note that the top of the results list contains matching entries from the modern Settings app, followed by results from the desktop Control Panel, with the latter identifiable by their colorful icons, as shown here:

- **The Control Panel search box.** The classic desktop Control Panel has its own search box in the upper right corner. Entering a word or phrase here returns results exclusively from the All Control Panel Items list, as shown here. Its index does not include options from the modern Settings app.

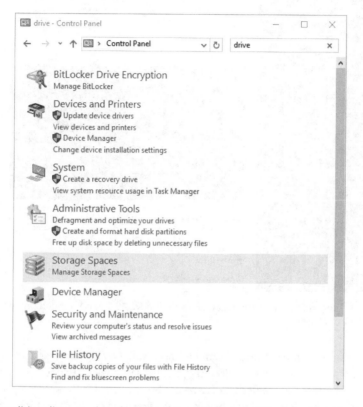

For traditionalists, one bit of local help is available on a Windows 10 device, courtesy of a Windows Store app called Get Started. The app, shown in Figure B-3, is installed with Windows 10 and updated through the Windows Store.

The content in the Get Started app is basic, offers an overview of core features, and is aimed primarily at nontechnical users. Most readers of this book will probably find little new information there, but it's an excellent resource to suggest to friends, family members, and coworkers who could benefit from it. Click Browse in the navigation pane to see a list of topic areas, and then click any topic to see text explanations and tutorial videos.

Figure B-3 The Get Started app is installed with Windows 10 and is intended primarily for beginners and nontechnical users.

You can open Get Started directly from the Start menu. An alternative entry point comes via pop-up tips that appear occasionally after you install Windows 10, suggesting that you try out new features. Those tips are designed to be unobtrusive and won't appear if you already used the feature the tip is intended to introduce. But if you want to eliminate them completely, go to Settings > System > Notifications & Actions. Slide the Get Tips, Tricks, And Suggestions As You Use Windows switch to the Off position and you won't be bothered by those pop-ups.

> ➤ An additional source of detailed help in Windows 10 is available through the Troubleshooting section of Control Panel. We cover these guided tools as well as online Fix It resources in Chapter 17, "Troubleshooting."

Online reference material from Microsoft

Microsoft's commitment to ongoing support of Windows 10 includes an enormous library of training aids and reference material. This section lists the most important of these resources.

Microsoft Knowledge Base

Knowledge Base (KB) articles are official support documents that provide details about known issues, workarounds, security updates, new features, and anything else that the Microsoft Support organization deems worthy of formal publication.

Every Knowledge Base article has a unique ID number you can use as a search term to locate a specific document. Security updates, for example, are documented with KB numbers so that IT pros can read details about what a specific update does.

To search for specific information in the Knowledge Base, start with this search term:

site:support.microsoft.com/en-us/kb "windows 10"

If your Windows 10 language is something other than US English, replace *en-us* with the prefix for your regional settings.

Save that search in your browser's Favorites bar or bookmarks and use it as the starting point for any future searches, appending your search terms in the search box. The results list will contain only documents that have been formally published in the Knowledge Base.

Microsoft TechNet

TechNet (*https://technet.microsoft.com*) is Microsoft's hub for technical information written primarily for IT pros. It includes news, technical articles, and downloads for all Microsoft products.

To focus exclusively on information about Windows 10, visit the Windows 10 TechCenter: *https://technet.microsoft.com/windows/dn798751*.

The TechNet library for Windows (*https://technet.microsoft.com/itpro/windows/index*) is continually expanding as new technical articles are added. The content, written for IT pros and experts, is thorough and sometimes extremely technical, in sharp contrast to the consumer-friendly general help pages. It's worth bookmarking that page and visiting occasionally to see what's new.

Microsoft Virtual Academy

This online learning resource (*http://microsoftvirtualacademy.com*) is an excellent source of free training on a wide range of topics, including Windows 10. Available content includes pre-recorded courses, live events (and archives of previous events), and books, with walk-throughs and demos bringing complex topics to life. New content is added regularly. You might even find videos featuring one of the authors of this book!

Getting technical support

If you can't find an answer in the Knowledge Base, or if a problem seems to be unique to your system configuration, you can turn to Microsoft's support forums for help.

Microsoft Community

Nontechnical users running consumer versions of Windows should start with the Microsoft Community forums at *http://answers.microsoft.com*. These threaded message boards are organized into categories—choose Windows, and then Windows 10 to find the most relevant answers.

It's tempting to start by firing off a question, but a much better strategy is to use the search box on the page to see whether anyone else has reported a similar issue. After entering the Windows 10 topic area, enter your search term in the box in the upper-right corner. If a relevant topic shows up in the Autocomplete list, go ahead and click it. Otherwise, choose Current Scope from the drop-down list, as shown in Figure B-4. That step ensures that you see only answers relevant to Windows 10.

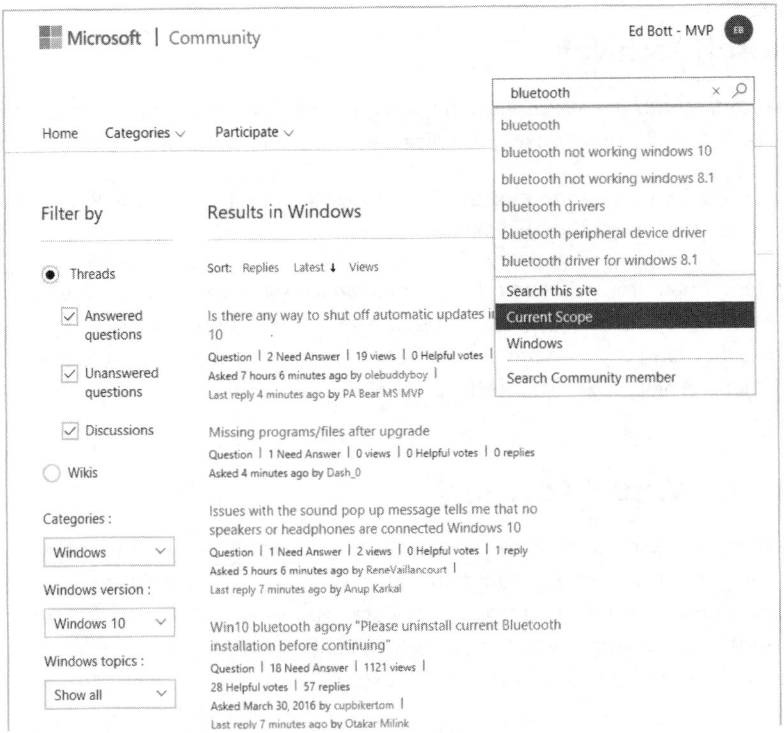

Figure B-4 Use the Current Scope option to limit search results to those matching the categories you selected from the lists on the left side of the Microsoft Community forums.

If your search doesn't turn up the answer you're looking for, click Ask The Community to begin composing a question of your own. (You can use this same form to start a discussion if you want to raise an issue that doesn't require an answer.) When posting to the Community forums, try to be as specific as possible, providing relevant details about your system configuration and hardware as well as any troubleshooting steps you already tried and their results.

Note that support in these forums is provided by community members as well as Microsoft support personnel. You're also likely to run into an occasional Microsoft MVP (Most Valuable Professional), including one of the authors of this book. There's no guarantee you'll get a satisfactory answer, but we can testify from personal experience that this route has been successful for many people.

To keep track of a discussion, sign in with your Microsoft account and use the notification options at the bottom of any message. You'll receive an email at the address associated with your Microsoft account whenever anyone replies to the message; this is true regardless of whether you started the discussion yourself or found an existing discussion that you want to follow.

TechNet forums

If you're an IT pro and have a question or want to start a discussion with other like-minded and experienced individuals, go to the TechNet forums, *https://social.technet.microsoft.com/Forums*. Topics available here include a much broader range of Microsoft products and technologies than those covered in the Community forums, with a special emphasis on deploying and using Windows in the enterprise.

The basic rules of these more advanced message boards are similar to those we recommend for the Microsoft Community forums: search first, and ask a new question only if you can't find an existing discussion that addresses your issue.

Search options for the TechNet forums allow you to select multiple forums, shown on the left in Figure B-5, and then find specific topics within that selection by using a search box above the message list.

Use the filtering and sorting options (above the message list) to narrow your search further or make specific answers easier to locate.

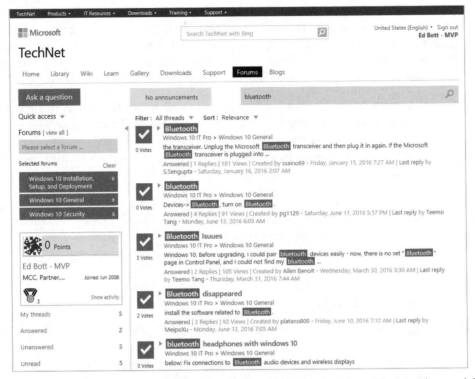

Figure B-5 Choose one or more TechNet forums from the list on the left, and then use the search box at the top of the message list to narrow your results.

Free and paid support from Microsoft

Getting answers from fellow Windows users has the advantage of being free and easily accessible, but sometimes you need formal support from Microsoft engineers.

Microsoft provides free support for security issues. If you suspect your computer has been infected with malware, for example, you can request and receive support at no charge. Other support options might be covered under a product warranty that's provided if you purchase Windows directly from Microsoft, or you can open a support ticket (called an "incident") for a fee.

Visit the Microsoft Answer Desk online at *http://support.microsoft.com/contactus* to see your support options. Listings on that page direct you to the appropriate technical support resources for different business categories.

As an alternative, use the Contact Support app, which is installed by default with Windows 10. Figure B-6 shows the options available for Windows support, which includes chat and telephone options.

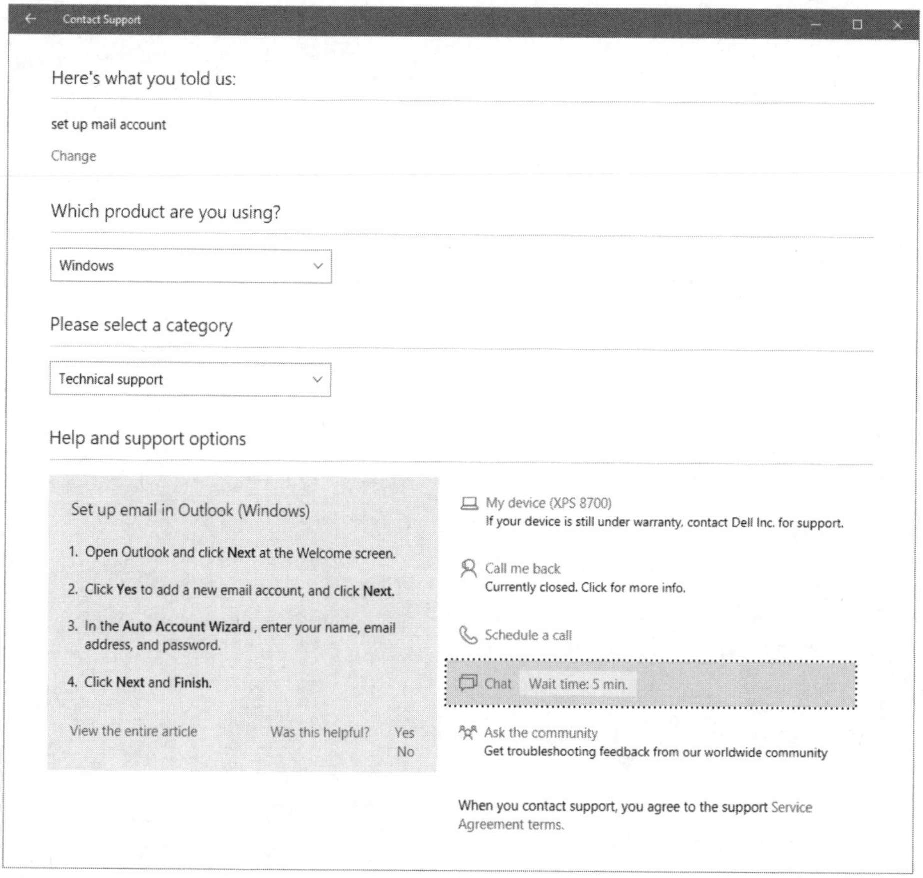

Figure B-6 Use the Contact Support app to chat online or talk with a support representative. Note that some options might require payment.

Index to troubleshooting topics

Index

About the authors

Ed Bott is an award-winning author and technology journalist who has been researching and writing about Windows and PC technology, in print and on the Internet, for more than two decades. He has written more than 30 books, all on Windows and Microsoft Office, which in turn have been translated into dozens of languages and read worldwide. You can catch up with Ed's latest opinions and get hands-on advice at *The Ed Bott Report* on ZDNet (*zdnet.com/blog/bott*). You can also follow his lively and occasionally irreverent Twitter feed (@edbott). Ed and his wife, Judy, live in northern New Mexico with two English springer spaniels, Mackie and Lucy, who were adopted with the help of English Springer Rescue America (*springerrescue.org*). Both of those lucky dogs make cameo appearances in this book.

Carl Siechert began his writing career at age eight as editor of the *Mesita Road News*, a neighborhood newsletter that reached a peak worldwide circulation of 43 during its eight-year run. Following several years as an estimator and production manager in a commercial printing business, Carl returned to writing with the formation of Siechert & Wood Professional Documentation, a Pasadena, California, firm that specializes in writing and producing product documentation for the personal computer industry. Carl is a coauthor of more than 20 books, covering operating systems from MS-DOS 3.0 to Windows 10 and productivity applications from Microsoft Works 3 to Office 2013. In a convergence of new and old technology, Carl's company now operates a popular website for hobby machinists, *https://littlemachineshop.com*. Carl hiked the Pacific Crest Trail from Mexico to Canada in 1977 and would rather be hiking right now. He and his wife, Jan, live in Southern California.

Craig Stinson, an industry journalist since 1981, was editor of *Softalk for the IBM Personal Computer*, one of the earliest IBM-PC magazines. He is the author or coauthor of numerous books about Windows and Microsoft Excel. Craig is an amateur musician and reformed music critic, having reviewed classical music for various newspapers and trade publications, including *Billboard*, the *Boston Globe*, the *Christian Science Monitor,* and *Musical America*. He lives in Bloomington, Indiana.

From technical overviews to drilldowns on special topics, get *free* ebooks from Microsoft Press at:

www.microsoftvirtualacademy.com/ebooks

Download your free ebooks in PDF, EPUB, and/or Mobi for Kindle formats.

Look for other great resources at Microsoft Virtual Academy, where you can learn new skills and help advance your career with free Microsoft training delivered by experts.

Hear about it first.

Get the latest news from Microsoft Press sent to your inbox.

- New and upcoming books

- Special offers

- Free eBooks

- How-to articles

Sign up today at MicrosoftPressStore.com/Newsletters

 Microsoft

Visit us today at

microsoftpressstore.com

- **Hundreds of titles available** – Books, eBooks, and online resources from industry experts

- **Free U.S. shipping**

- **eBooks in multiple formats** – Read on your computer, tablet, mobile device, or e-reader

- **Print & eBook Best Value Packs**

- **eBook Deal of the Week** – Save up to 60% on featured titles

- **Newsletter and special offers** – Be the first to hear about new releases, specials, and more

- **Register your book** – Get additional benefits

Now that you've read the book...

Tell us what you think!

Was it useful?
Did it teach you what you wanted to learn?
Was there room for improvement?

Let us know at http://aka.ms/tellpress

Your feedback goes directly to the staff at Microsoft Press, and we read every one of your responses. Thanks in advance!

 Microsoft